HE GAVE US STORIES

HE GAVE US STORIES

The Bible Student's Guide to Interpreting Old Testament Narratives

RICHARD L. PRATT, JR.

P&R PUBLISHING
P.O. BOX 817 • PHILLIPSBURG • NEW JERSEY 08865-0817

Manufactured in the United States of America

Library of Congress Cataloging-in-Publication Data

Pratt, Richard L., 1953–
He gave us stories : the Bible student's guide to interpreting Old Testament narratives / Richard L. Pratt, Jr.
p. cm.
Originally published: Brentwood, Tenn. : Wolgemuth & Hyatt, 1990.
Includes bibliographical references and index.
ISBN 0-87552-379-X (paper)
1. Bible. O.T.—Study and teaching. I. Title.
[BS1193.P673 1993]
220.6—dc20 93-1565

To my wife, Gena
and
my daughter, Becky

*"The things revealed belong
to us and to our children forever."*
(Deuteronomy 29:29)

CONTENTS

Part II: Investigating Old Testament Narratives

Part III: Applying Old Testament Narratives

ILLUSTRATIONS

PREFACE

When my wife and I decided that I should pursue an advanced degree in theological studies, we had a difficult choice. My personal interests and academic training were in philosophy of religion. But we became convinced that many serious problems in the church stem from a neglect of the Old Testament. With that conviction we committed ourselves to a lifetime of helping God's people understand and apply the Old Testament. *He Gave Us Stories* is one step toward reaching our goal.

This book focuses on interpreting Old Testament narratives. Many outstanding books on Biblical interpretation have appeared in recent years. Why another?

First, this book is not a scholarly study. Some of the best works on Biblical interpretation have been too technical for widespread use. My target audience is motivated lay people and beginning theological students. I have assumed very little knowledge of the Old Testament, theology, and interpretation. I have also avoided many complexities for the sake of inexperienced readers. For the most part, technicalities are addressed in the endnotes.

Second, this book specifically deals with Old Testament narratives. Many guides to understanding Scripture consider the whole Bible in general terms and neglect the unique challenges presented by Old Testament stories. Many of the perspectives of this book have implications for all Biblical interpretation, but I have concentrated on the special features of stories in the Old Testament.

Third, this book builds on the foundation of orthodox Protestant theology. To the best of my knowledge, the views presented in this study are thoroughly consistent with evangelical theological commitments. Beyond this, traditional Protestant doctrinal formulations frequently guide the discussion. In recent years I have become increasingly concerned that evangelical Biblical scholars often fail to integrate traditional systematic theology with their Biblical research. In response to this trend, I frequently refer to confessions, creeds, catechisms, and representative theological works from the past and the present.

Fourth, this book addresses the practical use of Old Testament narratives in the church. Church leaders have the responsibility to teach the whole counsel of God. Unfortunately, they are seldom well equipped to analyze, explain, and apply Old Testament narratives to the church. In order to meet this need, this book proposes practical guidelines for preparing, investigating, and applying Old Testament stories to the modern world.

This study is little more than an introduction to Old Testament interpretation. Countless issues are left for readers to pursue on their own. The chapters that follow represent the results of my own wrestling with Old Testament interpretation. This struggle has been a consuming academic pursuit for the past decade. But more than this, it has been a driving spiritual quest since I came to know the mercy of God in Christ and realized that He gave us stories.

Richard L. Pratt, Jr.

Reformed Theological Seminary
Orlando, Florida
31 December 1989

ACKNOWLEDGMENTS

A number of friends deserve special thanks for their help with this project. As usual, my wife, Gena, read through the text and offered many helpful suggestions. I also acknowledge John Farrar, whose enthusiasm and financial support made the project possible. Jane Sheppard and Diana Soule worked diligently on revising the manuscript. Many thanks to my colleague, Knox Chamblin, who read the book and encouraged me to complete it. Jon Balserak, Bob Cara, Ray Craig, Reeves Flint, Scott Lindsay, Kris Lundgaard, Greg Perry, Janie Pillow, Jerry Robbins, Tim Stewart, and John Van Dyke provided indispensable encouragement and feedback as my research assistants. Finally, I must thank all of my students at Reformed Theological Seminary whose interactions over the years have contributed significantly to this material.

Thanks a lot, friends. This book belongs to all of us.

INTRODUCTION

THREE PROCESSES OF INTERPRETATION

Several years ago I had the opportunity to work on an archaeological project. My professor had spent months digging up ancient potsherds and tools, which he meticulously cataloged and shipped back to the United States. After nearly a year, the crates arrived at the museum, where other students and I helped piece together the artifacts.

Many things came together to make that dig a success. The team prepared for the excavation well in advance and planned everything down to the last detail. But the hard work had only begun. The crew worked for weeks in the hot sun, digging through the mud and sand, careful not to overlook the smallest item. The dig itself was strenuous but getting the artifacts back home proved to be equally difficult. Government officials had to inspect all the packages, and the shipping lines were unreliable.

One lesson was plain to all of us aspiring archaeologists: To have a successful dig, you must prepare carefully, work hard at the site, and get your discoveries home. If you neglect any of these, the project will be incomplete.

In this book we are going on a dig into the ancient texts of Old Testament narratives. We will make preparations for our work, investigate the Old Testament in its ancient world, and apply our discoveries to modern life. If we overlook any of these steps, our work with Old Testament narratives will be incomplete.

To complete these processes, we must give attention to *hermeneutics*, the study of all that goes into interpreting the Bible.[1] We will speak of three major facets in the interpretation of Old Testament stories: *preparation*,

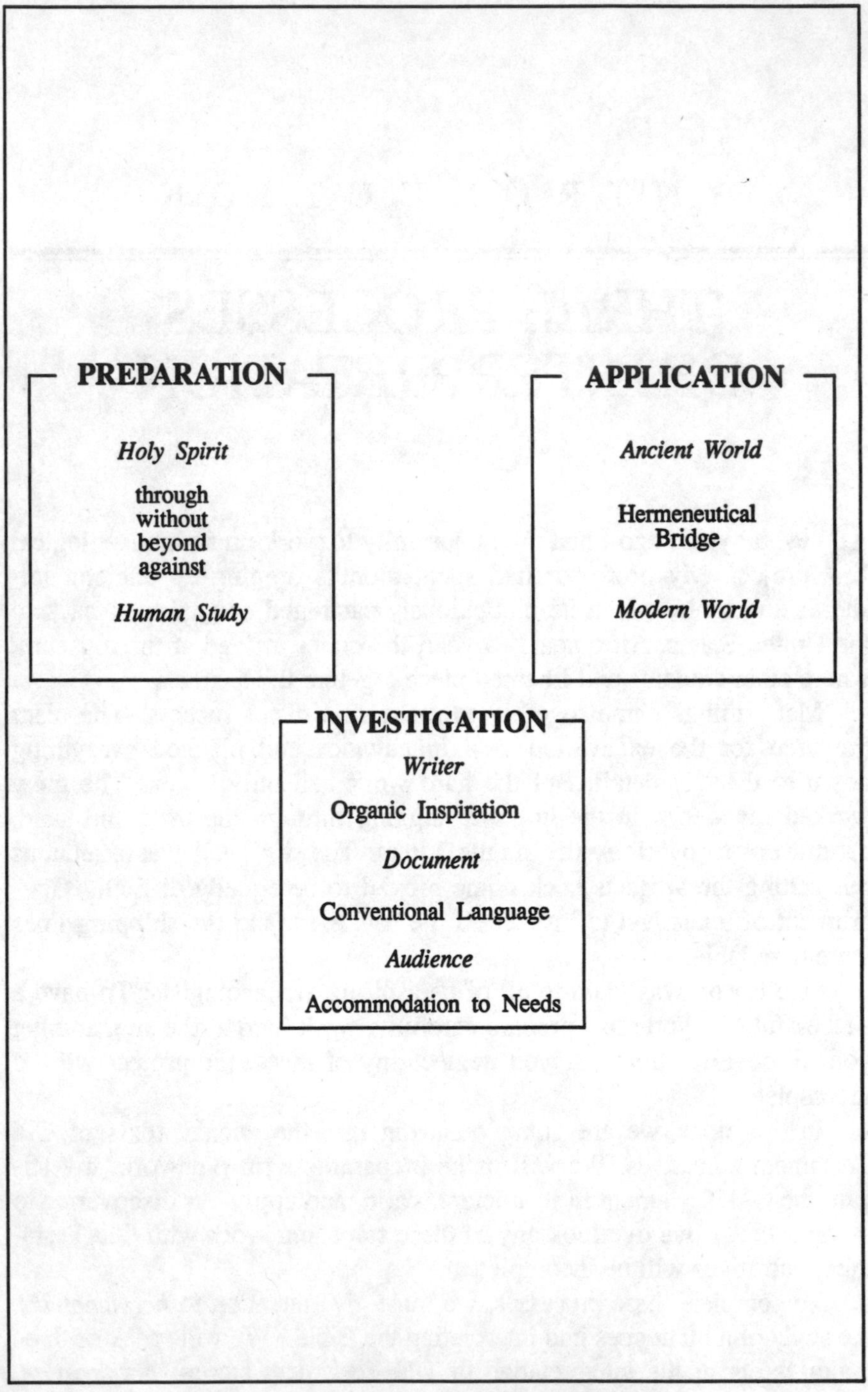

PREPARATION

Holy Spirit

through
without
beyond
against

Human Study

APPLICATION

Ancient World

Hermeneutical
Bridge

Modern World

INVESTIGATION

Writer

Organic Inspiration

Document

Conventional Language

Audience

Accommodation to Needs

Fig. 1: Three Processes of Interpretation

investigation, and *application* (see figure 1). These processes are not entirely separate; they depend on each other in countless ways. Yet each one is essential for understanding Old Testament narratives. In this chapter we will address several preliminary issues in each area.

Preparation

The first hermeneutical process is preparation—getting ready to interpret Old Testament narratives. Many issues come to the foreground as we approach this subject, but foundational to any discussion is a proper understanding of the relationship between human study and the Holy Spirit.

I have a friend who built his own cabin in the mountains of Vermont. Hoping to finish construction during a two-week vacation, he packed his truck with lathes, power saws, drills, and an assortment of other tools. When he arrived at his property, however, my friend discovered that he had no electricity. Without electrical power he could do no work; his wonderful tools were useless, so he spent the time fishing.

As we prepare to read Old Testament stories, we must realize that it takes tools and power to interpret these texts. Unless we have power, all of our tools will be useless. Likewise, power is of little use without tools.

What are the tools of hermeneutics? What is the power? Our hermeneutical tools are the vast array of human knowledge and skills we bring to interpretation. Hermeneutical power is the work of our divine Teacher, the Holy Spirit. Sadly, we often forget that we need both human tools and divine power to interpret Old Testament stories. Instead we rely too much on one or the other.

Overemphasis on the Spirit

Lay people commonly emphasize the ministry of the Holy Spirit and neglect careful study. They often appeal to the words of Paul, "No one knows the thoughts of God except the Spirit of God" (1 Corinthians 2:11).[2] Since the Spirit is our Teacher, these believers prepare themselves by searching exclusively for spiritual guidance.

I remember once talking with a friend who had given a lesson from the story of Jacob's ladder (Genesis 28:10–22). Most of his comments were helpful, but at one point he remarked that Jacob's ladder represented "the way we climb up to God through our diligence." Sometime later I suggested that a more careful reading would not have led to his conclusion. "The ladder was a symbol of God's grace," I contended. "The angels, not Jacob, went up and down the ladder." The distinction seemed obvious to me, so I was surprised when he disagreed.

"No," he insisted. "The Holy Spirit told me this is what it means, and that's good enough for me!" No amount of discussion or exegetical observation could move him from his position. He had rejected careful study for what he thought was spiritual enlightenment.

Not everyone goes to this extreme, but many lay people see little need for academic study of the Bible. "Understanding Scripture is a spiritual matter," they say. "If we depend on the Spirit, we don't need formal study." What causes Christians to take this perspective? Why do they turn from rigorous preparation for interpretation? By and large this tendency rests on a misunderstanding of the Spirit's work in *inspiration* and *illumination*.

Inspiration. Many Christians think that the inspiration of Scripture eliminates the need for human study.[3] The Spirit is the author of revelation (Isaiah 61:1–4) and the source of inspiration (1 Corinthians 2:9–10; 2 Timothy 3:16).[4] In His wisdom the Holy Spirit so inspired Old Testament narratives that many matters can be grasped through simple reading;[5] they are available to the "learned and unlearned alike."[6] The central message of salvation is easily discerned; we are able to grasp it without much effort.[7] Clarity extends to other teachings as well. For instance, it is obvious that Saul hated David (1 Samuel 18:7–12), and that Ruth loved Naomi (Ruth 1:8–18).

Considering only this side of inspiration, we might think that rigorous study of the Bible is not necessary. But the Spirit also intended Scriptures to require careful examination. Jesus purposefully spoke in obscure parables (Matthew 13:10–13), and Peter commented that many things written by Paul were "hard to understand" (2 Peter 3:15–16). In much the same way, large portions of Old Testament narratives are not easily understood. Why were the Israelite midwives blessed when they lied to Pharaoh (Exodus 1:15–21)? How do we reconcile the accounts of creation in the first and second chapters of Genesis? How should we relate parallel texts in Kings and Chronicles? The list goes on and on. The more we read Old Testament stories the more it is evident that "all things in Scripture are not alike plain in themselves."[8]

The difficulties that the Spirit placed in Scripture reveal the need for serious study. Despite the clarity of many matters in the Bible, the Spirit has been pleased to form portions of the Biblical message in ways that challenge us to vigorous investigation.

Illumination. Some believers also reject human study because they misunderstand the Spirit's illumination. Alongside the objective inspiration of Scripture, the Spirit gives us subjective enlightenment so that we may understand what has been written. Without His ministry we would be left in ignorance and darkness. This work of the Spirit is also vital to hermeneutics.[9] As John Owen reminds us:

> The principal efficient cause of the due knowledge and understanding of the will of God in the Scripture . . . is the Holy Spirit of God himself alone, for there is an especial work of the Spirit of God on the minds of men, communicating spiritual wisdom, light, and understanding unto them, *necessary unto their discerning and apprehending aright the mind of God in his word.* (Emphasis added)[10]

In a word, the Spirit illumines our minds so we may apprehend and appropriate Scripture (Romans 8:14–17; 1 Corinthians 2:10–16; 1 Thessalonians 1:5; 2:13; 1 John 2:27; 5:7–9). Without His enlightenment our interpretative efforts are hopeless.

But illumination does not rule out the need for human study. The Holy Spirit is not a hermeneutical *Deus ex machina,* solving all our interpretative problems. He does not miraculously grant us complete insight and thus remove the need for careful investigation. On the contrary, illumination varies from person to person, group to group, and time to time. We are sinful, finite human beings who always have more to learn.

To sum up, we must depend on the Spirit, who inspired Old Testament narratives and illumines our minds. But the Spirit's inspiration and illumination still require extensive human effort in interpretation.

Overemphasis on Study

While lay people often neglect serious study, Biblical scholars tend to set their hopes primarily on human effort. Many of them base their views on Paul's words to Timothy, "Do your best to present yourself to God as one approved, a workman who does not need to be ashamed and who correctly handles the word of truth" (2 Timothy 2:15). In this outlook preparation amounts to amassing an arsenal of knowledge and exegetical skills. Human efforts actually take the place of seeking help from the Spirit.

Critical scholars typically treat interpretation as a mere human affair. Correct understanding depends on academic research, not the Holy Spirit. Naive lay people, we are told, simply cannot understand the Bible properly. A priesthood of intellectuals rules critical hermeneutics. With rare exception this "'expert' ethos"[11] excludes conscious attention to the Holy Spirit.[12]

This outlook is also evident among evangelical scholars, who give a place to the personal ministry of the Spirit in their theology, but seldom apply these convictions consistently to interpretation. The extent of this neglect is illustrated by the paucity of writing on the Spirit in hermeneutics. On occasion older works focus a bit on the Spirit,[13] but most modern evangelical studies say precious little about Him.[14] To my knowledge the most recent work of substantial size on this subject was written over three hundred years ago by John Owen (1616–1683).[15]

The results of neglecting the Spirit appear all around us. No matter what we say theoretically, in practice evangelicals often treat hermeneutical preparation primarily as a matter of acquiring knowledge and skills. Our hope for understanding rests more on our abilities than on the personal ministry of the Holy Spirit.

Why do we neglect the Spirit in this way? Often human efforts are overemphasized because we assume that the Spirit always teaches through rigorous study. A. Thiselton reflects this conviction when he concludes: "The Holy Spirit may be said to work through human understanding, and not usually, if ever, through processes which bypass the considerations discussed under the heading of hermeneutics . . . "[16] This viewpoint is true as far as it goes, but it places too much importance on one way in which the Spirit teaches His people.

The Holy Spirit usually works through human study, so we must rely to a large extent on our efforts. But the Spirit also works *without, beyond,* and *against* our interpretative efforts.[17]

Without. We have all experienced times when the Spirit granted insight into a passage without formal study or rigorous reflection. Often the insights of untrained interpreters are more significant than anything derived from academic study. Why? Because the Spirit sometimes teaches without the creaturely means of academic investigation.

Beyond. Insights also go beyond human efforts. Pastors experience this work of the Spirit in their busy ministries. They often find themselves pushed for time and unable to study as much as they would like. Occasionally, however, their poorly prepared sermons actually have more depth than their well-prepared messages. Why? Their meager efforts are superseded by the work of the Spirit. This blessing should not be used as an excuse for neglecting study, but it is comforting to know that the Spirit gives us insight beyond what we gain through our own research.

Against. The Holy Spirit also works against us, enlightening our minds despite ourselves. Well-meaning believers frequently pursue Scripture to support erroneous preconceptions. Biases cloud our minds and hinder accurate understanding. From time to time, the Holy Spirit works against these tendencies and grants true insights, inspite of our distortions of the truth. In many different ways, the Spirit actually works against our efforts to teach us what He has revealed in Scripture.

In the chapters that follow, we will examine more thoroughly the relationship of human study to the Holy Spirit. For now we must simply recognize that preparation for interpreting Old Testament narratives involves both human and divine effort. We look to the Spirit as the power enabling us to interpret, and we look to hermeneutical skills as the tools of our trade. As we remember both of these elements, we will be better prepared to interpret Old Testament stories.

Investigation

As an archaeologist goes to a site to dig, so also must we go back in time to the ancient world of the Old Testament and investigate narratives in their historical contexts. What are the important issues involved in going back to the original setting of these stories? Is this time travel necessary? To answer these questions, we will examine two issues: *grammatico-historical investigation* and the *importance of historical investigation.*

Grammatico-Historical Investigation

"Look at this ad!" I shouted to my wife. "It's just what we've been looking for, and it's on sale tomorrow!"

My wife eagerly took the newspaper to look for herself. "It's a great price too," she added. But her smile quickly faded. "We can't buy it," she said as she pointed to the top of the page. "This is last week's paper!"

To understand written material, we have to look at the words on the page, but we also have to consider the time when the words were written. We deal not only with grammar but also with history. Unfortunately evangelicals often fail to apply this principle to reading Old Testament stories. We read these texts as if they dropped out of the sky right into our laps. How much difference does it make for most of us that Moses wrote Genesis?[18] Do we care that the book of Samuel was compiled after the division of the kingdom?[19] What does it matter that Kings was written during the exile and Chronicles after it?[20] Often we do not even know these facts, much less incorporate them into our interpretations. "After all," we think, "we are interested in what these stories mean for us today, not for people long ago."

In reaction to this outlook, academic hermeneutics has traditionally stressed the historical setting of the Bible. Formal instruction has been oriented toward learning ancient languages, history, customs, and religious beliefs. This orientation can be seen in L. Berkhof's summary of the goal of hermeneutics:

> Hermeneutics is usually studied with a view to the interpretation of the literary productions of the past. Its special task is to point out the way in which the differences or the distances between an author and his readers may be removed. It teaches us that this is properly accomplished only by the readers' transposing themselves into the time and spirit of the author.[21]

Evangelicals commonly call this hermeneutical outlook the *grammatico-historical method*.[22]

The basic elements of grammatico-historical investigation stem from the Reformers' rejection of allegorical interpretation in the medieval church.[23] The relationship between Protestant and medieval interpretation is complex, but early Protestant exegesis made significant strides toward emphasizing historical and grammatical investigation of the Bible.[24] This shift was deeply influenced by Renaissance studies of newly discovered classical Greek and Latin texts.[25] As techniques for interpreting these classical documents grew, scholars rejected allegorical methods in favor of meticulous philological and historical methods.[26]

The term "grammatico-historical" first appeared in the 1788 edition of K. A. G. Keil's treatise on interpretation.[27] Keil's hermeneutical approach can be traced directly to his influential teacher, J. A. Ernesti (1701–1781).[28] Ernesti in turn depended heavily on H. Grotius (1583–1645), who was steeped in Renaissance classical studies.[29] The works of these men reflected the growing conviction among orthodox theologians that the Bible should be read as an ancient document. As Ernesti put it, "The Scriptures are to be investigated by the same rules as other books."[30]

The resulting method was basically two-fold. As the term "grammatico-historical" suggests, grammar and history were central. Interpreters examined words and expressions and explored the historical circumstances in which the text was written, especially the writer's background and purposes.

Through the centuries this historical orientation has undergone a number of significant changes. We commonly distinguish historical-critical exegesis from more conservative grammatico-historical exegesis. The former builds on Enlightenment assumptions of the superiority of human reason over the Bible; the latter maintains belief in the authority of Scripture.[31] As different as these approaches are, both see grammar and history as the keys for unlocking the meaning of a passage.

Importance of Historical Investigation

As we begin our study of Old Testament narratives, the historical orientation of academic hermeneutics raises a vital question. Why is it necessary to go back to the original settings to interpret these texts properly? Three pillars undergird a concern for the historical contexts of Old Testament stories: *the conventional character of Biblical language, organic inspiration through Biblical writers,* and *accommodation to Biblical audiences.*

The conventional character of Biblical language. What allows two people to communicate, to understand each other? In many respects successful communication depends on shared conventions[32]—certain symbols, gestures, and expressions that have specific meanings. If we do not agree to some extent on the meanings of these signs, we cannot communicate.

For example, the word "house" often means "a dwelling" in English. But Spanish speakers have a different convention, *casa.* In other languages similar concepts are signified by *maison* and *Haus*. There is nothing inherent in these expressions that make them signify a dwelling; they are meanings agreed upon by the people who speak each language. Linguistic agreements change from people to people, group to group, and age to age, but the ability to communicate rests on these cultural conventions.[33]

It is no different with the language of Old Testament narratives. Everything from individual words to overarching literary style is fundamentally conventional. The assumptions that Biblical authors shared with their audiences become road signs directing us to the meaning of their texts. If we are unaware of these historical conditions, we cannot even translate the Bible, much less interpret it. The conventional character of Biblical language compels us to explore the ancient world of Old Testament stories.

Organic inspiration through Biblical writers. But isn't the Bible inspired by God and, therefore, above these cultural influences? This question brings us to a second reason for dealing with the ancient world of the Bible: the doctrine of *organic inspiration*—that God worked through the personalities and intentions of human writers when He inspired Scripture.[34] B.B. Warfield described the doctrine in these words:

> These books [of Scripture] were not produced suddenly, by some miraculous act—handed down complete out of heaven, as the phrase goes; but, like all other products of time, are the ultimate effect of many processes cooperating through long periods. . . . There is the preparation of the men to write these books to be considered, a preparation physical, intellectual, spiritual, which must have attended them throughout their whole lives, and, indeed, must have had its beginning in their remote ancestors, and the effect of which was to bring the right men to the right places at the right times, with the right endowments, impulses, acquirements, to write just the books which were designed for them.[35]

As Warfield pointed out, God ordained every detail of history so that Scriptures would come through human authors who had been perfectly designed to write them. In this way their personalities, outlooks, and intentions were not circumvented; rather, they were used by the Spirit to form the Biblical text.

The organic quality of inspiration explains many peculiarities of the Old Testament. For instance, in the book of Kings, Manasseh is an arch miscreant who finally seals the fate of Judah (2 Kings 21:10–16). In Chronicles, however, he is a model of repentance and restoration (2 Chronicles 33:10–17). These variations are not contradictory; they simply resulted from the different purposes of each writer. The writer of Kings wrote during the exile and focused on Manasseh's sin to explain why Judah had been taken to Babylon (2 Kings 21:12–17).[36] The Chronicler wrote after the return from exile to demonstrate the importance of repentance and prayer for the full restoration of the post-exilic community.[37]

The organic view of inspiration gives us another reason to pay attention to the original settings of Old Testament stories. Biblical revelation came through human authors whose circumstances, interests, and intentions gave each story its particular shape and content.[38] If we fail to return to their original historical settings, we cut ourselves off from proper understanding.

Accommodation to Biblical audiences. Exploring the world of the past also rests on the *accommodation of revelation* to ancient audiences. The doctrine of accommodation, which teaches that God revealed Himself by speaking to His people in ways they could understand, has been a longstanding belief among Protestants.[39] The form of many Old Testament texts illustrates accommodation. The book of Deuteronomy, for instance, resembles aspects of ancient Near Eastern treaties well known to the people of that day.[40] If God had given Israel this revelation in the form of modern business contracts or on a floppy disk, it would not have revealed anything; it would have been irrelevant.

Some Old Testament books focused on more specific audiences than others. Kings was written to a rather specific original situation, and we must acknowledge this accommodation if we are to understand the book.[41] However, the book of Job, which deals with the perennial issues of evil and suffering, appears to be directed to a more general audience.[42]

All books of Scripture accommodated their original recipients to some degree. We can understand these books more fully as we become aware of the ancient world of those to whom they were written.

As we have seen, grammatico-historical exegesis orients interpretation toward the original historical context. This orientation is essential because of the conventional language of the document, organic inspiration, and accommodation to the original audience. In the chapters that follow, we will explore these matters in much detail. At this stage we should simply note that the more we learn about the document, writer, and audience, the better we will be equipped to investigate Old Testament narratives.

Application

The third major concern of our study is application of Old Testament narratives. In this aspect of interpretation, we are interested in how passages should affect people today. We return from digging about in the ancient world and bring our discoveries back to modern life. To introduce this hermeneutical process, we will consider *the challenge of application*, *obstacles to application*, and *relevance and distance in application.*

Challenge of Application

As a child I was fascinated by H. G. Wells' *The Time Machine*. What would it be like to travel back in time? How would things be different? Along with this fascination was a constant dread. What would happen if I could not get back to my own time? Would I want to spend the rest of my life stuck in the past?

In many ways these are questions we need to ask ourselves as we interpret Old Testament narratives. It may be fascinating to go back to the ancient world of these stories, but what good is it if we do not come back to our own day? We must commit ourselves to returning to the modern world and applying what we have learned.

At first glance it might seem that evangelicals focus a lot on the application of Scripture. On an informal level, this is true. But formal studies in hermeneutics have been so concerned with the ancient world that they give little attention to the relevance of Old Testament narratives.[43] Some interpreters have shown marginal interest in application, but application has hardly occupied a prominent place in the history of academic discussions.[44]

This neglect of application has produced serious ill-effects. Theological students often reduce interpretation to an academic exercise. Reading Old Testament stories without a keen interest in the Spirit's transforming influence can turn these texts into relics of ancient history. This is a common malady among new students of hermeneutics; they substitute technical, detached examination for personal encounter with God.

Ignoring application also leads to poor teaching and preaching. Many church leaders, especially recent seminary graduates, devote their pulpit time to the historical background of a passage, word studies in the original languages, and summaries of its original meaning. These matters are important, but often application is entirely omitted. "Exegesis is what I do best," they say. "I trust the Holy Spirit to apply the Word." Ignoring explicit application can devastate the church. Congregations are left spiritually malnourished and with little ability to see how Old Testament stories have any bearing on their lives. This practice results in the lifeless orthodoxy plaguing many evangelical churches.

In recent decades evangelical interpreters have challenged this orientation of academic hermeneutics. The challenge has risen primarily out of recent hermeneutical perspectives that stress the vital interconnections between ancient texts and modern readers.[45]

This outlook has been stressed most successfully by Hans Georg Gadamer, who closely followed the lead of Martin Heidegger (1889–

1976).[46] While we must take exception to many of his viewpoints, Gadamer pointed out that understanding a text is always an encounter of two worlds: the ancient world of the passage and the contemporary world of the reader. Since interpretation always involves an interaction between the present and the past, neither world may be neglected without skewing, even forfeiting, proper understanding.

In response to this challenge, evangelicals have begun to see more clearly that we must give attention not only to the Bible's original meaning, but also to application to the modern world. Several recent evangelical works have pointed in this direction. Among others, E.A. Nida, A.B. Mickelsen, H.A. Virkler, and W. Kaiser have devoted much more space than older works to matters of application.[47] Thiselton also reflects this shift as he summarizes the goal of hermeneutics. He says, "the goal of Biblical hermeneutics is to bring about an active and meaningful engagement between the interpreter and text, in such a way that the interpreter's own horizon is re-shaped and enlarged."[48] In a word, contemporary trends in hermeneutics not only take the reader into the world of the Bible; they also strive to bring the Bible into the world of the reader. We do not interpret Old Testament stories merely to acquaint ourselves with the original writer, document, and audience; we are also set on reforming the modern world in light of these Scriptures.

Obstacles to Application

While interpreters have become more interested in application, a number of obstacles hinder us from extending this interest to Old Testament narratives. Perhaps the greatest difficulty we face is an acute sense of the historical distance between ourselves and Old Testament stories. We are at ease in the Gospels; we are comfortable in the New Testament epistles; we are even familiar with the Psalms and Proverbs. But Old Testament stories often seem very strange to us.

Reading Old Testament stories is like visiting a foreign country. The people speak a different language; their customs are perplexing. The literary forms of these stories often seem alien to us. The book of Esther is like a short novel,[49] but books like Samuel and Kings seem to have little coherence by our modern standards. Moreover, many Old Testament narratives offend our modern sensitivities. Who doesn't at least hesitate when Solomon rids the royal court of his political opponents (1 Kings 2:13–46)?[50] Most of us find it difficult to accept God commanding the execution of innocent women and children (Joshua 6:17, 24; 8:24–26).[51]

If we look closely at many Old Testament stories, we feel like strangers in a foreign land.

Despite these difficulties, we must affirm that Old Testament stories are relevant for the church today. God's revelation was designed to be passed down from generation to generation. As the Lord told Abraham about the destruction of Sodom, He said, "I have chosen him, *so that he will direct his children and his household after him* to keep the way of the Lord by doing what is right and just, so that the Lord will bring about for Abraham what He has promised him" (Genesis 18:19, emphasis added). In Old Testament days, God did not reveal Himself merely for the people who first heard. He gave His Word to be declared to future generations. As we read in Deuteronomy 29:29: "The secret things belong to the Lord our God, but the things revealed belong to us *and to our children forever,* that we may follow all the words of this law" (emphasis added). From a Biblical point of view, revelation has multi-generational significance.

Old Testament writers depended heavily on contemporary application of previous revelation. The writer of Kings applied the theological perspectives of Deuteronomy to his day;[52] Daniel wrestled with the meaning of Jeremiah's prophecy of seventy years (Jeremiah 25:1, 29:10, Daniel 9:2–22); the Chronicler drew extensively from Samuel and Kings and also referred to Jeremiah (2 Chronicles 36:21); Nehemiah was deeply concerned with the relevance of Deuteronomy 30 for his ministry (Nehemiah 1:8–9). Throughout the Old Testament, Biblical figures had much more than antiquarian interests in previous revelation. They applied revelation from long ago to their own day.

Similarly, the New Testament quotes the Old Testament over 320 times and alludes to it even more.[53] This dependence on the Old Testament illustrates the importance of contemporary application. Jesus built His entire ministry on applying Scripture to His day, arguing tenaciously for the authority and applicability of the Old Testament.[54] In a similar way, Paul informed Timothy that the Old Testament Scriptures are for every believer: "All Scripture . . . is useful for teaching, rebuking, correcting and training in righteousness" (2 Timothy 3:16). He also told the Roman Christians: "For everything that was written in the past was written to teach us, so that through endurance and the encouragement of the Scriptures we might have hope" (Romans 15:4). To treat the Old Testament as a relic of the past with no significance for today contradicts the Bible's own treatment of the Old Testament. We must strive to know how these texts relate to the modern world.[55]

Relevance and Distance in Application

When we interpret Old Testament stories, we should always remember that we are not hearing texts spoken directly to us; we are *overhearing* stories told to others. This fact creates tension, pulling us back and forth between the relevance and distance of these stories.

This tension can be found in the words of Paul in 1 Corinthians 10:1–10. In the early verses of this chapter, Paul referred to a number of episodes in the wilderness wanderings recorded in Exodus and Numbers: Israel's grumbling at Meribah, their syncretistic practices, sexual immorality, and the plague of snakes. After recounting these events, he added, "These things happened to them as examples and were written down as warnings for us, on whom the fulfillment of the ages has come" (1 Corinthians 10:11). Paul's comment illustrates the tension in applying Old Testament stories. He argued that these stories applied to the Corinthians, but they applied indirectly. Paul affirmed in no uncertain terms that Old Testament stories were relevant for the Corinthians. "These things were written for us," he insisted. He could hardly have put the matter more forcefully. The stories of tragedy in the wilderness had a message pertinent for Christian readers who lived over a thousand years after the events.

Even so, Paul qualified the applicability of these texts by referring to the situation of the Corinthians. These stories were not just "for us." He added the qualification, "for us *upon whom the fulfillment of the ages has come*" (emphasis added). In these words Paul acknowledged that the Corinthians did not live in the days of the Old Testament. They lived after the death and resurrection of Christ. The Corinthians stood in a different place in the history of redemption. While these Old Testament stories applied, the Corinthians had to read them not as the original recipients, but as Christians living in the eschatological age.[56] From Paul's perspective we have to keep in mind both the relevance and distance of Old Testament stories.

The tension between relevance and distance is not always pronounced. On a rudimentary level, we may not feel far from Old Testament stories. When we read that "the Israelites settled in Egypt" (Genesis 47:27a), we do not sense too much distance from the original setting. If we have some acquaintance with Egyptian geography and living conditions in ancient times, our understanding is very similar to that of the original audience. Moreover, when Moses replied sarcastically to Pharaoh, "Just as you say . . . I will never appear before you again" (Exodus 10:29), few of us have much problem getting the point. We chuckle much like the original audience must have. Even some theological perspectives easily apply to our day. Joseph's reply to his brothers speaks clearly: "You intended to harm me, but God intended it for good" (Genesis 50:20). We hear these words of confidence in God's providence much like the original audience did.

But many times tension is unavoidable. The complexities of applying Old Testament stories become pronounced when we move beyond the basics. For instance, how are we to apply a book like Kings, written to help the exiles maintain a hope of return, to modern Christians in the United States who have never been exiled? How do we take the book of Deuteronomy, written for Israelites about to make war in Canaan, and apply it to Christians involved in modern international politics? How should we appropriate Israel's celebration at the Red Sea when our "struggle is not against flesh and blood" (Ephesians 6:12)? Even if we have confidence that we understand the original meaning, it is difficult to extend that meaning into our world. We know these stories have something to say to us, but we know just as plainly that we live in a different world.

Application of Old Testament narratives involves building bridges from the ancient world to our day; we seek to span the gulf between ourselves and the Bible. On one side of the historical gulf, we carefully investigate Scripture. We do our best to understand Old Testament stories in terms of their original settings. On the other side, we become aware of our own situation. We learn of needs and opportunities for the Word today. At times bridging the gap will be easy, at other times extremely difficult.

To complete our hermeneutical project, we must focus on how texts apply today. In the chapters that follow, we will pursue a number of ways we may succeed in applying Old Testament narratives.

Conclusion

We began this chapter saying that interpreting Old Testament stories is like working on an archaeological dig. We prepare, work at the site, and bring our discoveries home. Following this analogy we will pursue our study of Old Testament narratives in three major parts. In chapters 1–4 we will explore how the Spirit prepares us to read Old Testament narratives. In chapters 5–12 we will learn how to investigate Old Testament stories in their ancient contexts. Finally, in chapters 13–16 we will find ways to apply Old Testament narratives to modern life. As we examine each area in detail, we will move forward in our understanding of Old Testament stories.

Review Questions

1. Define hermeneutics. What are the three hermeneutical processes which we will follow in this study?
2. Discuss the importance of dependence on the Spirit and human effort in hermeneutical preparation. How are these two activities interdependent?
3. Why has traditional evangelical hermeneutics been called "grammatico-historical exegesis?" Why is this method crucial to responsible interpretation?
4. How do academic interpreters often ignore application? What are the basic issues involved in applying Old Testament stories to the modern world?

Study Exercises

1. Glance at two books on the subject of Biblical exegesis. List the items they consider in hermeneutical preparation. Do you agree? How may the list be expanded? Why?
2. Quickly make a list of 10 issues you think should be pursued in the interpretation of the Tower of Babel story (Genesis 11:1–9). Review your list and divide the items between the "Ancient World" and "Modern World." Which side do you tend to stress? Why? How can you balance your questions more evenly between the ancient world and the modern world?
3. Take a look at three commentaries on Genesis 12:10–20 and answer the following questions: Are the commentaries concerned primarily with the ancient world or with the modern world? How does the central concern of the interpreter determine the kind of findings which are made in the passage? What sorts of questions would you add to broaden the scope of the interpretation?

PART I

PREPARING FOR OLD TESTAMENT NARRATIVES

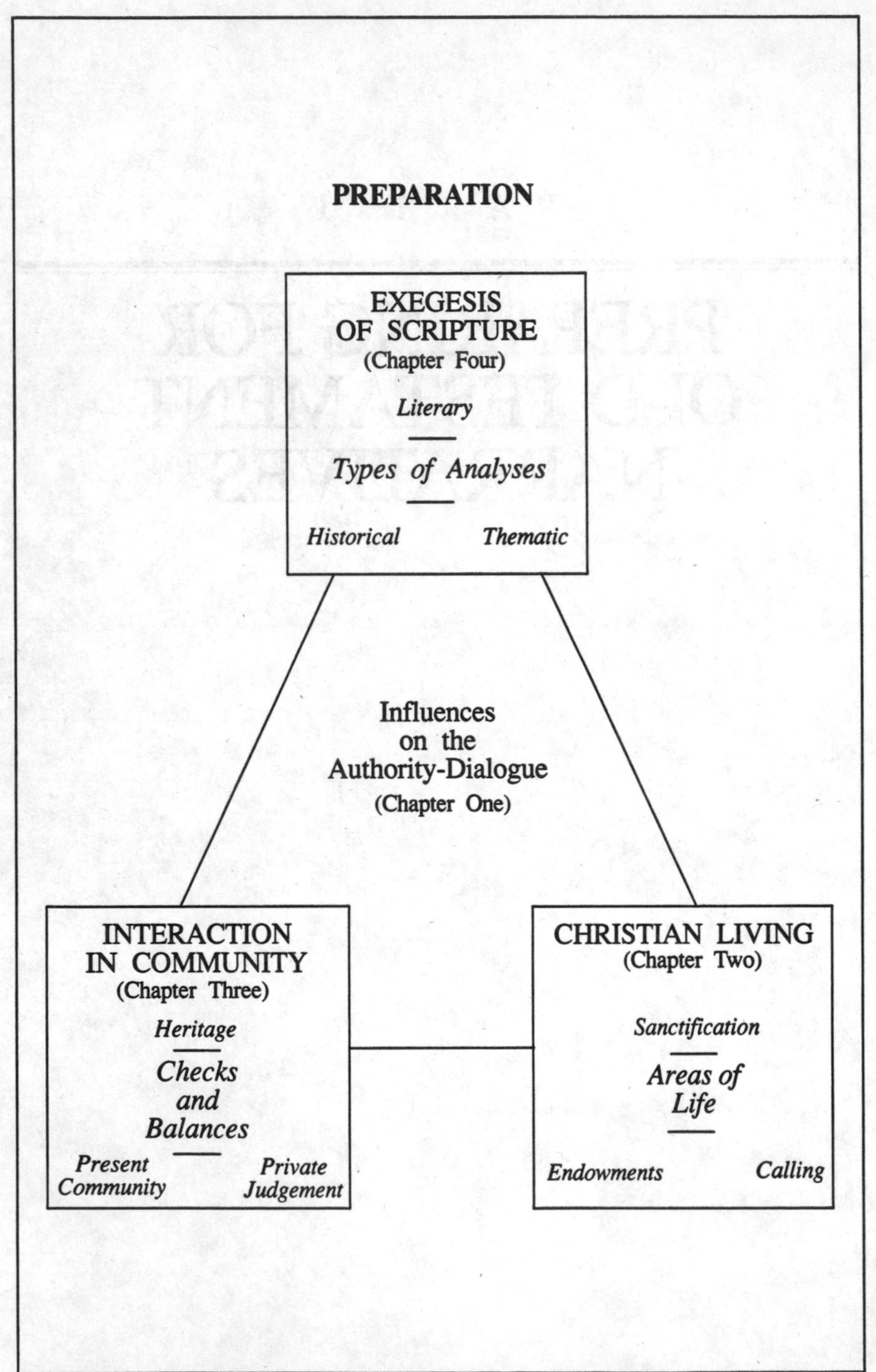

Fig. 2: Schema of Part I: Preparation

SYNOPSIS

In the first part of our study, we will look in some detail at the first hermeneutical process: preparation for reading Old Testament narratives (see figure 2). The Holy Spirit empowers us to interpret, but He uses many means to equip us. In these chapters we will examine some of the main ways in which the Spirit prepares us for interpretation.

In chapter 1 we will see that preparation involves becoming self-conscious of the predispositions we bring to the interpretative enterprise. Understanding Old Testament narratives always involves the interaction of our commitments, beliefs, and experiences with the authoritative presentation of the text. We come to Scriptures with presuppositions, but we also come ready to listen. We will speak of this interaction between ourselves and the text as an Authority-Dialogue.

Chapter 2 deals with the influence of individual Christian living on the Authority-Dialogue. Our sanctification, endowments, and sense of calling affect the way we interpret Old Testament stories. As the Spirit works in these areas of our lives, we are better equipped to understand as we ought.

Chapter 3 explores the influence of interaction in community. Preparation for interpretation also involves learning from others. Within the Christian community, the Spirit has given us a system of checks and balances. We pursue the interpretation of Old Testament narratives while interacting on the levels of our Christian heritage, present community, and private judgment.

Chapter 4 deals with a third major influence on the Authority-Dialogue: our exegesis of Scripture. We will see that the Spirit has led His people to approach Old Testament narratives in three basic ways. We look for themes that are of interest to us; we explore the historical events behind the stories; we treat the passages as literary works. As we become better acquainted with the benefits and limitations of these approaches, we will be equipped to use them in our investigation of Old Testament narratives.

This portion of our study is preliminary to other aspects of interpretation, but it is no less important. The matters covered in this section continually inform the discussions of later chapters on investigating and applying Old Testament stories.

1

ORIENTATION FOR PREPARATION

I didn't expect him to call on me! After all, he was the teacher; I was just a student. "You mean you didn't come prepared to discuss this material?" the professor asked. I sheepishly nodded my head. "At this school we expect you to be ready to contribute to classroom discussion. You don't expect me to do all the talking do you? Tomorrow *you* will lead the class."

To be frank, I did expect him to do the talking. I liked sitting back and taking notes. Classes were supposed to be professorial monologues, not teacher-student dialogues. But now I was in a real mess; I had to do *all* the talking the next day!

When you go to class, it's important to know who's going to talk. It makes a lot of difference in how you prepare. If the teacher is going to lecture, you come to listen; if you are going to lead the class, you get ready to speak. If you are going to be in a dialogue, you'd better be prepared to talk *and* listen.

The same issues confront us when we prepare to interpret. Is reading Old Testament stories like a student presentation in which we do all the speaking? Is it like a lecture in which we simply listen to the text? Or is it more like a classroom discussion where both we and Scripture make contributions to the final outcome? Our answers to these questions will affect our preparation for reading Old Testament stories.

In recent years all three viewpoints have been adopted. Some interpreters emphasize the reader's contribution; others stress the text; still others seek to give more balanced emphasis. We will speak of these viewpoints as the *subjective model*, the *objective model*, and the *authority-dialogue model* (see figure 3).

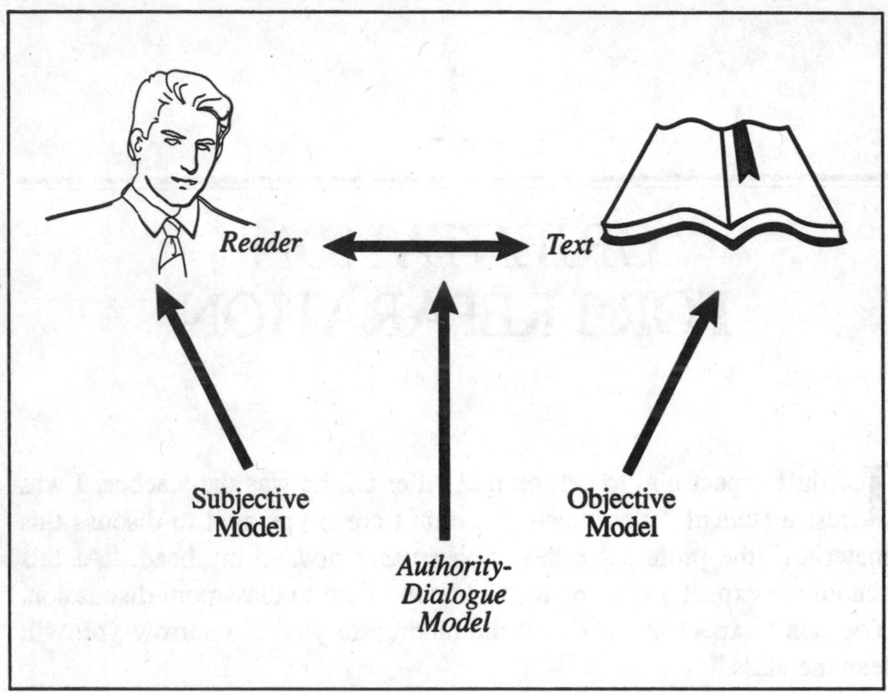

Fig. 3: Different Orientations Toward Preparation

The Subjective Model

"Beauty is in the eye of the beholder." Maybe so, but what is beautiful to one person may be plain, even ugly, to another. One popular hermeneutical model follows a similar motto: "*Meaning* is in the eye of the beholder." According to this view, understanding Old Testament stories is largely subjective—the interpreter's own viewpoint and life experience determines the meaning of Scripture.

This tendency is especially common in informal settings. I remember visiting a Bible study class once in which the leader read the Scripture and asked, "What does this passage mean to you?" Several initial observations seemed straightforward, but as we continued, it seemed that everyone had a different opinion of the passage's meaning. With a sigh of resignation, the leader concluded, "Well, I guess that goes to show you that we all interpret the Bible the way we want to." That was as far as we could go. Class dismissed.

Too often Christians read Old Testament stories as if they were empty canisters just waiting to be filled with meaning. We simply pour in our theological convictions. We shrug our shoulders and concede that these texts can mean just about anything we want them to mean.

Even formal hermeneutics has fallen prey to subjectivism. Serious scholars affirm that the text places some limits on interpretation. Even so, many formal approaches to hermeneutics find the primary locus of meaning in the reader's predispositions rather than in the objective, authoritative text. To one degree or another, interpretation has come to be viewed as a process of reading in terms of our subjective individual outlooks.

Philosophical Background

The philosophical background of subjectivity in Biblical hermeneutics is complex. Many aspects can be traced to the views of Immanuel Kant (1724–1804).[1] Kant opposed the radical skepticism of David Hume (1711–1776), who challenged the Enlightenment assumption that true knowledge of the world could be discovered through rational investigation. Hume doubted that the external world was ordered in ways that corresponded to the rational structures of the human mind. Kant could not ignore the wedge Hume and others had driven between the external world and the internal world of our mental conceptions.[2] Therefore, Kant postulated that knowledge always involves conceptualization of the world according to categories which the human mind brings to experience.[3] We look at the world through a mental grid. Our minds operate with certain categories through which we understand the world.[4]

From this point of view, knowledge itself does not entail simple apprehension of objective reality. We cannot know a *Ding an sich* (thing in itself); knowledge always involves significant interaction between external realities and our internal processing.

There is at least a kernel of truth in Kant's outlook. Many aspects of ordinary experience confirm it. For example, when you read this page what do you see? Photons bouncing off the page onto the rods and cones of your retina which send electrical impulses down the optical nerve to the brain (although that in itself would be a conceptualization in Kant's outlook)? Of course not! You see letters, words, and sentences. You even understand something of the thought patterns I am experiencing as I write. As a reader of English, you categorize what you see according to certain linguistic rules you have adopted. Moreover, your understanding of this page differs from that of a preliterate child or illiterate adult. Their mental categories are different, so their knowledge of the page is different.

Education, culture, psychological dispositions, and countless other factors influence the way we conceive the world. A measure of subjectivity in knowledge is unavoidable.[5]

These epistemological outlooks have highly influenced the interpretation of language and literature. Building on Kant through the work of such figures as Schleiermacher (1768–1834), Dilthey (1833–1911), and Husserl (1859–1938), recent philosophical hermeneutics has emphasized the importance of the reader's preconceptions in interpretation.[6]

In our century Martin Heidegger (1889–1976) brought the influence of preconceptions to the foreground of interpretation. In his early work *Being and Time,* Heidegger insisted that prior experiences in the web of life deeply affect our interpretation of life. He postulated, "Whenever something is interpreted as something, the interpretation will be founded essentially upon fore-having, fore-sight, and fore-conception. An interpretation is never a presuppositionless apprehending of something presented to us."[7]

Perhaps the most influential figure in this line of philosophical hermeneutics is Hans Georg Gadamer, who agreed with many of Heidegger's outlooks and also stressed the importance of the reader's input.[8] In *Truth and Method*, he rejected the Enlightenment's quest for rational objectivity as a "prejudice against prejudice."[9] In his view the Enlightenment's attempt to get rid of preconceptions was actually a prejudice in favor of poorly conceived rationalistic preconceptions. He argued that preconceptions in hermeneutics are not only inescapable but essential for understanding.[10]

The impact of these hermeneutical views has been felt in many ways. For instance, the growing literary school known as "Reader-Response Criticism" has turned attention to the reader as the main concern in interpretation.[11] From this viewpoint the locus of meaning lies less in the ancient writer or document (as in grammatico-historical methods) than in the understanding processes of the reader.[12]

Extremes in Subjectivism

While asserting a constant subjective element, Heidegger and Gadamer cautioned against arbitrary interpretation. Although interpretation rests on preconceptions, a reader should not haphazardly impose ideas onto a text. Gadamer sounded a stern warning: "All correct interpretation must be on guard against arbitrary fancies and the limitations imposed by imperceptible habits of thought and direct its gaze 'on the things themselves' (which, in the case of the literary critic, are meaningful texts)."[13]

Sadly, many followers of Heidegger and Gadamer have overemphasized the role of preconceptions and consequently have spawned a growing tendency toward extreme subjectivism in Biblical interpretation.

Several recent theological movements self-consciously read Old Testament narratives with a subjective model. They assume that the objective meaning of these texts, if it exists at all, is unattainable. Rather than submitting themselves to these passages, they boldly construe the texts in terms of their own ideals.

Some Liberation theologians openly admit that they emphasize the subjective side of interpretation.[14] On occasion, Liberationists have attempted to ground their views in more objective approaches, but the majority rely heavily on the importance of preconceptions to justify their approaches and conclusions. For example, Croatto states his approval of subjectivity with alarming clarity: "Exegesis is eisegesis, and anybody who claims to be doing only the former is, wittingly or unwittingly, engaged in ideological subterfuge."[15] Croatto does not deny a place for historical-critical analysis. He attempts to orient interpretation toward the text, but only by noting the manifold possible meanings which texts offer "through the unfolding of a surplus-of-meaning disclosed by a new question addressed to the text."[16]

Liberationists consciously select certain passages as normative and construe them in terms of Marxist ideology. The stories of the Exodus from Egypt lose their original significance and become stories of Marxist class struggle;[17] the narratives of conquest in Joshua are interpreted as proletarian revolution.[18] It comes as no surprise, then, that many others accuse Liberationists of using the Bible simply as a tool of their ideology.[19]

Similarly, many Feminist and Gay Liberation theologians also justify their exegetical conclusions by pointing to inevitable subjectivity in interpretation. They intentionally pick one part of Scripture over another according to the canons of liberation.[20] As Elizabeth Fiorenza has said, "Only the nonsexist and nonandrocentric traditions of the Bible . . . have the theological authority of revelation."[21]

When precommitments dominate hermeneutical discussions in these ways, radical forms of subjectivism follow. In fact, it is not long before interpretation becomes more a chance to expound our own beliefs rather than an opportunity to expound the text.

Descriptive Emphasis

How do these views affect hermeneutics? What difference does subjectivism make? Put simply, if we adopt a subjective model, we have little need to concentrate on rules for proper interpretation because our understanding stems mostly from the outlooks we bring to the text. Therefore, subjectivists concentrate more on describing what happens as people read texts, rather than prescribing how they should read. They are more concerned with the ways personal engagement, religious and philosophical commitments, and cultural traditions influence Biblical interpretation.

A few years ago I had the opportunity to play touch football with a group of Americans and Europeans. Although we had agreed to play football, we soon learned that the European and American conceptions of football are completely different. The biggest problem we had that afternoon was deciding whose rules to follow. Neither group wanted to impose their rules on the other. Who was to say that one way was better than the other? It was impossible to decide on the right set of rules.

Many interpreters who tend toward subjectivism think of rules for interpretation in much the same way. As far as they are concerned, exegetical methods are fundamentally conventional. One group follows one standard, and another group follows another. Westerners interpret in one way, Easterners in another; the powerful follow one set of rules, the oppressed another; men read the Bible with certain outlooks, women with others. In the end there is no way of deciding that one approach is better than another.

Gadamer, for instance, insisted that his hermeneutical reflections were not a new method.[22] He suspected that rules for interpretation merely attempted to reach the unattainable goal of detached, objective knowledge; so he focused his efforts on describing *how* interpretation occurs. We could argue that Gadamer's rhetoric against method is a method itself, but we would miss his basic purpose—to describe what happens as we read.

Liberationists often come near to prescribing a methodology for interpretation when they speak of the importance of *praxis,* or the involvement in the struggle against oppression. At times hermeneutical rules can be found in many of their discussions.[23] Even so, these directions are not usually cast in terms of right or wrong; they primarily point out how Scripture *may* be read by those who are committed to certain ideologies.

While most evangelicals reject extreme subjectivity in hermeneutics, we must be careful not to throw out the insights that this orientation offers. Perhaps more than anything else, the subjective model of hermeneutics has pointed out that preconceptions always influence our interpretation of Old Testament stories.[24] As we realize the impact of our presuppositions, we can be critical of them and learn to look at Scripture from a variety of perspectives.

Nevertheless, we must not be satisfied merely to learn what happens when we interpret Scripture; we must also learn from it how we *should* interpret Scripture. This need for prescriptive preparation brings us to a second major hermeneutical model.

The Objective Model

"Let the facts speak for themselves." These words urge us to make judgments on the basis of objective facts, rather than subjective opinion. As Sergeant Friday used to say, "Just the facts, Ma'am. Just the facts."

A similar desire for objectivity has inspired a prominent model for Biblical interpretation through the centuries: "Let the *Scriptures* speak for themselves." This hermeneutical model turns away from subjectivity to objective knowledge of the text.

Objectivism takes many shapes in informal hermeneutics. Lay people often assume that their interpretations are simply obvious facts. "All you have to do is to be objective and read what the passage says," we insist. "Then you will agree with me."

In formal hermeneutics, objectivism is the tendency to follow rigorous methods of empirical science as we analyze Scripture. Detached observation, hypotheses, and testing of hypotheses form the basis of academic hermeneutics in the English-speaking world. Interpreters try to determine and express exegetical conclusions with scientific precision and detached objectivity.

In one way or another, hermeneutical objectivism treats interpretation as a process of stripping away preconceptions and applying carefully conceived techniques, so that texts may make their own impression on us. The goal is for meaning to flow from the passage to an unbiased, receptive reader.

Philosophical Background

This hermeneutical tendency has a complex philosophical development. Recently, R. Lundin has pointed to several ties to the philosophical views of René Descartes (1596–1650), Francis Bacon (1561–1626), and Thomas Reid (1710–1796).[25]

Descartes began his inquiry into human knowledge by attempting to strip away all beliefs and opinions to base his knowledge on a self-evident, objective epistemic foundation.[26] His desire to build knowledge on a rational foundation was the cornerstone of the Enlightenment.[27] By ridding ourselves of prejudices in pursuit of objective, rational certainty, human beings could gain true knowledge of themselves and the world.

Hermeneutical objectivism has also been influenced by Francis Bacon's scientific procedure. In Bacon's conception the scientific method involved three "Tables of Investigation": 1) gathering all known examples of phenomena with similar characteristics, 2) observing phenomena that contrast in some way, and 3) comparing these observations.[28] Through these scientific means, an observer could study the data of the world without allowing biases to shape his or her conclusions.

After the Enlightenment the tendency toward objectivism was popularized in Britain and the United States through the Common Sense Realism of Thomas Reid (1710–1796).[29] Scottish Common Sense Realism continued the belief that human observers are capable of objective knowledge of the world. As Lundin comments: "As an epistemological theory Common Sense Realism . . . claimed that the human mind can know some things with certainty and without need of an outside authority. . . . In short, the basic laws governing moral and physical life can be discerned by all sincere, right-thinking men and women."[30]

Like Kant, Reid recognized that we understand the world through a conceptual grid. Yet he asserted that God had constituted the human mind in a way that corresponds to the objective world.[31] As we use our senses and rational capacities carefully, we know the real world. As far as Reid was concerned, the philosophical questions raised against these assumptions were simply denying the first and universal principles of common sense.[32]

Most of us recognize at least an element of truth in these philosophical traditions. We usually trust our senses to give us reliable knowledge. We believe our ability to reason will get us through the day. On the whole we think that we have experienced and understood the real, objective world.

Most Bible interpreters in the English-speaking world have applied this kind of thinking to Biblical hermeneutics, modeling their interpretations on rational-scientific objectivism. We strip away misconceptions and apply scientific procedures, so we can see Scriptures as they really are. From left to right on the theological spectrum, interpreters assume that proper methods can unveil the objective meaning of a text.

This tendency toward objectivism has especially influenced evangelical hermeneutics. In older works a generic objectivism prevails with little apparent self-consciousness.[33] This quest for objectivity through the grammatico-historical method prompted "a kind of *'tabula rasa'* approach to exegesis."[34]

The same tendency continues today. Recent studies on the role of preconceptions in hermeneutics have created more sensitivity to the subjective element. No responsible interpreter thinks that every vestige of subjectivity can be eliminated. Yet evangelicals often give little more than lip service to this side of interpretation, mostly emphasizing the objective text as the locus of meaning.

Prescriptive Emphasis

Objectivism leads to a predictable emphasis. Whereas subjectivism describes what happens when we interpret, objectivism *prescribes* the way in which we should read Scripture.

A survey of evangelical works on hermeneutics demonstrates this propensity toward rules for interpretation. Consider a couple of titles: *Principles of Biblical Interpretation* (Berkhof) and *The Science of Biblical Hermeneutics* (Chafer).[35] Sometimes we are warned against reducing interpretation to a science,[36] but the heartbeat of evangelical hermeneutics has been developing rules and guidelines which assure us of arriving at true understanding.[37]

Exegetical rules are valuable in preparing to read Old Testament narratives. We make many mistakes that good methodology can correct. But a focus on hermeneutical rules without careful consideration of the actual processes of interpretation can be misleading.

For example, a common interpretative principle is that the stories of Scripture must be evaluated in terms of the commands and doctrinal teachings of the Bible. No doubt this rule helps us look at one passage in light of others, but it presents only one side of the coin. If we look at what we actually do as we interpret narratives, we can see that our emphasis on didactic materials is out of balance. Narratives can help us understand the didactic portions of Scripture as well. For instance, Jesus understood the Sabbath regulations in the light of a story about David (Mark 2:23–27). We understand stealing, adultery, killing, and bearing false witness through stories involving these sins. In a word, narratives and doctrinal materials inform each other. Any hermeneutical principle that denies this reciprocity is abstract and misleading.

So it is that prescriptive preparation is valuable, if it is not divorced from thorough description. What we *should do* must always be set within the context of what we *in fact do*.

The Authority-Dialogue Model

In this study we will attempt to avoid the pitfalls of subjectivism and objectivism by adopting the "Authority-Dialogue" model. This model will steer us away from relativism and rationalism in interpretation.

Dialogue has been used as a hermeneutical model by a number of writers. Heidegger and Gadamer, who tend toward subjectivism, popularized the dialogical approach to interpretation. They described the reader and the text as involved in conversational give-and-take.[38] While this model is helpful in many ways, it has limited application for evangelicals. When we speak of interpretation as a dialogue, we must also keep in mind the doctrine of Biblical authority.

Dialogue with an Authority

In everyday life we converse with people under our authority, with peers, and with people who have authority over us. These conversations take on very different characteristics depending on our relationship with the other person. For instance, how we feel about the other person will greatly influence the dialogue. The tone and content of a conversation with a preschooler on medical questions will be different from talking with a doctor. We speak differently with a friend about legal questions than we do with a lawyer.

In line with historical Protestant orthodoxy, evangelicals affirm the unquestionable authority of Scripture in all matters of faith and life.[39] We are committed to the principle of authority that Biblical writers themselves affirmed.[40] This conviction deeply influences how we dialogue with Old Testament narratives.

Dialogues with authorities contain at least two common elements. On one hand, we come with our own expectations and questions that prepare us for meaningful dialogue. On the other hand, we come fully yearning for understanding beyond our own ideas.

Once when I was trying to find my way to a small town in rural Mississippi, I missed a turn and could not find my way back. After some time I came across a service station. "They'll know where it is!" I thought. I pulled over and went inside. "Can you tell me how to get to Duck Hill?" I asked. The attendant gave me directions. "Let me see if I got this right," I responded. "I go how far? I turn where?" Finally, after drawing a map, the attendant sent me on my way.

I pulled into that station with many assumptions about myself, my situation, and the station attendant: that I had taken the wrong turn, that the station attendant spoke English and could help me, that there was a way to get back to my destination. But even though I brought these and other ideas to the conversation, I needed more information. The attendant knew things I didn't know, and if I was going to find my way, I needed to understand his directions. So I listened to his words, watched his hands, and read his map. I even repeated his instructions to make sure I grasped them.

Likewise, when we dialogue with Old Testament narratives, we come with so many expectations and assumptions we cannot even list them all. We assume, for example, that Old Testament stories can be understood to some extent and that they have something valuable to say to us. From our past experiences, we even have ideas of what the passages will say. Without these and other preconceptions, we would not be able to enter a fruitful dialogue and begin interpretation.

Even so, the Old Testament narratives themselves are our unquestionable authority. We must not read our preconceptions into them; rather we must hear what *they* have to say. We are eager to see how they can help us. Because these stories are our inerrant and infallible rule, we use every tool available to help us understand what the texts themselves say.

In many ways only the model of an authority-dialogue protects us from treating Scripture and its readers as peers. Subjectivism tends to make us equal with Scripture by bringing the text down to our level. We critique the Bible as much as it critiques us. Objectivism tends to make us peers with Scripture by raising our understanding to the level of Scripture itself. Our interpretations are identified with the teaching of the text. Only the authority-dialogue keeps the Bible supreme and the reader a servant of the text.

The authority-dialogue model stands in contrast to both subjective and objective tendencies. In contrast to objectivism, it recognizes the constant influence of preconceptions on interpretation. Hermeneutics is fundamentally a dialogue in which we pose questions and make initial proposals. In contrast to subjectivism, the authority-dialogue model recognizes the importance of having methods that allow us to hear Old Testament stories speak authoritatively to our lives. Hermeneutics is a dialogue, but it is a dialogue with an *absolute authority*. It will help to look in detail at both of these contrasts (see figure 4).

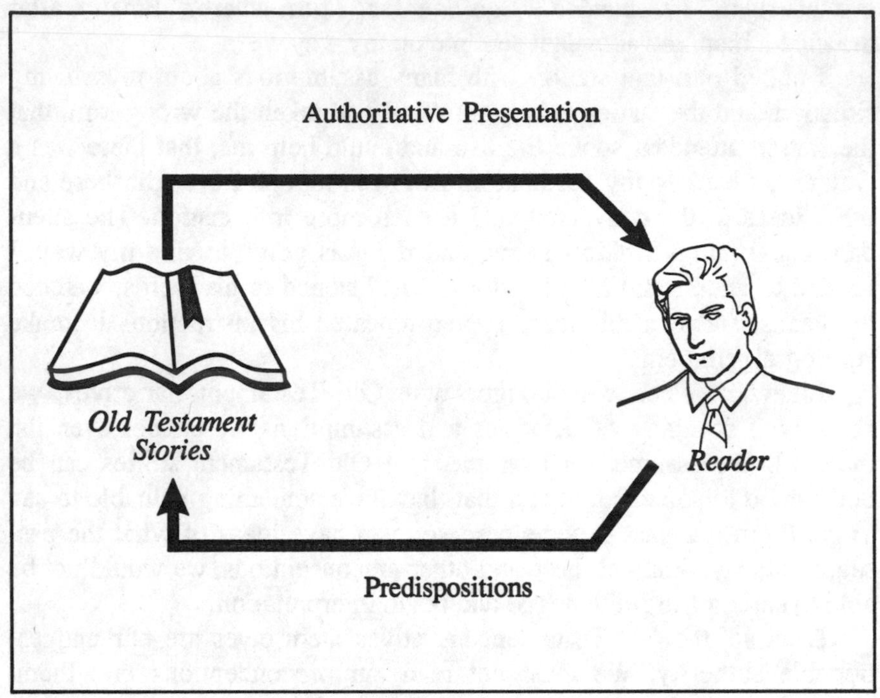

Fig. 4: Priorities in the Authority-Dialogue Model

Dangers in Objectivism

The goal of objectivity sounds attractive: to understand Old Testament stories *as they are*. No doubt we should try to overcome barriers to legitimate understanding, but, even so, serious problems lurk behind this attempt to rid ourselves of preconceptions.

I once visited an interdenominational Bible study led by a young man who professed, "No confession but the Bible, no creed but Christ." He took pride in the fact that he never used a commentary. "I get my messages straight from the Bible," he said. Sure of his own objectivity, he went on to explain what he felt was the true meaning of the passage. According to him we were merely listening to Scripture.

Toward the end of the study, however, a young woman from a different church background interrupted, "You're not teaching the Bible! You're teaching your denominational views!" She then proceeded to tell the group what the text really meant. As they argued back and forth, it was clear that neither person was objective at all. They both read the passage in the light of their denominational theology!

Every believer has experienced the impact of preconceptions in personal Bible reading. Think about your favorite verse. How many times have you read or recited it? Isn't it fascinating that we can read a verse, even memorize it, and still discover new insights nearly every time we come across it? It's remarkable how much more we find in passages when we return to them after a period of years. What makes the difference? The verse itself hasn't changed. Often our exegetical techniques haven't changed significantly. *We* are the variable that modifies our understanding. In His wise providence, God so orders our lives that many of our experiences, questions, and assumptions toward the text vary, creating remarkable differences in the way we understand even familiar passages.

These kinds of experiences should convince us that our interpretation of Old Testament narratives will always be influenced by our preconceptions. But sadly, evangelicals who lean toward objectivism often have the mistaken notion that they can simply read the Bible as it is. They blur the distinction between the Bible and their interpretation of the Bible.

This problem also comes up in academic hermeneutics. In contrast to their informal counterparts, formal interpreters usually admit that complete objectivity is unattainable. Yet, in practice, scholarly interpreters often overlook how much their predispositions influence their understanding. They may carefully scrutinize a few blatant misconceptions, but after some initial self-reflection, they too act as if their preconceptions are insignificant. They assume that readers are largely unbiased so long as they follow well-conceived methods. As a result they often treat their exegetical conclusions as objective statements of fact.

Ironically, this outlook often results in a backhanded subjectivism in which we allow unnoticed prejudices to ride roughshod over interpretation. Without realizing it, we read our own ideas into the text. So far as our constantly changing predispositions remain in the background of our unconscious, they remain misleading and dangerous. Our interpretations are inescapably affected by what we bring to the text.

Recent philosophical hermeneutics have influenced more evangelicals to begin questioning the objective model. The notion that readers may harness all of their influential prejudices through careful methodology has increasingly come under scrutiny.[41] In the future we will see even more distance between evangelical hermeneutics and objectivism.

Dangers in Subjectivism

The authority-dialogue model also stands apart from hermeneutical subjectivism. One of the most important differences lies in the evaluation of exegetical methods.

As we have seen, interpreters who emphasize the subjective side of hermeneutics shy away from prescribing rules for interpretation. They are suspicious of the traditional emphasis on rules, which give the impression that it is possible to set aside prejudices. But the authority-dialogue model stands in opposition to this outlook. Though exegetical methods are always influenced by our backgrounds, we are not free to approach Old Testament narratives any way we want. Because these texts are our authority, we must try to use interpretative methods that allow the texts to communicate their message to us.

Once again the issue of authority is central. In many circles where subjectivism rules, Scripture and readers are considered equals. Consequently, we find little reason for bringing our interpretative methods into submission to the text. Interpreters have every right to make the Old Testament narratives play by their rules.

In contrast, evangelicals view readers as subordinate to Old Testament stories, affirming the responsibility to interpret in compliance with the phenomena of these texts. Some methods are indeed better than others. In fact, some exegetical procedures are out of accord with Old Testament narratives. There is a definite "ethic" to evangelical hermeneutics.[42] We have not come to make Old Testament stories dance to our music; we have come to dance to their melody.

Seeking to submit ourselves to Scripture, we are concerned not only with arriving at an understanding from a particular viewpoint—whether tradition (Gadamer), some sort of life-engagement (Heidegger), or a socio-political ideology (Liberationists)—but we want our understanding to be appropriate for the way the stories of the Old Testament present themselves.

How do we decide which methods to use? On a basic level, many procedures are not difficult to discern. Even a cursory acquaintance with Scripture gives some guidelines. For example, no one would deny that Old Testament stories have literary qualities. To follow methods that ignore these features will muffle the voice of Scripture. Old Testament narratives were written with certain grammatical conventions; interpretation must observe these conventions. These texts are ancient documents; they must be handled as ancient books. To look at them as modern writings is to misconstrue them. The list of such basic rules of interpretation goes on and on. As Tracy has said, "Every text, after all, is a structured whole. Every subject matter comes to us with a claim to serious attention in and through its form and structure."[43]

Nevertheless, once we move beyond these basic considerations, it becomes plain that our exegetical techniques need to follow the framework of the authority-dialogue. We begin with methodological assumptions from our backgrounds and modify them as we interact with Scripture.

How do we decide the best way to understand someone in an ordinary conversation? From early childhood our conversational experiences begin to teach us many things about understanding other people. We begin our communications with a host of assumptions, but we also adjust our methods during the conversation. Someone may speak with a heavy accent, use sign language, or even seem totally incoherent. We accommodate ourselves to each situation as best we can. We ask questions, we make them repeat themselves, and we use every means available to adjust our techniques. As we continue in the dialogue, we refine our approach to match the presentation of the ones with whom we speak.

In a similar way, methods for interpreting Old Testament stories evolve through interaction with these texts. As Riceour put it, methodological guidelines for explanation (*Erklärung*) are helpful when we remember that they are a part of the process of understanding (*Verstehen*).[44] All attempts to establish and improve hermeneutical procedures are a part of our ongoing dialogue with Old Testament stories. Interpretative rules are not objective, fixed items. On the contrary, they are subject to improvement as our awareness of texts improves.

In contrast with tendencies toward subjectivism, the authority-dialogue model holds that we must work hard at developing methods to guide us toward legitimate understanding. Yet we must be willing to refine our methods as we become more familiar with Old Testament narratives.

Hermeneutical Progress

But doesn't the authority-dialogue model still leave us in a vicious circle? What assurance do we have that we can progress in our understanding when we develop methods and conclusions in the context of dialogue?

It is common to describe the hermeneutical process as a "hermeneutical circle," a constant cycle back and forth between the reader and the text.[45] As many have suggested, however, this term is unfortunate.[46] I prefer to think of interpretation as a "hermeneutical spiral."[47] This model recognizes the dialogical relationship between Scripture and its readers, but it also indicates that there is a forward movement of the dialogue toward the goal of fuller understanding.

What generates this forward spiraling toward better understanding? As we saw in the preceding chapter, hermeneutical progress ultimately rests in the hands of the Holy Spirit. Only His illumination can move us toward truth. But recent studies have pointed out that the Spirit uses many different resources to help us in this process.

Before Schleiermacher (1768–1834)[48] it had become common to speak of specialized hermeneutics for theology, literature, and law.[49] These were viewed as separate disciplines with their own interpretative procedures. Schleiermacher, however, argued that a common "art of understanding" (*Kunst des Verstehens*) operated for all language. Schleiermacher believed that the same general process of human understanding lies behind all specializations. One effect of this view has been to set Biblical interpretation against the backdrop of human knowledge in a variety of disciplines.[50]

In line with these modern interests, evangelicals must realize that Old Testament interpretation is influenced by nearly every discipline ranging from the physical sciences to the humanities.[51] Linguistics, literature, philosophy, psychology, sociology, anthropology, archaeology—to name only a few more prominent fields—open the way for progress in interpretation.

Inevitably, some evangelicals will feel uncomfortable with depending on resources outside of the Bible. Isn't it good enough just to read the Bible? Doesn't depending on other disciplines contradict belief in "Scripture interpreting Scripture" (*Sacra Scriptura sui ipsius interpres*)?[52]

On the contrary, Scripture interpreting Scripture has to do with the notion of infallible interpretation. Over against church tradition and private judgment, the Reformers insisted that the only unquestionable guide for interpretation is the Bible itself.[53] Evangelical circles continue to acknowledge this basic principle.[54] The Bible is its best interpreter, and the Holy Spirit uses Scripture to help us interpret Scripture. This formula, however, does not rule out the contribution of other disciplines.

Relying on other resources fits well with belief in the interdependence of special and general revelation. Evangelicals affirm the longstanding Christian view that God has revealed Himself through Scripture (special revelation) and in all of creation (general revelation).[55] These two sources of revelation work with each other and not against each other.[56]

Usually evangelicals think of the relationship between special and general revelation in only one direction. If we want insight into an aspect of life, we look at it through the Bible. Whatever the particular issue, the Bible is our guide to proper understanding. Historically, Protestants have emphasized Scripture as the spectacles through which we correctly understand general revelation.[57]

But it works the other way as well; general revelation helps us understand special revelation. What the Spirit teaches us from resources outside the Bible also equips us to interpret Scripture.[58]

The struggle between Galileo (1564–1642) and church authorities illustrates the importance of extra-Biblical resources for interpretation.[59] The church took Joshua 10:13 ("so the sun stood still") to mean that the sun stopped revolving around the earth for a time. This interpretation seemed rather obvious in that day. Today, however, scientific investigations have established that day and night are caused by the earth spinning on its axis. Consequently, most modern evangelicals understand this passage differently from their historical counterparts. We know that daylight was miraculously extended for Joshua, but we also know that the halting of the sun was an appearance relative to Joshua's position on earth. We now consider Joshua 10:13 as ordinary, non-scientific language much like we still speak of "sunrise" and "sunset."[60] Improved awareness of general revelation has not caused us to reject Scripture, but it has helped us adjust our interpretation of Scripture. In this case and many others, the Holy Spirit has used general revelation to enhance our understanding of special revelation.

We must remember that many factors hamper our ability to understand both forms of revelation. As a result, Biblical studies and other disciplines often seem to conflict. When these tensions arise, the two forms of revelation are not actually at odds; general and special revelation are never contradictory since both come from God. Our *understanding* is the problem. Sometimes our awareness of the Bible needs improvement. At other times our understanding of general revelation is inadequate. Then again, our perspectives on both may be wrong.

When such conflicts arise, evangelicals favor their understanding of Scripture until the evidence of general revelation is overpowering.[61] This course is the way of wisdom, but we must never go so far as to deny the value of insights from different fields. Compelling evidence from general revelation can persuade us to change our interpretation of the Bible without giving up our commitment to Biblical authority. J. I. Packer has summed up the matter nicely:

> It is not for scientific theories to dictate what Scripture may and may not say, although extra-Biblical information will sometimes helpfully

> expose a misinterpretation of Scripture. . . . For though exegesis must be controlled by the text itself, not shaped by extraneous considerations, the exegetical process is constantly stimulated by questioning the text as to whether it means this or that.[62]

In the chapters that follow, we will explore how the Spirit uses both the Bible and general revelation to influence our interpretation of Old Testament narratives. These influences may be divided in many ways, but for the sake of convenience, we will separate them into three major areas: *individual Christian living, interaction in community, and exegesis of Scripture*.

Individual Christian living. First, we will see that individual Christian living impacts our reading of Scripture. The Spirit uses our personalities, experiences, and callings in life to help us to understand Old Testament narratives. Suffering makes us aware of Biblical teaching on human pain; joyous events open us to other facets of Old Testament narratives; ethical life styles confirm and flesh out the guiding principles of these texts. Every ordinary and extraordinary aspect of our lives has the potential of moving us along the hermeneutical spiral. The Holy Spirit uses our individual Christian lives to influence our interpretation of Old Testament stories.

Interaction in community. Second, we will notice that the Spirit prepares us to read Scripture by our interaction in community. This aspect of general revelation reveals how the Holy Spirit helps us interpret Scripture through other people—teachers, books, friends, family members. Interaction with others who have learned from the Spirit prepares us to examine Old Testament stories.

Exegesis of Scripture. Third, the Spirit prepares us to interpret by involving us in the exegesis of Scripture. What we gain from exposure to the Bible deeply influences us. Nothing can replace looking at special revelation itself. Exploring the Bible also moves us along the hermeneutical spiral toward better understanding. As we will see, these hermeneutical resources offer us indispensable help for interpretation (see figure 5).

Conclusion

We began this chapter with the realization that a classroom dialogue requires us to prepare to speak and listen. Reading Old Testament narratives is like a classroom discussion. We always speak and listen as we examine Old Testament stories. Yet we are not left to our own devices

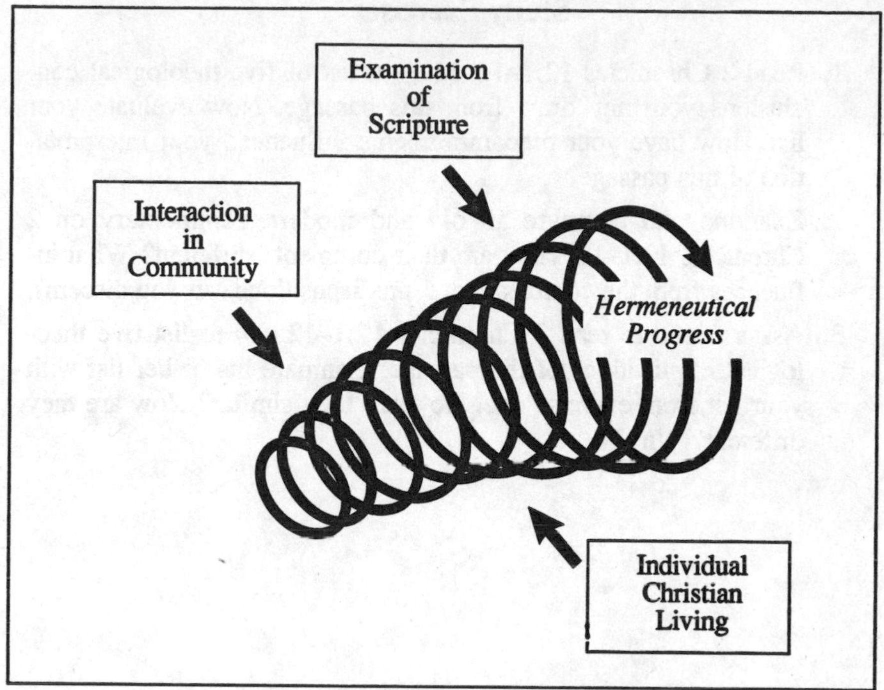

Fig. 5: Major Resources for Hermeneutical Progress

to prepare for this dialogue. The Spirit prepares us through individual Christian living, interaction in community, and examination of Scripture. By these means we are prepared to move forward on the hermeneutical spiral toward fuller understanding and appropriation of Old Testament narratives.

Review Questions

1. Describe the philosophical background of subjectivism in formal hermeneutics. Why has this outlook led to a descriptive emphasis? What are some dangers of subjectivism?
2. Describe the philosophical background of objectivism in formal hermeneutics. Why has this outlook led to a prescriptive emphasis? What are some dangers of objectivism?
3. What is an "authority-dialogue model" for Old Testament hermeneutics? How does it differ from subjectivism and objectivism? How may we hope for progress in understanding with this model?

Study Exercises

1. Read 2 Chronicles 12:1–12. Make a list of five theological conclusions you may draw from this passage. Now evaluate your list. How have your precommitments influenced your interpretation of this passage?
2. Examine and compare an old and modern commentary on 2 Chronicles 12:1–12. How are their comments different? What influences from the commentators' predispositions can you discern?
3. Ask a friend to read 2 Chronicles 12:1–12 and to list five theological implications of the passage. Compare his or her list with your list from exercise one. How are they similar? How are they different? Why?

2

THE INFLUENCE OF CHRISTIAN LIVING

Many dimensions of life affect a child's ability to learn. Skilled teachers and hard study are not the only factors. Family turmoil can cripple a student's performance; physical exercise and good eating habits can have a positive effect. If we want to know how to help children do well in school, we must consider many aspects of their lives.

Similarly, many things in life affect our interpretation of Old Testament narratives. Why do you look at a passage in one way instead of another? What causes you to understand an Old Testament story as you do? Our interpretations are influenced by many aspects of life that we seldom acknowledge. We must expand our vision to account for a wide range of influences.

In this chapter we will see how the Holy Spirit uses many dimensions of our individual Christian lives to prepare us for interpretation. We will look at three main areas: *sanctification, endowments, and calling*. We read Old Testament stories in the context of a spiritual struggle for maturity in Christ. We understand them in terms of the natural and supernatural gifts God has given to us. We also read according to the service to which God has called us. We will look at each of these areas to see how the Spirit uses them to help us understand Old Testament narratives (see figure 6).

These facets of our lives are interdependent. Sanctification extends to our gifts and callings; endowments include aspects of spirituality and vocation; our calling in service is bound to sanctification and gifts. Though we will discuss each area individually, we must always keep their interdependence in mind.

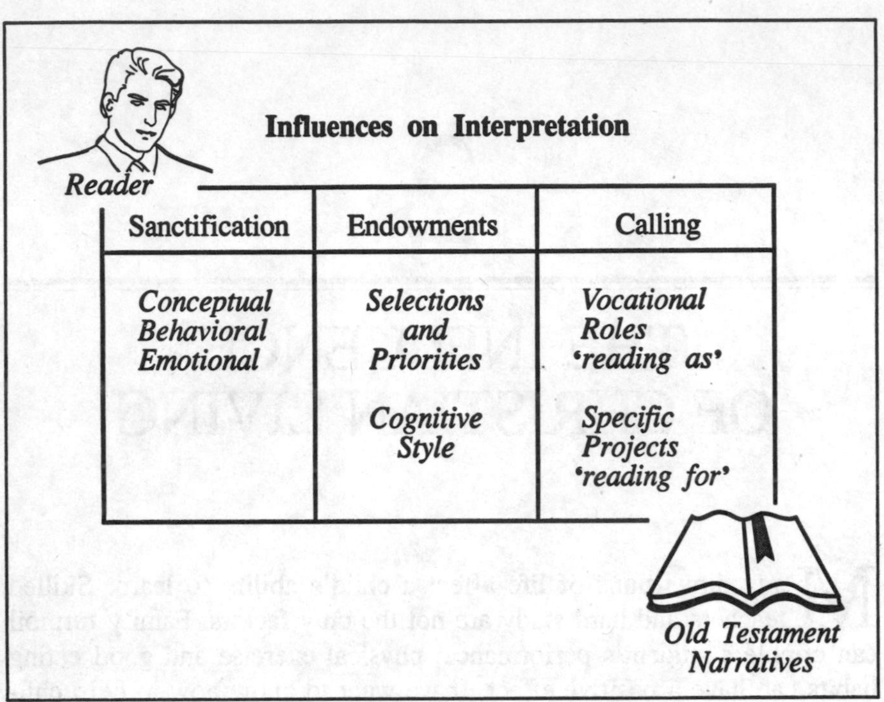

Fig. 6: Major Influences of Christian Living

Sanctification

Without exercise our bodies deteriorate. After a few months of inactivity, hard work becomes difficult. The same is true in our spiritual lives. Unless we develop ourselves in the power of the Holy Spirit, we will be hindered in our religious responsibilities. We may desire to interpret Old Testament stories properly, but we will fail unless we are growing strong through sanctification.

In this study we will speak of sanctification as a progressive struggle for spiritual growth in all areas of life.[1] As Hoekema recently put it: "We may define sanctification as that gracious operation of the Holy Spirit, involving our responsible participation, by which He delivers us as justified sinners from the pollution of sin, renews our entire nature according to the image of God, and enables us to live lives that are pleasing to Him."[2]

Growing in sanctification is one of the most important ways in which believers are prepared to read Old Testament narratives. To explore this vital connection, we will focus on two aspects of sanctification: its *progressive struggle* and its *extensive scope*.

Progressive Struggle

Sanctification is a progressive struggle that spans a lifetime. The Spirit works in our lives to conform us to the image of Christ (Romans 8:29), but in this struggle we are pulled back and forth between righteous and sinful living. As Paul put it:

> So I say, live by the Spirit, and you will not gratify the desires of the sinful nature. For the sinful nature desires what is contrary to the Spirit, and the Spirit what is contrary to the sinful nature. They are in conflict with each other, so that you do not do what you want. (Galatians 5:16–17; see also Romans 7:14–25)

No Christian escapes the tensions of this conflict. At every moment we are influenced by both sin and the Spirit. In different ways and at different times, our lives are torn between the frailties of the flesh and the transforming power of God's grace.

Evangelicals often acknowledge that Scripture plays a vital role in this struggle. Reading and meditating on Scripture is a means of grace, essential for Christian maturity. "All Scripture is God-breathed . . . so that the man of God may be thoroughly equipped for every good work" (2 Timothy 3:16–17). Without prayerful attention to Scripture, sanctification grinds to a halt. Even so, this is only half the picture. Not only does studying the Bible affect our spiritual condition, but our spiritual condition also helps and hinders our study of the Bible.

Sadly, evangelicals often ignore this side of the relationship between sanctification and Scripture. Older writings on hermeneutics occasionally mentioned the importance of an interpreter's spiritual condition, but most of these treatments were marginal.[3] And recent major evangelical works on hermeneutics virtually ignore the subject.[4]

We can see this same trend in our theological seminaries, where most curricula promote the ideal of a detached, erudite scholar. We act as if Scriptures are studied best by learned men and women who cloister themselves in their studies to do research in peaceful solitude. But this ideal is deceptive. Each of us reads the Bible in a foxhole surrounded by the fire of a cosmic war between evil and the Spirit (Ephesians 6:10–18). We deceive ourselves if we think we can read Old Testament narratives as detached, objective scholars; whether we acknowledge it or not, we actually interpret as warring soldiers, wounded by sin and strengthened by the Spirit.

This cosmic battle places a sobering responsibility on each of us. God does not want erudite interpreters; above all He desires *holy* interpreters. The New Testament focuses more on the moral character of teachers than on their vast knowledge.[5] Knowledge and skills are required for hermeneutics, but our major concern must be sanctification.

For this reason we must always tie our study of Old Testament narratives to self-examination. How am I weak? Where am I strong? How is my interpretation influenced by the flesh and by the Spirit? These are not questions that scholars typically ask themselves, but they are vital concerns for Christian men and women who know that they study Old Testament stories on a spiritual battlefield.

Self-evaluation of this sort will be negative and positive. Negatively, we are to "throw off everything that hinders and the sin that so easily entangles" (Hebrews 12:1b). To be sure, the Holy Spirit often works *despite* our sinful tendencies. His Word confronts us precisely in those areas of life in which we are failing. But in these cases, He works against us, not through us. Our responsibility is not to erect obstacles that the Spirit must overcome, but to mortify the flesh that we may be fertile ground for the seed of His Word. Through confession, repentance, and dependence on God, we must drive sinful tendencies from our lives. We never rid ourselves completely of these negative factors, but our goal is to be as free as possible from the power of sin as we interpret Old Testament stories.

Positively, we are to "make every effort . . . to be holy" (Hebrews 12:14). The Spirit's sanctifying work is a gift that helps us interpret. We want the work of the Spirit to influence, even dominate our study. Through self-reflection we may distinguish between the flesh and the Spirit, rid ourselves of the former, and build on the latter.

Extensive Scope

I once talked with a woman who was a teenager in Holland during World War II. "Everything we did was under the shadow of the war," she explained. "Day and night—the war affected everything." They woke up to the sounds of soldiers in the streets; they spent every waking hour wondering who would be arrested next; they went to sleep hungry because the soldiers had stolen their food. Living in the war zone affected every aspect of their lives.

Our war between sin and the Spirit is not limited to one corner of our lives; it reaches every aspect of our existence.[6] We will consider three levels of conflict: the *conceptual*—our thinking processes, the *behavioral*—our actions, and the *emotional*—our feelings and attitudes. When God created human beings, we were holy in all these ways. When we fell into sin, we became completely corrupted. Now in Christ our thoughts, actions, and feelings are involved in the process of sanctification.

These three aspects of our lives are inextricably woven together. What we think affects the way we act and feel. How we behave influences our thoughts and attitudes. Our emotions change the way we think and act. So we must look carefully at the ways each area affects our interpretation of Old Testament stories.

Conceptual. The Biblical portrait leaves no doubt that we struggle in sanctification on a conceptual level. We all have inconsistencies in the way we think. One believer may be fully aware of his responsibility to widows and orphans but misunderstand an important aspect of the doctrine of God. Another believer may have his "theology proper" in order but fall short of conforming his thinking on social justice to Scripture. Since no one is exempt from these kinds of conceptual inconsistencies, we must strive to submit our thinking to the Spirit. As Paul put it, "be transformed by the renewing of your mind" (Romans 12:2).

Conceptual sanctification affects our interpretations of Old Testament narratives in many ways. Sometimes the influence is obvious. For example, interpreters who read the crossing of the Jordan (Joshua 3:1–17) with the misconception that Biblical miracles did not occur will understand this passage differently from those who think that they did happen.[7] Racism has caused interpreters to twist passages such as the curse on Cain (Genesis 4:10–15) and Canaan (Genesis 9:24–25).[8] Conceptual shortcomings like these can lead to wretched interpretations of Old Testament stories.

Why does the conceptual tug-of-war play such an important role in the way we read Old Testament narratives? Because these stories are from the Spirit and are "spiritually discerned" (1 Corinthians 2:6–16). The more consistently we follow the mindset of the flesh, the more consistently we will distort Scripture (2 Peter 3:16). The wisdom of this world is antithetical to the wisdom of God (1 Corinthians 2:6–8); it is darkened, futile, and ignorant (Ephesians 4:17–18). It considers the heart of Biblical teaching, the death and resurrection of Christ, to be foolishness (1 Corinthians 1:23–24; 2:14). At the same time, the more we submit our thinking to the Spirit, the better we will understand these portions of Scripture. We must "think God's thoughts after Him"[9] if we are to interpret properly.

Behavioral. The behavioral level of sanctification also affects our interpretation of Old Testament narratives. Holiness of life does not merely mean right thinking; it involves moral action as well. Christianity is a religion of action, not just ideas. We may think correctly, but if we do not put our thinking into action, we inhibit our ability to understand Old Testament stories. We must "put to death the misdeeds of the body" (Romans 8:12–14).

One critical activity for Biblical interpreters is prayer. Communion with God through prayer brings us under His influence. It is no wonder that the apostles devoted themselves to "prayer and the ministry of the word" (Acts 6:4). Prayer and interpretation go hand in hand. Successful interpreters are those who gain the help of the Spirit through prayer.[10]

Sadly, we often neglect prayer in academic studies on hermeneutics. While evangelicals affirm the need for personal interaction with God in the Christian life, they do not stress its role in Biblical interpretation.[11] As a result, men and women trained in hermeneutics tend to overlook their need to pray. It seems that the more thoroughly trained we are the less we see the need for prayer as a hermeneutical resource.

How much do you pray when you read Old Testament stories? Most of us begin and end our study with a sentence or two to God. But the bulk of our time and energy is devoted to study. To the degree that we neglect prayer, we can expect our understanding to lack depth and significance. To heal this serious malady, we must learn how to talk with God as we study His Word.

My wife and I often sit together and discuss letters and papers we have written. As we read we do not sit in silence mulling over the pages to ourselves. We pause to ask questions and make comments. Often we get so involved in our discussions that it takes a long time to get through a short text. Reading together is worth the time because it offers us the opportunity to pay attention to each other.

The same should be true when we interpret Old Testament stories. Instead of sitting in silence, we must learn to ask God, the Author, for insights into particular aspects of a passage as we read. He is the Author of these texts; we must seek Him for understanding. We bow in confession of sin. We lift our hearts in praise. Whatever the case, we must approach Old Testament stories with a keen sense of entering the presence of God and giving Him our personal attention as we read. *Ora et labora* (prayer and work) must be our motto.[12]

Prayer is not the only action that influences interpretation. Everything we do affects our ability to understand correctly, but for the most part, we have overlooked the interconnections between our general behavior and interpretation. Several considerations demonstrate, however, that *all* our actions have a bearing on hermeneutics.

Beliefs and opinions are often formulated, confirmed, and modified in the context of practice.[13] Experiences of failure and success, benefit and harm help us form our beliefs. Actions even influence our basic religious commitments. Myers summarizes the Biblical perspective:

> Instructions on how to really understand the Bible are given over and over again in both Old and New Testaments. "He who does what is true comes to the light" [John 3:21]. The wise man—the one who built his house on the rock—differs from the foolish man in that he acts upon the word [Matthew 7:24–29]. The power of Jesus' words is known in the doing of them.[14]

Similarly, Liberationists point to the influence of praxis, active engagement in the world, on interpretative perspectives.[15] They insist that their interpretations cannot be adequately evaluated in the comfort of an air-conditioned study. They are right; struggling with social oppression leads interpreters to ask questions of the Bible in ways that others may never consider.[16]

On a more negative note, the Bible indicates that wicked behavior blinds our eyes and hardens our hearts to God's revelation (Isaiah 29:9–13; John 8:43–44; 1 Corinthians 3:1–3). When we disobey, our minds are corrupted. Wicked life styles create spiritual blindness. The worse the behavior, the deeper we plummet into darkness and depravity. Sinful behavior affects our interpretation of Old Testament stories in many ways. A person whose life style depends on the economic oppression of others may have a hard time grasping the significance of Israel's deliverance from slavery (Exodus 3:7–10). Persons living in sexual immorality often cannot understand why God treated David so harshly for his sin with Bathsheba (2 Samuel 11:2–12:12). Sin clouds our vision; we cannot see what these stories teach.

Yet as our behavior comes under the Spirit's influence, we are better equipped to understand. A reader who is faithfully praying in a time of trouble will read the account of Hannah's prayer (1 Samuel 1:3–2:11) with heightened sensitivity. A believer who shows courage in service to God will greatly appreciate Ehud's heroic character (Judges 3:12–30). Action and discernment go hand in hand; therefore, as we grow in behavioral sanctification we will understand Old Testament stories better than before.

Emotional. Finally, sanctification reaches to our *emotions*. Feelings are as much a part of our spiritual struggle as ideas and actions. In Biblical perspective emotions are a vital part of our growth in Christ.

Consider Paul's list of the fruits of the Spirit: "love, joy, peace, patience, kindness, goodness, faithfulness, gentleness, and self-control" (Galatians 5:22–23a). We must not reduce any aspect of this list to mere feelings, but each fruit of the Spirit is intensely emotional.[17] In contrast to "the passions and desires" of the sinful nature (Galatians 5:24), Christians are to have emotions that come from the Spirit. Roberts summarized the matter nicely:

> Whatever else Christianity may be, it is a set of emotions. It is love of God and neighbor, grief about one's own waywardness, joy in the merciful salvation of our God, gratitude, hope and peace. So if I don't love God and my neighbor, abhor my sins, and rejoice in my redemption, if I am not grateful, hopeful, and at peace with God and myself, then it follows that I am alienated from Christianity.[18]

We have to be careful not to oversimplify the complexities of emotional sanctification. Joy, peace, and happiness do not exhaust the list of proper feelings. Disgust, sadness, and anger are also fitting at times.[19] Whatever the case, growth in the Spirit also includes our emotions.

Our emotions also have a direct bearing on the way we understand Old Testament stories. How we feel will open and close us to different aspects of these texts. Above all, *reverent fear of God* must control our attitudes as we read Old Testament narratives. "The fear of the Lord is the beginning of knowledge, but fools despise wisdom and discipline" (Proverbs 1:7). Fear or reverence for God is essential to understand Scripture. To be sure, the term "fear" is not synonymous with "fright" or "terror."[20] It involves much more than an emotional experience; nevertheless, the fear of God *is* emotional. To understand Old Testament narratives beyond the most elementary level, we must come with reverence and godly fear. Those who try to interpret without submissive, humble spirits will twist and pervert the Scriptures.

Another indispensable set of emotions appears in the great commandments. Jesus' summary of the Law and Prophets must be foremost in the minds of all interpreters. "Love the Lord your God with all your heart and with all your soul and with all your mind" . . . . "Love your neighbor as yourself." All the Law and the Prophets hang on these two commandments (Matthew 22:37–40).

Love for God and neighbor is essential to hermeneutics. We must not reduce these commands to mere emotions, but the loyalty and service we are to give our Creator and fellow humans involves the deepest emotional commitments. Emotional preparation for interpreting Old Testament stories entails a delight in serving God and others. After all, what is the goal of our work with these texts if not to please the One who gave them and to use them for the benefit of our neighbors? If we come with hearts hardened against the mercies of God and indifferent to the needs of those around us, we will cut ourselves off from the motivations that undergird the investigation and application of Old Testament narratives.

Beyond this, the full range of our emotions affects interpretation. It influences our selections of passages. When we are sad, we may look for stories to make us happy. The way we feel also draws our attention to one aspect of a passage instead of another. A young couple in love will naturally delight in the wedding of Ruth and Boaz (Ruth 4:13–15) more than the other chapters of the story. Attitudes even help or hinder our ability to recognize the applications of a text to our lives. A malcontent may find it difficult to understand why Israel's grumbling against the Lord in the wilderness was such a serious offense (Numbers 14:26–35).

Emotional dispositions influence the way we read Old Testament stories. Unfortunately, the academic model of a staunch, detached scholar obscures the role of emotions in Biblical interpretation. We often think that understanding is just a matter of getting certain facts straight. But facts and feelings are partners in hermeneutics.

To sum up, the Spirit prepares us to interpret Scripture through sanctification. In our thinking, acting, and feeling, we struggle between the Spirit and the flesh. As we pursue the Spirit and grow in sanctification on all three levels, we will be better prepared to read Old Testament stories.

Endowments

What causes differences among teachers? Why does one interpreter emphasize aspects of a text that another ignores? Many differences among us do not result from our struggle with sin but arise from our different *endowments*—the natural and supernatural gifts God has given each of us.

For simplicity's sake we will restrict our discussion of endowments to certain psychological tendencies within each of us. We are not so concerned with physical and social abilities, though these endowments also affect our handling of Old Testament stories. Instead, we are more concerned with the area often called *personality*.[21]

Informally defined, personality is the psychological features that characterize a person's outlooks, behavior, and emotions. As we will see, these endowments have an unavoidable bearing on the way we interpret Old Testament narratives.[22]

Sources of Endowments

Where do we get our endowments? What aspects of life shape us into the kinds of people we are? God orchestrates countless influences to mold us as He desires. It is not possible to fathom all of the sources He uses. Yet as we explore these influences, we become more aware of how the Spirit prepares us for fruitful interpretation. We will look into three major sources of our psychological tendencies: *heredity, environment,* and *supernatural bestowal.*

Heredity. A perennial question in psychology has been the relative importance of heredity and environment for personality development.[23] Am I primarily a product of my genetic make-up or my experience? Are my psychological tendencies more a matter of nature or nurture? Although this debate is ongoing, modern psychologists are generally agreed that both nature and nurture, heredity and environment, exert powerful influences on us.

Most of us realize that the size of our ears, the texture of our hair, and the color of our eyes come from our parents. "She's got her mother's chin and her father's nose," we say, as we peek through the nursery window. But studies also show that heredity influences even our psychological endowments.

Research has suggested, for example, that inclinations toward depression and schizophrenia may be inherited.[24] Intelligence is also tied to genetics.[25] Common experience teaches us that special aptitudes such as musical and artistic ability are often passed from parents to their children. God has designed the world so that our genetic inheritance determines who we are in many ways.

Environment. Another powerful force behind personality is environment.[26] Early childhood experiences have a strong bearing on us. Parents can equip a child early in life for great good or great evil. Formal education, various traumas, and all kinds of social experiences determine to a great extent our values, outlooks, and behavior. God uses everything from profoundly memorable events to the basic contours of our cultures to prepare us for interpretation.

Supernatural bestowals. Finally, supernatural bestowals from the Holy Spirit influence our personalities. As head of the church, Christ grants different abilities to the various members of His body (Romans 12:6–8; 1 Corinthians 12:1–11; Ephesians 4:7–13; 1 Peter 4:10). Some believers teach while others listen; some show mercy in special ways while others demonstrate great faith. Some of us are gifted with discernment; others live relatively unaware of many of life's problems and solutions. Whatever the case, these gifts of the Holy Spirit influence our concepts, behavior, and emotions.

We have seen that we derive our endowments from heredity, experience, and supernatural bestowal. But what do these endowments have to do with Old Testament interpretation? We will focus on two ways in which endowments affect our treatment of Old Testament narratives.

Selections and Priorities

Human perception is always selective.[27] Without exception we pick and choose what we will acknowledge in our experience. As we encounter the world around us, we are never able to assimilate everything. Instead, we acknowledge some elements and exclude others. Cognitive selectivity is always at work.

I remember the first time I tried to find the George Washington Bridge near New York City. Cars were everywhere, horns were blowing, and signs were pointing in every direction. About halfway through the ordeal, I panicked. "I'm overloading!" I shouted to my wife. "Help me find the bridge!" From that point on, we ignored everything around us except the car just ahead and the signs pointing in our direction. As far as our field of attention was concerned, the skyline of the city no longer existed. Horns stopped blowing; exits, tunnels, and loops disappeared. We had to exercise radical cognitive selectivity.

Even in a calm, quiet setting, we exercise conscious and unconscious selection. What could be simpler than reading this page? Yet you cannot read it without selectivity. You do not randomly read words from anywhere on the page. You read from left to right and from top to bottom. You ignore some elements entirely; you handle others according to priorities you have established.

We are also selective when we interpret Old Testament stories. We consider one thing more important than another. We highlight some facets of a story and relegate others to the margin. Some of this selectivity is intentional. We zero in on one verse instead of another because of interpretative strategies. But our planned discrimination is only the tip of the iceberg. Our selections are unintended more than we can imagine.[28] How do these unconscious selections occur? Many unintentional choices stem from the genetic, environmental, and supernatural influences.

The story of David bringing the ark into Jerusalem (2 Samuel 6:1–23) provides a good example of how selectivity operates on the basis of endowments. In the opening paragraphs of the narrative, three scenes introduce different facets of the event. David brings the ark from Baalah with great celebration (vv. 1–5). Uzzah touches the ark, and the Lord strikes him down (vv. 6–7). David expresses fear over the event and sends the ark away (vv. 8–11). On which of these three scenes do readers tend to focus their attention?

If we took a poll, it would not be surprising to find musicians attracted to the first scene. "What were those instruments? How did they sound? What did the procession look like?" Even if they do not completely ignore other aspects of the story, musicians will often gravitate toward a scene that mentions music.

Suppose some other reader has recently lost a loved one to unexpected death. Many questions have been racing through his mind: "Why did God take him? What sense does it make?" This person might move quickly through the first scene only to be arrested by the sudden death of Uzzah. Experience has so traumatized him that his mind tends to focus on that segment of the story.

Finally, suppose a person has grown up in an unstable home. His or her personality has been shaped by repeated rejection and mistreatment of those who were supposed to care. Would we be surprised to find a focus on David's insecurity in the third scene? The same kinds of questions David asked plague the reader. "I can relate to that," the reader would think.

Each of these interpreters differs from the other, but none has strayed into error or been misled by sin. How can this be? Their endowments—their interests and talents—steered them in different directions.

Many interpreters are unaware of how much selectivity takes place as they read, and such a lack of self-awareness here breeds hermeneutical arrogance. We assume that careful study will keep us from excluding aspects of a text, but this can never be. Interpretation always involves selections based on our endowments.

On a practical level, then, as we read Old Testament stories we must do more than evaluate a text; we must also evaluate the influence of our endowments. How may I assess my psychological tendencies? How has my personality drawn me toward one aspect of this passage? As we become more aware of our natural tendencies, we can then reach in other directions. What areas of this passage have I left untouched? How can I see more than before?

Cognitive Style

Endowments also influence our *cognitive style,* the way in which we arrange the data of experience. Much psychological research has gone into cognitive style.[29] These studies suggest that people tend to follow one of two directions toward objects of knowledge. As Van Leeuwen has put it:

> Some people . . . function in a way that is characterized by objectivity, abstraction, and differentiation in the intellectual sphere, independence and achievement in the social sphere, self-containment and relative stoicism in the emotional sphere. Other people . . . function in a way that is characterized by intuition, concreteness, and global perception in the intellectual sphere, interdependence and affiliative concern in the social sphere, and freedom of expression in the emotional sphere.[30]

These two styles of cognition can be described as *analytic* and *global*. Basically, the analytic style is oriented toward detailed, critical, and factual knowledge. The global style is concerned with synthesis, intuition, and emotion.[31]

How would you answer the question "What is a flower?" If you tend toward an analytical, cognitive style, your answer would probably sound like a botany textbook: "A flower is the reproductive portion of a sporophyte that consists of a filament, anther, stigma . . . ." If you tend toward a global, cognitive style, your response would be different: "Flowers are the gift of spring." Both of these definitions are correct as far as they go. They differ according to cognitive style.

These styles are tendencies, not absolute distinctions. We tend to be more or less analytic or global in a given area, and we may operate globally in some tasks and analytically in others. Yet cognitive style can make a big difference in the way we understand Old Testament stories. Two ways in which cognitive style influences our reading of Old Testament narratives are *small and large units* and *hard and soft dimensions* of texts.

Small and large units. We can distinguish analytic and global styles of interpretation as tendencies toward microscopic and macroscopic outlooks, dealing with small and large units of a text. On the one hand, analytic approaches look at a narrative primarily in terms of small units. An interpreter with this orientation usually dissects and analyzes a passage in units of words, phrases, clauses, sentences, or verses.

On the other hand, a global approach looks at a narrative as a whole story. This outlook synthesizes the various elements of the story. Paragraphs, episodes, sections, and whole books occupy the foreground of global perspectives. The goal is to understand stories in terms of overarching motifs.

Most academic training in Biblical interpretation has favored microscopic analytic approaches. The use of Old Testament narratives for proof-texting doctrinal positions has led to analytic exegetical styles. The dominance of classical philology in grammatico-historical exegesis has guided theologians toward looking at small units of meaning. Even if students begin theological education with a global orientation, by the time they finish, most of them have been molded into microscopic interpreters.

This trend in theological academics trickles down to lay people, whose understanding of Old Testament stories often amounts to looking at a few verses here or there. Our Bible studies often consist of deriving a moral lesson from a verse or two. Since most of us learn to study Scripture in this atmosphere, we are prone to microscopic examination of Old Testament stories.

Microscopic techniques have much to offer us, but this represents only one exegetical approach. In addition, we must affirm the importance of global cognitive style. Becoming aware of large units is just as vital as focusing on smaller parts. Instead of always doing what comes naturally from our training, we must look for ways to deal with stories macroscopically. At least some of the time "What does this verse mean?" should be replaced by "What does this story, section, and book mean?"

Hard and soft dimensions. Cognitive style also affects our focus on the hard and soft dimensions of a text. Analytic approaches emphasize the harder, factual side of a story, while a global mentality deals with the softer, affective side. Neither of these outlooks excludes the other, but interpreters naturally lean in one direction or the other as they read Old Testament stories.

I faced this distinction in my first college biology class, in which we had to dissect a laboratory rat. The teacher instructed us to cut, but I just couldn't do it. Why not? Because I always thought of furry little animals as pets, not laboratory specimens. While other students were able to deal with their rats in a detached, factual manner, it was emotionally impossible for me. Medical doctors go through the same kind of tension. Several surgeons have told me they have to train themselves to think differently about the patient on the operating table than they do about people in everyday life. There is a lot of difference between the way we approach an object of scientific procedure and the way we relate to the same objects in common experience.

The same sort of tension exists in the interpretation of Old Testament narratives. As followers of Christ, we love these texts; they offer us words of life. As David loved and delighted in the Scriptures (Psalm

119:14, 16, 47, 48), they touch us on the deepest levels, too. But in sophisticated Biblical interpretation, we usually perform very impersonal analysis. Grammatico-historical methods have been oriented toward the logical, factual aspects of a text. As a result, most scholarly approaches to Old Testament narratives barely acknowledge the softer, emotional side.

A survey of commentaries on the first chapter of Jonah reveals this tendency. Commentators usually show a lot of interest in the peculiar Hebrew constructions and the structure of the passage. They make much of the question of historicity. With rare exception interpreters overlook the emotional aspects of the passage. Few mention, for instance, the striking irony at the heart of this story. While the prophet runs as hard as he can from God, he hypocritically claims, "I am a Hebrew and I worship the Lord, the God of heaven, who made the sea and the land" (Jonah 1:9). Few commentators dwell on how the writer ridicules Jonah by contrasting him with pagan sailors calling upon the Lord (Jonah 1:14), making sacrifices, and taking vows (Jonah 1:16). Personal and emotional tensions fill this passage, but our usual cognitive style turns us away from them.[32]

Recognizing this tension between the factual and emotional sides of a passage can help us balance our treatment of Old Testament narratives. It helps to evaluate the ways we naturally tend to interpret Scripture. Do I usually see the softer side of a text? Do I focus more on the harder side?

In the chapters that follow, we will explore ways to read with both cognitive styles. As we learn how to go beyond the natural tendencies of our endowments, our understanding of Old Testament stories will be enriched.

One final consideration deserves mention. God designed differences among Christians so that we may benefit from each other. "The eye cannot say to the hand, 'I don't need you'" (1 Corinthians 12:21a). Honoring the diversity of endowments in the church is a hard lesson to learn, especially for Christians with strong theological convictions. They nearly always assume that a difference in interpretation is a matter of right and wrong. Undoubtedly, this is often the case. But the differences between one interpreter and another can also be a matter of endowments rather than actual disagreement. Often these differences can be resolved if we recognize them for what they are.[33]

Although we have touched only briefly on two aspects of this matter, it is evident that endowments greatly affect our understanding of Old Testament narratives. We must become self-conscious of our selectivity and cognitive style. As we do so, we prepare ourselves more fully for the hermeneutical task before us.

Calling

A third aspect of Christian living that affects interpretation is our calling. In addition to sanctification and endowments, the Holy Spirit uses our responsibilities in life to prepare us to interpret. Calling refers to two aspects of our Christian experience: our *vocational roles* in church and society, and the *specific projects* we pursue in God's service.

Vocational Roles

There once was a young woman who was about to participate in her first public art contest. She was excited at the chance to have her work displayed. Unknown to her, however, the other participants were far better than she. Their work made her finest piece look like preschool scribbling. Fortunately, the director of the show was the woman's friend. The day before the contest began, she called her friend on the phone and said, "Sue, as the director, I have to tell you to be here tomorrow at 8:00 A.M. But as your friend, I have to tell you that you'd better not show up at all!"

As an official the director had one thing to say, but as a friend she had quite another. She was not contradicting herself, even though her words were very different. She simply spoke from the perspectives of two roles, director and friend. Happily, the young woman took her friend's advice and spared herself a lot of embarrassment.

We face similar circumstances when we read Old Testament stories. The roles we assume in life shape the way we interpret. Believers have many callings to fulfill in church and society. God has put us in various positions, each with its own responsibilities. We have vocations in the church. Pastors, elders, teachers, and deacons have certain jobs to do. Church committees assign tasks to their members. Some people lead; others follow. Some evangelize; others serve the needy (Romans 12:4–8; 1 Corinthians 12:27–31; Ephesians 4:11–13).

Our vocations also reach beyond the church. God calls us to fulfill our role as His image in every part of life. In family, school, business, politics and art, believers in Christ are called to serve. Some of us are community leaders, others ordinary citizens. Some are employees, others employers. Some are parents, others children. Whatever our calling, as followers of Christ we serve as "unto the Lord" (Colossians 3:18–24).

To complicate matters further, our stations in life are changing. For example, in the course of one day, my wife is not just a church member; she is also a wife, daughter, sister, friend, employee, neighbor, citizen, consumer, student, patient, traveler, cook, housekeeper, counselor, disciplinarian, teacher, and nurse, to name just a few. Each of us fulfills a multitude of roles and has many callings.

Whether or not we realize it, we always read Old Testament stories from the vantage point of our vocations.[34] Interpreters cannot completely disentangle themselves from their callings in life. We read as students, mothers, fathers, children, and pastors.

We must qualify this observation. While reading in one role or another always affects our interpretation of Old Testament stories, this influence varies. Basic levels of understanding are often the same, no matter what our vocation. A pastor's elementary understanding of a text may be very similar to that of a child. For instance, as they read Balaam's words, "Must I not speak what the Lord puts in my mouth?" (Numbers 23:12), both would agree that Balaam felt he must say what God told him to say. Both would also understand the words "Let there be light" (Genesis 1:3) in the same way on a rudimentary level. At this stage vocation makes little difference.

But the further we go beyond the basic levels of understanding, differences between reading in one role and another become more evident. Our vocation affects the methods we follow, the selections we make, the emphases we pursue, and the arrangement of our presentations.

One example will suffice. When I teach the book of Judges in seminary, I devote a whole class period to the rape of the Levite's concubine (Judges 19:1–30). My main purpose in this lecture is to show that Judges was written to demonstrate the need for a godly king in Israel.[35] This ancient horror story illustrated how social anarchy prevailed when "there was no king in Israel" and "everyone did what was right is his own eyes" (Judges 21:25 NASB). By the time this lecture is over, most of the students are completely convinced that Israel needed a king.

But when I taught through Judges in our family worship, I skipped right over the whole episode. I had many of the same intentions that I had in the classroom. I wanted my eight-year-old daughter to understand the purpose of Judges. Why, then, did I skip this passage? Because I was reading as a parent of a young girl. I feared the trauma that chapter 19 might cause her, so I made the same point to her using other passages in the book. Interpretative decisions of a parent are quite different from those of a professor.

Similar variations occur every time we interpret the Bible. We look for things, we leave things out, we explore avenues, and we handle materials in certain ways because of our sense of calling. Even the attempt to be detached from a particular calling is itself a vocation, reading in the role of an objective examiner. To deny the effects of vocation on interpretation does not safeguard us against misusing texts for our own purposes. In fact, failing to be conscious of our roles opens us to unintentional abuses of the text.

Young pastors fresh out of seminary often experience role confusion. The years spent in school watching academicians in action cause many pastors to act like academic scholars in the pulpit. But the pulpit is not a scholar's lectern. The hermeneutical practices of seminary teachers usually make poor models for pastoral interpretation. Unless pastors become more conscious of the vocation to which God has called them, they risk being academic instructors rather than shepherds of God's people.

We must therefore seek to be more aware of our callings as we interpret. What vocation am I fulfilling? What bearing should my sense of calling have on my approach to this passage? The more carefully we answer these questions, the more hope we have of handling Old Testament narratives responsibly.

Specific Projects

Within our various stations in life we also have many *specific projects*, or tasks, that affect the way we interpret Old Testament stories. We read passages differently as we move from one vocation to another, but we also interpret in light of the particular project at hand. As parents we use Old Testament narratives in many different ways for our children. As friends we share these texts for a variety of purposes. As pastors we use Old Testament stories to instruct, correct, comfort, lead, and encourage the people we serve. Our tasks influence the way we treat these passages. In this sense we do not simply read *as* someone; we also read *for* one purpose or another.[36]

To be sure, there are similarities in the ways we handle Old Testament stories, regardless of our specific project. But as we move beyond basic assessments of a text, our specific tasks have a great bearing on the methods and conclusions of our study.

A few years ago I had the opportunity to preach from Hezekiah's Passover celebration (2 Chronicles 30:1–27) in three different churches. This experience opened my eyes to the powerful influence of specific projects.

At the height of his efforts, Hezekiah invited the northern tribes to join with him in Jerusalem for the Passover (vv. 1–9). Many of them refused, but some accepted the invitation (vv. 10–12). The festival progressed splendidly until some of the participants became ill because they had failed to go through the ritual cleansing (vv. 15–18a). In the face of this catastrophe, Hezekiah prayed that God would look on the hearts of the people, forgive, and heal (vv. 18b-19). In response God healed the sick, and the feast continued in grand style (vv. 20–21).

This story fit well with the Chronicler's overall concern for the reunification of Israel in the post-exilic period.[37] North and South joined together to worship God at the temple. The Chronicler used this reunification under Hezekiah as a pattern for his readers to follow as they sought to restore the kingdom in their day.

As I studied this passage to preach in three different churches, many aspects of my work remained the same. My basic vocation was the same: I was a visiting minister called to bring a sermon. My methods were largely the same. Even so, I handled the passage differently for each congregation.

In the first church, I knew that the congregation was in need of a stronger commitment to the Word of God. As you can imagine, I looked closely at the ways Hezekiah was committed to the Law of God. From his youth he kept the commands the Lord had given Moses (2 Kings 18:6). He considered Judah's difficulties the result of disobedience of the Law (2 Chronicles 29:6–10). He purged Judah of idolatrous practices (2 Kings 18:4). He renewed the covenant, cleansed the temple, and reinstituted the Passover (2 Chronicles 29:3–10; 30:1–5).

In the second church, the congregation was committed to doctrinal purity but needed encouragement toward patience and unity. This consideration led me to look more closely at the king's desire for unity. I examined how Hezekiah sent letters inviting all the tribes to the Passover celebration (2 Chronicles 30:1). When those who came did not purify themselves, Hezekiah prayed for the Lord to pardon them (vv. 18–20). I saw how God blessed Hezekiah by giving a spirit of unity to the people (v. 12). Aspects of the passage that I had not emphasized in my first study suddenly moved to the center.

Finally, as I prepared for the third message, I had little idea of the needs of the congregation. So I determined to present a balanced picture. My preparation focused on the balance between purity and unity that Hezekiah displayed in his reform. My study and my presentation were equally focused on these two sides of the story.

To one degree or another, an interpreter's particular purpose always influences his or her examinations and discoveries. We pursue one line of thought and not another, explore one area and not another, emphasize one item and not another. We approach the same Old Testament stories for many legitimate purposes: worship, evangelism, doctrine, encouragement, and correction. We read Old Testament stories for different purposes in personal devotions, family worship, church, school, in sickness, at births, weddings, and funerals.

As we face different situations in life, our interpretations may seem unusual. But unusual need not imply illegitimate. Thiselton offers an analogy that illustrates the breadth of legitimate interpretations: "A piano can be used for firewood, and in most circumstances such actions would be irresponsible. But if one were dying of cold, stranded on an ice floe in the Arctic Ocean, it might conceivably become a responsible act to set fire even to a Steinway."[38] Of course, this is not to say that Old Testament stories can mean anything we want them to mean. Throughout this study we will develop safeguards against misunderstanding and abuse. But within the parameters of proper interpretation, we must recognize that the way we understand Old Testament stories depends to a great extent on our specific purposes in interpretation.

As a result, we need to be self-conscious when we come to Old Testament stories. We must examine not only the text before us but also what we are trying to do with this text. What are my specific purposes? How do I work with the text to reach this goal? What am I overlooking because of my project?

Conclusion

We began this chapter with the observation that Old Testament interpretation is influenced by many factors in life that we often overlook. Not only must we pay attention to matters ordinarily considered in Biblical studies; we also must recognize the influence of the broad range of our sanctification, endowments, and calling. As we examine how the Holy Spirit prepares us for interpretation in these areas, we will be better equipped to discover the treasures that await us in Old Testament stories.

Review Questions

1. What is sanctification? How do the conceptual, behavioral, and emotional dimensions of sanctification affect the interpretation of Old Testament narratives? Illustrate with a particular passage.

2. How is the term "endowments" used in this study? What are the sources of our endowments? How can they affect our interpretation of Old Testament stories?
3. What is an interpreter's calling? Why must we always acknowledge our calling as we interpret Old Testament narratives? Illustrate with a specific passage.

Study Exercises

1. Make a list of the five most important things you normally do to get ready to read a passage in the Old Testament. Categorize these items under conceptual, behavioral, and emotional sanctification. Where are you strong? Where are you weak? How should you expand your preparations?
2. Ask four people to identify an important aspect of Genesis 1:1–2:4. Compare their answers. What influence can you detect from their endowments? Can you expand the list of important features in the text?
3. Read Genesis 9:1–11. How should you vary your interpretative emphasis when preparing to teach this to preschoolers, a college history class, an adult Bible study, an inner city mission? Why?

3

THE INFLUENCE OF INTERACTION

"Never go into the water alone." That's one of the first rules I learned in swim class. "If you get into trouble, someone must be there to help." Of course, as a nine-year-old boy I had little idea how threatening the water could be. The rule didn't apply to me—not until one summer at the beach.

I stood speechless in the sand as strong currents pulled my older cousin out to sea. Jumping into the water, I swam out to help. But when I reached him, he grabbed me and we both went under. A few seconds later, I pushed him away and left him to drown. I can still remember him calling, "Don't go! Don't leave me!" Fortunately, as I came near the shore, two men ran past and rescued my cousin from certain death. I've never forgotten that day. I never swim alone.

Similarly, we should not try to interpret Old Testament narratives alone. There are dangers in interpreting these texts. Strong currents can drown us in a sea of misunderstanding. For safety we must learn to interpret in community, so that someone will be there to help if we get into trouble.

In the last chapter, we saw how the Holy Spirit prepares us to read Old Testament stories through different aspects of our individual Christian lives. In this chapter we will look at the second major influence on interpretation: *interaction in community*. As we examine interaction with others, we will address three main issues. What is the community within which we interact? What are the dynamics of interaction? How do interpretation and interaction relate? As we explore these subjects, we will see how vitally other people influence our interpretation of Old Testament stories.

Interaction in Community

Most evangelicals read Old Testament stories as if they need little help from others. "All I need is the Spirit, the Bible, and me." Although this viewpoint does identify the principal elements of interpretation, that is only part of the picture. We also need the help of a community as we interpret Old Testament narratives.

All of us live in some kind of community. We associate in families, friendships, clubs, neighborhoods, and nations for mutual support. God's first negative words about His creation reveal the importance of these communities. Everything He made was "good" (Genesis 1:25); in the end they were "very good" (1:31). But when He looked at the first man living by himself, He declared, "It is not good for the man to be alone" (2:18). God made us to live and work with others.

Community of Humanity

As followers of Christ, we work in two communities. First, we interact with the whole human race. In the sphere of common grace, we share many things with other people, despite our differing religious commitments.[1] We live in the same physical world, share many cultural ideals, and work together toward common goals. Though we must not fall prey to the sinful course of this world, we still involve ourselves with the rest of the human race.

Most of us recognize the need to interact with humanity in general. We seldom check out the religious commitments of a car mechanic. If he has a reputation for honesty and good work, we call on him. The exterminator does not have to be a Christian. We do not ask for a Christian officer when we call the police station. In daily life we constantly depend on people who do not share our faith commitments. Therefore, it should not surprise us that we must also interact with unbelievers in the study of Old Testament stories. Men and women who do not confess faith in Christ have done important work in many areas related to these texts. Much of their historical, linguistic, philosophical, even their theological work, contributes significantly to interpreting Old Testament narratives.

But how can non-Christians have insights into the Old Testament? Aren't they devoid of the Holy Spirit, who is so essential to interpretation? To answer these questions, we must realize that the Bible presents a two-sided portrait of unbelievers. At times Scripture describes them in terms of their system of unbelief, their basic loyalties, and tendencies. At other times it depicts unbelievers in terms of their actual life styles.[2]

On one side, Paul reveals the fundamental commitment of non-Christians in his warning to the Colossians: "See to it that no one takes you captive through hollow and deceptive philosophy, which depends on human tradition and the basic principles of this world rather than on Christ" (Colossians 2:8). Unbelievers have a basic loyalty to human tradition, or human autonomy.[3] This basic commitment shapes the way they think, act, and feel about everything. They suppress the truth of general revelation (Romans 1:18); they love darkness and hate light (John 3:19); their understanding is futile and darkened (Ephesians 4:17–18). The effects of sin reach even to the thinking processes.[4] In principle, unbelievers' rebellion against God removes all hope for true understanding of God, the world, and humanity. The more consistently they adhere to human autonomy, the more their efforts are worthless and vain.

On the other side, however, God does not abandon unbelievers to their own devices. In common grace He restrains their attempts to live consistently in their rejection of Christ. Non-Christians live inconsistently with their basic commitments and reflect their character as the image of God. As Paul put it, "Indeed, when Gentiles, who do not have the law, do by nature things required by the law, they are a law for themselves, even though they do not have the law" (Romans 2:14). All unbelievers fall short of their commitment to human autonomy. To one degree or another, they consciously and unconsciously rely on "borrowed capital,"[5] outlooks and beliefs that ultimately make sense only in a Christian view of life. These inconsistencies result from the common, non-redemptive operations of the Spirit.[6]

Scripture confirms this viewpoint. For instance, the book of Proverbs insists that knowledge and wisdom rest ultimately on "the fear of the Lord" (1:7). True knowledge belongs to a philosophy of life that submits to the claims of Biblical religion. Yet Proverbs depends extensively on the sayings of wise men from other cultures in the ancient Near East.[7] In fact, the proverbs of Agur (30:1–33) and Lemuel (31:1–9) probably originated outside of Israel altogether.[8] Wise people in the ancient world were blessed with common grace insights that were valuable for men and women of the true faith.

The New Testament also gives ample evidence of similar interaction with unbelievers. Jesus instructed His followers to learn as much as possible from their unbelieving Jewish teachers, though He cautioned against their hypocrisy (Matthew 23:1–12). Paul referred positively to the words of pagan philosophers. In Acts 17:28 he quoted from Aratus and Cleanthes.[9] In Titus 1:12 he alluded to Epimenides.[10] Similarly, in 1 Corinthians 15:33 he referred to Menander.[11] Clearly, God grants unbelievers many common grace insights.

Evangelicals go to extremes as they consider unbelievers' work with the Bible. On one side, some of us so fear their false ideas that we avoid their commentaries and theological writings completely. "Those writers are not Christians," we say. "Keep away from them!" But this denies the common operations of the Spirit. Consider Calvin's advice: "If we regard the Spirit of God as the sole fountain of truth, we shall neither reject the truth itself, nor despise it wherever it shall appear, unless we wish to dishonor the Spirit of God."[12]

On the other hand, however, some evangelicals forget that basic loyalties and religious commitments make a vast difference in interpretation. They handle unbelievers' opinions with little scrutiny. But interpreters' predispositions, especially their spiritual condition, deeply influence their interpretations.[13] We must never forget that commitment to human autonomy corrupts unbelievers' work with Old Testament stories.

Neither of these extremes is appropriate. We must acknowledge the insights of unbelievers without ignoring the dangers of their views. Interacting with unbelievers is like digging for gold. Nuggets of insight are mixed with tons of worthless rock and mud. We must not be tricked by fool's gold, but we must not be such fools that we pass over genuine gold, no matter where we find it. We are part of the human race, and we should be ready to interact with unbelievers as we seek to understand Old Testament stories.

Community of Believers

Christians also belong to a second community, the body of Christ. We have been incorporated into the new humanity of faith (1 Corinthians 12:13). In this special community, we enjoy a familial communion that transcends any bond we have with humanity at large. We share "one Lord, one faith, one baptism" (Ephesians 4:4–6). Most important for hermeneutics, we share the sanctifying and illuminating work of the Holy Spirit.

The Reformation doctrine of the priesthood of believers points to the need for extensive interaction among believers.[14] Sadly, this doctrine is often misunderstood to mean that interpretation of Scripture is purely a matter of private judgment. But nothing could be further from the original intent of this doctrine. The Reformers affirmed the priesthood of all believers to counter blind allegiance to official ecclesiastical authority. They insisted that understanding Scripture was the responsibility of all believers working together as the body of Christ. According to Eastwood's view, "The doctrine of the priesthood of believers, properly understood, transcends the distinction between clergy and laity, and, while allowing differences of function, unites them in the exercise of a priesthood which is common to all."[15] The priesthood of believers is not individualistic; it is something we hold in common with all believers. We interpret Scripture together.

When the New Testament speaks of our communion with other believers, it is often in the context of mutual service and cooperation (Philippians 2:1–4; 1 Corinthians 12:12–31). We do not stand alone; we work together for the kingdom of God. We join hands to serve each other in the body of Christ. In the same way, we join with each other to understand Old Testament stories. We study together at church, home, and school. We serve each other by exchanging ideas in the hope that the Spirit will orchestrate our individual contributions into a symphony of understanding.

In our day the need for interaction in the community of faith is greater than ever. We live in an age of information explosion. For years scholars have focused on either the Old Testament or the New Testament. Today the tendency is to narrow the focus even further to just small parts of the Old Testament and New Testament. As Biblical interpretation has become more complex, the scope of required study has grown enormously, and we are forced to specialize.

Increased specialization makes plain our need to cooperate. Pastors and teachers, for instance, simply cannot be experts in all the areas required for interpreting Old Testament narratives. We need general competence in a wide range of subjects, but time and talent limit our ability to delve firsthand into many areas. The only way to avoid working entirely from ignorance is to interact with those who specialize in other areas.[16]

How much do you interact with others as you interpret Old Testament narratives? From a Biblical perspective, responsible interpretation requires commitment to interaction in community. We need the help of others, both inside and outside the Christian faith.

Dynamics of Christian Interaction

A number of years ago a friend asked me to coach a basketball team. I'd never done it before, and I didn't know the boys; but I took the job anyway. First, I assessed the abilities of each player—who could dribble, who could rebound, who could shoot from the outside. Then I formed a team; I taught the boys how to work together. We spent weeks running drills and practicing plays. I didn't know much about coaching, but I knew this much: you have to recognize each player's talent and mold the players into a team.

Interaction in the Christian community is a team effort. If we are going to work together, we must do at least two things. First, we must become familiar with the various players on our team. What jobs are to be done? Who fulfills them? Second, we must learn how to coordinate each player's contributions with the rest of the team. How are we to cooperate with others?

Elements of Interaction

What elements of interaction must we consider as we approach Old Testament stories? What players make up our team? For the sake of convenience, we will speak of three basic elements: *heritage, present community,* and *private judgment.*

Heritage. The first element of interaction is heritage, the historical expressions of the Christian faith to which we trace our spiritual ancestry. To some degree we all operate under the influence of believers who have gone before us. What we consider acceptable interpretation is largely determined by what our theological heritage has passed down to us.

Why should we be concerned with heritage as we interpret Old Testament narratives? What has the past to do with our understanding today? Heritage contributes to our understanding because it shows us how the Holy Spirit has taught His people in the past. Contrary to the way we often act, the Holy Spirit did not begin His illuminating work in our generation. He has always taught the church.

Believers in the past struggled with sin and finitude just as we do. We must use discretion as we explore their views (1 John 4:1). We learn what to avoid from their mistakes, but we also learn what to do from their successes. As we consider our Christian heritage, we are "not [to] imitate what is evil but what is good" (3 John 11). We must become familiar with our theological heritage and draw upon it as we interpret.

A theological heritage may be conceived broadly or narrowly. In the broadest terms, the ecumenical councils of the early church reflect beliefs that we share with all followers of Christ. Documents such as the *Nicene Creed,* the *Council of Chalcedon,* and the *Apostles' Creed* have established parameters for orthodoxy.[17] The divinity and humanity of

Christ, the Trinity, and the historical reality of our redemption in Christ provide a solid orientation toward interpretation. If we find ourselves drawn toward an analysis of a passage that contradicts these and other foundational Christian views, we discard it as heretical.

Protestants also think of the major tenets of the Reformation as non-negotiable. Doctrines such as *Sola Fide* (Faith Alone), *Sola Scriptura* (Scripture Alone), and *Sola Gratia* (Grace Alone) were pillars of reform.[18] These summaries of vital Biblical doctrines continue to be held by orthodox Protestants to this day. Any interpretation that seems to violate these common Protestant views is held in suspicion.

Heritage also takes more distinctive forms in the creeds of denominations. Many churches have formal documents that represent the classical expressions of their distinctive traditions. Reformed churches endorse documents such as the *First Helvetic Confession* and *Second Helvetic Confession,* the *Heidelberg Catechism* and *Belgic Confession,* as well as the *Westminster Confession of Faith* and catechisms. Lutheran views are summarized in the *Book of Concord,* containing the *Augsburg Confession,* the *Formula of Concord* and *Luther's Catechism.* Anglicans look to the *Thirty-Nine Articles.* Baptists find a creedal heritage in the *Philadelphia Confession,* which first appeared as the *London Confession.*[19] Some longstanding denominations do not have written creeds, but oral traditions have formed sets of common beliefs, and these doctrines define orthodoxy for their churches.

Both written and unwritten ecclesiastical standards change through the centuries, but their major tenets have remained stable theological guides for successive generations. These formulations within our particular denominations also guide our interpretation of Old Testament stories.

On a less formal level, heritage includes the works of important individuals from the past. Each branch of the church has particular people who have exerted long-lasting influence on the beliefs of that tradition. Lutherans look to Martin Luther and Philipp Melancthon. Calvinists think of John Calvin and an assortment of continental, British, and American figures. Methodists find their roots in John and Charles Wesley. Every church has leaders from the past whose commentaries, sermons, and theological writings are highly respected. These individuals' opinions usually carry less weight than officially endorsed creeds and confessions, but their viewpoints are often used as important aids to interpretation.

Why should we let the beliefs of the past inform us? Why not simply read these texts for ourselves? In a word, ignoring heritage is the first step toward heresy. Consider some modern heretical groups.

Jehovah's Witnesses, the Church of Jesus Christ of Latter-Day Saints, and other heterodox groups ignore the theological heritage of historical Christianity. Although for the most part they do not blatantly deny the authority of Scripture itself,[20] they refuse to draw upon the Spirit's work in the church. To disregard heritage as we read Scripture invariably leads to serious error.

Present community. The second member of our hermeneutical team is the present community. This term refers to interpretative work within the contemporary church. The Holy Spirit not only gives us a rich heritage; He also blesses us with a living community of believers who contribute to our understanding of Old Testament stories.

Interaction at this level involves many different groups. In the first place, the present community appears in formal church courts. Just as the apostle Paul submitted himself to the Jerusalem council to gain the wisdom of other church authorities (Acts 15:6–29), we too have the privilege of looking to duly established authorities in our churches. Many denominations have official channels through which the collective wisdom of the church expresses itself. We must carefully evaluate these pronouncements. Constitutional documents, position papers, advisory letters, and disciplinary cases often reflect the teaching of the Spirit today. We are wise to take advantage of these expressions of collective wisdom.

At other times our present community takes the form of contemporary scholarly societies, theological schools, and other para-church associations. In these cases ecclesiastical authority is lacking, but the work of such groups represents the prayerful research of sincere, well-trained interpreters. Their judgments are not infallible by any means, but their views should at least make us hesitate to endorse contrary interpretations. Positions endorsed by many people who earnestly seek to follow the Spirit deserve serious consideration as we explore Old Testament stories.

Interaction with the present community also includes proper respect for the teaching ministry of individuals within the church. The Spirit has been pleased to equip some believers with special abilities to understand and explain Scripture (Ephesians 4:11–12). In many cases these abilities are acknowledged officially through ordination. At other times the gift of teaching becomes evident through informal means. Whatever the case, responsible interpreters will not turn away from the teaching of others. We must devote ourselves to reading contemporary commentaries and theologies, and listening to others as we interpret Old Testament narratives.

Even informal discussions of Scripture are an important part of the present community. As we participate in Bible studies, talk around the dinner table, and travel in the car, we are involved in interaction that helps us interpret Old Testament narratives. At times the Spirit grants us profound insights through people we least expect to teach us. Students teach their professors, parishioners teach their pastors, and children teach their parents. The Spirit gives insights at His discretion. Whenever we talk about a text with other believers, we are involved with people who are taught by the Spirit. The more sensitive we are to this fact, the better we will be able to draw on His ministry.

In addition to different levels of formality, interaction in the present community also ranges between narrow and broad associations. Discussions within the narrow confines of a tradition offer opportunity for in-depth study. The outlooks we share in particular affiliations make it possible to explore new areas of interest together. Moreover, within the bounds of relatively narrow communities, we are more accountable to each other; we watch and protect each other from error.

Even so, we must be careful not to withdraw from exposure to a broader range of Christian groups. Limiting ourselves to a particular denomination can truncate our exploration of Old Testament stories. Believers from other traditions have different perspectives as they come to these texts; they notice things that we never see on our own. If we interact only within comfortable theological boundaries, we will miss much of the Spirit's work in the present community. Broad and narrow expressions of the contemporary church are vital to interpretation.

So it is that the present community forms the second element of interaction. The work of the Spirit in our contemporaries is a rich resource for our own interpretative efforts.

Private judgment. Private judgment, our understanding of Old Testament stories apart from conscious interaction with others, is the third major element in interaction.[21] Of course, we never completely escape the influence of our heritage and present community. Yet we often go to Old Testament narratives with little concern for what others have said. We read primarily from our personal vantage point.

Private judgments may be informal or formal. At times we form impressions as we read a text and intuit its meaning. At other times we determine the meaning of an Old Testament story on the basis of careful study. Whatever the case, in private judgment we are concerned with what we, not others, think of a passage.

Despite the importance of heritage and present community, God holds each believer responsible for searching out his or her own understanding of the Bible. The warning of Scripture is clear: We will give an account for what we do with the Word of God as individuals. As Paul said, "So then, each of us will give an account of himself to God" (Romans 14:12). Interpreters of the Word cannot hide behind their communities; we will all answer for the way we handle Old Testament stories.

Evangelicals often go to extremes in private judgment. On the one hand, some believers feel so inadequate that they give themselves blindly to the opinions of others. I have heard many people comment, "I can't understand the Bible; I just believe what the pastor says." Some pastors are themselves afraid to venture out on their own. They cling to their commentaries, merely parroting what others have said.

For the sake of personal integrity, sometimes we ought to hold fast to our private judgments despite the viewpoints of others. Where would we be today if our forebears had simply followed the status quo of their heritage and present community? Imagine the effects on the church had Paul not resisted Peter by standing against the error of the Judaizers (Galatians 2:11–21). What would the church be like if Martin Luther had not stood alone against Rome? We must cling to private judgment when others stray from the truth.

On the other hand, some evangelicals go to the other extreme. Presuming that they have more insight from the Spirit than anyone else, they turn every interpretation into petrified dogma. Every opinion is fixed and absolute. No matter what others have said in the past, no matter what contemporary believers say, many of us never question our own views of a text. We forget how easily we fall into misunderstanding.

Personal interpretations always need improvement. Even the simplest text offers more than our minds can exhaust. We must interpret humbly, ready to learn from others, in order to interact effectively within the Christian community.

Checks and Balances

An important working principle of democratic governments is the concept of checks and balances. In order to protect against tyranny, branches of government keep watch over each other. But this system has its drawbacks. Since no one has absolute power, few decisions can be made quickly and easily. Dictators get more done in much less time. In less than a decade, Adolf Hitler transformed Germany into a powerful war machine. Pol Pot reshaped Cambodia overnight. Concentrated power works efficiently. Yet, as history warns us, only a system of checks and balances can protect us from tyranny.

Community interaction also needs a system of checks and balances. While heritage, present community, and private judgment make important contributions, one is not necessarily better than the others. Each is blessed by the Spirit, and each is influenced by sin. As those outside the church are quick to point out, our heritage is riddled with failure. The present community has problems, too. If we are honest about ourselves as individuals, we recognize how we quickly stray into error. Because of these limitations, the elements of interaction must keep watch over each other.

Many believers prefer to subject themselves uncritically to one element rather than deal with all of these checks and balances. Our work with Old Testament stories would be simpler if we didn't have to adjudicate among different viewpoints. Yet, just as concentrated political power leads to oppression, too much reliance on one element of community interaction leads to hermeneutical tyranny.

On occasion evangelicals subject themselves to the tyranny of heritage. These well-meaning believers look at the church today, see its many weaknesses, and are tempted to idealize some historical period. We isolate a particular creed or group of people and insist that all interpretation must fully conform to their viewpoints. The outcome of these tendencies is not difficult to see. When heritage tyrannizes hermeneutics, we lose touch with our contemporary world. Our interpretations become irrelevant, unable to deal with today's questions.

The issues of our day force the church beyond the findings of heritage. Today we must interpret Old Testament narratives in the light of nuclear war, world hunger, human rights, euthanasia, genetic engineering, abortion, and a host of relatively modern issues. Our heritage can help only indirectly. Total dependence on heritage turns our eyes away from contemporary needs.

The present community can also tyrannize interpretation. Many of us tend to follow every theological trend that comes our way. As the church explores an issue, we jump on the bandwagon and find nearly every story in the Old Testament speaking to it. Yet we can press attention to current concerns too far. Without the restraint of heritage, our pursuit of relevance can actually distract us from authentic Christianity. As Paul warned, we are not to be "blown here and there by every wind of teaching" (Ephesians 4:14). We must not allow the present community to dominate interpretation.

Finally, we sometimes crown private judgment as absolute monarch over hermeneutics. This problem is acute in academic circles. The ideal modern scholar, we are told, is a person who follows the truth wherever it leads, despite tradition and popular opinion. Some pastors and church leaders imitate this scholarly ideal, always looking for something unique to say. But placing too much importance on creativity and individual insight can be dangerous. When we forget the checks and balances of heritage and present community, individualistic interpretations can lead to error and fragmentation in the church. Private judgment, like the gifts of the Spirit, should be used for edification (Ephesians 4:11–13). The pursuit of truth is not an individual journey; it is a goal toward which we strive with others. The Christian scholar's task is not to invent idiosyncratic approaches to Old Testament stories. Rather, it is to interpret these texts while participating in the full range of community interaction.

All of us tend to fall prey to hermeneutical tyranny. If we are to escape this problem, we must correct our natural proclivities. Am I too inclined to submit my views to my heritage? Do I blindly pursue contemporary trends? Am I prone to follow my own judgments too much? How can I balance my normal practice by giving more attention to the other elements of interaction?

But a balanced approach creates a lot of red tape. When we give all three members of our hermeneutical team the attention they deserve, tensions will inevitably arise. Heritage, present community, and private judgment can be in harmony and disharmony.

At times the various elements confirm each other; we often find that our own convictions agree with those of the contemporary church and our heritage. When we find this harmony, we have confidence and a high level of cognitive rest.[22] Of course, harmony does not ensure that we have proper understanding, but convictions grow stronger as we hear confirmation from all sides.

At other times, however, discord within our hermeneutical team sounds a warning. We should be cautious when the church moves away from its heritage. If individuals come to conclusions at odds with the rest of the church, we should hesitate. The less concurrence we discover, the less confidence we should have.

Each member of our hermeneutical team has a role to play. Heritage keeps us in touch with the work of God's Spirit in believers of the past. Present community holds us accountable to the work of the Spirit in believers of our own day. Private judgment keeps us looking for personal illumination from the Spirit. In the light of the complexities of interpreting Old Testament stories, we need each of these elements to watch over the others (see figure 7).

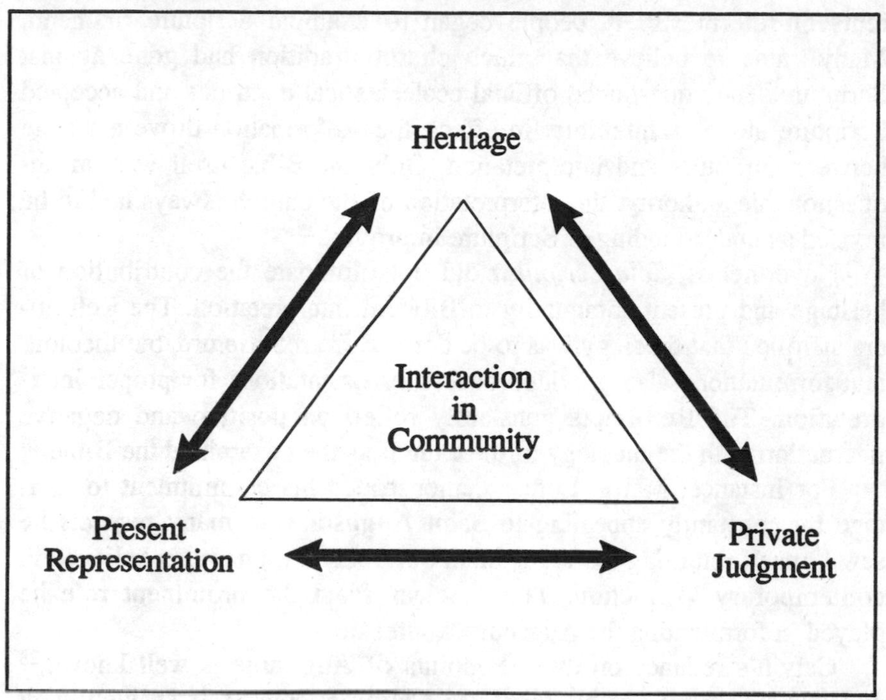

Fig. 7: Checks and Balances in Interaction

Interpretation and Theology

This concern with the influence of interaction in the Christian community will make many evangelicals uncomfortable. It raises an issue that concerns all of us. Is the theology of the church supposed to govern our interpretation of the Bible? Are we to allow theology to affect our understanding? Isn't that putting the cart before the horse? After all, theology is to be derived from the Bible, not the other way around.

Sola Scriptura

For many evangelicals the Protestant slogan *Sola Scriptura* (Scripture Alone) settles the issue. "First things first!" we say. "Scripture is to determine our theology; theology does not come before Scripture." As the Reformation motto states, Scripture is the only sufficient rule for theology.[23] Yet this basic commitment does not settle every aspect of the interplay between theology and interpretation.

The Reformers developed this doctrine in response to the medieval church's tendency to treat Scripture and tradition as equals.[24] As currents of reform stirred, people began to examine Scripture firsthand. Many came to believe that much church tradition had gone against Scripture. They questioned official ecclesiastical doctrines and accepted Scripture alone as infallible. In effect, the Reformation drove a wedge between Scripture and interpretation. Only the Bible itself was an unquestionable authority; the interpretation of the church always had to be revised as understanding of Scripture improved.[25]

Nevertheless, *Sola Scriptura* did not eliminate the contribution of heritage and present community to Biblical interpretation. The Reformers affirmed that theology was to be derived from Scripture, but theological formulations also provided necessary orientations for proper interpretation. The Reformers constantly relied on positive and negative interaction with the theology of the church as they examined the Bible.[26]

For instance, Martin Luther demonstrated his commitment to heritage by constantly appealing to Saint Augustine. In many respects he saw himself returning to Augustinian outlooks.[27] Luther also believed in contemporary interaction. This is clear from the prominent role he played in formulating the Augsburg Confession.

Calvin's reliance on the viewpoints of Augustine is well known,[28] and in later editions of his *Institutes,* Calvin interacted extensively with numerous other figures in the ancient and medieval church.[29] Calvin never failed to rely on the guidance of ecclesiastical tradition, so long as it was subordinated to the authority of Scripture.[30]

For the Reformers, *Sola Scriptura* did not imply that Biblical interpretion should be isolated from traditional theology. Instead, it set the Scriptures as the supreme authority for theological formulations. The Scriptures alone are the unquestionable rule of faith and life.

In recent years a number of evangelicals have lost sight of the value of traditional theology for interpreting Old Testament narratives. Fearing the domination of perspectives foreign to the Bible, they argue that traditional views, especially those of systematic theology, must be suppressed in interpretation. At first glance this outlook has a certain appeal. No one wants to impose illegitimate philosophical categories on the Bible. We struggle to conform our interpretation to the text itself. But this perspective has been taken to extremes and has led to significant hermeneutical problems.

Biblical Theology

One influential trend away from systematic theology may be traced to the Biblical Theology movement in the second half of our century. This movement began outside evangelical circles, but it has significantly shaped the way we study Old Testament narratives. In the following sketch, we will look at two major perspectives in the Biblical Theology movement.

First, from its inception Biblical Theology was committed to reading Old Testament narratives with a *historical orientation.* The historical qualities of the Old Testament had been recognized through the centuries in a number of ways, but Biblical Theology highlighted these as never before. Modern Biblical Theology was deeply influenced by the philosophical outlooks of Hegel (1770–1831),[31] who believed that historical progress brought unity to all creation. History held the key to understanding all reality.[32] In this view interpreters sought not so much for abstract theological ideas as for historical developments behind the text. This historical orientation was modified by several important figures who looked at the Bible as special redemptive history (*Heilsgeschichte*).[33] But the focus of interpretation was still on historical development. The stage was now set to discard the scholastic concept of the Bible as a resource for doctrine and to treat Scripture primarily as a resource for reconstructing God's progressive redemption of humanity.[34]

The redemptive-historical outlook grew rapidly in Europe after World War I.[35] In one way or another, many prominent figures continued to emphasize the history of revelation.[36] American theologians followed suit, especially after World War II.[37] Many leading twentieth-century critical interpreters focused their efforts on understanding the mighty acts of God recorded in the Bible.[38]

Second, Biblical Theology assumed that this redemptive-historical orientation was central to the Bible itself. Traditional systematic theology derived its categories from Aristotelian philosophy,[39] but the dynamic, historical orientation of Biblical Theology was thought to be the heartbeat of Biblical texts themselves. This conviction was frequently linked to a distinction between Greek and Hebrew mindsets. As it was described, the Greeks looked at the world in abstract, static categories, but Middle Easterners thought in terms of concrete history. Beegle's words represent the typical view, "The Hebrews and the other Semites did not think in speculative philosophical terms. . . . The Hebrew language was one of action, and the God of the Hebrews was understood as One who acted."[40]

During the 1960s the Biblical Theology movement came to an abrupt halt among critical scholars, who raised questions against the concept of divine activity in history.[41] Barr and Gilkey pointed out the inconsistency of theologians speaking as if God actually acted in history, while explaining the majority of such records in natural scientific terms. As Gilkey argued, critical Biblical theologians tried to "have their cake and eat it too."[42]

Another objection rose against the concept of the Hebrew mindset. In his monumental work, *Semantics of Biblical Language*, Barr demonstrated that linguistic evidence did not support a sharp distinction between eastern and western thinking.[43] Middle Easterners often thought as abstractly as westerners, and westerners often thought just as dynamically as easterners. This insight proved to be a decisive blow against Biblical Theology.[44]

While critical Biblical Theology is nearly obsolete, it continues to influence evangelicals today. The most important figure in the evangelical branch of the movement was Princeton's first professor of Biblical Theology, Geerhardus Vos (1862–1949). His *Biblical Theology: The Old and New Testaments* has been one of the most influential evangelical works in Old Testament hermeneutics in this century.[45] We find the two tendencies of critical Biblical Theology in Vos. On the one hand, Vos made redemptive revelatory acts of God his central concern. He divided Old Testament history into five epochs: 1) the Pre-Redemptive era, 2) the Noahic period and the developments leading up to it, 3) the period between Noah and the great patriarchs, 4) the Mosaic period, and 5) the Prophetic period. He focused on the form and content of divine revelation unique to each era.

On the other hand, Vos affirmed that redemptive history was the Bible's "own revelatory structure" and the "main stem of revelation."[46] Following the distinction made by J. S. Gabler (1753–1826),[47] Vos argued that Biblical Theology was descriptive of the Bible.[48] A redemptive-historical approach is not imposed on Scripture; it comes from the Bible itself. Vos warned against going too far with this view.[49] But many of his followers have gone beyond him to suggest that the historical orientation of Biblical Theology represents the Bible's own theological patterning. Contrary to the logical categories of systematic theology, they assume that historical categories reflect the Bible's own inner coherence.[50]

When a redemptive-historical approach is so closely identified with the Bible's own "categories and thought forms,"[51] it raises a serious question about the relationship between interpretation and traditional theology. Most Biblical theologians insist that systematic theology must embrace the discoveries of a redemptive-historical approach, but they seldom argue as strongly that the logical constraints of systematic theology must restrain redemptive-historical analysis. They occasionally mention the need for both of these approaches, but mutual dependence is not their emphasis.[52] Instead, Biblical Theologians usually treat the relationship as a one-way street, giving redemptive-historical analysis priority over systematic-theological analysis.[53]

This one-sided emphasis did not present serious problems in evangelical circles for several decades. It appears that traditional theological outlooks restrained Biblical Theologians from straying too far. But as the movement has gained momentum in recent decades, Biblical interpreters have felt free to ignore systematic theology more and more. It is common to find Biblical Theologians overlooking the relevance of systematic theological questions for the interpretation of Old Testament stories. "Biblical writers were not giving us a system of doctrine," they say. "We must look for the redemptive-historical focus, not an abstract system of ideas."

To avoid this dangerous tendency, we must first recognize that redemptive history is not the central concern of many portions of the Old Testament.[54] Wisdom literature—Job, Proverbs, Ecclesiastes, some Psalms—for instance, has little interest in redemptive history. Although a connection between history, law and wisdom appears in covenantal structures,[55] the fact remains that wisdom books hardly devote themselves to reporting redemptive history.

Beyond this, as Vos himself noted, Biblical Theology does not reflect the Bible's most dominant organizing principle. Biblical Theology uses an historical model as opposed to a logical model, but it still reorganizes the Old Testament.[56] The extent of this rearrangement can be seen when we recognize that the basic units of Scripture are not historical epochs, but books. We do not find the Old Testament organized "First Chapter of History," "Second Chapter of History," and so on. On the contrary, it is arranged in literary units: Genesis, Exodus, Leviticus. . . . Operating out of a redemptive-historical framework, Vos derived three epochs in Old Testament history from the first unit of the Bible, the book of Genesis.[57] He then went on to include four books in the period of Moses and the rest of the Old Testament books in the single prophetic period. This kind of analysis hardly appears to coincide with the pattern of revelation given in Scripture.

Beyond this, the many ways in which evangelical Biblical Theologians divide the Old Testament into periods lead us to suspect that Biblical Theology does more than simply uncover the internal structures of the text. There is little agreement as to how Old Testament history should be viewed. Vos divided the history of the Old Testament and New Testament into seven periods. Some follow his pattern,[58] but others deviate significantly.[59]

With so many different arrangements, we can see how much Biblical Theology reorganizes the Bible.[60] Biblical Theology follows a historical pattern that reorganizes the Bible just as much as, if not more than, the logical patterns of traditional theology.

The great value of a redemptive-historical approach is its ability to help us reassess the meaning of Old Testament narratives. It is easy to be so preoccupied with systematic theological questions that we miss much of what these stories teach. We force them into our theological system, never noticing how they challenge our preconceptions. Nevertheless, we must be careful not to go to the extreme of ignoring traditional theological concerns. The writers of Old Testament narratives gave their readers a system of beliefs through their texts. They were concerned with logical patterning of beliefs as well as with the history of revelation.[61] To understand their stories properly, we must set them within the framework of logical parameters as well as historical development.

As a result, we must not set either Biblical Theology or systematic theology above the other; we must put them on equal footing. Both can misrepresent Scripture and both can reflect the teaching of Scripture. Both outlooks are ways of synthesizing material into useful formats, each with its own strengths and weaknesses. As we learn to employ both methods, we will grow in our understanding of Old Testament narratives.

Reciprocity

When builders construct a house, they begin with the groundwork. They lay the foundation; they build the first and second floors; finally they put on the roof. They build from the ground up. Or so it seems from a distance. But every experienced builder will tell you that it is not quite so simple. Constructing a multi-story house is not just a one-two-three-step project. A closer look reveals a more complicated procedure.

Throughout the construction process, builders have to deal with more than one level at a time. They build each floor in anticipation of the levels that go on top of it. They pour the foundation anticipating what will rest on it. The shell of the first story has to match the second floor. The second story is built on top of the first, but its shape and size are determined by the kind of roof the house will have.

Beyond this, builders do not complete one level before moving to the next. Once the roof is intact, the workers return to the first and second floors to do the interior work. So although construction may seem to follow a simple vertical movement, the workers actually go from level to level throughout the project.

Many evangelicals act as if the relationship between Biblical interpretation and theology is a simple one-two-three-step process. We first go to the text to get some basic information. Next, we put this information into some kind of theological format. Finally, we put our theology into practice. Exegetical theology comes first, systematics second, and practical theology third. But this model is too simple and often misleading.

From the outset we should affirm that this outlook is correct as far as it goes. We learn from Scripture and bring what we have learned into theological discussion. We go through this kind of process every time we read Scripture. For instance, we read the words of Joseph in Genesis 50:20, "And as for you, you meant evil against me, but God meant it for good in order to bring about this present result, to preserve many people alive" (NASB). We often take this statement to mean that God was controlling the evil actions of Joseph's brothers, working their evil for the good of Joseph and the nation. We put this concept alongside other passages and construct a doctrine of divine providence. In effect, we have developed our theology from the ground up.

Nevertheless, information does not simply flow from exegesis to theology. Biblical, systematic, and practical theology are not just derived from exegesis. They also inform our exegesis of Scripture.

Every branch of theology prepares us for interpretation. We always approach Scripture in light of prior theological reflection. These prior considerations may be informal or formal, but they always influence our approach to specific passages.

For instance, what causes most of us to zero in on the providential hand of God as we read Joseph's words in Genesis 50:20? Why not use the passage to understand the psychology of forgiveness? Why not reconstruct the personality of Joseph and his brothers on the basis of the passage? Why not concern ourselves with the intra-patriarchal relations? These matters are also in the passage. But most of us see the providence of God because our theological systems emphasize this doctrine. At some point this particular passage may have shaped our understanding of the doctrine, but our theological reflection also directs us as we approach the passage.

Building a house involves upward movement, but it also entails going back and forth among the various levels of construction. In a similar way, hermeneutics always involves reciprocity between the various theological disciplines and interpretation.[62]

The pendulum swings back and forth in the emphasis we give to firsthand exegesis and theological reflection. At times we give theological discussions precedence over exegetical work; at other times we give priority to looking at specific texts. Both tendencies present benefits and dangers.

If theology dominates our exegetical work, the qualities of individual texts tend to fade into the larger picture of a theological system. If we follow this approach too long, our exegesis can become little more than the servant of our preconceived notions. No room is left for discovery; texts simply confirm what we already believe.

On the other side, however, we can give exegetical work too much precedence over theology. For a variety of reasons, many evangelicals insist that interpreters must keep the influence of theology to a minimum. As good as this viewpoint may sound, it opens interpreters to significant danger. Ignoring the guidance of theology does not free us from the influence of theological preconceptions; they will always be present. But ignoring theology can cut us off from well-formed theological preconceptions.

So it is that theology and interpretation must inform each other. Fresh investigation of the Bible often challenges the theological structures of the church. We always want to test and evaluate theology according to our examination of particular passages of Scripture. But theology protects us from misconstruing individual texts. It constrains our interpretation by shedding light on the passage at hand. Interpretation and theology are mutually dependent; they must inform and control each other.

Conclusion

We began this chapter saying that we must read Old Testament narratives in community. Interaction with people in general, and with other Christians in particular, is essential for responsible interpretation. As we interpret Old Testament narratives, we are influenced by the checks and balances among heritage, present community, and private judgment. Despite current tendencies to overlook the importance of theology for exegesis, traditional theological systems are crucial for interpreting Old Testament stories. As we interact with theological perspectives developed within the church, we will be equipped for better understanding of Old Testament stories.

Review Questions

1. Why must we think of interpretation as a community enterprise? What two communities help believers understand Old Testament narratives? What are two advantages and disadvantages of involvement with each community?
2. What are the three major elements of interaction in the Christian community? Explain how interpreters fall victim to hermeneutical tyranny. How can this danger be avoided? Give an example.
3. Describe the basic tenets of the Biblical Theology movement. What is the danger of giving priority to redemptive-historical analysis over systematic theological analysis? How should Biblical and systematic theology relate to each other?

Study Exercises

1. Look at the Scripture index of a major ecclesiastical confession or systematic theology. Note three or four cases where Old Testament narratives are used. How can you benefit from these uses? Can you spot a misuse of an Old Testament narrative?
2. Write your theological family tree (include persons, books, confessions, etc.). Identify the present community of your theological tradition. List five ways your theological convictions have been shaped by these forces.
3. Read Genesis 2:5–3:24. What systematic theological issues does this account address? What Biblical Theological issues does it address? What is the value of each perspective on this passage?

4

THE INFLUENCE OF EXEGESIS

As I walked into the college chapel one sunny afternoon, I looked up at a large stained glass window. But clouds racing across the sky played tricks on me. At first all I could see was my own reflection. The sky outside had darkened, turning the window into a mirror. Suddenly the clouds moved, and the mirror dissolved. At that moment the light shifted, and I could see outside through the glass. Turning to go, I glanced back at the window once more. This time I saw something I had missed before—a colorful picture formed by the tinted panes. That afternoon I had looked at the same stained glass window in three different ways: as a mirror, a window, and a picture.

In much the same way, the Holy Spirit has led the church to look at Old Testament stories as: *mirrors, windows,* and *pictures.*[1] In *thematic analysis* we treat Old Testament stories as mirrors that reflect our interests and concerns. In *historical analysis* we see these texts as windows to historical events. In *literary analysis* we look at Old Testament stories as pictures, appreciating form and content together. As we explore how the Spirit prepares us to interpret Old Testament narratives, we must see how each of these exegetical approaches influences us (see figure 8).

Of course, these approaches do not operate independently. Thematic analysis includes historical and literary appreciation; historical analysis looks at themes and literary features; literary analysis cannot ignore thematic and historical concerns. In one way or another, these approaches always depend on each other.

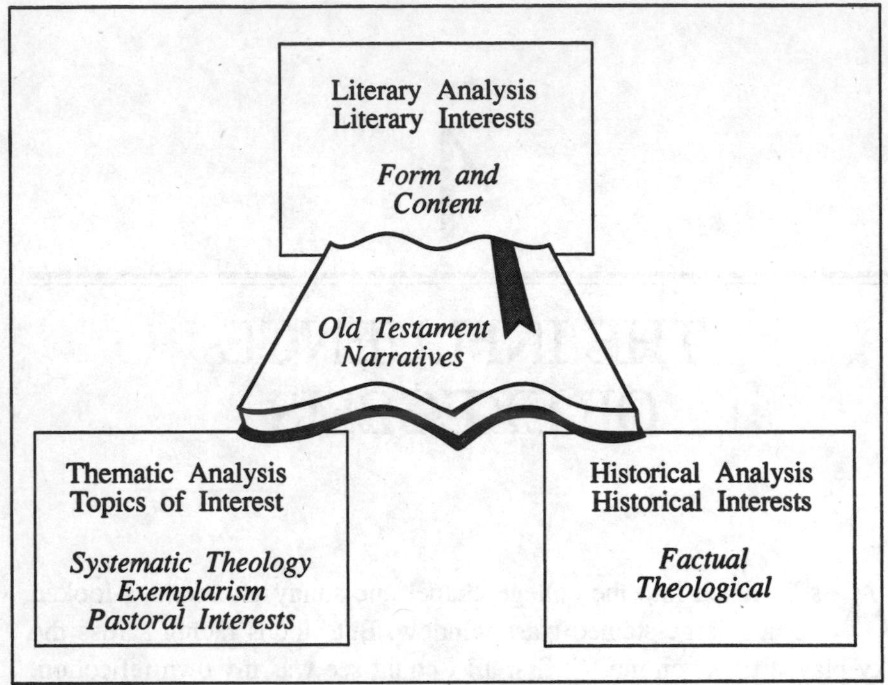

Fig. 8: Major Exegetical Approaches

Thematic Analysis

On occasion my wife and I host a night at the movies for seminary students. We watch a film and then discuss it. I often start the discussion by asking, "What was the most important part of the movie?" As you can imagine, we usually get as many answers as there are people. What is critical to one person may be ignored by another. Certain scenes stand out because they stir a memory or speak to a personal interest. We all tend to focus on the aspects of the movie that are particularly important to us.

Through the centuries the Holy Spirit has led the church to take a similar approach to Old Testament narratives. We concentrate our attention on elements in a passage that seem particularly relevant to us. Rather than honing in on historical events behind stories or on their prominent literary focus, we hold a story up as a mirror and search for the themes that speak to our own concerns. As a result, thematic analysis often majors on minors, highlighting secondary themes in a passage. We concentrate on our theological, philosophical, or personal interests, even if they are not prominent in the texts themselves.

Thematic analysis has a strong appeal because Old Testament stories say so many things. Take the simple sentence, "In the beginning God created the heavens and the earth" (Genesis 1:1). How many ideas does this passage convey? Is it only the concept that God made everything? This aspect of the passage is certainly prominent, but what about other facets? If we slow down and read it again we spot several kernels of thought:[2] 1) there is a God, 2) there are heavens, 3) there is an earth, 4) there was a beginning, 5) God created, 6) and creation included all things. The list goes on and on. Any of these kernels may become the focus of a thematic approach. We may decide to stress God, the world, the act of creation, the beginning of time, or any other facet of the text. We concentrate on a particular motif, not because of its prominence in the text, but because of our interests.

If such variety characterizes one verse, imagine the number of items in a whole story. The familiar story of Abraham's sacrifice of Isaac serves as a good example (Genesis 22:1–19).[3] How many concepts are conveyed by this passage? We cannot number them all. Some are more important than others. Most readers would agree that God's command to sacrifice Isaac is more important than the fact that two servants went with Abraham and Isaac. The substitute ram is more significant than the fact that Abraham saddled his donkey. Even so, the more central themes may not be *our* primary concerns. We may ask about the use of donkeys in travel, servants, or any other minor aspect of the story. The possibilities are endless.

The profusion of themes in Old Testament stories offers many focal points for exegesis. While we are not free to read into a passage what is not there, in thematic analysis we are free to attend to minor motifs, if they are important to us.

Basis of Thematic Analysis

Is it appropriate to highlight minor themes? Shouldn't our exegesis always concentrate on the central motifs of a passage? At times studies in hermeneutics suggest that we must always identify the main idea in a text and make it central in our interpretation.[4] As important as this approach is, we need not limit ourselves to it.

Biblical writers themselves often majored on minor themes. For example, when we compare the Chronicler's account of David's life to the book of Samuel, we see that the Chronicler approached the book of Samuel thematically. Samuel divides David's reign between his time under God's blessing and under God's curse.[5] It reports the king's grand accomplishments and his horrible sins. It shows him to be both the great king of Israel and also a troubled, frail human being. In fact, the writer of Samuel blamed David for many of the ills that plagued his house for generations (2 Samuel 12:10).[6]

Even though the Chronicler relied heavily on the book of Samuel, he approached David's life from a different perspective. The Chronicler idealized David.[7] David is by no means free of shortcomings (1 Chronicles 13:5–13; 15:11–15; 21:1—22:1; 22:7–8), but by comparison the Chronicler's portrait of David is remarkably unblemished. The Chronicler omitted several key passages from Samuel:

1 Samuel 1:1—2 Samuel 4:12	Pre-Davidic History
2 Samuel 6:20b–23	Michal's Reproach of David
2 Samuel 9:1–13	David's Concern for Saul's House
2 Samuel 11:1–21:14	Bathsheba and Ensuing Troubles

He ignored the checkered history leading to David's rise, omitted the substance of Michal's reproach, and avoided David's troublesome relationship with Mephibosheth. Most pointedly, he did not record David's acts of adultery and murder.[8]

In this sense the Chronicler read Samuel thematically. He did not hide David's weaknesses, but his interests in presenting David as an ideal for his post-exilic audience led him to focus on the positive side of the monarch. The Chronicler's method of interpretation validates the basic approach of thematic analysis.

Types of Thematic Analysis

Thematic analysis has been applied in many ways through the centuries. For our purposes we will describe three important ways: *systematic theology, exemplarism,* and *pastoral interests.*

Systematic theology. The most dominant form of thematic analysis is traditional systematic theology. Older confessions and catechisms frequently used Old Testament stories as proof-texts to define and support doctrinal beliefs.[9] This has been the case in recent systematic theologies as well.[10]

Unfortunately, however, systematic theologians have misused texts. At times the passages they cite have little to do with the doctrines in view. This has turned many modern interpreters against proof-texting.[11] But we must be careful not to reject proof-texting altogether. When done with care it is "a useful form of theological shorthand."[12]

Old Testament stories touch on many traditional theological themes. Under the rubrics of systematic theology, we may ask questions such as, "What does this story say about the character of God?" "How does it shed light on the doctrine of sin?" "What does it contribute to the doctrine of salvation?" "What insight does it give into ethics?" Searching Old Testament stories with such questions in mind will enrich our theological system.

Exemplarism. At other times thematic analysis amounts to exemplarism. In this form interpreters explore passages for illustrations of religious life. David as shepherd (1 Samuel 17:34–36) and warrior (1 Samuel 17:37–51) becomes a model of faith and courage. Solomon's justice (1 Kings 3:16–28) becomes a paradigm of wisdom.

Exemplary approaches sometimes go to extremes. For instance, there is the obvious temptation to psychologize characters beyond the limits of the text. We must be wary of such abuses.[13] Yet we must not entirely reject the exemplary approach because of these errors. Old Testament narratives offer many examples of what to do and not to do. We should be ready to appropriate these aspects of the texts.

Good exemplary thematic analysis may be found in several popular treatments of Nehemiah as a model of leadership.[14] The major concern of the writer of Ezra-Nehemiah is the continuation of Nehemiah's reforms.[15] Nevertheless, Nehemiah did exhibit expert leadership. He laid careful plans, delegated responsibility, managed conflict, and showed courage and persistence. Although these features of Nehemiah's life are secondary to the main purpose of the book, we may draw attention to them through exemplary thematic analysis.

Many different questions can be answered through exemplarism. "What was the struggle this character faced?" "How did he or she overcome the problem?" "What can I learn from this example?" These matters may not be central to the stories, but they may still be important to us.

Pastoral interests. Sometimes readers come to texts thematically because of pastoral interests. As we examine our churches, we grow concerned with a particular issue. Old Testament stories often address these modern struggles.

Topical sermons are usually based on thematic exegesis. The pastor surveys the congregation, notes a need, and develops a sermon to address that need.[16] Charles Spurgeon (1834–1892) is known for using Old Testament stories thematically. In his sermon on 1 Samuel 12:17, he took the words "Is it not wheat harvest today?" as a starting point for a sermon on Christian evangelism. He acknowledged, however, the thematic character of his approach: "I shall not note the connection [to the larger context], but I will simply take these words as a motto, and my sermon will be founded upon a harvest field."[17] This extreme example illustrates that Old Testament narratives can profit the church when viewed thematically.

Thematic analysis may take these and many other forms. It may be informal or scholarly, practical or theoretical. Whatever the case, thematic analysis holds up Old Testament stories as mirrors that reflect the interests of readers. We must guard against abuses, but we should also recognize that thematic analysis is a major way the Spirit has taught us to approach these texts.

Historical Analysis

Several years ago I visited Auschwitz, the notorious Nazi concentration camp. As I walked under the entry sign, *"ARBEIT MACHT FREI"* (Work Makes Free), I wondered what the prisoners must have felt as they passed by. I stood on the spot where whole families were executed daily. I visited the crowded dormitories, cramped starvation cells, and a gas chamber. Horrible images from the past haunted me.

On the way out of the camp, I bought a copy of *Auschwitz: Nazi Extermination Camp*.[18] As I read the book, I noticed that it lacked tight organization; it was riddled with typographical errors; the translation was poor. But none of this stopped me from reading. The events described were so gripping that I could not put the book down until I had read it twice.

What drew me to the book? What caught my interest? I was not impressed by its literary quality; no themes related to events in my life. Rather, it was primarily the history behind the book that held me captive. The book had become my portal to the past.

The Holy Spirit has led the church to take a similar approach to Old Testament narratives. Old Testament stories become our windows to the historical events they describe. Themes and literary qualities fade into the background as we concentrate on events behind the passages through historical analysis.

Basis of Historical Analysis

Although evangelicals generally affirm the historical reliability of Old Testament narratives,[19] the precise relationship between actual history and Old Testament texts is hardly settled. In the past decade or so, discussions on the hermeneutical implications of Biblical inerrancy have raised many questions related to historical analysis.[20] As a result, two extremes have emerged among evangelicals.

Some evangelicals have begun to move away from believing in a close connection between real history and Bible stories. This tendency is understandable; Old Testament narratives present many historical difficulties.[21] In the past, evangelicals usually dealt with these problems by assuming that further research would yield solutions.[22] In the face of continuing questions, however, a different strategy has developed.

In this more recent view, Biblical narratives present historical problems because they were intentionally cast in genres that did not follow the canons of historical reliability. In other words, at least some Biblical writers never meant for their audiences to take their accounts as historical. If this is the case, our concern for historical reliability is misplaced.

We can hardly disagree with this position in theory. If Jonah is indeed a fable, we would be wrong to interpret it as reliable history. If the Chronicler did not want his book to be taken as a record of historical events, we should not treat it as such. We must read poetry as poetry, proverbs as proverbs, laws as laws, and tales as tales.[23]

We must also admit that this approach has a certain appeal. Genre considerations help us seek the original meaning of the text instead of imposing our modern scientific agenda onto it. In addition, emphasizing genre avoids an outright denial of inerrancy. Instead of attributing error to Biblical writers, we may say that they simply followed the literary conventions of their day. This direction may be appealing, but we must exercise extreme caution.

First, before we discount the historical reliability of a Biblical narrative on the basis of genre, we must find some precedent for this in the Bible itself. To my knowledge, however, Biblical writers themselves never treated Old Testament stories as anything but reliable history. At times the historicity of events is essential to the perspectives of New Testament writers (Romans 5:12–14; Romans 9:6–18; Luke 1:1–4; Hebrews 11:17–40). Critical interpreters may discount these Biblical witnesses as precritical and naive, but evangelicals must look at the Bible's own testimony to its historicity as normative.

Second, we must remember that genre criticism is plagued with difficulties. From the time of Gunkel's foundational work on Genesis and the Psalms, genre studies have seen many significant revisions.[24] Attempts to pin down the features and functions of Biblical genre are rife with uncertainties.

Third, we always face the problem of knowing when to stop. Once a single example of history-like material has been deemed non-historical, what keeps us from treating other portions of Scripture in the same way? Although it may not seem theologically significant to treat some Biblical narratives as fabrications or fables, once we accept this practice without solid, clear criteria, it becomes dangerously easy to deal with other unresolved historical problems in the same way. How many major historical events will we end up sacrificing? Will we treat the pillar of fire, the crossing of the Jordan, the defeat of Jericho, the Davidic promises, even the Gospels themselves, as fables or legends?

Nevertheless, it is appropriate to explore the question of genre and history. This is an important ongoing project, but several issues must be kept in mind.

What features might indicate that history-like narratives in the Old Testament were not intended to be taken as historical? The mere presence of historical problems is not a sufficient criterion, since further research may always uncover solutions. Next, critical interpreters often reject historicity because a text reports supernatural events, but evangelicals do not question the historicity of supernatural occurrences. In addition, similarities between Biblical stories and non-historical texts outside the Bible do not provide solid criteria. Similarities do not necessarily imply the same level of historical truth.

A better way of working at these issues is to look within the stories themselves for markers that indicate genre. If we can identify vocabulary, style, or structures peculiar to a genre, we are on our way to more secure conclusions. But at this point, there are no well-established markers of fables, sagas, tales, and legends in ancient Near Eastern literature, much less in Old Testament narratives.[25] For instance, can it be established from the text that the opening of the Tower of Babel should be translated, "Once upon a time . . ." (Genesis 11:1, NEB)?[26] Such a translation rests on theological and historical presuppositions, not on evidence from the text itself.

We must handle genre considerations with care. The witness of the Bible itself, the complexities of genre criticism, and the difficulty of setting limits caution against drawing hasty conclusions. Though further research may shed light on some of these matters, a heavy burden of proof lies on those evangelicals who argue that history-like narratives in the Old Testament were not intended to be reliable, inerrant historical accounts.

Nevertheless, many evangelicals have gone to the other extreme and simply identify Biblical narratives with history. They act as if historical portions of the Bible give an exacting, meticulous account of history. They treat Old Testament stories as instant replays or candid camera accounts of the past.

Evangelicals affirm the inerrancy of Old Testament narratives in the sense that they do not intentionally or unintentionally misrepresent history, but these accounts may not give the detailed historical record modern readers often demand. As Murray put it, we should not expect "pedantic precision" from Scripture. He mentions, "The Scripture abounds in illustrations of the absence of the type of meticulous and pedantic precision which we might arbitrarily seek to impose as the criterion of infallibility."[27]

With the *Chicago Statement on Biblical Inerrancy*, we must reject the notion that

> Inerrancy is negated by Biblical phenomena such as a lack of modern technical precision, irregularities of grammar or spelling, observational descriptions of nature, the reporting of falsehoods, the use of hyperbole and round numbers, the topical arrangement of material, variant selections of material in parallel accounts, or the use of free citations.[28]

Throughout Old Testament narratives, we find history written in ways that do not follow our modern penchant for exacting precision.

All reports of history involve some interpretation from the writer's perspective.[29] But the level of precision and creativity ranges over a wide scale. One end of the scale nears speculation, as seen in many historical novels and biographies. These histories focus on a few well-established events, but writers also fill the gaps with fabrications. Often the reader cannot differentiate between truth and fiction. On the other end of the scale, the interpretative dimension is present but not obtrusive. Responsible writers of history textbooks and newspaper reports, for example, avoid speculating and hypothesizing as much as possible. At least they openly admit when the level of reliability varies. Finally, historical writings may fall anywhere along the scale between these two extremes.

Evangelicals believe that what the Old Testament narratives say about historical events is true and reliable; there are no errors in God's revelation. Yet these texts present "history from a prophetic point of view."[30] On the one hand, we must not say that Old Testament writers fabricated their stories. Biblical writers were inspired by the Spirit of truth and did not present fiction as fact. On the other hand, ideological purposes determined which events the writers chose and how they presented them. Old Testament narratives do not give us a second by second, detailed account of the past. They were written from a point of view, but without error and misrepresentation.

We should avoid both extremes. We must not allow genre considerations to separate Biblical text from real history. At the same time, however, we must remember that all Biblical narratives are interpretations of history from ideological perspectives. Historical analysis is possible because these stories are inerrant, but historical analysis must always consider the purpose for which Old Testament narratives were written.

Types of Historical Analysis

As with thematic analysis, historical analysis takes many forms; two of which have been prominent: *factual* and *theological*.

Factual. In factual historical analysis, we look through the window of the text and ask, "How should we reconstruct events in the light of the text and other historical data?" Evangelicals are especially concerned with this approach in apologetic endeavors. We have spent much energy trying to establish the historical reliability of the Bible. A quick survey of major evangelical Old Testament introductions from the late nineteenth century through recent years illustrates the prominence of this sort of historical analysis.[31] Until recently evangelical commentaries have also been preoccupied with factual historical reconstruction.[32]

Challenges to inerrancy have not faded in recent years. People will always ask, "Is the first chapter of Genesis historical?" "Was there a flood?" "How do we reconcile the apparent discrepancies between Chronicles, Samuel, and Kings?" Factual historical analysis will always be an important part of interpreting Old Testament stories.

Theological. Theological historical analysis has risen to prominence in evangelical circles through the influence of Biblical Theology. We have already looked at this interpretative outlook in some detail.[33] This approach is more conceptual than factual, but it is still oriented toward the events that lie behind Old Testament stories. Biblical Theologians primarily use Old Testament narratives to reconstruct the character of revelation and religious life in different periods of redemptive history. They ask several key questions: "What are the distinctive periods of Biblical history?" "What are the unique features of these periods?" "How do the epochs relate to each other?" These questions also form an important avenue for exploring Old Testament narratives.

Historical analysis may be oriented toward facts or theology. Whatever the case, we use Old Testament stories as windows to past events.

This is another major way the Holy Spirit has taught the church to approach Old Testament narratives.

Literary Analysis

On a shelf at home, we have an album full of photographs of my wife. Occasionally I show these pictures to our guests. They thumb through the pages, politely glancing at one snapshot after another. Most of these pictures are "grins and snaps." As they turn to the last page, however, it never fails that someone exclaims, "Now that's a picture!" The last photo was taken by a professional photographer with an artistic bent. It's a lovely picture. Usually people pause, comment on the expert lighting, the focus, the balance, and say, "She's beautiful!"

The Holy Spirit has led the church to this kind of appreciation for Old Testament stories. Instead of looking at minor themes or historical events, we approach these texts through literary analysis. Literary analysis treats Old Testament narratives as skillful works of art, maintaining the integrality of form and content. We study literary features of a text the way we appreciate the colors, textures, contrasts, lines, and balance of a fine portrait. By this means we are able to distinguish major and minor aspects of the text. As we have seen, thematic and historical analyses often focus on relatively minor dimensions of stories. Literary analysis, however, helps us discern the central motifs of a passage.

Basis of Literary Analysis

Literary analysis is the current trend in Biblical hermeneutics. But should evangelicals devote themselves to this approach? Three considerations undergird the value of literary analysis: the *literary units* of the Old Testament, the *literary qualities* of Old Testament texts, and the *insights* this approach yields.

Literary units. First, literary analysis is important because the Old Testament consists of literary units, not historical or theological units. The literary structure of the canon stands in contrast to the way we often think about the Old Testament. Our propensity toward historical analysis might lead us to expect Scriptures to come divided into the great epochs of redemptive history: Book 1—"Before the Fall," Book 2—"From the Fall to the Flood," Book 3—"Patriarchal Period" and so on. Our interest in thematic analysis might have led us to expect the categories of systematic theology: Book 1—"The Doctrine of God," Book 2—"The Doctrine of Humanity," Book 3—"The Doctrine of Salvation."

But the Old Testament does not come to us in either of these formats. Neither history nor theological themes structure the Bible. Instead, single books like Genesis cover several major periods of redemptive history, and large groups of books like the prophets cover a single epoch. Similar theological themes appear repeatedly in various combinations within the books of Scripture. The canon of Scripture is primarily structured according to literary units, not history or themes. We must pursue literary analysis because the Old Testament comes to us in literary units. To ignore this approach is to overlook how God structured the Scriptures.

Literary qualities. Beyond this, literary analysis is necessary because Biblical texts exhibit literary qualities.[34] In His wisdom the Spirit inspired Scripture in the forms of poems, songs and—most important for our work—narratives. These texts exhibit many literary characteristics such as imagery, figures of speech, and intricate structures. Had God wanted us merely to concentrate on historical events and theological themes, He would not have given us revelation with literary qualities. We must learn how to incorporate literary outlooks into our interpretative efforts.

Insights. Third, literary analysis is important because it often offers insights that thematic and historical approaches overlook. Consider the well-known episode of Abram's sojourn to Egypt (Genesis 12:10–20). Commentators from all sides of the theological spectrum have focused on historical and thematic dimensions of this text to the neglect of literary analysis. J. Skinner, for instance, commented that the "speech of Abram to his wife (vv. 11–13) is an instructive revelation of social and moral sentiments in early Israel."[35] He also argued that the text is full of ethical reflection on the topic of Abram's lie (vv. 18–19).[36] G. von Rad was interested with the arrival of Asiatics in Egypt and the reported beauty of Sarai at such an old age (v. 14).[37] He also focused on the theme of God's intervention and the moral issue of Abram's lie.[38] For both of these commentators, the text served primarily as a window to history and a mirror of their ethical interests.

Conservative interpreters have examined the passage with similar concerns. Keil and Delitzsch surprisingly suggested that the historical problem of Sarai's beauty could be solved by a comparison with Egyptian women, who were "generally ugly and faded early."[39] They also venture into the ethical problem and wonder how Abram expected to save honor and retain possession of his wife.[40] More recently Kidner has attempted to solve the problem of Sarai's beauty by arguing that the "key . . . lies with patriarchal life span."[41] His other interest is predictably with Abram "using one half of the truth to conceal the other."[42] Each of these commentaries focused on historical and thematic dimensions of the story. Although these reflections are legitimate and important, they ignore the integrality of form and content so vital to literary analysis.

Let us taste the value of literary analysis by sketching a few structural observations of this story. First, we will make an intrinsic inquiry,[43] looking at the passage itself without reference to a specific writer or audience. Second, we will set this text in the extrinsic context of its original writer and audience. For the sake of convenience, we will look at the dramatic structure of this passage in a standard description of dramatic flow[44] (see figure 9).

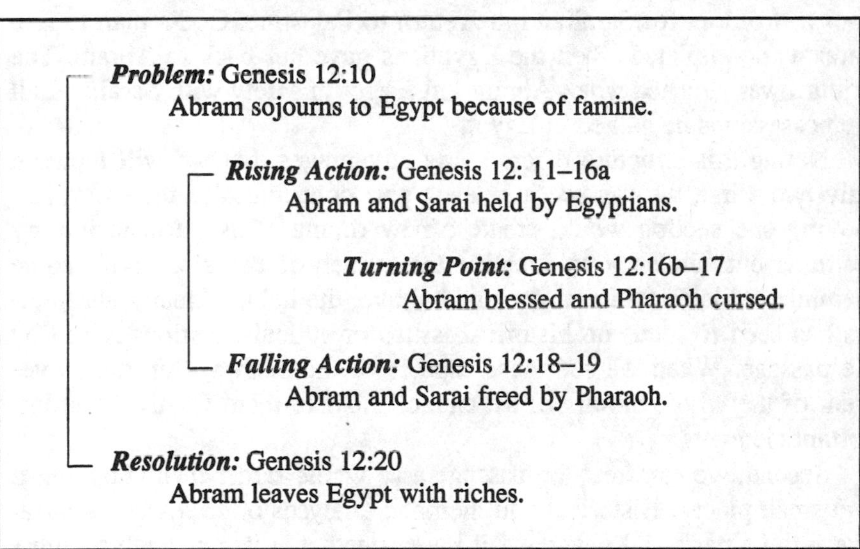

Fig. 9: Dramatic Flow of Genesis 12:10-20

Genesis 12:10 may be called the *dramatic problem;* it introduces the context out of which the narrative flows. Abram goes to Egypt because of a famine and intends to stay there temporarily. The *resolution* (v. 20) balances with the beginning of the story. The writer contrasts the poverty of famine with the riches of Abram as he completes his sojourn. Genesis 12:11–16a contains the *rising action.* The plan to lie is carried through but leads Sarai into Pharaoh's harem. This section is balanced by the *falling action* of Genesis 12:18–19. Both portions are predominantly dramatic dialogue and contain similar expressions—"you are my sister" (v. 13) and "she is my sister" (v. 19). Finally, the middle portion of Genesis 12:16b-17, the *turning point* of the story, forms a skillful interlocking of perspectives. Abram prospers but Pharaoh is cursed.[45] These verses both foreshadow future action in the text and reflect on the previous events of the story. Genesis 12:16b anticipates what will happen to Abram; he will leave with many riches from the Egyptians. Genesis 12:17 deals with the problems that arose for Pharaoh "because of Sarai." In this way the turning point of the drama looks forward and backward, adding to the symmetry.

We can summarize the story in the light of this structural pattern. Abram intended to sojourn in Egypt. His plan to lie about Sarai succeeded in part but was complicated by Sarai's abduction. To resolve the problem, God distinguished between Abram and Pharaoh. He blessed Abram but sent plagues on Pharaoh. The curse on Pharaoh opened the door to freedom for Sarai and the return to Palestine. God's plan to free Sarai was completed when the Egyptians gave her back to Abram. The sojourn was finished when Abram left Egypt in safety with Sarai and all the possessions he gained in Egypt.

Noting this structure offers many advantages, but we will mention only two. First, we can see how each part contributes to the story. Removing one section would create a new drama. This intrinsic inquiry restrains our tendency to identify the center of the story with some thematic or historical item. As noted above, the habit of many interpreters has been to focus on historical issues or ethical questions raised by the passage. When we see these aspects of the story within the movement of the whole narrative, we cannot mistake them for the most important elements.

Second, we can treat the passage as a whole rather than chopping it into small pieces. Historical and thematic analyses often dissect a narrative into its parts and never put it back together. Literary analysis presents the story as the conceptual unit, so we can probe into its meaning and relevance. The movement of sojourn/captivity/intervention/release/return becomes the focus of our interpretative reflection, anticipating other portions of Scripture and countless realities in the life of faith. As we give our attention to the whole story, we will find material for theological contemplation often ignored in other approaches.

When we set these observations in the extrinsic context of the original writer and audience, the story comes to life. Moses told this story to the children of Israel in a way that spoke directly to their situation.[46] It is not difficult to see the connection of this narrative with Moses in the

Exodus. When we consider Israel's experience and its correspondence to Genesis 12:10–20, it becomes clear that Moses reported this story from Abram's life to parallel the deliverance of Israel from Egypt.

Abram sojourned in Egypt because of a famine in Canaan; a famine drove Jacob and his sons into Egypt for food. Deception was characteristic of Abram; Joseph's brothers were known for their lies. While in Egypt Abram prospered, but his hope for a progeny faded because Pharaoh had taken Sarai; Israel flourished in Egypt, but slavery and the slaughter of male infants threatened their posterity. God drew a line between Abram and Pharaoh by His blessings and curses; divine intervention in the Exodus protected the Israelites but brought plagues on Pharaoh. Freedom came through open confrontation between Pharaoh and Abram; Moses and Pharaoh met several times before the king finally said, "Go!" The Egyptians sent Abram away in safety and riches; the Egyptians sent Israel away with their riches.

From these parallels between the Exodus event and the Abram story, we see that Moses intended to use this story as a paradigm to teach Israel the nature of her departure from Egypt and return to Palestine.[47] Moses faced disbelief and discouragement among the tribes. By relating this story from patriarchal history, he presented a relevant word to his fellow Israelites. We can imagine Moses commenting on the story, "Do not give up! No mistake has been made. What you are going through has already been experienced by your father, Abraham. Follow him away from Egypt and have confidence in the power of the Lord!" Similarly it is not difficult to hear the faithful among the tribes responding, "Abraham's exodus is our exodus!"

From this brief example, we can see why we must go beyond thematic and historical interests and apply literary analysis to Old Testament narratives. As we focus on form and content together, the way is open for us to see more of what God has given us in these stories.

Types of Literary Analysis

Literary analysis is not new. Through the centuries the Holy Spirit has led his people to maintain the integrality of form and content as they read Scripture.[48] But frequently literary concerns have been overshadowed by theological and historical issues.

During the Reformation doctrinal controversies with Rome dominated exegesis. The Reformers looked to the Scriptures primarily as theological resources, not as literary works. Yet the Reformers were not without literary sensitivities. For instance, Calvin frequently noted figures of speech, dramatic tension, and vivid imagery. He recognized the differences between narrative and law, wisdom and prophecy.[49] Calvin's commentaries are packed with literary observations, even though his concern with doctrine was primary.

Since the Enlightenment, evangelical interpreters have been preoccupied with historical questions.[50] We have explored Old Testament stories primarily to prove their historicity. Even so, every major work on Biblical hermeneutics has acknowledged literary features of Scripture.[51]

In Old Testament hermeneutics today, the spotlight has shifted to literary analysis. Doctrinal and historical battles continue, but concern with literary approaches has grown significantly. A thorough survey of these developments is beyond the scope of our study, but it will help to trace several major steps.[52]

Source criticism. Near the end of the nineteenth century, literary criticism amounted largely to *source criticism.*[53] In this approach interpreters looked for written sources behind Scripture as we now have it. The familiar documentary hypothesis of the Pentateuch (J, E, D, P) was one of the earliest efforts in this direction. Since then interpreters have reconstructed hypothetical sources for many Old Testament books.

Form criticism. A second major step rose in the early 1900s in *form criticism.*[54] The distinctive focus of form criticism was to identify genre and reconstruct the oral *Sitz im Leben* (cultural situation) in which Old Testament stories were originally used. By comparing the Old Testament with literature from other ancient Near Eastern cultures, they proposed early forms, settings, and uses behind the texts of Scripture.

Redaction criticism. The third major stage of literary analysis came to the foreground in the 1950s under the title *redaction criticism.*[55] Redaction critics traced the developments of Biblical texts from their oral and literary sources to their present shape. They went beyond the concerns of source and form criticism to the full development of passages. This outlook focused on the redactor's purposes by observing the developments of texts.

By and large modern evangelicals remain skeptical of these diachronic approaches. We must distance ourselves from these methods in many ways.[56] For the most part, they are based on commitments radically opposed to evangelical outlooks on the inspiration and authority of Scripture. Nevertheless, as we will see in later chapters, literary appreciation from an evangelical point of view must take sources, forms, and authorial arrangements into consideration.[57]

In the last two decades, however, a major shift has begun in literary approaches to Old Testament narratives. Instead of focusing on sources and developments, interpreters are increasingly more interested in the final form of Old Testament stories.

Rhetorical criticism. One decisive move in this direction occurred in *rhetorical criticism* during the late 1960s and 1970s.[58] Instead of concentrating on the developments of a text, rhetorical critics looked at passages as completed works of art designed to persuade readers. Rhetorical critics dealt primarily with small units in a Biblical book—one story, one poem. But the structures, aesthetic qualities, and rhetorical patterns of these texts became the central concern of interpretation.

Structuralism. During the same time frame, *structuralism* made its mark on Biblical studies.[59] Structuralism represented a number of philosophical and linguistic viewpoints.[60] Structuralists differed from each other in many ways, but they all agreed that the meaning of a text is found primarily within the inner-coherence of the text itself.

Canonical criticism. In recent years these tendencies have been developed further into a theological program known as *canonical criticism.*[61] Canonical critics agree that most Biblical texts developed through time, but they focus on the final, canonical form of the text. Canonical criticism looks at structural and rhetorical patterns but goes beyond other approaches to examine larger contexts.

Evangelicals generally feel more at home with these contemporary literary methods. We can benefit in many ways from rhetorical, structural and canonical analyses, so long as we do not fall prey to their underlying critical assumptions.

Literary analysis is a third major way the Holy Spirit has taught us to understand Old Testament narratives. As we give attention to the integrality of form and content, we gain many insights into the meaning of these texts.

Conclusion

As we prepare to interpret Old Testament narratives, we must be aware of the ways in which the Holy Spirit influences us through exegesis of Scripture. Throughout history three major directions have been taken toward Old Testament narratives. Various forms of thematic, historical, and literary analyses have proven to be indispensable to the people of God.

Each form of analysis relies on the others. Thematic analysis easily moves into eisegesis without the restraint of historical and literary perspectives. Historical analysis loses its theological moorings without thematic and literary controls. Literary analysis becomes speculative without the constraints of thematic and historical outlooks. We will miss many of the blessings that await us if we limit ourselves to just one or two of these approaches. Following the lead of the Spirit, we must deal with Old Testament narratives as mirrors of our concerns, windows to historical events, and literary pictures.

Review Questions

1. What is thematic analysis? Why is it a legitimate approach to Old Testament narratives? What are some common types of thematic analysis?
2. What is historical analysis? Why is it a legitimate approach to Old Testament narratives? What are some common types of historical analysis?
3. What is literary analysis? Why is it a legitimate approach to Old Testament narratives? What are some common types of literary analysis?

Study Exercises

1. Read the story of Abram's call (Genesis 12:1–9). What themes do you find for these theological categories: 1) the doctrine of God, 2) the doctrine of humanity, and 3) the doctrine of sin and salvation?
2. Look at Genesis 12:1–9 again. What historical items stand out? How does this passage let you reconstruct what God was doing at that time in redemptive history?
3. Examine a nineteenth-century, early twentieth-century and modern evangelical commentary on Genesis 12:1–9. Do these commentaries focus more on thematic, historical, or literary analysis? How?

PART II

INVESTIGATING OLD TESTAMENT NARRATIVES

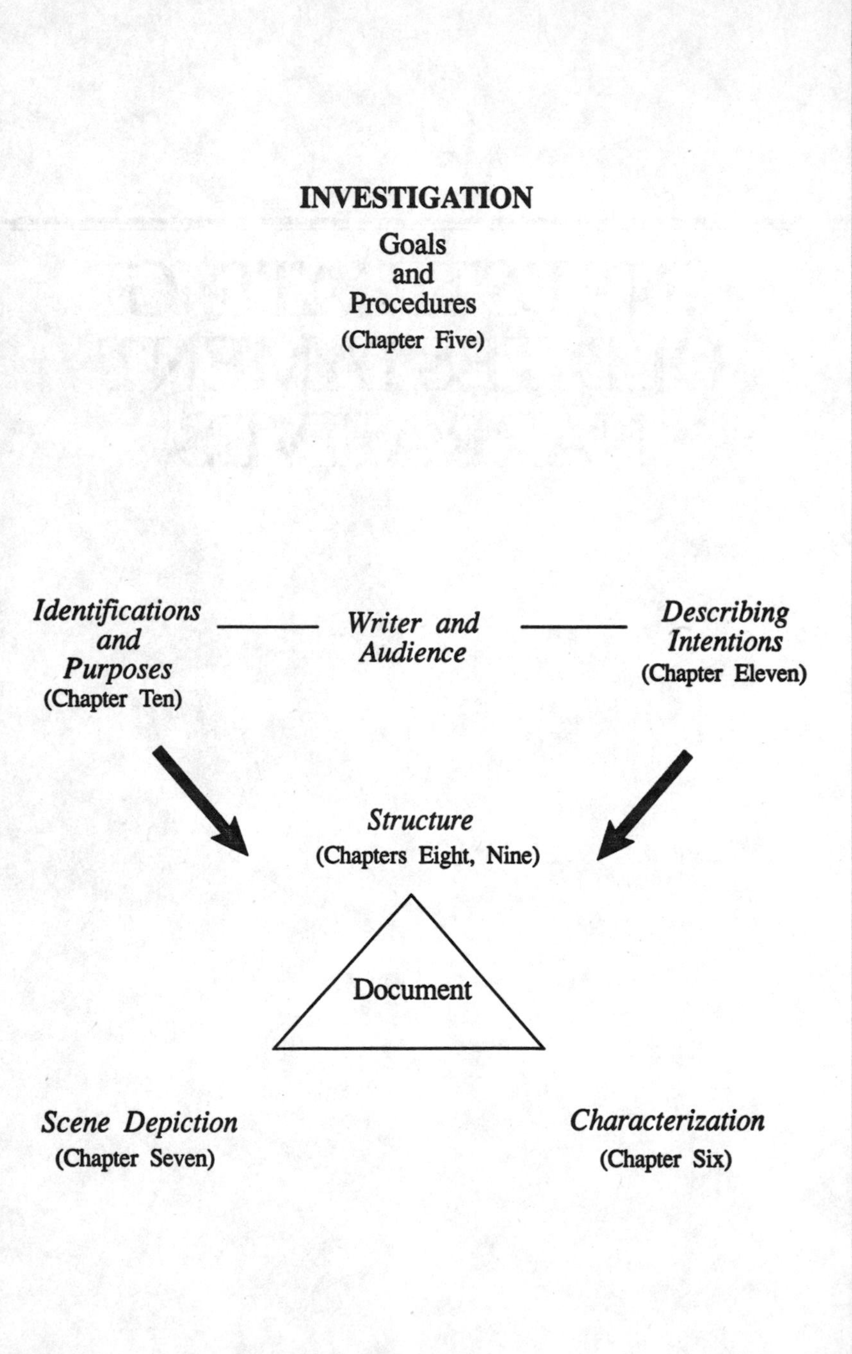

Fig. 10: Schema of Part II: Investigation

SYNOPSIS

In part one we examined some of the principal ways in which the Holy Spirit prepares us to read Old Testament narratives: individual Christian living, community interaction, and examination of Scripture. The more we become aware of this side of the hermeneutical process, the better we will be able to understand Old Testament stories.

In part two we will investigate the original meaning of Old Testament stories. We will discover what the Spirit did when He first inspired Old Testament narratives in their ancient historical contexts.

Investigating original meaning is a complex task. We will begin by setting forth the goal of investigation and several procedural guidelines (chapter 5). We will then explore features found within the documents of Old Testament narratives: characterization (chapter 6), scene depiction (chapter 7), individual episodes (chapter 8), and large narrative structures (chapter 9). Chapters 10 and 11 will focus on the writers and audiences of Old Testament narratives. Chapter 12 will provide a brief overview of all the Old Testament books that are predominantly narrative.

By applying the methods introduced in this part of our study, we will discover a general framework for further detailed investigation.

5

ORIENTATION FOR INVESTIGATION

As archaeologists investigate the past, they face many difficulties. In addition to the strain of digging, the heat, rain, and wind can so distract them that even experienced researchers pass over important discoveries. If a dig is to be successful, archaeologists must be single-minded, fixing their minds on the goal before them and paying careful attention to the procedures that will help them reach their goal.

In this part of our study, we will dig for the original meaning of Old Testament narratives by investigating Old Testament stories in their historical contexts. Many difficulties will easily divert our attention. If we hope to succeed, we must have a clear concept of what we are trying to find and pay careful attention to the procedures that help us reach our end.

We will begin our investigation of Old Testament narratives with two preliminary questions: 1) What is the *goal of investigation?* 2) What *procedures for investigation* help us achieve that goal?

Goal of Investigation

I was once told about an exchange between a homiletics teacher and a student. The student had preached on the eternality of God from Genesis 1:1. Afterward, the instructor began, "Tell me in just a few words what you think this passage means." The student responded quickly, "It means that God is eternal."

"No," the teacher insisted, "You've missed the point. It means that God created everything."

"I think it means both," the student objected.

"Impossible," chided the teacher, "every passage has only one meaning."

Every seminary student goes through the ordeal of homiletics class. Waiting your turn to preach is like sitting on death row. No matter what you say, the teacher always finds something wrong. But this particular conversation raises an important issue for us as we dig for the meaning of Old Testament stories. What is the goal of our investigation? Are we searching for one or many meanings?

Polyvalence

John was walking downtown one afternoon when he saw a small piece of paper blowing down the sidewalk. He picked it up and read, "GET HELP!" John was a competent reader of English; he had a basic understanding of what "get" and "help" mean. At first, John thought he knew what the note meant.

But two strangers suddenly came up to him. The first one pointed at a passing car and said, "I saw where that note came from. A little boy dropped it as he was pulled into that car. You'd better call the police."

But the second person interrupted. "Don't listen to him," she insisted. "I wrote the note for a friend and dropped it by accident. My friend is sick, and I want him to get some help."

Now John was completely confused. Was the note a call for help or friendly advice? John could not be certain, so he wadded the note in his hands and threw it back onto the sidewalk. "I don't know what to do," he exclaimed angrily. "This note can mean many things."

John had stumbled onto a perspective that many students of Old Testament narratives have affirmed through the centuries. In one way or another, they have said that Biblical texts are polyvalent; they have many meanings.

Before the Reformation most Biblical interpreters assumed that Old Testament stories had more than one meaning. The main line of rabbinic exegesis insisted that every text held multiple meanings.[1] Philo's uninhibited use of allegorical methods continued momentum toward polyvalent methods of interpretation.[2] The Alexandrian school—Clement, Origen, Ambrose, and others—also emphasized multiple meanings.[3]

By the time of Thomas Aquinas (1225–1274) the medieval church had largely adopted John Cassian's fourfold method of interpretation (*Quadriga*).[4] Authorial intention was important, but the meaning of a text went far beyond this *sensus literalis* (literal sense).

As Steinmetz summarizes the matter:

> From the time of John Cassian, the church subscribed to a theory of the fourfold sense of Scripture . . . [beyond the literal sense] . . . the allegorical sense taught about the church and what it should believe . . . the tropological sense taught about individuals and what they should do . . . the anagogical sense pointed to the future and wakened expectation.[5]

In general, belief in the divine authorship of Scripture undergirded early and medieval views of polyvalency. Because God was the principal Author of the Bible, the Scriptures held many meanings that went beyond the intent of their human writers. Augustine's words summarize the prominent outlook prior to the Reformation. He said, "What more liberal and more fruitful provision could God have made in regard to the Sacred Scriptures than that the same words might be understood in several senses?"[6] This emphasis on divine authorship led most pre-Reformation interpreters to affirm that Old Testament narratives were polyvalent.

Polyvalency has gained wide acceptance once again in our day. For the most part, however, these modern views have been based on a different consideration: the inherent polyvalency of language itself.[7] In many respects the roots of this outlook in modern hermeneutics can be traced to Friedrich Schleiermacher, who asserted that the language of a text serves only a limiting function (*die Grenzen angebende*). It sets parameters on possible meanings, but within those boundaries the same text can mean many things.[8] Looking at a document alone cannot always give readers enough to determine a specific meaning. In order to specify the meaning, they have to look outside the text to the psychological experience of the writer.[9]

Today most literary and Biblical interpreters accept the notion that language alone cannot fix meaning. The same expressions can mean many things, as long as we have no other reference point. But in some circles, Schleiermacher's appeal to the author has been replaced by a dependence on the reader.[10] In this view the meaning of a text is specified by the ideological outlooks of the reader.[11] As readers view a passage from various viewpoints, different meanings emerge. As Wittig has put it, "Freudian and Jungian psychology, Marxist economic theory, and structural and semiotic criticism can find various significations in a single work, supplying as they do stable explanatory systems with their own comprehensive philosophies and methodologies."[12] Similar views have become widespread in recent years.[13]

Through the centuries countless interpreters have viewed Biblical texts as polyvalent. Earlier views were based on the assumption of divine authorship. Modern views appeal more often to the inherent polyvalency of language itself. Whatever the case, from these viewpoints interpreters must search for many meanings in Old Testament stories.

Univalence

In opposition to these ancient and modern forms of polyvalency, other interpreters have viewed Scripture as univalent: a text has only one meaning—that which was intended by the original human author. A univalent view parallels much of our daily experience. More often than not, we assume that our statements have the one meaning we intend them to have.

As Joey was on his way out to play, his mother called out, "I'd like for you to put on your shoes." He heard her but went out barefoot anyway. After a couple of hours, Joey came in, but his mother stopped him at the door. "I thought I told you to put on your shoes!" she exclaimed. Joey responded indignantly, "No you didn't. You said you'd *like* for me to put on my shoes." "Yes," she admitted, "but you know what I meant!"

Joey focused on his mother's words and interpreted them within the framework of his own desires. Technically he was right; she said she would *like* for him to put on shoes. The words themselves did not rule out Joey's interpretation. Given the right circumstances, they could have meant just what Joey suggested. But his mother insisted that her statement should be understood in terms of what he knew she meant. Her intentions specified the meaning of the statement. She meant for him to put on his shoes, and he should have done it.

We think this way in most conversations. When we do not understand a friend, we ask, "What exactly did you mean?" When someone misunderstands us, we add, "No, what I meant was . . . ." We often assume that a statement has one meaning—the meaning the speaker intended.

As we have seen, before the Reformation most interpreters believed that Old Testament stories had many meanings, many of which were not accessible through ordinary reading. So interpreters needed special spiritual enlightenment. Who could gain these privileged insights? The answer of the Roman church was forthright: God granted special illumination to the ecclesiastical hierarchy. Understanding Scripture was the prerogative of an enlightened priesthood.[14]

In response to these developments, the Reformers prized the *sensus literalis* as the norm for all interpretation. As Calvin put it in his comments on Galatians 4:22, "the true meaning of Scripture (*verum sensum scripturae*) is the natural and simple one."[15]

The normativity of the one plain sense of Scripture has remained central to major Protestant works on interpretation.[16] William Ames (1576–1631) wrote in no uncertain terms: "There is only one meaning for every place in Scripture. Otherwise the meaning of Scripture would not only be unclear and uncertain, but there would be no meaning at all—for anything which does not mean one thing surely means nothing."[17]

This view was so widely accepted among seventeenth-century scholastics that it was codified in the *Westminster Confession of Faith*. The full sense of every Biblical text "is not manifold, but one."[18]

Macpherson's comment on this confessional statement represents the mainstream of orthodox thinking during the nineteenth century: "If we are not to bring complete confusion into the contents of divine revelation, we must maintain only one sense for Scripture, and that the literal sense, reached by careful examination of the text itself."[19]

Many modern evangelicals have reaffirmed the importance of one meaning for each text. Berkhof, Ramm, Virkler, and Mickelsen are just a few who have followed this traditional viewpoint.[20] Kaiser has been the most avid defender of traditional univalency in recent years. Depending heavily on the work of Hirsch,[21] he insists that the only way to avoid a sea of uncertainties is to identify the meaning of a passage with the "author's truth-intention."[22] As Kaiser put it:

> A literary work like the Bible can have one and only one correct interpretation and that meaning must be determined by the human author's truth-intention; otherwise, all alleged meanings would be accorded the same degree of seriousness, plausibility and correctness with no one meaning being more valid or true than the others.[23]

Belief in the univalence of each text is so widespread among modern evangelicals that it appears in the *Chicago Statement on Biblical Hermeneutics*. It reads, "We affirm that the meaning expressed in each Biblical text is single, definite and fixed."[24]

In line with the Reformation's focus on the plain sense, most evangelicals today view meaning as univalent. Every passage has one meaning. In this outlook the goal of exegetical investigation is to discover the single author-intended meaning.

Meaning and Full Value

Which view is correct? Does a text have one or many meanings? In recent years a great deal of confusion has arisen because a number of evangelicals have used the term "meaning" more broadly than the traditional Protestant sense. In one way or another, they have spoken of many meanings for a single text.[25] These variations have drawn attention to a number of complexities, but they have also raised concerns over the traditional concept of a fixed normative meaning.[26]

Many believers are left asking a serious question. If a text can mean more than one thing, how can we be sure we have understood it properly? How can we distinguish between correct and incorrect interpretations? If meaning is not restricted to the original intention of the writer, are we not set adrift in a sea of indeterminacy?[27]

To avoid these difficulties, we will affirm the traditional view of univalence, but we will also distinguish other facets of a text's full value. In this study we will speak of a story's *original meaning, Biblical elaborations, legitimate applications,* and *full value*. These distinctions are somewhat artificial; the categories overlap in a number of ways. Yet they help us avoid confusion in our investigation of Old Testament narratives.

Original meaning. We will speak of the most basic aspect of a story's value as its original meaning. Original meaning is the sense of a text in the setting of its original writer and audience. Why did the writer compose this passage? What was his purpose for this story? Since this setting is the frame of reference in which the Spirit first inspired and accommodated Scripture, the original meaning is normative for all other interpretative work. But we must remember that the original meaning does not exhaust a text's value.

Biblical elaborations. Biblical elaborations are also part of a text's value. Elaborations include all that Scripture says about an Old Testament story. How does the Bible expound on this narrative? Elaborations may focus on an entire story or part of it; they may speak directly or indirectly of the passage.

Whatever the case, Biblical elaborations are always true and reliable. They never contradict the original meaning, because God is the ultimate Author of both. But elaborations often go beyond the original meaning, bringing out implicit dimensions of a text that remained hidden in the writer's day. Nevertheless, even Biblical elaborations do not exhaust a story's value; they too represent only a portion of what a text offers.

Legitimate applications. Legitimate applications are a third facet of a story's value. Applications are those proper understandings which uninspired interpreters—past, present, and future—derive from the original meaning and Biblical elaborations. How has this story been applied? How should it be applied today? How may it be applied in the future? Proposed applications are always subject to refinement because they are not inerrantly inspired by God. But insofar as they are correct, legitimate applications also form an aspect of a story's value.

Full value. We will speak of the entirety of a text's communicative potential as its full value—the sum of its legitimate uses. It includes the original meaning, all Biblical elaborations, and every proper application.[28] In this sense, full value is any divinely authorized use of a passage. The evangelical's ultimate goal is to know and apply what God Himself intended His people to receive from Old Testament stories.[29] Why did the Spirit have this text written? What was God's intention for His people? Each time we discover an aspect of the original meaning, Biblical elaborations, and legitimate applications, we have uncovered a portion of that full value.

To sum up, the original historical meaning of Old Testament narratives is the guide to the full value of a text. Although elaborations and legitimate applications may go beyond the author's intended meaning, they will never contradict it. Therefore, if we hope to understand the full value of Old Testament stories, we must begin with investigating the original meaning (see figure 11).

Procedures for Investigation

With our attention focused on the original meaning of Old Testament stories, we are now in a position to lay some procedural groundwork for investigation. What must we consider to uncover the meaning of these texts? What approach will enable us to arrive at the fixed, normative sense? We will touch on three preliminary issues that set parameters for our work: *multiple controls on original meaning, multiple angles on original meaning,* and *multiple summaries of original meaning.*

Multiple Controls

Many things affect a symphony performance. The conductor leads the orchestra, the musical score guides the players, the performers work their instruments, and the audience encourages with applause. Even the

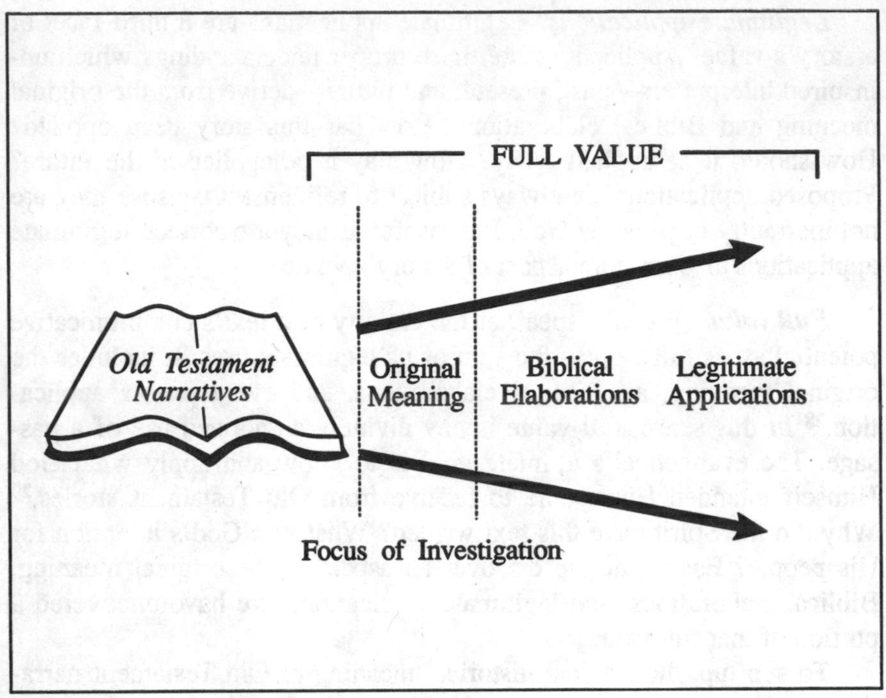

Fig. 11: The Goal of Investigation

physical setting of the concert influences the performance. These and countless other factors control the quality of a symphony concert.

Many factors also work together to produce the original meaning of Old Testament stories. From an evangelical perspective, the ultimate control on original meaning was the Holy Spirit; every Old Testament story is God revealing Himself. But God used many creaturely instruments as secondary controls. What were these controlling factors?

Ferdinand de Saussure's *Cours de linguistique générale (Course in General Linguistics)* has set the pace for many recent studies on this topic.[30] One of Saussure's most important contributions to the study of meaning was his attention to the interconnections between *parole*—particular linguistic expressions, and *langue*—the system of linguistic conventions shared by speakers and listeners. As Saussure put it:

> [*Langue*] is . . . a collection of necessary conventions that have been adopted by a social body to permit individuals to exercise that faculty . . . [*Parole*] is the executive side of speaking . . . an individual act.[31]

Saussure argued that the meaning of a statement (*parole*) depends on an assortment of linguistic conventions (*langue*) out of which speakers and listeners operate. The community of people who speak a given language share an elastic but consistent set of linguistic structures. Every time they communicate they employ these conventions.

We will follow suit by thinking in terms of three major controls on original meaning: the *document*, the *writer*, and the *audience*. We cannot discover the meaning of a story in the text alone; the document is but *parole*. We must also consider the *langue* of the writer and the audience.

Many interpreters of literature have followed this threefold focus,[32] although at times they may not have stressed the elements equally. Overemphasis on the writer's intentions as the key to meaning may be dubbed "the intentional fallacy;" [33] insisting that the document alone is necessary to provide meaning may be called "the graphic fallacy;"[34] and thinking that meaning is merely a matter of influence on the reader may be called "the affective fallacy."[35] We will attempt to avoid these extremes and give due attention to all three controls on meaning.

In one way or another, we always give some attention to each of these controls. We cannot understand a text without an examination of the document itself. Our study may bc cursory, but we must know something about the text if we hope to understand it. Similarly, we may not think much about the writer, but we always make some assumptions about him. We assume that the writer had some level of linguistic ability, intelligence, and awareness of life. Likewise, we may not examine the audience extensively, but we generally assume that readers could understand the basic elements of the text and had some level of interest. Whenever we investigate the meaning of a note, letter, paper, story, or book, we reflect to one degree or another on all three controls on meaning.

Several examples of the Bible interpreting itself illustrate the importance of these controls. Biblical writers were deeply concerned with the document of the Old Testament. They examined it carefully, sometimes appealing to specific wording (Galatians 3:16–18; Romans 4:18–25). In addition, they occasionally tied their interpretations to the original writer and audience (2 Chronicles 36:22; Nehemiah 1:8–9; Daniel 9:1–3; Matthew 22:44–46; Acts 2:26–36; 2 Peter 3:15–16; Hebrews 4:6–11). The level of interest in each control varied from case to case with Biblical writers. But the Bible itself indicates the need to consider all three controls as we assess the original meaning of Old Testament stories.

Multiple Angles

Many people like to go to the stadium to watch a football game. It's exciting to be there in the middle of all the action. But from the bleachers, you see the play from only one perspective. In this respect, watching the game on television has an advantage. You see from one side; then through instant replays you look from the left, right, front, and from behind. These various perspectives form a more complete picture than a view from the stands. Apparently, lots of people agree; I've even seen fans watching portable televisions at the stadium!

In much the same way, a single perspective limits our perception of the original meaning. Writers, documents, and audiences interact with each other in many ways. The intentions of the writer influence the audience; the needs of the audience shape the document; the document facilitates the writer's desire to communicate. The interconnections are complex.[36] Learning how to look at these interactions from different vantage points gives a fuller picture of what the Holy Spirit originally gave His people through these stories.

What perspectives should we take to grasp the interconnections between writers, documents, and audiences? It helps to take three basic perspectives: *paradigmatic, syntagmatic,* and *pragmatic*.[37] These vantage points are fully interdependent and deal with numerous issues, but for simplicity's sake, we will think in terms of three basic questions. The paradigmatic angle asks *what* the writer chose to say; the syntagmatic perspective looks at *how* he arranged his composition; the pragmatic outlook asks *why* he wrote for his readers.

Most semanticists have applied these vantage points primarily to the level of words, phrases, and sentences. What words did the speaker choose? How does the structure of a phrase or sentence bear on the meaning? What significance does the extra-linguistic context of an expression have on its meaning?[38] In our study, however, we will use these categories to examine the meaning of whole stories, series of stories, and whole books in the Old Testament. How do paradigmatic, syntagmatic, and pragmatic considerations help us understand original meaning on these levels?

Paradigmatic. The paradigmatic vantage point analyzes the meaning of an expression by comparing it with the available options. What did the writer choose to say and not to say? Meaning is viewed as a matter of choice. From single words to whole discourses, writers always make selections. Looking at what they decide to include and exclude helps us determine the meaning of what they express.

The meaning of a particular word must be assessed in terms of other words in the person's vocabulary stock.[39] Languages provide many words from which to choose. Why do we choose one word over another? Sometimes choices are arbitrary, but often they result from perceived differences among the words. Two important differences are *denotations* and *connotations*.[40]

We often choose one word instead of another because it denotes the concept we desire to communicate. If I want to tell my family that I went to the supermarket, I may say, "I went to the store." I would not say, "I went to the movies." Why? Because the word "store" denotes the concept of supermarket, but "movie" does not. We do not call a hat, "book"; we do not call a car, "Christmas tree." Unless we are using a special figure of speech, we do not intentionally choose a word that denotes something other than the concept we want to communicate.

At times we choose one word over another because of its denotative advantage. For instance, "store" can be too ambiguous. It can denote a clothing, hardware, or auto parts store. Instead of saying, "I went to the store," I may choose to say, "I went to the grocer's." We may decide to say "ocean" instead of "water," "daughter" instead of "child," because the terms better suit our purposes. Denotative advantage can be specific or ambiguous, playing off of the breadth of terms.[41] Yet we still choose words in the light of their denotative advantage.

Second, we choose words because of associated connotations. There are countless types of connotations,[42] but emotional connotations often play a vital role. What is the difference in describing someone as "bureaucrat," "government official," and "public servant"? The denotation may be the same, but the emotional connotations of the words are quite different.[43] I may describe myself as "firm," another person as "obstinate" and a third person as "a pig-headed fool."[44] Again, my choice is based on the emotive connotations of the terms.

The writers of Old Testament narratives chose their words because of their denotations and connotations. Consider one verse from the story of the Tower of Babel: "But the Lord came down to see the city and the tower that the men were building" (Genesis 11:5). What did Moses mean when he wrote that God "came down" (*yrd*)? We find clues by considering the other words he might have selected. For instance, why did he say "came down" (*yrd*) instead of "went up" (*'lh*)? Apparently he wanted a word that denoted a downward movement. Why did he say "came down" (*yrd*) instead of "came" (*bw'*)? "Came" (*bw'*) would have sufficed since the readers knew that God dwells in heaven. But Moses chose "came down" (*yrd*) because of its denotative specificity. Finally, the word "came down" (*yrd*) may also have been chosen because of its emotive connotation. In the previous verse, Moses had said that the tower "reaches to the heavens" (Genesis 11:4). It is likely that he chose "came down" (*yrd*) for its satirical connotations. The people building the tower thought they had reached heaven, but the Lord had to come down just to see it.[45]

Noting the options that writers had before them helps us understand the meaning of the words they chose. We must consider antonyms, synonyms, metonyms, and the like in order to clarify the meaning of the words that they used.[46] By examining the selections of a writer, we acquire insight. As Thiselton put it, "The interpreter cannot know how much significance to attach to an author's use of word x until he also knows what alternatives were available to him at the same time."[47]

In this study we will assess original meaning by taking a similar perspective on larger units of material. In an ultimate sense, the Holy Spirit determined what was included in Old Testament stories. But in the light of organic inspiration,[48] we must ask ourselves what the human writers chose to include and exclude in order to comprehend more clearly the original meaning of the text.

Evangelicals often fail to consider the selectivity Old Testament writers exercised. "They wrote about those events because that's what happened," we say. This is certainly true, but Old Testament writers could have described the same events in countless ways without misconstruing the facts.[49] What is reported, emphasized, de-emphasized, and omitted is largely a matter of choice.

How many options do writers have for composing a scene of a man walking down a road? They can tell us the year, month, day, or hour; they can report the name of the state, the town, or the road; they may choose to describe the weather, the condition of the road, the people with the man, or the people not with him. The writers may describe his physical appearance, clothing, or stride; they may focus on his purposes, thoughts, or feelings. Of course, the availability of information eliminates some of these options. But these and many other choices face writers who want to compose a simple scene of a man walking down a road. How many more choices did Old Testament writers face in composing whole stories and books? And, if Old Testament writers had so many choices to make, how did they decide what to include in their stories? Again they based their selections on denotations and connotations.

Old Testament stories were designed to denote certain states of affairs. Writers reported what they wanted their readers to consider. Why, for instance, does the writer of Samuel say, "And the boy Samuel continued to grow in stature and in favor with the Lord and with men" (1 Samuel 2:26), instead of "Samuel was twelve years old and stood about five feet tall"? Why does the writer of Judges tell his readers that Eglon was "very fat" (Judges 3:17) instead of reporting that the king "had a beard"? In the first place, these writers wanted their audiences to consider the elements they reported and not others. Choices in Old Testament stories were often based on the concepts the writers wanted to denote. Old Testament writers also chose what to include and exclude based on connotations. Samuel's reputation was reported to evoke appreciation for him and disdain for the sons of Eli. The description of Eglon's obesity mocked the ruler.

In the chapters that follow, we will focus on choices writers made. It will be evident that we must ask what these writers chose to report. They did not say everything they could have said; they withheld information as they gave it. Noticing these selections allows us to explore the meaning of their stories.

Syntagmatic. The second major angle on original meaning is syntagmatic arrangement—how a word is used in relation to other words in the text. As Saussure put it:

> In discourse . . . words acquire relations based on the linear nature of language because they are chained together . . . a term acquires its value only because it stands in opposition to everything that precedes or follows it or to both.[50]

Often syntagmatic context determines the word to be used, but it also causes the same word to have different meanings.[51] The phrase, clause, or sentence within which a word appears determines its meaning. Take, for instance, the preposition "on." If I asked you whether the words you are reading are "on" or "next to" this page, your response would be a confident "on." In this context "on" and "next to" are quite different. But let's change the syntagmatic context. If you ask me, "Where do you live?" I will answer, "I live on Wekiva Cove Road." In this context "on" is synonymous with "next to." The word's meaning is influenced by its syntagmatic context.

Larger literary contexts also have an effect on the meaning of a word.[52] The paragraph or whole discourse may help a reader discern the meaning of a particular word. For example, if we use the expression "full house" in a paragraph describing a party in a friend's home, it probably denotes many people in a family dwelling. If, however, we write "full house" in a passage describing a poker game, it probably denotes a certain arrangement of cards.

The same is true in Old Testament stories. The meaning of a particular word may vary within a single passage because of its syntagmatic context. One striking example is the use of the word "house" (*byt*) in 2 Samuel 7:1–16. This one word is used eight times in the passage, but it has at least three different meanings. "House" denotes the concept of David's "palace" (vv. 1, 2), "God's temple" (vv. 5, 6, 7, 13) and "David's dynasty" (vv. 11, 16). How can we distinguish among these various meanings? We discern the differences by noting the syntagmatic contexts within which each occurrence takes place. If the context speaks of where David lived, "house" is his palace. If the passage is talking about David or Solomon building "a house," it is God's temple. If God is speaking to David about his future, "house" is David's dynasty. In each case the syntagmatic context gives clues to the meaning of the word.

In the following chapters, we will consider how syntagmatic context affects meaning on a larger level by examining the arrangement of narratives. As we consider how a story is arranged, we find more clues to the original meaning.

Unfortunately, many evangelicals fail to see the importance of the arrangement of Old Testament stories. We often say to ourselves, "Stories are simply arranged as the events took place." No doubt historical realities constrained Biblical writers; they neither fabricated nor misrepresented events. Yet Old Testament writers arranged the same series of events in many different ways in their stories. At times Old Testament writers followed historical sequence; at other times they did not. Events adumbrate later scenes and recollect previous materials. Some stories arrange scenes symmetrically, others asymmetrically. Actions heighten and relax dramatic tension. These are but a few of the ways in which Old Testament writers arranged their stories.

As we dig for original meaning, we will be concerned with *how* Old Testament writers arranged their accounts. We will explore single stories, series of stories, and whole books from a syntagmatic angle.

Pragmatic. Saussure's distinction between *parole* and *langue* points to one more vital angle for assessing the meaning of a text: the *pragmatic context*. In recent years much attention has been given to the pragmatics of human language. It has become evident that factors other than language itself affect the meaning of an expression. The situation of the speaker and listeners significantly determines the meaning of a discourse. Meaning not only depends on paradigmatic choices and syntagmatic arrangements; it also depends on the extra-linguistic, pragmatic context in which an expression occurs.[53]

The pragmatic angle consists of a wide range of considerations, including general historical and cultural settings. The meaning of an expression will differ from place to place and time to time. The word "dinner" refers to the third meal of the day when used in the context of New England, but it generally refers to the noon meal in the deep South. Even within the same geographical and temporal context, a word can have various meanings as it is used in different social settings. "I'm going to the *court*" could refer to a place to play tennis or a place where alleged criminals are tried. Without syntagmatic clues the only way to distinguish these possibilities is to consider the pragmatic setting.

Extra-linguistic context also consists of the purposes for which an expression is chosen. Take, for instance, the meaning of an imperative. Theological students often assume that an imperative verb always expresses a command, and in many instances this is the case. When God speaks on a moral issue, an imperative is clearly a command (Exodus 19:10). When a king tells his servants what to do, the imperative is an order (2 Samuel 11:14–15). But some pragmatic contexts make it plain that the imperative does not always indicate an authoritative command. When a servant speaks to a king in the imperative, it is not intended as a decree (2 Samuel 14:4). Similarly, when a worshipper offers prayers in the imperative, they are imperatives of entreaty, not commands (Psalm 51:10).[54]

The importance of extra-linguistic considerations is evident when we consider the relation between a speaker's thoughts and his grammatical expressions. Evangelicals often assume that grammatical forms in a text directly correspond to the intentions of the writer.[55] We assume, for example, that if a writer wants to tell us facts, he composes declarative sentences; if he wants to ask a question, he writes interrogative sentences; and if he wants to tell us of our obligations, he writes in the imperative.

But upon reflection, logico-grammatical isomorphism cannot be sustained.[56] The thoughts of a writer and the surface grammar of his text do not correspond directly. Indeed, often the grammar of a text will closely parallel the intentions of the writer. But given the right circumstances, a declarative sentence can be a command, an interrogative sentence can be an order, and an imperative sentence can be a statement of fact.

For example, what does the sentence "It's cold in here" mean? At first glance it appears to be a mere description of the temperature. But the right pragmatic conditions can point us toward different understandings. If, for instance, the speaker is sick, it could be an appeal for sympathy, the equivalent of "Help me; I have a fever." When students say this as they walk into the classroom, they may mean, "Please turn up the heat!" If it is a sweltering summer day, the sentence could even be uttered sarcastically and mean, "It's hot in here." How is this variety possible? Because the meaning of an expression is not determined solely by the structures of surface grammar. Grammar must be read in terms of the extra-linguistic circumstances and intentions of the speaker.

Pragmatic considerations are essential for interpreting Old Testament narratives. If we assume a strict parallel between the thoughts of Biblical writers and their grammatical expressions, we would have to conclude that most Old Testament stories do not teach moral or theological principles. After all, most texts simply report facts. But the surface presentation does not exhaust the meaning.[57] To be sure, Old Testament stories inform the audience of facts, but they do much more. Other dimensions of meaning lie beneath the surface and can be seen only in the light of the pragmatic circumstances in which the story was written.

For instance, the surface presentation of a passage like the story of Shadrach, Meshak, and Abednego (Daniel 3:1–30) merely reports events. The writer never explicitly does more than state facts. Yet given the pragmatic context of the exile in which the original audience received this story, we can see that it communicated much more than the surface presentation might suggest. Among many other things, it served to guide readers into faithful living; it instilled a sense of pride in the courage of the young men; it inspired faith in the readers; and it offered doxology. None of these things were stated explicitly in the grammatical forms, but when we consider *why* the story was written, we come face to face with these aspects of the original meaning.

Old Testament stories were used for many purposes. We will explore the pragmatics of these accounts in detail later in this study. At this point, however, it should be evident that if we are to understand the original meaning of these texts, we must do more than merely look at what appears on the page. We must also consider the circumstances of composition and determine why the account was written.

To sum up, we will take three perspectives on the interactions among the document, writer, and audience: the paradigmatic angle (What did the writer choose to say?), the syntagmatic angle (How did the writer arrange his material?), and the pragmatic angle (Why did the writer present his material?). As we apply these outlooks to Old Testament stories, we will be in a better position to comprehend the original meaning of these texts (see figure 12).

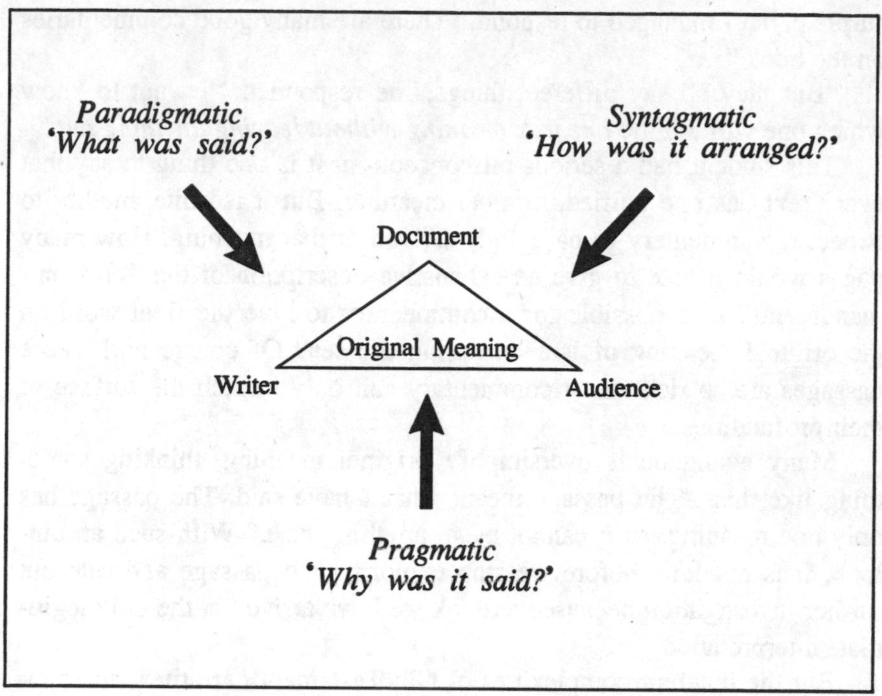

Fig. 12: Angles on Original Meaning

Multiple Summaries

We all know there is only one Atlantic Ocean; it is a single objective reality. Yet this one reality is an intricate conglomeration of numerous elements. Wide assortments of chemical compounds, animal and plant life, and countless other factors form the Atlantic Ocean. This complexity makes it impossible to give an exhaustive description. The best we can do is to make many different descriptions.

As we have seen, Old Testament authors wrote univalent, coherent texts for their audiences. Each passage has one original meaning. But *univalence is not the same as simplicity*. Writers, documents, and audiences interacted in numerous ways to produce the original meaning. Paradigmatic, syntagmatic, and pragmatic angles reveal just how complex these interactions were. Consequently, as we investigate Old Testament stories, the best we can do is to make many different summaries of the one original meaning.

I once had a student come up to me and ask, "Which commentary will give me the true meaning of Exodus?" The question took me by surprise, but I managed to respond, "There are many good commentaries on the book."

"But they all say different things," he responded. "I want to know which one will tell the *one true meaning without leaving anything out.*"

This student had a serious misconception. It is one thing to say that every text has one unified, original meaning. But it is quite another to expect a commentary to have fully arrived at that meaning. How many pages would it take to give an exhaustive description of the Ten Commandments? Is it possible for a commentary to give the final word on the original meaning of Israel crossing the sea? Of course not! These passages are so rich that a commentary can only scratch the surface of their profundities.

Many evangelicals oversimplify original meaning, thinking something like this: "The passage meant what I have said. The passage has only one meaning, so it cannot mean anything else." With such an outlook, it is not long before we stop exploring the passage and rule out further investigation because we think we have arrived at the only legitimate interpretation.

But the inherent complexities of Old Testament narratives make investigation an ongoing process. We may discover aspects of the original meaning, but there is always more to be unearthed. We may exhaust ourselves as we investigate Old Testament narratives, but we will never exhaust the texts themselves.

As we begin to investigate Old Testament stories, we must remember that *there is one original meaning, but there are many legitimate summaries of that one meaning*. Careful examination can rule out incorrect assessments, but many correct descriptions can be made. Our goal is not to formulate the *only* proper description of original meaning. It is to formulate an *assortment* of legitimate descriptions.

In the chapters that follow, we will learn how to make many different summaries of Old Testament narratives. In chapters 6 through 9, we will focus on *intrinsic summaries*.[58] We will deal primarily with the characterization, scenes, and structures in the document. In chapters 10 through 12, we will turn attention to *extrinsic summaries*. We will be more specifically concerned with the writers and the pragmatic goals they had toward their audiences. Because the original meanings of Old Testament narratives are complex realities, no single summary will suffice. We must learn how to make these different kinds of summaries, so that our understanding of the Old Testament stories can grow (see figure 13).

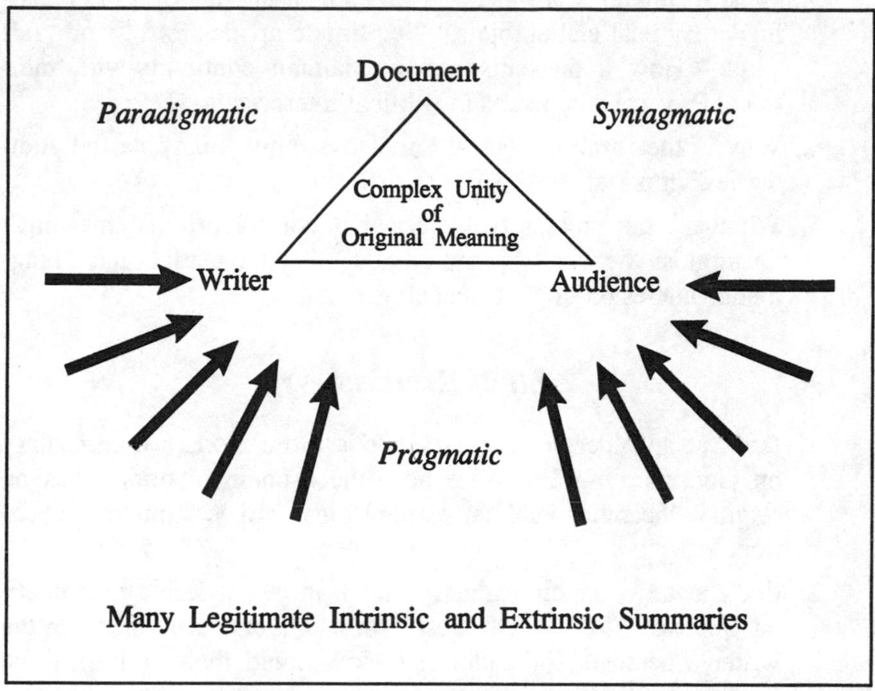

Fig. 13: Multiple Summaries of Original Meaning

Conclusion

In this chapter we have introduced the basic approach we will follow as we investigate Old Testament stories. The goal of investigation is to discover the original meaning—the sense the document had in the context of its writer and audience. This meaning is historically fixed, singular and normative for all interpretative work. Yet we must remember the complex interactions among the writer, document, and audience and give attention to paradigmatic, syntagmatic, and pragmatic angles on the meaning. As we learn how to make these kinds of summaries, we can discern what these stories first meant when God gave them to His people.

Review Questions

1. What is a polyvalent view of meaning? How do ancient and modern views of polyvalency differ?
2. What is a univalent view of meaning? What are some of the historical roots of this view in Biblical interpretation?

3. What distinctions are made in this study among "original meaning," "Biblical elaborations," "legitimate applications," and "full value"? How do these distinctions maintain continuity with traditional Protestant concerns in Biblical interpretation?
4. Why is the formula "one original meaning—many partial summaries" important?
5. What are the creaturely factors that control original meaning? Distinguish between "paradigmatic," "syntagmatic" and "pragmatic" angles on original meaning.

Study Exercises

1. Look at an older commentary and a more modern commentary on Genesis 1:1—2:4. Note how these commentators focus on original meaning, Biblical elaborations, and legitimate application.
2. Look at an older commentary and a more modern commentary on Genesis 1:1—2:4. Do these commentators focus more on the writer, document, or audience? How could their comments be improved if they were to broaden their focus?
3. Look at an older commentary and a more modern commentary on Genesis 1:1—2:4. Do these commentators concentrate more on paradigmatic, syntagmatic, or pragmatic issues? Can you fill in some of the gaps in their approaches?

6

CHARACTERS IN OLD TESTAMENT STORIES

I remember the time when my fourth grade teacher read Charles Dickens' *A Christmas Carol* to our class. "What did you like best in the story?" she asked as she closed the book.

"I liked tiny Tim," replied the little girl sitting next to me. "He was so sweet."

Like a typical young boy, I couldn't stand for that. "No way!" I objected. "The best part was in the middle of the night. So many scary things happened."

The class divided down the middle. The girls agreed that tiny Tim was most important; all the boys sided with me. We never came to a consensus. I realize now that the girl and I were focusing on two basic elements of stories. The plot caught my attention; a character fascinated her.

We are all drawn in one direction or the other when we read books or watch movies and plays. In fact, the relative importance of characters and plots has been a longstanding controversy among literary critics.[1] Some argue that stories revolve primarily around characters, while others urge that plot is central. Some passages depend more on one element than the other. But in the final analysis, both characters and plot are crucial.[2]

As we begin to investigate the original meaning of Old Testament narratives, we will focus first on characters. Three major issues stand out: the *presentation of characters,* the *techniques of characterization,* and the *purpose of characterization.* What characters appear in these passages? How did Old Testament writers form their characterizations? Why did they give so much attention to these matters?

Presentation of Characters

Understanding the role of characters in Old Testament stories begins with two basic considerations. What characters are included? How are they portrayed? To answer these questions, we will make some general observations on the roster of characters and the portraits of characters in Old Testament narratives.

Roster of Characters

We often summarize stories in terms of the persons they include. Hemingway's *The Sun Also Rises* is about Jake Barnes, Lady Brett Ashley, and Bill Gorton. Faulkner's *Absalom, Absalom!* focuses on Thomas Sutpen and Quentin Compson. As we recall these literary works, the roster of characters helps us remember a lot about the stories.

In much the same way, we can gain many insights into Old Testament narratives simply by noting their characters. Genesis 11:10—25:10 is about the life of Abraham. The book of Jonah focuses on the prophet Jonah. The book of Samuel deals with Samuel, Saul, and David. The roster of characters gives us a basic orientation with which we can examine these texts more fully.

Characters are persons or groups of persons in a story. But what kinds of characters do Old Testament narratives include? Who is usually on the roster? Most recent studies of characters in the Bible limit attention to human figures.[3] Humans are prominent in the Old Testament, but Old Testament writers also focused on *God, supernatural creatures,* and *human beings.*

God. When we read the Bible, we frequently think that God is always the most important character. Old Testament writers did not simply describe human affairs; their ultimate purpose was to reveal God and His will to Israel.[4] In this sense Old Testament narratives always disclose the character of God. Nevertheless, God is not always in the foreground of Old Testament stories. The intensity of His presence varies from passage to passage.

God plays a central role in many texts, interacting extensively with His creatures and directing events. In the record of the expulsion from the Garden of Eden, God questions and curses (Genesis 3:9–24). In the account of Solomon's prayer for wisdom, God speaks to Solomon and answers his prayer (1 Kings 3:1–15). These and many other stories place God at the heart of the action.

But in other texts, human affairs dominate, and God plays a less prominent role. The account of the Tower of Babel (Genesis 11:1–9) focuses first on humanity's attempt to build an invincible city.[5] God appears after construction is well under way (Genesis 11:5–9). At times God simply appears as an intervening *Deus ex machina* (God from a machine).[6] A problem develops, God corrects it, then He immediately retreats from view. In the account of Abram's exodus from Egypt (Genesis 12:10–20), God is not explicitly mentioned except in Genesis 12:17, "But the Lord inflicted serious diseases on Pharaoh and his household." Having reversed Abram's trouble, God disappears from the story. Beyond this, many passages make only brief mention of God. For instance, God played no active role when David learned of Saul's death (2 Samuel 1:1–16). In much the same way, the record of David's adulterous affair (2 Samuel 11:1–27) does not mention God, except in the closing sentence, "But the thing David had done displeased the Lord" (2 Samuel 11:27b).

Finally, there are passages in which God fades completely into the background. The account of David's time among the Philistines (1 Samuel 27:1–12) does not mention God. Sheba's rebellion against David (2 Samuel 20:1–26) omits any reference to divinity. Most remarkably, God is absent from the entire book of Esther.[7]

We have to be careful here. Although God is not specifically mentioned in some passages, He was never absent from the outlooks of Old Testament writers. He was presupposed as the providential Controller of events even when He did not appear on the surface of the text.

God's hidden presence is acknowledged in the opening scenes of Samson's marriage to the Philistine woman (Judges 14:1–4). Samson falls in love with the young woman at Timnah. His father and mother object to the marriage, but Samson insists upon having her. Up to this point, God is not mentioned, but in a parenthetical remark the writer of Judges lets his readers know that God was operating behind the scenes: "His parents did not know that this was from the Lord, who was seeking an occasion to confront the Philistines" (v. 4). The writer of Judges informed his audience of a fundamental belief held by all Old Testament authors. The events of their stories always reflect the providence of God. In this sense God is an implicit character in every Old Testament story, even if He is secretly working behind the scenes.

Supernatural creatures. A number of Old Testament passages include supernatural creatures on their roster of characters. Angels play important roles in various texts; even Satan appears from time to time. Old Testament writers believed that these supernatural beings actively participated in Israel's history.

The destruction of Sodom and Gomorrah (Genesis 18:1—19:29) presents a well-known example of supernatural characters. Heavenly visitors meet with Abraham and tell him of the coming judgment (Genesis 18:16–33).[8] Later the story focuses on angelic messengers rescuing Lot and his family from the city (Genesis 19:12–22). Similarly the opening chapters of Job (Job 1:6—2:7) focus on Satan's role in Job's troubles. In the Chronicler's account of David's census (1 Chronicles 21:1—22:1), Satan appears as the one who incited David to sin (1 Chronicles 21:1). An angel from God also steps into the story to punish Israel (1 Chronicles 21:15). Many stories mention supernatural creatures performing tasks: Jacob's ladder (Genesis 28:12), Jacob at Peniel (Genesis 32:24–30), the test of Abraham (Genesis 22:11–18), Saul's demonic torment (1 Samuel 16:14–16, 23)—to name only a few.

Human beings. As important as God and supernatural creatures may be, Old Testament stories focus primarily on human beings. Some passages deal with only a few people (Genesis 4:1–16; 9:1–17; 29:14b-30; Ruth 3:1–18), while others bring groups, whole cities, nations, and all of humanity into focus (Genesis 11:1–9; 19:1–29; Exodus 12:31–42; Judges 16:23–31; 1 Kings 17:7–24). Unfortunately evangelicals easily overlook the human focus of Old Testament stories. But we must never forget that these texts are about humanity as well as God. By concentrating on people, these passages reveal much about human life. Old Testament writers taught profound theological truths, but they expressed their views by focusing on the ways human beings lived. They taught theological concepts largely through records of human experiences.

Old Testament stories present a variety of characters. As we investigate the original meaning of these passages, it helps to identify the roster of characters. Does God appear? What supernatural creatures are mentioned? What human beings are included? Noting which characters appear in Old Testament narratives will help us gain a basic orientation toward the original meaning of these passages.

Portrayal of Characters

Two young women were discussing a mutual acquaintance. The first woman commented, "I think he's a great guy. He's so polite and helpful."

"I don't think he's like that at all," answered the second. "Are you sure we're talking about the same person?"

"We're talking about the same guy," the first woman responded. "I think we've just seen two different sides of him."

People often have different perspectives on the same person. Human beings are complex creatures; we never fully comprehend them. We may form true opinions, but our judgments are always partial at best. We must never fully identify a person with our outlook on that person.

A similar distinction should be made as we interpret Old Testament stories. Old Testament writers dealt with real figures from the past, but they gave limited portraits of these characters. They formed characterizations, profiles of the "habits, emotions, desires, [and] instincts"[9] of characters. They did not offer detached, comprehensive assessments. Instead, they characterized God, supernatural creatures and humans to lead their readers to particular perspectives and responses. Characterization in Old Testament stories follows many different patterns. We will discuss several features later in this chapter, but at this point, we will mention two qualities of characterization: *honesty* and *selectivity*.

Honesty. Old Testament writers demonstrated remarkable honesty in characterization. They did not fabricate qualities for their characters. Their figures often present faults as well as virtues. In the book of Kings, for example, Elijah stands out as Israel's greatest prophet. The writer of Kings presented him as God's man in desperate times. He performed miracles (1 Kings 17:7–14, 17–23; 18:18–46; 2 Kings 1:12), challenged royal authority at God's command (1 Kings 18:15–46), and courageously withstood the priests of Baal (1 Kings 18:16–40). We might expect the writer of Kings to conceal the flaws of such an important figure, but he did not. After Elijah demonstrated great courage at Mount Carmel, we read:

> Elijah was afraid and ran for his life. When he came to Beersheba in Judah, he left his servant there, while he himself went a day's journey into the desert. He came to a broom tree, sat down under it and prayed that he might die. "I have had enough, Lord," he said. "Take my life; I am no better than my ancestors." Then he lay down under the tree and fell asleep (1 Kings 19:3–5a).

Similar revelations of shortcomings appear in the lives of other important figures. Noah became intoxicated after the flood (Genesis 9:20–21); the heads of Israel's twelve tribes were a sorry lot (Genesis 35:22; 34:1–31; 37:12–35; 38:1–26); Aaron fashioned the golden calf (Exodus

32:2–6); Nathan called David to account for his adultery (2 Samuel 12:1–14); Solomon permitted and practiced idolatry (1 Kings 11:1–8).

Old Testament writers presented a forthright portrait of God as well. They never questioned divine perfection, but neither did they hesitate to show their readers difficult truths about the character of God. God's long-suffering and forgiveness stand out in many stories (see Exodus 32:9–14; 33:12–17; 2 Samuel 12:13; Jonah 2:1–10; 3:4–10); but God's anger and wrath, even against His own people, comes to the foreground in other passages (2 Samuel 12:11–12, 14; 1 Kings 11:9–13; 2 Kings 17:1–23; 1 Chronicles 21:1—22:1). God sends evil spirits (1 Samuel 16:14–16, 23; 18:10) and calls for a "lying spirit in the mouths of these prophets" (2 Chronicles 18:18–22). Old Testament writers characterized God as He is, not as their readers may have wanted Him to be.

The honesty of Old Testament writers heightens our sense of confidence in their characterizations. When human failure played an important role in their stories, they did not hide it. If any aspect of God's character was vital to their purposes, they did not refrain from reporting it. In the light of their frank disclosures, we can be assured that Old Testament characterizations are true.

Selectivity. Nevertheless, Old Testament writers also demonstrated a high degree of intentional selectivity. They chose to say some things about their characters and to omit others. As we read their accounts, it becomes evident that Old Testament writers felt little obligation to form comprehensive characterizations. They reported only those facets of their characters that suited their purposes.

As we have seen, the book of Judges was written to demonstrate Israel's need for a king;[10] the writer used intentionally selective character portraits to communicate this message. The middle section of his book covers many major characters: Othniel (3:7–11), Ehud (3:12–30), Shamgar (3:31), Deborah (4:1—5:31), Gideon and his son Abimelech (6:1—9:57), some minor judges (10:1–5), Jephthah (10:6—12:7), other minor judges (12:8–15), and Samson (13:1—16:31). As the following diagram indicates, the writer characterized these figures with a definite arrangement in mind (see figure 14).

As this chart suggests, the series of judges begins with three major figures whom the writer characterized as ideals. Othniel, Ehud (Shamgar), and Deborah fulfilled their duties without a flaw, and Israel experienced peace for many years.

A shift in characterization occurs in the account of Gideon and his son Abimelech. Gideon began his ministry much like the preceding

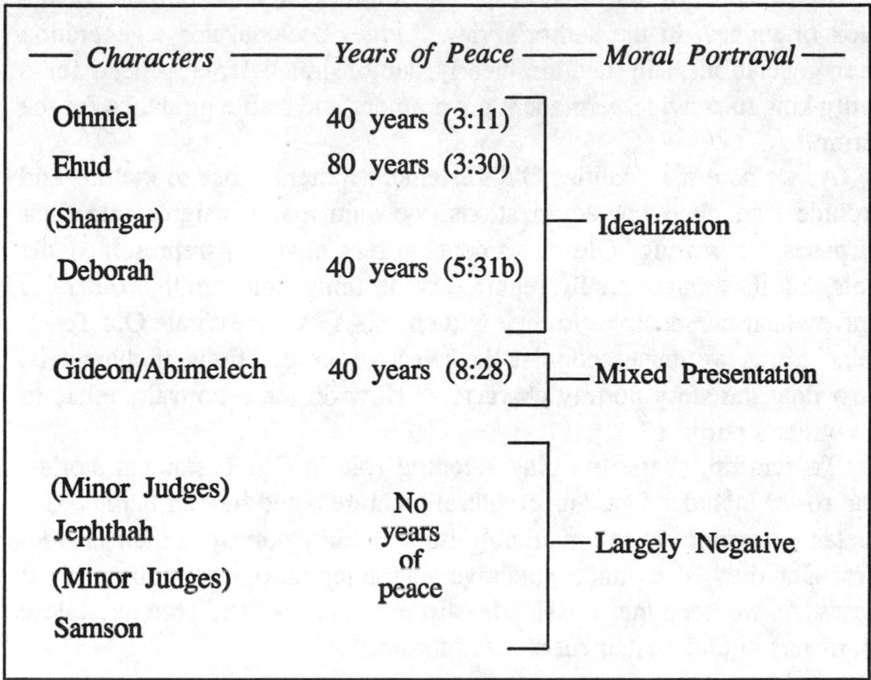

Fig. 14: Declining Character Among Judges

judges; he obeyed and succeeded. Near the end of his life, however, Gideon faltered and worshipped the golden ephod he had made (Judges 8:27). Following this event Gideon's son declared himself king, rebelled against God, and oppressed the people. Gideon and Abimelech present a mixture of good and bad.

This turn for the worse is carried further by the stories of Jephthah and Samson.[11] Jephthah's episodes are introduced with an important variation in the cycle of apostasy, repentance, and deliverance. In Judges 10:10 the people cry out for mercy as they had previously, but this time God refuses to respond to their request (Judges 10:11–14). Only after intense supplication does He succumb to their pleas (Judges 10:16b). Jephthah accomplishes victories, but his deliverance is marred by the rash vow to sacrifice whoever came out of his house (11:29–39).[12]

Samson also appears as a man of questionable moral character. Although a Nazirite set apart to God (13:5), he marries a Philistine woman (14:1–20) and is lured into divulging the secret of his strength to Delilah (16:1–22). He finally succeeds in overcoming the Philistines, but at the cost of his own life (16:23–30). In his presentation of Samson's life, the writer came to the low point in his characterizations of the judges.

This pattern of selective characterization served the purpose of the book of Judges. In the author's view, judges became worse generation after generation. This decline clearly demonstrated Israel's need for a godly king to provide permanent government and stable guidance for the nation.

As we note the qualities Old Testament writers chose to include and exclude from their characterizations, we gain many insights into their purposes for writing. Old Testament writers never misrepresented the facts, but they intentionally reported some things and omitted others to convey their perspectives to their audience. As we investigate Old Testament stories, we must recognize the selective presentations of characters. How does the story portray characters? How do these portraits relate to the writer's purpose?

To sum up, characters play a central role in Old Testament stories. The roster includes God, supernatural creatures, and human beings. Old Testament writers were remarkably frank as they portrayed their characters. But they also made selective characterizations to convey their views. As we keep these basic ideas in mind, we will be able to explore characters in Old Testament stories more fully.

Techniques of Characterization

I have a friend who is an accomplished glass artist. I have always admired his work, but recently I gained even greater appreciation when he took me to his workshop and demonstrated many of the techniques he uses to produce his art. I was amazed at the complexity of the process. Now I look at his work with new admiration. Knowing the process of production makes me able to see the beauty of his glass more clearly.

In many ways the same is true of characterization in Old Testament stories. Most of us intuitively sense the importance of character portraits. But our appreciation of this aspect of Old Testament narratives is enhanced as we understand the techniques Old Testament writers used to form their characterizations.

The techniques used in characterization are complex, but three factors are particularly important: *clues for characterization, depths of exposure,* and *character arrangement*. What hints did Old Testament writers give to disclose their perspectives on characters? What insights did they reveal? How did Old Testament authors arrange characters in relation to each other?

Clues for Characterization

In one sense every aspect of Old Testament texts contributes to our understanding of characterizations. But Old Testament writers revealed their outlooks in four main ways: *appearance and social status, overt actions, direct speech and thought,* and *descriptive comments.*[13]

Appearance and social status. First, Old Testament writers laid the groundwork for characterizations in the appearance and social status of their characters. Old Testament writers focused primarily on inward qualities, concentrating on "the motives, the attitudes, (and) the moral nature of characters."[14] But external factors often provided clues for their viewpoints on inward character traits.

Old Testament stories differ from much world literature in their lack of attention to external appearance; physical descriptions occur only occasionally. Goliath is said to be "over nine feet tall" (1 Samuel 17:4); Saul stood "a head taller than any of the others" (1 Samuel 9:2b); Esau was "red" and "hairy" (Genesis 25:25); Sarai was "very beautiful" (Genesis 12:14); Moses' face "was radiant" after he had spoken with God (Exodus 34:29). These clues for characterization occur so infrequently that they deserve special attention when they appear.

Social status also hints at character traits. Old Testament writers frequently noted the background and rank of human figures to form an orientation toward their characters. David is called the "king" (2 Samuel 2:4); Elijah is deemed "a man of God" (1 Kings 17:24); Rahab is "a prostitute" (Joshua 2:1); and Naaman is "commander of the army of the king of Aram" (2 Kings 5:1). These facts did not reveal specific insights into the qualities of these characters, but they set up initial expectations for the readers upon which other clues build.

The story of Eglon's assassination (Judges 3:12–30) illustrates the value of appearance and social status in characterization. The writer of Judges oriented his readers toward the two principal characters, Ehud and Eglon, in two ways. First, he called Ehud "a deliverer," and described Eglon as a "king of Moab." These designations immediately prejudiced the readers in favor of Ehud. Second, the writer mocked Eglon noting that he was "very fat." This physical description added to the negative orientation already established toward the king.

Appearance and social status are relatively vague clues. We must infer the character traits associated with these descriptions,[15] since they do not contribute much in themselves. Yet they often set forth vital outlooks toward characters that find fuller explication as the story proceeds.[16] As we look at Old Testament narratives, we must take note of these clues.

Overt actions. Old Testament writers relied much more on overt actions to convey their characterizations. These clues take at least three forms: the actions of the characters themselves, other human characters, and God and His representatives.

The behavior of characters themselves reveals their inner qualities. We may learn a great deal about a character by noting the specific actions the writers chose to mention. What sorts of moral and immoral actions did the character perform in the story? These factors are critical, but they do not state character traits explicitly. We must infer inward qualities from these external realities.

Second, the behavior of other human characters exposes a character's inner traits. What did other figures do? How did they react to the character? Again we must infer traits from these external realities. Moreover, we must evaluate the actions of other human characters; they often made mistakes. Yet if their reactions reflected correct assessments, we can learn a great deal about the writer's perspective.

Third, Old Testament writers often relied on the actions of God and His representatives to characterize other figures. Divine blessing and judgment demonstrate how the audience was expected to evaluate a character. We are often left to infer why God acted as He did, but His reactions are never mistaken. His responses reveal the true nature of other characters.

It will help to look again at the story of Eglon's assassination in Judges 3:12–30. The writer of Judges used the actions of Ehud and Eglon, other humans around them, and God to portray the judge and the king. Eglon is characterized as an oppressive ruler prone to excess and stupidity. His tyrannical heart is revealed in his first actions, in which the Moabite ruler attacked Israel and dominated the territory surrounding Jericho. His rule was so oppressive that "the Israelites cried out to the Lord" (v. 15). God's willingness to send a deliverer also indicates the writer's outlook on Eglon's moral nature.

The writer of Judges ridiculed Eglon's excesses by noting that "the fat closed" over the handle of Ehud's sword (v. 22). He mocked Eglon by stating that his guards waited "to the point of embarrassment" (v. 25) before entering the king's chamber because they thought he was "relieving himself" (v. 24).

Finally, the writer of Judges characterized Eglon as an absolute fool. Imprudently leaving himself unguarded, Eglon rises to his feet as Ehud approaches, totally unaware of his pending doom (v. 20). The writer even cast dispersions on the king when he noted how his select guards stood by as Ehud locked the doors and escaped (v. 23).

Overt actions form the opposite portrait of Ehud. The writer of Judges portrayed him as an extraordinary person, full of courage, wisdom, and strength. We are given an indication of Ehud's outstanding character when God chooses him to deliver the people (v. 15). He shows technical skill by preparing his own "double-edged sword" (v. 16). The Israelites recognize his exceptional qualities when they entrust their tribute to his care (v. 15).

Ehud's character also becomes apparent as he deals with the Moabites. He sends his company away and returns to face Eglon alone (v. 18). Ehud cleverly tricks Eglon into granting him a private audience by speaking of his "secret message" for the king (vv. 19–20). Ehud's strength stands out as he thrusts his sword all the way into Eglon's body (vv. 21–22). He escapes (v. 23) and courageously leads Israel in victory over the Moabites (vv. 26–30).

The writer of Judges used these overt actions to reveal his perspectives on Eglon and Ehud. Although we must rely on inferences, these clues give significant insights into his characterizations.

Direct speech and thought. Clues to characterization also appear through direct speech and thought. Old Testament writers revealed the traits of their characters by recording what they spoke and thought. Once again it helps to think of the characters themselves, other human characters, and God and His representatives.

First, characters themselves often comment on their own motivations, attitudes, and moral nature. These disclosures are more explicit than those drawn from appearances, social status, and actions. We do not have to infer the inward qualities in view. Of course, we must always assess whether the self-reflections of ordinary human beings are accurate. David's confession to Nathan, "I have sinned against the Lord" (2 Samuel 12:13), was obviously correct, revealing what the writer wanted his audience to think about David. But Aaron falsely represented himself when he claimed, "Do not be angry, my lord . . . they gave me the gold, and I threw it into the fire, and out came this calf" (Exodus 32:22–24). Aaron was lying; he himself had made the golden calf (Exodus 32:2–4). Since Old Testament writers reported false ideas and lies, all such statements must be examined carefully within their contexts.

Second, human characters often make statements about other characters. Sometimes their comments are true. Judah, for instance, is correct when he concludes that Tamar "is more righteous than I" (Genesis 38:26), but Pharaoh is certainly wrong when he claims that the Israelites "are lazy; that is why they are crying out, 'Let us go and sacrifice to our God'" (Exodus 5:8b). Even so, Old Testament writers often used the words and thoughts of other people to unveil the inward qualities of certain characters to their readers.

Third, Old Testament writers reported the words and thoughts of God and His representatives for the sake of characterization. For instance, at Sinai God declared, "I have seen these people . . . and they are a stiff-necked people" (Exodus 32:9). Moses expected his readers to accept this insight into the moral qualities of the previous generation without question. The assessments God, His prophets, or supernatural messengers express are totally reliable.

Direct speech plays a vital role in the account of Jacob's preparations for meeting Esau (Genesis 32:1–32). Prior to this chapter Moses had shown how Jacob lived as "the supplanter" (*y'qb*) by deceiving his father and stealing his brother's birthright (Genesis 25:19–34; 27:1–40).[17] But as Jacob contemplates Esau's approach, he expresses his personal sense of moral deficiency to God: "I am unworthy of all the kindness and faithfulness you have shown your servant" (Genesis 32:10). He also admits to his fear and helplessness: "Save me, I pray, from the hand of my brother Esau, for I am afraid" (32:11). Through Jacob's self-reflection, Moses alerted his readers to the developments that had taken place within the patriarch.

Jacob's character is further disclosed in the conversation between Jacob and the "man" with whom he wrestled at Peniel (32:26–30).[18] Jacob confesses that his name is indeed Jacob (32:27), but the man responds, "Your name will no longer be Jacob, but Israel, because you have struggled with God and with men and have overcome" (32:28). Through the words of this messenger from God, Moses disclosed Jacob's new character to his readers. No longer is he the supplanter; he is now the one who has overcome and attained the blessing of God.

Words and thoughts often help to form characterizations. Through the comments and reflections of the figures themselves, other humans, and God and His representatives, Old Testament writers offered many insights into the qualities of characters within their stories.

Descriptive comments. Old Testament writers also made their own descriptive comments on characters' inward traits. These clues are usually brief, but they are relatively clear and certain. For instance, when Lot settled near Sodom, Moses commented, "Now the men of Sodom were wicked and were sinning greatly against the Lord" (Genesis 13:13). Moses stated explicitly that "Jacob was in love with Rachel" (Genesis 29:18); the writer of Judges reported how "the Israelites grieved for their brothers, the Benjamites" (Judges 21:6); and the writer of Samuel recounted that "David was angry because the Lord's wrath had broken out against Uzzah" (2 Samuel 6:8). Such direct descriptions appear in many Old Testament stories and help us understand the writers' characterizations.

Old Testament writers presented many different clues to form their characterizations. What is said about the appearance and status of each character? What actions reveal inner qualities? How do direct speech and thoughts expose figures in the story? What descriptive comments does the writer offer? As we investigate characterization in Old Testament stories, we must examinc all of these clues.

Depths of Exposure

Old Testament writers also portrayed characters by offering various depths of exposure. Some figures appear as full persons; we learn about the complexities of their attitudes and qualities. Others remain largely obscure. It helps to examine the depth of exposure for each character. We will use the following well-known literary categories: *round characters, flat characters,* and *functionary characters.*[19]

Round characters. Round characters are persons whose portraits are multifaceted. The writers presented them as thinking, feeling, and choosing persons who function in a story by "manifesting a multitude of traits and appearing as 'real people.'"[20] In most cases characters gain depth when they appear many times in large sections of Scripture. The information in individual episodes forms cumulative portraits. For example, the chapters of Samuel devoted to David's life reveal his courage (1 Samuel 17:1–58), devotion to God (2 Samuel 6:12–15), adultery (2 Samuel 11:1–26) and humble repentance (2 Samuel 12:13). They show him pleasing to God and under divine judgment.

Smaller episodes usually do not present very full portraits. Yet, even within the confines of a single story, some characters are more fully developed than others. For example, the writer of Kings portrayed Solomon as a round character in his account of his request for wisdom in 1 Kings 1:3–15. Although Solomon was characterized primarily as an obedient man, he nevertheless had a serious fault. Solomon "showed his love for the Lord . . . except that he offered sacrifices and burned incense on the high places" (v. 3). At the same time, Solomon's prayer reveals his humility: "I am only a little child and do not know how to carry out my duties . . . who is able to govern this great people of yours?" (v. 9). God's reaction to Solomon demonstrates his moral qualities even further: "The Lord was pleased that Solomon had asked for this" (v. 10). To show development in Solomon's character, the writer of Kings ended the account with a note that the king left the high place in Gibeon and went "to Jerusalem, stood before the ark of the Lord's covenant and sacrificed burnt offerings and fellowship offerings" (v. 15). In this one episode, the writer of Kings presented Solomon as a round character through actions, words, and descriptive comments.

Flat characters. Old Testament writers also presented flat characters in their narratives who appear relatively plain and colorless. For the most part, flat characters are "built around a single quality or trait."[21]

Persons who are disclosed in depth over large portions of Scripture may appear rather flat in a particular episode. For instance, Isaac is a very rich character on a large scale (Genesis 21:1—35:29). In the episode of Abraham's test (Genesis 22:1–19), however, Isaac appears as a flat figure—a submissive son—but little more can be said of him.

The depth of exposure in a particular episode is not an indication of that individual's theological importance. A character may be very important on a large-scale but relatively flat in a particular passage. Consider again the account of Solomon's prayer for wisdom (1 Kings 3:1–15). The writer of Kings disclosed less about God than Solomon. God's activity in Solomon's life is a chief concern of the writer, but in this episode God is a relatively flat character. He simply grants Solomon the privilege of asking for whatever he wants and approves of his request. No mention is made of God's attitude toward Solomon's marriage to Pharaoh's daughter or Solomon's sacrifices at the high places. The divine character is relatively uncomplicated.

Functionary characters. Many persons in Old Testament stories have the status of functionary characters. These figures are mentioned in the text, but their personalities are barely disclosed at best. Writers include them to give their stories coherence and realism, but these agents are "mere functionaries and not characterized at all."[22] Once again, however, we must distinguish between large sections and single episodes, since characters may be flat or round in some passages and merely functionary in another.

Functionary characters appear throughout the Old Testament. For example, in the story of Abraham's test (Genesis 22:1–19), the two servants are merely functionaries. Although they are mentioned several times in the story (Genesis 22:3, 5, 19), their personalities are barely disclosed. In much the same way, the account of Solomon's prayer for wisdom (1 Kings 3:1–15) mentions Pharaoh's daughter, and we may assume certain traits on the basis of her identity. Yet the writer of Kings did not disclose her further.

Characters may be round, flat, or functionary. As we investigate characterizations in Old Testament stories, we should note the depth of disclosure for each character. Which characters are round, flat, or functionary?

Character Arrangement

To understand characterization we must also look at how characters are arranged in relation to each other. Old Testament writers did not present characters haphazardly but often arranged them into groups. As we discern these configurations, we can grasp more fully the role of each character in the original meaning.

We will consider three companies of characters: *protagonistic, antagonistic,* and *ambivalent*. Stories do not always include each group, but all characters tend to fall into one of these companies.

Protagonistic. Protagonistic characters include the protagonist and less important, supporting figures. The protagonist of the story is the first struggler from whose viewpoint we go through the action.[23] This character may be good or evil, hero or miscreant. Whatever the case, the protagonist is the main character of the story.

But we must be cautious. Evangelicals have a natural tendency to identify God as the protagonist in every story. This is certainly true in a metaphysical sense; these stories reflect His good purposes and sovereign will at work. But as we saw earlier in this chapter, God is not always in the foreground.

Old Testament stories usually have human protagonists. For instance, in the record of Abram's sojourn to Egypt (Genesis 12:10–20), Abram is the protagonist. The account of Solomon's prayer for wisdom (1 Kings 3:1–15) presents the king as the main character. In the Tower of Babel account (Genesis 11:1–9), all of humanity is the protagonist.

Frequently Old Testament stories gather around the protagonist a number of characters whom we will call *the protagonist's entourage*. This entourage may be small or large; it may include humans, supernatural creatures, and God. Whatever the case, this group supports the protagonist through the events of the story. Isaac and the two servants are supporting characters in the account of Abraham's testing (Genesis

22:1–19), making it possible for Abraham to succeed in his task. Moses received help from God and Aaron as he faced Pharaoh (Exodus 5:1–21). Joshua supported the two spies he sent to Jericho (Joshua 2:1–24). The Israelites helped David bring the ark into Jerusalem (2 Samuel 6:1–19). These characters do not occupy the center stage, but they aid the protagonists in their tasks.

Antagonistic. Old Testament stories also present antagonistic characters. The antagonist is the major character who is "arrayed against the protagonist."[24] Antagonists may be evil or good; they may intend harm or benefit to the protagonist. But in one way or another, the antagonist represents the opposite side of dramatic tension in the story. Personal antagonists are not essential for well-formed stories; opposition may come from impersonal obstacles as well.

Even so, most Old Testament stories have personal antagonists. God resists humanity at the Tower of Babel (Genesis 11:1–9); Pharaoh troubles Abram (Genesis 12:10–20); and God challenges Abraham by calling him to sacrifice his son (Genesis 22:1–19). The tensions these antagonists introduce differ in many ways, but they stand on the side of action opposite the protagonist.

In many passages characters gather to form the *antagonist's entourage*. These persons play relatively minor roles, but they support the antagonist. The heavenly host joins God in opposing the Tower of Babel (Genesis 11:7); Pharaoh's men side with Pharaoh in troubling Abram (Genesis 12:10–15); Eglon is attended by his guards (Judges 3:18–19, 24–25).

Ambivalent. Stories also present some persons as ambivalent characters who do not clearly support the protagonist or the antagonist. Pharaoh's daughter hardly enters the drama in the account of Solomon's request for wisdom (1 Kings 3:1–15). She neither strongly supports nor challenges Solomon in this passage. At other times ambivalent characters shift from one side to the other. Rahab begins as an opponent of Joshua's spies, but as the story progresses she becomes their key supporter (Joshua 2:1–24).

As we investigate the original meaning of Old Testament stories, we should take notice of the ways in which Old Testament writers arranged characters into groups. Who is the protagonist? What characters offer him or her support? Who is the antagonist? Who sides with him or her? What characters are ambivalent in their association?

In this section we have seen how Old Testament writers formed characterizations, offering clues to their characterization through appearance and status, actions, direct speech and thought, and descriptive comments. Their characters appear round, flat, and functionary; they fall into protagonistic, antagonistic, and ambivalent groups. As we keep these basic ideas in mind, we will be able to discern this aspect of Old Testament narratives more clearly (see figure 15).

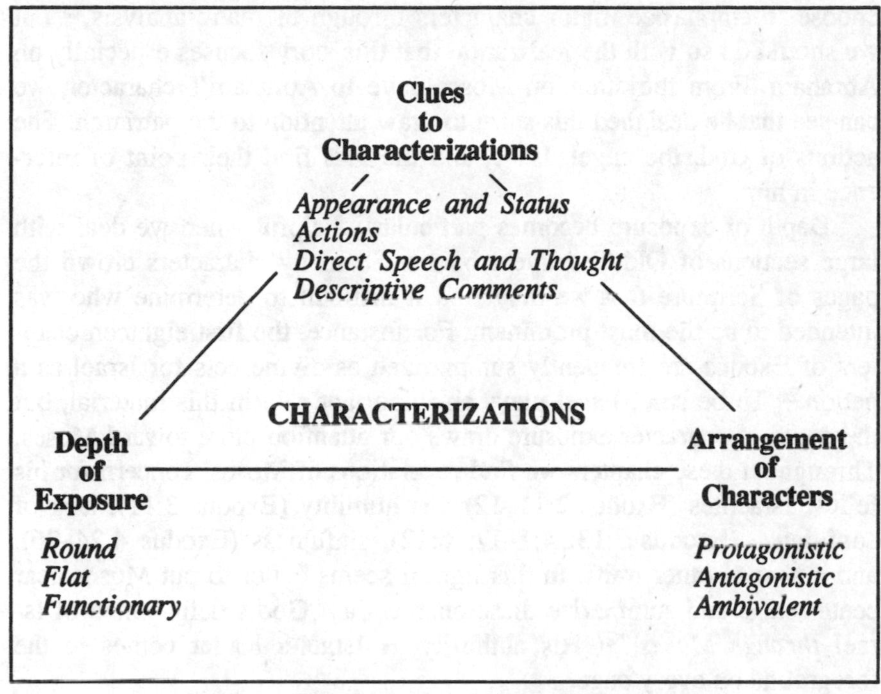

Fig. 15: Techniques of Characterization

Purpose of Characterization

Why should we investigate characterization in an Old Testament story? What value does such analysis have? Characterizations help us assess several vital dimensions of Old Testament narratives. We will touch on three facets of these texts that become clear as we investigate characterization: *prominent concerns, basic drama,* and *reader responses.*

Prominent Concerns

In many stories the writer's central concerns emerge as we take note of which characters are more fully exposed. Functionary characters are usually the least significant. Flat characters may play more important roles but normally do not stand in the foreground. Round characters are the principal figures in most stories. The fuller the exposure, the more importance a character has in a particular passage.

For example, in the story of Abraham's test (Genesis 22:1–19), God, Abraham, and the angel stand out as developed characters. As we have seen, however, Abraham is certainly the most fully exposed. We may choose to emphasize minor characters through thematic analysis,[25] but we should do so with the realization that this story focuses especially on Abraham. From the attention Moses gave to Abraham's character, we can see that he designed this story to draw attention to the patriarch. The actions of God, the angel, Isaac, and the lads find their point of reference in him.

Depth of exposure becomes particularly helpful when we deal with large sections of Old Testament books. So many characters crowd the pages of Scripture that we may find it difficult to determine who was intended to be the most prominent. For instance, the first eighteen chapters of Exodus are frequently summarized as divine acts for Israel as a nation.[26] To be sure, Israel plays an important role in this material, but the depth of character exposure draws our attention more toward Moses. Throughout these chapters we find revelations of Moses' concern for his fellow Israelites (Exodus 2:11–12), his humility (Exodus 3:11), lack of confidence (Exodus 3:13; 4:1–17; 6:12), sinfulness (Exodus 4:24–26), and a host of other traits. In this light it seems better to put Moses near center stage and summarize these chapters as "God's deliverance of Israel *through Moses*."[27] His authority as Israel's leader comes to the foreground on every page.

As we investigate Old Testament narratives, we should follow this guide to prominence: "What characters are exposed more fully?" "How does the depth of exposure point to the prominent aspects of the story?"

Basic Drama

Old Testament stories weave many strands of action together. Large sections present innumerable plots and sub-plots.[28] Even single episodes report more than a simple chain of events. Frequently these complexities make it difficult to discern the basic drama of a text. In these cases we can gain insight by observing the arrangement of characters. Identifying the associations of characters orients us to the fundamental structures of a story.

The protagonist and the opposition of the antagonist reveal the critical concerns of Old Testament writers; events come together in the ways that relate to their struggle. All elements of a story have some bearing on the problems, challenges, projects, failures, and accomplishments of the main character.

A case in point is the story of Abram's sojourn to Egypt (Genesis 12:10–20). Moses reported that God "inflicted serious diseases on Pharaoh and his household." Of what significance was this event? Did Moses write primarily to depict the misery of the Egyptian king and his family? Was the major purpose of this event to inform us of the nature of God? Abram is the main character of this story, and Pharaoh is his antagonist. The primary reason Moses reported this event was to show its effect on the relationship of these characters. God sent diseases to reunite Abram and Sarai, and to deliver them from Pharaoh.

In much the same way, the tension between protagonists and antagonists of large sections displays the central plot. Many events take place in the book of Jonah. How did the writer pull these events together? For example, how are we to understand the Ninevites' repentance (Jonah 3:4–9)? What was its significance? The writer of Jonah was not primarily concerned with teaching about the city of Nineveh. Rather his foremost interest was in Jonah and his struggle with God. The reaction of the people of Nineveh challenged Jonah's self-righteousness and failure to comply with God's purpose for this life. This focus was the dramatic center of the account.[29]

Exploring characterization often helps us understand the basic drama of a text. As we identify the protagonist, the events of the story fall into placc. To understand the central dramatic tension of a passage, we may ask, "Who is the protagonist?" "Who is the antagonist?" "How do the events of the story relate to their struggle?"

Reader Responses

Investigating characterization also lends insight into the kinds of reactions Old Testament writers expected from their readers. Old Testament authors did not present characters simply to tell their readers about people in the past but to evoke responses. The interactions of characters and readers were complex and varied. We will explore several aspects of this interaction in later chapters.[30] At this point, however, we will merely point out how characters were designed to elicit three main types of reactions: *sympathetic, antipathetic,* and *mixed.*

Sympathetic. Old Testament writers intended for many of their characters to elicit sympathetic responses of approval. Characters take on the qualities of heroes or models of appropriate attitudes and behavior that the audience was expected to appreciate and admire. Needless to say, audiences were always to respond with admiration for God. All His ways are holy and right. God stands out as the perfect character everywhere He appears. Beyond this, sympathetic responses were also appropriate for many human characters. Readers were never expected to give unqualified approval of human figures, but Old Testament writers designed many of their accounts to elicit largely positive reactions toward human characters.

For example, Ehud appears without fault (Judges 3:12–25). He performs his service to God with skill and courage. The writer of Judges emphasized this facet of Ehud's life to call his readers to appreciation and admiration. Similarly, in the account of Abraham's testing (Genesis 22:1–19), the patriarch follows the command of God without hesitation. Despite the anxiety that grips Abraham's heart, he is willing to sacrifice his son.[31] As God approves of the patriarch's obedience, Moses expected his readers to do the same.

Antipathetic. Old Testament writers also designed some characters to evoke antipathetic responses. They behave in ways that the audience was to reject and, in extreme cases, they aroused contempt in the hearts of readers.

Satan and his agents consistently appear as antipathetic characters. Their ways are opposed to all that is good and holy. Old Testament writers always expected their readers to have antipathy toward them. Beyond this, many human characters also elicited disapproval. Eglon appears as a villain without a single redeeming quality (Judges 3:12–25). In the stories of deliverance from Egypt (Exodus 1:1—15:21), Pharaoh emerges as an antipathetic character who resists God and threatens Israel's future. In the account of Naboth's vineyard (1 Kings 21:1–29), the writer of Kings portrayed Jezebel as a murderous miscreant. He wanted his readers to be repulsed by her character.

Mixed. In many cases, however, characters combine positive and negative qualities, requiring mixed responses from the original audience. Few characters are perfectly balanced between good and evil. For the most part, the writers presented either positive figures tainted by negative qualities or negative figures softened by some positive characteristics.

Solomon's prayer for wisdom (1 Kings 3:1–15) presents Solomon as basically a positive figure. The story focuses on how he prayed and received approval from God (1 Kings 3:7–14). Yet the writer of Kings also presented imperfections in Solomon's character. His marriage to Pharaoh's daughter (v. 1) foreshadows the syncretism which led to the division of the kingdom. Moreover, the writer also explicitly noted that

Solomon "offered sacrifices and burned incense on the high places" (v. 3). These aspects of Solomon's characterization evoked mixed reactions from the original readers.

The story of Abraham and Abimelech (Genesis 20:1–18) presents Abimelech as a negative character who took Sarai from Abraham and threatened the promise of the seed. These actions aroused contempt from the audience. Yet Moses reported that God warned Abimelech in a dream, and Abimelech recognized his error (Genesis 20:4–5). As a result he returned Sarai to Abraham, saying, "What have you done to us? How have I wronged you that you have brought such great guilt upon me and my kingdom?" (v. 9). Abimelech's response to Abraham elicited positive attitudes from the original audience. They too wondered how Abraham could have done this. Moses portrayed Abimelech in a way that aroused mixed reactions.

As we investigate characterization in Old Testament stories, we must look for the kinds of reactions the writers expected from their audiences. What are the positive and negative qualities of the character? Would the original audience have reacted with sympathy, antipathy, or mixed attitudes? As we understand these matters, we will find ourselves challenged to respond appropriately as well.

Conclusion

In this chapter we have examined several basic features of characters and characterizations in Old Testament stories. Old Testament writers selectively revealed the traits of characters and arranged them in dramatic tension with each other. These characterizations alert us to the important aspects and basic drama of their accounts. We can also gain an understanding of how the writers wanted readers to respond to their texts. In these ways characters form a vital dimension of the original meaning of Old Testament stories.

Review Questions

1. Describe the different types of characters in Old Testament stories. Why do we speak of honesty and selectivity in characterization?
2. How do Old Testament writers give clues to their outlooks on a character? Give an example of each technique.

3. What are round, flat, and functionary characters? Give an example of each.
4. Define the following terms: protagonist, antagonist, protagonistic entourage, antagonistic entourage, ambivalent character.
5. How does characterization help us see prominence, drama, and expected reader responses? Illustrate.

Study Exercises

1. Make a list of the roster of characters in Genesis 2:4—3:24.
2. Categorize the characters in Genesis 2:4—3:24 as round, flat, and functionary. Describe the traits of the round characters. What responses did Moses want his readers to have toward each character?
3. Arrange the characters of Genesis 2:4—3:24 into protagonistic, antagonistic, and ambivalent groups. Then describe the basic drama of the story in terms of this arrangement.

7

SCENE DEPICTION

Walking along the Charles River early one spring morning, a friend and I came upon an artist painting a portrait of wild daisies. With just a few strokes, she had captured the beauty of the scene on her canvas. "Remarkable," I commented. But my friend did not agree. "I don't think it's so good," he whispered. "She didn't paint it like it *really* is . . . I'd rather have something more precise."

In Western culture today, we put such a premium on precise, scientific knowledge that we often fail to see the value of artistic depictions of reality. We prefer a photograph to a painting, a video tape to a photograph. With these ideas embedded so deeply within us, it can be difficult to appreciate an artistic portrait.

But we must gain an appreciation for artistic depictions if we are to investigate Old Testament stories. Old Testament narratives are neither straightforward photographs nor surveillance videos; they do not give comprehensive, detailed accounts of events. On the contrary, Old Testament stories present creative portraits of Israel's history.

In the previous chapter, we saw how Old Testament stories present characters artistically; in this chapter, we consider the ways Old Testament writers depicted scenes. For our purposes scenes may be defined as batches of closely related circumstances, actions, and characters that form the basic building blocks of Old Testament stories.[1] As we look into these narrative units, we will examine three major issues: *scene divisions, space and time in scenes,* and *imagery in scenes*. How can we distinguish one scene from another? What attention should we give to their spatio-temporal qualities? How did Old Testament writers use imagery in their scenes?

Division of Scenes

"Divide and conquer" is an effective strategy. If a job is too big to do all at once, we can still accomplish it one step at a time. The same is true for interpreting Old Testament stories. Most texts are far too complex for us to handle everything at once. For this reason we will divide them into their basic units and walk through them scene by scene. We will consider *obstacles to dividing scenes, clues for divisions,* and some *examples.*

Obstacles to Dividing Scenes

We face at least two significant obstacles when we divide Old Testament stories into their basic units. One barrier comes from us; the other resides in the texts themselves.

The first problem lies in our hermeneutical orientation. Put simply, we seldom think of scenes as the basic units of Biblical stories. Church background and formal training usually orient us toward smaller units. We think primarily in terms of words, phrases, clauses, and sentences. At best we venture to the level of verses. These elements are important, but we often fail to see the value of larger portions of Old Testament stories.

To overcome this obstacle, we will approach Old Testament narratives much as we do other stories. For instance, when we read *Robinson Crusoe,* or a more recent work such as Potok's *Davita's Harp,* a special word or the turn of a phrase may arrest our attention on occasion. But for the most part, we reflect on these stories in terms of scenes. We recall Crusoe's first sighting of human footprints in the sand; we remember the tragic scene in which Davita learned of her father's death.

There are times when we need to focus on smaller details in Old Testament stories. But understanding these texts depends more on an ability to think in terms of scenes. Therefore, we must break with our usual microscopic orientation as we investigate.[2]

The second problem with establishing scene divisions lies in Old Testament stories themselves. Unlike other forms of storytelling, these texts do not explicitly mark where scenes begin and end. A comic strip indicates scenes by separate frames; each box presents a distinct batch of interactive circumstances, actions, and characters.[3] Plays distinguish scenes by performance on different parts of the stage, rearranging props, lowering and raising the curtain. In contrast, Old Testament narratives tend to move smoothly from one scene to the next. Boundaries are seldom abrupt.

As a result, readers may disagree over precisely how to divide a text. Some will be prone to make scenes larger; others will make them smaller. Some will divide the text at one spot; others will vary by a verse or two.[4] We must be flexible as we divide Old Testament stories into scenes.

Clues for Divisions

Whatever obstacles we face, Old Testament stories offer many clues for establishing scene divisions. As we become familiar with these clues, we will discover many boundaries more easily. We can separate one scene from another by noting significant changes in *time, setting,* and *mode of narration.*

Time. Significant shifts in time often indicate scene boundaries. Old Testament stories do not always present tightly interlocking events in precise chronological order. Instead, they often interrupt the chain of events through *subsequent, simultaneous,* and *antecedent breaks* in the sequence.

First, these temporal shifts appear as gaps between *subsequent events.* One block of action stands apart from the next because of a relatively large lapse of time.

Sometimes Old Testament writers indicated these gaps explicitly. References to "the next day" (*mmḥrt*),[5] "morning" (*bqr*),[6] "evening" (*'rb*),[7] "months" (*ḥdš*),[8] "years" (*šnh*),[9] and "after" some period of time[10] frequently designate the beginning of a new scene. The expressions "and he (they) rose up" (*škm*)[11] and "and it came to pass" (*wyhy*)[12] typically indicate a break.

But gaps in subsequent time do not always appear so plainly. For instance, the typical "and/then" (*waw* consecutive) construction, so prominent in Hebrew narrative, marks both immediate action and action after a significant passage of time.[13] In many cases Old Testament writers did not make explicit temporal remarks because they expected their audiences to recognize the break.

Second, Old Testament writers distinguished scenes by shifts to *simultaneous action.* Cinema often presents simultaneous events on a split screen or by rapidly switching back and forth between scenes. In a play two or more events may take place on stage at the same time. But events that happened at the same moment in the real world follow each other in the narrative world.[14] As a result stories retrace the same period of time, though the text moves forward on the page.[15] This retracing often indicates a new scene.

Shifts to simultaneous events occur frequently in Old Testament stories. At times Hebrew constructions (often simple *waw*) indicate simultaneous action.[16] For example, after describing Hannah's prayer and vow (1 Samuel 1:10–11), the writer of Samuel mentioned that Eli had been watching: "As she kept on praying to the Lord, Eli observed her mouth" (*w'ly šmr 't pyh*) (1 Samuel 1:12). Similarly, as Pharoah took Sarai into his palace, "He treated Abram well for her sake" (*wl'brm hytyb b'bwrh*) (Genesis 12:16a). Abram received good treatment *while* Sarai continued in the royal harem.[17] In these and similar passages, the grammar indicates simultaneous events.

In many cases, however, grammar does not explicitly denote simultaneity. Only by assessing the contents do we notice such a shift. For instance, after Jonah preached to Nineveh, all of the city believed and joined in a fast (Jonah 3:5). It seems unlikely that the next scene, in which the king declared a fast (Jonah 3:6–7), was entirely subsequent to the city-wide repentance. Some overlap probably occurred between the events.[18] In these situations the original readers simply supplied "meanwhile . . ." from their assessment of the content.

Third, temporal shifts occur when scenes regress to *antecedent actions*—events completed before the current scene. On occasion Hebrew grammar reveals these antecedent actions, and English translations often make these shifts clear as well. Sometimes, however, we must rely on content to tell us we are dealing with action that occurred beforehand.

Antecedent scenes often amount to vignettes of background information.[19] After mentioning that Shishak had laid siege against Jerusalem (2 Chronicles 12:2), the Chronicler retraced Shishak's preceding campaign throughout Judah (2 Chronicles 12:3–4). Antecedent shifts like this usually indicate the beginning of a new scene.

In sum, temporal breaks between scenes occur in three ways: gaps between subsequent events, shifts to simultaneous actions, and regressions to antecedent events. As we take note of these changes, we will be able to identify many scenes in Old Testament narratives.

Setting. Changes in setting also help us define scene boundaries. We will speak of three important changes in setting: *place, environmental features,* and *characters.*

First, variations in *place* mark scenes. For instance, the account of Sodom and Gomorrah moves from the city gate (Genesis 19:1–2) to inside Lot's home (Genesis 19:3). As Abram and Sarai travelled toward Egypt, Genesis 12:11 places them on the border, but Genesis 12:14 puts them in Egypt itself. After God came down to see the Tower of Babel

(Genesis 11:5), He returned to heaven and called the heavenly host to action (Genesis 11:6–7).

We must add one qualification. Frequently a single scene will contain *teichoscopies*—the mention of events offstage.[20] The scene may be oriented toward one place but refer to something in another setting. Teichoscopy occurs most frequently in direct discourse where characters are speaking of events that take place elsewhere. For instance, when God commissioned Moses at the burning bush, He referred to events in Egypt, even though the scene itself was located in the desert (Exodus 3:7–10). As Michal rebuked David for his behavior before the ark, she referred back to what she had seen outside her window (2 Samuel 6:20–23). Teichoscopy does not indicate a scene division but should be treated simply as part of the larger scene.

Second, significant changes in *environmental features* also divide one scene from another. Frequently several scenes, even whole stories, will occur in one place.[21] Yet we must still watch for the external surroundings to vary.

Environmental variations may include darkness to light, cold to heat, or drought to rain.[22] A writer may simply give new facts about geography, animals, plant life, and buildings.[23] Environmental features can also include variations of space and time. The first scene may be panoramic and the next narrowly focused; one scene may be fast and the next slow.[24] Old Testament writers frequently indicated boundaries of scenes by changing environmental features.

Third, Old Testament writers divided scenes by changing the *characters* who occupy the stage.[25] These shifts closely resemble changes in environment but involve persons: human beings, supernatural creatures, and Deity. A story's stage may be crowded in one scene and nearly empty in the next.[26] Sometimes a scene with one or two characters precedes a scene with innumerable participants.[27] At other times the number of characters remains equal, but their identities change.[28] These clues also help us separate scenes. We must be alert to these variations in place, environmental features, and characters as we look for scenes in Old Testament stories.

Mode of narration. Scenes also divide as the mode of narration changes. Narrative mode is determined by the degree to which the writer's presence is felt,[29] whether he has walked out to center stage or remained backstage, allowing the characters themselves to tell the story through their own thoughts, words, and actions. Shifts from one mode to another give important clues for scene divisions. For our purposes we will distinguish four modes of narration: *authorial comments, description, straight narration,* and *dramatic depiction.*

First, writers directly addressed their audiences through *authorial comments,* scenes in which they evaluated or explained something in the story.[30] For instance, after reporting Adam's joy at seeing Eve, Moses stepped forward and commented, "For this reason a man will leave his father and mother and be united to his wife, and they will become one flesh" (Genesis 2:24). Similarly, at the end of Jacob's wrestling at Peniel (Genesis 32:22–32), Moses explained, "Therefore to this day the Israelites do not eat the tendon attached to the socket of the hip, because the socket of Jacob's hip was touched near the tendon." In both verses the story itself stopped, and Moses inserted his own commentary. Usually authorial comments like these form their own scenes.

Second, Old Testament writers often wrote in the mode of *description.* They took one step back from center stage but stopped the progress of the account to add descriptive details. The descriptive mode resembles authorial comments, but it is less explanatory. It adds information that highlights some feature of the narrative.[31] For instance, the story of Abram's migration (Genesis 12:1–9) contains two descriptive scenes. After reporting that Abram departed for the land, Moses added, "Abram was seventy-five years old when he set out from Haran" (Genesis 12:4b). After Abram had entered the land of Canaan, Moses pulled his readers to comment, "At that time the Canaanites were in the land" (Genesis 12:6b). Moses asserted himself to give some descriptive details, but not as strongly as an authorial comment.

Third, scenes appear in *straight narration.* In this mode the writer allowed his readers to look more directly on the action taking place. We recognize that the events are mediated through the author, but we are more directly in contact with the drama than in his descriptions and comments. For example, after Jacob died we read, "Then Joseph directed the physicians in his service to embalm his father Israel" (Genesis 50:2a). In this verse Moses did not allow Joseph himself to speak; he merely reported that the event took place. We will call such reporting straight narration.

Fourth, in the *dramatic mode,* the author moved far into the background. Instead of reporting that something happened, he permitted his characters to speak, think, and interact for themselves. This mode occurs most commonly in Old Testament narratives through direct discourse.[32] Though Moses merely reported Joseph's instructions to the physicians (Genesis 50:2a), just a few verses later he allowed Joseph to speak and say:

> If I have found favor in your eyes, speak to Pharaoh for me. Tell him, 'My father made me swear an oath and said, "I am about to die; bury me in the tomb I dug for myself in the land of Canaan." Now let me go up and bury my father; then I will return' (Genesis 50:4b–5).

Apart from a brief introduction, Moses is absent from this passage. He presented Joseph's words through dramatic narration.

In the Tower of Babel story (Genesis 11:1–9), we see all four modes of narration. Consider the following examples:

> [Comment] That is why it was called Babel—because there the Lord confused the language of the whole world. From there the Lord scattered them over the face of the whole earth (Genesis 11:9, NASB).
>
> [Description] They used brick instead of stone, and tar for mortar (Genesis 11:3b, NASB).
>
> [Straight] As men moved eastward, they found a plain in Shinar and settled there (Genesis 11:2, NASB).
>
> [Dramatic] They said to each other, "Come, let's make bricks and bake them thoroughly" (Genesis 11:3a, NASB).

As these examples illustrate, Moses' presence was unavoidable in his comment (Genesis 11:9); he asserted himself a little less in his description (Genesis 11:3b); he moved further away in straight narration (Genesis 11:2); and he nearly disappeared as the characters talked to each other in dramatic narration (Genesis 11:3a).

These modes are not absolutely distinct. They form a continuum and often appear mixed with each other.[33] Nevertheless, changes in the mode of narration often form boundaries for scenes within Old Testament stories. As we account for these shifts, we find another set of clues for scene divisions.

Figure 16 shows the three main ways of discerning scene boundaries in Old Testament stories: changes in time through subsequent, simultaneous, and antecedent breaks in the action; changes in setting through varying place, environmental features, and characters; and changes in narrative mode through comments, description, straight, and dramatic narration. These features help us divide Old Testament stories into their basic units.

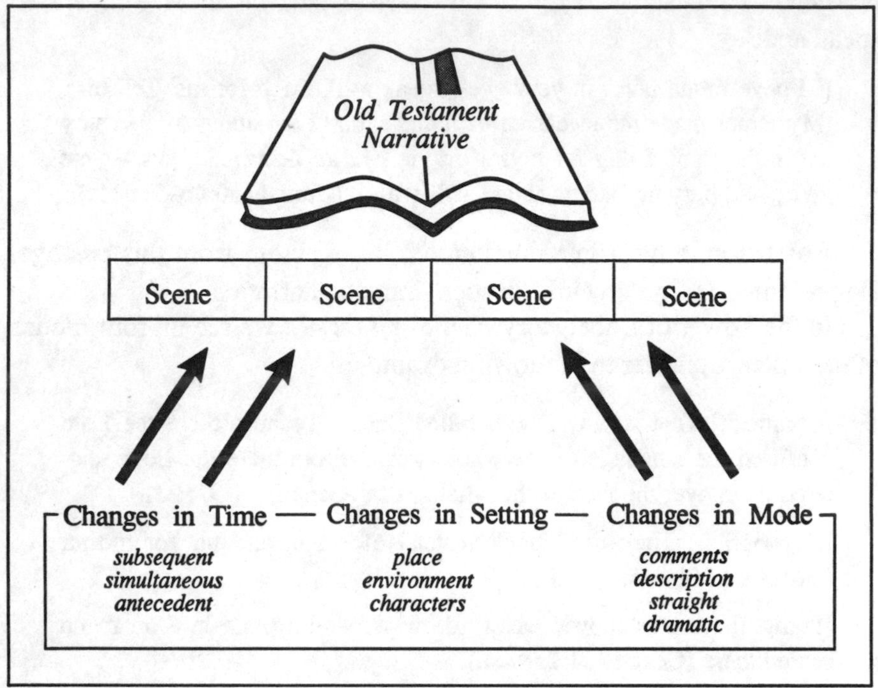

Fig. 16: Clues for Scene Divisions

Examples

To illustrate the process of dividing scenes, we will look at two passages: Genesis 15:7–21 and 2 Chronicles 12:1–12, which will provide examples of several clues for scene divisions.

Genesis 15:7–21. Let us look first at the story of God's covenant with Abram.

Scene One

> He also said to him, "I am the Lord, who brought you out of Ur of the Chaldeans to give you this land to take possession of it." But Abram said, "O Sovereign Lord, how can I know that I will gain possession of it?" So the Lord said to him, "Bring me a heifer, a goat, and a ram, each three years old, along with a dove and a young pigeon." (vv. 7–9)

Scene Two

> Abram brought all these to him, cut them in two and arranged the halves opposite each other; the birds, however, he did not cut in half. (v. 10)

Scene Three

Then birds of prey came down on the carcasses, but Abram drove them away. (v. 11)

Scene Four

As the sun was setting, Abram fell into a deep sleep, and a thick and dreadful darkness came over him. Then the Lord said to him, "Know for certain that your descendants will be strangers in a country not their own, and they will be enslaved and mistreated four hundred years. But I will punish the nation they serve as slaves, and afterward they will come out with great possessions. You, however, will go to your fathers in peace and be buried at a good old age. In the fourth generation your descendants will come back here, for the sin of the Amorites has not yet reached its full measure." (vv. 12–16)

Scene Five

When the sun had set and darkness had fallen, a smoking firepot with a blazing torch appeared and passed between the pieces. (v. 17)

Scene Six

On that day the Lord made a covenant with Abram and said, "To your descendants I give this land, from the river of Egypt to the great river, the Euphrates—the land of the Kenites, Kenizzites, Kadmonites, Hittites, Perizzites, Rephaites, Amorites, Canaanites, Girgashites and Jebusites." (vv. 18–21)

Significant changes in time mark several breaks between scenes. The beginning of Genesis 15:12 states, "As the sun was setting." This temporal remark indicates rather plainly that a new scene has begun. In verse 17 "when the sun had set" separates the verse from what went on before. The temporal reference in verse 18, "on that day" suggests that the last verses form a new simultaneous scene.

This story also contains at least one example of a less explicit temporal break. We have placed a scene division at verse 10. The text says nothing about Abram getting the animals, inspecting them, and preparing them for the ceremony before he brought them to God. The omission of these events from an otherwise tightly woven series presents a significant gap between subsequent events.

These shifts in time are confirmed by changes in setting. No major variation in place occurs in this story; all of the action takes place in the same geographical spot. Even so, changes in environmental features appear. In the second scene (v. 10), animals, blood, and carnage surround Abram. In the third scene (v. 11), birds of prey intrude. The mysterious grey of dusk, the inward darkness of Abram's mind, and the teichoscopies of the future comprise the environment of the fourth scene (vv. 12–16). The outward darkness of the world illumined by the flaming torch and smoking pot[34] set the stage for the next scene (v. 17). Finally, references to all the lands promised to Abram characterize the last scene (vv. 18–21).

Shifts in characters coincide with these divisions. In the first scene, God and Abram are both active participants (vv. 7–9). In the second scene, Abram is in focus (v. 10), and God is barely mentioned. The third scene presents only Abram (v. 11). The fourth scene deals with Abram, God, and Abram's descendants (vv. 12–16). The fifth scene portrays God alone in theophany (v. 17). In the last scene, God, Abram, and Abram's descendants all occupy the foreground (vv. 18–21).

Finally, changes in mode of narration help us divide the story into its basic units. The first scene is predominantly a dramatic dialogue between God and Abram (vv. 7–9). The next two scenes are straight narrative, reporting Abram's preparations for the covenant ceremony (vv. 10–11). In scene four we turn primarily to a dramatic monologue within Abram's dream (vv. 12–16). The fifth scene is straight narration depicting God's action in theophany (v. 17). The last scene presents a dramatic divine monologue (vv. 18–21).

These observations permit us to summarize the basic story line as follows:

- *Scene One (Genesis 15:7–9)* [Dramatic] [S5, T1][35]
  God promised Abram the land and responded to his request for assurance by ordering a covenant ceremony.
- *Scene Two (Genesis 15:10)* [Straight] [S10, T10]
  As a result Abram obeyed by preparing for the ceremony.
- *Scene Three (Genesis 15:11)* [Straight] [S10, T8]
  Also Abram kept the ceremony sanctified by driving away birds of prey.
- *Scene Four (Genesis 15:12–16)* [Dramatic] [S1, T1]
  At dusk Abram received revelation in a dream.
- *Scene Five (Genesis 15:17)* [Straight] [S10, T8]
  Later that night a theophany passed between the carnage.

- *Scene Six (Genesis 15:18–21)* [Dramatic] [S5, T1]
  At that time, God established His covenant of land possession to Abram and his descendants.

2 Chronicles 12:1–12. A second story, the invasion of Shishak in the reign of Rehoboam, divides into ten scenes.

Scene One

After Rehoboam's position as king was established and he had become strong, he and all Israel with him abandoned the law of the Lord. (v. 1)

Scene Two

Because they had been unfaithful to the Lord, Shishak, king of Egypt, attacked Jerusalem in the fifth year of King Rehoboam. (v. 2)

Scene Three

With twelve hundred chariots and sixty thousand horsemen and the innumerable troops of Libyans, Sukkites, and Cushites that came with him from Egypt, he captured the fortified cities of Judah and came as far as Jerusalem. (vv. 3–4)

Scene Four

Then the prophet Shemaiah came to Rehoboam and to the leaders of Judah who had assembled in Jerusalem for fear of Shishak, and he said to them, "This is what the Lord says, 'You have abandoned me; therefore, I now abandon you to Shishak.'" (v. 5)

Scene Five

The leaders of Israel and the king humbled themselves and said, "The Lord is just." (v. 6)

Scene Six

When the Lord saw that they humbled themselves, this word of the Lord came to Shemaiah: "Since they have humbled themselves, I will not destroy them but will soon give them deliverance. My wrath will not be poured out on Jerusalem through Shishak. They will, however, become subject to him, so that they may learn the difference between serving me and serving the kings of other lands." (vv. 7–8)

Scene Seven

When Shishak, king of Egypt, attacked Jerusalem, he carried off the treasures of the temple of the Lord and the treasures of the royal palace. He took everything, including the gold shields Solomon had made. (v. 9)

Scene Eight

So King Rehoboam made bronze shields to replace them and assigned these to the commanders of the guard on duty at the entrance to the royal palace. (v. 10)

Scene Nine

Whenever the king went to the Lord's temple, the guards went with him, bearing the shields, and afterward they returned them to the guardroom. (v. 11)

Scene Ten

Because Rehoboam humbled himself, the Lord's anger turned from him, and he was not totally destroyed. Indeed, there was some good in Judah. (v. 12)

Changes in time are complex in this story.[36] In the second scene (v. 2), we read an explicit designation of time: "And it came about in King Rehoboam's fifth year" (NASB).[37] This scene presents Shishak and his army in siege "against Jerusalem" (NASB). The siege is not picked up again until the seventh scene (v. 9), "When Shishak . . . attacked Jerusalem."[38] Instead, the third scene (vv. 3–4) regresses to the antecedent campaign against the cities of Judah.[39] Verse 5 begins the fourth scene with an event that occurred simultaneously with Shishak's campaign.[40] Shemaiah the prophet gave an oracle of judgment against the nobility of Judah. The fifth scene (v. 6) reports the nobles' repentance. Scene six (vv. 7–8) records that simultaneously the Lord sent word of hope through the prophet. Scene seven (v. 9) moves to the siege and the plunder taken by Shishak. The eighth scene (v. 10) follows the aftermath of defeat, showing that all was not lost. Scene nine (v. 11) extends the narrative to the ongoing practices of the king. The last scene (v. 12) summarizes the continuing experience of Rehoboam and Judah.

Two basic settings arise in this story. The first and second scenes are located in and around Jerusalem (vv. 1–2). But scene three switches to the campaign against Judah (vv. 3–4). From the fourth through the last scene, we return to Jerusalem—in the palace, at the guards' room, and in the temple (vv. 5–12).

Changes in characters are also significant. In scene one Rehoboam, Israel, and the Lord are mentioned (v. 1). Scene two and three focus primarily on Shishak and his innumerable army (vv. 2–4). The number of characters shifts abruptly in scene four with Shemaiah, the leaders, and the Lord (v. 5). Shemaiah is omitted in the fifth scene (v. 6), but scene six returns to the prophet along with the Lord, the king, and the leaders (vv. 7–8).

Finally, this story also contains changes in mode of narration. Scene one is straight narrative; scene two contains a slight authorial comment ("Because they had been unfaithful . . . ") but is primarily straight narrative. Scene three is largely descriptive, reporting the size of Shishak's army, and scenes four through six are dramatic discourse. The prophetic warning (v. 5) contains teichoscopies that recollect antecedent events. God's response to the repentance reports what will happen. Scenes seven through the end present straight narration of Shishak's plunder and Rehoboam's continuing practices.

By dividing this story into these scenes, we can summarize its basic flow.

- *Scene One (2 Chronicles 12:1)* [Straight] [S10, T10][41]
  Although Rehoboam was established, he and Judah forsook the Law of God.
- *Scene Two (2 Chronicles 12:2)* [Straight] [S6, T6]
  Because of Rehoboam's rebellion, Shishak laid siege against Jerusalem.
- *Scene Three (2 Chronicles 12:3–4)* [Descriptive] [S9, T9]
  Before the siege Shishak's massive army had ravaged the cities of Judah.
- *Scene Four (2 Chronicles 12:5)* [Dramatic] [S1, T1]
  During this time Shemaiah announced a warning to the nobility of Judah.
- *Scene Five (2 Chronicles 12:6)* [Dramatic] [S1, T1]
  As a result the leaders of Judah and Rehoboam repent.
- *Scene Six (2 Chronicles 12:7–8)* [Dramatic] [S1, T1]
  Meanwhile, Shemaiah announced a measure of deliverance.
- *Scene Seven (2 Chronicles 12:9)* [Straight] [S8, T8]
  As a result of the siege, Shishak took a heavy tribute from Jerusalem, including the gold shields of Solomon.

- *Scene Eight (2 Chronicles 12:10)* [Straight] [S4, T4]
  Nevertheless, Rehoboam had not lost all; he replaced the gold shields with bronze replicas.
- *Scene Nine (2 Chronicles 12:11)* [Straight] [S4, T4]
  Moreover, Rehoboam frequented the temple after this time and his shields were carefully protected.
- *Scene Ten (2 Chronicles 12:12)* [Straight] [S10, T10]
  As Rehoboam continued to humble himself, conditions were good.

Two considerations. These two examples demonstrate that dividing and summarizing scenes are vital steps in our investigation of Old Testament stories. As we summarize the content of scenes, it helps to keep two considerations in mind.

First, summaries should be as simple as possible without misrepresenting the material. Scenes usually contain a number of details, and boiling them down to their salient elements allows the interpreter to handle the material more adequately. When we state these elements as plainly as possible, our summaries serve as useful shorthand for identifying the building blocks of the story.

Second, it also helps to formulate our summaries so that they make the interconnections between one scene and the next as explicit as possible. A linking expression will usually suffice. One or two words help make these relations explicit: "because of," "before," "meanwhile," "nonetheless," and so on. As we set scenes alongside each other in this way, we gain a sense of the interconnections that form the chain of events in the story.

By looking for significant changes in time, setting, and mode of narration, we are able to divide a story into its fundamental units of thought. Then, through careful summaries, we can understand more fully the ways Old Testament writers put their stories together.

Space and Time in Scenes

A number of years ago I took a class on filmmaking. For my class project, I had to write a story and make it into a short, animated film. A friend and I worked many evenings putting the eight-millimeter film together. Before we began, I knew absolutely nothing about making a movie. I assumed a three-minute film would not take much thought, but I quickly discovered I was wrong. Among other technical decisions, we had to determine which scenes needed a close-up shot and which required a wider angle. We had to decide whether to use slow motion, normal speed, or fast motion. These decisions proved to be crucial to the quality of the final product.

Writers of Old Testament stories made similar decisions about space and time in their scenes.

Spatial Variations

Spatial orientation can make a big difference in our perceptions. Old Testament writers influenced their readers' perception of Israel's history by magnifying some events more than others. Their spatial strategy drastically influenced the original impact of their stories. As we explore Old Testament narratives, we will look for ways to evaluate the spatial focus of each scene.[42]

Like photographers, Old Testament writers gave panoramic views and moved in for close-ups of outward events. But this is only half the picture. Unlike photographers, they also depicted the inward world of their characters' thoughts and feelings.[43] They provided close-up and panoramic perspectives on these inward realities as well. We will look briefly at both sides of this spectrum.

Old Testament narratives generally presented a panoramic view of the outward world. These broad outlooks often brought together events that happened in several different places. In just one verse, for instance, Asa destroyed the high places and altars in every city of Judah (2 Chronicles 14:5).

But Old Testament writers also zoomed in for a close-up view of the outward world. Sometimes close-ups involve interaction among several characters. Moses focused on Abraham and Isaac on Mount Moriah (Genesis 22:6–9). At other times writers viewed only one person in private. After running for his life, Elijah sat alone under a broom tree (1 Kings 19:3b–5). In close-up scenes like these, Old Testament writers usually gave more attention to detail.

Old Testament authors also varied their spatial focus on the inward world. For instance, Micaiah ben Imlah painted a panoramic portrait of his vision of heaven (1 Kings 22:19–23), but when Saul ordered his armor-bearer to kill him, Saul focused only on what might happen to himself (1 Samuel 31:4)—a close-up view.

Whether outward or inward, the spatial orientations of a scene can be crucial to interpretation. Often a shift from one focus to another indicates that a particular scene is prominent in a story. A panoramic scene stands out in a context of close-ups; a close-up among panoramic scenes also draws attention to itself.[44] As we note the spatial variations within a story, we can grasp the writer's outlook more fully.

Temporal Variations

Filmmakers slow and speed up time for dramatic effect. Older movies relied heavily on fast motion to depict humor and the passage of time.[45] Today directors use slow motion to make a romantic moment linger, to enhance the horror of an event, and to give viewers an opportunity to look carefully at crucial action.[46]

Old Testament writers manipulated time in similar ways. Although they did not speed up or slow down images on a screen, they reported events in fast and slow time frames.[47] Just as spatial variations occur in both the outward and inward world, so time varies in the description of external realities and inward thoughts.

First, time in the outward world may vary. Fast action tends to characterize Old Testament stories. Direct speech approximates the pace of real time, but scenes usually report events much faster than they actually occurred, resulting in a faster-than-reality quality. Yet significant variations still occur. In many texts, one or two scenes accelerate beyond the rest of the story. When this occurs the rapid scenes deserve special attention. On the other hand, some scenes decelerate significantly,[48] occasionally slowing to a snail's pace. Often these portions of a story are especially crucial.

Consider the temporal variations in the account of the assassination of Eglon (Judges 3:14–26). For the most part, time moves quickly. It slows a bit as dialogue ensues between Ehud and Eglon (vv. 19–20). But in the crucial scene, when Ehud assassinates the king, we have nothing less than frame-by-frame slow motion.

Ehud reached with his left hand, drew the sword from his right thigh, and plunged it into the king's belly. Even the handle sank in after the blade, which came out his back. Ehud did not pull the sword out, and the fat closed in over it (vv. 21–22).

We see each fraction of a second: the hand reaching for the sword, the sword drawn, the sword plunging into the king, the handle going in after the blade, and the fat closing over the handle.[49]

The sacrifice of Isaac has a similar temporal variation. Until Abram and Isaac arrive at Moriah, the story moves rather rapidly. But when Abram prepares the altar, we read, "He bound his son Isaac and laid him on the altar, on top of the wood. Then he reached out his hand and took the knife to slay his son" (Genesis 22:9–10). Once again time has almost come to a standstill,[50] suspending the tension of the moment.

Second, the inward world also varies in temporal rate. If the pace increases dramatically, it often reflects the character's sense of urgency and intensity. For instance, Saul cried out to his armor-bearer, "Draw your sword and run me through, or these uncircumcised fellows will come and abuse me" (1 Chronicles 10:4). The rapid pace with which Saul thought through his situation reflected his panic. Inward scenes also may be slow. At times the inner thoughts of a character barely creep along. For example, Joshua's spies go into great detail in their instructions to Rahab (Joshua 2:17–20). The writer of Joshua reported this material in detail to draw attention to specific elements in the oaths between Rahab and the spies.

Old Testament narratives have a general tendency toward rapid temporal progression as they depict the inward and outward worlds of the past. Yet we must take account of scenes in which time speeds forward even faster. More than this we must watch for time to slow down. Such temporal variations often indicate that a scene has special importance in a story.

Examples

One convenient way to assess spatial focus is to rate scenes on a numerical scale. First, identify the scenes with the most panoramic focus as "S(pace)10." A scene that rates "S10" in one story may not have the same breadth as an "S10" in another passage. But relative to other portions of its own episode, an "S10" rating represents the widest angle. Second, rate the scenes with the closest focus "S1," relative to other scenes within the same story. Once we have identified the extremes, we can rate all the other scenes "S2–S9." This technique permits us to recognize patterns in spatial focus at a glance.

We may describe temporal acceleration and deceleration in a similar way. Identify the fastest scenes as "T(ime)10" and the slowest scenes as "T1," then place other scenes along the scale. Following such a procedure enables us to review quickly the temporal variations in a story.

Let us illustrate this technique with Genesis 15:7–21 and 2 Chronicles 12:1–12. The temporal variations of Genesis 15:7–21 are not drastic. The story's fastest portion (T10) is scene two (v. 10), when Abram initiates the covenant cutting ceremony. Scenes three (v. 11) and five (v. 17) are rated "T8"; they fall about mid-range in the spectrum of outward actions. The slowest scenes in this story involve speech. Scene one (vv.

7–9) is a dialogue over the certainty of the promise (T1). The final scene parallels this slow pace as God vows to give Abram the land (vv. 18–21). The fourth scene (vv. 12–16) also slows to "T1." The pace of this central scene forms a temporal pivot in the story.

Spatial variations in Genesis 15:7–21 parallel the temporal pattern. The widest angles are found in scenes two (cutting the animals), three (chasing the birds of prey), and five (the smoke and torch). We have rated these three scenes "S10." Scene four has the lowest spatial focus (vv. 12–16), narrowing to a close-up of Abram falling asleep in terror.

Time and space variations in this story help us see which scenes Moses highlighted. The spotlights shine brightly on scenes one and six. God's promise, Abram's question, and God's response in the beginning (vv. 7–9) parallel God's covenant oath at the end (vv. 18–21). Space narrows and time slows because these scenes are so important. But the combination of temporal and spatial focus in scene four (vv. 12–16) highlights God's promise to bring Israel out of Egypt and back to the land. This scene spoke directly to Moses' audience; they had seen these promises take place in their own lives and could now take courage in the future.

The spatio-temporal variations in 2 Chronicles 12:1–12 form a different pattern. Scene one (v. 1) opens with a quick panoramic view of the fourth year of Rehoboam's reign (S10, T10). In scene two (v. 2), space narrows to the vicinity of Jerusalem and the period of the siege against the city (S6, T6). The third scene (vv. 3–4) moves back up the scale in space and time as it quickly retraces Shishak's campaign through Judah (S10, T10). In scenes four through six (vv. 5–8), the Chronicler gave the slowest and most narrowly focused portion of the entire story (S1, T1). Compared with the rest of the drama, the actions of the prophet and the nobles are close-up and in slow motion. As a result these scenes of confrontation and repentance stand out in the story. Scene seven (v. 9) shifts back to a rapid, panoramic view (S8, T8), and quickly recounts the end of the siege. The next two scenes (vv. 10–11) move to the middle range (S4, T4), and the final scene (v. 12) returns to a fast pace and broad focus, balancing with the opening scene (S10, T10).

These observations offer a number of insights into the story. The breadth of the third scene and the detailed account of the size of Shishak's army give a sense of the severe threat against Jerusalem. Then the slow, narrow focus of the fourth, fifth, and sixth scenes arrests the readers' attention as Judah's nobles face the prophet. The spotlight intensifies and the volume rises as we hear oracles from God and Judah's nobility responding.

Our brief examination of these stories shows that assessing space and time offers many benefits. We are alerted to the writer's focus, the relative prominence of scenes, and the balance between various sections of a story. As we note temporal and spatial variations, we can perceive many facets of Old Testament narratives that may otherwise go unnoticed.

Imagery in Scenes

The sign read "Scenic View." I was tired of driving, so we pulled over to take a look. But one of our passengers wasn't excited about the idea. "All you're going to see is a bunch of hills and farms," he grumbled from the back seat.

He was right, but he was also wrong. As we stood on the mountainside, we could see for miles in every direction. We noticed ant-like cars below speeding down the highway, picturesque farms just beyond them, rolling hillsides in the distance, and the hazy outline of a city on the horizon. Our friend had given us fairly accurate information, but his information was nothing compared to looking at the sight itself.

Old Testament writers gave their readers scenic views of Israel's history. They related much more than a list of bare facts and abstract principles. Through the use of vivid imagery, they invited their readers to have imaginative, sensory experiences of the past.[51]

Obstacles to Imagery

Many evangelicals have a difficult time appreciating the sensory dimensions of Old Testament stories. At least three factors keep us from investigating this aspect of the text. First, compared to other literature, Old Testament narratives do not spend much time in imaginative detail.[52] They hardly compare to elaborate depictions in modern literature to which we are accustomed. We seldom find detailed descriptions of the sights and sounds of morning; the texts simply tell us it was morning (Joshua 3:1). We do not discover extensive discussions of smell, taste, or touch; Old Testament stories simply report that people ate (1 Kings 19:21). Because most Old Testament narratives use imagery sparingly, we easily overlook it.

But we must not allow the scarcity of imagery to keep us from appreciating what *is* there. Old Testament writers were not frivolous in their descriptions of scenes, so when they mentioned a sensory detail, we may assume that they had a purpose. We must pay careful attention to the slightest hint of imagery in Old Testament narratives.[53]

Second, we often miss imagery in Old Testament stories because we are unfamiliar with the historical realities they describe. We do not know what images to associate with the words. If a modern story mentions the roar of a jet plane or the beat of rock and roll, we immediately associate the words with familiar experiences. But we pass over many vivid descriptions in Old Testament stories because we do not know enough to appreciate them.

For instance, the Chronicler's original audience would have relished the sights and "the sounding of rams' horns and trumpets, and of cymbals, and the playing of lyres and harps" (1 Chronicles 15:28). But our lack of familiarity with ancient music can keep us from reading these words for all they are worth. Consequently, as we investigate the use of imagery, we must try to identify with the original audience. How would *they* have understood these words? What would *they* have experienced? We must not allow our ignorance of the ancient world to obscure this facet of Old Testament stories.

Third, we miss vivid imagery because of our hermeneutical orientations. For the most part, we look to these texts primarily for facts and theological principles. For many of us, the meaning of an Old Testament story consists primarily, if not exclusively, in its contribution to our historical, theological, and moral understanding. We treat imagery as little more than ornamentation.

But God did not give us stories just to have us eliminate their imagery. Had He desired to give us only facts and theological principles, He would have done so. On the contrary, the Spirit inspired Old Testament writers to compose stories that contained imagery, and we must learn to appreciate this dimension of their texts.

Why concern ourselves with imagery? How does imagery help us understand Old Testament stories? What advantages does it offer? First, looking for imagery causes us to *think*. Becoming aware of the imaginative power of a scene will cause us to contemplate the details of the text more thoroughly. Second, reflection on imagery gives our understanding *vitality;* the text comes alive and engages us. Rather than merely cataloguing events from the dull, grey past, Old Testament narratives now explode in living color. Third, imagery affects us *emotionally* as we contemplate the imagery of a scene. It is difficult not to be affected on a visceral, emotional level.

Imagery contributes significantly to the power of Old Testament stories. As we investigate their original meaning, we must look for the full range of sensory experiences they offered their original readers.

Types of Imagery

Old Testament stories touch all of our senses. In many different ways, writers depicted the circumstances, actions, and characters of their stories so that they offered *visual, auditory, tactile, olfactory,* and *gustatory* experiences to their audiences.

Visual. Old Testament writers relied on visual imagery more than any other. They depicted scenes so that their readers could see the past in their mind's eye. We may look for visual imagery in the three principal elements of a scene: circumstances, actions, and characters. How did the setting appear? What did the characters look like? How did the actions take place? As scenes tell us more details, we are able to reflect further, but even the slight mention of such matters presents visual images to contemplate.

Consider the simple example of Joshua 3:1: "Early in the morning Joshua and all the Israelites set out from Shittim and went to the Jordan, where they camped before crossing over." This short verse presents a number of vivid sights. The circumstances of early morning evoke visions of dawn breaking through the darkness. We see the camp at Shittim and the Jordan River. The principal characters also appear: the warrior Joshua and the mass of men, women, and children with him. We also see people rising from bed, breaking camp, organizing for the journey, marching forward, and setting up camp at the Jordan. These impressions form a vital dimension of the story's original meaning.

Auditory. As Old Testament writers composed their scenes, they also presented auditory imagery. Sounds played a vital role in their stories. What sorts of auditory imagery appear in Old Testament stories? What sounds did the original audiences hear?

Once again we may think in terms of circumstances, actions, and characters. Circumstances in a scene often entail sounds, even if they are not highlighted explicitly. Many actions produce noise. Characters also make sounds when they speak, cry, or shout.

First Kings 22:34 provides a good sample of auditory images: "But someone drew his bow at random and hit the king of Israel between the sections of his armor. The king told his chariot driver, 'Wheel around and get me out of the fighting. I've been wounded.'"

Some of the sounds of this scene are more explicit than others. The most obvious auditory image comes from the character Ahab. His desperate cry rings out. But many other noises are conveyed by this scene. Ahab was in a battle—hardly a quiet place. Clamoring and shouting, clashing swords and shields, screams of anger and pain form constant background noise. In particular, the writer focused on the action of one man firing his bow. The arrow whistles through the air and punctures the king's body. Even these few specifics give us many auditory experiences.

Tactile. We can also find tactile imagery in Old Testament stories, both external and internal.[54] External tactile imagery is the experience of touching things outside ourselves and feeling their texture, weight, or temperature. Internal tactile imagery is inward sensation: the beating of the heart, breathing, tension, relaxation, pain, and pleasure. These images of touch also function in conjunction with circumstances, actions, and characters.

A striking illustration of tactile imagery comes in one scene from the story of Samson: "Then the Philistines seized him, gouged out his eyes and took him down to Gaza. Binding him with bronze shackles, they set him to grinding in the prison" (Judges 16:21). We fail to catch the significance of this passage if we reduce it to a statement of fact: "The Philistines captured Samson," or a principle: "Sin brings divine punishment." Tangible imagery cast the original audience into the gruesome horrors inflicted on their hero: the piercing pain of Samson's gouged eyes, the cuts and bruises he suffered as the Philistines dragged him to Gaza, the weight of bronze chains, the hardship of pushing a massive stone grinder. We must appreciate Samson's pain if we are to read this story as the writer of Judges intended.

Some scenes contain more explicit tactile images than others. Yet the mere mention of certain settings, characters, and actions brought inescapable tactile experiences to the minds of their readers.

Olfactory. Old Testament narratives also present olfactory imagery. Smells occur less frequently than visual, auditory, and tactile imagery, but they do appear and are also associated with circumstances, actions, and characters. An obvious example of olfactory imagery may be found in Genesis 27:27–28:

> So he went to him and kissed him. When Isaac caught the smell of his clothes, he blessed him and said, "Ah, the smell of my son is like the smell of a field that the Lord has blessed. May God give you of heaven's dew and of earth's richness—an abundance of grain and new wine."

We see Jacob coming near his father, feel his kiss, and hear the words of blessing. But we also smell Jacob. Isaac's love for Esau is highlighted by his delight in the smell of his son. At the same time, the depth of Isaac's treachery is depicted by this olfactory deception.

The original audiences of Old Testament stories were keenly aware of the smells of animals, wounds, death, flowers, perfumes, and oils. Smells may be more or less explicit, but they provide important insights into Old Testament stories.

Gustatory. Gustatory imagery, the imaginative experience of taste, also occurs in Old Testament stories. When food and drink appear, we may be confident that the writer wanted his audience to associate the events with taste. At times the predominance of this kind of imagery is striking. For example, at the end of the celebration of the ark coming to Jerusalem we read: "Then he gave a loaf of bread, a cake of dates and a cake of raisins to each person in the whole crowd of Israelites, both men and women. And all the people went to their homes" (2 Samuel 6:19).

Why did the writer of Samuel include this scene? Did he merely want his readers to see the sights and hear the sounds of celebration? Apparently not. He was also interested in having them experience the gustatory delight of the event. The wonder of the celebration broke through as original readers imagined the taste of cakes given to all. After this festive imagery, the account of Michal's reproach (2 Samuel 6:20–23) is even more shocking.

Once again we must recognize that gustatory imagery may be more or less explicit. Old Testament writers did not emphasize it in detail every time it appears. Yet, as we come upon taste in Old Testament narratives, we must acknowledge it as a facet of the writer's original meaning.

Throughout Old Testament narratives, scenes touch on all five of our senses. Visual, auditory, tactile, olfactory, and gustatory imagery comprises essential facets of scene depiction. As we investigate Old Testament narratives, we must ask, "What do I see?" "What do I hear?" "What do I touch and feel within?" "What do I smell?" and "What do I taste?" Asking these questions will open up many dimensions of Old Testament stories to us (see figure 17).

Examples

To illustrate we will look again at Genesis 15:7–21 and 2 Chronicles 12:1–12. Our summaries of the imagery in these stories will be brief, but they will show the importance of scene imagery for interpretation.

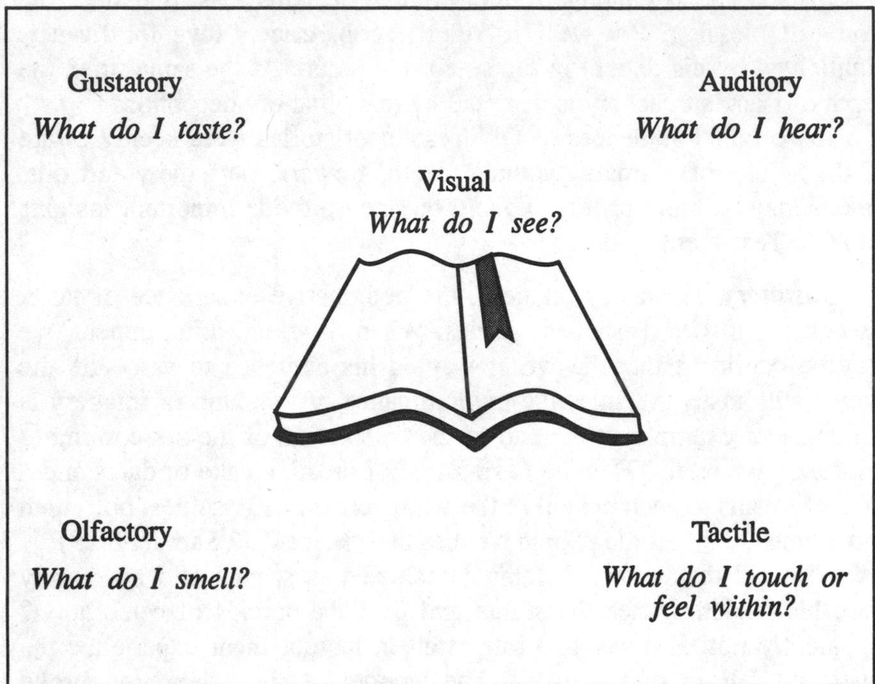

Fig. 17: Imagery in Scenes

Genesis 15:7–21 is packed with imagery. Scene one (vv. 7–9) has several layers. The primary focus is auditory. We overhear a dialogue between God and Abram concerning the possession of the land of Canaan. In the dialogue the imagery of several sub-scenes stands out. In verse 7 we can imagine the memories of Ur and the migration with its sights, sounds, and smells. In Abram's question (v. 8), we not only hear and see Abram ask for assurance, but we also have a tactile sense of his tense yearning. Finally, in God's command to gather the animals, Moses listed each animal separately so that his readers would imaginatively visualize, hear, touch, and smell them (v. 9).

In the second scene (v. 10), we see Abram once again before God with the animals. The primary focus of this scene is on the action of cutting. Abram draws a knife, cuts the animals in half, and arranges the halves in two rows. Many modern readers easily overlook the sensory dimensions of this scene. But those familiar with the slaughter of animals know the sounds of struggle, the ripping of the flesh, the pulling the warm halves apart, even the smell of the carnage.

Scene three is primarily visual (v. 11). We see Abram, the carnage, and approaching birds of prey. Abram drives them away, perhaps running, shouting, and waving his arms.

The fourth scene draws attention immediately to the horizon where a setting sun is barely visible (vv. 12–16). Abram lies down to sleep. As we look inside his mind, we see a dreadful darkness. We sense his tension as terror came upon him. We also hear God speak to Abram in his dream. His words create sights and sounds of the future. Tensions mount until God tells Abram what will happen to him and his descendants.

Scene five (v. 17) remarks that the sun has gone down. The dark of night surrounds Abram. Breaking through that darkness, a smoking pot and flaming torch appear. The fiery orange and red glow of the torch and smoke, the shadows cast over the carnage as they pass between the pieces, and the crackling of the flames stand out in this scene.

Finally, scene six portrays the last divine speech (v. 18). We hear God speaking to Abram as He expounds the promise that opened this story. We see Abram before God and the sights of the rivers and lands that God promised to Abram.

Second Chronicles 12:1–12 begins with a visual glimpse of the fourth year of Rehoboam's reign, in which he and the people turned away from the Law of God. In the second scene (v. 2), we see Rehoboam and Jerusalem surrounded by Shishak. Without a doubt the visual and auditory imagery of the sounds of a siege would have come to the minds of the original readers.

Scene three (vv. 3–4) focuses primarily on the sights and sounds of Judah's defeat. The whole of 2 Chronicles 12:3 is devoted to giving the audience the overwhelming sight of Shishak's chariots, horsemen, and soldiers. We see Shishak's massive, innumerable army moving with little trouble right to the gate of Jerusalem.

In the fourth, fifth, and sixth scenes (vv. 5–8), the horizons narrow. We see Shemaiah the prophet, Rehoboam, and the nobles from Judah together in the confines of Jerusalem. We have a glimpse of the Lord in heaven. More central to these scenes, however, are the sounds of the prophetic proclamations and the repentance of the nobles. We should note the specific attitude of humility and the associated bodily reaction. The horror of hearing the initial oracle of judgment and the relief of reprieve also form important imagery in this scene.

The seventh scene (v. 9) mentions the removal of royal treasures. We can see the glistening gold shields in our mind's eye. Implicitly we sense the sounds associated with these events and the tactile experience of grief as the characters saw the royal treasuries emptied.

In the eighth scene (v. 10), we see Rehoboam order his men to make bronze replicas of the shields and to protect them. The ninth scene (v. 11) presents the sights of Rehoboam going to the temple and the guards taking bronze shields to the guard room.

In the tenth scene (v. 12), we see and hear Rehoboam humbling himself periodically in the temple. A wide range of imagery comes to mind as we contemplate the good conditions in Judah that resulted so long as Rehoboam continued to humble himself.

As we reflect on the imagery of this text, our hearts and minds are drawn into the story, and we can understand more fully what the Chronicler sought to communicate to his original audience.

Investigating scene depiction in Old Testament stories involves much more than correctly assessing the facts and principles. We must also take account of the vivid imagery—the sights, sounds, touch, tastes, and smells—that contribute significantly to their original meaning.

Conclusion

We began this chapter suggesting that we must learn to appreciate the artistic design of Old Testament narratives. To begin this dimension of interpretation, we have looked into three aspects of scene depiction. We noted how to divide texts into scenes, and we explored the importance of spatial and temporal variations. We also saw the value of reflection on scene imagery. These considerations open the way for us to see the artistry of Old Testament narratives and to comprehend more fully the original meaning of their most basic units.

Review Questions

1. What is a scene in Old Testament stories? Why is dividing a story into scenes so important? What clues help us divide a story into its scenes? How may we summarize a story in terms of its scenes?
2. What do we mean by space and time variables in scenes? Describe the process for giving scene spatio-temporal ratings. How do these variables help us notice the emphases of a writer?
3. What is imagery in scenes? What kinds of imagery may be found in Old Testament narratives? Give an example of each. What is the value of taking note of these facets of Old Testament stories?

Study Exercises

1. Look at Exodus 1:22—2:10. Divide this episode into its scenes. Specify the features of the text that indicate a shift in scenes; summarize each scene in one sentence.
2. Examine the spatio-temporal variations of each scene in Exodus 1:22—2:10. Rate each scene as outlined in this chapter. From your analysis, which scenes seem to be emphasized?
3. Summarize the explicit and implicit imagery in Exodus 1:22—2:10. What insights does your summary of the imagery afford you?

8

STRUCTURE IN INDIVIDUAL EPISODES

A couple of years ago I was visiting friends whose preschool daughter made me feel at home by showing me all her toys. One toy in particular caught my attention: a large, five-piece puzzle. Put the pieces together one way, and they made a man; a second way and a duck appeared; a third way and they formed a tree. The pieces remained the same, but they formed different pictures as the little girl rearranged them.

Old Testament writers arranged the pieces of their stories in many different ways, focusing in detail on some elements and passing quickly over others. They switched from one mode of narration to another. They moved to subsequent, simultaneous, and antecedent events as they wished. These arrangements did not affect the historical veracity of their accounts, but they had a great effect on the literary portrait their stories produced.

Aristotle referred to the "the arrangement of incidents" as the plot (*muthos*) of a story.[1] We will follow this definition and speak of plot, or dramatic flow, as the heightening and lessening of tension through the arrangement of scenes.[2]

Dramatic flow may be approached in many different ways.[3] In this chapter we will look into *types of dramatic flow, symmetry of dramatic resolution,* and *typical patterns of dramatic resolution.* What kinds of plots do we encounter in the Old Testament? What basic symmetries appear in these texts? What patterns did Old Testament writers tend to follow?

Types of Dramatic Flow

We can analyze dramatic flow in Old Testament narratives on many levels.[4] Whole books and large sections within books contain many plot structures. We will look into these larger structures in the chapter that follows. At this point, however, we will begin our investigation of dramatic flow with individual episodes.

We will define an episode as the simplest unit of narrative material displaying a significant level of independence from its context. For instance, "The Abrahamic Story" (Genesis 11:27—25:11) contains a number of episodes: "The Call of Abram" (Genesis 12:1–9), "Abram's Exodus" (Genesis 12:10–20), "Abram and Lot Separate" (Genesis 13:1–18), and so on. Similarly "The Story of Joseph" (Genesis 37:2—50:26) consists of "Joseph's Dreams" (Genesis 37:1–11), "Joseph Sold into Slavery" (Genesis 37:12–36), "Judah and Tamar" (Genesis 38:1–30), and the like. These episodes vary in length and complexity, but they form relatively self-contained units.

A well-formed episode requires at least one sentence with two temporally related actions or states of affairs.[5] Few episodes in the Old Testament are as small as one sentence, but this minimal definition permits us to look into the types of dramatic flow we encounter in the Old Testament. Consider the following sentences:

- "I saw the book; it stood out on the table."
- "I wanted the book; it sat on the top shelf."
- "I wanted the book; I bought it."

Each of these scenarios contains two temporally related elements that form simple stories, and each reflects a different type of dramatic flow. We will speak of the first as an episode of *report,* the second as an episode of *unresolved tension,* and the third as an episode of *resolution.*[6] These types of dramatic flow are not entirely distinct; they represent points on a continuum. Yet they provide models that help us see how Old Testament writers structured their individual episodes.

Report

"I saw the book; it stood out on the table" is a report containing two scenes: 1) The storyteller saw the book; 2) the book stood out. Apart from a larger context, however, this episode does not create much dramatic tension. No initial conflict occurs; no resolution appears. In itself the episode basically gives notice that something has happened.

Reports primarily describe situations. Their temporal arrangement makes them more than a plain list of facts, but not much more. At times they contribute to the structure of a larger context, but within themselves these episodes display little dramatic tension. We do not ask, "What will be the resolution of this problem?" No problem exists to be resolved.

Episodes tending toward mere report occur frequently in the Old Testament. For the most part, they are very brief. For instance, the reports of Keturah's children (Genesis 25:1–4) and Solomon's international trade (1 Kings 9:26–28) consist of fewer than five verses each. These passages describe a series of events, but they do not reveal a problem and resolution. There is at best only slight tension.

At times reports can be lengthy. Judges 1:27–36 is a longer series of reports in which the writer recorded the tribes' failure to drive out the Canaanites.[7] Genealogies and other lists often form lengthy episodes of report as well.[8] In the larger context of the book, these reports contribute to dramatic tension, but the passages themselves do not involve a significant problem or resolution.

Unresolved Tension

"I wanted the book; it sat on the top shelf" moves away from mere report. The words "I wanted" create a sense of expectation. Will the narrator get the book? Will something stand in his way? However, the final clause falls short of completing the drama; we never know if the narrator got the book. While we have more than a mere report, we do not have a complete sense of conflict and resolution.

Similar structures occur throughout the Old Testament. For example, the brief account of Reuben's immorality reads: "Israel moved on again and pitched his tent beyond Migdal Eder. While Israel was living in that region, Reuben went in and slept with his father's concubine Bilhah, and Israel heard of it" (Genesis 35:21–22). Tension rises in this short episode. Reuben sins against his father, and his father hears about it. But what will happen to Reuben? What will his father do? The episode itself does not tell us; the drama is unresolved.[9]

Another example of unresolved tension appears in the story of the floating axhead.[10]

> The company of the prophets said to Elisha, "Look, the place where we meet with you is too small for us. Let us go to the Jordan, where each of us can get a pole; and let us build a place there for us to live." And he said, "Go." Then one of them said, "Won't you please come with your servants?" "I will," Elisha replied. And he went with them.

They went to the Jordan and began to cut down trees. As one of them was cutting down a tree, the iron axhead fell into the water. "Oh, my lord," he cried out, "it was borrowed!" The man of God asked, "Where did it fall?" When he showed him the place, Elisha cut a stick and threw it there, and made the iron float. "Lift it out," he said. Then the man reached out his hand and took it (2 Kings 6:1–7) (see figure 18).

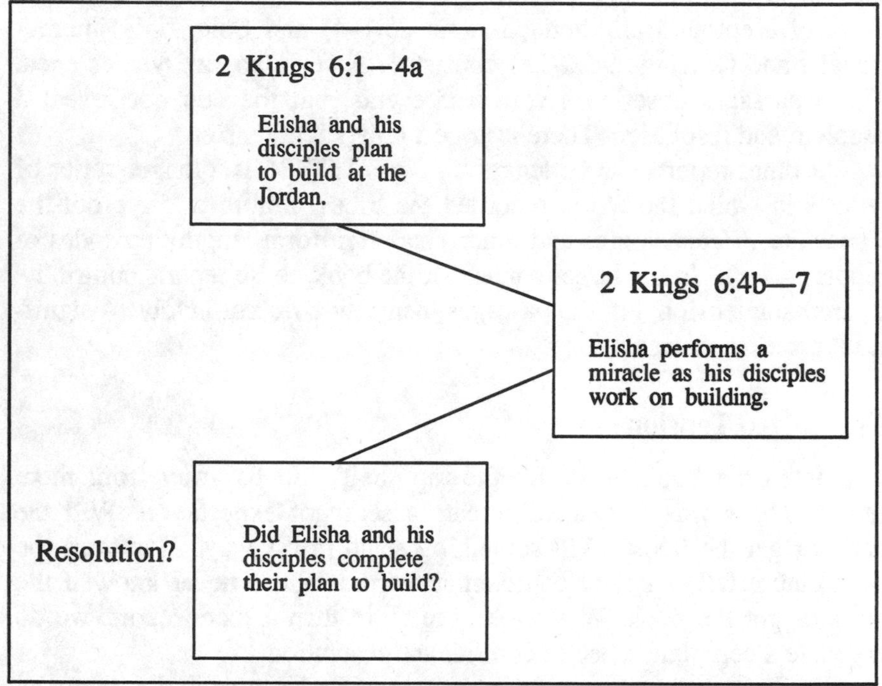

Fig. 18: Unresolved Tension in 2 Kings 6:1–7

This story opens with Elisha agreeing to go with his disciples to build a dwelling near the Jordan (vv. 1–4a). These verses lead us to ask, "Will they succeed? Will they build a new dwelling?" They reached the Jordan and began to cut down trees (v. 4b). But a difficulty arose when one of the disciples dropped a borrowed axhead in the water (v. 5a). He cried out, and Elisha miraculously retrieved the axhead (vv. 5–7). At this point we might expect the episode to describe how Elisha and his disciples completed their building project. This would resolve the dramatic tension begun in 2 Kings 6:1–4a.[11] But the account ends abruptly with the retrieval of the axhead. We are left to wonder if the disciples completed their new dwelling. The writer of Kings did not give his readers a resolution to the episode.[12] Why this lack of resolution? Apparently the writer had little interest in the building project itself; he merely used that information to give a setting for the miraculous event. After reporting the miracle, he ended his episode and left the matter of building unresolved.

Resolution

Dramatic flow works out more fully in the third scenario, "I wanted the book; I bought it." Instead of a flat report or unresolved tension, the drama distinctly rises and falls. We find a problem and a resolution. The narrator wanted the book. What will happen? Success or failure? The second clause reveals that the narrator fulfills his desire. In this brief account, tension does not rise to great heights, but the story poses a problem and unravels it.

A brief narrative of resolution occurs in Joshua 15:16–17, which consists of three short scenes.

Scene One

And Caleb said, "I will give my daughter Acsah in marriage to the man who attacks and captures Kiriath Sepher." (v. 16)

Scene Two

Othniel son of Kenaz, Caleb's brother, took it. (v. 17)

Scene Three

So Caleb gave his daughter Acsah to him in marriage (see figure 19).

Despite its brevity this episode has a definite problem and resolution. The dramatic problem occurred when Caleb offered his daughter to a valiant warrior (v. 16). Will someone respond to his offer? Will he give her in marriage? The next scene (v. 17a) tells us of a decisive event that moves the story toward resolution. Othniel conquered the city, thus fulfilling the requirements of the offer. Caleb then gave his daughter to Othniel (v. 17b), resolving the initial problem.

Stories of resolution possess a level of inner coherence not found in reports, and we can evaluate their meaning more in terms of their own structures. The presentation of a problem and its resolution form an arena of action that requires focused attention. The dramatic arrangement conveys an episode whose inner structure significantly displays its meaning.

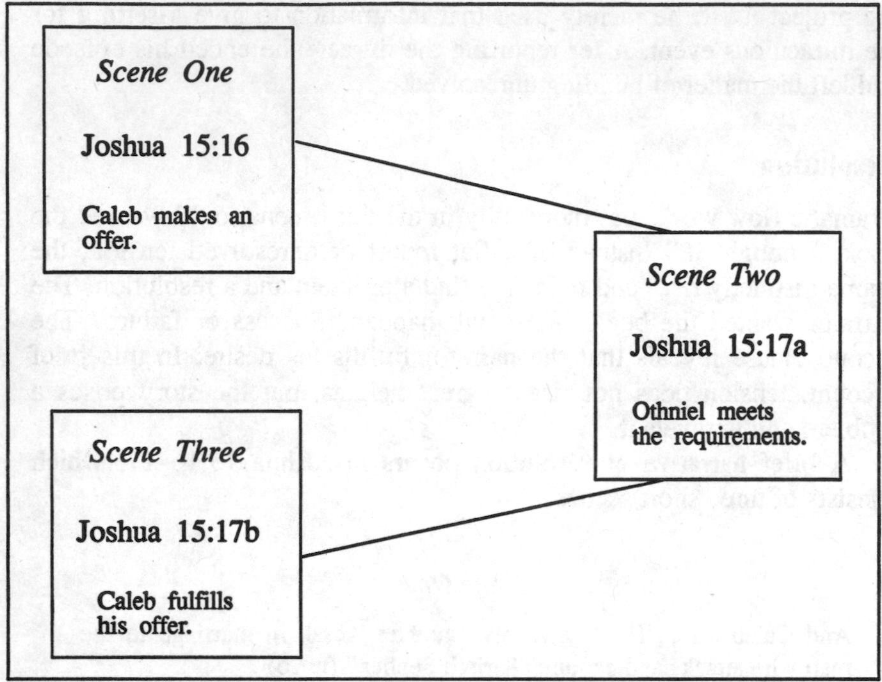

Fig. 19: Dramatic Resolution in Joshua 15:16–17

These categories represent three types of dramatic flow we encounter as we explore individual episodes in the Old Testament. In this chapter we will concentrate on narratives of resolution. They present a number of complexities that must be addressed in detail. As we understand this plot format more thoroughly, we will also be able to explore episodes of report and unresolved tension more effectively.

Symmetry of Dramatic Resolution

When we examine episodes of resolution, we discover that Old Testament writers tended to arrange these passages symmetrically. Though some stories have less extensive balance than others, symmetry is nevertheless a fundamental feature of plot in episodes of resolution.

To understand these essential structures, we must work through three basic considerations: *beginnings and endings*, *tripartite design*, and *phases*. Once we understand these features, we will be in a position to look further into the details of dramatic resolution.

Beginnings and Endings

How does basic structural symmetry operate in episodes of resolution? In a word, symmetry builds on a conceptual balance between the beginning and the ending of a story. This is not to say that the opening and closing of a passage are equally long or important, but they do balance each other conceptually. One part recalls or anticipates concepts found in the other part. Three types of conceptual balance stand out prominently in Old Testament narratives. Beginnings and endings may reflect *circular, contrasting,* or *developmental* patterns.[13]

Circular. Stories of resolution often present a predominantly circular pattern; the closing returns to the situation with which the passage began. The body of the story introduces some contrasts and developments, but the text does not highlight them. Instead, a sense of dramatic resolution comes when the final portion takes us full circle.

Many narratives present a predominantly circular symmetry. For example, the story of Abraham's test (Genesis 22:1–19) begins with him living in Beersheba (Genesis 21:33) and ends with him returning to the same place. Similarly, in Genesis 15:7–21, God promises land to Abram at the beginning (v. 7) and affirms His promise at the end (vv. 18–21). We sense that these stories have ended largely because we have returned to a situation similar to the beginning.

Contrasting. Opening and closing scenes also contrast with each other. In these texts the ending stands in opposition to the opening. If the first portion is positive, the last is negative. If conditions are bad initially, they become good in the end. Emphasis falls on an antithetical balance between the opening and closing.[14]

Many Old Testament narratives present a contrasting pattern. For example, the account of Elisha's healing the water (2 Kings 2:19–22) begins with the men of Jericho telling Elisha that "the water is bad" (2 Kings 2:19). Elisha "heals" the water, and the episode concludes: "And the water has remained wholesome to this day" (2 Kings 2:22). The ending reverses the initial situation. The account of Eglon's assassination (Judges 3:12–30) also portrays contrast. Judges 3:12 reads, "the Lord gave Eglon king of Moab power over Israel," but the story ends, "That day Moab was made subject to Israel."

Developmental. Finally, development may occur between the initial and final portions of an episode. In these cases the story ends by describing a different—though not an opposite—state of affairs. The main character may face a problem or conflict in the beginning, but the resolution moves him or her to a new situation. These linear developments may have undertones of reversal and circularity, but the drama primarily develops toward new ends.

For example, Genesis 12:1–9 begins with God calling Abram to go to the land of promise. The final scene depicts the patriarch completing the call by continuing to the Negev. We sense a slight contrast between Abram outside the land and in the land, but the predominant balance is a development from commission to fulfillment. The episode of Abram and Lot's separation (Genesis 13:1–18) begins with the patriarch entering the Negev and ends with him moving on to Hebron. In both of these passages, the episodes close by moving the main character to new circumstances.

As we work toward understanding dramatic flow, it helps to note the conceptual balance that connects the beginning and ending. What is the opening dramatic problem? How does the ending bring about a resolution? What circular, contrasting, and developmental patterns stand out?

Tripartite Design

The symmetry of most episodes of resolution follows a threefold design, although some stories have only two parts. As Aristotle suggested most dramatic accounts consist of "a beginning, a middle, and an end."[15]

Consider the following tale of three simple scenes:

> [Scene One] Fido longed for the bone across the yard, but his chain was too short to reach it. [Scene Two] So he barked and barked until his master came and released him from the chain. [Scene Three] At that Fido raced for the bone and chewed his way to doggie heaven.

The first and last scenes balance as expected. The first scene introduces the problem: Fido wants the bone but cannot reach it. The third scene resolves the problem: Fido reaches the bone and satisfies his longing. These scenes contrast as delight replaces desire, and they develop as the dog moves from one spot in the yard to another.

What then is the function of the middle portion? This section bridges the gap between the beginning and ending, telling the reader what actions took place to make the symmetry possible. Fido reached the bone because he barked, and his owner released him from his chain.

Similar tripartite structures appear in most Old Testament episodes of resolution. They begin with a problem, end with a resolution, and the body of the story traces the developments in between. This threefold structure takes different forms, but it appears in most episodes.

Consider once again God's covenant with Abram (Genesis 15:7–21). As we noted in the preceding chapter, this story divides into six scenes (see figure 20).

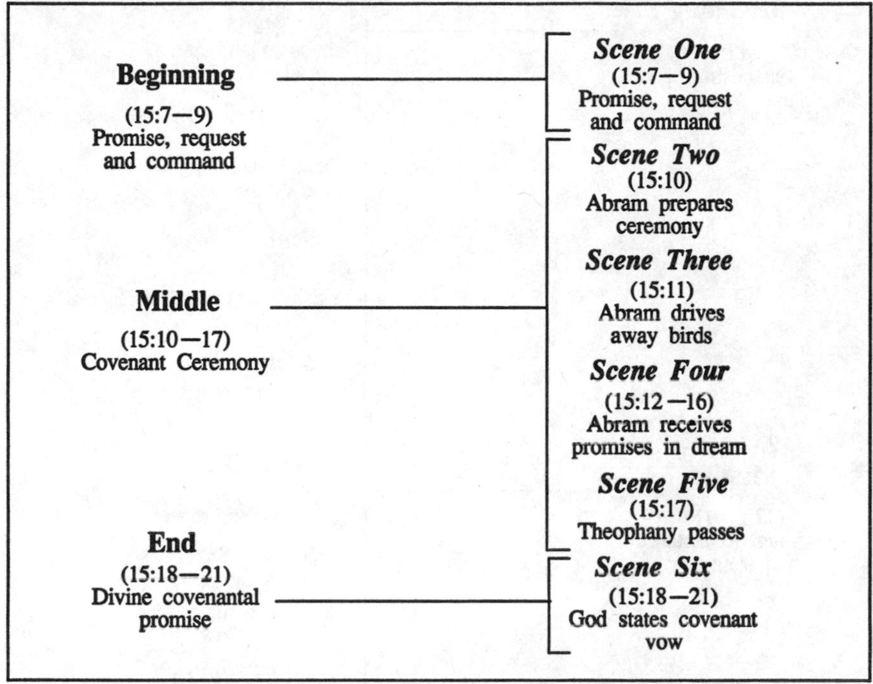

Fig. 20: Tripartite Design of Genesis 15:7–21

The first scene begins with a divine promise, Abram's request for assurance and God's order to prepare for a covenant ceremony. This initial problem is balanced by the last scene, where God states His covenant vow to give Abram the land. The intervening scenes explain how God came to speak again, how Abram's doubt dissipated, and how the promise was transformed into a covenant oath. The story reached these ends through the covenant ceremony found in scenes two through five.

A similar situation holds for the story of Shishak's invasion in 2 Chronicles 12:1–12. As we saw in the preceding chapter, this passage has ten scenes (see figure 21).

Scene one speaks of the establishment of Rehoboam's kingdom and the problem of apostasy. The last scene circles back to Rehoboam's kingdom and reverses apostasy with Rehoboam's continuing humility. How did this closure occur? Scenes two through nine tell us the threat

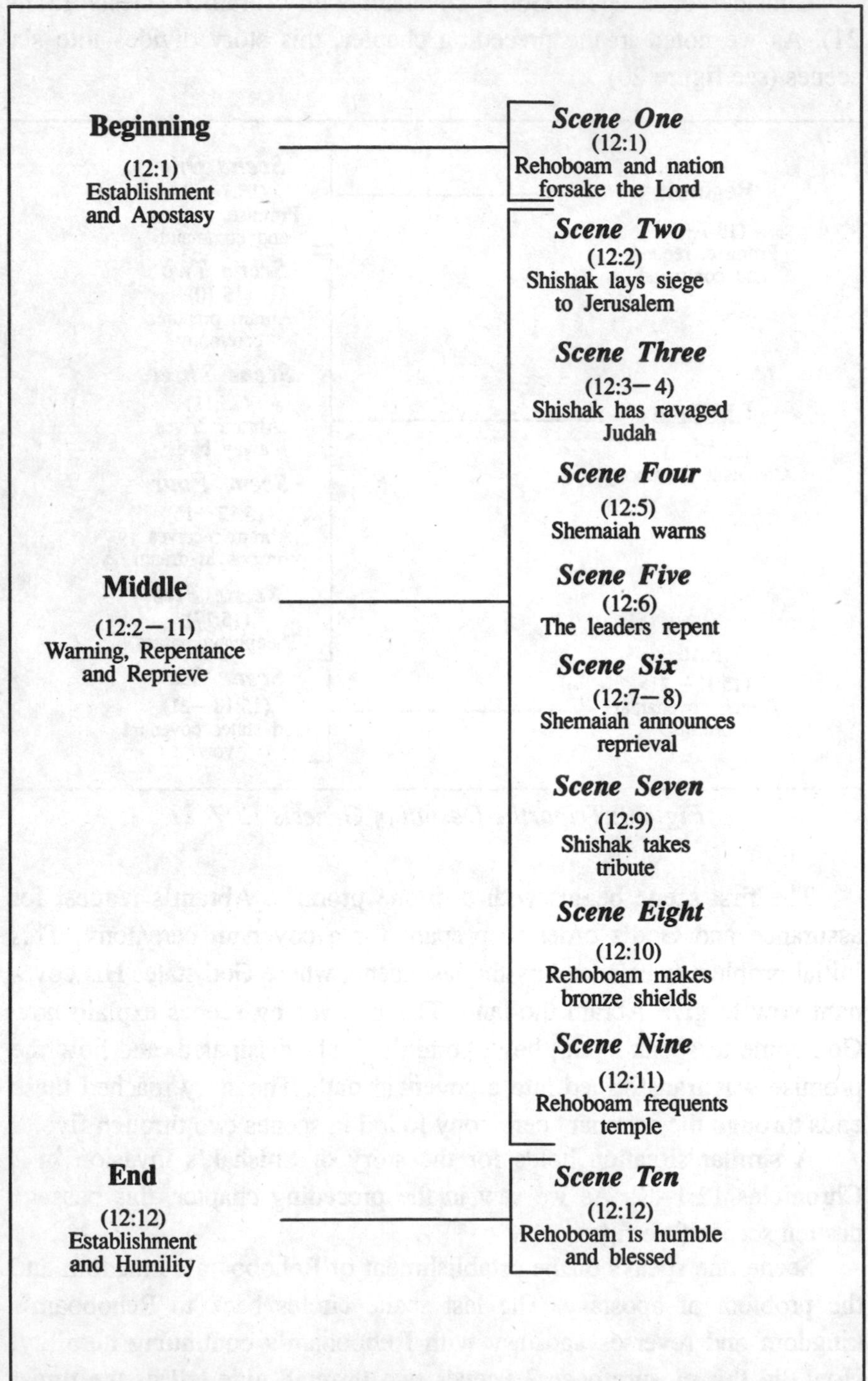

Fig. 21: Tripartite Design of 2 Chronicles 12:1–12

of Shishak's invasion, repentance by the nobility, and the kingdom's partial deliverance.

As we examine the structure of dramatic episodes, we must take note of this basic threefold structure. After establishing the conceptual balance between the beginning and end, we should then note the developments of the middle portion.

Phases

To see the basic symmetry of a story more clearly, it often helps to batch a text into units larger than scenes. As we observe the overall dynamics of a story, two, three, or four scenes often fall together into *phases*. At times these scenes deal with the same characters; at other times the same setting, action, or theme draws them together. Whatever the case, gathering scenes into phases helps us discern the episode's structure more clearly.

The account of the Tower of Babel (Genesis 11:1–9, NASB) illustrates the value of grouping scenes into phases.[16]

Scene One

Now the whole earth used the same language and the same words. (v. 1)

Scene Two

And it came about, as they journeyed east, that they found a plain in the land of Shinar and settled there. (v. 2)

Scene Three

And they said to one another, "Come, let us make bricks and burn them thoroughly." (v. 3a)

Scene Four

And they used brick for stone, and they used tar for mortar. (v. 3b)

Scene Five

And they said, "Come, let us build for ourselves a city, and a tower whose top will reach into heaven, and let us make for ourselves a name; lest we be scattered abroad over the face of the whole earth." (v. 4)

Scene Six

And the Lord came down to see the city and the tower which the sons of men had built. (v. 5)

Scene Seven

And the Lord said, "Behold, they are one people, and they all have the same language. And this is what they began to do, and now nothing which they purpose to do will be impossible for them. Come, let Us go down and there confuse their language, that they may not understand one another's speech." (vv. 6–7)

Scene Eight

So the Lord scattered them abroad from there over the face of the whole earth; and they stopped building the city. (v. 8)

Scene Nine

Therefore, its name was called Babel, because there the Lord confused the language of the whole earth; and from there the Lord scattered them abroad over the face of the whole earth. (v. 9)

While these scenes represent the basic building blocks of the story, some of them have affinities with each other. If we bring these scenes together into phases, the following arrangement appears (see figure 22).

As this diagram suggests, scenes one and two come together to provide the background for the building project. Scenes three, four, and five deal with the construction of the tower. Scenes eight and nine focus on God scattering the people and confusing the language. Only scenes six and seven stand alone. We will treat these scenes as phases in themselves. As a result the nine scenes of this episode form five phases.

Up to this point we have seen several basic structural features. All episodes of resolution display conceptual balance between the beginning and end. Most of them have a threefold structure. If we group closely related scenes into phases, many texts become more manageable. With these features in mind, let us now look more closely at several typical patterns that occur in episodes of resolution.

Typical Patterns of Dramatic Resolution

In Old Testament narratives, a number of different symmetrical configurations emerge—so many, in fact—that we cannot deal with them all.

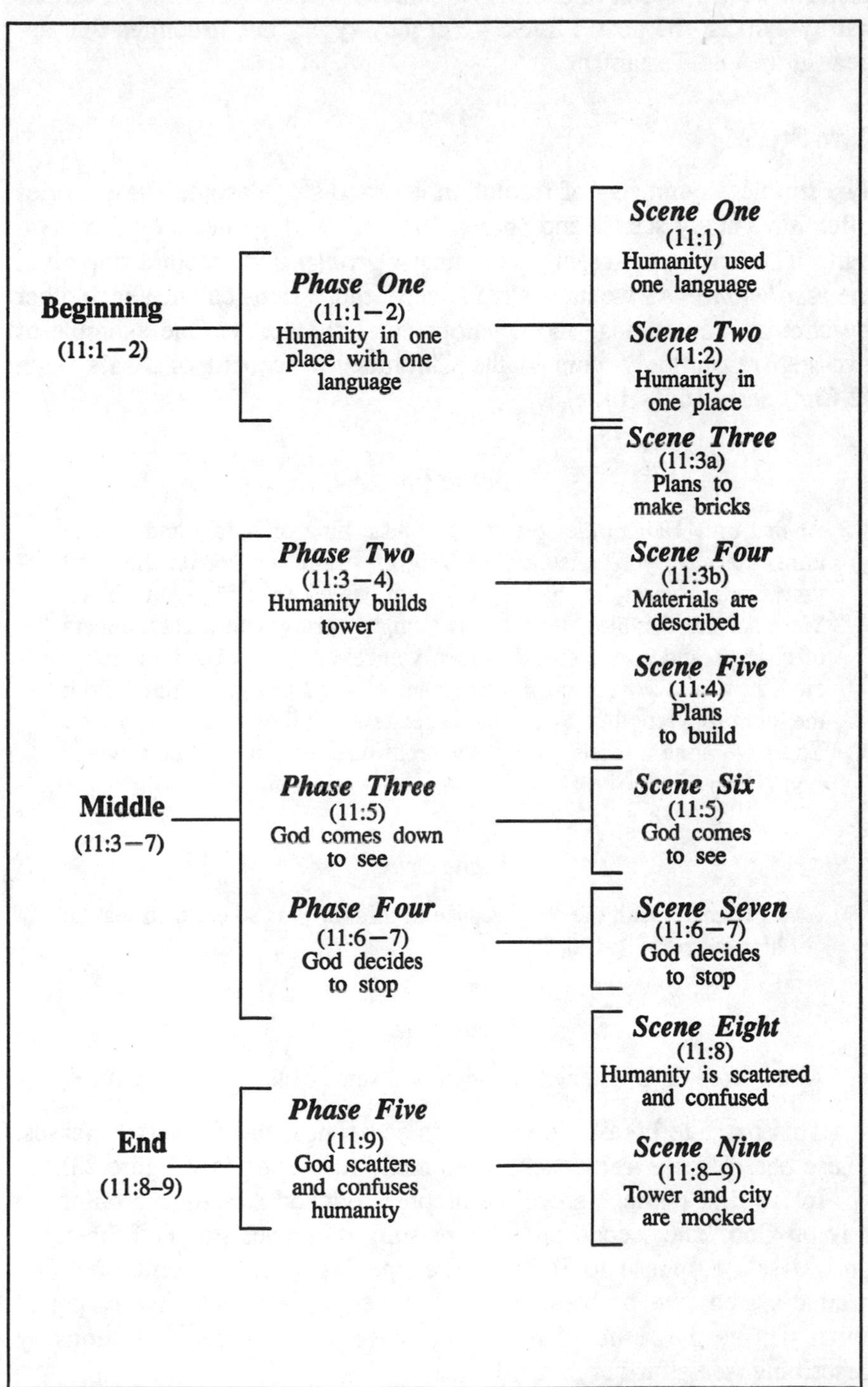

Fig. 22: Phases in Genesis 11:1–9

Instead, we will speak of four usual patterns that occur. These variations hardly exhaust the possibilities.[17] Yet they typify the structures that appear in the Old Testament.

Two Steps

The simplest symmetry of resolution is a two-step design. These stories often have many scenes and phases, but batched together they form two parts. The first step presents the dramatic *problem;* the second step gives the *resolution.*[18] As we have already seen, these steps balance each other by circular, contrasting, and developmental symmetry. One example of two-step resolution occurs in the Chronicler's account of Asa's reign (2 Chronicles 16:7–10).[19]

Scene One

> At that time Hanani the seer came to Asa, king of Judah, and said to him: "Because you relied on the king of Aram and not on the Lord your God, the army of the king of Aram has escaped from your hand. Were not the Cushites and Libyans a mighty army with great numbers of chariots and horsemen? Yet when you relied on the Lord, he delivered them into your hand. For the eyes of the Lord range throughout the earth to strengthen those whose hearts are fully committed to him. You have done a foolish thing, and from now on you will be at war." (vv. 7–9)

Scene Two

> Asa was angry with the seer because of this; he was so enraged that he put him in prison. (v. 10a)

Scene Three

> At the same time, Asa brutally oppressed some of the people. (v. 10b)

This passage breaks down into three scenes that form two phases. These phases serve as the steps in dramatic resolution (see figure 23).

In the first phase, Hanani the prophet rebuked Asa for his failure to rely on God. The second phase, consisting of scenes two and three, reports Asa's response to Hanani. The opening phase presents the first dramatic step, the problem of the prophecy. How will Asa respond? What will be the result? The closing phase answers these questions by describing Asa's further disobedience.

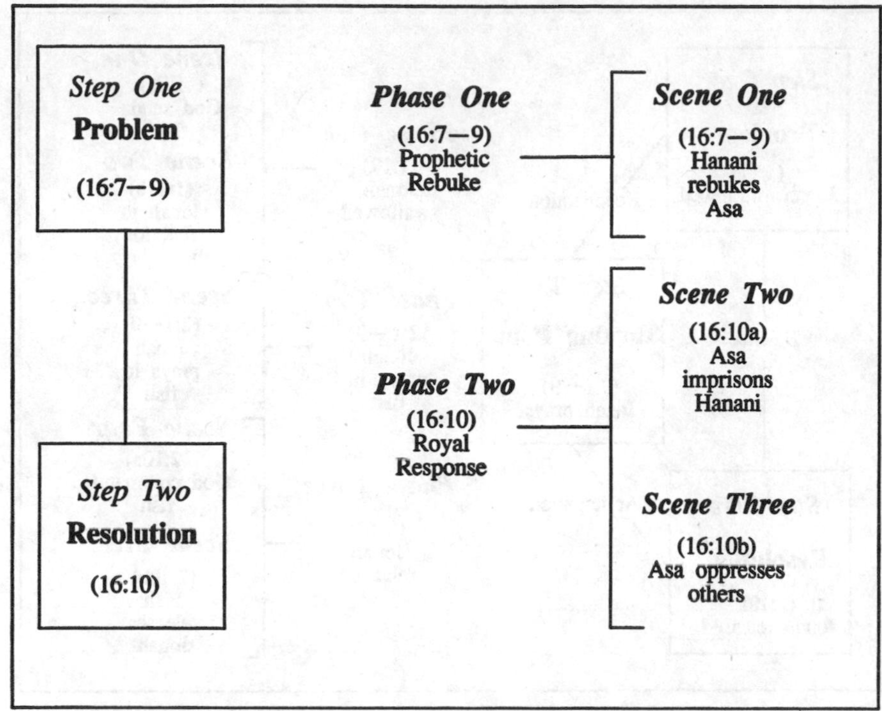

Fig. 23: Dramatic Flow of 2 Chronicles 16:7–10

Three Steps

More frequently, episodes of resolution present at least three steps. These stories may also contain many scenes and phases, but grouped together they present a three-part drama: a *problem*, a *turning point*, and a *resolution*.

In this pattern concepts balance in two ways. The problem and the resolution are symmetrical as in all narratives of resolution, but in addition, the turning point often recalls some aspect of the problem and/or anticipates dimensions of the resolution.[20] The second episode in the book of Jonah (Jonah 1:17—2:10) follows a three-step pattern[21] which may be depicted as follows (see figure 24).[22]

Balance between the problem and resolution of this story is straightforward. The introductory step contains two scenes of straight narration: God appointed a fish to swallow Jonah, and Jonah was in the fish for three days and nights. The final step also consists of two scenes of straight narration. God commanded the fish, and it vomited Jonah onto the shore. The first and last steps balance circularly; both the problem

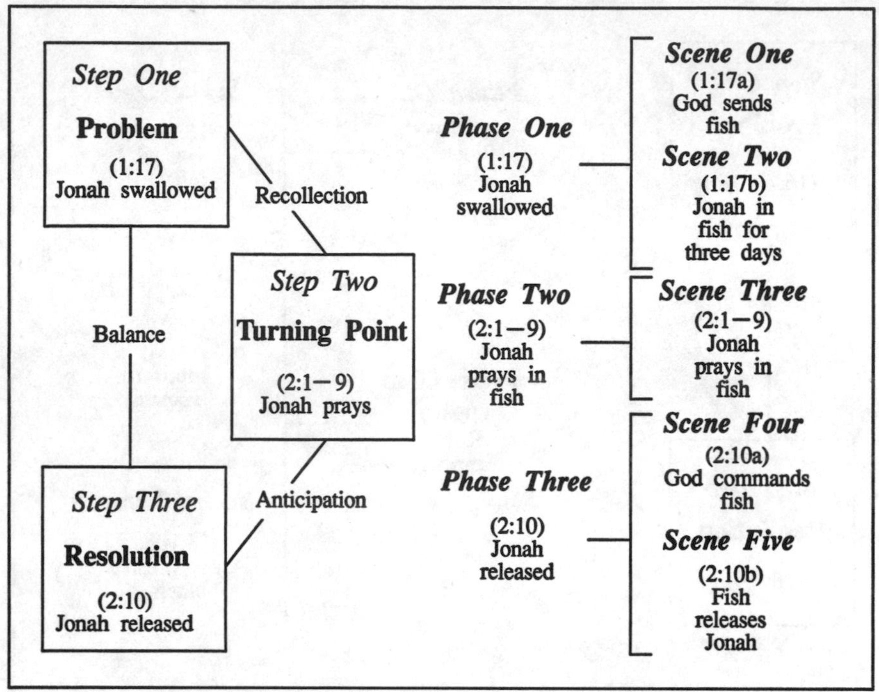

Fig. 24: Dramatic Flow of Jonah 1:17–2:10

and resolution report a divine decree and an ensuing action. Contrast also occurs as the fish first swallowed and then vomited.

The turning point (2:1–9) consists of Jonah's psalm of thanksgiving within the fish.[23] As with many turning points, this step recollects the problem and anticipates the resolution. The first portion of the prayer looks back to Jonah's hopeless condition as he sank into the depths of the sea (2:2–6b). The second part of the prayer expresses Jonah's hope for the future (2:6c-9),[24] thus anticipating his release from the fish.

Four Steps

Dramatic resolution also appears in four steps. In effect, the middle of the episode breaks into two balancing sections, resulting in a *problem, rising action, falling action,* and *resolution.* A specific turning point cannot be isolated. Again, the problem and resolution balance each other and the rising and falling actions tend to recollect and anticipate aspects of the problem and resolution. Beyond this, the rising action and falling action frequently display conceptual balance between each other as well.

Consider the account of God's confrontation of Adam and Eve (Genesis 3:8–21).

Scene One

Then the man and his wife heard the sound of the Lord God as he was walking in the garden in the cool of the day, and they hid from the Lord God among the trees of the garden. (v. 8)

Scene Two

But the Lord God called to the man, "Where are you?" He answered, "I heard you in the garden, and I was afraid because I was naked; so I hid." And he said, "Who told you that you were naked? Have you eaten from the tree that I commanded you not to eat from?" The man said, "The woman you put here with me—she gave me some fruit from the tree, and I ate it." Then the Lord God said to the woman, "What is this you have done?" The woman said, "The serpent deceived me, and I ate." (vv. 9–13)

Scene Three

So the Lord God said to the serpent, "Because you have done this, cursed are you above all the livestock and all the wild animals! You will crawl on your belly and you will eat dust all the days of your life. And I will put enmity between you and the woman, and between your offspring and hers; he will crush your head, and you will strike his heel." To the woman he said, "I will greatly increase your pains in childbearing; with pain you will give birth to children. Your desire will be for your husband, and he will rule over you." To Adam he said, "Because you listened to your wife and ate from the tree about which I commanded you, 'You must not eat of it,' cursed is the ground because of you; through painful toil you will eat of it all the days of your life. It will produce thorns and thistles for you, and you will eat the plants of the field. By the sweat of your brow you will eat your food until you return to the ground, since from it you were taken; for dust you are and to dust you will return." (vv. 14–19)

Scene Four

Adam named his wife Eve, because she would become the mother of all the living. (v. 20)

Scene Five

The Lord God made garments of skin for Adam and his wife and clothed them. (v. 21)

As the following diagram indicates, the five scenes of this episode fall into four steps (see figure 25).

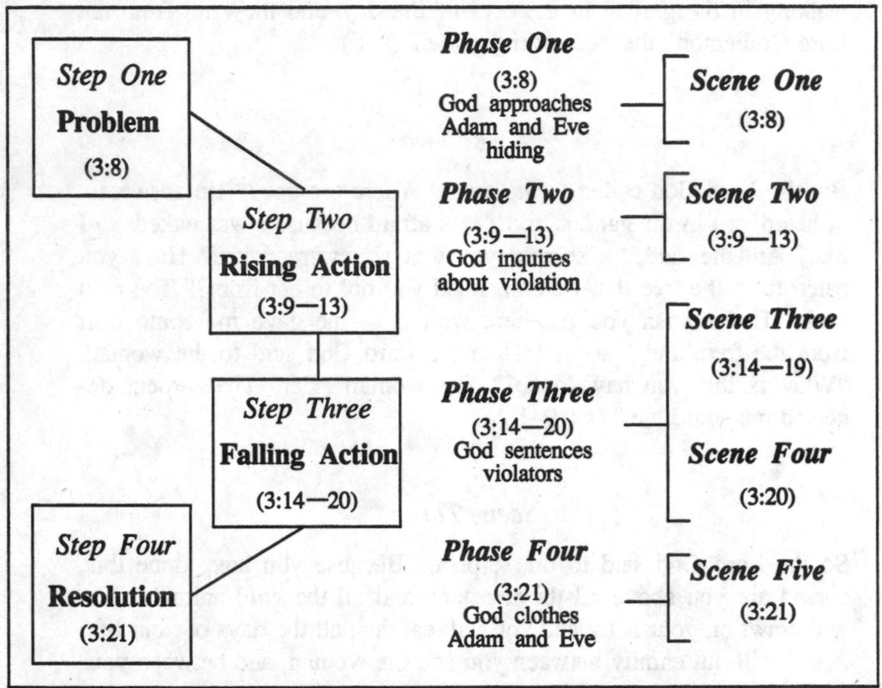

Fig. 25: Dramatic Flow of Genesis 3:8–21

Most of the scenes in this episode remain separate, but the brief authorial comment in scene four combines with the lengthy pronouncement of judgment in scene three, resulting in a four-step pattern of resolution.

These four phases reflect the typical characteristics of a four-step account. The problem balances with the resolution. Both present relatively fast temporal movement; they also focus on the same characters. The shame of nakedness in the initial step contrasts with the final step where God clothed Adam and Eve.

But how do we get from shame to covering? Rising and falling action bridge the gap. These steps each focus on dramatic narration and involve similar characters. In the second step, God inquired about the guilt of Adam and Eve; in the third step, He sentenced the guilty parties.

The well-known sacrifice of Isaac (Genesis 22:1–19) is also a four-step drama in twelve scenes.

Scene One

> Some time later God tested Abraham. He said to him, "Abraham!" "Here I am," he replied. Then God said, "Take your son, your only son, Isaac, whom you love, and go to the region of Moriah. Sacrifice him there as a burnt offering on one of the mountains I will tell you about." (vv. 1–2)

Scene Two

> Early the next morning Abraham got up and saddled his donkey. He took with him two of his servants and his son Isaac. When he had cut enough wood for the burnt offering, he set out for the place God had told him about. (v. 3)

Scene Three

> On the third day, Abraham looked up and saw the place in the distance. He said to his servants, "Stay here with the donkey while I and the boy go over there. We will worship and then we will come back to you." (vv. 4–5)

Scene Four

> Abraham took the wood for the burnt offering and placed it on his son Isaac, and he himself carried the fire and the knife. (v. 6)

Scene Five

> As the two of them went on together, Isaac spoke up and said to his father Abraham, "Father?" "Yes, my son?" Abraham replied. "The fire and wood are here," Isaac said, "but where is the lamb for the burnt offering?" Abraham answered, "God himself will provide the lamb for the burnt offering, my son." And the two of them went on together. (vv. 7–8)

Scene Six

> When they reached the place God had told him about, Abraham built an altar there and arranged the wood on it. He bound his son Isaac and laid him on the altar, on top of the wood. Then he reached out his hand and took the knife to slay his son. (vv. 9–10)

Scene Seven

But the angel of the Lord called out to him from heaven, "Abraham! Abraham!" "Here I am," he replied. "Do not lay a hand on the boy," he said. "Do not do anything to him. Now I know that you fear God, because you have not withheld from me your son, your only son." (vv. 11–12)

Scene Eight

Abraham looked up and there in a thicket he saw a ram caught by its horns. He went over and took the ram and sacrificed it as a burnt offering instead of his son. (v. 13)

Scene Nine

So Abraham called that place The Lord Will Provide. And to this day it is said, "On the mountain of the Lord it will be provided." (v. 14)

Scene Ten

The angel of the Lord called to Abraham from heaven a second time and said, "I swear by myself, declares the Lord, that because you have done this and have not withheld your son, your only son, I will surely bless you and make your descendants as numerous as the stars in the sky and as the sand on the seashore. Your descendants will take possession of the cities of their enemies, and through your offspring all nations on earth will be blessed, because you have obeyed me." (See verses 15–18)

Scene Eleven

Then Abraham returned to his servants, and they set off together for Beersheba. (v. 19a)

Scene Twelve

And Abraham stayed in Beersheba. (v. 19b)

The scenes of this passage gather into four phases (see figure 26). Scenes one and two deal with the call to leave and the beginning of the journey. Scenes three, four, and five take place "on the third day" within sight of the mountain. Scenes six through ten cover events that took place on the mountain. Scenes eleven and twelve narrate the return and the end of the journey.

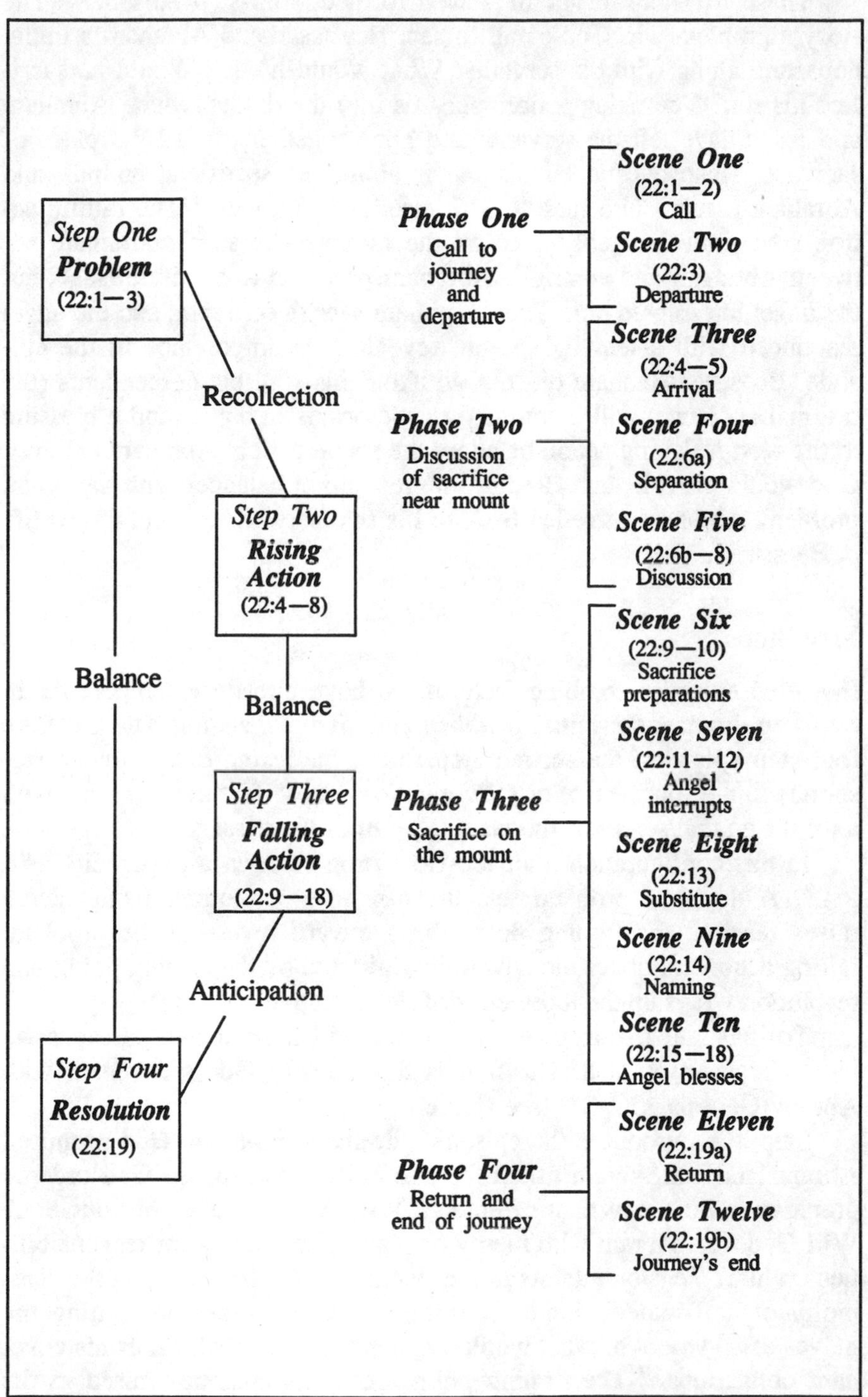

Fig. 26: Dramatic Flow of Genesis 22:1–19

These divisions result in a well-formed, four-step episode.[25] The story's problem was God's call to sacrifice Isaac and Abraham's initial departure along with his servants. What would he do? Would he sacrifice his son? The rising action takes us into the drama, where Abraham and Isaac have left the servants and gone together toward the place of sacrifice. Isaac questioned his father about the sacrificial animal, and Abraham assured him that "God himself will provide." The falling action covers all that took place on the mount. The scenes alternate between Abraham and an angel. Abraham prepared to sacrifice Isaac, but the angel interrupted him. Then Abraham sacrificed a ram, and the angel responded with a lengthy speech, revealing its importance in the episode. Because Abraham did not withhold his son, his descendants (the original audience) will be numerous, victorious in battle, and a blessing to the world. Falling action balances the rising action. Abraham believed God would provide, and He did. The resolution balances with the initial problem. Abraham travelled back to his two servants and continued life in Beersheba.

Five Steps

Five-step episodes combine features we have already examined. As in two-step dramas, the initial *problem* and final *resolution* balance. Like four-step episodes, the second step forms the *rising action* that corresponds to the fourth step, or *falling action*. These features combine with a third step that serves as the *turning point* of the passage.

In this configuration dramatic flow progresses in a pyramidic fashion.[26] A dramatic problem sets the narrative in motion; rising action raises tension; the turning point shifts toward reversing the problem; falling action continues the unwinding initiated by the turning point; and resolution wraps up the loose ends of the narrative.

To illustrate five-step resolution, we will look at two passages we have already examined. The first is the story of God's covenant with Abram (Genesis 15:7–21) (see figure 27).

Step one introduces the episode's dramatic problem. God promised Abram land and Abram asked for assurance. In response God ordered preparation for a covenant ceremony. What will come of this situation? Will God treat Abram with mercy or place heavy covenant responsibilities on him? Tension mounts in the rising action. Abram began the ceremony of self-malediction by cutting the animals and separating the halves as a symbol of what would happen to the one who fails his covenant obligations.[27] The turning point recollects anxieties raised in the

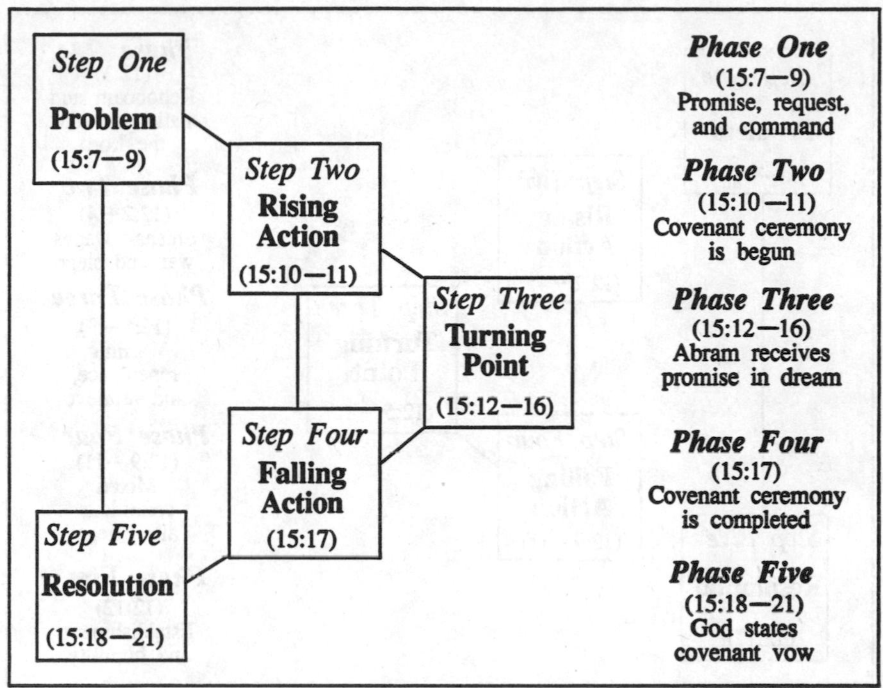

Fig. 27: Dramatic Flow of Genesis 15:7–21

first steps as Abram fell into nightmarish darkness. But it also lessens the tension because God assured Abram He would give his descendants the land after a period of slavery. The falling action unravels the tension further. God appeared swearing to His own destruction.[28] The ceremony begun in the second step now reaches completion. To Abram's relief securing the land depended on God, not Abram. The resolution closes the matter; God confirmed His promise with a solemn covenant oath. Abram's need for assurance was met.

The invasion of Shishak (2 Chronicles 12:1–12) follows a similar pattern. Consider the following outline (see figure 28).

The dramatic problem initiates the story with Judah's apostasy. What will be the fate of the kingdom? Will the rebellion result in judgment? Tension of the rising action mounts as we read of Shishak's incredible army. Will the holy city fall prey to the same fate as the rest of Judah? The turning point recollects this tension. The prophet delivered a stinging oracle of judgment; surely Judah's fate was sealed. But the nobles of Judah repented of their apostasy. Anticipating the final phases, the prophet spoke of partial deliverance. The falling action shows how the prophetic word proved to be true. Conditions were not perfect;

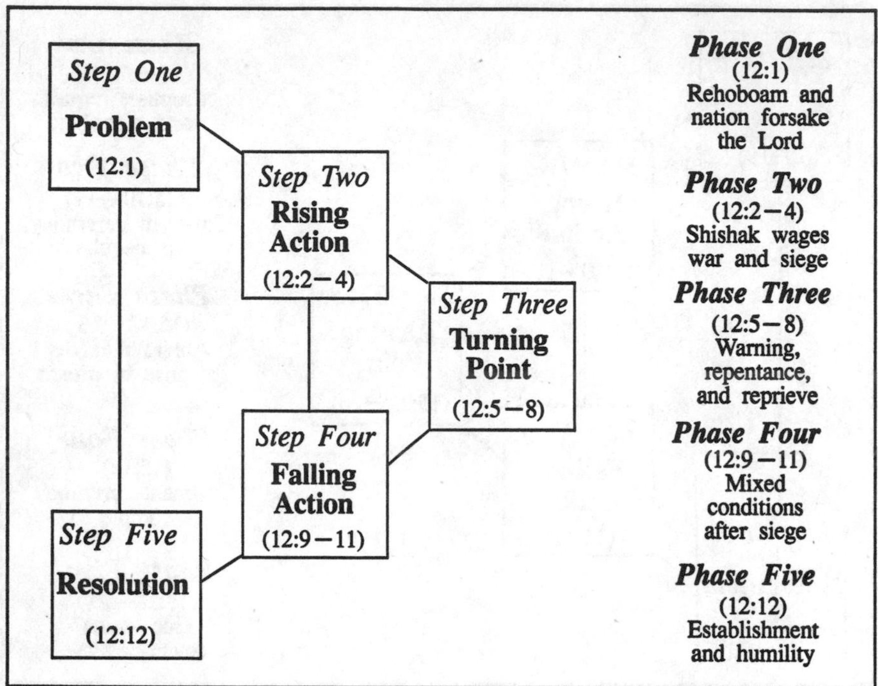

Fig. 28: Dramatic Flow of 2 Chronicles 12:1–12

Shishak evoked a heavy price from Judah. But the kingdom was not in total ruin. Finally, the resolution of the story returns us to Rehoboam's kingdom in peace. Good conditions prevailed as the king continued to humble himself.

Episodes of resolution take many forms in the Old Testament. They may break down into more than five steps, but the two-, three-, four-, or five-step patterns outlined here suffice for most passages.

Conclusion

When we examine the plots of individual episodes, we face countless varieties. The passages vary the degree to which they convey dramatic tension, ranging from simple report to unresolved tension and full resolution. Episodes of resolution exhibit symmetries of different sorts. We may summarize most of them in two to five steps. By this means we will be able to see the structure of these stories more clearly and investigate their original meaning more thoroughly.

Review Questions

1. What are the three basic types of plot found in Old Testament narratives? What distinguishes them from each other? Give an example of each.
2. What is the difference between a scene and a phase in a story? Why is phasing helpful?
3. What patterns of dramatic flow occur in narratives of resolution? Name and describe the functions of phases in each pattern. What is the difference between a simple and complex narrative of resolution?

Study Exercises

1. Read 1 Chronicles 10:1–6. Divide it into scenes and batch the scenes into phases. Explain how this story may be outlined as a three-step episode of resolution. What symmetries can you discern?
2. Read 1 Samuel 2:12–17. Divide it into scenes and batch the scenes into phases. Explain how this story may be outlined as a four-step episode of resolution. What symmetries can you discern?

9

LARGE NARRATIVE STRUCTURES

"Comc up here if you want to get the lay of the land!" my friend shouted from the observation tower. We had walked through the forest for hours and were completely lost. Down among the trees we could only see a few yards in any direction. "Where is the lake? . . . the river? . . . the town?" We needed to see the big picture. So I joined my friend on the tower platform.

In many ways the same is true of interpreting Old Testament stories. Up to this point, we have been primarily concerned with the inner workings of single episodes. But to understand a particular text, we must get the big picture of large narrative structures. Larger contexts help us determine the meaning of individual stories.

In this chapter we will examine two features of large narrative structures: the relative importance of *chronology and topics* and *typical configurations* that occur in lengthy accounts. How did Old Testament writers balance temporal sequence and topical concerns? What typical structures do we find in large sections of Old Testament stories?

Chronology and Topics

If we were assigned to write a history of the United States, we could take at least three strategies. First, we could arrange the data primarily according to temporal sequence. In this approach our account would look something like this: chapter 1—"The 17th Century," chapter 2—"The 18th Century," and so on.

But a purely chronological account would not be possible. So many events occurred at the same time that we would have to arrange the data into topical subheadings. A chapter dealing with the eighteenth century might cover "Events in the North," "Events in the South," "Life in the City," and "Life on the Frontier." Even if chronology dominates our history, we must still organize events into topical sub-categories.

Second, we could orient our historical record toward topics instead of dividing the past into periods. With this emphasis our chapter divisions might be: chapter 1—"American Wars," chapter 2—"Politics of Peace," chapter 3—"Architecture in America," and other subjects of interest.

A purely topical approach would not be possible either. We must include temporal developments as subheadings. A chapter on "American Wars" might divide into: "The Revolution," "The French and Indian War," "The War of 1812," and "The War Between the States."

Third, our history of the United States might mix chronological and topical concerns. Parts of our report could be chronological, while other parts follow a more topical arrangement.

Old Testament writers faced similar choices. As they dealt with the history of Israel, they arranged their accounts chronologically, topically, and in various combinations. In order to understand their texts, we must explore the relative importance of chronological and topical concerns. What were the dominant interests behind the arrangement of Old Testament stories? How do topics and chronology present themselves in the structuring of large sections?

Chronological Dominance

Overall, Old Testament narratives basically follow a chronological order. Just as scenes in individual episodes tend to move forward through time, series of whole stories and sections of books present chronological sequence. Shifts between simultaneous and antecedent events occur, but the major movement is toward successive action.

Old Testament writers often indicated their interest in the sequence of events explicitly. For instance, the Abrahamic stories mention the aging of the patriarch (Genesis 12:4; 16:16; 17:1). The book of Joshua also records Joshua's increasing years (Joshua 14:10; 24:29). The books of Kings and Chronicles remark on the dates of many events (1 Kings 15:1, 9; 2 Chronicles 15:10; 16:1).

The overarching outlines of most books indicate an interest in chronology. Genesis is structured largely by historical sequence: chapters 1—11 covering the primeval history and chapters 12—50 dealing with the subsequent patriarchal period. Exodus divides into events prior to Sinai (chap. 1—18) and events at Sinai (chap. 19—40). Numbers traces Israel's travels: at Sinai (1:1—10:10), from Sinai to Kadesh (10:11—12:16), at Kadesh and in the Wilderness (13:1—20:13), from Kadesh to Moab (20:14—22:1), and finally at Moab (22:2—36:13).

Topical Concerns

If chronology dominates the landscape of Old Testament narratives, what place is there for topical concerns? Many evangelicals assume that topical interests had little to do with the large-scale arrangements of Old Testament stories. We see these books merely following the sequence of events. Why does the battle of Ai follow Jericho? Why does Hezekiah's Passover follow his reforms? Our usual response is simple; the events happened that way.

This view is true as far as it goes, but mere chronology cannot account for all the arrangements we find in Old Testament narratives. Old Testament writers often selected and arranged their materials according to topical interests. We will look at three ways topical interests influenced large sections of Old Testament narratives: *selection, simultaneous events,* and *dischronologized events.*

Selection. Even when Old Testament writers followed historical sequence, they had to select their material. Often these selections rose out of topical considerations. A simple example occurs in Genesis 15:1–21. This passage consists of two episodes. The first (vv. 1–6) presents God's promise of a son to Abram; the second (vv. 7–21) deals with the promise of land.[1]

Why are these episodes set alongside each other? No doubt one reason is the chronological proximity of the events. The absence of an explicit subject at the beginning of Genesis 15:7 (*wy'mr* "He also said . . . ") suggests that the events of Genesis 15:7–21 followed immediately after the events of Genesis 15:1–6.[2] But we must remember that Moses did not have to keep both these episodes. He could have easily omitted one or the other. What explains his choice to put them together?

Topical affinities caused Moses to structure his text in this way. Consider the following thematic similarities between the passages (see figure 29).

The uniqueness of each event is apparent, but at least five topical connections stand out:[3] 1) both deal with promises from God; 2) each presents Abram requesting confirmation of God's promise; 3) in both passages God responds to Abram's request; 4) in each passage God

Genesis 15:1–6	*Genesis 15:7–21*
God promises Abram reward (v. 1).	God promises Abram land (v. 7).
Abram requests confirmation of promised seed (vv. 2–3).	Abram requests confirmation of promised land (v. 8).
God confirms promise of seed (v. 4).	God confirms promise of land (vv. 9–16).
God demonstrates reliability by pointing to stars (v. 5).	God demonstrates reliability by passing through carnage (v. 17).
Abram believes promise (v. 6).	God reaffirms promise; Abram is without doubts (vv. 18–21).

Fig. 29: Topical Affinities Between Genesis 15:1-6 and 7-21

demonstrates that He will fulfill His Word; and 5) by the end of each episode, God meets Abram's need for confirmation.

These episodes follow chronological order, but Moses' prominent interests become clear as we see the topical connections. Together the passages cover the two principal elements in Abram's hopes: seed and land. By placing them alongside each other, Moses affirmed that both hopes were certain because of the reliability of God's promises.

A more striking example of topical selection appears in the Chronicler's account of Asa's reign (2 Chronicles 14:1—16:14) (see figure 30).

The Chronicler refers to dates in four of these six episodes. The early prosperity of the kingdom extended "for ten years;" reforms took place in "the fifteenth year;" and prosperity continued "until the thirty-fifth year." In the "thirty-sixth year," Asa failed in battle. During the "thirty-ninth year," the king became ill; he finally died in the "forty-first year." The Chronicler's account of Asa's reign is dominated by concern for temporal sequence.[4]

But historical order was not the only factor influencing the arrangements of these materials. Out of all the things that took place in Asa's reign, why did the Chronicler select these six episodes? The Chronicler himself noted that many other events could have been mentioned (2 Chronicles 16:11). Why these? He selected them on the basis of topical interest: the importance of seeking and relying on the Lord.

Chronology	Topics
Episode One	
Asa's early years of prosperity (14:1–7)	
"for ten years" (v. 1)	"at peace" (vv. 1,5,6)
	"built and prospered" (v. 7)
	"we sought" (v. 7)
Episode Two	
Victory in war with the Cushites (14:8–15)	
	"for we rely" (v. 11)
	"much booty" (v. 14)
Episode Three	
Prophetic encouragement and royal reforms (15:1–19)	
"fifteenth year" (v. 10)	"if you seek" (v. 2)
"until the thirty-fifth year" (v. 19)	"rewarded" (v. 7)
	"seek the Lord" (v. 12)
	"rest on every side" (v. 15)
	"no more war" (v. 19)
Episode Four	
Failure in war with Israel (16:1–6)	
"thirty-sixth year" (v. 1)	"treasuries of the Lord's temple" (v. 2)
Episode Five	
Prophetic condemnation and royal rebellion (16:7–11)	
	"relied on the king" (v. 7)
	"not on the Lord" (v. 7)
	"from now on you will be at war" (v. 9)
Episode Six	
Asa's last years of sickness and death (16:12–14)	
"thirty-ninth year" (v. 12)	"did not seek help from the Lord" (v. 12)
"forty-first year" (v. 13)	

Fig. 30: Chronology and Topics in 2 Chronicles 14:1-16:14

Each episode contributes to the development of this theme. In the first three episodes, conditions in the land were positive. The land was "at peace" (14:1, 5, 6); the people of Judah "built and prospered" (14:7); Judah defeated the Cushites and acquired "much booty" (14:14); the prophet Azariah promised that Judah would be "rewarded" (15:7); the king was granted "rest on every side" (15:15) and faced "no more war" (15:19) for many years.

Why were conditions so positive for the nation? The Chronicler's answer to this question stands out in several key terms: "seek" (*drš*), "rely" (*š'n*), and "forsake" (*'zb*).[5] In the first episode (14:1–7), Asa remarked that the blessing of his reign occurred "because we have sought (*drš*) the Lord our God; we sought him (*drš*) and he has given us rest on every side (14:7)." A similar topic resounds in the second episode (14:8–15) when Asa cried out in prayer, "we rely (*š'n*) on you" (14:11). In the third episode (15:1–9), Azariah declared that Judah's status depended on a basic principle: "If you seek (*drš*) him, he will be found by you, but if you forsake (*'zb*) him, he will forsake (*'zb*) you" (15:2). The episode goes on to describe how the people of Judah "entered into a covenant to seek (*drš*) the Lord" (15:12). All of Judah rejoiced because they had "sought (*drš*) God eagerly, and he was found by them" (15:15). From the repetition of these concepts, the Chronicler made his viewpoint plain. The prosperity of the first half of Asa's reign was reward for seeking and relying on God.

The last three episodes tell a different side of the king's reign. In the fourth episode (16:1–6), Asa allied himself with the Syrian king Ben-Hadad against Baasha of Israel. As a result he fell short of complete victory. Moreover, in the fifth episode (16:7–11), Hanani the seer declared to Asa, "from now on you will be at war" (16:9). The sixth episode (16:12–14) reports Asa's illness and eventual death.

Why did conditions in Asa's reign change so drastically? We get the first hint when Asa bought Ben-Hadad's support with silver and gold taken from "the treasuries of the Lord's temple" (16:2).[6] Hanani condemned this turn of events, explaining that Baasha escaped Asa's army because "you relied (*š'n*) on the king of Aram and [relied] (*š'n*) not on the Lord your God" (16:7). The prophet also reminded the king that his earlier victory against the Cushites occurred because "you relied (*š'n*) on the Lord" (16:8). A similar theme appears in the sixth episode. Asa died from his illness because he "did not seek (*drš*) help from the Lord, but only from the physicians" (16:12).[7] Unfavorable conditions existed in Judah because the king failed to seek and rely on the Lord.

From this brief examination, we see that the Chronicler arranged Asa's reign according to both chronological and topical interests. He followed the order of history but selected only a few events to emphasize a theme: Blessings come to those who seek and rely on God, but curses fall on all who forsake Him.

Simultaneous events. Topical interests also governed the arrangement of simultaneous events. When different episodes deal with events that took place at or near the same time, topical concerns were often guiding the writer. The stories of Judah and Joseph in Genesis 38:1—39:23 offer a good example. The following outline points to topical affinities between these two chapters (see figure 31).

Episode One
Judah and Tamar (38:1–30)

Chronology	*Topics*
"At that time" (v. 1)	[deceit, immorality] "She is more righteous than I" (v. 26)

Episode Two
Joseph in Potiphar's house (39:1–23)

Chronology	*Topics*
Joseph sold in Egypt to Potiphar (v. 1)	[honesty, morality] "How then could I do such a wicked thing . . . ? (v. 9)

Fig. 31: Chronology and Topics in Genesis 38:1–39:23

These episodes report simultaneous events. The last scene of chapter 37 develops the story of Genesis to the time when Joseph entered Potiphar's house. We pick up there again after the story of Judah and Tamar, when Moses recalled that Joseph had been sold to Potiphar in Egypt (Genesis 39:1). The story of Judah and Tamar (Genesis 38:1–30), therefore, reports an event that took place in Canaan near the time Joseph was in Potiphar's house.

Why does Moses digress to events in Canaan when he had already shifted attention to Egypt (Genesis 37:36)? Why did he include the story of Judah and Tamar here? His main reason was topical affinity.

In Genesis 38 Judah and his sons had relations with Canaanite women. Judah's sons were judged by God, leaving Judah's daughter-in-law, Tamar, without a husband (vv. 6–11). When Judah failed to deal fairly with Tamar, she disguised herself and seduced him (vv. 12–19). Judah heard that Tamar was pregnant and condemned her to death. Upon investigation, however, it became apparent that Judah was the father of the child, and he rightly confessed, "She is more righteous than I" (vv. 24-26).

The familiar story of Joseph in Potiphar's house (Genesis 39:1–23) presents a striking contrast. Joseph behaved in exemplary fashion. He served Potiphar well and resisted the seduction of Potiphar's wife. By his own words, he declared his innocence, "How then could I do such a wicked thing and sin against God?" (v. 9). Joseph was falsely accused and was sent to prison; but God was with him, and he rose to prominence.[8]

These stories have been juxtaposed to develop the theme of patriarchal morality.[9] Judah fell into sin and suffered severely. Joseph remained pure, and God rewarded his righteousness. This topical connection is vital to understanding why these chapters appear together.

Dischronologized events. In some cases topical concerns were so influential that the episodes were *dischronologized,* arranged with little or no interest in temporal order. These texts do not misrepresent historical facts; they are structured according to topics rather than sequence of events.[10] An impressive example of dischronologization occurs in the last four chapters of 2 Samuel.

- Episode One: David Intervenes (21:1–14)—Royal intervention
- Episode Two: Accomplishments in Battle (21:15–22)—Royal warfare
- Episode Three: David's Song of Praise (22:1–51)—Royal words
- Episode Four: Oracle of David's Wisdom (23:1–7)—Royal words
- Episode Five: Accomplishments in Battle (23:8–39)—Royal warfare
- Episode Six: David Intervenes (24:1–25)—Royal intervention

These events are not in chronological order. David's first intervention is closely connected to 2 Samuel 19;[11] the second episode covers David's dealings with the Philistines; the third episode is dated by the text itself to David's deliverance from Saul; the fourth episode begins with "the last words of David"; the fifth section covers a broad range of dates; and the sixth episode probably occurred after the events of 2 Samuel 15—20.

What organizational principle did the writer of Samuel follow? He grouped these materials topically. This section in Samuel follows the account of trouble in David's household. Without this final series, David would have been presented as an utter failure. Yet this dischronologized finale reminds the readers of the benefits David brought to Israel and the blessings offered through his permanent dynasty.[12]

Typical Configurations

No two sections of Old Testament narrative follow precisely the same pattern; each passage has unique features. But as we survey Old Testament texts, we come across several patterns that appear again and again. At this point we will turn our attention to these typical structures. The configurations suggested here provide an orientation for analyzing many large sections of material.

We will speak of three typical arrangements: *clusters, parallels,* and *dramatic accounts*. These categories overlap and interconnect in many ways. For the sake of simplicity, however, we will deal with them separately.

Clusters

Clusters are episodes that illustrate different facets of a common theme. They have few structural parallels among them and little or no overarching dramatic unity. They merely provide perspectives on a topic.

One example of clustering occurs in the early periods of Solomon's reign (1 Kings 3:16—4:34). This material comes between the well-known story of Solomon's prayer for wisdom (1 Kings 3:1–15) and the accounts of Solomon's building projects (1 Kings 5:1—8:66). Its four episodes have few structural similarities and no all-encompassing dramatic flow (see figure 32).

These episodes differ from each other in many ways. The well-known judicial case (1 Kings 3:16–28) is a five-step narrative of resolution. The other episodes are narratives of report dealing with Solomon's bureaucracy (4:1–19), economic successes (4:20–28), and superior wisdom (4:29–34).

Why are these texts set alongside each other? A clue appears in the preceding account of Solomon's prayer (3:5–15), in which the writer drew attention to Solomon's wisdom. Solving the case of two prostitutes proved Solomon "had wisdom from God to administer justice" (3:28). The same theme appears in the last episode of this section, where we are told that "God gave Solomon wisdom and very great insight" (4:29).

Episode One [resolution]

Solomon's Case of Two Prostitutes (3:16–28)

I. Two Prostitutes Stand Before the King (3:16)
II. Prostitutes Accuse Each Other (3:17–22)
III. Solomon Gives Preliminary Ruling (3:23–25)
IV. Prostitutes React to Ruling (3:26)
V. Solomon Gives Final Ruling (3:27–28)

Episode Two [report]

Solomon's Bureaucratic Order (4:1–19)

I. Chief Officials (4:1–6)
II. District Governors (4:7–19)

Episode Three [report]

Solomon's National Economy (4:20–28)

I. Extent of Economy (4:20–21)
II. Daily Royal Provisions (4:22–26)
III. Monthly Supplies (4:27–28)

Episode Four [report]

Solomon's Supreme Wisdom (4:29–34)

Fig. 32: Clustering of Episodes in 1 Kings 3:16–4:34

These passages cluster around the topic of Solomon's administrative wisdom. He was wise in court (3:16–28), in political organization (4:1–19), in economic policies (4:20–28), and in comparison with other wise men (4:29–34). To understand this section of Kings, we must take this clustering structure into account.

The last chapters of Numbers reveal another cluster. In Numbers 33:1–49 we find a summary of the travels covered in the first thirty-two chapters. This recapitulation introduces the last portion of the book, a cluster of events that occurred in the plains of Moab (see figure 33).

These passages differ in many ways. The first three episodes are reports; the last is an episode of resolution. They deal with different subjects: driving out Canaanites, drawing tribal boundaries, establishing cities, and ordering intra-tribal marriages. Why, then, do they appear together? These units cluster around two topical concerns. First, as the summary indicates, each episode took place in the plains of Moab (36:13). Second, these passages teach how Israel was to handle the inheritance of the promised land. The first episode (33:50–56) portrays Moses receiving divine instructions for the people to dispossess the Can-

Episode One [report]
Instructions to Dispossess and Divide (33:50–56)

Episode Two [report]
Instructions on Boundaries (34:1–29)
I. Boundaries (34:1–15)
II. Leaders to Divide (34:16–29)

Episode Three [report]
Instructions for Levitical Cities (35:1–34)
I. General Instructions (35:1–5)
II. Cities of Refuge (35:6–34)

Episode Four [resolution]
Instructions for Zelophehad's Daughters (36:1–12)
I. Heads of Gileadites Approach Moses (36:1)
II. Gileadites Make Proposal (36:2–4)
III. Moses Responds to Proposal (36:5–9)
IV. Moses' Order is Obeyed (36:10–12)

Summary (36:13)

Fig. 33: Clustering of Numbers 33:50–36:13

aanites and divide the land. The second episode (34:1–29) examines this topic further by specifying the outer boundaries of the land and the appropriate procedures for assigning each family its share. The third episode (35:1–34) shifts attention to the special concerns of Levitical possessions and cities of refuge. The fourth episode (36:1–12) concerns the marriage of land-owning women.

These episodes appear disjointed at first glance, but upon reflection we can see that they form an assortment of perspectives on land distribution and possession that the audience of Numbers had to remember as they moved toward conquest of the promised land.

Parallel Accounts

Old Testament writers also arranged large sections of topically related material into parallel accounts—episodes that closely resemble each other in one way or another. These stories hold together more tightly than clusters, but they fall short of a unified, dramatic account.

Parallel episodes confirm or contrast with each other. If two passages primarily confirm each other, they amplify a particular point of view. By reporting two events in similar ways, the second account echoes the outlook of the first. A contrasting parallel, however, clarifies the writer's point of view by offering a second episode which somehow qualifies the first. This distinction is not absolute; it is often a matter of emphasis. Parallel accounts form many different arrangements. We will look into three patterns that emerge frequently: *simple parallels, inclusions*, and *chiastic parallels*.

Simple parallels. Simple parallels consist of confirming or contrasting episodes that are directly adjacent to each other. We have already seen one example of simple parallels in the stories of Judah and Joseph (Genesis 38:1—39:23). As our discussion suggested, Moses arranged these episodes around the issue of patriarchal morality. On one level, these passages have many similarities; they both concern a patriarch and focus on sexual behavior. But the dominant feature of their relationship is contrast (see figure 34).

Judah (Genesis 38:1–30)	***Joseph (Genesis 39:1–23)***
Association with Foreign Women (38:1–3)	Separation from Foreign Women (39:6b–12)
Sexual Immorality (38:12–18)	Sexual Morality (39:6b–12)
Victimizer (38:24)	Victimized (39:13–20a)
Judgment of God (38:6–10)	Blessing of God (39:20b–23)
True Accusation of Woman (38:25)	False Accusation of Woman (39:13–20a)
Confession of Sin (38:26)	Rejection of Sin (39:10)

Fig. 34: Contrasting Parallels Between Judah and Joseph

The dissonance between these accounts makes Moses' purpose evident: to contrast the moral character of the heads of Israel's tribes. The head of Judah failed to maintain his integrity; but Joseph, the head of Ephraim and Manasseh, remained pure. This contrast played a vital role in the meaning of this section for Moses' original audience. It explained why God treated the tribes of Judah and Joseph as He did and how these tribes should relate to each other.

Another example of simple parallels appears in the stories of Solomon's court in 1 Kings 2:13–46. This section of Solomon's reign is separated from its surrounding context by repetition in 1 Kings 2:12b ("and his rule was firmly established"), and 1 Kings 2:46b ("the kingdom was now firmly established in Solomon's hands"). Between these two verses, the writer described in four episodes how Solomon dealt with his principal political opponents (see figure 35).

Episode One [resolution]

Execution of Adonijah (2:13–25)

I. Adonijah Approaches Bathsheba (2:13a)
II. Adonijah and Bathsheba Converse (2:13b–18)
III. Bathsheba Approaches Solomon (2:19)
IV. Solomon and Bathsheba Converse (2:20–24)
V. Solomon has Adonijah Executed (2:25)

Episode Two [report]

Expulsion of Abiathar (2:26–27)

I. Solomon's Declaration (2:26)
II. Authorial Explanation (2:27)

Episode Three [resolution]

Execution of Joab (2:28–35)

I. Joab Flees to the Altar (2:28)
II. Execution Delayed (2:29–30)
III. Execution Accomplished (2:31–34)
IV. Benaiah Replaces Joab (2:35)
(Zadok Replaces Abiathar)

Episode Four [resolution]

Execution of Shimei (2:36–46)

I. Shimei under House Arrest (2:36–38)
II. Servants Leave and Shimei Follows (2:39–40)
III. Solomon Is Told of Violation (2:41)
IV. Solomon Interrogates Shimei (2:42–45)
V. Shimei Is Executed (2:46a)

Fig. 35: Confirming Parallels in 1 Kings 2:13–46a

These four episodes are alike in a number of ways. They all deal with Solomon's treatment of his opponents. Three of the four mention Benaiah as the one carrying out Solomon's decrees. But the parallels go further than this. In one way or another, each episode justifies Solomon's actions. No doubt Solomon seemed ruthless to many Israelites. From all appearances he simply destroyed anyone who got in his way. But each of these episodes explains why Solomon was justified in his actions. Adonijah was executed because he asked for David's concubine (1 Kings 2:22–25; see also 1 Kings 1:3).[13] Abiathar was rejected to fulfill a prophecy against the house of Eli (1 Kings 2:27). Joab was executed to rid the house of David of innocent blood (1 Kings 2:31–33). Shimei was put to death because he broke the generous terms of his house arrest (1 Kings 2:36–46).

These confirming parallels reveal that the primary focus of this text is not only to report what Solomon did but also to form an apologetic for his actions.[14] Solomon's own words highlight the central focus of this section. Three times Solomon himself declared that God had chosen and established his house (1 Kings 2:24, 33, 45). By reporting a series of similar events, the writer defended the manner in which Solomon overcame opponents and showed his support for the Davidic-Solomonic line.

Inclusions. An inclusion is formed by parallel episodes that frame, or set boundaries on a section.[15] Short or long intervening materials may appear between the parallels. Sometimes they exhibit detailed similarities; at other times there are only a few connections. Whatever the case, the parallels form the material into one unit.

National Glory (3:1–9:25)

Pharaoh's Daughter and Sacrifices (3:1–3)

Solomon's Wisdom (3:4–9:23)

Pharaoh's Daughter and Sacrifices (9:24–25)

International Glory (9:26–10:29)

International Trade (9:26–28)

Queen of Sheba (10:1–13)

International Trade (10:14–29)

Fig. 36: Inclusions in Solomon's Glorious Reign

In the book of Kings, two inclusions help organize the account of Solomon's reign. After reading about Solomon's rise to power, we come upon a long section focusing on Solomon's glorious kingdom (1 Kings 3:1—10:29). Inclusions divide this material into two major parts (see figure 36).

As the outline suggests, this portion of Solomon's reign breaks into two sections: his national and his international glory.[16] Both of these sections are marked by inclusions.

First, a brief narrative of report introduces Solomon's national glory (1 Kings 3:1–3). Solomon married Pharaoh's daughter and kept her in the city of David until he had finished the palace and temple (v. 1). Moreover, the people and Solomon sacrificed at the high places (vv. 2–3). This brief narrative introduces the account of Solomon's sacrifices at Gibeon (v. 4), but it also serves a much larger purpose.

Six chapters later a similar notice appears (9:24–25). After lengthy accounts of Solomon's administrative wisdom (3:16—4:28) and his great building projects (5:1—9:9), the writer of Kings returned to the matter of Pharaoh's daughter and sacrifices (9:24–25). At this point, however, he drew a contrasting parallel by reporting that Pharaoh's daughter now lived in the palace and that Solomon sacrificed three times a year at the temple in Jerusalem. Through this parallel to 1 Kings 3:1–3, the writer formed an inclusion around all the intervening material. In effect, he told his readers that his account of Solomon's domestic wisdom had come to an end.

Immediately following the closure of Solomon's national glory, the writer included three episodes: a narrative of report (9:26–28), resolution (10:1–13), and a second report (10:14–29). The first and last episodes form another inclusion. These narratives of report (9:26–28; 10:14–29) rehearse Solomon's accomplishments in international trade in glowing terms. Between these two episodes, the queen of Sheba visited Solomon (10:1–13). The inclusion reveals the purpose of this section: to concentrate on the effects of Solomon's wisdom in the international realm. Once again, by means of inclusion, the writer marked boundaries and characterized a section of his book.

Inclusions appear frequently in Old Testament narratives, and the ability to identify them is crucial for interpretation. As we read through long accounts, we can easily get lost among individual episodes. Inclusions help us find sections within these materials and understand their focus.

Chiastic parallels. Parallel episodes in Old Testament stories also appear in chiastic patterns. Chiasm is an arrangement of multiple inclusions (A B C//C'B'A'). Chiastic arrangements also occur in a concentric pattern when episodes parallel around a pivotal episode (A B C B'A').[17] The first episode parallels the last, the second parallels the next to last, and so on. These patterns appear on both small and large scales. Whatever the case, chiastic structures often limit the boundaries of a section and help us understand the writer's interest.

We have already noted that the last four chapters of Samuel contain six dischronologized episodes. If we look at these chapters once again, we can see that they form a chiasm (see figure 37).

Why this arrangement? As we have seen, this material demonstrated the value of the Davidic line for Israel.[18] Yet the parallels in this passage reveal several more specific topics. The first and last episodes are similar in a number of ways. God pours out His anger against Israel's sin (21:1 and 24:1), but the last verses indicate the most striking parallel between them: a reference to relief from God's anger through answered prayer (21:14 and 24:25). In this light both stories illustrated David's efficacious intervention in the face of God's wrath against Israel.

The second and fourth episodes parallel each other throughout in subject matter. Both recount David's military accomplishments. The second reports the outcomes of battles. The fifth deals with the accomplishments of David's military heroes.

Both the innermost episodes are reports of David's words. The psalm of praise ends with the confidence that David's family will be established forever by God (22:51). The oracle of David contains a series of rhetorical questions announcing that divine favor had been given him through an everlasting covenant (23:5). In both cases David expressed assurance of God's choice and protection.

By repeating themes in each parallel episode, the writer revealed his focus. Hope remains in the Davidic line despite troubles for three reasons: the sons of David intervene effectively (A, A'); they are victorious military leaders (B, B'); and they are protected and established by divine covenant (C, C').

Noticing this chiastic arrangement offers at least two benefits. First, the parallels establish boundaries for the section. How do we know that the last four chapters of Samuel should be separated from the rest of the book? One way is to recognize the extent to which they parallel each other. Second, chiastic structures help us discern the primary concerns of each section. Corresponding portions of a section confirm and/or contrast with their counterparts in ways that cause prominent dimensions of the text to stand out. For example, the story of David's census (24:1–25) may appear at first glance to emphasize David's failure.[19] But comparing this passage with its parallel in 2 Samuel 21:1–14 shows that David's positive role as mediator was most important to the writer. Similarly, David's two poetic speeches (22:1–51; 23:1-7) in this section have many facets that

A: Episode One
David Intervenes (21:1–14)

Royal intervention: "After that, God answered prayer in behalf of the land." (21:14)

B: Episode Two
Accomplishments in Battle (21:15–22)

Royal warfare

C: Episode Three
David's Praise (22:1–51)

Royal words: "He gives his king great victories; he shows unfailing kindness to his anointed, to David and his descendants forever." (22:51)

C': Episode Four
David's Wisdom (23:1–7)

Royal words: "Is not my house right with God? Has he not made with me an everlasting covenant, arranged and secured in every part? Will he not bring to fruition my salvation and grant me my every desire?" (23:5)

B': Episode Five
Accomplishments in Battle (23:8–39)

Royal warfare

A': Episode Six
David Intervenes (24:1–25)

Royal intervention: "Then the Lord answered prayer in behalf of the land, and the plague on Israel was stopped." (24:25)

Fig. 37: Chiasm in 2 Samuel 21:1–24:25

could be emphasized, but in comparing them, the focus on divine support for the Davidic line stands out most prominently.

Dramatic Accounts

Large sections of narrative also form unified dramatic accounts, which resemble individual stories in a number of ways.[20] First, large sections of material range between incomplete and full dramatic resolution, just as episodes vary between unresolved tension and full resolution. Second, as with single stories, the minimal requirement for resolution is two parts—a beginning and an end. Third, as individual narratives consist of different kinds of scenes, these large dramatic accounts may consist of different kinds of episodes. Some passages contain multiple narratives of resolution; others include narratives of unresolved tension and report. At times even sections of poetry are interspersed among the prose. Finally, as phases in individual narratives form two, three, four, or five dramatic steps, the episodes of large dramatic accounts constitute similar configurations.

By way of illustration, we will look at dramatic accounts that contain two, three, four, and five episodic steps.

Two episodic steps. Two adjacent episodes often form two episodic steps. The individual episodes stand on their own to some extent, but together they form a unified presentation. In these cases the first episode presents a problem, and the last conveys its resolution. For example, the account of Ishmael's birth in Genesis 16:1–16 contains two episodes (see figure 38).

The first episode presents a five-step narrative of resolution. Hagar begins in Sarai's company (I). Sarai and Abram agree to have her serve as a surrogate mother (II). Matters turn for the worse when Hagar conceives and ridicules Sarai (III). Sarai plans to expel Hagar from the family (IV). The problem of Hagar in Sarai's company is resolved as Hagar leaves to wander in the wilderness (V).

The second episode follows a three-step pattern. The resolution of the preceding episode leads to the problem of this passage. An angel finds Hagar in the wilderness (I). He assures her of protection and orders her to return to Sarai (II). The initial problem is resolved when Hagar returns to the clan and gives birth to Ishmael (III).

While these episodes maintain their individuality, they also work together in a dramatic pattern of problem and resolution. The first story leaves us with a problem: Hagar is with child, but Sarai has driven her

1. Problem

Hagar Conceives and Is Expelled (16:1–6)

I. Barren Sarai Has Hagar as Handmaiden (16:1)
II. Sarai and Abram Talk about Substitution (16:2)
III. Hagar Conceives and Ridicules Sarai (16:3–4)
IV. Sarai and Abram Talk about Ridicule (16:5–6a)
V. Sarai Expels Hagar (16:6b)
[Hagar conceives but goes away]

2. Resolution

Hagar Returns and Gives Birth (16:7–16)

I. Angel Finds Hagar in Wilderness (16:7)
II. Angel Assures and Commands Hagar to Return (16:8–14)
III. Hagar Gives Birth to Ishmael (16:15–16)
[Hagar is sent back and gives birth]

Fig. 38: Two Step Account in Genesis 16:1–16

away from the family. The second story resolves the problem; Hagar returns and gives birth in the presence of the family.

Three episodic steps. A dramatic account may also consist of three episodic steps. The first episode presents a problem, the second forms a turning point, and the third forms a resolution. The Old Testament contains many examples of this arrangement.

Genesis 15:1—17:27 forms a three-step dramatic account and deals with three principal subjects: covenant promises to Abram (15:1–21), Abram's failure with Hagar (16:1–16), and Abraham's covenant fidelity (17:1–27) (see figure 39).

In this passage the dramatic problem consists of Abram receiving divine assurance of a seed and land. Genesis 15:1–21 consists of two confirming parallel accounts. The first tells of God's assurance to Abram regarding the seed; the second reports the covenant ceremony that assured Abram of possessing the land.

The resolution of this dramatic problem occurs in Genesis 17:1–27. While Genesis 15:1–21 emphasizes the promissory side of the Abrahamic covenant, this chapter emphasizes the obligatory side.[21] God speaks once again about covenant and reward, but Abraham's obligation ("walk before me and be blameless") moves to the foreground as well. God reminds Abraham of what He will do for him,[22] but God then turns attention to the ways Abraham must keep covenant obligations.[23] The knife appears in this chapter as it did in Genesis 15:7–21, but Abraham, not God, must go

1. Problem
God's Covenant Promises (15:1–21)

Abram Assured of Seed (15:1–6)

I. God Promises Reward (15:1)
II. Abram Requests Confirmation of Seed (15:2–3)
III. God Confirms Seed Promise (15:4)
IV. God Assures by Pointing to Stars (15:5)
V. Abram Believes God's Promise (15:6)

Abram Assured of Land (15:7–21)

I. God Promises Land; Abram Requests Confirmation (15:7–9)
II. Covenant Ceremony is Prepared (15:10–11)
III. God Confirms Land Promise (15:12–16)
IV. God Demonstrates Reliability by Covenant Ritual (15:17)
V. God Swears Oath for Land (15:18–21)

2. Turning Point
Abram's Failure with Hagar (16:1–16)

Hagar Becomes Surrogate but is Expelled (16:1–6)

I. Barren Sarai has Hagar as Handmaiden (16:1)
II. Sarai and Abram Talk about Substitution (16:2)
III. Hagar Conceives and Ridicules Sarai (16:3–4)
IV. Sarai and Abram Talk about Ridicule (16:5–6a)
V. Sarai Expels Hagar (16:6b)

Hagar Returns and Gives Birth (16:7–16)

I. Angel Finds Hagar in Wilderness (16:7)
II. Angel Assures and Commands Hagar to Return (16:8–14)
III. Hagar Gives Birth to Ishmael (16:15–16)

3. Resolution
Abraham's Covenant Fidelity (17:1–27)

I. God Instructs Abraham on Covenant Requirements (17:1–21)
II. God Departs (17:22)
III. Abraham Fulfills Covenant Requirements (17:23–27)

Fig. 39: Three Step Account in Genesis 15:1–17:27

through the cutting ritual. Just as God had sworn an oath of self-malediction, so now Abraham is required to do the same. The passage then goes on to explain that the promise belonged to Isaac, not Ishmael (Genesis 17:15–21). After God leaves Abraham, the patriarch responds to divine instructions by circumcising himself and his family.

The beginning and end of this account balance each other in a number of ways. The opening mentions promises and covenant (Genesis

15:1–21); the closing also mentions promises and covenant (Genesis 17:1–27). But the first story deals primarily with the divine promises, and the last episode speaks primarily of Abraham's obligations. In the opening account, God obligates Himself through a cutting ritual; in the closing episode, Abraham and his household undergo the cutting ritual of circumcision.[24]

How does the account move from an emphasis on promise to an emphasis on obligation? The turning point bridges the gap. The middle portion (Genesis 16:1–16) consists of Sarai and Abram striving to fulfill the promise of a seed through Hagar. Surrogate motherhood of this sort was acceptable in the culture of that day.[25] But as the apostle Paul pointed out, Sarai and Abram had turned away from the promise and sought a child "according to the flesh" (Galatians 4:23, NASB).[26] The patriarch took God's promises as license for sin. He and Sarai became impatient and sought to secure the future for themselves. This turning point recollects the beginning and anticipates the end. Chapter 16 recalls the concern for the seed promised in chapter 15. Also, chapter 16 anticipates God's exhortation to obedience and Ishmael's role in chapter 17.

Four episodic steps. Four-episodic-step accounts also function in ways that resemble individual stories. The section begins with a problem made up of one or more episodes that anticipate the ending. The second batch of materials forms the rising action balanced by the third section of falling action. The fourth step resolves the initial problem.

We have already seen an example of a four-episodic-step dramatic account in the Chronicler's record of Asa's reign. As the following outline indicates, the king's reign breaks down into four parts (see figure 40).

This outline reveals a rather elaborate structure. Earlier in this chapter we saw that the Chronicler organized the reign of Asa into two main parts: the early period in which Asa sought God and was blessed (2 Chronicles 14:1—15:19), and the later period when the king failed to seek God and was cursed (2 Chronicles 16:1–14). But the configuration of this material is even more elaborate.

The account breaks down into four main steps.[27] The problem consists of two narratives of slight tension: an account of Asa's reforms and safety, and a record of his building projects and prosperity. This aspect of the account is balanced by the final step covering Asa's last years. Early on, Asa prospered as he sought God; in the end he failed to trust God and died.

1. Problem
Asa's Early Years of Prosperity (14:1–7)
I. Religious Reforms and Safety (14:2–5)
II. Building Projects and Prosperity (14:6–7)

2. Rising Action
Victory, Approval, and Obedience (14:8–15:19)
Victory in War with the Cushites (14:8–15)
I. Asa's Army (14:8)
II. Battle Lines Drawn (14:9–10)
III. Asa's Prayer (14:11)
IV. Cushites Routed (14:12–14)
V. Return to Jerusalem (14:15)
Prophetic Approval and Reforms (15:1–19)
I. Prophetic Approval (15:1–7)
II. Royal Reforms (15:8–19)

3. Falling Action
Failure, Disapproval, and Sin (16:1–11)
Failure in War with Israel (16:1–6)
I. Baasha's Fortifications (16:1)
II. Asa's Alliance with Ben-Hadad (16:2–3)
III. Baasha Flees Ben-Hadad (16:4–5)
IV. Asa Destroys Baasha's Fortifications (16:6)
Prophetic Condemnation and Sin (16:7–11)
I. Prophetic Disapproval (16:7–9)
II. Royal Sins (16:10–11)

4. Resolution
Asa's Last Years of Sickness and Death (16:12–14)
I. Asa's Illness (16:12a)
II. Asa's Failure (16:12b)
III. Asa's Death and Burial (16:13–14)

Fig. 40: Four Step Account in 2 Chronicles 14:1–16:14

The middle portion is easily organized into two steps: the rising action and the falling action. Both of these middle steps consists of a battle narrative (2 Chronicles 14:8–15; 16:1–6) followed by a prophetic encounter and royal response (2 Chronicles 15:1-19; 16:7–11). In the rising action, Asa sought God's help in battle, received prophetic approval, and obeyed. In the falling action, Asa sought the help of Ben-Hadad, received prophetic disapproval and disobeyed God. The two halves of the middle portion contrast with each other.

As we may expect, the middle portion both recollects the beginning and anticipates the end. The rising action recalls the blessings which Asa had received for his piety. The falling action adumbrates the troubles to come in his later years.

Five episodic steps. Although dramatic accounts in the Old Testament come in six and more steps, for the sake of convenience, we will limit ourselves to only five episodic steps. As with individual stories, these passages consist of a problem, rising action, turning point, falling action, and resolution.

An interesting example of this configuration may be found in the story of the garden of Eden (Genesis 2:4—3:24). Many commentaries are so dominated by traditional thematic concerns that they often ignore the overarching pattern.[28] Yet Moses portrayed these events in an intricate five-step structure (see figure 41).

As the outline suggests, these two chapters consist of five episodes.[29] Each episodic step consists of three-, four-, or five-step narratives of resolution. Some interconnections within the individual narratives themselves have been noted in the outline, but we will limit our comments to the relationships that form the individual stories into a unified account.

Thc first and last episodes reflect each other in many ways. Both focus on the relationship of humanity to the garden. In the first Adam is put into the garden to cultivate it. In the last he and Eve are expelled to cultivate the earth. Both episodes deal with trees. God forms the garden with trees for man; Adam and Eve are excluded from the garden and its tree of life.

The second and fourth episodes serve as rising and falling actions. The second episode intensifies the problem of Adam's service in the garden by introducing a partner to help him. Adam could not fulfill his task alone, so God created the woman to join him in the project. The two of them live harmoniously as one. The falling action anticipates the end of the story. As Adam and Eve are cursed, we are given glimpses of exclusion from paradise.

Beyond this the rising and falling actions also correspond with each other. As the rising action puts man and woman together in a common commission, the falling action of the fourth episode focuses on Eve's curse in childbearing and Adam's futility in working the land. Moreover, the unity of the man and woman is replaced by disharmony.

1. Problem

Adam in Garden Commissioned to Cultivate (2:4–17)

I. No Trees Because No Man to Cultivate (2:4–6)
II. Man Created and Garden with Trees Planted (2:7–14)
III. Man Commissioned to Cultivate (2:15–17)

2. Rising Action

God Improves Conditions for Commission (2:18–25)

I. Adam Needs Partner (2:18)
II. Animals Not Suitable Partners (2:19–20)
III. God Takes Adam's Rib (2:21)
IV. Partner Found in Eve (2:22–24)
V. Adam and Eve in Partnership (2:25)

3. Turning Point

Adam and Eve Violate Commission (3:1–7)

I. Eve Tempted to Violate for Knowledge (3:1–5)
II. Eve and Adam Violate Commission (3:6)
III. Adam and Eve Know Their Shame (3:7)

4. Falling Action

God Confronts Humanity with Violation (3:8–21)

I. God Approaches Shameful Adam and Eve (3:8)
II. God Questions about Violation (3:9–13)
III. God Curses for Violation (3:14–20)
IV. God Covers Shame of Adam and Eve (3:21)

5. Resolution

Adam and Eve Expelled from Garden (3:22–24)

I. God Fears Further Problems (3:22)
II. God Drives Humanity from Garden (3:23)
III. Angel Placed to Guard (3:24)

Fig. 41: Five Step Account in Genesis 2:4–3:24

The turning point of the account is the episode of violation, eating the forbidden fruit. This turning point recalls the original commission and anticipates the following episodes. Adam and Eve wanted their eyes to be opened to know good and evil, but ironically the first thing they see is their shame.

From these observations we may summarize the dramatic flow as follows: The garden is planted, and man is created to keep it; the man's situation is perfected with the creation of a partner; the man and woman violate their commission; the harmony of their partnership is cursed, and their task turns into severe hardship; and finally, the gardeners are expelled from the garden of God to cultivate the earth.

So it is that large sections of Old Testament narratives form dramatic accounts. As with single stories, these presentations may follow many different configurations. But in every case, as we recognize the structure, we are afforded insights into the purposes for which they were written.

Conclusion

In this chapter we have investigated a number of ways in which Old Testament writers structured large sections of narrative material. Although chronology was an important consideration, Old Testament writers also arranged their texts according to topics. These motivations formed large segments of narratives into clusters, parallels, and dramatic accounts. Investigating these large narrative structures is a vital aspect of Old Testament interpretation.

Review Questions

1. How do large sections of Old Testament texts display the influence of chronological and topical interests?
2. What is a cluster? Give an example.
3. What are parallel accounts? Distinguish simple parallel, inclusion, and chiasm. What is the importance of noting parallel accounts?
4. What are large-scale dramatic accounts? How are they similar to the dramatic flow of individual stories?

Study Exercises

1. Look again at Genesis 2:4—3:24. Examine the dramatic flow of each episode. What observations can you make that go beyond the discussion in this chapter?
2. Look at 1 Samuel 2:27—3:19. How would you analyze the structure of this large section of narrative material?

10

WRITERS AND THEIR AUDIENCES

One afternoon I walked down the hall leading to my office and found a note lying on the floor. "Thanks for your hard work in our class," it read. I looked for an address and signature, but there were none. I put the note on my desk and forgot all about it.

A few days later a student came up after class. Many times during the semester he had objected strongly to my lectures. Dread came over me as I anticipated another confrontation. To my delight, however, he asked, "Did you get my note thanking you for your class?"

"Did *you* write that note to *me?*" I replied in disbelief.

"Yes," he grinned. "I wanted you to know that my attitude has changed. I really appreciate what you are teaching."

You can imagine what I did when I got back to my office. I found the note and read it again, this time with much more interest. Once I knew who had written it and that he had written it specifically for me, the note meant much more than before.

Similarly, many dimensions of Old Testament narratives are so plain that we can understand and apply them to our lives with little idea of when they were written. But our understanding is greatly enriched when we learn about the writer and original audience.

Up to this point, we have focused primarily on intrinsic inquiry into Old Testament narratives. Nothing can substitute for careful examination of the inner workings of these texts. Now, however, we must turn to *extrinsic inquiry*—looking at a text in the light of its writer and audience. We are not concerned simply with the texts themselves; we are now more interested in the pragmatic dimensions of original meaning.

Why did Old Testament writers compose their stories as they did? What purposes did they have toward their readers?

Two preliminary issues come to the foreground as we embark on this aspect of investigation: *identifying writers and audiences* and *discerning a writer's intentions*. How can we discover the extrinsic agents of Old Testament stories? How may we uncover the purposes for which these texts were written?

Identifying Writers and Audiences

A friend of mine once called a neighbor to talk about a personal matter. She talked for about a minute, but suddenly realized she had dialed the wrong number. My friend was telling her secrets to a complete stranger! Terribly embarrassed, she slammed the receiver down. "I learned my lesson," she said. "I always ask who's on the other end of the line!"

As we interpret Old Testament narratives, we also need to find out who is on the other end of the line. With whom are we talking as we investigate these texts? We must do our best to find out who wrote these stories and who received them. We will examine some *problems with identification* and some *clues for identification*.

Problems with Identification

Many students are shocked when they discover how difficult it is to identify the writers and audiences of Old Testament narratives. Most of us enter this subject expecting the Old Testament to be like the New Testament. We are accustomed to thinking of Paul's letters to the Romans, Galatians, or Ephesians. But the relative certainty we have in much of the New Testament highlights uncertainties we face with many Old Testament books.

Evangelicals affirm a crucial guiding principle: belief in the *reliability of the Biblical witness*.[1] This stance goes hand in hand with a commitment to Biblical inerrancy. Because Scripture does not misrepresent the facts, it correctly identifies authors and audiences.[2] When a New Testament epistle states that it was written by Paul (for example, Romans 1:1; 1 Corinthians 1:1), it is true. When Jesus referred to Psalm 110:1 as "David speaking by the Spirit" (Matthew 22:43–44), His words form a trustworthy witness to the authorship of the psalm. In a word evangelicals accept every claim to literary origins made by Scripture. As *The Chicago Statement on Biblical Inerrancy* puts it: "Being wholly and verbally God-given, Scripture is without error or fault in all its teaching, no less in what it states about God's acts in creation, about the events of world history, and about its own literary origins under God, than in its witness to God's saving grace in individual lives."[3]

As we work to identify authors and audiences of Old Testament narratives, we will follow the Bible's own testimony.

Trusting the Biblical witness does not solve all our problems, however. At least three obstacles still complicate matters. As we look for the extrinsic agents of Old Testament stories, we must also deal with *developments of the texts, transmission of the texts,* and *lack of information in the texts.*

Developments of the texts. One difficulty we face is that most Old Testament narrative books were not written all at once; some developed over years, decades, even centuries before reaching their final form. Critical approaches toward the Old Testament have focused primarily on compositional history,[4] taking into account developments over a period of time. But most of these analyses remain speculative and unreliable.[5] Many methods used in these endeavors are incompatible with evangelical perspectives on Biblical authority.[6] We must exercise extreme caution as we consider diachronic reconstructions offered by critical interpreters.

On the other hand, many evangelicals minimize the value of diachronic analysis. "We take the text as we have it today," they often say. "We are not interested in how Old Testament narratives developed." As attractive as this viewpoint may appear, several considerations make it imperative that we take note of the developments behind Old Testament narratives.

To begin with, Old Testament writers often acknowledged that they used sources (for example, 1 Chronicles 9:1; 1 Kings 14:19). It is apparent from duplicate accounts that complicated historical developments lie behind many texts (compare 2 Kings 18:13–37 with Isaiah 36:1-22, and 2 Chronicles 36:22–23 with Ezra 1:1–4).[7] Collecting, copying, and editing written and oral sources was one dimension of the organic process of inspiration.[8] From the Chronicler's use of Samuel and Kings, we can see that Old Testament writers followed their sources closely at times, but freely reworked them at other times.[9] These explicit features of Old Testament texts require us to acknowledge that many Old Testament narratives had extensive compositional developments.

Investigating compositional history also helps us understand many literary features of Old Testament books. These texts sometimes seem disjointed and uneven because of diachronic developments. For example, the stories of Elijah and Elisha (1 Kings 17:1—2 Kings 8:15) exhibit a measure of stylistic difference from other portions of the book of Kings.[10] The stories of Joseph (Genesis 37:2—50:26) exhibit a literary unity that other portions of Genesis do not share.[11] Often these kinds of literary features can be explained in terms of diachronic developments.

The compositional history of Old Testament narratives also complicates our attempt to identify the writer and audience. Occasionally Old Testament writers incorporated sources into their books without completely adjusting the source materials to their own circumstances. Geographical, political, and stylistic features often betray an earlier source. If we overlook these features, we easily confuse the date of a source with the date of final composition.

One striking example appears in 1 Kings 8:8. This passage states that the poles used to carry the ark of the covenant "were so long that their ends could be seen from the Holy Place in front of the inner sanctuary, but not from outside the Holy Place; *and they are still there today*" (emphasis added).

Apart from compositional history, this passage could lead us to conclude that the book of Kings was written before the destruction of the temple. The text affirms that the poles used to carry the ark are "still there today" (1 Kings 8:8), but the rest of the book of Kings demonstrates that this dating is not possible. The final chapters of the book cover historical events well beyond the destruction of the temple. How, then, do we explain "still there today" in 1 Kings 8:8? Apparently the final compiler of Kings followed an earlier source and let the temporal reference stand as he received it. "Today" referred to the time of the source, not to the days of the writer.[12] If we fail to notice this diachronic dimension of the text, we will be misled as we try to establish the identities of the writer and audience of Kings.

Transmission of the texts. In addition to our consideration of a text's compositional history, we must be alert to editorial activity in transmission after final composition. Minor editorial adjustments have entered many Old Testament narratives.[13] The majority of these modifications can be identified through textual criticism.[14] Glosses, expansions, omissions, and the like appeared as Old Testament narratives were passed from generation to generation. In most cases, however, the earlier reading of the text can be reconstructed through traditional text-critical methods.

Moreover, evangelicals have occasionally identified editorial changes in a passage for which there is little or no textual evidence. These editorial activities usually involved updating language, geographical names, lists, and similar details.[15] Identifying these changes in a text can also be crucial for determining the extrinsic agents of a book. Later additions can give a false impression of late composition.

For instance, in Genesis 14:14 we read that Abram chased his enemies "as far as Dan." From Judges 18:29 we know that this site was called Laish in the days of Moses. Its name was changed only after the tribe of Dan left its original territory and moved north (Judges 18:1–31). How can we reconcile the reference to "Dan" in Genesis 14:14 with Mosaic authorship of Genesis? Most evangelicals treat the reference as a later editorial adjustment.[16]

In 1 Chronicles 3:1–24 the royal genealogy extends two to five generations beyond Zerubbabel. If the original form of the book contained this complete list, the final composition of Chronicles could have taken place no earlier than c.478 B.C.[17] Yet, the style of the last portion of the genealogy calls into question the originality of 1 Chronicles 3:21b-24. As Keil put it, "the list from . . . v. 21b, to the end of the chapter, is a genealogical fragment, which has perhaps come into the text of the Chronicler at a later time."[18] When we identify the date of the Chronicler, we must acknowledge that this genealogy may have been extended beyond its original form. This raises the possibility that Chronicles was written earlier than the genealogy would suggest.[19]

In much the same way, E.J. Young notes that Jaddua (351–331 B.C.), high priest during the time of Alexander the Great, appears in Nehemiah 12:1–22. He then suggests that this "list of priests and Levites . . . may have been a later addition."[20] This observation greatly affects the date we assign to the author and audience of Nehemiah.

We must always exercise caution when identifying editorial activity, especially when there is no textual evidence to support theories. The burden of proof lies on those who propose that a passage has been reworked or expanded. Yet we must not fail to acknowledge the possibility of such changes as we try to identify the writer and audience.

Lack of information. Once we have isolated sources and later editorial activity in Old Testament stories, we are left with the level of final composition. This material is the locus of original meaning. But all our problems are not resolved. We still face a lack of information. Old Testament stories explicitly identify only a few writers and audiences. All Old Testament narrative books remain anonymous, except the books of Moses.

Traditional viewpoints on extrinsic agents have grown around each book.[21] Some of these designations are possible, even likely. But most have little merit and tend to overlook contrary evidence in the books themselves.[22]

So it is that many problems confront us as we try to identify Old Testament writers and audiences. The use of sources and the presence of editorial activity complicate matters. Beyond this the lack of explicit designations in the texts themselves also present us with problems that must be overcome. These difficulties raise an important question. What can we hope to know about the writers and audiences of Old Testament narratives? How much should we expect to discover?

Clues for Indentification

Since we have little explicit information available, we must establish a range of possible extrinsic agents based on an assortment of clues. By looking carefully at the evidence, we find a number of indications of the likely times and circumstances of the original writer and audience. What are these clues and how do they help us establish the earliest and latest dates for extrinsic agents?

Earliest likely date. Three main considerations help establish the earliest likely date of final composition: the *latest events of a book, anachronisms,* and *authorial comments*.[23]

First, the final form of an Old Testament book cannot have been written earlier than the *latest events* mentioned within it. For the most part, Old Testament narratives report events that have already occurred. This consideration helps us establish the earliest possible date for many books.

For instance, the last event in the book of Kings is the release of Jehoiachin (2 Kings 25:27–30). The book as a whole must have been written after this event. From the Chronicler's closing verses (2 Chronicles 36:22–23), we can see that Chronicles reached its final form no earlier than the Cyrus Edict in 538 B.C. In every Old Testament narrative book, the latest historical event mentioned gives an initial orientation toward the earliest possible date of final composition.

While this factor deserves careful consideration, it does not settle the question for every book. Some Old Testament books were composed long after the events they reported. We know, for instance, that Moses wrote Genesis at least four hundred years after the last event in that book. As we will see, similar circumstances seem likely for other books as well.

Until recently, evangelicals have tried to place writers and audiences as close as possible to the events of a book. This perspective rose from the belief that temporal proximity made historical accuracy more likely.

But this assumption seems less than adequate. Historical distance often permits a writer to see the facts of history more accurately. Moreover, temporal proximity is not the basis of historical reliability in Old Testament narratives; they are historically inerrant because the Holy Spirit of Truth inspired them. Historical distance was no problem for Him. Years, decades, or centuries may have transpired between the events and the stories that report them without compromising historical reliability.

Second, Old Testament writers give us clues to their times through *anachronisms*—placing an expression or concept from their own day into the earlier setting of the story. Anachronistic descriptions of the characters, places, or events reveal the times of the writer.

For instance, in 1 Chronicles 29:7 the heads of the tribes are reported to have contributed "ten thousand darics (*'drknym)* of gold" to the temple construction. This reference to "darics," or "drachmas" as the case may be, is clearly anachronistic,[24] since neither darics nor drachmas existed in David's day. This term must then reflect the currency used in the Chronicler's own day. If we accept this term as original to the book, it forms an important clue for dating of the final composition of Chronicles. The Chronicler wrote after the currency had begun to be used.[25]

Anachronisms often indicate the earliest date of an Old Testament narrative. Taken together with other clues, they help to limit the possibilities.

Third, *authorial comments* sometimes suggest the earliest possible date. Writers reveal their times by their explanations and observations. For example, before the ritual in which Boaz received a sandal from Naomi's nearest kin (Ruth 4:8), the author supplies a parenthetical explanation:[26] "Now in earlier times in Israel, for the redemption and transfer of property to become final, one party took off his sandal and gave it to the other. This was the method of legalizing transactions in Israel" (Ruth 4:7). Apparently, by the time of final composition, this custom had been forgotten. So the writer explained why the practice occurred "in earlier times." A significant amount of time had passed between the events of the book and its final composition. This understanding is confirmed by the genealogy at the end of the book, which goes well beyond the days of Ruth (Ruth 4:18–22).

Latest reasonable date. Old Testament texts also present clues that help us establish the latest reasonable date for final composition. This limit on extrinsic agents is more difficult to determine, but at least three hints are available: *external references, absence of important events,* and the *ideology of the book.*

First, in some cases we may appeal to the *earliest reference* to the book in other material. Many times Old Testament books refer to each other, permitting us to draw some limits on the range of extrinsic agents. We assume, for instance, that Samuel and Kings were written before Chronicles, because the Chronicler used them extensively. We may be assured that Deuteronomy was written before the days of Nehemiah because he referred to it (Nehemiah 1:8–9). This criterion helps at times, but we must remember that a quotation may reflect a common source or a reference to a book before it reached its final form. The evidence of an external reference must always be used in conjunction with other clues.

Second, the *absence of important events* in Israel's history also provides clues for the latest likely date of final composition. When an event had major significance for the nation of Israel and the writer did not include it in his history, its omission may indicate that the event had not yet occurred.

It is highly probable, for instance, that the writer of Kings wrote before the Cyrus Edict, because he did not include this crucial event in his history. The abrupt ending of the book also suggests that Cyrus had not yet issued the edict.[27] In much the same way, the genealogy of Ruth stops with David (Ruth 4:18–22). It does not go on to Solomon, Rehoboam, and the other descendants of David. It would appear, therefore, that the book was composed during David's lifetime.[28]

Nevertheless, this guideline must also be used with caution. Old Testament writers were under no obligation to record everything that occurred up to their day. A writer may have omitted events for any number of reasons.

Third, often the best way to establish the latest date of final composition is to examine the *ideology* of the book.[29] With broad parameters in place we may ask several helpful questions. What is the theological focus of the book? What setting in Israel's history seems best suited for its message? As we better understand the prominent issues of a book, we are more able to suggest a likely time for its composition.

Some interpreters have argued, for instance, that the book of Chronicles focuses on kingship and temple with a programmatic emphasis.[30] It provides detailed models for the role of king as a supporter of Israel's worship. To the degree that this evaluation is correct, it provides evidence for dating the Chronicler before the disappearance of Zerubbabel, while the conjunction of king and temple was still an imminent possibility for the post-exilic community.

In a similar way, the book of Judges supports the need for a king by pointing to the failures of judges and Levites.[31] Needless to say, this argument worked best before the failures of monarchs became so evident to Israel. This consideration raises the possibility that the book was written before the troubles in David's house had become pronounced.

Ideological clues are not indisputable. Texts can speak to a variety of settings. Moreover, our assessment of a book's message depends to a great extent on the extrinsic setting we presume for that book. Yet, taken together with other hints, these clues help us establish some parameters for the date of final composition.

For many Old Testament books, we must be satisfied with little certainty on the latest date of final composition. In most cases, however, we can identify some reasonable limits based on clues in the text (see figure 42).

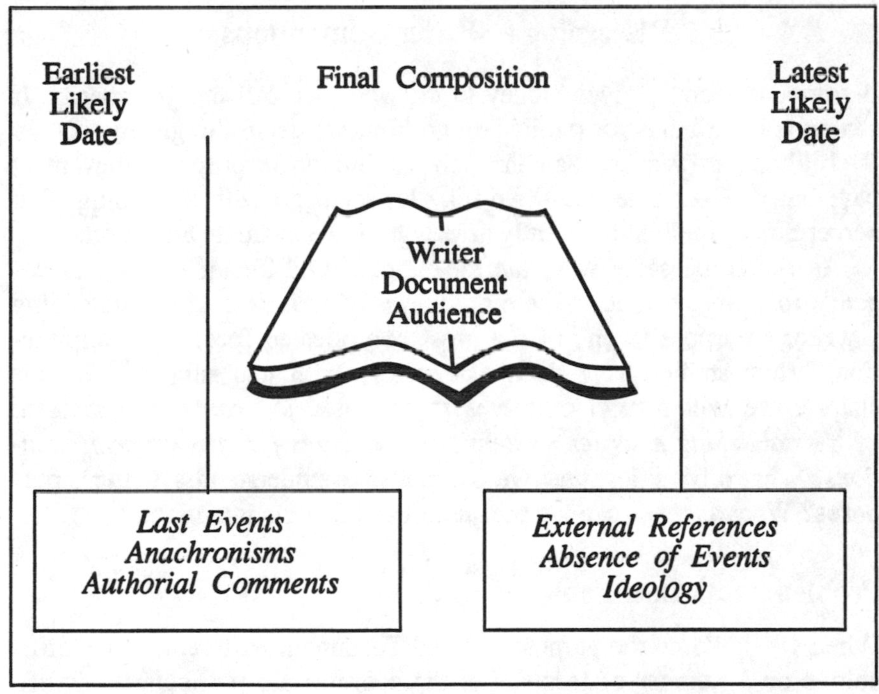

Fig. 42: Establishing a Range of Extrinsic Agents

Establishing a range of extrinsic agents in this way offers at least two advantages. First, a range of possibilities keeps us mindful of what we actually know about a book's author and audience. The Holy Spirit has withheld knowledge of precisely who wrote most Old Testament narratives. We can arrive at general orientations on the basis of clues He has given us, but in many cases the Spirit apparently did not want us to have specific knowledge of the author and audience. We must humbly accept what He has given us.

Second, operating with expanded extrinsic perspectives keeps us from limiting the meaning of a text to a narrow hypothesis. If we tie our interpretations too closely to one set of extrinsic agents, we risk obscuring aspects of the meaning.

Identifying writers and audiences is a vital dimension of interpreting Old Testament narratives. We run into problems of developments, transmission, and paucity of information. Yet, by exploring available clues, we can determine the earliest and latest likely dates of a book's final composition. Investigating Old Testament narratives within this range helps us to understand their original meaning more fully.

Discerning a Writer's Intentions

If someone secretly gives money to the poor, we call the gift charity. If someone contributes for public recognition, we deem the gift hypocrisy. If children throw a baseball through a window on purpose, they must pay; but if it is an accident, we may let them go with a warning. Our perception of motivation greatly affects how we evaluate an action.

In much the same way, the meaning of Old Testament stories depends to a large extent on the motivations of writers. But understanding a writer's purpose is one of the most complicated facets of interpretation. Many studies have dealt extensively with this subject.[32] In this chapter we will restrict ourselves to two issues: *problems associated with establishing a writer's intentions* and *clues for the writer's intentions*. What difficulties must we overcome to understand a writer's purposes? What avenues can we pursue to establish his intentions?

Problems with Intentions

When we look into the purposes of Old Testament writers, we face difficulties on a number of fronts. But three issues are particularly significant: the *complexity* of their intentions, the *historical distance* between us, and the *subtle style* of Old Testament writers.

Complexity. The difficulty of understanding a writer's purpose becomes evident when we consider the complexity of intentions. Contrary to the way we often treat them, Old Testament authors did not simply think about one or two ideas as they wrote. They had many aims on a variety of levels.[33]

On a basic level, Old Testament writers focused on the mechanics of composition. They selected certain letters, words, phrases, and sentences. They intentionally used characterizations, scene depictions, and structural arrangements. These and other fundamental writing strategies were part of the writers' intentions.

In our study, however, we are primarily concerned with Old Testament writers' ideological intentions—the set of beliefs they wanted their readers to accept.[34] But even within these limits, we run into complexities.

First, Old Testament writers operated with a hierarchy of ideological goals, placing more importance on some concerns than on others. For instance, in the account of Abram's migration to the promised land (Genesis 12:1–9), Moses was more concerned with God's call than with the fact that "Lot went with him" and that "Abram was seventy-five years old." The mention of Lot prepares us for episodes to follow; Abram's age adds a vivid detail. But we sense a greater emphasis on God's call and Abram's faithful response. As we assess an author's intentions, we must look for the relative importance of elements in his message.[35]

Second, each part of a text has a unique contribution to make to the overall ideological purpose. Writers constructed scenes, episodes, larger sections, and whole books to accomplish their ends in a cumulative fashion. As a result we must look for the objectives behind smaller and larger units. Sadly, interpreters often ignore one side or the other. Sometimes we identify the purpose of a small portion and ignore the larger context. At other times we grasp the big picture and ignore the intentions behind smaller units.

For example, interpreters commonly focus exclusively on Deborah's exemplary behavior (Judges 4:1—5:31). But what did the writer intend? Did he want his readers to believe that Deborah was exemplary or that the office of judge failed? He meant both. In his view Deborah was flawless. But even the greatest judges could not give Israel sufficient leadership. Both motifs were vital to the writer's purpose.

Third, Old Testament writers often intended to address diverse segments of their audience.[36] The original audiences of Old Testament books consisted of many kinds of people: young and old, rich and poor, men and women, nobility and commoners, believers and unbelievers, Israelites and sojourners, to name just a few. As a result the writers' intentions were often multifaceted. In seeking to address the strengths, weaknesses, interests, and responsibilities of people within the audience, they had to concern themselves with many different issues.

For instance, the writer of Kings commented that Solomon "replaced Abiathar with Zadok the priest" (1 Kings 2:35). Diversity within his audience caused him to have at least three ideological intentions: his words encouraged the Zadokites, warned other priestly families against usurping the place of the Zadokites, and instructed worshipers to accept only Zadokites as legitimate high priests.

Every Old Testament writer had to deal with some degree of diversity. Various segments of the audience moved to the foreground of their concerns from time to time. In some instances a multiplicity of needs were addressed at once.

Fourth, in the light of these sorts of complexities, we must assume that Old Testament writers had varying degrees of psychological awareness of their purposes. As Polletta observes:

> All artful writing is some sum or product of what Coleridge called "spontaneous impulse and voluntary purpose," but the precise quantities of the combination, and even the distinctive make-up of each faculty, will vary almost without limit from writer to writer. . . . Behind any voluntary purpose may be the force of the author's whole mental outlook, his vision, his way of perceiving and ordering experience and reality; voluntary purpose may be an impulse from those parts of the mind which, to use Freud's own definition of "unconscious," are "outside of awareness."[37]

Some motivations of Old Testament writers were at the forefront of their minds. But many aspects of what they were doing remained at best in the back of their minds. In this sense Old Testament writers often said more than they realized.[38]

A simple illustration will make this clearer. Consider the sentence "I am thinking of you." Was I conscious of the full range of intentions that went into writing this sentence? Of course not. As I wrote I had a rather vague notion of thinking about you. But I was entirely unconscious of moving my fingers, spelling the words correctly, and using a particular syntactical structure. These choices came to me without conscious reflection. Moreover, I was not thinking of who you are, what I have written to you, what I will write, and countless other aspects of the meaning of my sentence. These and other determinations come to my awareness only as I look back on the sentence. Upon reflection I can see many more things than I did as I wrote.

Similarly, as Old Testament writers composed their stories, they too were unaware of much they accomplished. When we remember that these authors were inspired by the Holy Spirit, we see even more clearly that their understanding was limited. We must always "take into account the intention of the divine author, as well as the intention of the human author."[39] Many elements of texts went beyond what Old Testament writers consciously thought as they wrote. Was Moses fully conscious of the complex configuration we proposed for Genesis 2:4–3:24 as he composed the story?[40] We cannot know for certain, but it seems unlikely. The interconnections in this text are so intricate that they probably were not fully planned by Moses. His conscious understanding of the text was not exhaustive. His writing experience was more like the experience of musicians as they play instruments. Some elements were studied choices, but many were not as deliberate. Moses said more than he was able to keep in the forefront of his mind.

We can never be absolutely certain how much Old Testament writers understood their texts, so we must not limit ourselves to their conscious intentions. We must also explore matters of which writers may not have been fully aware.

Historical distance. Another major problem we face is the historical distance between us and Old Testament authors. Whenever we attempt to assess their motivations, we run into numerous historical barriers.

First, as we have seen, we do not know precisely who wrote most of the books. For books like Joshua, Judges, and Samuel, the range of possible extrinsic agents extends over more than a century.[41] It is difficult to reconstruct a writer's intentions when we can only get within several hundred years of his actual date.

Second, a chasm of more than two thousand years of cultural differences stands between us. For the most part, we are unfamiliar with the backgrounds and circumstances of Old Testament writers. How much do we know about Moses' education in Egypt? How familiar are we with the political environment of the Chronicler's post-exilic situation? We have a difficult time reconstructing the writer's purposes because we are unfamiliar with the life styles, standards, and expectations they shared with their audiences. Careful research into a writer's culture can eliminate some historical barriers. But for every wall research topples, a thousand others still stand strong. We are not assessing the motivations of our next door neighbors; we are reconstructing over millennia.

Subtle style. The third major difficulty we face is the subtle style of Old Testament writers. For the most part, they did not state their ideological goals explicitly.[42] Moses did not write down why he composed Exodus; the writer of Esther did not state his purpose. Generally, we are left to infer writers' motivations. We study their texts and determine the intentions that best explain the form and content of their stories. The subtle style of Old Testament writers also makes assessing their purposes difficult.

As we explore the aims of an Old Testament writer, we must keep in mind the many problems we face. The complexities of intentions, historical distance, and subtle style make this a difficult task. These challenges should make us careful and humble as we interpret (see figure 43).

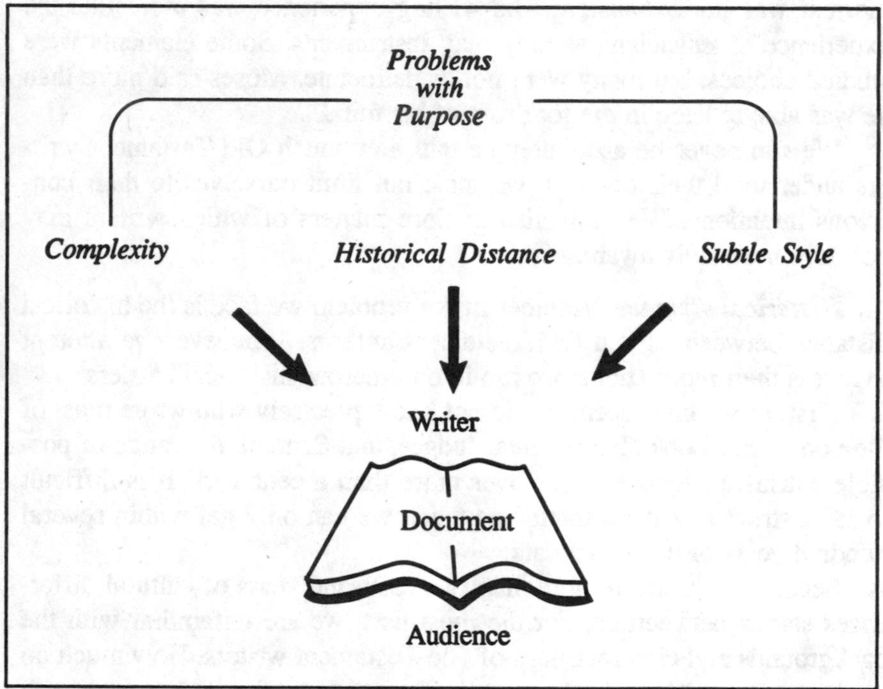

Fig. 43: Problems with Discerning Intentions

Clues for Intentions

Detectives delight in putting together bits of evidence to solve a mystery. If you like sleuthing, you'll love exploring the intentions of Old Testament writers and collecting the widely scattered clues. A number of hints help us discern a writer's ideological point of view. We can look for them *in the text* and *in the writer's circumstances*.

In the text. In the preceding chapters, we looked at a number of *clues in the text* that help discern a writer's purpose. Let's review them briefly and then look more closely at several special techniques found in Old Testament stories.

First, characterization opens the writer's purpose to us.[43] Old Testament writers wanted their audiences to approve, disapprove, and have mixed reactions to their characters. As we take note of the presentations of characters in stories, we uncover the ideological intentions of the writer.

Second, scene depiction also reveals aspects of the writer's ideology.[44] Variations in narrative mode highlight certain scenes. Authorial comments also make his viewpoint evident. Detailed imagery raises issues important to the writer. Shifts in temporal and spatial variables draw attention to the scenes that are more crucial to the writer's perspective.

Third, structures help us discover the writer's purposes.[45] The rise and fall of dramatic tension gives a sense of problem and resolution. Confirming and contrasting parallels, inclusions, and chiastic arrangements juxtapose scenes, episodes, and sections. In these structures Old Testament writers revealed their ideological aims.

Fourth, Old Testament writers employed many special techniques to disclose their point of view. We have mentioned some of these features in passing, but it will help to describe them now in more detail. This list represents only a sampling of the more important features of stories that reveal ideological intentions.

Repetition

Perhaps the most common technique Old Testament writers employed was *repetition.*[46] At times it may be inadvertent or focused on a minor theme. But similar motifs appearing several times in a passage usually indicate that these concerns were prominent in the author's outlook.

For example, in 1 Chronicles 10:1–14 we have two episodes of resolution followed by an explanatory report. Repetitions show us the Chronicler's prominent ideological motivation in this passage (see figure 44).

What was the Chronicler's chief concern? In each episode he mentioned the motif of death. In the first episode (vv. 1–7), the Chronicler repeated the theme of death several times: Saul's sons died (v. 2); Saul asked to be killed (v. 4); Saul killed himself (v. 4); and the armor-bearer killed himself (v. 5). Then the entire affair is summed up: "Saul and his three sons died" (v. 6). The second episode deals with Saul's burial. His body found rest but only after severe defilement. In the third episode, the Chronicler commented on the reason for this disgraceful death. Saul died because "he was unfaithful to the Lord" (v. 13).

Saul and Sons Die (10:1–7)

I. Philistines Battle Israel (10:1)
II. Saul and Sons Die (10:2–6)
III. Philistines Occupy Cities (10:7)

Bodies Defiled and Retrieved (10:8–12)

I. Philistines Defile Bodies (10:8–10)
II. Gileadites Retrieve Bodies (10:11–12)

Kingdom Given to David (10:13–14)

I. Saul's Death Explained (10:13–14a)
II. Transfer to David (10:14b)

Fig. 44: Outline of 1 Chronicles 10:1–14

How do these repetitions help us understand the Chronicler's purpose? They demonstrate that he was not primarily concerned with warfare, nor with the trouble the Philistines caused Israel. These were relatively minor aspects of his story. Rather, he was primarily interested in the death of Saul and his sons.

The repetition of the death motif gives a clue that the Chronicler wanted his readers to focus on the significance of Saul's disgraceful death. Accordingly, he concluded, "*So the Lord put him to death* and turned the kingdom over to David son of Jesse" (v. 14b, emphasis added). The Chronicler intended to teach how Saul's ignominious death demonstrated God's utter rejection of Saul and the exaltation of David's line.[47]

Allusion

Allusion may be defined as a reference in one passage to another.[48] This technique is similar to repetition but usually involves separate episodes that have few other connections. As we spot allusions, we discover important dimensions of the writer's intentions.

For example, in the story of the Levite and his concubine (Judges 19:1–30) we find a scene that reminds us of another well-known story:

> While they were enjoying themselves, some of the wicked men of the city surrounded the house. Pounding on the door, they shouted to the old man who owned the house, "Bring out the man who came to your house so we can have sex with him." The owner of the house went outside and said to them, "No, my friends, don't be so vile. Since this man is my guest, don't do this disgraceful thing. Look, here is my

> virgin daughter, and his concubine. I will bring them out to you now" (Judges 19:22–24).

This horrifying scene alludes to a similar event in the story of Sodom and Gomorrah:

> Before they had gone to bed, all the men from every part of the city of Sodom—both young and old—surrounded the house. They called to Lot, "Where are the men who came to you tonight? Bring them out to us so that we can have sex with them." Lot went outside to meet them and shut the door behind him and said, "No, my friends. Don't do this wicked thing. Look, I have two daughters who have never slept with a man. Let me bring them out to you, and you can do what you like with them. But don't do anything to these men, for they have come under the protection of my roof" (Genesis 19:4–8).

The similarities are striking; in both scenes wicked men stand outside and call for a male guest, but the host offers females in his place. Even the language is similar at points: "No, my friends, don't be so vile" (Judges 19:23); "No, my friends. Don't do this wicked thing" (Genesis 19:7).

Why did the writer of Judges allude to Sodom and Gomorrah in this scene? In effect, he did so to demonstrate that Israel had become as corrupt as the notorious cities of Abraham's day, utterly wicked and deserving the judgment of God (Judges 19:30). Through this allusion he supported his overarching viewpoint that Israel needed a king. Without a king God's people were no better than the citizens of Sodom and Gomorrah.

Dramatic Irony

The term "irony" has many different uses.[49] We may speak of verbal irony, in which "the implicit meaning intended by the speaker differs from that which he ostensibly asserts."[50] A writer or character in his story says just the opposite of what he or she means. Another form of irony is litotes, or understatement. Writers often use this device to create within their audience the sense that "a thing means more than it says."[51]

At this point, however, we are more interested in *dramatic irony,* a situation in which "the audience shares with the author knowledge of which a character is ignorant."[52] This technique was an effective way in which Old Testament writers disclosed their ideological outlooks. Dramatic irony occurs both explicitly and implicitly. At times Old Testament writers clearly stated information that gave the audience insights beyond characters. In this way the writer created tension in the audience as they wrestled with the characters' ignorance.

Explicit irony. Explicit irony is at the heart of the book of Job. In the opening chapters, the readers learn of a heavenly contest between God and Satan (Job 1:1–12). Job and his friends, however, are kept ignorant of these events. Throughout the dialogues of the book, Job wants to learn why he suffers, but no heavenly access is granted. In fact, God rebukes Job (Job 38—41), telling him he has no right to such knowledge.

As the original audience read the friends' simplistic solutions and Job's struggle for wisdom, they possessed knowledge hidden from the characters. Their knowledge alerted them to the plight of the one who suffered and the difficulties of those who tried to help in ignorance. This explicit dramatic irony forms a vital dimension of understanding the author's ideological intentions.

Implicit irony. Old Testament writers also presented their outlooks through implicit dramatic irony. Most Old Testament stories were not entirely new to their original audiences. Some readers had experienced the events themselves and knew other pertinent information. Beyond this, the original audience had the opportunity to hear a story more than once. When they returned to the text a second or third time, they did so with an awareness of outcomes that the characters did not possess.[53] By these means, dramatic irony occurred even when the writer did not specifically offer special information to the reader.

For example, in the division of land between Abram and Lot (Genesis 13:1–18), Lot chose the land that was "like the garden of the Lord," settling near Sodom and Gomorrah. After mentioning the cities, however, Moses commented, "Now the men of Sodom were wicked and were sinning greatly against the Lord" (v. 13). This brief comment says nothing explicitly of events to follow, but to an audience that knew of the destruction of Sodom and Gomorrah, it posed poignant dramatic irony. Lot thought he was going to a land of prosperity, but the audience knew he was moving to a place of judgment. Relying on this knowledge, Moses disclosed his own viewpoint. Far from losing the blessing of the good land to Lot, Abraham was now on his way to becoming the one to intercede for Lot (Genesis 18:22–33).

Direct Discourse

The importance of *direct discourse* in Old Testament narratives has been noted by many interpreters in recent years.[54] As we have seen, speech functioned significantly in characterization, scene depiction, and structure.[55] Beyond this, however, direct discourse is one of the clearest ways Old Testament writers presented their own ideological point of view.

When we examine the direct speech of human characters, we must exercise caution. As we have seen, Old Testament writers often presented the frailties of their characters, giving their faulty or false evaluations of an event.[56] For instance, when Michal rebuked David for dancing before the ark, she said, "How the king of Israel has distinguished himself today, disrobing in the sight of the slave girls of his servants as any vulgar fellow would!" (2 Samuel 6:20).

Even so, characters frequently reflect the writer's own ideological point of view. David responded, "It was before the Lord, who chose me rather than your father or anyone from his house when he appointed me ruler over the Lord's people Israel—I will celebrate before the Lord" (2 Samuel 6:21). Undoubtedly, David spoke for the writer. The audience was to evaluate the event as David had.

We could mention countless other techniques for discovering clues into the writer's ideological viewpoints. But with these aspects of the text in mind, interpreters can make strides toward understanding why Old Testament stories were written.

The writer's circumstances. In addition to clues within the text, an author's ideological intentions become clearer as we pay attention to the writer's circumstances—the historical context in which a passage was written. The text by itself limits the possibilities, but to determine more precisely what a text meant, we must know something about the surrounding circumstances.[57]

For the sake of convenience, we will speak of only two major factors in the writer's historical situation: *divine interventions* and the *writer's culture*.

First, Old Testament writers were deeply influenced by *divine interventions* in their day. They composed their accounts to give original readers perspectives on what God was doing in their times. Ostensibly, they wrote about ancient events, but their accounts were also designed to explain acts of God in the audience's contemporary world.[58] To understand a writer's ideological intentions, we must consider how God had intruded into the course of history in the writer's day.

For example, let us assume that the book of Genesis was written late in the exodus from Egypt.[59] What was God doing at that time? He had brought the Israelites out of slavery, caused them to wander in the wilderness, and had placed the second generation on the verge of Canaan.

In this light we can see how a passage like Abram's deliverance from Egypt (Genesis 12:10–20) spoke to the original audience.[60] Moses wrote this story to mirror the audience's exodus experience so they could understand what God was doing for them. God was acting in their day the same as He had acted earlier for Abram.

Similarly, the writer of Kings lived in a time when God had exiled the people from the land. This divine act greatly influenced the writer's ideological intentions. For example, near the end of Hezekiah's reign, the writer of Kings reported a visit by envoys from Babylon (2 Kings 20:12).[61] Hezekiah foolishly displayed his wealth to the envoys, and Isaiah reproached him:

> Hear the word of the Lord: The time will surely come when everything in your palace, and all that your fathers have stored up until this day, will be carried off to Babylon. Nothing will be left, says the Lord. And some of your descendants, your own flesh and blood, that will be born to you, will be taken away, and they will become eunuchs in the palace of the king of Babylon (2 Kings 20:16–18).

Why did the writer of Kings include this blemish on Hezekiah's reputation? He did so to explain that even Hezekiah's reign gave cause for God to send the nation to Babylon.[62]

As we assess an author's intentions, we must pay careful attention to the redemptive-historical events surrounding the writing of a book. Old Testament writers were deeply influenced by what God was doing in their day.

Second, the *writer's culture* also influenced his ideology. Old Testament writers were not only concerned with divine intrusions but also with the human dimension of their times. These aspects of life were not entirely distinct from divine interventions. Cultural circumstances grew out of God's activity. But everyday political, religious, and economic conditions contributed to their point of view.

For example, in Genesis 48:1–22 we have an account of Joseph visiting his dying father. Joseph brought his sons to Jacob. Jacob received a directive from God to treat the sons of Joseph as his own sons. Jacob blessed the two, but crossed his hands so that the younger Ephraim received his right hand. The account closes with Jacob's words to Joseph: "I am about to die, but God will be with you and take you back to the land of your fathers. And to you, as one who is over your brothers, I give the ridge of land I took from the Amorites with my sword and my bow" (Genesis 48:21–22).

Why did Moses spell these matters out in such detail? Was this just a sentimental family record? Was he simply concerned with the past? No, Moses intended to instruct the people of his day on their circumstances. The amount of space given to tribal relations in Exodus, Numbers, Deuteronomy, Joshua, and Judges indicates that the tribes had many questions about their place in the national structure. Genesis 48:1–22 anticipates these problems. Why should Ephraim and Manasseh be treated as equals of the other tribes? Why should Joseph's tribe receive a rich, double portion? These contemporary cultural questions were answered by this passage: the place of Joseph's tribes was established by Jacob's blessing.

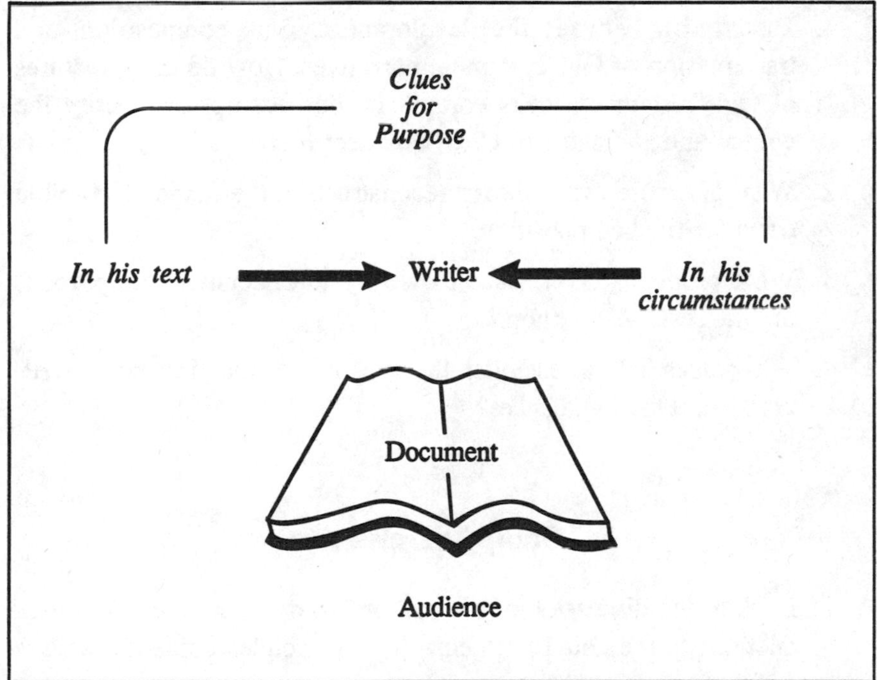

Fig. 45: Clues for a Writer's Purposes

Many problems confront us as we reconstruct the ideological intentions of Old Testament writers, but clues are available in the texts themselves and in the conditions of the writers' day. As we piece these clues together, we will be able to discern the original purposes for Old Testament stories (see figure 45).

Conclusion

In this chapter we have looked briefly at two basic considerations. In order to understand why Old Testament stories were written, we must identify the earliest and latest reasonable dates for the final composition of each book. Within this framework we can begin to search for the writers' purposes by examining their texts and circumstances. As we move forward in our extrinsic investigation of Old Testament narratives, these basic guidelines will prove indispensable.

Review Questions

1. Distinguish between the development, final composition, and transmission of Old Testament narratives. How do these features of Old Testament books complicate our attempt to identify the writers and audiences of Old Testament narratives?
2. What clues are available for reconstructing the range of possible dates for final composition?
3. What problems do we face as we try to understand the purpose of Old Testament writers?
4. What clues help us establish the purposes of Old Testament writers toward their audiences?

Study Exercises

1. Look at the discussion of the authorship of Genesis in two introductions to the Old Testament. What principles guide the writers as they determine who wrote Genesis?
2. Examine the book of Ruth. What clues can you discover for dating its final composition? Focus especially on the genealogies in the last chapter.
3. Read Genesis 1:1—2:3. Make a list of five specific ways this passage was designed in particular for Israel in the days of Moses. What Mosaic themes are present in the passage?

11

DESCRIBING A WRITER'S INTENTIONS

My sophomore literature class went out one evening to see *Gone with the Wind*. When we discussed the picture the next day, the teacher asked, "What do you think the movie was about?"

For a moment I thought the question was odd. "Obviously, the movie was about the Civil War." Some of my classmates felt the same way. "The Civil War was horrible!" "Slavery was unjust!" "Scarlet got what she deserved!" they called out.

But other students saw much more than we did. They thought the movie dealt with modern life. "The movie shows that all war is evil," one young man argued. Another commented, "Selfish love is no love at all."

As we offered our suggestions, the teacher jotted them on the board in two columns: "That World" and "Our World."

When the discussion drew to a close, she asked, "Which world was the movie *really* talking about? The world of the Civil War or our contemporary world?" After a moment's silence, she volunteered an answer, "I think it tells us about both worlds."

Old Testament writers also focused on two worlds: the world of the past and their own world. They made historical observations, affirming that certain events took place in particular ways. But they also wrote to teach their audiences contemporary applications.

This two-sided purpose leads us to consider a third dimension of the writers' intentions. How did Old Testament authors connect their historical observations to contemporary implications? How did they help the audience move from the past to the present?

In one way or another, Old Testament stories anticipated the circumstances of their audiences by showing how past events addressed current issues. These connections took many forms, but Old Testament writers always anticipated the present as they composed stories about the past.

In this light we will speak of three dimensions of an Old Testament writer's intentions: *observations, anticipations,* and *implications* (see figure 46). What observations of the past did Old Testament writers want

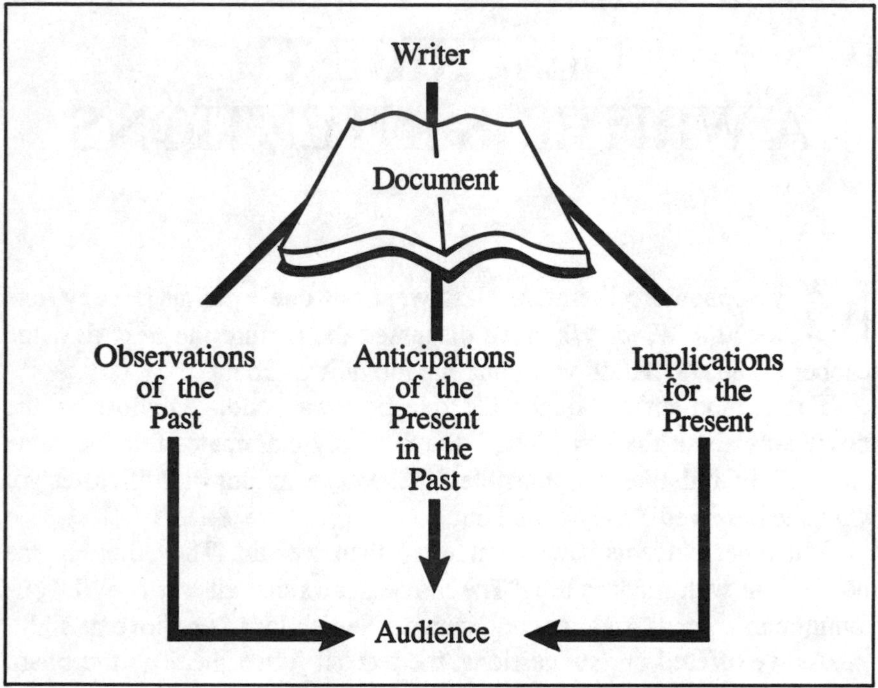

Fig. 46: Three Dimensions of a Writer's Intentions

their readers to grasp? How did they describe events long ago so that they anticipated the audience's contemporary concerns? What ramifications did their stories have for the times of the readers?

Observations

I once heard of a fourth grade teacher who loved to tell stories about the American Revolution. She sat in a big rocking chair in front of the room and told her students about Washington, Jefferson, and her favorite patriot, Patrick Henry. She always took the same approach. She leaned back in her chair, stared into the distance, and gave a detailed account of something special these men had done. At the end of her story, she rocked forward, looked straight at the children, and said, "Boys and girls, if you do the same, you can be heroes, too!" That fourth grade teacher was obviously concerned with her students; she wanted them to be "heroes." But she never mentioned contemporary events in her stories. She never directly addressed issues facing those boys and girls. Instead she spent all of her time talking about the past. Her students had to listen carefully to her stories and draw out the implications for their lives.

Old Testament writers also taught their readers how to live by giving them observations of the past. If we are to understand the original implications of Old Testament stories, we must first look carefully at their presentations of history. We will explore three dimensions of historical observations: *factual, moral,* and *emotional*. What factual historical data did Old Testament writers want their audiences to know? What past moral issues did they bring to the foreground? What emotional aspects of that world did they want their original readers to consider (see figure 47)?

Factual Observations

A television newscast recently reported that 20 percent of 1985 high school seniors were unaware that the United States fought a war in Vietnam. When I heard this news, I commented to a friend, "We will never remember the lessons of that war if we don't remember that there was a war." Factual knowledge is the starting point for drawing any implications from the past for our lives today. If we do not know what happened, we cannot apply what happened to our present concerns.

Old Testament writers understood this principle. That is why they reported many historical facts to their audiences. We can categorize these facts in terms of *circumstances, people,* and *God.*

Circumstances. Old Testament writers told their readers about historical circumstances. What was the situation? What happened? They reported such things as dates (1 Kings 15:1), customs (Ruth 4:7–8), famines (Genesis 41:53–57), victories (Joshua 6:1–27), and defeats (Joshua 7:1–5).

The Old Testament is a book of redemption, but this redemption did not simply occur in the hearts of people. Nor did it take shape primarily in the theological traditions of the believing community. On the contrary, redemption occurred in the context of real historical events. The hope of Israel rested in the fact that God had acted in space and time.

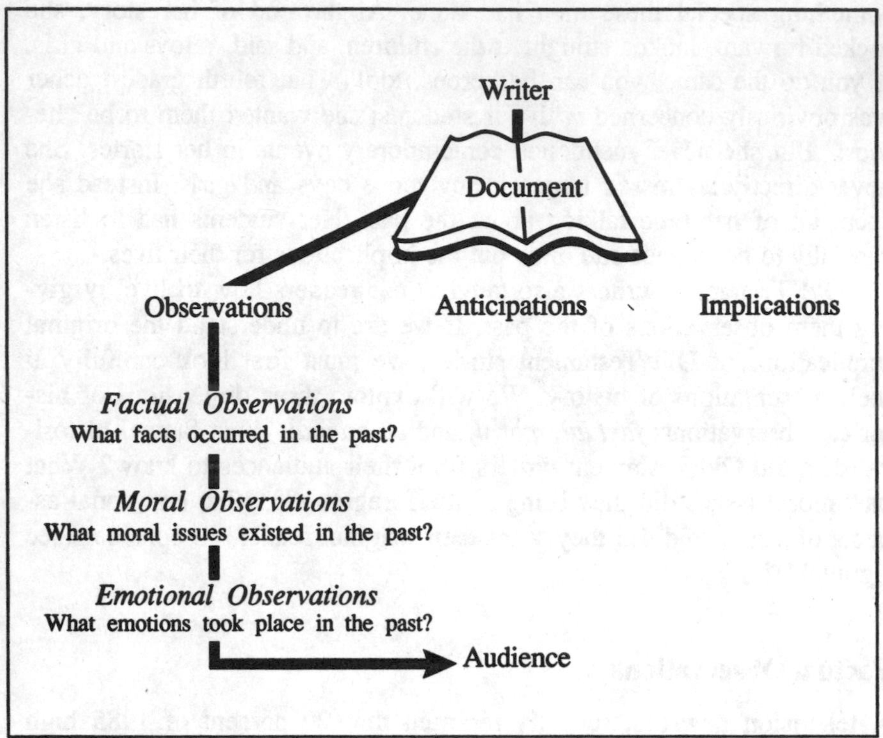

Fig. 47: Three Facets of Observations

For this reason general historical conditions formed a vital facet of writers' observations.

Descriptions of circumstances often contributed significantly to a story's meaning. As we saw in an earlier chapter, several historical circumstances are central to the story of Abram's exodus from Egypt (Genesis 12:10–20).[1] For instance, the opening scene mentions a famine in the land. On the surface this bit of history seems merely to give background to the scenes that follow, but it actually forms a crucial facet of Moses' intentions. The famine that drove Abram to Egypt foreshadowed the famine that drove all the sons of Jacob to Egypt. Similarly, the story reports that Abram left with "everything he had" (Genesis 12:20). This datum also appears to be insignificant, until we recall that Israel departed from Egypt only after they had "plundered the Egyptians" (Exodus 12:36).

At times writers emphasized numerous details; at other times, they mentioned only a few generalities. Whatever the case, we must take into account the author's descriptions of historical circumstances. What situations did the writer include? What elements did he leave out? How did he describe conditions?

People. Old Testament writers also concerned themselves with facts about people. Human beings occupy a central place in most Old Testament stories.[2] Who were these people? What were they like? These facts also formed a crucial dimension of historical observations.

At times the mere identity of a character points to a writer's intentions. Consider the account of Michal's rebuke of David (2 Samuel 6:16–23). We are not told that "one of David's wives" scolded him. The writer of Samuel was very specific. Three times he identified the woman as "Michal daughter of Saul" (vv. 16, 20, 23). This simple historical detail reveals an important dimension of the writer's point of view. This event was more than a quarrel between David and one of his wives; it was a struggle between David and *Saul's daughter*. In the writer's mind, this argument symbolized the conflict between the house of David and the house of Saul. As David himself noted: "It was before the Lord, who chose me rather than your father or anyone from his house when he appointed me ruler over the Lord's people Israel—I will celebrate before the Lord" (2 Samuel 6:21).

Why did the writer want his readers to keep Michal's familial identity in mind? He was addressing a matter of concern in his own day. Was Saul's royal line to continue? Was his family a viable alternative to the line of David? The final verse of the episode makes the writer's outlook clear: "And Michal daughter of Saul had no children to the day of her death" (2 Samuel 6:23). The union of Saul and David's house produced no progeny. Saul's line had been entirely rejected by God, and David's family had exclusive right to the throne.[3]

Along these same lines, the book of Samuel begins with an interesting observation about Elkanah, father of Samuel. The writer observed that he was "from Ramathaim, a Zuphite from the hill country of Ephraim" (1 Samuel 1:1). This fact may seem trivial, but upon reflection we can see that it conveyed an important dimension of the writer's purpose. Why did he tell his readers that Samuel's father was from Ephraim? He did so to establish that the Davidic dynasty was not a Judahite scheme. A prophet from the *north* had anointed David.[4]

God. Old Testament writers also made factual observations about God. They observed revelations of His character and purposes in the past.

For example, in Genesis 17:10 God ordained the rite of circumcision. "This is my covenant with you and your descendants after you, the covenant you are to keep: Every male among you shall be circumcised."

This historical observation had direct implications for the audience. God had established circumcision for His people in the days of Abraham. As a result the rite was to be observed by Moses' audience as they continued in the Abrahamic covenant.

Similarly, in the story of Abram's exodus (Genesis 12:10–20), Moses reported, "But the Lord struck Pharaoh and his house with great plagues because of Sarai, Abram's wife" (v. 17, NASB). This historical fact allowed the original audience to understand the significance of this passage for their lives. God had struck Pharaoh's house in their day as He had in the days of Abram.

Whether a story places God at center stage or leaves Him hidden as the providential Controller of events, God is one of the principal focal points of Old Testament accounts.[5] Whatever God established endures. His reactions to events revealed their true character. The original meaning of a text depended to a great extent on the facts writers reported about God.

Moral Observations

Facts raise moral questions. How should I respond to my neighbor's insults? What should I do about the homeless in my city? The particulars of our lives bring up all sorts of ethical considerations.[6] Old Testament writers reported historical facts to raise issues of conscience. They designed accounts so that their readers would be faced with moral dimensions of the past. As they read these texts, they were to ask, "Was that circumstance good or bad?" "What should those people have done?" "How was the righteous character of God demonstrated in those events?"

All facets of an Old Testament story work together to present moral observations. Scene depictions, structures, characterizations, and numerous other special features reveal all sorts of ethical issues in the past.

In many cases these aspects of texts are plain to us. We have little problem understanding how Moses wanted his audience to view the murder of Abel (Genesis 4:2b–16) or how the writer of Kings evaluated Manasseh's infidelity (2 Kings 21:1–18; 23:26; 24:3–4).

But at other times, we have difficulty knowing what to make of the moral dimensions of a passage. Why was Ahab wrong in offering to buy Naboth's vineyard (1 Kings 21:1-3)? Why did God break out in judgment against Uzzah when he saved the ark from falling (2 Samuel 6:7)? To grasp these more puzzling stories, we must set aside our own standards as much as possible and adopt the norms that Old Testament writers shared with their audiences. Two important standards of morality allow us to understand more clearly: *the Mosaic Law* and *later special revelation.*

Mosaic Law. With the possible exception of Genesis, every Old Testament narrative was written after God gave the Mosaic Law at Sinai.[7] Consequently, the Law of Moses was the touchstone by which Old Testament writers expected their audiences to evaluate the past. The principles set forth in the Ten Commandments and other Mosaic legislation were normative for all moral judgments.

At the same time, we must remember that God revealed His will to Israel progressively. Events before Sinai must not be evaluated fully in terms of Mosaic legal codes.[8] Some actions inappropriate after Sinai may have been permitted at an earlier time. The readers of Genesis would not have condemned Abel for offering his own sacrifices rather than calling on Levitical priests (Genesis 4:4). At the time there were no such priestly restrictions. Also, Abram did not violate cultic regulations by building numerous altars rather than having only one (Genesis 12:1–9). Before the tabernacle was established, this practice was perfectly acceptable.

In contrast, when Lamech boasted "I have killed a man for wounding me, a young man for injuring me" (Genesis 4:23), Moses called on his audience to react in horror. Murder had always been sin; self-glorification had always been rebellion against God. Likewise, when Moses recalled Abram's relationship with Hagar (Genesis 16:1–16), he expected his audience to evaluate it negatively. Despite the customs of Abram's culture,[9] failing to trust God's promises had been wrong from the beginning. The Law of Moses simply confirmed these creation principles.[10]

Many times Old Testament writers approved of events by referring explicitly to Mosaic legislation. In reporting early progress in the postexilic community, the writer of Ezra commented that sacrifices were offered "in accordance with what is written in the Law of Moses the man of God" (Ezra 3:2).[11] Writers also disapproved of events by mentioning that they violated the Law of Moses. For instance, when the Chronicler described the sickness that interrupted Hezekiah's Passover, he mentioned that many people ate in a manner "contrary to what was written" (2 Chronicles 30:18).[12] These kinds of comments gave the audience an explicit starting point for their own moral reflections.

At other times writers only hinted that a violation had occurred. For example, in the story of Naboth's vineyard (1 Kings 21:1–29), the author made no express reference to Mosaic inheritance laws (Leviticus

25:23–28; Numbers 36:7). But he subtly reminded his audience that Ahab had no regard for the legislation.[13] Naboth called his field an "inheritance" (*nḥlh*) (1 Kings 21:3), the technical Mosaic term for a permanent family possession.[14] But Ahab and Jezebel referred to it simply as a "vineyard" (*krm*) (1 Kings 21:2). Relying on his readers' acquaintance with Mosaic Law, the writer indicated the proper evaluation of this event.

Later special revelation. Old Testament writers also based their moral observations on later special revelation through prophets and leaders. For example, the writer of Kings presented the exclusion of Abiathar (1 Kings 2:26-27) as proper because it fulfilled the prophecy uttered against Eli's family (1 Samuel 2:27–36).[15] The writer of Ezra appealed to Haggai and Zechariah to give his readers a proper outlook on the restoration program (Ezra 5:1; 6:14).

As God revealed His moral guidelines beyond Moses, these regulations also formed standards for reflection on history. Old Testament writers expected their readers to make moral evaluations in light of these revelations.

Old Testament writers did more than remind their audiences about the facts of the past. They also designed their stories to convince them of certain moral features of history. As we investigate a writer's purposes, we must take careful note of these observations.

Emotional Observations

Nothing is more boring than a story without emotion. If you want to put your audience to sleep, just list fact after fact after fact after fact. But the same events come to life when we infuse them with feelings. As we describe the emotions of a character, his doubts, fears, joys, and pleasures give the story power.

Old Testament writers drew their readers into a world full of emotions. They described scenes, portrayed characters, structured accounts, and used every other literary tool available to help their readers see the affective dimensions of history. They wanted their readers to hear laughter and sobbing, taste pleasure and bitterness, and sense the excitement and discouragement of past events.

Old Testament stories depict both *human emotions* and *divine emotions*. How did Old Testament writers describe the sentiments of human characters? How did they observe God's attitudes?

Human emotions. Old Testament writers frequently pointed to the emotions of their human characters. Of course, readers had to evaluate these feelings; the people often reacted inappropriately. Yet what people in the past thought, said, and did gave the readers a starting point for grasping the emotional power of events.

Observations of human emotions occur in many ways. First, examples of *explicit descriptions* include Abram's terror (Genesis 15:12), Isaac feeling comforted (Genesis 24:67), and women singing and dancing for joy (1 Samuel 18:6). Such portrayals are rare, so when they occur, they usually form a significant dimension of the writer's emotional observations.

Second, a *character's words* give off emotive qualities as well. When Sarai overheard the three visitors promise she would have a child, she laughed, saying to herself, "After I am worn out and my master is old, will I now have this pleasure?" (Genesis 18:12). Sarai's skepticism was inappropriate, but Moses' report of her words pointed out how the promise seemed absolutely impossible. By doing so he highlighted God's grace toward Sarai and the miraculous character of Isaac's birth.

Third, *outward actions* sometimes reveal the emotional impact of an event. In Genesis 17:1–2 God confronted Abram after his failure with Hagar saying, "Walk before me and be blameless." In reaction "Abram fell facedown." He did not object or offer excuses; he simply prostrated himself in humility. Moses reported this response so that his readers could see the emotional force of Abram's frightening, convicting, and humbling encounter with God.

Fourth, many times the emotional reactions of characters were so ordinary and predictable that Old Testament writers saw little need to state them explicitly. Instead they expected their audiences to see these attitudes through *sympathetic reading* by asking, "What would I be feeling if I were in that situation?" In many cases few clues were needed for audiences to see the emotional qualities of an event.

For example, when God called Abraham to sacrifice Isaac, we have little difficulty reconstructing his initial heart-rending reaction. Although the text says nothing explicitly about his feelings, we are given several clues.[16] For instance, God commanded Abraham, "Take your son, *your only son*" (Genesis 22:2, emphasis added), reminding us that Isaac was precious to Abraham. Sympathetic reading gives us a glimpse of what Abraham must have felt.

When we read that Eli's sons "had no regard for the Lord" (1 Samuel 2:12), we do not have to be told about their attitudes to have some awareness of their emotional condition. Disregard of the sort they exhibited always entails a hardness and indifference—even disdain—for God.

We know that these feelings were present in Eli's sons because of the rest of Scripture and our own experiences.

With a bit of sympathetic reading, the original readers could transfer themselves into the situation of a story to encounter the joys and sorrows, enchantments and horrors of the past.

Divine emotions. Old Testament writers also pointed out God's emotions. Descriptions of His attitudes, words, and actions uncovered the affective qualities of the past. Unlike human responses, God's reactions were always appropriate. His love, joy, sadness, regret, and anger were central to the writer's emotional observations.

God's emotions stand out in several ways. First, writers often stated how God felt. For example, when the writer of Kings recalled Solomon's syncretistic practices he mentioned, "The Lord became angry with Solomon because his heart had turned away from the Lord" (1 Kings 11:9). This information gave the readers a starting point for their own reactions.

Second, God's words revealed how He felt. In the days of Noah, God said, "I am grieved that I have made them" (Genesis 6:7). These words disclosed how God felt about humanity at the time. People had become so corrupt that God regretted having made them. His emotional reaction formed a vital dimension of the flood story.

Third, in many cases Old Testament writers implied that God reacted emotionally. In these passages they did not have to state how God felt. The rest of Scripture and the readers' own religious experiences made His emotional reactions clear enough. When God granted David His Spirit and removed His Spirit from Saul (1 Samuel 16:13–14), we can see divine approval and disapproval. Similarly, the writer of Samuel reported that "The sin of the young men was very great in the Lord's sight" (1 Samuel 2:17). He did not explicitly mention God's feelings or words. Nevertheless, his audience could easily discern how God reacted to sin; it stirred Him to anger.

As we investigate the observations that writers made of the past, we must give attention to more than facts and moral concerns. Throughout these texts Old Testament authors communicated emotional dimensions of history and challenged the audience on an affective level.

Anticipations

I have had many history teachers, but one stood out for his keen ability to show how events in the past were relevant for contemporary life. He did not just teach us dates, names, and events. He took the time to tell us how history anticipated issues we faced in our own day. By drawing connections between the past and present, this teacher gave me a life-long love for history.

Old Testament writers were great history teachers. They presented observations on Israel's past with a deep interest in the circumstances of their readers. Consequently, Old Testament authors described history in ways that anticipated issues their audiences faced.

For the sake of simplicity, we will speak of three main kinds of anticipation. Old Testament writers described the past in ways that *established* the historical origins of beliefs and practices. Their narratives presented *models* for the audience to imitate and avoid. And their accounts of past events foreshadowed, or *adumbrated,* aspects of their readers' lives (see figure 48).

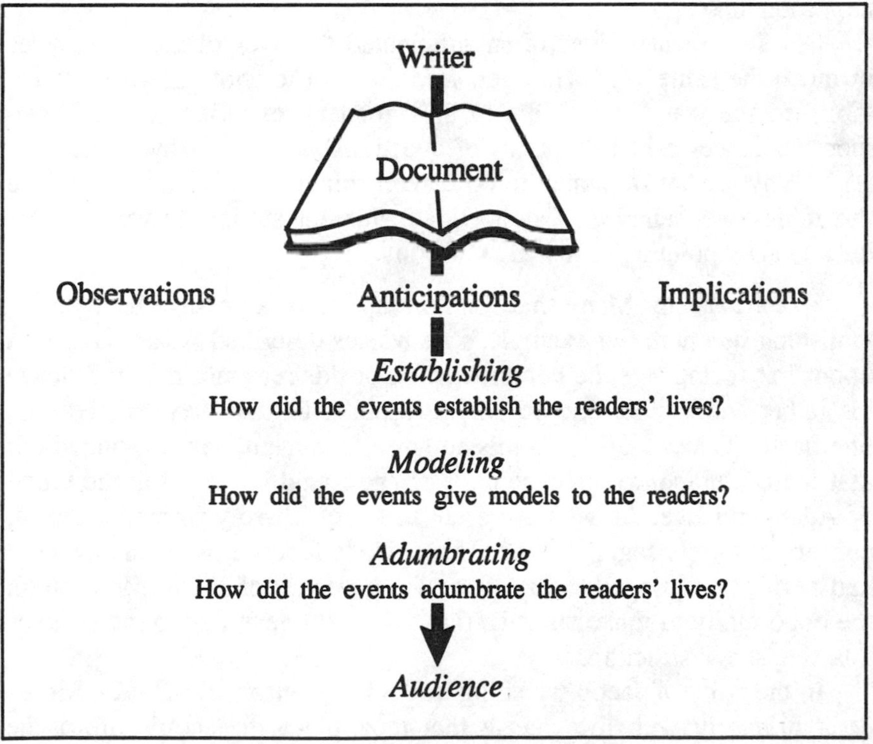

Fig. 48: Three Facets of Anticipations

These forms of anticipations are not mutually exclusive; most Old Testament narratives present a mixture of anticipations. As we identify how lines were drawn between the past and contemporary life, we will gain significant insights into the original meaning of these stories.

Establishing

We often use historical facts to establish or explain how life came to be as it is. When someone asks us why we face certain situations, we often appeal to historical origins.

"Daddy," the five-year-old asks her father, "Why does the American flag have thirteen stripes? I think it would look better with a lot more."

"The flag has those stripes because of something that happened long ago," he explains. "When our country first began, we only had thirteen colonies. Those colonies formed the United States. We have thirteen stripes on our flag to represent our thirteen original colonies."

This father showed his little girl how history established the present by explaining that current practices had their origins in something that happened long ago.

Old Testament writers often anticipated the lives of their audiences in much the same way. They reported the past to show how events established the way things were in their readers' experience. Old Testament audiences asked the kinds of questions we ask. "Why is life as it is?" "Why are we obligated to do certain things?" "Why do we believe the things we believe?" Often Old Testament stories answered these questions by pointing to historical origins.

Minor aspects. Many times minor aspects of a passage have an establishing function. For example, after Moses described Adam's reaction upon first seeing Eve, he commented, "For this reason a man will leave his father and mother and be united to his wife, and they will become one flesh" (Genesis 2:24). In this authorial comment, Moses pointed out that the contemporary practice of marriage found its origin in the union of Adam and Eve. As we have seen, this motif hardly formed a central concern of the passage.[17] Rather, this episode focused more on how God had perfectly equipped Adam to be the gardener of Eden. Moses took the opportunity to make an aside that this event gave rise to marriage as a lasting social structure.

In the story of Jacob wrestling at Peniel (Genesis 32:22–32), Moses dealt primarily with the change that took place in Jacob's life as he prepared to meet Esau.[18] In the context of this more central focus, he also mentioned that Jacob's hip was wrenched. Spotting the opportunity to explain a contemporary practice, Moses then commented, "Therefore to this day the Israelites do not eat the tendon attached to the socket of the hip, because the socket of Jacob's hip was touched near the tendon" (v. 32). Once again we find historical background given to a current practice outside the central focus of an account.

More central aspects. The intention to provide historical background can be more central to a passage. Rather than forming a sideline or afterthought, establishing the origins of current realities occupied a vital role in some passages. For example, the discussion of Purim in Esther 9:18–32 had a central establishing function.[19] The text describes how the people celebrated God's deliverance and openly insists that Purim must be continued. This declaration is hardly an insignificant aside. One of the writer's main concerns was to establish the basis of the observance of Purim.

Very often the establishing function of an Old Testament story was not stated explicitly. The writer relied on the audience to make connections between the past and their situation. For instance, in 2 Samuel 7:1–17 the writer reported how Nathan announced God's promise that David's descendants would be the permanent dynasty over Israel. The prophet declared that chastisement would come to individual sons of David who proved to be unfaithful, but God would never take His love away from David as He had from Saul (2 Samuel 7:15). How did this event connect with the original audience? How did it anticipate their day? It established the claims of the Davidic line by explaining the historical origins of David's permanent dynasty. What right did the sons of David have to sit on the throne in the days of the readers? The observations of 2 Samuel 7:1–17 gave the answer: God had promised that David's family would rule forever over Israel. This historical fact confirmed current practices and obligations.

In one way or another, every narrative in the Old Testament anticipated its audience's world by establishing some historical origins. Why should the people of Israel worship God alone as the Creator? Why should they think that the land of Canaan belongs to them? Why should they live in harmony? Moses answered these kinds of questions by providing historical background in Genesis.[20] Why should the Israelites follow Moses? Why should they obey the Mosaic social order? Why worship in Moses' tabernacle? The book of Exodus established the historical basis for these practices.[21] In a similar way, every other Old Testament narrative book established an historical background for realities that the original audience experienced.

To see the establishing function of a text, we may ask several diagnostic questions. What lasting order did events in the passage erect?

How did these life-structures extend to the original audience? How could this background have helped the audience respond properly to their current circumstances? As we ask these sorts of questions, it becomes evident that Old Testament writers often pointed to historical background to help their readers deal with contemporary issues.

Modeling

A second way in which we often see the relevance of history is to search for models—examples from the past that guide our decisions.

"But Mom," Johnny objects, "Why do I have to study? It's not important."

"Don't you remember the story of Abraham Lincoln?" his mother asks. "He worked hard all day, but when evening came, he sat in front of the fire and studied until he fell asleep. Do you think he could have become president if he had not studied?"

Obviously Johnny's mother was appealing to history to address a contemporary issue. But how did she connect the past to the present? Lincoln's study habits did not erect lasting life-structures for academic pursuits. They did not establish an historical background to Johnny's responsibilities. Instead, Johnny's mother appealed to Lincoln as a model. By learning from Lincoln's example, Johnny could see how important it was for him to study.

Minor aspects. Many times Old Testament writers met the needs of their audiences by providing them with examples from the past. Some of these examples were to be imitated; others were to be avoided. Sometimes this connection was a relatively minor aspect of a passage. While an episode or section of a book may have anticipated, the audience more by establishing or adumbrating their lives, it may still have offered the audience a model.

For example, the story of Adam and Eve's expulsion from the garden (Genesis 2:4—3:24) had the overarching purpose of establishing why the image of God suffers pain and futility.[22] Our first parents' violation cast the human race into sin and death. Moses composed this story to explain the origins of suffering and trouble.

Within this larger purpose, Adam and Eve served as negative models for the audience. Why should the readers take to heart the commandments of God in their day? Why is obedience to the Law so important? One answer lies in the paradigm of Adam and Eve. When the first humans violated the Law of God, consequences were severe; the same would be true for the people of Moses' audience who violated God's requirements.[23]

The writer of Kings also reported the reign of Manasseh primarily to establish an historical basis for the exile (2 Kings 21:1–18). Mannasseh's sins sealed the fate of Judah.[24] As the prophet said, God was "going to bring such disaster on Jerusalem and Judah that the ears of everyone who hears of it will tingle" (21:12). But this was not the only way in which this story was helpful for the lives of the readers. Manasseh's life served as a negative example to the exiles. Only as they avoided Manasseh's syncretism and rebellion could they look forward to the possibility of return.

More central aspects. Sometimes modeling was a more central concern. Some stories connected the past and present primarily by offering examples. For instance, throughout the first chapters of Daniel, young Israelite men are set forth as paragons of faith. They do nothing wrong; they serve faithfully in the kingdom of Babylon, but they never compromise their devotion to the God of Israel. The story of Shadrach, Meshach, and Abednego (Daniel 3:1–30) presents these young men as examples of pious living in exile. Their acts of faith in the face of certain death demonstrated the kind of piety expected of all who served God outside the land.[25] What is the result of their fidelity? God blesses them and brings glory to Himself. The connection with the original audience is plain. What were they to do when tempted to worship other gods? How could they serve a foreign power and still maintain loyalty to the God of Israel? The writer of Daniel answered these questions in the examples of these three men.

The story of the golden calf (Exodus 32:1—33:6) offers another example of modeling. This episode appears after God gave regulations of tabernacle worship on Mount Sinai, but before their actual application among the tribes. In this intervening passage, Moses reported God's horrifying judgment against Israel's corrupt worship. What did this account have to do with Moses' audience? How did it envisage their situation? Moses reported this account to give his readers a model of what happens to those who neglect the regulations of the cult. If the audience turned away from the purity of God-ordained worship, it would incite God's wrath just as it had at the foot of Sinai.

Anticipation through modeling also extends to large sections and whole books. The Chronicler's idealized presentation of David and Solomon provided the post-exilic audience with representative illustrations for their lives.[26] Esther's behavior taught by precedent how the Israelites were to serve the interests of their own people outside the land.[27]

Throughout the Old Testament, we find stories that provided models for the original audience. Several questions help us identify this connection. First, did a character fail or succeed at a critical juncture and experience significant results from his or her actions? Second, did the actions of the character relate to choices that the audience had to make in their day? Third, what results could the audience have expected to see in their time if they imitated or avoided the character's actions? As we ask these kinds of questions, we will see the modeling function of many Old Testament narratives.

Adumbrating

"History repeats itself" is a popular slogan among historians. Few modern Westerners mean this literally; we normally think of history moving forward in a linear fashion. Yet we also know that events in our day can be surprisingly similar to events in the past.

Old Testament writers knew this to be true of Israel's past. Events that occurred in bygone eras were often analogous to the situations their audiences faced. Therefore, they composed their accounts to show how the past adumbrated the present. By reading Old Testament stories with these analogies in mind, the audience could see their own existence mirrored in history.

How do adumbrations differ from stories that establish and model? The main difference is the degree of similarity set up between the past and the present. Narratives establish the origins of current practices by building on a few similarities. Models tend to parallel the lives of the audience a little more, but the correspondence does not have to be extensive. Adumbrations, however, build on sustained analogies between history and the audience's experience; events are reported so that they closely resemble the situation of the audience.

While adumbrations function on the basis of analogies between the past and present, Old Testament writers did not fabricate or force these parallels; they gave true reports. Consequently, the analogies are never complete or perfect. Prefiguring passages will be similar to the situations of the audience in significant ways, but never identical.

Minor aspects. On occasion, minor adumbrations of the audience will appear in a story that primarily establishes or models. For instance, the account of God's covenant with Abram (Genesis 15:1–21) served to establish the covenantal basis of Israel's hope for the land of Canaan.[28]

Moses' audience could expect to inherit the land because God confirmed His promise with an oath to Abram. But within this establishing function, Moses pointed out a small foreshadowing of the audience's experience. In Genesis 15:17 God appeared before Abram as a "smoking firepot with a blazing torch." Moses reported this visual image of smoke and fire to show how this event in Abram's life anticipated his own day. As Moses told this story, the Israelites could see God appearing before them once again as a pillar of cloud and fire.[29] In effect, Moses alerted his readers to the fact that the God who promised to bring Abram's descendants to the land was the same God who now appears before them and will lead them into that land.

More central aspects. Adumbrations can be more central to a passage. For example, the Chronicler's account of Manasseh's reign (2 Chronicles 33:1–20) foreshadowed the experience of his audience.[30] Manasseh sinned greatly before the Lord and was exiled to Babylon. While in Babylon he repented and cried out for help. God heard his cry and brought him back to Jerusalem. Upon his return Manasseh purified the worship of Israel and rebuilt the city of Jerusalem.

The similarities between this series of events and the post-exilic experience are striking. The Israelites had sinned against God, gone to Babylon, sought the favor of God, returned to the land, and were in the process of restoring worship and rebuilding the city of Jerusalem. Why did the Chronicler present Manasseh's reign in this manner? To encourage his readers in their efforts. Their exile had been God's response to sin; their deliverance had been an act of grace based on their repentance. If the wicked King Manasseh demonstrated his repentance by establishing the cult and city, how much more must they do the same?[31]

To one degree or another, many Old Testament narratives connected the world of the past to the present world of the audience by adumbrating dimensions of their experience. As we look for these anticipatory events, it helps to ask several questions. Do elements in the passage parallel the experiences of the audience? What extensive analogies appear? How did the actions of the story clarify the audience's past experience and future responsibilities?

As we discern the ways Old Testament writers established current circumstances, modeled proper and improper behavior, and adumbrated the situations their audiences faced, we will move further in our understanding of the original meaning of Old Testament stories.

Implications

I know a number of teachers involved in higher education. Most of them agree that we live in a day when knowledge for knowledge's sake no longer motivates most students. Professors have to show that their subjects have practical benefits. Students of science, business, the humanities—even theology—insist on knowing how a subject bears on life.

Interest in practical living is not new. Old Testament writers had similar concerns. They did not write simply to introduce their readers to the past, but to teach their audiences how to live in their day. Old Testament stories were full of many relevant implications for their readers.

The implications of Old Testament narratives take many forms. They too are complex and interrelated, but for the sake of convenience, we will speak of three main types of implications: *informative, directive,* and *affective*. What information did the story give the readers about their world? What moral directives did the passage offer for their lives? How did the story touch on the feelings of the readers toward their world? (See figure 49)

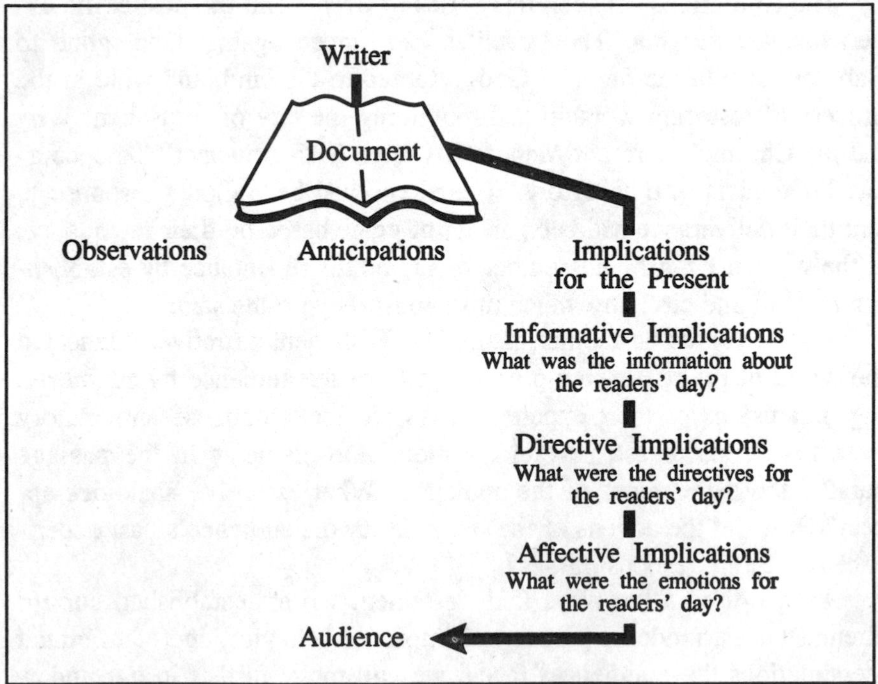

Fig. 49: Three Facets of Implications

Informative Implications

Unless we have true information about our world, it is nearly impossible to live in fidelity to God. Without accurate data we cannot make proper moral decisions or have appropriate emotional reactions. To a great extent, everything we do depends on getting the facts straight.

The same was true for recipients of Old Testament stories. As they struggled to live before God, they needed reliable facts about their world. Sin and finitude had clouded their minds so that they often misconstrued reality. They could hope to live honorably before God only as they gained genuine knowledge of their day. To meet this need, Old Testament writers composed accounts to serve as eyeglasses by which the recipients could see life as it really was.

We may think of a story's informative implications in terms of *circumstances, people,* and *God.* Of course, different passages tend to emphasize one category, but Old Testament stories informed their readers of proper perspectives on all three aspects of reality.

Circumstances. Old Testament stories told the audiences about their circumstances. We have seen several examples of this focus already. Many within the audience of Genesis thought they had made a mistake in coming out to the wilderness. Egypt seemed more desirable than the life Moses had given them. The story of Abram's exodus (Genesis 12:10–20) offered Moses' readers a proper perspective on their circumstances.[32] It was no mistake to leave Egypt; the exodus was a blessing from God, just as it was in Abram's day.

Similarly, many who heard the stories of Genesis were convinced that the cities of Canaan were invincible. They had heard discouraging reports from the spies and thought that they could never conquer the land (Numbers 13:26–33). Moses wrote the Tower of Babel story (Genesis 11:1–9) to correct this false viewpoint.[33] He told how the people of Babel wanted to build a tower "that reaches to the heavens" *(wr'šw bšmym)* (Genesis 11:4). The people of Israel thought the same was true of the cities of Canaan. In Deuteronomy 1:28 Moses recounted how the spies had reported that the Canaanite cities were "fortified up to heaven" *(wbṣwrt bšmym)* (RSV). He therefore exhorted the Israelites to be confident because God had guaranteed that they would indeed take cities "fortified up to heaven" *(wbṣwrt bšmym)* (Deuteronomy 9:1, RSV).

This connection between Moses' speeches in Deuteronomy and the Tower of Babel hardly appears coincidental. As the original audience heard this story, their false viewpoints were challenged. The famous primeval city seemed invincible, reaching to the heavens, but God conquered it and scattered the people.[34] Surely He could defeat the lesser cities of Canaan.

People. Old Testament writers also wrote to give proper information about people in the audience's world. Their stories made observations about human beings in the past, but by implication they also informed the readers about themselves and other people who lived in their day.

We have already seen that the episode of David and Michal (2 Samuel 6:20–23) did not merely tell the audience about Saul's daughter. By implication it informed them about Saul's family in the audience's day; Michal was left childless, and the house of Saul had no claim to royalty.

The stories of Abraham and Lot, Isaac and Ishmael, and Jacob and Esau reported facts about these people. But these chronicles also said something about people living in the days of Moses' audience. Lot was the father of the Moabites and Ammonites (Genesis 19:36–38); Ishmael was the father of the Arab nations (Genesis 25:12–18); Esau was the father of the Edomites (Genesis 36:9–43). As Moses' audience heard these stories, they not only learned about the historical relations between their patriarchs and the heads of these nations; they also learned how they were to view the nations in their own times.[35]

God. Old Testament writers informed their readers about God in their day. Many factual observations were made about God, and these facts instructed the audience about the ways of God in their contemporary situation.

For example, we have noted on several occasions that the promises God gave to Abraham applied to the audience of Genesis. The promises of seed, land, protection, and blessing (Genesis 12:1–3) revealed how God was treating the nation of Israel in the days of Moses. In much the same way, God's promise to David (2 Samuel 7:1–17) had implications for the audience of Samuel. God could be trusted to keep this covenant promise.

Divine reactions to events also had contemporary implications. God's displays of mercy in history told the audience of divine mercy in their day. The deliverance of Jerusalem in the days of Rehoboam (2 Chronicles 12:1–12) informed the Chronicler's audience of God's willingness to assist the post-exilic community against their enemies.[36] God's reaction to sin in the past also informed the audience of His view of sin in their time. God's anger toward Adam and Eve (Genesis 3:16–19) taught Moses' audience about God's contemporary disposition toward sin.[37] God's judgment against Uzzah (2 Samuel 6:6–7) informed the readers of Samuel that He would not treat violations of worship lightly. These events revealed aspects of God's character relevant to the lives of the readers. They could expect God to act in their day as He had before.

Directive Implications

Just as Old Testament narratives focused on moral issues in the past, they also communicated directive implications to the audience. Old Testament writers helped their readers to see how they ought to live—what moral obligations applied to them and what they should do with their lives.

We must remember the standard of morality that guided directive implications for the audience to prevent misunderstanding. For the most part, the moral implications of Old Testament stories can be understood in terms of Mosaic precepts and further revelation between the time of Moses and the final composition of the story.[38]

The directive implications of a passage are vast and thoroughly intertwined with the informative and affective implications. As usual, it helps to consider them in terms of *circumstances, people,* and *God.*

Circumstances. Old Testament stories directed their audiences to live in certain ways in relation to their circumstances. Just as they learned information about the world, they also learned their obligations in certain situations. For example, the Chronicler's account of Asa's reign offered a model of response to military threat (2 Chronicles 14:2—16:14).[39] When Asa trusted God in warfare, he gained the victory. But when he took from the temple treasures to gain Ben-Hadad's help, he suffered severely (16:1–9). From this account the Chronicler directed his post-exilic readers to deal properly with contemporary military threats. He instructed them to avoid foreign alliances and to trust in God.[40] Every narrative book in the Old Testament directed its readers to deal properly with the circumstances they faced in their own day.

People. The directive implications of Old Testament narratives also extended to the audiences' relations with other people. These passages told them how to handle the inter-personal dimensions of their lives. For instance, the story of Moses' restrictions on the marriages of land-owning women (Numbers 36:1–13) applied to human relations in the promised land.[41] Women who owned land were required to marry within their own tribe.

In a similar way, the stories of Joseph and his brothers had many directive implications for the ways the readers of Genesis were to relate to each other. The animosity and jealousy that characterized the brothers were to be avoided in the interaction of the tribes of Israel.[42]

God. Old Testament writers also composed stories to direct readers in their obligations toward God. Examples of these implications abound. When David told Michal, "I will celebrate before the Lord" (2 Samuel 6:21), the design for the audience was evident. They were to worship with hearts centered on God. When Abraham responded in faith to God's command to sacrifice Isaac (Genesis 22:1–19), by implication the audience also learned their obligation to respond faithfully to God in times of testing.

Affective Implications

Old Testament writers were not just interested in informing and directing their audiences; they also wanted them to have proper emotional responses to their times. Joy, sadness, fear, and confidence—the full range of human emotions—were touched by their stories. As we consider the ideological intentions of Old Testament authors, we must also take into account the affective implications of their stories.

We must be careful to distinguish between affective implications and emotional observations in a passage. Old Testament writers observed emotional dimensions of the past so that their readers would respond emotionally to those events. They felt good or bad, happy or sad about something that happened long ago. These emotional considerations form an essential facet of the writer's purposes. But at this point, we are more interested in how Old Testament writers wanted their readers to feel about *their own times*. How should they feel about their own lives? Excited? Discouraged? Frightened? Strengthened? We will think of affective implications in the same three ways: *circumstances, people,* and *God.*

Circumstances. Once more let us note that the readers of Old Testament stories faced many different kinds of circumstances. Some of them were encouraging, others frightening. Some situations built up confidence in the readers; others caused them to doubt.

For example, we have seen that the writer of Kings taught his readers in a number of ways that the exile of the North and South was just.[43] Did he devote himself to this theme simply to give his audience information? Did he do this simply to obligate them to obedience? It would appear that the writer of Kings was also interested in the visceral response of his audience to the exile. As they heard of one historical event after another demonstrating the justice of their expulsion from the land, they were to feel regret, sorrow, and sober humility over their present circumstances.

When the audience of the book of Numbers heard of the fears that gripped those who spied in the land (Numbers 13:31–33), what affective implications did this event have for them? It called those who feared to gain confidence and strengthened the convictions of those who were determined to take the land of Canaan.

People. Old Testament stories also contained many implications for the ways audiences were to feel about people. The readers of Old Testament narratives had to deal with themselves and with other nations. Many passages taught them how to react emotionally to the people with whom they interacted.

One example appears when Solomon ruthlessly emptied his court of all political opponents (1 Kings 2:13–46). How were the readers to feel about Solomon's descendants who claimed leadership in their day? As we saw earlier, the writer of Kings demonstrated that Solomon's actions were completely justified.[44] As a result the exilic audience was to have high regard for Solomon's progeny who would one day lead them back to the land.

A striking example of affective implications toward people appears in the last chapter of Jonah (Jonah 4:1–11). When the vine that had sheltered the prophet withered, Jonah told God, "I am angry enough to die" (Jonah 4:9). God responded, "But Nineveh has more than a hundred and twenty thousand people who cannot tell their right hand from their left, and many cattle as well. Should I not be concerned about that great city?" (Jonah 4:11) Through God's rebuke the writer of Jonah taught his readers that they too must learn to have compassion and love for the lost among the nations. Jonah's hardness of heart must be rejected in favor of hearts that rejoiced to see repentance and faith in other nations.[45]

God. Old Testament stories conveyed implications for the ways their readers were to feel about God. At different times and places the readers were to have a variety of attitudes toward God. Reverence and submission were always expected, but Old Testament narratives highlighted particular emotional dispositions toward God from time to time.

When God struck Uzzah for touching the ark and David responded, "How can the ark of the Lord ever come to me?" (2 Samuel 6:9), the ramifications for the audience were obvious. Those who took the holiness of God in worship lightly had every reason to fear His wrath. When the same account reported that the ark finally entered the city in proper order and with great celebration, it also instructed the readers that those who worshipped should do so with joy and pleasure in the grace of God.

Similarly, as Moses' audience heard of the destruction in Noah's day, their hearts were filled with fear of God's destructive power against sinners even in their day. At the same time, however, God assured Noah "As long as the earth endures, seedtime and harvest, cold and heat, summer and winter, day and night will never cease" (Genesis 8:22). Moses' audience found delight in God in this part of the story; the stability of life was God's wondrous gift to them.

Conclusion

In this chapter we have described ideological intentions in three major categories: observations, anticipations, and implications. These facets of original meaning are inextricably interrelated. But as we uncover these facets of a writer's purposes, we will have a better grasp of the original meaning of his story.

Review Questions

1. Distinguish a writer's observations, anticipations, and implications.
2. What were the three main types of observations Old Testament writers made?
3. What are the three main ways in which Old Testament writers anticipate their audiences?
4. What are the three principal kinds of implications Old Testament writers expected their audiences to derive from their stories?

Study Exercises

1. Examine Genesis 12:1–9 and outline its five-step dramatic flow.
2. Go through each step of Genesis 12:1–9 and make notes on the factual, moral, and emotional observations Moses made.
3. Go back through each step of Genesis 12:1–9 and summarize any establishing, modeling, and adumbrative anticipations for the original audience you find (keep in mind that Abram was called

to migrate to the promised land just as Moses had called Israel to migrate).

4. In light of your research, summarize some of the prominent informative, directive, and affective implications of Genesis 12:1–9 for the original audience of Genesis (keep in mind the struggles faced by the original audience as they heard this story).

12

OVERVIEW OF OLD TESTAMENT NARRATIVES

The bigger the pond, the thinner the ice,"—a helpful rule of thumb for beginning ice skaters. The more area the ice has to cover, the thinner it tends to be.

In this chapter we will be skating on thin ice. We will quickly survey all the major Old Testament books consisting predominantly of narratives. Because this presentation is so broad, it must remain superficial. Our goal in this chapter is merely to suggest basic orientations for further investigation. More information and alternative views may be found in standard introductions and commentaries.

Most Old Testament narrative books fall into groups of literary families, even though each book retains its own features and purposes. Four families stand out:

1. The *Mosaic History* (Genesis, Exodus, Numbers, and Deuteronomy)
2. The *Deuteronomistic History* (Joshua, Judges, Samuel, and Kings)
3. The *Chronistic History* (Chronicles, Ezra, and Nehemiah)
4. Other Books (Ruth, Esther, and Jonah).

In this survey we will begin with a few observations on each corpus and then look briefly at the individual books within them.

The Mosaic History

Old Testament narratives first appeared in the Mosaic History (*Genesis, Exodus, Numbers, and Deuteronomy*).[1] Jewish and Christian interpreters have long recognized significant connections among these books. Genesis begins the history, Exodus builds on the events of Genesis, Numbers extends the history further, and the events of Deuteronomy follow the incidents of Numbers. As such the Mosaic History extends from creation to the death of Moses.

Nevertheless, the Mosaic History is not a single unified work. The books exhibit features that suggest they were relatively independent compositions.[2] After Genesis ends with the death of Joseph (Genesis 50:22–26), Exodus briefly recaps the Joseph story (Exodus 1:1–7). Exodus closes with a reference to the tribes "during all their travels" (Exodus 40:38), and Numbers opens at Sinai (Numbers 1:1). Numbers traces the march of Israel toward the promised land and discusses numerous events on the plains of Moab (Numbers 21:10–36:13); Deuteronomy presents Mosaic speeches given in Moab and a few events following the speeches. While we must keep in mind the overall unity of the Mosaic History, we must not overlook the diversity reflected in the individual books.

In keeping with the Biblical witness, evangelicals affirm fundamental Mosaic authorship of the Pentateuch.[3] Critical interpreters have long discounted this traditional view in favor of the well-known documentary hypothesis (J, E, D, P).[4] It is likely that Moses used sources[5] and employed amanuenses;[6] Deuteronomy gives evidence of posthumous publication.[7] Yet we cannot deny the formative authorial role of Moses without questioning the authority of Scripture and the words of Jesus Himself.[8]

Most evangelicals affirm Mosaic authorship of the Pentateuch, but they seldom consistently apply this extrinsic frame of reference in interpretation. For the most part, interpretation is disconnected from Moses' ministry. In this survey, however, we will examine how each book fits within the times of Moses. Why did he compose these stories? What messages did he convey to his readers? This approach will shed light on the original meaning of the Mosaic History.

Genesis

The book of Genesis records selected events that occurred from creation to the death of Joseph. All of these events pre-date Moses. Yet the influence of Moses' mother (Exodus 2:8–9), his education in the Egyptian court (Exodus 2:10), and special revelation from God prepared him to give this history to Israel.

Some passages reveal minor editorial activity.[9] The orthography of the Hebrew text also suggests that the language of the book has been updated. But there is no compelling evidence that Genesis reached its final form after Moses. Nevertheless, we cannot be certain precisely when Moses composed Genesis. He may have written in Egypt, during the wilderness wanderings or on the plains of Moab. In fact, the book may have developed throughout these circumstances. Moses may have composed this book any time from his call (Exodus 3:1—4:31) to his death (Deuteronomy 34:5) (see figure 50).

Many interpreters have suggested that Genesis is structured by the "generations" (*twldwt*) formula (Genesis 2:4; 5:1; 6:9; 10:1; 11:10; 11:27; 25:12; 25:19; 36:1; 37:2).[10] But this outlook attributes too much prominence to the generations of Ishmael (Genesis 25:12–18) and Esau (Genesis 36:1–43), which play only minor roles in the book. It seems better to treat these formulas as indicating sources, genre designations, or functions of particular passages.[11] Instead, Genesis breaks down more easily into three major parts:

I. Primeval Times (1:1—11:9)
II. Early Patriarchal Times (11:10—37:1)
III. Joseph's Times (37:2—50:26)[12]

Moses wrote the book of Genesis to teach his readers that *leaving Egypt and possessing Canaan was God's design for Israel.* The primeval acts of bringing creation from chaos to sabbath rest, recreating the fallen world through waters of judgment, choosing Shem's descendants to dispossess Canaan, and defeating the city of Babel explained what God was doing for Israel in the exodus from Egypt (I). The lives of Abraham, Isaac, and Jacob anticipated Israel's interest in their numerical expansion, possession of the promised land, and relationships with surrounding nations (II). The interaction among the tribal patriarchs in the Joseph story established proper inter-tribal relations in Moses' day and assured Israel of her destiny in Canaan (III). Moses' observations of ages past encouraged his readers to turn away from Egypt and to pursue the conquest of Canaan with confidence. Joseph's final words clearly reveal Moses' purpose: "But God will surely come to your aid and take you up out of this land to the land he promised on oath to Abraham, Isaac and Jacob" (Genesis 50:24).

This major theme fits well within the entire range of likely dates for final composition. If Genesis reached its final form early in Egypt,

Moses wrote to exhort the Israelites to leave Egypt for the promised land[13] because: 1) God will work for them as He worked in the primeval history (I); 2) God promised the patriarchs He would richly bless their descendants (II); 3) God will form the tribes of Israel into a nation and bring them to Canaan as He demonstrated in Joseph's day (III).

However, if Genesis was written in the wilderness or on the plains of Moab, Moses encouraged the people to move forward into conquest.[14] Israel could be confident in conquest because: 1) God's actions in the primeval history reveal His plan to give them possession of Canaan (I); 2) God promised, led, and protected the patriarchs, and He will do the same for the nation as they move toward Canaan (II); 3) God ordered the twelve tribes in the days of Joseph in order to bring them to the land (III).

The book of Genesis reports history from the beginning of time to the death of Joseph. But this history had significant implications for Moses' readers. As they heard these stories, they learned the significance of their experiences, their responsibilities, and their hopes for the future.

Exodus

The book of Exodus covers events from the birth of Moses to the arrival of the nation in the plains of Moab. It focuses especially on Israel's deliverance from Egypt under Moses' leadership, and the legal and cultic order he mediated in the Sinai covenant.

The range of likely dates for final composition of Exodus is rather narrow. The text reports that Israel ate manna "until they reached *the border of Canaan*" (Exodus 16:35, emphasis added). It closes with the observation that the pillar of cloud and fire was "in the sight of all the house of Israel *during all their travels*" (Exodus 40:38, emphasis added). These passages push the earliest likely date of final composition to the plains of Moab.

We also know that Exodus reached its final form before the death of Moses. A few passages may reveal later additions,[15] but larger framing and reworking after Moses' death does not seem likely. Therefore, the latest reasonable date for final composition is shortly before the death of Moses (see figure 50).

Exodus breaks into three basic parts:

I. Deliverance under Moses (1:1—18:27)
II. Covenant under Moses (19:1—24:18)
III. Worship under Moses (25:1—40:38)[16]

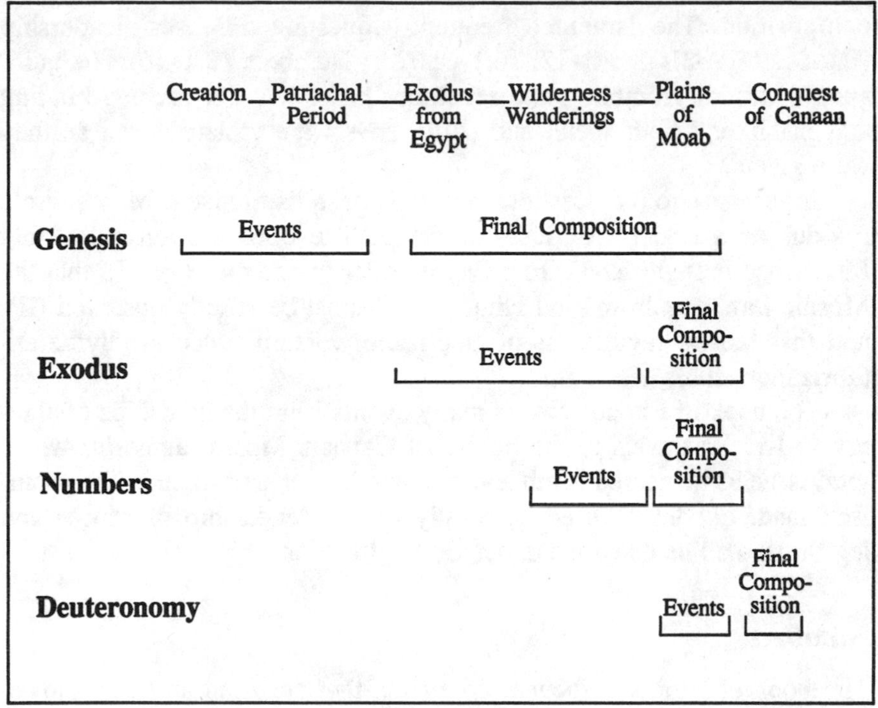

Fig. 50: The Mosaic History

Exodus contains many important themes for the original audience, but its most dominant concern is *the divine authorization of Moses' covenant order for the nation.*[17] While God's mighty works on behalf of His people are repeated throughout the book, we must not overlook the central role that Moses' leadership plays. Moses' miraculous deliverance as a child, his concern for fellow Israelites, his call from God, the miracles in Egypt, and the wonders he performed in the wilderness demonstrated that God had established Moses as the leader of Israel (I). Moses' authorization also extended to the Law he mediated to the nation. The Law was of divine origin, and Moses alone had been permitted to enter the holy presence on Sinai to receive it (II). Similarly, the tabernacle was not Moses' invention; he received instructions in worship from God on the mount (III).

In many ways Exodus explains and legitimates Moses' ministry much like the Gospels support the work of Christ.[18] In his first adult encounter with an Israelite, Moses was asked a vital question: "Who made you ruler and judge over us?" (Exodus 2:14). The book of Exodus answers that God ordained Moses as Israel's leader.

Concern with Moses' authority fits well within the time of final composition. The Israelites frequently questioned Moses' leadership (Exodus 5:19–21; 14:10–12; 16:1–3; 32:1; Numbers 12:1–16). His guidance met with grumbling and rebellion, his new order seemed binding and harsh, and both social and cultic laws were violated even as they were given.

In response to the questions raised against his ministry, Moses wrote Exodus as a defense of his leadership. The book demonstrated that Moses had brought Israel from Egypt under divine direction (I), that the Mosaic Law was from God Himself and must be strictly observed (II), and that Moses' regulations of tabernacle worship rested on divine authorization (III).

The book of Exodus covers many events from the hardships of slavery to Israel's travels to the border of Canaan. Moses' authority was a vital issue as he neared death and the people prepared to enter the promised land. Exodus focused especially on the leadership of Moses and legitimized all he had done under God's direction.

Numbers

The book of Numbers focuses on events that occurred as Israel moved from Sinai to the plains of Moab. It deals with this journey in several stages and reports times of obedience leading to blessing, and rebellion leading to judgment.

The final composition of Numbers occurred on the plains of Moab. With the exception of a few verses, there is little evidence of editing after Moses' death.[19] The last historical events recorded in the book set the tribes in Moab "across from Jericho" (Numbers 22:1; 26:3; 26:63; 31:12; 33:48, 50; 34:15; 35:1; 36:13). Repeated references to Jericho suggest that the book may have been written very near the end of Moses' life as Israel looked ahead to the conquest of the land (see figure 50).

The book of Numbers breaks down into three main sections:

I. Constituting the First Army (1:1—10:10)
II. Failures in the March (10:11—25:18)
III. Constituting the Second Army (26:1—36:13)[20]

Moses composed the book of Numbers to *call the second generation of Israel to arms as the holy army of God*. The book begins with the formation of the first generation army and the regulations of holiness it must observe (I). It then moves to the march of the first generation from

Sinai to the plains of Moab. Along the way the army rebels and loses heart. God protects His people but ultimately rejects the first generation (II). The final major section describes the constitution of the next generation into a holy army. The new generation is organized, tested, and given regulations (III).

Numbers spoke directly to the needs of the original audience. These stories called Israel, camped on the plains of Moab, to see themselves as the holy army of God. They focused on 1) how magnificently God had formed the first generation into an army (I); 2) God's blessing on the first army, its failures, and God's chastisement (II); and 3) the merciful reorganization of the second generation into a mighty army with instructions for war and life in the land after victory (III).

The book of Numbers taught Moses' audience that God had called them to be a holy army. The first generation failed in its march. Soon the people of the second generation had to march forward into Canaan. What would they do?

Deuteronomy

Deuteronomy reports a brief sequence of events that took place on the plains of Moab. It focuses on Moses' farewell addresses to the nation and the transfer of authority to Joshua, and it closes with Moses' death. Within this narrow historical setting Moses' speeches reflect on the history of the entire Exodus and anticipate events in the promised land.

The time of Deuteronomy's final composition is difficult to establish. The majority of the book came from Moses himself; there is no reason to doubt his role as the substantial author of the book. Nevertheless, the book itself suggests that Deuteronomy reached its final form shortly after Moses.[21] The strongest evidence for this point of view is the record of Moses' death (Deuteronomy 34:1–12). This substantial account is not a minor editorial addition but forms an interpretative framework for the whole book. Deuteronomy presents Mosaic instructions to an audience after his death.[22]

The affinities of Deuteronomy with international covenant treaties of the second millennium suggest that Deuteronomy reached its final form in the days of Joshua.[23] Deuteronomy focuses on Joshua as the faithful keeper of the Mosaic Law (Deuteronomy 1:38; 31:7–8; 34:9), and it deals with the need for the nation to appropriate the book as it enters Canaan (Deuteronomy 11:29–32). A lengthy passage contains detailed instructions on how the Mosaic covenant was to be renewed at Mount Ebal and Gerizim (Deuteronomy 27:1–26). As the book of Joshua reports, these directives were kept in meticulous detail (Joshua 8:30–35). It seems likely that the book came to its final form at least by the time of this covenant renewal under Joshua[24] (see figure 50).

Deuteronomy consists of several major addresses by Moses and an account of the final events in Moses' life.[25] These materials were arranged in a topical structure that roughly paralleled the order of ancient Near Eastern covenant treaties.

I. Preamble (1:1–4)	First Address (1:5—4:43)
II. Historical Prologue (1:5—4:43)	Second Address (4:44–28:68)
III. Stipulations (4:44—26:19)	
IV. Blessings, Curses, and Ratification (27:1—30:20)	Third Address (29:1—30:20)
V. Succession (31:1—34:12)[26]	

The book describes events in the time of Moses *to guide the nation in covenant renewal under Joshua*. It establishes the origins of the covenant relationship (I); rehearses the historical background of God's mercy (II); outlines the expectations of covenant life (III); presents blessings, curses, and ratification of the covenant (IV); spells out the continuation of covenant administration (V).

As the nation moved forward into the land of Canaan, it faced many difficulties and temptations. Deuteronomy impressed upon it the need to remember: 1) the God who had established a covenant with it through Moses (I); 2) what God had done on its behalf throughout history (II); 3) His requirements for life (III); 4) the blessings, curses, and ratification of the covenant relationship (IV); and 5) the need to follow Joshua as the leader of the covenanted nation (V). In this manner Deuteronomy spoke directly to the needs of the original audience.

The Mosaic History forms the first corpus of narrative materials in Scripture. It deals with issues that addressed the needs of Israel in the early decades of her life as a nation. It explained and justified the exodus program (Genesis), established Moses' authority and the legitimacy of his national order (Exodus), directed the nation to move forward as a holy army (Numbers), and taught the need for covenant fidelity in the land (Deuteronomy). The Mosaic History formed a foundational document for all the stories God would give His people in the future.

The Deuteronomistic History

The second major division of the traditional Hebrew Canon is the prophets *(nby'ym)*. The prophetic material divides into two groups: the "former prophets," (*Joshua, Judges, Samuel, Kings*) and the remaining or "latter prophets."[27] At this point we will survey the former prophets, or Deuteronomistic History, as it has come to be called in recent years. This division of the canon gives a prophetic evaluation of Israel's history from the conquest of Canaan to the exile in Babylon.

Critical approaches to the authorship of the former prophets have taken many directions, but two outlooks have dominated the field. On the one hand, older critical interpreters continued the search for the documentary sources of the Pentateuch in some of these books. Overall, however, this approach has not received broad support.[28]

On the other hand, Martin Noth proposed a view that has gained widespread acceptance.[29] He argued that the final form of Deuteronomy through Kings, excluding Ruth, was the work of an exilic editor whom he called the Deuteronomist. Noth recognized that the individual books in this history were different from each other. He explained these differences in style and content as variations in the sources upon which the Deuteronomist relied.[30] Even so, from Noth's outlook one principal theological perspective ran through all of these books: that Israel had violated the laws of Deuteronomy to such an extent that the nation had been justly condemned to exile.[31]

While agreeing that these books reflect a basic unity, von Rad modified Noth's negative assessment of the history's purpose. He focused on the messianic hope, especially in Samuel and Kings, and argued that the Deuteronomist emphasized hope for the continuation of the Davidic line.[32] Despite sin and judgment, the Davidic promise was not lost.

In recent years the tendency has been to give both themes more equal footing. Cross argues that judgment and hope reflect different redactional levels.[33] The positive hope in the Davidic line stems from an editor (Dtr_1) who wrote during the times of Josiah's reforms (2 Kings 22:1—23:30). The negative theme of condemnation was then added by an exilic editor (Dtr_2).

Wolff approached the negative and positive elements of the history in a more helpful manner. In his outlook the justice of exile and hope in the Davidic line finds a connection in the theme of repentance. If the exiles would fully repent of their violations of the covenant, then their return from exile would occur.[34]

Modern evangelicals have taken different stances on the date and purpose of the former prophets. Two issues have been of particular concern: *the place of Deuteronomy* and *the unity of the history*.

The Place of Deuteronomy

Critical interpreters typically treat the final form of Deuteronomy as a part of the Deuteronomistic History.[35] As we have already seen, evangelicals affirm fundamental Mosaic authorship of Deuteronomy, ruling out any later date for the book.

Even so, it cannot be denied that Deuteronomy played an important role in the books of Joshua through Kings, even though the Deuteronomistic History relied on other books in the Pentateuch as well. Theological terminology, covenantal structures, and many other theological motifs stem largely from Deuteronomy.[36] From this perspective Deuteronomy served the dual function of closing the Mosaic History and providing a theological foundation for the Deuteronomistic History.

The Unity of the History

A second major concern has been the distinctive characteristics of each book. Despite his attempts to the contrary, Noth's concept of an exilic edition of the history tended to minimize the differences among the books. As we will see, however, Joshua, Judges, Samuel, and Kings reflect significant diversity. To understand these books properly, we must deal with them individually.

In light of the evidence of diversity and unity among these books, it seems best to assume that the Deuteronomistic History represents the work of different writers within a single theological family. The harmony of the history stems primarily from its extensive dependence on Deuteronomy. Yet the books reflect distinctive perspectives that rose out of the diverse situations each writer addressed.

Joshua

The book of Joshua reports the events of Israel's initial conquest of Canaan: the division of the land, the early days in Canaan, and the death of Joshua. The fact that many passages have features of eyewitness reports (Joshua 2:21; 5:1, 6; 7:21; 8:26; 14:6–12; 15:16–19; 17:14–18) indicates that portions of the book were written near or during this time.[37] Rahab is said to have lived "among the Israelites to this day" (Joshua 6:25).[38] The city of Sidon was reported as the chief city of Phoenicia (Joshua 19:28).[39] The Jebusites still occupied Jerusalem (Joshua 15:8; see 2 Samuel 5:6ff), and the Gibeonites were still servants in the sanctuary (Joshua 9:27; see 2 Samuel 21:1–6). But in the light of other portions of the book, these references seem to reflect sources used by the final compiler.

A number of passages indicate that the date of final composition was much later than most of the events in the book. On several occasions the writer thought it necessary to give the modern equivalents for older names of places (Joshua 15:9, 49, 54). Several incidents noted in the book occurred after the time of Joshua. For instance, the writer mentions the conquests of Hebron by Caleb (Joshua 15:13; Judges 1:8–10), of Debir by Othniel (Joshua 15:15–17; Judges 1:11–13) and the migration of the Danites to the extreme north of Israel (Joshua 19:47; Judges 18:27–29). The last chapter records the death of Joshua (Joshua 24:29–30) and Eleazar (Joshua 24:33). The book even gives a retrospective evaluation on the elders who outlived Joshua (Joshua 24:31).[40] In the light of these evidences, we may conclude that the book of Joshua came to its final form no earlier than a generation or two after Joshua's death.

The best indication of the latest likely date is found in the book of Kings. First Kings 16:34 alludes to Joshua's curse on anyone who rebuilt Jericho (Joshua 6:26).[41] The book of Kings may be dated between the release of Jehoiachin (561 B.C.) and the Cyrus Edict (538 B.C.).[42] Consequently, the latest reasonable date for the final composition of Joshua is during the exile (see figure 51).

Joshua divides into three main parts.

I. Conquest of the Land (1:1—12:24)
II. Inheritance of the Land (13:1—22:34)
III. Covenant Life in the Land (23:1—24:33)[43]

The book of Joshua focuses on the days of conquest to teach its readers *how to live in the land God had given them.* The successes and failures of Joshua's warfare demonstrated how Israel was to continue to fight for the land (I). The establishment of land distribution and intertribal relations taught how Israel was to manage the inheritance of the land (II). The covenant renewal ceremony at the end of Joshua's life showed the necessity of living in fidelity before God by commitment to the covenant (III).

These prominent motifs fit well within the range of dates for final composition. If the book was written before the monarchy, it exhorted the audience: 1) to continue holy war as Joshua had pursued it (I); 2) to respect tribal possessions and unity (II); 3) and to continue covenant renewal and fidelity (III).

If the book was finally composed in the exile, it 1) offered the exiles hope of victory over their enemies (I); 2) reminded them of their national inheritance in the promised land (II); 3) and called them to covenant renewal and fidelity (III).

The book of Joshua looks back to the days when Israel first took the land to teach the readers about their own times, outlining the way to victory, security, and covenant fidelity in the land of Canaan.

Judges

The book of Judges records events between the conquest and the rise of Israel's monarchy. As in Joshua, a number of passages were written very near the events that are reported. The Jebusites are said to live in Jerusalem "to this day" (Judges 1:21); Sidon is treated as the chief city of Phonecia (Judges 18:28).[44] These passages probably reflect sources used by the final compiler.

Several passages indicate that the earliest likely date for the final composition is the monarchical period.[45] Four times the writer contrasts his own day with the historical events of the book saying, "In those days Israel had no king" (Judges 17:6; 18:1; 19:1; 21:25). Judges 18:30 may suggest that the exile of Israel had occurred. But the expression "the captivity of the land *(h'rṣ)*" (Judges 18:30), may be a corruption of "until the captivity of the ark *(h'rwn)*."[46] The evidence of this verse is uncertain, but it at least points to the early years of monarchy in Israel (1 Samuel 4:1b–11).[47]

A few clues suggest the latest likely date for Judges. The book of Samuel picks up the historical sequence of Judges. In fact, it models the account of Samuel's birth after the birth of Samson.[48] This evidence suggests that Judges was written at least by the time Samuel was finally composed. The promonarchical character of the book may suggest a date prior to the great failures of kingship in Israel, but the nation placed high hopes in its kings even after David and his descendants led it into trouble. The apparent presence of kings in the writer's day (Judges 17:6; 18:1; 19:1; 21:25) may suggest that the final composition occurred before the exile. But the maintenance of royal hopes during the exile could explain these passages as well. While a time in the early monarchy seems more likely, we may not rule out the possibility of a later date (see figure 51).

The book presents its material in three main sections.

I. Faltering Conquest (1:1—2:4)
II. Cycles under the Judges (2:5—16:31)
III. Anarchy under the Levites (17:1—21:25)

The book of Judges is an *apologetic for Israel's monarchy.*[49] Why does Israel need a godly king? The book gives three answers: without a

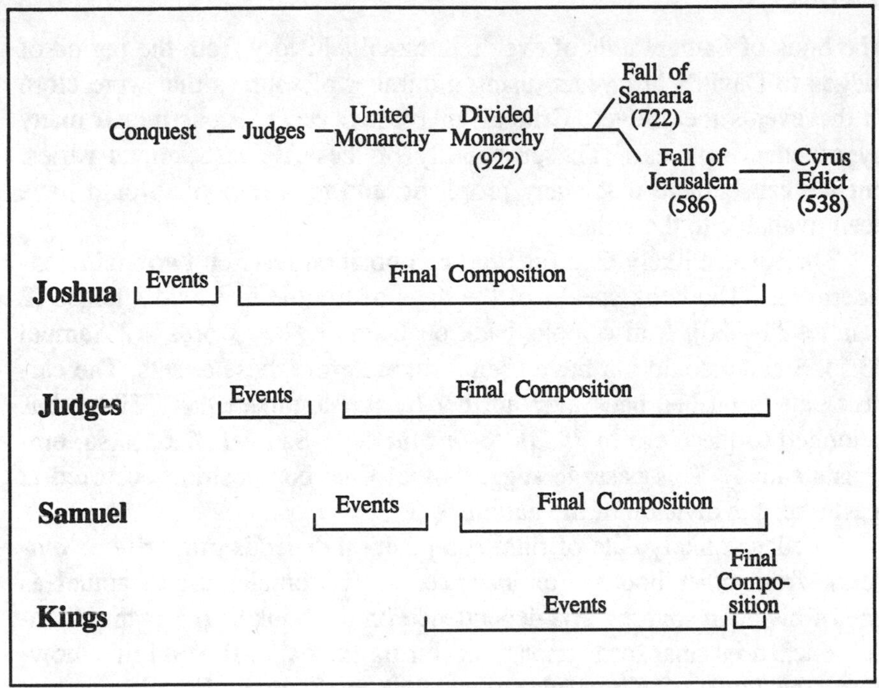

Fig. 51: The Deuteronomistic History

king the tribes faltered in the conquest (I); the office of judge could only bring sporadic relief from cycles of apostasy (II); and when there was no king, the Levites failed to provide stability in the cultic and social life of Israel (III).

These prominent themes fit well within the range of dates for final composition. If Judges was written as early as David's rise to power, it spoke to the need for a Judahite leader to guide the people in battle (I), a king to provide peace and security (II), and a king to enforce cultic and social standards of the Mosaic Law (III).

If the book was finally composed during the exile, it instructed the people of their need for a Davidic king to lead the people (I), the inadequacy of returning to premonarchical tribal leadership (II), the need for a new Davidic king to keep Israel from cultic and social anarchy (III).

The book of Judges covers a dark period in Israel's history. Failure and trouble appear on nearly every page. The writer reported these difficulties to demonstrate the need for a godly king. From the early days of David to the latter days of exile, this message spoke directly to the experiences of the people of God.

Samuel

The book of Samuel tells of events in Israel's history from the period of judges to David's last years, using a number of sources that were close to the events themselves. Critical interpreters have reconstructed many hypothetical sources.[50] The probability of these reconstructions varies, but we can be sure that many prophetic and royal records would have been available to the writer.

The earliest likely date for final composition rests on two main considerations. The book speaks of the days of trouble in David's house (2 Samuel 11—20). It also looks back on David's "last words" (2 Samuel 23:1). Samuel could not have been written before these events. The earliest date is pushed back even further by the comment that "Ziklag has belonged to the *kings of Judah to this day*" (1 Samuel 27:6, NASB, emphasis added). This passage suggests that final composition occurred at least after the division of the nation.[51]

The latest likely date of final composition depends primarily on evidence from other books. For instance, the Chronicler used Samuel as one of his main sources. His dependence on the book suggests that Samuel reached its final form prior to or during the exile. Beyond this, however, the book of Kings also depended on Samuel. For instance, it picked up the history of Israel's monarchy where Samuel left off (2 Samuel 23:1–7; 1 Kings 1:1). It also referred to the fulfillment of prophecy given in Samuel (1 Kings 2:27; see 1 Samuel 2:27–36). Since we know that Kings was written during the last years of exile, we may set this date as the parameter for the latest likely date of final composition for Samuel as well (see figure 51).

The book of Samuel may be outlined as follows:

I. Foundation of the Kingdom (1 Samuel 1:1—7:17)
II. Saul's Kingdom (1 Samuel 8:1—15:35)
III. David's Kingdom (1 Samuel 16:1—2 Samuel 20:26)
IV. Future of the Kingdom (2 Samuel 21:1—24:25)[52]

Central to this book is the theme that *Israel should hope in the Davidic line, despite the trouble caused by David's shortcomings.*[53] God's blessing on Samuel established the legitimacy of David's line because he anointed David as king (I). Saul and his family forfeited kingship by turning away from God (II). God blessed David as he was faithful but cursed him with trouble when he failed (III). Nevertheless, the last chapters demonstrate that David's house was still the legitimate dynasty in which Israel must put its hope for all generations (IV).

In the divided monarchy, these themes would have spoken directly to the needs of the nation. David's family had been the primary cause of Israel's division (1 Kings 11:9–13) and had led the people astray many times. Despite these shortcomings, however, the Davidic line was still the legitimate dynasty because: 1) Samuel established it (I); 2) Saul's kingdom was rejected (II); 3) David's house was founded as Israel's permanent dynasty (III); 4) God chose David's house to benefit the nation in many ways (IV). In a period when strong objections could be raised against David's house, this book spoke a sober but desperately needed message of hope.

In the exile, the same themes would have spoken to the need for maintaining hope in the Davidic line. Despite the fact that blame for the exile fell largely on David's house (2 Kings 21:10–15), the hope of the nation was still in David's seed who would rise and lead the kingdom to its glorious restoration.

Kings

The book of Kings deals with the history of Israel from David's death to the release of Jehoiachin from prison in Babylon. On many occasions the writer refers explicitly to specific sources that came from the days of the events themselves. He mentions "the book of the annals of Solomon" (1 Kings 11:41), "the book of the annals of the kings of Judah" (1 Kings 14:29; 15:7, 23), and "the book of the annals of the kings of Israel" (1 Kings 14:19; 15:31).[54] At times the writer maintained the formula "to this day" to refer to the time of his source material, but occasionally he had his own present day in view.[55]

The range of extrinsic agents for this book is relatively narrow. The earliest likely date for final composition is the release of Jehoiachin (2 Kings 25:27–30) (561/2 B.C.). The expression "for the rest of [Jehoiachin's] life" (2 Kings 25:29) is ambiguous. It may or may not indicate that Jehoiachin was dead by the time of composition.[56] Since the writer of Kings did not mention Cyrus, the latest likely date is just before the Cyrus Edict (538 B.C.) when the Israelites received permission to return to the land (see figure 51).

The outline of Kings is straightforward:

I. Failure and Hope in Solomon's Years (1 Kings 1:1—12:24)
II. Failure and Hope in the Divided Years (1 Kings 12:25—2 Kings 17:41)
III. Failure and Hope in Judah's Final Years (2 Kings 18:1—25:27–30)

The book of Kings demonstrated that *the nation deserved the exile, but restoration was possible through full repentance.*[57] The writer conveyed this message by focusing on Solomon's glory when he was faithful and on the division and ruin his rebellion brought to the nation (I). He then turned to the examples of fidelity and apostasy in the divided period, highlighting especially the failure of northern Israel and the justice of their exile (II). Finally, he turned to the disobedience that led Judah into exile and closed with a flicker of hope in Jehoiachin's release (III).

If Kings was written before Jehoiachin's death, it encouraged the people to commit themselves to full repentance because: when Solomon served God, his kingdom was glorious, but his syncretism brought curses on the kingdom (I); in the divided kingdom obedience brought rich blessings, but infidelity resulted in curses and exile (II); and in the remaining Judahite kingdom, the same principle of blessing and cursing applied (III). Jehoiachin's release was taken as a sign that blessings may be coming. Perhaps now God would remove the curse if the people repented.

If the book of Kings was written after the death of Jehoiachin, it addressed the disappointments that rose with his demise. It demonstrated that God was just to keep His people in exile and that return depended on full repentance and faith.

The Deuteronomistic history represents the second major corpus of Old Testament narratives. Its various books took the Mosaic law, especially Deuteronomy, and evaluated different segments of Israel's history from the conquest to the release of Jehoiachin in Babylon. Taken together these books form a joint perspective. Yet we must not lose sight of the unique perspectives each book presented. They taught basic guidance for life in the land of promise (Joshua), the need for a king (Judges), the continuing legitimacy of the Davidic line (Samuel), and the cause and remedy of the exile (Kings).

The Chronistic History

The Chronistic History, the third major family of Old Testament narratives, consists of *Chronicles, Ezra,* and *Nehemiah.* These books appear in the Septuagint and our English Bibles immediately after the book of Kings. In the Hebrew canon, however, they appear in a different order (Ezra, Nehemiah, Chronicles) at the end of "the writings" (*ktbym*).

Jewish traditions assign the scribe Ezra a dominant role in the authorship of all three books. Critical and evangelical interpreters have interacted with this traditional outlook in different ways.[58] The possibility that Ezra was involved with the final composition of this material cannot be ruled out entirely, but there is little positive evidence. To be sure, Ezra's memoirs (Ezra 7:1—10:44)[59] are autobiographical, but these sections may simply have been one of many sources.

Apart from the question of Ezra's involvement, the working assumption for most interpreters in recent centuries has been that a single person was responsible for the final composition of all three books. Similar to Noth's concept of the Deuteronomist, "the Chronicler" was presumed to have composed Chronicles, Ezra, and Nehemiah.[60]

It is no wonder that interpreters have been prone to see a single hand behind this history. The books have significant interconnections. For instance, Ezra duplicates and elaborates on the account of the Cyrus Edict in Chronicles (2 Chronicles 36:22–23; Ezra 1:1–4).[61] All the books were written in Palestine within a short span of time. They share a deep interest in the temple and the purity of the people of God. The books exhibit a significant degree of unity. Yet this unity must not obscure their differences.

For the most part, recent research continues to point to the original unity of Ezra and Nehemiah. Some interpreters have argued that Ezra and Nehemiah were originally separate books,[62] but most would agree with Williamson that "there is good reason to approach Ezra and Nehemiah as two parts of a single work."[63]

At the same time, however, recent studies have tended to drive a wedge between Chronicles and Ezra-Nehemiah.[64] A number of ideological differences strongly suggest that they came from different authors. For instance, the book of Chronicles emphasizes the doctrine of divine retribution and the Davidic covenant; these themes are largely absent in Ezra-Nehemiah.[65] The book of Chronicles is more irenic toward northerners than Ezra-Nehemiah.[66] Chronicles holds out the hope for reunification of North and South; Ezra-Nehemiah has no place for the participation of northerners.[67] The most impressive difference, however, is the treatment of Solomon's foreign wives.[68] Chronicles omits 1 Kings 11:9–13, where the division of the kingdom is attributed to Solomon's intermarriages. This omission is remarkable in light of the problems with intermarriage during and after the ministries of Ezra and Nehemiah (Ezra 10:1–44). Moreover, Nehemiah 13:26 explicitly discredits Solomon because of his intermarriages.[69] These ideological differences offer strong evidence for presuming a separate authorship for Chronicles and Ezra-Nehemiah.

In many respects the Chronistic History exhibits unity and diversity similar to that of the Deuteronomistic History. The similarities allow us to speak of a Chronistic corpus, a family of books that build on each other and represent similar points of view. But Chronicles and Ezra-Nehemiah were probably separate works dealing with different issues.

Chronicles

Chronicles covers a wide span of history beginning with Adam (1 Chronicles 1:1) and ending with the Cyrus Edict (2 Chronicles 36:22–23). The Chronicler skimmed events prior to David by way of genealogies, lists, and short narratives (1 Chronicles 1:1—9:44) but dealt with history from David to the Cyrus Edict in great detail.

The Chronicler used many sources,[70] principally Samuel and Kings.[71] Yet he also referred to a number of other sources:[72]

- portions of the Pentateuch, Judges, Ruth, Psalms, Isaiah, Jeremiah, and Zechariah;
- several unknown royal sources: "the book of the annals of King David" (1 Chronicles 27:24), "the book of the kings" (2 Chronicles 24:27), "the book of the kings of Israel" (1 Chronicles 9:1; 2 Chronicles 20:34), "the book of the kings of Judah and Israel" (2 Chronicles 27:7; 35:27; 36:8);
- several prophetic sources: the writings of Samuel (1 Chronicles 29:29), Nathan (1 Chronicles 29:29; 2 Chronicles 9:29), Gad (1 Chronicles 29:29), Ahijah (2 Chronicles 9:29), Iddo (2 Chronicles 9:29; 12:15; 13:22), Shemaiah (2 Chronicles 12:15), Isaiah (2 Chronicles 26:22), and anonymous "seers" (2 Chronicles 33:19);
- other unspecified sources.

The earliest possible date for the final composition of Chronicles is difficult to determine. The Cyrus Edict is the last event recorded. But how soon after the edict did the Chronicler write? In recent years a growing number of interpreters have argued for an early date near Zerubbabel's effort to reconstruct the temple (c. 520–515).[73] Early dating is not without problems. For instance, the royal genealogy in 1 Chronicles 3:17–24 appears to extend at least two generations beyond Zerubbabel.[74] As we have seen, however, the possibility of editorial expansion in this passage cannot be ruled out.[75]

Several considerations point positively to a Zerubbabelian date. First, the omission of Solomon's intermarriages (1 Kings 11:9–13) suggests that the book was written before the problems of syncretism grew in the post-exilic community. Second, the closing of the book depicts Cyrus explicitly stating that God had appointed him "to build a temple for him at Jerusalem in Judah" (2 Chronicles 36:23), a theme vital to the early reconstruction effort. Third, the Chronicler combined programmatic interest in kingship and temple in a way appropriate for the days of Zerubbabel. Throughout his account Israel's blessing depended on having the Davidic king and the Jerusalem temple in proper order. These motifs fit best in the days before Zerubbabel had vanished from the scene. For these reasons we will assign the earliest possible date for final composition to the time of temple reconstruction.

The latest date is very difficult to determine.[76] The lack of Hellenistic influences suggests that the book was composed before the dark years of the intertestamental period. If the full genealogy of 1 Chronicles 3:17–24 is accepted as original, it suggests a date around 400 *B.C.*[77] We will, therefore, set the limit of the likely extrinsic agents in the early fourth century (see figure 52).

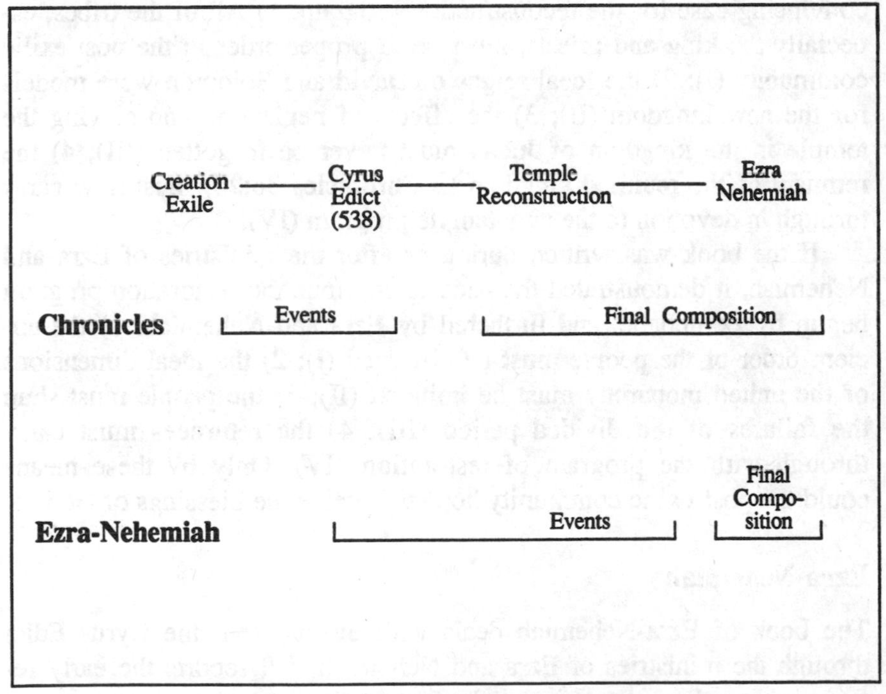

Fig. 52: The Chronistic History

The Chronicler wrote his history to *direct the restoration of the kingdom during the post-exilic period.*[78] His record divides into four main parts:

I. Genealogies of God's People (1 Chronicles 1:1—9:44)
II. United Kingdom (1 Chronicles 10:1—2 Chronicles 9:31)
III. Divided Kingdom (2 Chronicles 10:1—28:26)
IV. Reunited Kingdom (2 Chronicles 29:1—36:23)

The Chronicler began his history with an account of the people who belonged in the restored nation, tracing the background of Israel and the extent of all of the tribes and the families among the early returnees (I). He then presented an idealized account of the reigns of David and Solomon, who ruled over all the tribes and dedicated themselves to temple construction (II). The Chronicler continued by showing how Judah's prosperity and trouble depended on the nation's trust in God, obedience, and commitment to the temple (III). Finally, he traced the kingdom reunited under Hezekiah as it moved toward exile and finally returned to the land of Israel (IV).

If Chronicles was written in the days of Zerubbabel, it presented a convincing case for the reconstruction program: 1) All of the tribes, especially the king and priests, must be in proper order in the post-exilic community (I); 2) the ideal reigns of David and Solomon were models for the new kingdom (II); 3) the effects of neglecting and serving the temple in the kingdom of Judah must never be forgotten (III); 4) the remnant of the reunited kingdom (2 Chronicles 36:20) must now carry through in devotion to the new temple program (IV).

If the book was written during or after the ministries of Ezra and Nehemiah, it demonstrated the need to continue the restoration program begun by Zerubbabel and furthered by Ezra and Nehemiah: 1) the ancient order of the people must be observed (I); 2) the ideal dimensions of the united monarchy must be imitated (II); 3) the people must shun the failures of the divided period (III); 4) the returnees must carry through with the program of restoration (IV). Only by these means could the post-exilic community hope to receive the blessings of God.

Ezra-Nehemiah

The book of Ezra-Nehemiah deals with events from the Cyrus Edict through the ministries of Ezra and Nehemiah.[79] It reports the early return and temple construction under Zerubbabel and gives an account of the reforms and building projects years later under Ezra and Nehemiah.

Several sources for the book come from the times of the events.[80] The memoirs of Ezra and Nehemiah stem from the period.[81] Documents such as the Cyrus Edict given in Aramaic (Ezra 6:3–5), letters between Tattenai and Darius (Ezra 5:6–17; 6:3–12), correspondence from

Artaxerxes (Ezra 7:12–26), and letters to Artaxerxes (Ezra 4:8-22) reflect early sources. Lists of various sorts within the book may also have been independent sources.[82]

The range of likely dates for final composition is fairly narrow. When establishing the earliest reasonable date, we must note that the genealogy of Nehemiah 12:1–26 extends at least to 400 B.C. and perhaps to the Hellenistic period.[83] Yet, as we have seen, the possibility of editorial expansion cannot be excluded.[84] Apart from this genealogy, however, the earliest likely date is after the last events of the book during the later years of Nehemiah's governorship.[85]

Two considerations support a late date beyond the lifetime of Nehemiah. First, on two occasions the writer looks retrospectively on events that occurred "in the days of Nehemiah" (Nehemiah 12:26, 47).[86] Second, as we have already mentioned, the genealogical material suggests a date beyond him (see figure 52).

The book of Ezra-Nehemiah divides into five parts:

I. Struggle and Success for Zerubbabel (Ezra 1:1—6:22)
II. Struggle and Success for Ezra (Ezra 7:1—10:44)
III. Struggle and Success for Nehemiah (Nehemiah 1:1—7:7)
IV. Celebration of Successes (Nehemiah 8:1—12:47)
V. Continuing Struggle for Restoration (Nehemiah 13:1–31)[87]

The book of Ezra-Nehemiah was designed to *defend the legitimacy of the Ezra-Nehemiah program and the need to continue it.*[88] Each major portion of the book contains an apologetic quality. It begins with the divine authorization of Zerubbabel's temple reconstruction, traces the opposition that occurred, and recounts the prophetic and royal support that made the rebuilding succeed in grand celebration (I). Then attention turns to the divine authorization of Ezra's reforms, the opposition he received, and his success in challenging intermarriage (II). Nehemiah's mission to rebuild and repopulate Jerusalem also received divine authorization, faced human opposition, and was finally successful (III). These successes climax in worshipful confession and celebration (IV). But in the end, the book stresses the need for continuing the restoration program by reporting Nehemiah's further reforms (IV).

If we locate the book of Ezra-Nehemiah in the latter days of Nehemiah's ministry, it indicates the need for: 1) support for the new temple and its order (I); 2) restrictions on intermarriage (II); 3) repopulation and fortification of Jerusalem (III); 4) joyous celebration of this new community order (IV); and 5) continuing religious and social reforms in Judah (V). Since the new order had not brought the prosperity many expected, this book defended the continuation of the restoration program.

If the book was finally composed sometime after Nehemiah's death, its message was needed more desperately. Despite years of continuing trouble and hardship, the restored community must: 1) center itself on the new temple (I); 2) affirm the restrictions on intermarriage (II); 3) support the city of Jerusalem (III); 4) celebrate the goodness of the restoration (IV); and 5) continue these reforms even in the face of disappointments (V).

The Chronistic History represents a unified but diverse body of material stemming from and responding to Israel's experiences during the restoration. Chronicles and Ezra-Nehemiah provided essential instruction for the restoration and reform of the nation in the post-exilic period.

Other Books

A number of Old Testament narrative books do not belong to a particular theological tradition. In the Hebrew canon, they appear both within "the writings" and "the prophets." We will not comment on Jeremiah, Ezekiel, and Daniel; even though they contain large sections of narrative, the interpretative issues involved with these prophetic books are beyond the scope of this study. We will focus on just three other Old Testament books: *Ruth, Esther,* and *Jonah.*

Ruth

The book of Ruth deals with historical events that took place during the period of the judges. Ruth has been rightly characterized as a *novella.*[89] No evidence exists for extensive reliance on diverse written sources. It is possible that the final compiler relied on oral traditions, but it is unlikely that the book has gone through much compositional development. With the exception of the genealogical note in Ruth 4:17b and the fuller genealogy at the end of the book (Ruth 4:18–22), the story moves in a straightforward manner.

The range of extrinsic agents is not very broad. The earliest likely date for final composition is early in the beginning of David's reign. While the events took place much earlier, the genealogies at the end of the book trace Ruth's ancestry to David (Ruth 4:17b, 22).

The latest likely date is less certain. Some critical interpreters have placed the book in the post-exilic period on the basis of linguistic and theological analysis, but these evidences are questionable.[90] It seems most likely that the genealogies in Ruth extended to the king who reigned in the time of final composition. If this is so, the book came to its final form before Solomon's rise to the throne (see figure 53).

The book of Ruth has many important themes: the introduction of a Moabitess into Israel, the providence of God, the practice of levirate marriage, calamity, and blessing.[91] But all of these themes work together as part of an overarching concern. As the closing genealogies suggest, the book *established the legitimacy of David's kingship despite his Moabite ancestress.*[92] The law of Moses taught explicitly that the king of Israel must be "from among your own brothers" (Deuteronomy 17:15). The book of Ruth admits that David had a Moabitess in his line. But she was a convert (Ruth 1:16). She came into Israel through the providence of God (Ruth 1:1–7), and the legal practice of levirate marriage (Ruth 3:1–8). Moreover, she was approved by God's blessing (Ruth 4:13–17).

The book follows a simple outline forming a five-part narrative of resolution and an appendix:

I. Naomi's Bitterness (1:1–22)
II. Ruth Discovers Potential Kinsman Redeemer (2:1–23)
III. Boaz Agrees to be Kinsman Redeemer (3:1–18)
IV. Boaz Acquires Right to be Kinsman Redeemer (4:1–12)
V. Naomi's Blessing (4:13–17)
Genealogical Appendix (4:18–21)[93]

The book of Ruth could have served the cause of David early or late in his reign. If it was finally compiled as David rose to power, it supported him against those who opposed his leadership. If it was written after his establishment, it defended his right to continue to reign against those who sought to discredit him.

Esther

The book of Esther recounts events that occurred during the post-exilic period.[94] Unlike Ezra-Nehemiah, however, the story is not located in Palestine, but in Persia. While some of the exiles returned, many remained outside the promised land. The book of Esther deals with what happened to some of these people.

On several occasions the writer of Esther referred to written sources that came from the time of the events. He employed official Persian records (Esther 2:23; 8:8; 9:32; 10:2) and referred to Mordecai's writings (Esther 9:20).[95] Nevertheless, the compiler shaped his sources into a well formed *novella*.[96]

The book forms a five-part narrative of resolution:

I. Esther and Mordecai in the Persian Court (1:1—2:23)
II. Trouble for the Jews (3:1—4:17)
III. Esther's Intervention (5:1—7:10)
IV. Victory for the Jews (8:1—9:17)
V. Esther and Mordecai in the Persian Court (9:18—10:3)[97]

The range of final composition for Esther cannot be established with much certainty. The book was written at least after the death of Xerxes (c. 465 B.C.) since the writer refers to the official state history of Xerxes (Esther 10:2).[98] The author's interest in the details of Persian culture suggests that he lived in the district and may have written near the time of the events.[99] Nevertheless, the explanation of Purim (Esther 9:18–32), the discussion of the term "pur" (Esther 9:24), and the emphasis on the need for continued celebration (Esther 9:28) suggest that considerable time may have passed between the events and final composition. For lack of extensive Hellenistic influences on the book, we will assign the latest likely date prior to Alexander the Great (c. 330 B.C.).

Interpreters have suggested several major themes for the book. Many have seen the book as an explanation of the Feast of Purim.[100] Others have stressed the providence of God for Israelites remaining in exile.[101] These motifs are certainly close to the heart of the book, but the overarching theme seems to lie in a different direction.

One helpful way to approach Esther is in terms of the similarities among Esther, the story of Joseph in Egypt, and the opening chapters of Daniel.[102] All three accounts deal with Israelite figures in foreign lands who overcome trials through divine assistance. In one way or another, they come in contact with the foreign royal court and rise to positions of authority that enable them to influence national policies. This pattern suggests that the book of Esther offered the original audience *a model for living in fidelity to God outside of the land.*

This theme fits well with the range of likely extrinsic agents. Whether near the death of Xerxes, the time of Alexander, or sometime in between, the people of God outside the theocracy needed guidance on how to live faithfully, successfully, and influentially in foreign lands. The book of Esther provided them with such instruction.

Jonah

The events in the book of Jonah occurred sometime in the mid-eighth century B.C. Jonah, son of Amittai, ministered during the reign of Jeroboam II (783–743 B.C.) (2 Kings 14:25).[103]

The book of Jonah gives little evidence of extensive compositional history and few clues for the time of final composition. The earliest possible date is slightly after the events of the book. Evangelicals often assign authorship to Jonah himself.[104] While this possibility cannot be ruled out, the book offers little positive support for such a view.

One suggestion of temporal distance between the writer and the events appears in Jonah 3:3 where he comments, "Now Nineveh was a very important ('exceedingly great' [*NASB*]) city." The past tense suggests that by the time of writing Nineveh was no longer a great city.[105] If this is correct, we may date final composition after the fall of Nineveh to the Babylonian emperor Nabopolassar (612 B.C.). The ambiguity of the internal evidence for dating this book has made it virtually impossible to identify the latest likely date. Therefore, we must recognize a very wide range of possibilities (see figure 53).[106]

Jonah focuses on the theme of *Israel's prophetic role to the nations.* The book mocks Jonah for his self-righteousness and hypocrisy. It demonstrates that God receives other nations, even the Assyrians, and expected the Jewish people to serve as mediators to them. The universality of God's mercy and the mediatorial role of Israel are the central themes of the book.[107]

The book of Jonah divides into two main parts:

Part One
- I. First Commission and Jonah's Reaction (1:1–16)
- II. God's Response to Jonah (1:17—2:10)

Part Two
- III. Second Commission and Jonah's Reaction (3:1–10)
- IV. God's Response to Jonah (4:1–11)[108]

While the book of Jonah implicitly concerns all Gentile nations, it is helpful to read Jonah in terms of its particular focus on Jewish-Assyrian relations. Before the destruction of Nineveh, the Assyrians troubled Israel and raised hatred against them. If the book was written in this period, it spoke clearly to the need for Israelites to recognize: 1) God's call for Israel to minister to the Assyrians (I); 2) the need to repent of neglecting this call (II); 3) the power of prophetic ministry among As-

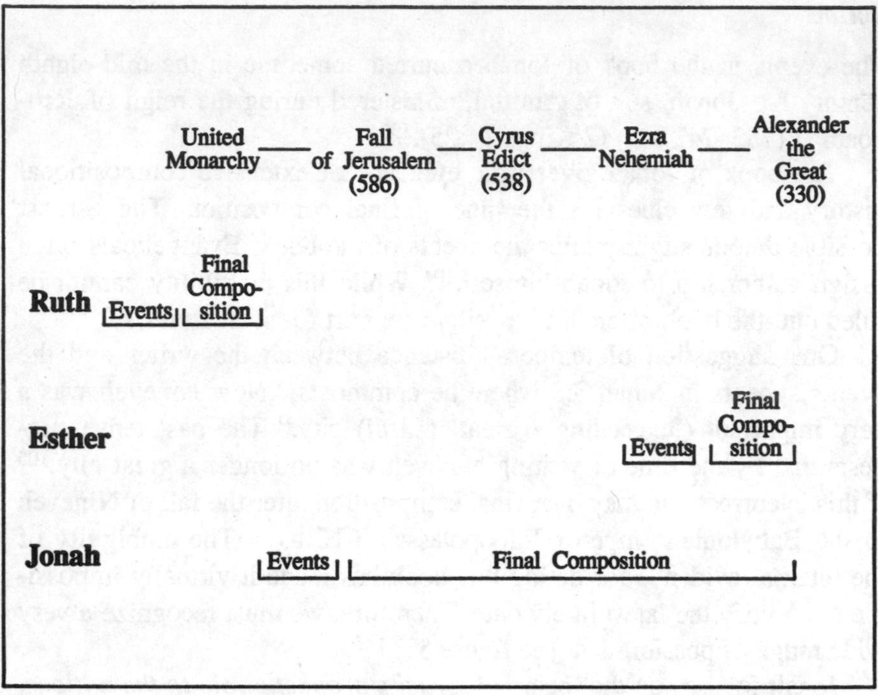

Fig. 53: Other Narrative Books

syrians (III); and 4) the need to have compassion even as God had compassion (IV).

If the book was written after the destruction of Nineveh, it spoke to the attitude that Israelites should have toward the war-torn nation. They were to: 1) accept their call to minister to the Assyrians (I); 2) repent of past attitudes (II); 3) seek to bring about repentance among Assyrians (III); and 4) rejoice in God's compassion toward their former enemies (IV).

Conclusion

Old Testament narrative books cover many periods of history and speak a variety of messages to the people of Israel. The Mosaic History, Deuteronomistic History, Chronistic History, and other narrative books were written to teach their readers how to serve God. We have barely scratched the surface of these sacred texts, but this survey of their original meaning gives us insights that permit us to apply these Old Testament stories to our own lives.

Review Questions

1. What factors unify the Mosaic History? Compare and contrast the dating and purpose of each book.
2. What factors unify the Deuteronomistic History? Compare and contrast the dating and purpose of each book.
3. What factors unify the Chronistic History? Compare and contrast the dating and purpose of each book.
4. Summarize the dating and purpose of Ruth, Esther, and Jonah.

Study Exercise

Choose one episode out of each book covered in this survey. How does it fit within the overarching outline presented here? How does the episode contribute to the overarching purposes proposed for the book?

PART III

APPLYING OLD TESTAMENT NARRATIVES

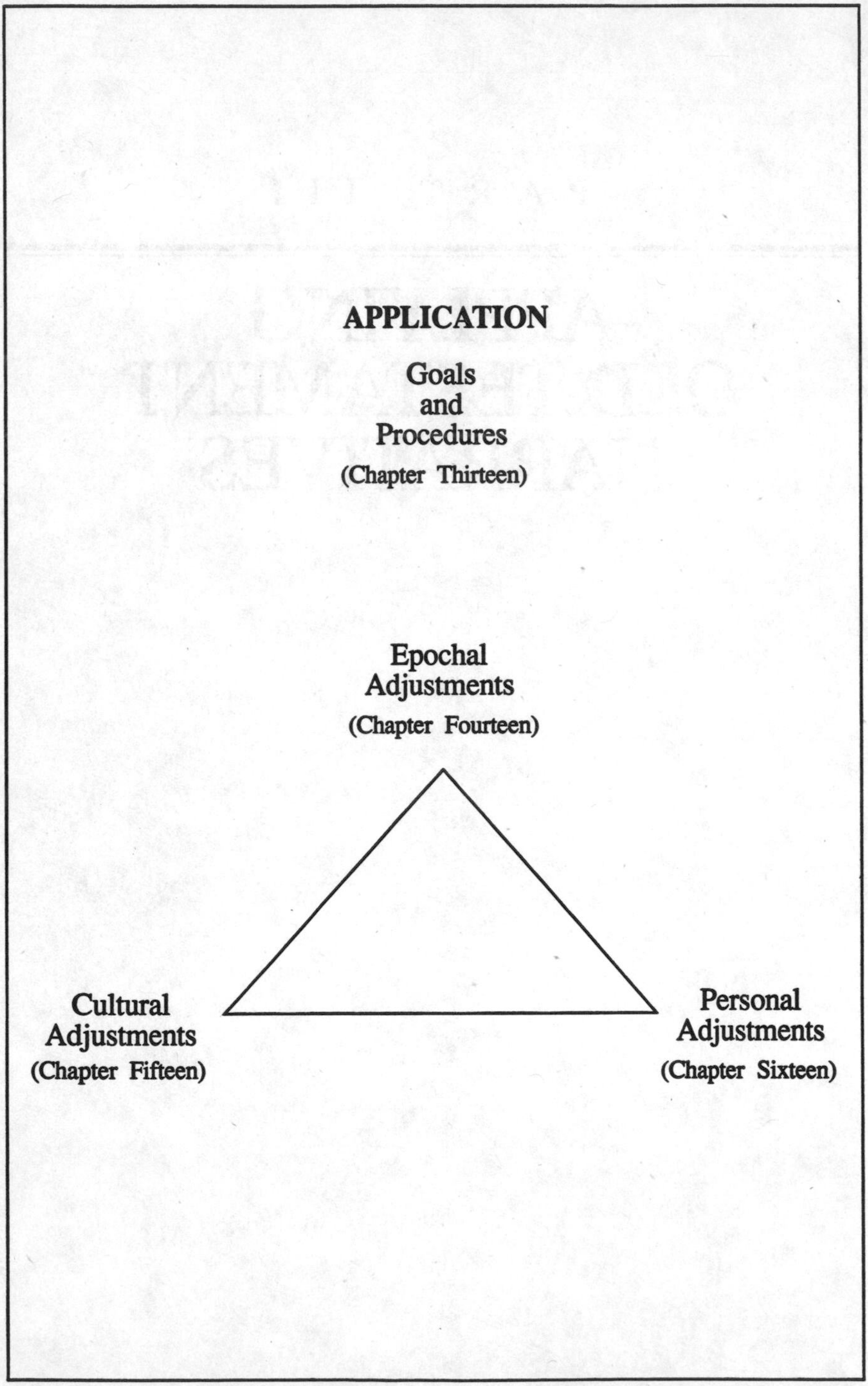

Fig. 54: Schema of Part III: Application

SYNOPSIS

In part one of this study, we explored the preparations necessary for interpreting Old Testament narratives. In part two we sketched a number of procedures for investigating the original meaning of these texts. Proper preparation and investigation are essential to understanding Old Testament stories.

In part three we will turn to the last major concern of this book, application to modern life. We will move beyond exploration into the Spirit's work in the original settings of Old Testament narratives to focus on what they mean for us today.

Application to our day involves many considerations. We will begin by outlining the basic goals and procedures of application (chapter 13). This discussion will provide a number of important definitions and set parameters for the chapters that follow.

The remainder of part three will explore three variations that we must always remember as we bring Old Testament stories to the modern world. Chapter 14 deals with epochal adjustments—the effects of redemptive-historical changes on application. Chapter 15 concerns cultural adjustments—recognizing cultural differences between ourselves and the Old Testament. Finally, chapter 16 focuses on personal adjustments—the ways in which we must apply Old Testament stories to the particular needs of groups and individuals today.

13

ORIENTATION FOR APPLICATION

My wife and I have lived in many places. Whenever we prepare to move again, we go through our closets and get rid of everything we have not been using. I guess I'm a pack rat; I always object when I see my worn-out shoes and broken tools carried away. But my wife usually insists, "What's the use in keeping these things if we're not going to use them?"

We have to ask the same question about Old Testament narratives. What's the use in having them if we don't use them? God did not give us Old Testament stories to hide them away in the closets of our lives. He inspired these accounts to address the challenges of life. "All Scripture is God-breathed . . ." (2 Timothy 3:16a). But to what end? ". . . so that the man of God may be thoroughly equipped for every good work" (2 Timothy 3:16b-17). Unless we apply Old Testament stories to contemporary life, we have no reason to keep them.

In an earlier chapter, we identified legitimate applications as part of the full value of Old Testament stories.[1] The original meaning of a text sets the parameters of interpretation. Biblical elaborations give us further authoritative insights. Applications are the appropriate ways in which the original meaning and Biblical elaborations speak to modern life.

Applying Old Testament narratives entails many complex issues. In this chapter we will deal with two preliminary matters: the *goal of application* and the *basic process of application*. What is our goal? What processes will help us reach this goal? Our answers to these questions provide an orientation that will guide all of our work in this aspect of interpretation.

Goal of Application

I was once told a story about a couple who planned a weekend getaway. They packed the car and started out of the neighborhood. As the husband turned north, his wife commented, "I think you're going the wrong way!" "No I'm not," he replied. "I know how to get there." They drove on until they came to another turn. "You're going the wrong way!" she protested. "I know how to get there!" he retorted. After an hour his wife could take it no longer. "We will never get to the beach going this way!" she insisted. "The beach?" he shouted. "I thought we were going to the mountains!" Then the woman mumbled sarcastically, "Well, I guess you can't know how to get there, if you don't know where you're going."

As we apply Old Testament narratives to modern life, we have to know where we're going. What do we hope to accomplish as we apply Old Testament narratives to our modern world?

The goal of application may be approached in many ways.[2] One helpful outlook is to compare our goals in modern application with the original goals of Old Testament writers. As we have seen in earlier chapters, Old Testament writers faced a situation similar to ours. They had the revelation of God's actions from the past and applied that revelation to their contemporary readers. In much the same way, we have the revelation of God in Scripture before us and we apply that revelation to our world.

We can press the analogy further. Old Testament writers had three principal purposes in writing. They offered their readers observations, anticipations, and implications.[3] These categories form a helpful way to think about our goal in contemporary application. We make *observations for our day*, recognize *anticipations of our day*, and point to *implications for our day*.

Observations for Our Day

Application entails making observations of the original meaning for our day. Every attempt to bring out the relevance of a text must be based solidly on observations of what the writer intended to convey to his original audience. Otherwise, a text can mean anything we want it to mean.[4] The writer's ideological point of view sets the standard for contemporary relevance. If we contradict or deviate from this standard, our attempts to bring the text to bear on contemporary life will be illegitimate.[5]

Nevertheless, we always select from the original meaning as we apply Old Testament narratives. Application is partial at best. To understand the selection process, we will consider the *need for selectivity* and the *guide for selectivity*.

Need for selectivity. Whenever we apply an Old Testament narrative, we face the need for selectivity. Old Testament authors designed their stories to have one coherent meaning, but this single meaning always consisted of countless interwoven motifs that presented an elaborate tapestry to the original audience.[6] Some ideas were more important than others; writers were also more conscious of some of their intentions than others. Under the direction of the Spirit, their texts had far-reaching impact on the lives of their readers.

A few years ago I asked a pastor how he applied Old Testament stories in his sermons. "How do you decide what to leave out?" I asked. His response shocked me. "I would never pick and choose what to say," he argued. "I apply the *whole message* of the passage to my congregation!"

You have to admire the determination of a pastor who tries to get every applicable element out of a passage. Too many of us just skim the surface for a simple point or two. But serious dangers lurk behind a failure to realize the need for selective application.

First, we miss the rich potential of these passages. Interpreters who think they can apply the whole message of an Old Testament narrative in just a few sermons have little idea how much those passages have to offer. The original meaning of Old Testament stories overflows with potential applications. No sermon or series of sermons can apply everything.

Second, if we think we have applied the whole message of a passage, we may end our analysis prematurely. Assured that we have applied what the passage teaches, we may fail to see other facets that are actually more relevant to modern readers.

To avoid these dangers, we must acknowledge that all of our applications are selective. We have limited time and insights. There is always more to apply to our lives than we have uncovered.

Guide for selectivity. What, then, is the guide for selectivity? How do we decide what to emphasize in our applications? In a word, we must select those aspects of Old Testament stories that are most relevant to our needs.

We have to be careful here. In one way or another, everything in Old Testament stories applies to us, no matter what our immediate circumstances may be. But some aspects of a passage speak more poignantly than others to the situations we face at a particular time. As we approach Old Testament stories we must ask what we need to get from this passage at this point in life. What are the issues we face? What challenges confront us? To be effective in applying Old Testament narratives, we must learn to coordinate the priorities of our contemporary needs with the vast array of motifs that these texts present.

To succeed in application we must not only exegete the text; we must also exegete our world.[7] Unfortunately this is precisely where many church leaders fall short. Pastors and church leaders often know a lot about Scripture but very little about the currents of contemporary life. Locked away in their studies, they live in relative isolation, largely unacquainted with the lives of people to whom they minister.

Consequently, pastors and teachers often pursue relatively unimportant issues as they apply Scripture. Since they know little about the matters that confront modern believers, they end up approaching the Old Testament with their own needs in mind. Teenagers hear sermons that actually speak to the interests of their middle-age pastor. Maturing believers hear what is important to their young teacher. Business people learn esoteric theological distinctives and never hear how to live for Christ in the marketplace. Nothing could be more debilitating to application than to be isolated from the world of those to whom we minister.

Students often ask me to recommend practical commentaries on the Old Testament. As strange as it may sound, the most practical commentary on Old Testament stories is *contemporary life*. It teaches us about people's strengths and weaknesses, their beliefs and doubts, their priorities and concerns. Effective application requires that we know people. Personal involvement, magazines, books, television, popular music, movies, and the like are indispensable resources for effectively applying Old Testament narratives. If we are to bring Old Testament stories to modern life, we must give careful attention to the world in which we live.

In an earlier chapter, we saw that the Holy Spirit has led the church toward three basic approaches to Old Testament narratives: literary, historical, and thematic analysis.[8] These exegetical approaches offer different strategies of selection. How do we decide which form of analysis to use? When is one more appropriate than another? While all three approaches are highly interdependent, we may emphasize literary, historical, or thematic analysis according to the specific needs of our contemporary situation. At times a story's central focus speaks forcefully to our circumstances; literary analysis is most appropriate at these moments. At other times historical observations touch our lives more directly; historical analysis helps us meet these needs. On other occasions a minor theme of a passage will be appropriate to our circumstances; thematic analysis then becomes crucial.

As we select facets of Old Testament narratives to apply to our day, we must ask what kind of analysis is required. Do the needs we are addressing fit with a literary approach? Does historical analysis speak more effectively to our circumstances? Should we take up a thematic angle on the passage in the light of problems we are facing? These questions will guide our selective observations in application.

Anticipations of Our Day

To show how past revelation affected their times, Old Testament writers also pointed out how these events anticipated their readers' circumstances. Revelation from the past *established* the historical background of current realities, offered *models* to be imitated and avoided, and *adumbrated* the present experiences of their readers. In much the same way, as modern interpreters of Old Testament stories, we must look for ways in which these texts *establish* dimensions of our lives, provide *models* for our lives, and *adumbrate* our lives.

Establish. Old Testament narratives are relevant to the modern world because they establish dimensions of our lives. They deal with events and issues that form historical and ideological backgrounds to our contemporary experience. What events have shaped our day? Why are we under certain obligations? We can often answer these questions by examining Old Testament stories.

It is not difficult for us to apply Old Testament stories that were designed to establish aspects of the original audience's experience. For example, one intention behind Genesis 1:1—2:3 was to show that God had ordained the Sabbath as a part of His created order.[9] By focusing on the Sabbath, Moses established the responsibilities of his readers. Sabbath rest was still to be observed as an integral part of life. As modern readers we can see that this creation ordinance establishes Sabbath observance for us as well. This Old Testament event erected structures for human life that extend to our day.

At other times the establishing function of a passage may be relatively minor. For example, Moses designed the story of Abram's call to the promised land (Genesis 12:1–9) to foreshadow Israel's call to take the land of Canaan.[10] But this passage also established Abram as the patriarch of Israel and the hope of blessing for all the nations. It was through him that all the nations of the earth would be blessed (Genesis 12:3).[11] This aspect of the story also establishes realities for us today.

Why are Gentile believers today adopted into the family of Abraham? Why must we follow a Jewish Savior? The answer from this passage is obvious: God ordained that salvation for all nations would come through the family of Abraham.

As we apply Old Testament stories, we may ask, "Does something in this story provide an historical background to my life today?"

Models. When applying Old Testament narratives to our world, we must also look for ways in which they provide models for our lives. Old Testament writers frequently wrote their stories to show a pattern of choice and consequence that would guide their readers in their own moral decisions. This modeling function was based on significant analogies between the circumstances of characters in the text and the situation of the original audience.

Modern interpreters will find significant analogies between our lives and the situations addressed by Old Testament writers.[12] We must beware illegitimate moralizing, but as long as we base contemporary modeling on an original modeling function, application of this sort is valuable.[13]

When modeling is a prominent motif in an Old Testament story, the passage can offer an example for contemporary believers as well. For instance, the Chronicler designed Hezekiah's reign as an example for his audience.[14] He downplayed the king's pride and failure (compare 2 Kings 20:1–21 and 2 Chronicles 32:24–33) and emphasized his cultic reforms.[15] In his grand Passover celebration, Hezekiah successfully reunited a remnant from the Northern Kingdom with the Southern Kingdom through intercessory prayer (2 Chronicles 30:17–20). This event established Judah as the representative of the entire nation during the exile and restoration,[16] but Hezekiah's prayer on behalf of the ailing Northerners also depicted him as a model for the post-exilic community.[17] The Chronicler offered an example of proper attitudes and actions toward the North as his readers faced the trials of the post-exilic situation.

Contemporary believers should emulate Hezekiah in responding to divisions and separations among the people of God today. What can we do to build the unity of Christ's kingdom?

Even when modeling is not central to the original meaning of a passage, we may find a connection with our lives. For example, the account of Nathan's rebuke of David (2 Samuel 12:1–14) was originally designed to explain why David's house suffered under God's judgment but remained the legitimate ruling family of Israel.[18] Nathan said that God would severely punish David but would not utterly reject him. While this establishing function may have been central in the purposes of the writer, David's repentance also served as a model. David did not resist Nathan's rebuke; he humbly submitted to the words of judgment. The readers of Samuel had many opportunities to hear words of prophetic judgment and to follow David's example. This passage is a model worthy of imitation today. David's broken spirit and willing acceptance of God's judgment serve as a portrait of repentance for our lives as well.

As we apply Old Testament narratives to the contemporary world, we must not only look for ways in which they establish the background of present realities. We must also ask, "Does this passage offer us a model to follow or avoid?"

Adumbrate. Old Testament stories also adumbrate our lives. Old Testament writers often developed extensive parallels between events in their stories and the experiences of their readers. Similarly, a story may foreshadow modern life today. To avoid illegitimate allegorizing, we must base these applications on the original meaning of the text.[19] But in line with the practices of Old Testament writers themselves, we may often discover significant adumbrations of our lives in Old Testament stories.

When Old Testament writers foreshadowed their readers' circumstances, we can easily see the same connection with our day. For example, the story of Abram's sojourn to Egypt (Genesis 12:10–20) paralleled Israel's sojourn to Egypt.[20] The analogies between Abram's experience and Israel's exodus are extensive. On the basis of this original anticipation, we may look for similarities with our own lives. Just as God miraculously delivered Abram from captivity in Egypt, He has delivered us from slavery to sin through the death and resurrection of Christ. Abram's exodus pictures our exodus.

Even minor aspects of a passage can foreshadow dimensions of our lives. We noted earlier that Moses treated the "smoking firepot with a blazing torch" (Genesis 15:17) as a prefiguring of the pillar of fire before Israel.[21] This theophany anticipates our day as well. Christ has gone before us into battle leading the way to our inheritance of eternal life (Hebrews 5:7–10; 9:11–15).

Many great themes of Old Testament history adumbrate our day. The typologies can be found throughout the Bible. Adam foreshadows Christ, the second Adam; Moses the lawgiver reflects Christ our Lawgiver; David the king anticipates our King Jesus; the land of promise foreshadows the new heavens and new earth. The list of parallels is enormous. Whenever we come upon these and similar themes, we are in a position to see adumbrations of our existence today.

In contemporary application we must imitate Old Testament writers by looking for anticipations of our day in their stories. As we examine the original meaning of Old Testament stories, we find that they establish, model, and adumbrate aspects of our contemporary lives.

Implications for Our Day

The third goal in contemporary application is to point out the implications for our day. Old Testament writers wanted their readers to understand life in the light of Old Testament stories. They shaped texts to convey many informative, directive, and affective implications for their readers. In the same way, we must view our world in light of Old Testament stories, looking for contemporary *informative, directive,* and *affective* implications.

Informative. Old Testament narratives offer many contemporary informative implications. They provide information about circumstances, people, and God in our day. For example, we have seen that God's defeat of the Tower of Babel (Genesis 11:1–9) taught Moses' audience about the enemies they feared.[22] Just as Babel could not withstand the army of heaven, so the cities of Canaan could not resist God's attack. The circumstances of Moses' readers were not as desperate as they thought; their Canaanite enemies were not as strong as they believed; their God was not impotent, as they had feared.

We too face obstacles that hinder the full possession of our inheritance in Christ. The barriers seem insurmountable at times, but this story reminds us that, no matter how great our difficulties, we can rest assured of victory. Our circumstances are not desperate; our enemies are not invincible; God has power over His enemies today as He did in the days of Babel.

When the writer of Samuel reviewed David's accomplishments at the end of his book (2 Samuel 21:1—24:25), he informed his readers of many things in their contemporary experience.[23] David's interventions, military accomplishments, and words of confidence demonstrated the benefits the original readers could expect from the line of David. Despite troubles in David's house, Davidic kings were chosen by God. God would bless His people through David's line.

These original informative implications offer us information about our own times. All around us the kingdom of God is weak and divided. We may be tempted to wonder if Christianity has failed. But these stories teach us that, despite the troubles that plague the Kingdom in our day, the Son of David—our King Jesus—reigns by God's decree. His kingdom has accomplished much and holds many blessings for the future. He who now sits on the throne is our hope today. These implications inform us of the true nature of life in the Kingdom of God.

We live in a world full of false information that needs to be corrected by Old Testament stories. When we approach these texts we must ask, "What information about our lives does this story offer?"

Directive. We must also search Old Testament stories for directive implications for our day. Old Testament writers taught their readers more than information; their stories also implied moral obligations. What obligations do these stories impress upon our lives? How does this passage tell us to respond to our contemporary circumstances, the people around us, and our God?

We have seen that the Chronicler composed his account of Asa's reign (2 Chronicles 14:2—16:14) to teach his readers how to respond to military threats during the post-exilic period.[24] When Asa trusted God, he defeated his enemies. When he trusted in human alliances, his kingdom failed. As the post-exilic readers of Chronicles dealt with military threats, they learned from Asa's life to trust fully in the power of God to protect them.

When we apply these directive implications to our lives, we learn that we have similar obligations. The Chronicler teaches us that in threatening circumstances we must not turn to human power. Trusting in human ingenuity and strength will ultimately lead to failure. As people of faith we must trust in God during our times of trouble.

The story of humanity's expulsion from the Garden of Eden (Genesis 3:1–24) had many directive implications for Moses' original audience.[25] One of his chief concerns was to demonstrate the absolute necessity of obedience to the commands of God. When Adam and Eve disobeyed, they were exiled from the garden and the tree of life. The directive implications of this motif were obvious to the original readers: they must observe God's commands. Disobedience would result in futility and death.

It is not difficult to see the modern directive implications of this passage. We too are under obligation to obey God's law. He has blessed us richly and given us law that benefits us. Yet if we turn away we can expect to see His chastising hand against us.

Responsible application to the modern world includes looking for contemporary directives, acknowledging that these texts place obligations on us just as they did on the original readers. When we apply Old Testament stories, we must ask, "What directives does this passage prescribe for our lives?"

Affective. We must also strive to apply the affective implications for our day. Old Testament writers composed their texts to touch their readers' emotions. Their stories brought sadness, happiness, encouragement, discouragement, and a host of other dispositions.

The story of God's covenant with Abram (Genesis 15:1–21) contained many affective implications for the original audience.[26] As the readers worked their way through the early portions of the passage, they were filled with fear and anxiety. But by the end of the story they had heard the promises of God and found joy and assurance. God promised to bring Abram's seed out of slavery and to give them the land of Canaan. Moses wanted enthusiasm and confidence to replace all doubts.

As we read through this story, our hearts are also moved to fear. But the end of the passage helps us look anew at our circumstances. God has not left us to find our own salvation; He has promised us eternal life in the new creation just as He promised the inheritance of Canaan to Israel. These truths should fill our hearts with confidence and joy, even as they should have influenced the original audience.

The opening chapter of the book of Jonah depicts the prophet in shameful disobedience while pagan sailors prove themselves more pious (Jonah 1:14, 16). Jonah is hurled into the sea under the judgment of God for his refusal to go to Nineveh. The writer of Jonah intended for hypocrites in his audience to experience anxiety and conviction for their sins. As you and I apply this passage to our lives, we must face the fact that we are like Jonah, ready to respond to God's call only when it is comfortable, and unwilling to reach to our enemies with the gospel. As a result this story should bring anxiety, conviction, and fear to our hearts as well.

Application of Old Testament narratives involves observations, anticipations, and implications. We observe the aspects of the text that are most important for our day. We discover the establishing, modeling, and adumbrating anticipations of our lives. We infer the informative, directive, and affective implications. Only when we incorporate all three dimensions have we applied Old Testament narratives to the modern world (see figure 55).

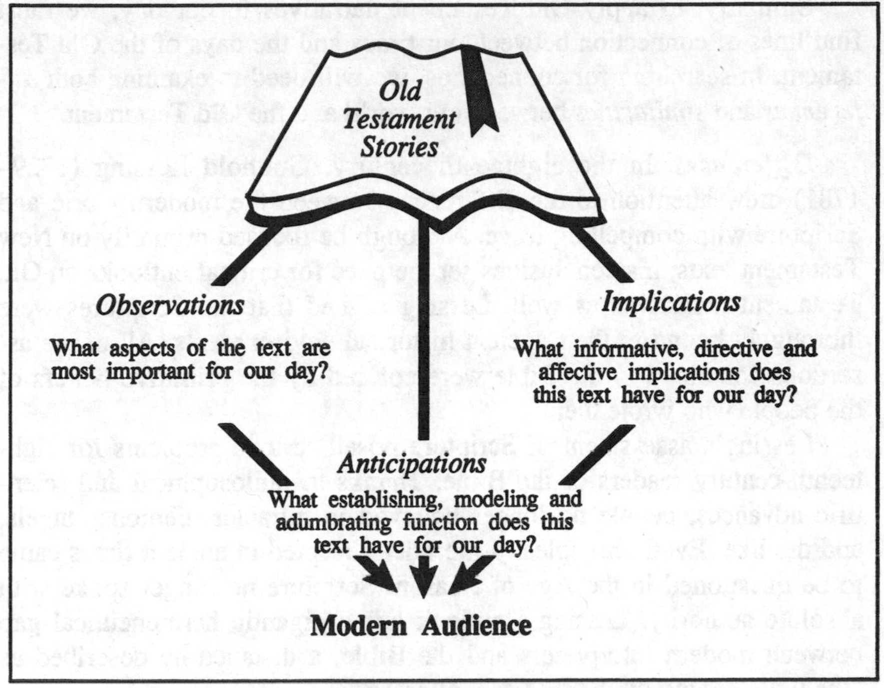

Fig. 55: Goals of Contemporary Application

Process of Application

Applying Old Testament narratives is the greatest challenge of interpretation. It presents more obstacles than any other hermeneutical process. In order to meet this challenge, we must deal with a number of difficulties. At this point we will focus on two considerations that are crucial in application: *connections between the past and present* and *adjustments for the present*. How can we connect the world of the Old Testament with our modern world? What adjustments are necessary as we pursue these connections?

Connections

My wife and I have some good friends in Eastern Europe. Every holiday we call them on the phone, but it usually takes a long time to get through. Normally a recording comes on the line, "We're sorry, but there are no lines connecting with the country you are calling. . . . Please call again." We have no choice but to try later. We have to find a connecting line.

Similarly, to apply Old Testament narratives to our day, we must find lines of connection between our times and the days of the Old Testament. In searching for connections, we will need to examine both *differences* and *similarities* between our world and the Old Testament.

Differences. In the eighteenth century, Gotthold Lessing (1729–1781) drew attention to the differences between the modern world and Scripture with compelling force. Although he focused primarily on New Testament texts, his conclusions set the pace for critical outlooks on Old Testament narratives as well. Lessing argued that the Scriptures were thoroughly bound to their ancient historical environments. All of the assertions contained in the Bible were colored by the primitive beliefs of the people who wrote them.

Lessing's assessment of Scripture posed serious problems for eighteenth-century readers of the Bible. Thanks to philosophical and scientific advances, people no longer believed in miracles, demons, angels, and the like. Even principles of morality accepted in ancient times came to be questioned in the Age of Reason. Scripture no longer spoke with absolute authority. Lessing's outlook left a gigantic hermeneutical gap between modern interpreters and the Bible, a distance he described as "the ugly, gaping ditch that I cannot cross."[27]

Centuries have passed since Lessing espoused this view, but his ditch has never disappeared from the thinking of critical interpreters. By and large they still operate on his basic premise: the Bible is a product of its day, presenting all sorts of primitive beliefs that modern people have discarded. It cannot speak authoritatively to the contemporary reader. As Barr has recently summarized the matter:

> Any work or text composed in an ancient time and an ancient culture has its meaning in that time and that culture, and in our time or culture may have a different meaning, or indeed may have no meaning at all. . . . A work like the Bible, which is the product of one particular cultural situation (or more correctly, which is a compilation of works, the products of a group of such situations over a long period of change) cannot therefore be authoritative in any decisive sense for other cultures; the idea is so absurd as not to be worth discussing.[28]

Evangelicals do not agree with this outlook, but we must not completely ignore the problem of Lessing's ditch. His observations have raised challenges to the process of application that are inescapable. On the one hand, Old Testament narratives were closely tied to the historical conditions in which they were originally written.[29] The form and content of every Biblical text reflect the conventions shared by the ancient writers and readers. God employed the writers' personalities, experiences, and cultural backgrounds as vehicles of revelation. He also accommodated Scriptural revelation to the capacities and needs of the original readers.

On the other hand, our day is different from the world of the Old Testament. Technological advances create distance. We do not use chariots and swords; we use nuclear missiles and satellite defense systems. Sociologically, we are not twelve tribes living in Palestine; we are countless congregations throughout the world. Even the supernatural character of many Old Testament events makes them seem distant from us. Evangelicals believe that miracles recounted in the Bible actually occurred. Elijah's axhead literally floated on the water (2 Kings 6:1–7); fire from heaven actually fell on Solomon's temple sacrifice (2 Chronicles 7:1). But when was the last time you saw an axhead float or fire fall from heaven? Events like these seem foreign to our twentieth-century experiences.

As modern readers we must acknowledge the differences between ourselves and the Old Testament world. As this distance becomes clearer, we will see the necessity of bridging the gap to make legitimate applications to our day.

Similarities. To overcome the distance between our world and the Old Testament, we must find significant similarities that connect the past and present. What are the continuities between the Old Testament to our day? What routes may we follow in application?

Critical interpreters impose modern criteria to determine the applicability of the Old Testament. Above all, human reason serves as the litmus test for evaluating the value of Bible teaching. Aspects of the Bible that pass the test of reason are accepted; other dimensions are cast aside or opposed.

For instance, Troeltsch (1865–1923) set the pace for many critical interpreters by searching for universal truths in light of developments in world religions.[30] In our century Bultmann (1884–1976) proposed a hermeneutic of demythologization, stripping the Bible of its primitive mythology to discern the kernel of human existential value.[31] In more recent years, many critical interpreters have turned to process philosophy[32] and social liberation[33] to discern the modern value of Scripture.

These are but a few of the ways critical interpreters determine a degree of relevance for Old Testament narratives. The variations are countless. In every case, however, the underlying assumption is the same. Modern thinking has so discredited the original meaning of Scripture that it is largely irrelevant and at times even repugnant to contemporary readers. As a result the only valid connections are those that are imposed on Scripture by the spirit of modernity.

This hermeneutical practice is not new. People in every age have limited the applicability of God's Word by some external standard they find more palatable. As early as the Garden of Eden, Eve evaluated revelation by noticing for herself "that the fruit of the tree was good for food and pleasing to the eye" (Genesis 3:6). The Israelites refused to obey the call to take Canaan because of their own ideas of what seemed reasonable (Numbers 13:1—14:10a). The people of Israel and Judah refused to hear the prophets because they judged prophetic pronouncements by their own standards. Jesus Himself was rejected for the same reason (Matthew 26:57–68). Yet Scripture repeatedly condemns this approach to revelation in the strongest terms as rebellion against God Himself.

Evangelicals must look for lines of connection that stem from the Bible, not from our own standards of judgment. What hermeneutical links did Old Testament writers use? How did they overcome the distance between their world and the past?

From the outset we must remember that Old Testament writers depended on the Holy Spirit to empower their efforts. Their most skillful and compelling applications fell on deaf ears apart from the Spirit of grace at work in the hearts of their readers. As the Spirit moved, however, even the worst of sinners in the most distant times and places could understand their stories and apply them to their lives.

We also depend entirely on the Spirit to make application possible.[34] The Spirit who inspired Old Testament narratives in their original settings also illumines modern readers. He has the power to overcome any obstacles Lessing's ditch may present to contemporary application. Without His blessing our efforts are in vain, but with His blessing we can overcome the difficulties of application.[35]

Beyond this it is apparent that Old Testament authors relied on several specific lines of connection between the past and the present. They based their applications on the fact that the past and present always involved the *same God,* the *same world,* and the *same kind of people*.

Same God. Old Testament writers applied the past to their contemporary situations because both the past and present were under the sovereign control of the same God.[36] They did not focus primarily on the acts of other gods; they looked instead to what their God had accomplished. Why? Because His will in the past revealed His will for the present.

God forms a vital line of connection because He is *immutable*.[37] The doctrine of immutability teaches that God is "devoid of all change, not only in His Being, but also in His perfections, and in His purposes and promises."[38] God is actively involved in the course of history, but His involvement never violates His ever-consistent, never-changing character and Word (Numbers 23:19; Isaiah 14:24; 41:4; 48:12; Romans 1:23; Hebrews 1:11–12; James 1:17). In an ultimate sense, God never reverses Himself, even though from a human perspective He may appear to change (e.g., Exodus 32:7–14). God never violates His nature, decrees, or promises.

Closely connected with immutability is *God's covenant fidelity*. The covenantal relationships God has established remain in effect for all time.[39] As Robertson comments:

> By creation God bound himself to man in covenantal relationship. After man's fall into sin, the God of all creation graciously bound himself to man again by committing himself to redeem a people to himself from lost humanity. From creation to consummation the covenantal bond has determined the relation of God to his people. The extent of the divine covenants reaches from the beginning of the world to the end of the age.[40]

The Scriptures teach that God is faithful to His covenant bonds throughout history (Genesis 17:7; Deuteronomy 29:13; 2 Samuel 7:13–16; 1 Kings 8:15–16, 56; Hebrews 6:16–20). This fidelity undergirds the applicability of His Word from generation to generation.

Although many differences exist between the past and present, God has remained the same. The structures He ordained long ago apply to our time. The promises He made in the past continue to our day. We can move from the original meaning of a passage toward modern application because we serve the same God.

Same world. Old Testament writers also applied ancient events to their readers' lives because both took place in the same world. Despite the fact that the external world of past revelation differed from the world of Old Testament writers and their readers, significant physical, cultural, and ideological continuities remained. These connections made it possible for Old Testament writers to apply their stories to their readers in at least two ways.

First, Old Testament writers pointed to events that made *indelible marks on the lives* of their audiences. Joshua had led Israel in conquest of the land (Joshua 1:1—12:24); the readers of the book of Joshua could apply this material because they lived in that land. The sins of Manasseh sent the nation into exile (2 Kings 23:26–27; 24:3–4); the audience of Kings could apply this event because they were in exile. In many cases, the original readers could relate past events to their lives because they experienced the impact of those incidents on their contemporary world.

We may apply Old Testament stories to our lives for the same reason. The Old Testament has left a lasting mark on many aspects of the modern world. Biblical events did not take place in a vacuum; they happened in real history and shaped the course of the world for all time. What historical events could be more essential to the world as we know it than the creation and fall? What set of religious beliefs have affected life more than those of ancient Israel? There is no place where events in the Old Testament have not left some mark on contemporary life.[41] These influences on life today make it possible for us to see similarities between our lives and Old Testament stories.

Second, Old Testament writers relied on *analogies between ancient times and their times.* Their readers' lives paralleled Biblical events in significant ways,[42] allowing the original audience to relate their lives to Old Testament stories. Just as Moses and the people entered into covenant with God at Sinai (Exodus 19:1—24:18), the readers of Exodus were to reaffirm their covenant commitments. In the same way that David provided for the temple (1 Chronicles 29:1–9), the Chronicler's audience was required to support the new temple.

Upon reflection we can see many parallels between our situations and those of Old Testament times. We live in a world created by God, but fallen into sin; we face opposition to our faith; we struggle for justice and mercy in society. The parallels are extensive. "There is nothing new under the sun" (Ecclesiastes 1:9). Once we look beneath superficial dissimilarities, we can see that we live in circumstances much like those of Old Testament writers and their audiences. Because of these parallels we can reach back to the ancient stories of the Old Testament and apply them to our lives today.

Same kind of people. Old Testament writers also found a line of connection between the past and present because they were dealing with the same kind of people. In Biblical perspective all people are the image of God fallen into sin (Genesis 1:27; 9:6; Isaiah 53:6; Romans 3:9–18, 23; 1 Corinthians 11:7; Colossians 3:10). These universal characteristics of humanity made it possible for Old Testament writers to connect the past with the present.[43] Although Old Testament writers knew that people were different in various historical periods, they also recognized that we have basic similarities as the fallen image of God. Among other things, we share *linguistic abilities, mental capacities,* and a *moral nature.*

First, Old Testament authors relied heavily on their readers' *linguistic abilities.*[44] The simple fact that the Old Testament was written at all demonstrates that its authors believed language could communicate across space and time and that their readers could understand and apply their messages.[45]

Our linguistic abilities enable us to apply Old Testament stories today. To be sure, we do not speak the ancient languages of Old Testament writers. Yet, as recent research increasingly suggests, beneath the particularities of individual languages are common linguistic structures that make significant trans-cultural and trans-historical communication possible.[46] In this sense our God-given linguistic abilities permit us to apply Old Testament narratives to the modern world.

Second, Old Testament writers also relied on the *mental capacities* of their readers. As the image of God, human beings reason, exercise their will, and experience emotions.[47] We ask questions, solve problems, pursue logical implications, imagine situations and respond emotionally to life. All of these abilities come from our character as the image of God. When Old Testament writers composed stories, they depended on their readers to exercise these capacities. Old Testament authors seldom explicitly stated their ideological intentions, because they assumed that readers could infer the implications of texts for themselves.

In much the same way, our attempts to apply Old Testament stories to the modern world rest on our mental capacities. As the image of God, we have been endowed with the ability to grasp the original meanings of these texts, to reflect on the differences between our world and the world of the Old Testament, and to understand how the ideology of these texts has a bearing on our lives today. Our interpretations always need improvement, but our mental capacities equip us to make advances in understanding.

Third, Old Testament writers relied on the *moral nature* common to all humans.[48] Authors of Old Testament stories viewed all people as the image of God made to serve as God's vice-regents in the world (Genesis 1:26–30).[49] They also recognized that humanity had failed its task (Genesis 3:1–13) and desperately needed God's redeeming grace (Genesis 3:1–20; 1 Kings 8:46–61; Ezra 9:5–15). Unlike other creatures, we were created with the capacity for religious life and with the responsibility to respond obediently to the revelation of God. This moral character made it possible for Old Testament writers to take events in the past and apply them to their contemporary readers.

The same is true for us.[50] Human beings today have the same moral character as people in the days of the Old Testament. We have the obligation to serve as God's image; we fail as Old Testament believers failed; we need God's grace as they did. We may bridge the gap between the Old Testament and our day because we remain moral creatures.[51]

So it is that Old Testament writers found lines of connection between the past and the present. They relied on the same God, the same world, and the same kind of people. We can meet the challenge of application by following their examples (see figure 56).

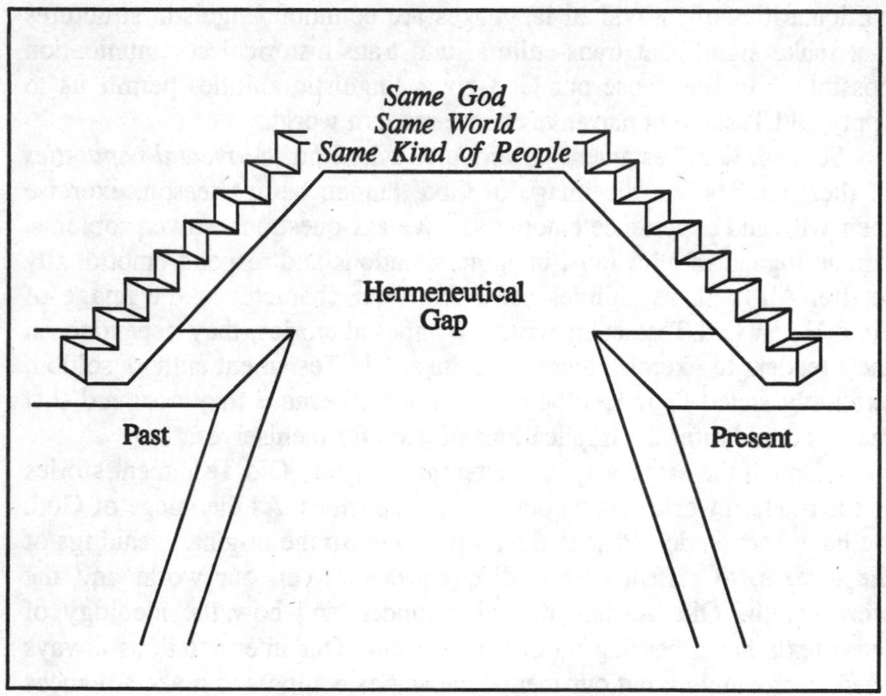

Fig. 56: Lines of Connection

Adjustments

As we apply Old Testament narratives to the modern world, we follow the routes of the same God, the same world, and the same kind of people. But these roads are not straight paths. As they pass through the centuries from the Old Testament to our day, they turn to the left and right. To succeed in application, we must take these variations into account. In the following chapters, we will examine these variations in some detail. For now we will merely touch on three basic issues: the *need for adjustments*, the *guides for adjustments*, and the *types of adjustments* we must make.

Need for adjustments. Why do we need to make adjustments as we apply Old Testament stories? Why don't we merely follow the original meaning as it is? Put simply, we must adjust our applications because we are not in precisely the same situation as the readers of Old Testament narratives; we have different needs and strengths. We experience different accomplishments and challenges. Facile imitation of the original readers will not suffice. In fact, if we apply Old Testament stories precisely as the original readers should have applied them, we could actually disobey God.

For example, the story of the golden calf (Exodus 32:1–35) taught Moses' original audience that they should worship God according to the design of Mosaic Law.[52] Their appropriate response was to shun idolatry and to worship in the tabernacle Moses had built for them. What would be the result if we simply imitated what the original readers were to do? If we erect a Mosaic tabernacle and follow the procedures ordained for that structure, we have not obeyed God. We have actually rebelled against Him because Christ has superseded Moses' tabernacle. As the writer of Hebrews argued, to worship at such a shrine in our day is to deny the work of our Savior (Hebrews 9:1—10:18).

The book of Numbers was designed to inspire Israel to fight as a holy army in the land of Canaan.[53] Should we simply follow ancient Israel's appropriate response to this book? If so, we would all be in Canaan today fighting the occupants of that land. Of course, we must not apply this book to the modern world through facile imitation!

Guides for adjustments. If adjustments are necessary in application, what guides can show us what variations to follow? Three signposts help us see where the lines of connection turn.

First, we find direction from our *individual Christian living*.[54] Our sanctification, endowments, and calling have much to offer as we explore adjustments in application. Prayer, worship, and personal attention to the Spirit enhance our sensitivity to His leading. Experience helps us to see our failures and successes. Commitment to our life work guides our application.

Second, we learn from *interaction in community*.[55] Our brothers and sisters in Christ have much to teach us about adjusting to the modern world. Through the centuries believers have worked hard at applying Old Testament stories to the needs of their day. We can benefit from their approaches. The modern church at large is also engaged in the process of application. As we interact with various viewpoints and practices in the church, we can gain insights from the ways in which others have applied Old Testament narratives to modern life.

Third, the only infallible guide for adjustments in application is *Scripture itself.* As the *Westminster Confession of Faith* puts it: "The infallible rule of interpretation of Scripture is the Scripture itself: and therefore, when there is a question about the true and full sense of any Scripture . . . it must be searched and known by other places that speak more clearly."[56] Legitimate applications must be based on original meaning *and* Biblical elaborations.[57] The Bible frequently comments on itself, providing modern readers with an infallible guide for adjustments in application. We should follow the lead of inspired Biblical writers who applied previous revelation to their situations.[58]

Biblical elaborations take many forms. In the Old Testament, the book of Deuteronomy is applied to a variety of circumstances in the Deuteronomistic History (Joshua, Judges, Samuel, and Kings).[59] The Chronicler applied the books of Samuel and Kings to his post-exilic situation. The prophets elaborated on events in the Pentateuch and historical books. Interconnections can be found throughout the Old Testament. As we understand how Old Testament writers varied the themes of other portions of the Old Testament to their situations, we find guidance for the adjustments we must make for our day.

We must also look to the adjustments made in the New Testament. New Testament writers did not discard Old Testament stories.[60] Nevertheless, when we examine how they handled Old Testament narratives, we find that they made a number of adjustments as they applied them to their circumstances.

In the chapters that follow, we will look into specific dimensions of variations within the Bible. At this point, however, let us simply acknowledge that the comments of Biblical writers form an infallible guide for the adjustments we must make in modern application. As much as possible, we must always tie our variations to the patterns that Biblical writers themselves used.

Types of adjustments. What, then, are the types of adjustments we must make? We have seen that our lives connect with Old Testament narratives because we are dealing with the same God, the same world, and the same kind of people. We must also deal with three corresponding variations: *epochal, cultural,* and *personal adjustments.*

First, in order to apply Old Testament narratives to our lives we must make *epochal adjustments.* Epochal variations occurred in Scripture because God progressively revealed Himself to humanity; the doctrine of progressive revelation is crucial to legitimate application.[61] God has remained the same throughout history, but He has displayed his nature, requirements, and the way of salvation little by little. Later revelation never contradicts previous revelation, but further disclosures develop and go beyond what was given beforehand.[62]

We must always take epochal shifts in progressive revelation into account. You and I live after the death and resurrection of Christ. We are in a different period of redemption from Moses, the writer of Kings, and the writer of Ezra-Nehemiah. This variation requires many significant adjustments. We are not a franchised national theocracy situated among other international powers. Our holy war is not "against flesh and blood, but against . . . the spiritual forces of evil in the heavenly realms" (Ephesians 6:12). We do not worship in a tabernacle or temple; we worship in "spirit and in truth" (John 4:24). These are important kinds of variations that we must carefully assess as we apply Old Testament narratives.

Second, we must make *cultural adjustments*.[63] We live in the same world as Old Testament believers, but social customs, sociological structures, and technological advances make our responsibilities and needs different. Although these variations have been affected by progressive revelation, they have resulted primarily from the diversity of natural resources, skills, and ideals. Even believers living in the same epoch of redemptive history live in different cultures and speak different languages. Some nations are at war, others at peace. Some are technologically advanced, others are developing. These cultural variations must be considered as we apply Old Testament narratives.

Third, we should also make *personal adjustments*. People are different from each other. Each person has qualities that makes him or her a unique individual.

Application is often aimed at the specific needs of individuals. On a general level, a text may have the same application for different kinds of people, but the more specific our application, the more variation in individual application. The same Old Testament text applies differently to a father and a child. It has different bearing on the life of an obedient believer than it does on a rebellious apostate. It applies differently to a businessman and a housewife. The needs and responsibilities of these people require adjustments in application.

We must consider these epochal, cultural, and personal differences as we search for the relevance of Old Testament narratives (see figure 57).

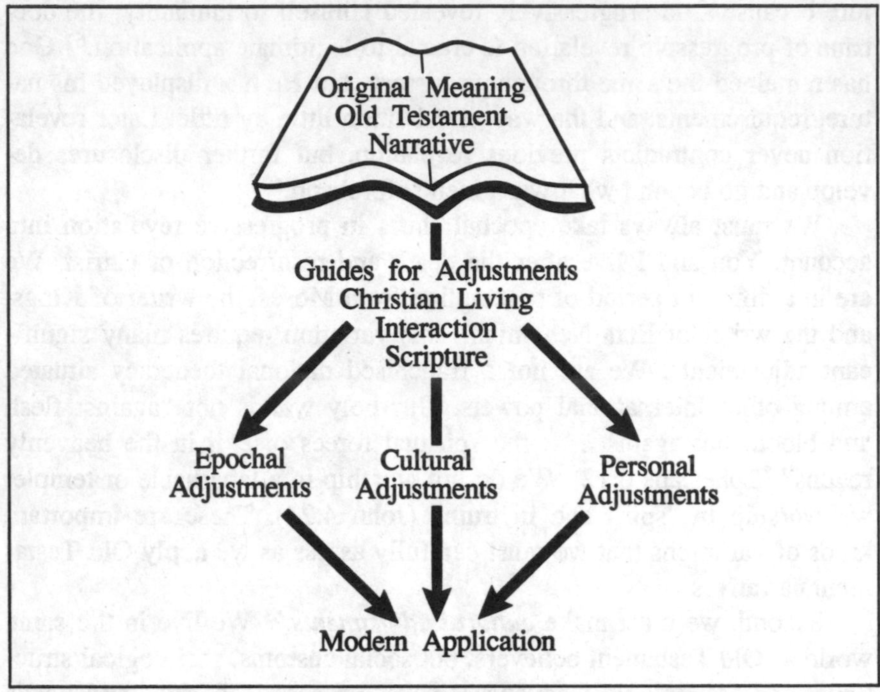

Fig. 57: Types of Adjustments in Application

Conclusion

In this chapter we have laid the groundwork for application. Our goal is to observe relevant motifs in Old Testament narratives, discover how they anticipate our lives, and recognize the implications for our day. To reach this goal, we must adjust our application according to the differences and similarities between the historical settings of Old Testament narratives and today. With these basic concepts in mind we will be able to apply these texts to the modern world.

Review Questions

1. How are observations, anticipations, and implications facets of our goal in application? Distinguish these purposes and give an example of each.
2. What are the three types of anticipations and implications we may derive from Old Testament narratives?

3. What are the lines of connection between the Old Testament world and our day? Illustrate how they are useful in application.
4. Why must we adjust the original meaning of a text in order to apply it to modern life? What are the three major types of adjustments we must consider?

Study Exercises

1. Examine the story of the Tower of Babel (Genesis 11:1–9). Choose one theme from the passage. How does this theme anticipate our day? Give a sentence summary of an informative, directive, and affective application.
2. Reflect on the modern implications you derived from Genesis 11:1–9. How did you adjust the original meaning for modern life? What epochal, cultural, and personal considerations controlled your adjustments?

14

FROM AGE TO AGE

When I get ready to drive on a long trip, I always check a map. But I don't immediately reach for a map showing secondary roads and residential streets. Too many details at first can be confusing. Instead I look for the major routes to my destination and get a broad perspective on the whole trip. Then I pull out the maps with more details.

In the previous chapter, we saw that applying Old Testament narratives to the modern world requires epochal, cultural, and personal adjustments. These considerations are like maps of varying scales that guide our efforts. Epochal adjustments give a broad overview, cultural considerations focus on more details, and personal variations treat more specific individual concerns. In this chapter we will outline the large-scale adjustments to be made as we apply Old Testament motifs across the great epochs of redemptive history. In the two next chapters, we will set cultural and personal considerations within this broad framework.

Application across the ages entails a number of important issues. We will touch on three: the *epochal structure of redemptive history, Old Testament narratives and Christ,* and *the Christian theocracy*. How does Scripture describe the ages of redemptive history? What place does Christ have in modern application? How should we apply Old Testament stories to our age?

Epochs of Redemptive History

It is difficult to conceive of life apart from historical categories. We nearly always think in terms of past, present, and future. The Bible also reflects a keen awareness of history; Biblical writers concerned themselves with the origin, development, and destiny of the world. They had individual perspectives, but their viewpoints contributed to a unified overarching outlook. We will briefly focus on two dimensions of this Biblical perspective: *divisions among the epochs* and *unity among the epochs*.

Divisions Among the Epochs

Pediatricians and parents alike will tell you that children do not mature at a steady pace. They go through surges of growth and develop much faster at some ages than others. In many ways the same is true of Biblical history. God revealed Himself to His people throughout the centuries, but dramatic developments occurred on a number of occasions. These swells in redemptive history took place as God decisively intervened in the world to bring His people into new ages of blessing.

What were these strides of development? Scripture divides redemptive history into *divisions within Old Testament history* and the *decisive division in Christ*.

Divisions within Old Testament history. New Testament writers took many perspectives on divisions within Old Testament history. As we examine their outlooks, we can see that they divided the Old Testament in different ways. But these diverse outlooks contribute to an overarching plan. By way of illustration, we will contrast Old Testament epochal structures outlined by Paul, Peter, and Luke.

In Romans 5:12–21 Paul divided the Old Testament into two periods. He spoke of "the trespass of the one man (Adam)" (v. 17), and then moved to the time when "the (Mosaic) law was added so that the trespass might increase" (v. 20). This two-fold division corresponded to "the obedience of the one man (Christ)" (v. 19) and its result that "grace increased all the more" (v. 20). In this passage Paul focused on the periods before and after Sinai.

In 2 Peter 3:5–7 we find a different pattern. Peter did not speak of Sinai as the crucial event in Old Testament history. Instead, he tied his epochal divisions more directly to Noah's flood. After God created the earth, "the world of that time" (v. 6) continued until the deluge. After the flood, history entered the period of "the present heavens and earth" (v. 7). This world continues until the formation of "a new heaven and earth" at the second coming of Christ (v. 13). Peter did not contradict Paul's emphases on Adam's fall into sin and Sinai, but he divided redemptive history differently into eras before the flood, after the flood and the new world to come.[1]

Luke's report of Stephen's speech (Acts 7:2–53) offers a third approach to Old Testament history. In response to the charge that he was "speaking against this holy place and against the law" (Acts 6:13), Stephen reviewed several high points in the Old Testament. He mentioned the time of the patriarchs (Acts 7:2–16), the exodus and conquest (Acts 7:17–45a), and the reigns of David and Solomon (Acts 7:45b—47). Stephen identified three periods in the Old Testament: the patriarchal, Mosaic, and monarchical.

At least two factors explain why Paul, Peter, and Luke looked at Old Testament history from complementary perspectives. On the one hand, the Old Testament is vast and complex, lending itself to many different patterns of division. Imagine how many ways we could categorize the periods of a child's growth. The possibilities are innumerable. Similarly, no single scheme can adequately explain all the developments within the Old Testament.

On the other hand, differences among New Testament writers also resulted from their specific intentions. In Romans 5:12–21 Paul contrasted Adam and Christ by emphasizing the similarities between Adam's initial disobedience and Christ's obedience, as well as the increase of sin after Sinai and the increase of grace and righteousness after Christ. Peter, however, addressed those who scoffed at the promise of Christ's return (2 Peter 3:3–13), pointing to the parallels among creation, the flood, and the final judgment. Luke reported how Stephen responded to questions about the temple by focusing on Abraham, Moses, and the monarchy (Acts 7:2–50). The specific intentions of each person brought about their distinctive outlooks on redemptive history.

One of the most helpful ways of outlining Old Testament epochal developments combines the periods which Paul, Peter, and Luke highlighted in the passages we have just mentioned. This scheme focuses on the major covenant events in the days of Adam, Noah, Abraham, Moses, and David. These periods of time are viewed primarily in light of the covenant relationships established during those times. The period of Adam focused on humanity's fall from the perfections of Eden; the period of Noah concerned God's judgment against evil and the promise of a stable world; Abram opened the patriarchal period's concern with the promise of a seed, land, and blessing; the Mosaic covenant emphasized the Law and Israel's constitution into a nation; and the Davidic period dealt with the establishment of David's dynasty over Israel. A number of interpreters have followed this basic pattern.[2]

Whatever particular scheme we follow, epochal developments within the Old Testament influence application in at least three ways.

First, we must assess the period of redemptive history in which the events took place. What were the peculiar features of the period? How are the characteristics of that epoch reflected in the text? Second, the period of the writer and his audience must be remembered. What were the distinctive features of the writer's epoch? How did they influence the text? Third, we must examine how the rest of the Old Testament traces similar motifs through other epochs. How have the shifts from one era to another influenced the presentation of a theme throughout the Old Testament? These considerations enable us to discern the abiding value of the original meaning of Old Testament stories for our day.

For example, in the Garden of Eden, God told Adam, "You are free to eat from any tree in the garden; but you must not eat from the tree of the knowledge of good and evil, for when you eat of it you will surely die" (Genesis 2:16–17). We cannot properly understand this command apart from considering the epoch of Adam and Eve. At that time they were sinless servants in God's holy garden. God placed them on probation to test their fidelity. Would they fulfill their commission or rebel against their Maker? In this sense the command to Adam and Eve was specifically tied to their redemptive-historical period.[3]

We live in a fallen, corrupt world. What can we learn from an event that took place in the age of perfection? Clues for modern application appear in the epoch of the writer. Moses wrote this story for people who lived long after the fall into sin. His Israelite readers did not face precisely the same choices as Adam and Eve. But Moses wrote to warn the Israelites of the dire consequences of disobeying the Word of God even in their day. Turning from God's command cast humanity out of paradise. In a similar way, disobeying the commands of God in their day would lead Israel even further away from the ideals of paradise.

The same theme occurs in other epochs of the Old Testament. In Abraham's day obedience to God's call led to blessing for the patriarchs; disobedience brought pain and trouble. In the Davidic period, the prophets called Israel to repentance and offered prosperity and blessing for devotion to God's commands. In all ages God's people either obeyed His Word or suffered severely for their disobedience.

Tracing the motif of disobedience in the garden through Old Testament epochs gives us direction as we apply this passage to our own day. We do not face the test of the tree of the knowledge of good and evil, but we still have the Word of God. We must obey or suffer severe consequences. The only way to the paradise of the new heavens and earth is through submission to our Creator.

We must always recognize the divisions of redemptive history within the Old Testament. We consider a motif as it functioned in the era of the events themselves, explore how the writer applied the motif to his day, and trace the manner in which the theme appears in other Old Testament periods. These considerations offer vital guidance for any attempt to apply Old Testament narratives (see figure 58).

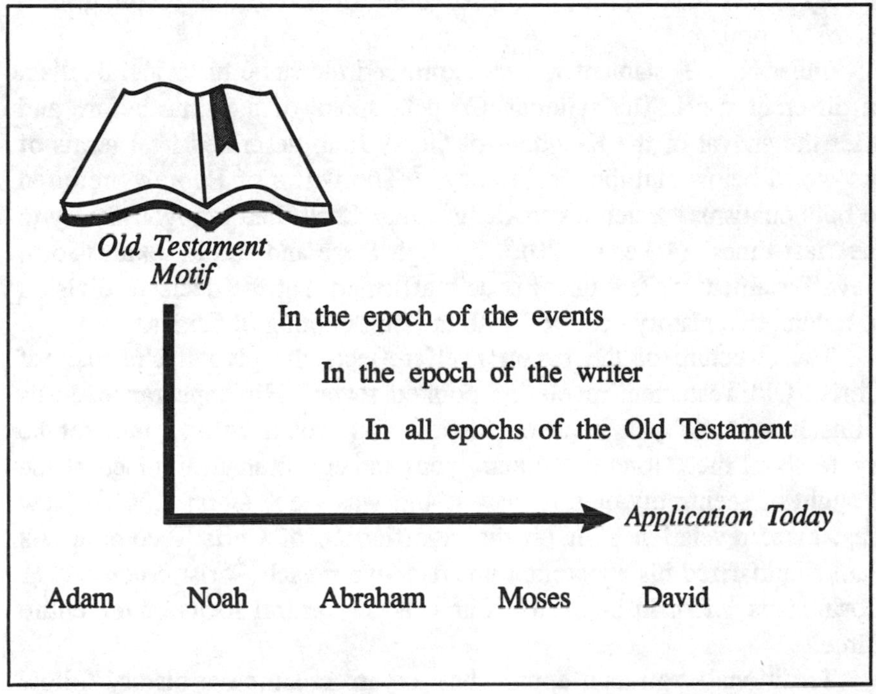

Fig. 58: Epochal Considerations in Old Testament History

Decisive division in Christ. The Bible also attests to a decisive epochal division in Christ. Although New Testament writers recognized that God revealed Himself in many waves of activity throughout the Old Testament, they identified the life, death, resurrection, and ascension of Christ as the central turning point of history. This fundamental epochal division appears succinctly in Ephesians 1:18–21,[4] where Paul identified the power at work in believers as the same power that raised Christ from the dead and seated Him in the heavenly realms. To elaborate on the wonder of that power, Paul explained that God had exalted Christ above all authorities not only in "the present age but also in the one to come" (v. 21).

With these words Paul divided all of history into two periods: "the present age" and "the one to come." His meaning is unlike our modern use of these terms. Paul did not refer to our current time and the time after Christ's return. Instead, he followed the common Rabbinic use of these categories to describe the time before the coming of Messiah ("this age") and the time introduced by the appearance of the Messiah ("the age to come").[5] For Paul "this age" referred to all that had happened in history before Christ; "the [age] to come" referred to everything after His first coming.

Other New Testament writers expressed the same historical dualism in different ways. The synoptic Gospels spoke of the time before and after the arrival of the Kingdom of God.[6] John described it in terms of the world below and the world above.[7] The writer of Hebrews referred to both dualisms.[8] Peter acknowledged that Christ had brought history to the "last times" (1 Peter 1:20).[9] Through these and similar expressions, New Testament writers unanimously affirmed that the decisive division in redemptive history occurred with the first coming of Christ.[10]

The structure of the canon itself reflects the pivotal character of Christ. Old Testament revelation pointed toward His appearance. Jesus Himself said, "If you believed Moses, you would believe me, for he wrote about me" (John 5:46) and "your father Abraham rejoiced at the thought of seeing my day; he saw it and was glad" (John 8:56).[11] New Testament revelation built on the significance of Christ's coming. As Paul summarized his apostolic ministry, "we preach Christ crucified" (1 Corinthians 1:23). In this sense Christ is the central focus of the entire Bible.[12]

Traditional Protestant approaches toward redemptive history follow this outlook as well. Major confessions and catechisms have viewed the first coming of Christ as the apex of Biblical religion. Typically, history before Christ has been described as the age of "Law," and history after Christ has been known as the age of "Gospel."[13] The centrality of Christ in salvation history has been a hallmark of orthodox Christian theology.

The epochal shift that Christ introduced is absolutely essential to applying Old Testament narratives. Christ brought about changes that compel modern interpreters to consider Old Testament stories in a new light.

Consider Uzzah's tragic death in 2 Samuel 6:6–7. The writer of Samuel first penned these words for God's people living in the period of the divided kingdom.[14] In that context God's judgment against Uzzah instructed them about the sanctity of the ark and the need for careful adherence to the regulations of temple worship.

Without considering the epochal changes that occurred in Christ, we will never arrive at a legitimate modern application of this passage. Uzzah's death warned Old Testament believers not to defile the sacred ark, but we have no physical ark to defile. Christian worship is before the heavenly mercy seat that we cannot even see, much less touch.

Nevertheless, this passage has powerful implications for New Testament worship. God's wrath against Uzzah warns us against irreverence in our approach to the heavenly throne of God. If His anger burned against Uzzah for mishandling the Old Testament ark, how much more will His wrath be kindled against those who defile the heavenly mercy seat through insincerity and irreverence in worship?

To put the matter simply, Christ always stands between Old Testament stories and the church. Whenever we search for modern applications, we must trace Old Testament motifs through the decisive revelation that took place in Christ. The content of His teaching, the effects of His life, death, resurrection, and ascension, and the instructions of His apostles lead us to significant adjustments of the original meaning for our day.

Unity Among the Epochs

Assessing the epochal structure of redemptive history is a difficult balancing act. Many important changes took place in Biblical religion, but these changes did not eliminate significant unity among the epochs. Rather, epochal shifts within Biblical history may be described as *organic developments*.[15] Biblical faith is like a tree growing from seed to full maturity. As an acorn gradually becomes an oak tree, Biblical religion grew from seminal form early in the Old Testament to fuller expression in Christ.

This outlook recognizes both discontinuities and continuities among the ages. On the one hand, the organic model acknowledges the striking differences between eras of redemptive history. To a casual observer, an oak tree hardly looks the same as an acorn. Apart from close scrutiny, it is difficult to see many similarities between the early stages of Biblical faith and the ages that followed.

On the other hand, the organic model draws attention to the unity of Biblical history. Careful examination of an oak tree through its growth reveals that the acorn and tree are one in the same. The seed had the potential of the whole plant within it; the mature tree is the realization of that potential. In much the same way, the early epochs of redemptive history contained immature structures and patterns that came to fuller realization as God revealed more of Himself to His people. The principles of faith we hold dear as Christians grew out of the preceding eras of Biblical revelation.

Unfortunately evangelicals go to extremes in the way they approach interconnections among the epochs. Some groups focus too much on disunity and others overemphasize unity. An organic outlook stands opposed to both of these extremes. It will help to compare approaches to Biblical history that emphasize *discontinuities, continuities,* and *organic developments.*

Discontinuities. Many evangelicals emphasize discontinuities among the ages. They view the epochs of redemption as fundamentally distinct, as if God planted a tree, allowed it to grow for a time, uprooted that tree, and replaced it with another. Dispensationalism is well known for emphasizing discontinuity among the epochs. For instance, the popular *Scofield Bible* divided Biblical history into discrete segments. The period from creation to the fall was a time of innocence; in this era Adam and Eve were responsible to maintain their innocence by abstaining from the fruit. The time from the fall to the flood constituted the age of conscience; in this era Adam and Eve acquired and transmitted the knowledge of good and evil, or natural conscience. From the flood to the dispersion at Babel comprised the era of human government; in this period God established government and three racial lines through Noah's sons. From the call of Abram to the giving of the law, we have the period of promise, dealing with the promises to Abram. Next, God gave His Law, but the Jewish people disobeyed. Following this age came the age of grace, extending from the cross to the return of Christ. According to standard dispensational thought, we are currently living in this age. The last and final dispensation is the eschatological age of the Kingdom.[16]

In this perspective very little continuity existed between one age and the next; interpreters must rightly divide the word of truth (2 Timothy 2:15) by keeping the principles of each epoch separate from the others.[17]

In its more extreme expressions, Dispensationalism has rejected the authority of Mosaic standards for Christians. As L.S. Chafer put it:

> Since law and grace are opposed to each other at every point, it is impossible for them to co-exist, either as the ground of acceptance before God or as the rule of life. Of necessity, therefore, the Scriptures of the New Testament which present the facts and scope of grace, both assume and directly teach that the law is done away. Consequently, it is not in force in the present age in any sense whatsoever. This present

> nullification of the law applies not only to the legal code of the Mosaic system and the law of the kingdom, but to every possible application of the principle of law.[18]

This outlook strikes at the heart of Old Testament narratives. As we have seen, all Old Testament writers presupposed the validity of Mosaic Law.[19] If Mosaic standards have no authority over New Testament believers, it is difficult to imagine how Old Testament stories can apply to our lives.

In recent decades Dispensationalists have softened the barriers between epochs; many of them are beginning to see more continuity. Nevertheless, even moderate Dispensationalists still tend to deal with the periods of redemptive history as separate entities, allowing relatively few principles of faith to transfer from one age to another.

With all the variations that exist in dispensational circles, it is difficult not to caricature the movement. For the most part, however, it is safe to say that Dispensationalists *presume discontinuity among the ages unless the revelation of a later period specifically reaffirms a principle of an earlier period.* From this outlook some branches of an earlier epoch may be grafted onto the tree of a later epoch, but the new tree must expressly accept the limbs of the uprooted tree. Again, before a principle from an earlier epoch can apply in a later era, it must be explicitly reaffirmed in Scripture representing a later period. Otherwise the teaching of the earlier period is presumed obsolete.

Continuities. Other evangelicals go to the opposite extreme, overemphasizing continuities among the ages. These groups tend to neglect the importance of epochal developments for the application of Old Testament themes. They acknowledge that the history of redemption consists of one tree that has grown through the ages. Yet, in their view some branches of the tree have never matured, as if stunted limbs appear here and there, mixed in with mature branches that have grown up in Christ.

One recent movement tending in this direction is Theonomy, or Christian Reconstruction.[20] It is difficult to generalize without misrepresenting some individuals, but we may safely say that Theonomists limit the maturation of the tree of redemption in particular areas. They tend to acknowledge significant developments between the Old Testament and New Testament in some but not all aspects of the faith.

For example, Theonomists admit the ceremonies of the tabernacle and temple are radically adjusted for New Testament believers, but the penal codes from Mosaic Law remain largely unchanged for the modern world.[21] Incorrigible children and blasphemers must still be executed

(Exodus 21:15, 17; Leviticus 24:16); Sabbath breakers should still be subject to civil criminal prosecution (Exodus 31:15). By and large the working assumption of Theonomists is that, *unless Old Testament standards have been specifically altered by New Testament revelation, they abide without significant change.*

Organic developments. Both of these extremes stand in contrast with the model of organic developments. The *Westminster Confession of Faith* contains one of the best summaries of an organic view of revelation: "There are not therefore two covenants of grace differing in substance, but one and the same under various dispensations."[22]

As opposed to Dispensationalism, this outlook emphasizes that one covenant of grace extends throughout all ages, uniting both the Old Testament and New Testament. The Old Testament was not a period of works and the New Testament a period of grace; the covenant made between the Father and the Son extends throughout salvation history.[23] The same God has been faithful to this one covenant throughout all ages.[24]

Admittedly, significant differences exist among the epochs. Details of religion in Abraham's day hardly seem the same as those of David's time. Moses' teachings appear very different from the teachings of the writer of Hebrews. Epochal variations are striking at times. Even so, we must be careful not to overestimate these dissimilarities. We must evaluate all differences in light of the covenantal unity of Scripture.

Placing impermeable barriers between epochs stands in direct opposition to the practices of Old Testament writers. They rested their efforts on the presumption of significant continuities, freely instructing their readers through revelation that had occurred in previous epochs. In the book of Genesis, for instance, Moses covers events that occurred during the period of innocent Adam, fallen Adam, Noah, and the patriarchs. As we have seen, he did not simply report this history to tell his readers about life during those bygone periods; he taught about life in his own age.[25] Moses wrote Genesis assuming major continuities between previous epochs and his own.

The presumption of continuity demonstrated by Old Testament writers has significant hermeneutical implications for us. Put simply, Old Testament themes do not have to be specifically reiterated to be authoritative for the people of God in a later epoch. On the contrary, we may presume the abiding validity of the original meaning of Old Testament narratives. Unlike Dispensationalists, we are not looking for a few branches from Old Testament faith to graft onto a different Christian tree. We find shade under the same tree as Old Testament believers; the tree is simply more mature.

In contrast with Theonomists, however, we understand that no Old Testament themes remain unaffected by the developments of later epochs. As the *Westminster Confession of Faith* acknowledges, the one covenant of grace has "various dispensations."[26] While Old Testament revelation remains authoritative for all generations, we must remember that it was accommodated to the people of God in their particular redemptive-historical setting. As Calvin put it:

> If a householder instructs, rules, and guides, his children one way in infancy, another way in youth, and still another in young manhood, we shall not on this account call him fickle and say that he abandons his purpose. Why, then, do we brand God with the mark of inconstancy because he has with apt and fitting marks distinguished a diversity of times? The latter comparison ought to satisfy us fully. Paul likens the Jews to children, Christians to young men. What was irregular about the fact that God confined them to rudimentary teaching commensurate with their age, but has trained us through a firmer and, so to speak, more manly discipline? [27]

For this reason all earlier revelation must be reinterpreted in the light of the principles of later revelation.[28]

But isn't adultery always adultery? Isn't blasphemy always blasphemy? Isn't stealing the same in all ages? Don't these Old Testament principles simply remain the same in all ages? In one sense, yes, but in another sense, no. When we summarize the original meaning of these motifs in general terms—relatively divorced from their specific Old Testament connotations—we need to make few adjustments as we move from one age to another. But when we define these Old Testament themes in terms of the specific connotations they held in the Old Testament age, we see plainly that even applications of these moral principles must undergo adjustments to our epoch.

Adultery is always wrong, but for Old Testament writers this principle could not be entirely separated from the penalties prescribed in the Mosaic Law (Leviticus 20:10). In the light of New Testament teaching, adultery within the church is no longer to be associated with capital punishment, but with ecclesiastical excommunication (1 Corinthians 5:1–13). Blasphemy in the Old Testament included the desecration of Mosaic tabernacle rituals (Leviticus 19:5–8), but not in our age. Prohibitions against stealing in the Old Testament included respect for a fellow Israelite's permanent land inheritance (1 Kings 21:1–19), but not in our time. If we summarize Old Testament principles in categorical, ahistorical terms, we have unwittingly already begun to make epochal adjustments. But if we define them according to their original setting, the need for epochal adjustments in all matters becomes evident.

To apply Old Testament stories to our day, we must always view the original meaning in terms of the organic developments of redemptive history. All motifs in Old Testament stories remain authoritative for us because our age builds on the revelation of earlier ages. We do not discard or deny the authority of any teaching in Old Testament stories. But the tree of divine revelation has matured. Epochal variations between the immature and mature stages affect the modern application of every dimension of these stories.

Old Testament Narratives and Christ

A friend of mine recently went through a serious illness; several times he even came near death. But God answered prayer and brought him back to health. The experience of illness dramatically changed him. "I have a new outlook on life," he commented one day. "I see everything differently because of what happened in the hospital." All of us have dramatic experiences that change our perspectives: an illness, the birth of a child, marriage, the loss of a loved one. These experiences become eyeglasses through which we view the rest of our lives.

In much the same way, the lordship of Christ colors everything we read in Old Testament stories. The basic Christian confession "Jesus is Lord" (Romans 10:9; 1 Corinthians 12:3) forms a pivotal hermeneutical consideration whenever we direct these texts to modern life. Christ brought the world into existence (Colossians 1:16); He sustains it day by day (Colossians 1:17); He is the end of all things (Romans 11:36). As followers of Christ, we must strive to see how every Old Testament narrative reveals His lordship over us. Every application is a personal response to Christ Himself.

How can we make Christ the center of our applications? Interconnections between the original meaning of Old Testament narratives and Christ are vast. No single approach will cover all relevant issues. Yet one helpful strategy is to ask how Old Testament stories anticipate Christ's three offices: *Prophet, Priest,* and *King*.[29]

The three offices of Christ rose out of Old Testament theocratic structures. Prophets spoke the Word of God, instructing in righteousness. Priests mediated between the people and God, providing the way for communion with Him. Kings administered justice and led Israel into battle, securing its victory and inheritance. These offices were so vital to the life of Israel that they required special anointings from God. As "the Christ" ("anointed one") Jesus fulfilled each of these anointed offices.

Prophet

As our Prophet, Jesus revealed God to His people.[30] He taught the Law in His words and deeds (Matthew 5:17–20; 22:34–40; Mark 1:44; 7:9–13). He proclaimed judgment against sin and called for repentance and faith (Matthew 5:21–22; 12:36–37; 4:17; Luke 13:3, 5; John 3:16, 18, 36; 9:39). He even went beyond Moses to give new revelation. Through His teaching Jesus revealed more about God than had ever been known before (Luke 10:22; John 1:17–18).

The prophetic dimension of Christ's lordship sheds light on Old Testament passages in two ways. First, if a passage refers explicitly to an Old Testament prophet, it directs us to Christ's prophetic work. For example, throughout the book of Exodus, Moses acted as a prophet instructing the Israelites. Because of this focus on Moses' prophetic ministry, we may apply this book to Jesus' prophetic ministry. He too warned against hypocrisy and insisted that His people live faithfully before God. As Christians we see Moses both as a historical figure in the book of Exodus and as a prefiguring of Christ, the great Prophet.

In the story of Naboth's vineyard (1 Kings 21:1–29), God called Elijah the prophet to condemn King Ahab and his wife Jezebel (1 Kings 21:17–29) for their mistreatment of Naboth. Christians recognize Elijah's authority as God's prophet, but his ministry also points us to the work of Christ. Matthew's account of the Mount of Transfiguration illustrates that Christ stood in continuity with Elijah, applying the Law of God to His day (Matthew 17:1–3). As we apply the story of Naboth's vineyard to our age, we must give attention to the prophetic ministry of Christ.

Second, even when a passage refers to divine revelation apart from a specific prophet, we may relate the material to Christ's prophetic office. Many Old Testament stories touch on the proclamation of God's Word. In every case we must turn our attention to Christ as Prophet. For example, in Genesis 12:1–3 God calls Abram to the promised land. No human mediator is mentioned; nevertheless, this event foreshadows Christ's call for all His followers to leave this world and to follow Him.

Old Testament stories reveal the lordship of Christ by focusing on the revelation of God. At times prophets explicitly came to the foreground. At other times God spoke His Word through other means. In either case Christian interpreters must draw the connection to Christ as Prophet whenever the authority of God's Word appears in Old Testament texts.

Priest

As our Priest, Jesus brings us into communion with God.[31] He offered Himself as a perfect sacrifice in payment for our sins (John 1:29; Romans 8:1–4; 2 Corinthians 5:21; Hebrews 9:28). Our sins are forgiven (Romans 6:18); we are justified (Romans 3:24; 5:1; 8:30) and sanctified (1 John 1:7; 3:6–10) in the service of God by Christ's priestly work.

Many Old Testament stories reveal the priesthood of Christ in at least two ways. First, many texts refer explicitly to priests. For example, in 1 Samuel 2:12–17 Eli's sons defiled worship rituals. God condemned their rebellion and provided a replacement for the sake of Israel (1 Samuel 2:34–36). The original readers of this story learned about Old Testament priests and sacrifices. As we apply this passage to our day, we learn of Christ, our Priest. In Jesus' day God rejected the defiled worship of Israel, but Jesus opened the way for blessings from God through His own priestly sacrifice and intercession.

Similarly, in Chronicles, Abijah rebuked the northern kingdom for rejecting the priestly order in Jerusalem, "But didn't you drive out the priests of the Lord, the sons of Aaron, and the Levites, and make priests of your own as the peoples of other lands do?" (2 Chronicles 13:9). This passage taught the Chronicler's original audience of their need to establish the Old Testament priesthood in proper order during the post-exilic restoration.[32] Christian interpreters, however, must go beyond this understanding and apply the passage to Christ as Priest. He is the divinely ordained Priest in our age. To respond in obedience to this passage today, we must turn to Him as our mediator.

Second, many Old Testament stories touch on themes associated with the priestly function without specifically mentioning priests. Forgiveness of sins, sacrifices, worship, prayer, and communion with God come to the foreground in many passages. Whenever these motifs appear, we must draw connections with the priestly office of Christ.

For example, the story of Jacob at Bethel (Genesis 28:10–22) deals with the special presence of God in Jacob's life. Jacob responds to his vision of the stairway to heaven saying, "This is none other than the house of God; this is the gate of heaven" (v. 17). He also worships and vows to pay a tithe. Moses' original readers associated this story with their tabernacle worship, but we also learn of Christ in this passage. He is our Mediator, our stairway to heaven. As Jesus Himself put it, "I tell you the truth, you shall see heaven open, and the angels of God ascending and descending on the Son of Man" (John 1:51).

Old Testament narratives reveal the lordship of Christ as they deal with motifs that anticipate His priestly office. Through their specific focus on priests and general treatments of worship, forgiveness, and other priestly functions, we can see how central Christ must be in our application of Old Testament stories.

King

As our King, Jesus rules over all things,[33] calling His people to submit to His rule (Psalm 2:10–12). He defends us and goes before us into battle (Psalm 72:4; John 10:28–29; Revelation 19:11–14), conquering evil and securing an eternal inheritance for His people (John 14:2–3; Ephesians 1:13–14, 18–19a; Hebrews 2:14; 12:28; 1 John 3:8).

Christ's kingship bears upon Old Testament narratives in two ways. First, Christ is the fulfillment of *divine kingship*. Throughout the Old Testament, God alone is the absolute Monarch in Israel (1 Samuel 12:12; Psalm 24:7–8; 29:10; 44:4; 47:2–8; 48:1–2; 89:18; Daniel 4:34; 6:26). Human kings ruled as His vice-regents but never as His substitutes.[34] As the second person of the Trinity, Christ is the supreme expression of divine rule over the people of God.

First Samuel 8:5 reports that Israel asked for "a king to lead us, such as all the other nations have." Their desire for the security of a human king with absolute power was a rejection of God as King.[35] "It is not you they have rejected," the Lord said to Samuel, "but they have rejected me as their king" (1 Samuel 8:7). This passage reminded the original readers of God's kingship over Israel. For Christian interpreters it points to Christ, the divine King. Israel's renunciation of reliance on God as King parallels our failure to rely on Christ. When we turn to other sources of security and strength, we repeat their failure.

Second, Christ is the *perfect human King*. Jesus was born the Son of David and fulfilled the hope of a permanent Davidic dynasty (Matthew 1:1; Mark 11:10; Luke 1:32–33). Consequently, Old Testament accounts of human kings in Israel also point to the Kingship of Christ.

For instance, the Chronicler's account of Asa's reign (2 Chronicles 14:1—16:14) focused on the king's obedience and failure.[36] As long as Asa was faithful to God, he experienced great victory; but when he turned to his own way, he failed miserably. These passages drew the attention of the original readers to their Davidic kings, but as Christian interpreters, we can also see the connection with Christ. Christ was entirely faithful in His royal calling, securing an eternal victory for His people. Where all other kings failed, He succeeded.

Beyond this the Kingship of Christ is anticipated whenever Old Testament stories deal with peace and war, victory and defeat, punishment and reward. These motifs were always closely associated with kingship and point to the work of Christ as King. For instance, when Abram conquered his enemies and rescued Lot (Genesis 14:1–16), God's blessing of victory was a demonstration of His royal power. Moses' readers gained confidence for their conquest of Canaan from this story. As Christian interpreters we are reminded of the great victory over sin and death accomplished by our King, Jesus Christ.

We should always view Old Testament narratives in the light of Christ's lordship. To accomplish this goal, we may begin with a simple question. How does the passage before us focus on prophetic, priestly, and royal dimensions of Old Testament life? As texts touch on these motifs, they lead us to consider the three offices of Christ (see figure 59).

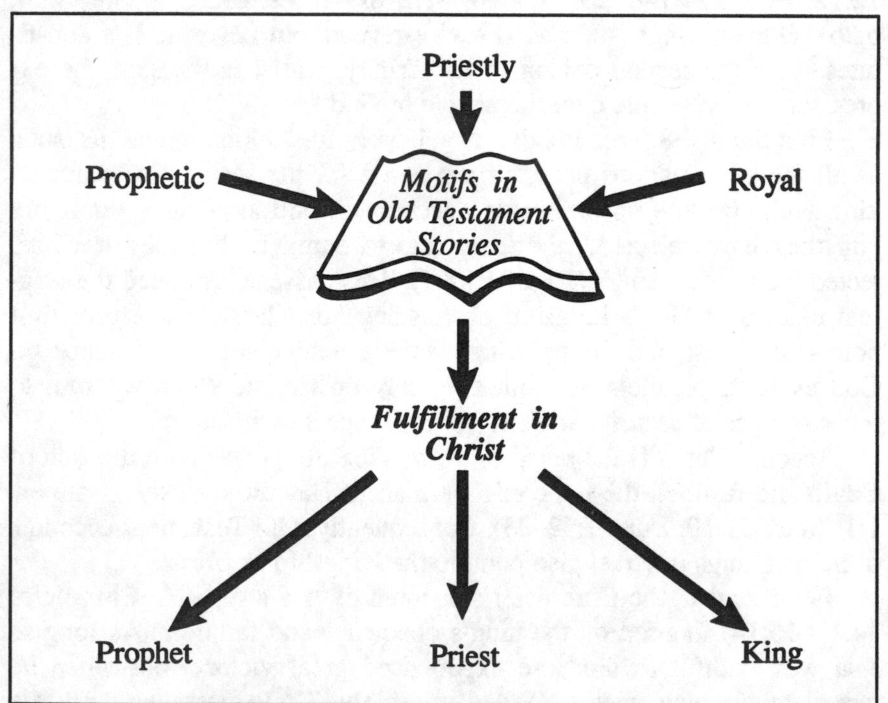

Fig. 59: Three Offices of Christ's Lordship

The Christian Theocracy

As we have noted on several occasions in this chapter, shifts among the epochs of redemptive history have made faithful living before God today different from faithful living in Old Testament times. These differences result from the character of our Christian theocracy. To account for these variations, we will look at the *theocratic ideal and Christ, phases of the Christian theocracy,* and *adjustments to the Christian theocracy.*

Theocratic Ideal and Christ

One motif unites all Old Testament narratives: the ideal of Israel's national theocracy. The Mosaic History dealt with its establishment; the Deuteronomistic History examined its continuation and decline; and the Chronistic History focused on the restoration of Israel as a theocracy. Despite obvious differences these traditions all dealt with the rule of God over Israel as a national unit.

Old Testament writers concentrated attention on the Kingdom of God in national Israel. Their concept of the theocracy was closely tied to geographical and political realities. The land of Canaan was the place of the inheritance; Jerusalem was the home of God's appointed king; the temple was the place of worship. In one way or another, Old Testament writers designed their books to instruct Israel about this national theocratic ideal.

Nevertheless, the Old Testament vision of the theocracy was not limited to a nationalistic focus. From the call of Abram, Israel was given a worldwide calling: "All peoples on earth will be blessed through you" (Genesis 12:3b). Throughout the Old Testament, the hope of extending the theocracy to the nations of the earth grew in intensity. From time to time Gentiles were incorporated into the nation (Joshua 6:25; Ruth 4:13–22). David and Solomon annexed Gentile nations (2 Samuel 22:48; 1 Kings 4:21; 2 Chronicles 8:1–8). Solomon prayed specifically for the blessing of Gentiles coming to the temple (1 Kings 8:41–43). The hope of expansion to other nations grew to a feverish pitch in the prophetic visions (Isaiah 2:2; 11:10; 51:4–5; 65:1). With increasing revelation in the Old Testament period, it became evident that this expansion of the Kingdom to all the world would ultimately be accomplished by the glorious intervention of the Messiah.

The New Testament confirms that these Messianic expectations were fulfilled in Christ. With His coming the theocratic ideal did not disappear; it was enlarged and lifted to a higher plane. The land of Canaan, the Jerusalem throne, and the temple were but foreshadowings of a new world introduced by Christ—small matters in comparison with the new state of the theocracy He introduced. The New Testament teaches that salvation came through the blood of Christ sprinkled on the heavenly mercy seat (Hebrews 9:11–14; 10:19; 1 Peter 1:1–2), not through animal sacrifices. Instead of an ordinary son of David, the eternal Son of David took his seat in heaven (Acts 2:22–36). Instead of a single nation, the New Testament speaks of the celestial city (Revelation 21:1–4) and the eternal reign of Christ over the new heavens and new earth (Isaiah 9:6–7).

The theocratic ideal of the Old Testament explodes into its fullest expression in Christ. All types and shadows disappear, and heavenly realities replace them. The tiny, failing national theocracy is transformed into a universal, victorious theocracy through the intervention of Christ.

Phases of the Christian Theocracy

When a person takes a single step forward, we usually think of it as a simple movement. But looking closer we can see that a step actually consists of many movements. We lift our foot from the floor, carry it through the air, and put it back down on the floor.

In much the same way, the expansion of the theocracy in Christ is a single step in redemptive history. Yet our epoch is not a simple, solitary event. Like an ordinary human step, it consists of several phases: the *inauguration,* the *continuation,* and the *consummation.*

Inauguration. The inauguration of the eschatological age took place in the first coming of Christ. When Jesus appeared He began His work as our Prophet, Priest, and King. As our Prophet, Jesus proclaimed "the year of the Lord's favor" (Luke 4:19). His teaching and miracles brought relief to the poor, healing for the blind, release and restoration for the captives (Luke 4:18). As Priest He came and "made his dwelling among us" (John 1:14). His suffering and death paid for the sins of His people, granting forgiveness to all who believe in Him. As King, Jesus was born the son of David; His resurrection and ascension were His coronation—the time when He sat on the throne of David with all authority.

The inauguration of our age also extended to the work of the Holy Spirit among the apostles. When Christ ascended on high, He granted the gifts of the Holy Spirit to His church (Ephesians 4:7–13). His apostles waited in Jerusalem for the empowerment of the Spirit (Luke 24:49; Acts 2:1–4), that they might become Christ's witnesses to the nations.

The Spirit came at Pentecost (Acts 2:1–11), and the apostles spread the Kingdom to Judea, Samaria, and to "the ends of the earth" (Acts 1:8).

All of these incidents formed a unified complex of events that began the new theocratic age of which we are a part. As one Pauline metaphor put it, we are "God's household, built on the foundation of the apostles and prophets, with Christ Jesus himself as the chief cornerstone" (Ephesians 2:19b–20). Just as a building rests on its foundation, we look back to the work of Christ and the apostles as the foundation of our age.

In His earthly ministry, Jesus drove a wedge between the Kingdom of God and all political institutions of this world order, including national Israel. Jesus taught His disciples, "Seek first his kingdom and his righteousness, and all these things will be given to you as well" (Matthew 6:33). Material gains in this world were to take second place to the advancement of Christ's Kingdom. When Pilate questioned Jesus, He responded plainly, "My kingdom is not of this world" (John 18:36). In line with Old Testament expectations, Jesus began an utter transformation of the national theocracy. He cut the Kingdom free of its geo-political moorings in the Old Testament as it set sail for the theocracy extending to all nations.

Continuation. The New Testament also teaches that the Kingdom of God goes through a lengthy phase of continuation. The Jews of Jesus' day expected the Messiah to set up a glorious worldwide Kingdom immediately upon His arrival.[37] Even John the Baptist assumed that the Messiah would bring salvation and final judgment simultaneously (Matthew 3:10–12; 11:3).[38] But Jesus revealed that God had a different plan. The Gospel of Matthew reports Jesus' Kingdom parables, which emphasize the extended, progressive nature of our age.[39] We live during the sprouting of the wheat and tares (Matthew 13:24–30, 36–43); the mustard seed is still growing (Matthew 13:31–32).

Jesus continues to be our Prophet, Priest, and King. As our Prophet He teaches through the faithful preaching of the Word (2 Peter 3:2). As our Priest He intercedes on our behalf before the throne of grace. As our King He leads us into battle, protecting, and providing for our needs.

Nevertheless, the continuation of the Kingdom must be described as the "already but not yet."[40] We live with many blessings from the age to come. We have the earnest of the Holy Spirit (2 Corinthians 1:21–22), inward renewal (2 Corinthians 4:16; Colossians 3:10) and an expanding church (Colossians 1:6). But the Kingdom has not come in its fullness. The ship of the Christian theocracy has left the old port of Jewish nationalism but has not reached its final destination of worldwide dominion. As a result followers of Christ are not citizens of a geo-political theocracy. Rather, "our citizenship is in heaven" (Philippians 3:20). The people of God now live as a disenfranchised theocratic remnant, a subculture scattering throughout the nations of the earth. We are passing through this world, engaged in spiritual warfare (Ephesians 6:12), and looking for the new world to come (1 Peter 1:7; 2:11). At the present time, we are blessed more than any age in the past; old theocratic types and shadows have passed away. But we still wait for the consummation of the theocracy in Christ's second coming.

Consummation. The return of Christ in glory will bring about the consummation of the Christian theocracy. Jesus promised to return to this world (John 14:1–4; Acts 1:11), and the apostles affirmed this hope (1 Corinthians 4:5; 1 Thessalonians 1:10; 3:13; Revelation 22:12). At Christ's return the whole of the universe will be utterly transformed into the Kingdom of God (2 Peter 3:10–12). This last phase of our epoch plays a vital role in the lives of believers today, coloring our present existence in many ways. Christ's return is the comfort and desire of the people of God (1 Corinthians 1:7; 1 Thessalonians 4:15–18; 2 Timothy 4:8; Philippians 3:20–21).

When Christ returns we will see the Christian theocracy come to its final phase. God's people will possess the earth as Christ reigns over every inch of it. As our Prophet He will reveal God to us. As our Priest He will welcome us into the glorious presence of God. As our King He will defeat our enemies and grant us "a new heaven and a new earth" (2 Peter 3:13).

Distinctions among the inauguration, continuation, and consummation of the Christian theocracy present us with three options every time we apply Old Testament stories to our day. We may look at the past, present, or future work of Christ on our behalf. We may ask: 1) How does the passage offer insight into Christ as Prophet, Priest, and King in His first coming? 2) How does it apply to the present continuation of Christ's prophetic, priestly, and royal offices? 3) How does the passage shed light on the consummation of Christ's prophetic, priestly, and royal ministry at His second coming?

For example, we have mentioned that Christians must relate Moses' prophetic activity to Christ, but three options lie before us. We may draw attention to Christ's teachings while He was on earth; we may focus on the continuation of His ministry through the preaching and teaching of the Word; and we may point to the revelation of God in the second coming. The implications of a given text for modern audiences include all phases of Christ's prophetic work.

In a similar way, we have suggested that the removal of Eli's sons from priestly service in 1 Samuel 2:12–36 anticipated the perfection of sacrifice and worship in Christ. This story reminds us of the wonder of Christ's perfect sacrifice on the cross, draws our attention to His continuing intercession before the throne of grace, and keeps us ever hopeful of the forgiveness and communion with God that Christ will grant to us in the second coming.

We may handle passages that focus on kingship in a similar manner. As we have suggested, the Chronicler's account of Asa's reign (2 Chronicles 14:1—16:14) applies to the victory and security provided by Christ the King. To apply this text to the Christian theocracy, we must remember the establishment of the Kingdom in the first coming of Christ. We turn to the power of Christ displayed for us day after day as His Kingdom continues, and we are reminded of the glory of His victory when the Kingdom will find universal expression in the second coming. Passages that speak of kingship may be applied to all the phases of our age.

As we assess the needs of modern believers, we may emphasize one dimension of modern application over another. Nevertheless, every Old Testament story directs us to consider how Christ is our Prophet, Priest, and King in the inauguration, continuation, and consummation of the Christian theocracy (see figure 60).

Adjustments to the Christian Theocracy

The ideology of Old Testament writers must be adjusted in the light of the shifts in the Christian theocracy. These modifications can be complex. It will help to comment briefly on the kinds of realignments that must take place in order to make applications of specific Old Testament stories.

The Mosaic History. The Mosaic History originally focused on Israel's formation into a national theocracy.[41] Moses wrote Genesis to guide Israel's departure from Egypt to the conquest of Canaan; Exodus legitimated Moses' social and cultic order for the new nation; Numbers exhorted the nation to be morally and ritually prepared to rout the Canaanites from the land; Deuteronomy called the people to reaffirm the Mosaic covenant as they entered the land of promise. These books instructed the people about vital dimensions of establishing the theocratic nation of Israel.

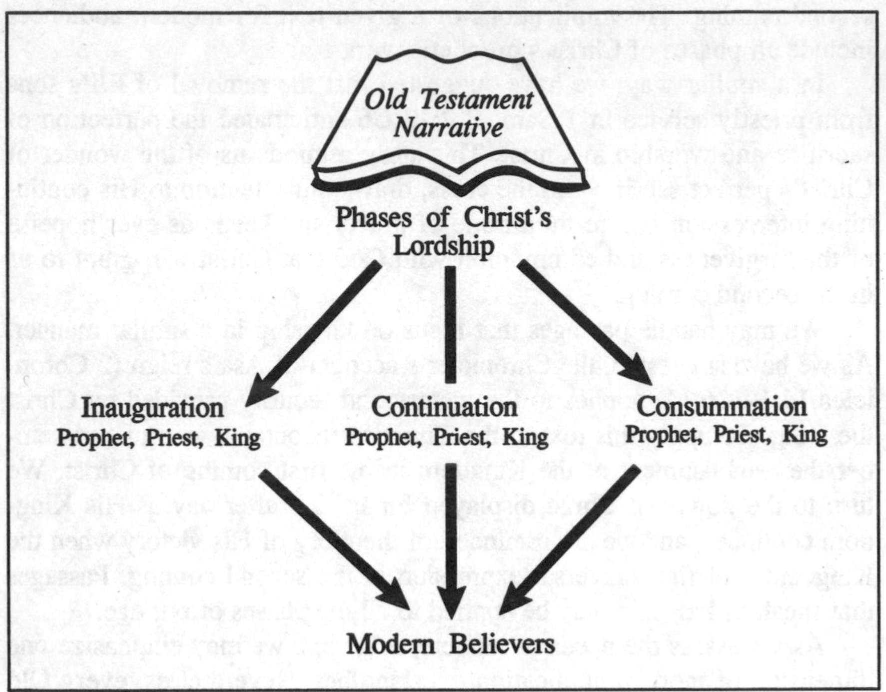

Fig. 60: Application to the Christian Theocracy

How do these books apply to people living in the Christian theocracy? When we adjust the outlooks of Pentateuchal texts to the form of God's Kingdom in our age, we find countless implications for responsible living in Christ. We are not following Moses through the desert to Canaan, but Genesis teaches us how Christ brought us out of slavery to sin and death. It explains the necessity of following Him in our daily lives away from sin and toward our ultimate destiny. Genesis also encourages us to continue with the confidence that Christ will one day bring us into the promised land of a new heaven and a new earth.

Exodus exhorted the people to submit to Moses' social and cultic order. Again we are no longer bound to the types and shadows of Moses' age, but Exodus instructs us to acknowledge the authority of Christ as He applied Moses' Law to His Kingdom.

Numbers called the second generation of Israel to follow God into conquest as His holy army. It teaches us "to keep [ourselves] from setting our hearts on evil things as they did" (1 Corinthians 10:6). We must devote ourselves to holiness as those who struggle "against the rulers, against the authorities, against the powers of this dark world" (Ephesians

6:12). Our only hope for victory in the spiritual battles ahead is devotion to Christ.

Deuteronomy called the nation to covenant renewal in the land of Canaan. As twentieth-century believers, we do not commit ourselves to the nationalistic types and shadows of Mosaic Law. Still Deuteronomy challenges us to remember that Christ fulfilled covenant requirements and calls us to daily fidelity as God's people. Finally, we hope for the fulfillment of covenant promises of peace and prosperity throughout the earth at the return of Christ.

The Deuteronomistic History. The Deuteronomistic History instructed the people of God about the continuation and decline of the theocratic nation.[42] The book of Joshua taught the nation how to succeed in holy war, divide the land in mutual respect, and renew covenant obedience. Judges defended the need for a king by pointing to the faltering conquest, cycles of good and bad under the judges, and the inadequacies of the Levites. Samuel declared Israel's hope in the Davidic line despite David's failures. Kings demonstrated the justice of the exile and offered hope of return to the land upon repentance.

Just as Israel learned about the Old Testament national theocracy in these books, we may find many implications for life in the Christian theocracy. Joshua instructs us to see our responsibilities as people who have been brought into our inheritance by the death and resurrection of Christ. We are to continue in spiritual warfare, in cooperation with others who share the inheritance, and in covenant renewal. We look forward to the day when our conquest will be completed by the second coming of Christ.

Judges teaches us of our need for Christ our King; without Him our conquest will falter. Other leaders can provide only temporary relief at best. With Christ our King, we are assured of victory and blessing.

Samuel teaches us to affirm our commitment to King Jesus, the Son of David, despite the troubles that riddle His Kingdom. Christ was without fault, but His Kingdom experiences difficulties. Even so, we know that the promises of God rest in Him.

The book of Kings reminds us not to take the accomplishments of Christ as a license for sin; God chastises His children when they stray. Even as the writer of Kings held out hope of restoration, we, too, can be restored through repentance and faith.

The Chronistic History. The Chronistic History focused on the restoration of the national theocracy after exile.[43] Chronicles emphasized the need to have the people of God, temple, and royal family in proper order to receive the blessing of God. Ezra-Nehemiah focused on God's requirement of holy living and devotion to the program of Kingdom restoration.

When we look at these books as Christians, we find that they speak powerfully to our responsibilities in the Christian theocracy. We are the remnant of the people of God. Just as the Chronicler called the people to return to the ideals of the national theocracy, we are exhorted to renew our commitment to the ideals of the Kingdom of Christ. The unity of the people of God, the centrality of Christ as King, and the importance of proper worship are essential to receiving God's blessing in our day. As Ezra-Nehemiah focused on the importance of holiness and practical efforts to restore the kingdom, we can see the vital importance of separation from the evils of the world and devotion to building the Kingdom of Christ.

Other books. The remaining narrative books also speak a relevant word to our theocratic duties.[44] The book of Ruth supported the legitimacy of David's line despite the presence of a Moabitess in his ancestry; as Christians we follow Christ, whose claim to Kingship is constantly challenged. The book of Esther taught the people of Israel how to serve God faithfully in a foreign land; we must learn to serve God in our sinful world. The book of Jonah impressed upon its original readers the importance of bringing God's Word to other nations. Today Christians are commissioned to carry the Word of Christ throughout the world as well.

These comments barely touch on the significance of these Scriptures for our epoch. Yet they point in the direction of the adjustments we must make in applying the original meaning of these books to our present age. Old Testament narratives are authoritative for our age, but we must respond to them as the people of God living between the first and second coming of Christ. Leaving the nationalistic ideals of Israel behind, we travel through this fallen world, looking for Christ's return and the full realization of the worldwide theocracy in Him.

Conclusion

In this chapter we have outlined several vital aspects of applying Old Testament stories to our age. Redemptive history consists of many epochs, but the advent of Christ brought about the most significant shift in Biblical religion. As a result Christ is the hermeneutical focal point of all attempts to bring these passages to our era. We must view Old Testament narratives in the light of His prophetic, priestly, and royal offices. As the people of God living between the first and second advents of Christ, we should also take into account the differences between the Old Testament theocracy and the present state of the Christian theocratic sub-culture. With these large-scale considerations in mind, we will be able to move toward more effective application of Old Testament stories to our age.

Review Questions

1. Describe the divisions and unity of redemptive history as it has been discussed in this chapter. How have evangelicals gone to extremes in these matters? What is an organic view of redemptive history?
2. What are Christ's theocratic offices? How may we make Christ's three offices central to modern application of Old Testament narratives?
3. How is the theocratic ideal of the Old Testament expanded in Christ? What are the phases of the Christian theocracy?

Study Exercises

1. Make a list of ten major themes that appear in Old Testament stories. Reflect on how each theme was modified as redemptive history progressed in the Old Testament and in Christ.
2. Examine 2 Chronicles 12:1–12. List three original implications of this story. Draw connections from each implication to the offices of Christ in the three phases of the Christian theocracy.
3. Examine Genesis 11:1–9. Repeat the steps in exercise 2.

15

FROM CULTURE TO CULTURE

I grew up in a small city and had little contact with people from other parts of the world. I had learned in school that other cultures were different from mine, but everyone I knew was like me. We shared the same customs and pursued the same dreams. When I moved to a large city, however, I learned quickly that people from other cultures can be very different. Diverse cultural backgrounds give people different outlooks and directions in life.

Culture may be defined as "the integrated system of learned patterns of behavior, ideas and products characteristic of a society."[1] As this definition suggests, culture influences every facet of human existence. Our ideas, customs, and expectations of life take shape in our social context. No one escapes its power.

Even Old Testament writers reflect the social milieu of their day. The inspiration of the Holy Spirit kept them from error, but the authors' outlooks grew out of their world.[2] They did not think like modern people, but looked at life largely in terms of ancient Near Eastern culture.

For this reason Old Testament stories reflect cultural perspectives and traditions that are different from ours in many ways. These differences challenge every serious interpreter. What can we do to overcome the culture gap? How can we apply these ancient stories to modern life?

Many topics arise as we deal with these matters. We will touch on three: *evaluating cultural variations, culture in the Old and New Testaments,* and *application to modern culture*. How should we evaluate the differences between one culture and another? What effect should the coming of Christ have on our view of culture? What cultural adjustments must we make when we apply Old Testament narratives to the modern world?

Evaluating Cultural Variations

I once knew a man who never showed tenderness to his family. He was always distant and cold toward his wife and children. "It's just his background," my friend explained. "That's the way men act in his country." But I was still troubled. "It may be his custom," I responded. "But is it *right?*"

This conversation reflects a tension many of us experience from time to time. We want to respect people from other parts of the world. We try not to impose our cultural expectations on them. But we still believe that some things are right or wrong no matter where a person lives.

When we apply Old Testament narratives to modern life, both the Bible and contemporary experience confront us with a vast array of cultural ideals. Is there a way to judge among these norms? How should we evaluate the customs of Old Testament days? How can we distinguish between good and bad in modern cultures?

To answer these questions from a Biblical perspective, we must recognize that cultures stem from two principal sources: *religion* and *nature*. As we understand these influences, we will discover vital guidelines for evaluating cultural variations.

Religion and Culture

Religion is a primary influence on every society. In many respects culture and religion are inseparable:

> Throughout human history, religion and culture have been inextricably connected. There has never yet been a great religion which did not find its expression in a great culture. There has never yet been a great culture which did not have deep roots in religion.[3]

Social interactions flesh out our basic loyalties and faith commitments. What we believe about God and our relationship with Him establishes the values that shape our societies. The fundamental structures of all cultures stem from religious beliefs.[4]

The powerful influence of organized religion has been evident throughout history. Societies in the past relied explicitly on religious ideals. The Babylonians and Egyptians self-consciously structured their societies according to the order their gods had established. Feudalism in medieval Europe was significantly patterned after the mixture of Christian and pagan belief so prominent at that time.[5] In contemporary western civilization, we bury our Judeo-Christian heritage under the rhetoric of religious neutrality. But many of our basic social values—justice, honor, equality, and the like—find their roots in this religious tradition.

To one degree or another, religious beliefs have determined the patterns and expectations of all cultures. But cultures do not simply grow out of the belief systems people consciously endorse. The roots of our life styles extend beyond organized religion to the inescapable accountability of all nations to the true God of heaven and earth.

Paul points in this direction in Romans 1:18–32. He argues that throughout history all people have known the "eternal power and divine nature" of God. This general revelation has been "understood from what has been made." As societies developed, however, they rebelled against this knowledge of God. The nations "neither glorified him as God nor gave thanks to him." So God abandoned the peoples of the world to "the sinful desires of their hearts."

But Paul's outlook is not entirely negative. Although sin permeates our existence, human beings have been unable to eradicate their knowledge of God. The nations fail to be consistent in their rebellion against Him and follow standards obtained through general revelation: "Gentiles, who do not have the law, do by nature things required by the law. . . . They show that the requirements of the law are written on their hearts, their consciences also bearing witness, and their thoughts now accusing, now even defending them" (Romans 2:14–15).

No one can escape the effects of general revelation, so many dimensions of our societies comply at least externally with God's will.[6] In different ways the nations exhibit both rebellion against God and compliance with His order.[7]

Paul stands opposed to popular outlooks on culture today. We live in a day of cultural relativism, where no universal standard holds for all people. We view all social norms as equally legitimate.[8]

In comparison Paul was a cultural absolutist. The apostle insisted that all nations are obligated to honor God and that the practices of every society in every age are subject to evaluation by the standard of God's revelation. Paul's perspective alerts us to an essential guideline for exploring variations among nations. Put simply, we must evaluate all cultural practices by the standard of God's revelation. God's holy will stands above both *culture in Old Testament stories* and *contemporary cultures.*

Culture in Old Testament stories. Reflections of culture in Old Testament stories are subject to divine revelation. Old Testament passages faithfully describe many common practices of the ancient Near East. These patterns of life either conformed to God's will or violated it. For this reason we must never mistake customs in the Old Testament as indications of God's will but should always ask if they met with divine approval.

Old Testament writers approved of many cultural practices. For example, in 1 Chronicles 18:15–17 the Chronicler reported that David established a political bureaucracy very similar to other nations of his day: "Joab . . . was over the army; Jehoshaphat . . . was recorder; Zadok . . . and Ahimelech . . . were priests; Shavsha . . . was secretary; Benaiah . . . was over the Kerethites and Pelethites; and David's sons were chief officials at the King's side."[9] As far as we know, God did not specifically command David to follow this form of government; David exercised his own judgment and adopted a practice of his time for the kingdom of Israel. How should we evaluate the king's policy? Was it right? In this case the Chronicler explicitly approved of David's actions by noting that they benefited Israel (1 Chronicles 18:14). David fulfilled his responsibility as the king of Israel, so following this cultural norm proved to be a positive choice.

At the same time, however, many customs that appear in the Old Testament did not conform to God's will. For instance, when Abram fathered a child through Hagar, he followed a common social norm.[10] But as Paul tells us, "The son by the bondwoman was born according to the flesh, and the son by the free woman through the promise" (Galatians 4:23, NASB). By adopting this ancient practice, Abram had turned from God's promise to his own fleshly efforts and violated the revelation of God. Abram's actions were wrong, despite the fact that they were culturally acceptable.

Old Testament stories report many cultural dimensions of Israel's day, some which conformed to God's will and others which violated it. Some matters are more difficult to evaluate than others, but we must always try to judge every custom reported in Old Testament texts by the standard of divine revelation.

Contemporary cultures. As we apply Old Testament stories to our day, we must also evaluate contemporary cultures. The practices of the modern world also stand under the rule of revelation.

Evaluating contemporary society is two-sided. On one side practices that are contrary to the revelation of God must be viewed negatively, as rebellion against God. Oppressive political policies, sexual perversion, thievery—all are wrong no matter what a society's standards may be. To apply Old Testament narratives to modern life, we must recognize these practices for what they are in God's sight.

On the other side, when modern societies accord with God's revelation, we must evaluate them positively. Evangelicals often find it easier to be more negative than positive about contemporary culture. We see rebellion against God all around us and tend to overlook positive cultural values, such as laws that restrain evil and social patterns that promote justice and mercy. We should affirm practices that bring honor to God. As we evaluate modern culture, we should always look for the good as well as the evil.

Evaluating culture must begin by recognizing the religious character of human existence. General revelation has obligated all people to respond obediently to God. The practices of people in ancient and modern times exhibit positive and negative responses to God's revelation. As we apply Old Testament narratives to contemporary life, we must evaluate culture by the standard of God's Word.

Nature and Culture

Evaluating culture requires a balanced perspective. Although religion plays an important role in forming the character of nations, it is not the only factor to consider. Variations in nature also shape human life. Cultures result from an interaction of religious values and natural diversities.

My wife and I once lived in an apartment above an artist. Her work was remarkable in many ways, but I was most impressed by her love for diversity. She worked well with a host of art forms: weaving, sewing, drawing, painting, and ceramics. I remember commenting one day, "I think she can make art out of anything."

When we examine the world God has made, it becomes evident that He also loves diversity. He did not create a monolithic social order for His image. On the contrary, God established countless natural diversities that spawn many differences among us. As Paul put it, "From one man he made every nation of men, that they should inhabit the whole earth; and he determined the times set for them and the exact places where they should live" (Acts 17:26).

Cultural anthropologists have pointed to many natural causes behind cultural diversities,[11] three of which seem especially influential. *Physical environment* plays an important role in culture. Weather patterns, geography, and natural resources shape vital dimensions of human life.

Groups that settle near the sea develop means of livelihood different from their counterparts in the desert; people living among the mountains invent different modes of transportation than those in the plains. Many cultural patterns grow out of the physical circumstances in which people live.

In addition God has endowed human beings with *diverse natural gifts and abilities*.[12] Ordinary observation tells us that both individuals and groups of people tend to have different strengths. Some possess keen artistic abilities; others are gifted in technical skills. Some are highly pragmatic; others are more reflective and philosophical. As these various kinds of people dominate a society, they lead their cultures in different directions.

Finally, cultural diversity results from the *passage of time*. Historical changes cause many differences among us. As generations build on the past and face the challenges of their changing world, their cultural patterns change again and again. Temporal changes also create many diversities.

The influence of nature raises a second guideline for evaluating culture. Since God did not intend all societies to be exactly the same, we must acknowledge legitimate differences among cultures. The natural diversities among people demonstrate that many cultural practices are not inherently right nor wrong. In themselves these social patterns have no moral value. For example, it is not necessarily better to ride horses instead of camels, to wear sandals instead of shoes, or to eat with a fork instead of your fingers. These facets of life result largely from the natural diversities God has ordained.

Natural differences are not beyond all evaluation, however. On the contrary, we must still assess these matters according to the general principles of Scripture. Does the practice violate broad moral directives found in the Bible? Does the custom pass the test of God's commandments? The motivations and results of all cultural patterns stand or fall in the light of divine moral standards.

The influence of nature on culture helps us clarify our task as we apply Old Testament stories. Natural variations caution us to respect diverse practices in *Old Testament culture* and *modern cultures*.

Old Testament culture. Many features in Old Testament culture resulted from natural diversities. Old Testament believers often responded to God in ways that were customary for their times. Consequently their practices were never intended to be normative for all believers.

For instance, Abraham traveled to Mount Moriah on a donkey (Genesis 22:3); David tended sheep (1 Samuel 17:15). No doubt, these actions were moral choices for these men. Abraham was responding to God's call to sacrifice Isaac; David was serving as an obedient son. These actions were cultural practices appropriate to accomplishing their divinely ordained responsibilities. All believers must obey the Biblical principles of fidelity and service as these men did. But we do not have to travel by donkey or become shepherds. These Old Testament expressions of obedience resulted from adherence to religious beliefs in the context of natural cultural diversities.

Modern cultures. In much the same way, legitimate differences exist among modern cultures. All believers must follow the principles of Scripture, but the expression of obedience will differ from time to time and place to place.[13] Allowing for modern cultural variations can be difficult. Our preconceptions of appropriate behavior often obscure the need for diverse applications. We assume that a text must be used in every cultural setting, just as we have applied it in our own. As Conn has said, "Our Western values have led us to expect both a single right answer to every question and the superiority of answers developed by Western academicians to the answers developed by the members of any other culture."[14]

For example, the Chronicler insisted on proper music in worship in the post-exilic community (see 1 Chronicles 6:31–47; 15:19–22, 28; 16:4–36; 2 Chronicles 7:6).[15] Most of us realize that we do not have to adopt ancient Near Eastern instrumentation and rhythm to apply the Chronicler's teaching. We focus on the principle, not the specific actions. Yet church leaders often believe that only traditional styles of music please God. We play organs and pianos; we sing traditional hymns. But we rule out other musical forms—folk, jazz, reggae—because of our cultural biases. We assume they do not please God because they do not please us. Cultural bigotry of this sort appears all around us.

The same moral standards may be fulfilled in different circumstances by different but equally legitimate means. Language is a gift that should be used according to the will of God, but this does not mean we must all speak the same language. Governments should exercise the power of the sword against evil, but the precise means to accomplish this end will vary. In different times and places, the standards of divine revelation require different expressions of obedience.

To sum up, cultures develop out of religion and nature. The religious character of life compels us to evaluate the moral quality of all practices in the Old Testament and our day according to the Word of God. But the natural diversities among cultures teach us to recognize legitimate varieties both in the Old Testament and in the modern world. As we keep these principles in mind, we will be better equipped to evaluate cultural variations (see figure 61).

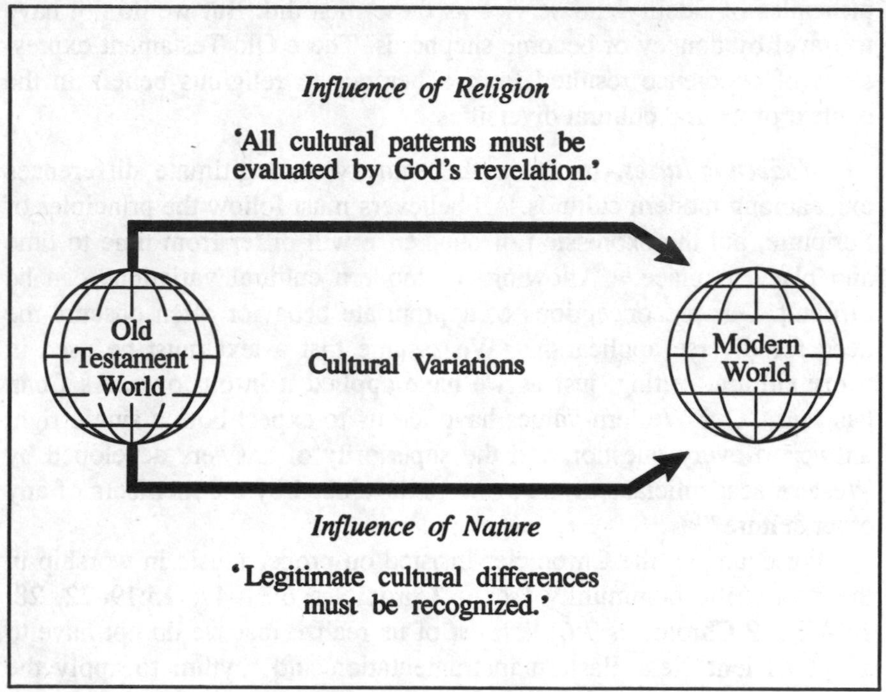

Fig. 61: Evaluating Cultural Variations

Culture in the Old Testament and New Testament

When we compare Old Testament stories with modern culture, we quickly realize that we are dealing with more than ordinary historical developments. The redemptive-historical changes that took place in the first coming of Christ have caused dramatic differences between us and the Old Testament. To explore these changes, we will examine *culture in both the Old Testament and the New Testament.*

Culture in the Old Testament

I remember a young woman coming up to me after a lecture. "I wouldn't want to live in the Old Testament days," she said. "People back then had so many rules they could hardly breathe." That's how most evangelicals perceive the Old Testament—as a period of legalism and confinement. Is this impression accurate? What was Old Testament culture really like?

A cursory reading of Old Testament stories reveals that Mosaic Law regulated the entire Israelite society. Our distinctions between secular and religious spheres of life were inconceivable to Old Testament writers. In one way or another, the Law of Moses governed every facet of the national theocracy: worship, political and legal arrangements, and interpersonal affairs. No area of life was unaffected by the precepts of revelation.

Nevertheless, Old Testament Law did not strictly regulate every facet of life. God addressed some aspects of Israel's culture more specifically than others. On one end of the scale, He permitted Israel to follow ancient customs as long as they did not violate the principles of His revelation, but on the other end, He ordered specific regulations to govern some aspects of Israel's cultural life. Every dimension of the national theocracy fell somewhere along this range. It will help to look at both ends of the spectrum: *cultural flexibility* and *cultural legislation.*

Cultural flexibility. Ancient Israelites experienced many areas of cultural flexibility. They could fulfill their responsibilities before God through various means. The moral principles of Biblical commandments set parameters, but within those limits, the people of God experienced great freedom.

As a result many aspects of the Old Testament theocracy were very similar to other ancient Near Eastern cultures. Israel's technological skills, art forms, domestic practices, and the like developed out of the historical context in which Israel lived. Old Testament writers treated these patterns as legitimate natural diversities. They did not prescribe specific instructions on matters such as dining etiquette, the color of clothing, forms of entertainment, or modes of transportation.

Israel's cultural freedom resulted from a number of factors. First, many of God's commands were negative prohibitions that allowed for a great deal of diversity. "You shall not murder," "You shall not commit adultery," "You shall not steal" (Exodus 20:13–15), told the people of God what they were *not* to do, but these commands did not specify in a positive way what the Israelites were to do in every circumstance.

Second, many positive directives in the Old Testament were general principles. For instance, "Remember the Sabbath day by keeping it holy" (Exodus 20:8) affirmed the necessity of faithful Sabbath observance.[16] Some specific items were addressed in other laws and stories. But these decrees did not clarify many of the particulars of Sabbath keeping. Many facets of Sabbath observance remained matters of conscience.

Third, there were very few specific laws in the Old Testament. While the lists may seem long from a modern outlook, they addressed only a few areas of daily life.[17] They did not deal with enormous portions of Old Testament culture.

For these reasons we may conclude that in many facets of life God permitted cultural flexibility. The nation was always limited by God's commands, but many particular practices were not legislated.

Cultural legislation. While God did not legislate everything in the Old Testament theocracy, He gave Israel wide-ranging cultural legislation. God did not permit His people to pursue any pattern of life they desired. He prescribed many directives that governed daily practices. For instance, Old Testament believers were specifically forbidden to allow their animals or servants to work on the Sabbath (Exodus 23:12). The Law also regulated dimensions of divorce (Deuteronomy 24:1–4), aspects of military service (Deuteronomy 20:1–9), punishments for specific crimes (Leviticus 20:1–27), and the consumption of particular foods (Deuteronomy 14:1–21).

Why did God regulate Israel's society in such detail? Did He bind His people in a cultural straight jacket? The answer to these questions appear in God's words to Moses: "You yourselves have seen what I did to Egypt, and how I carried you on eagles' wings and brought you to myself. Now if you obey me fully and keep my covenant, then out of all nations you will be my treasured possession" (Exodus 19:4–5).

Put simply, Old Testament theocratic Law was designed to glorify God and to benefit Israel. It separated the theocracy from other nations and made Israel God's "treasured possession" (*sglh).* The Law of Moses taught Israel how to please and honor God. Moreover, it protected Israel from sin's destructive power and pointed to the way of fruitful living (Joshua 1:7–8). Through the course of time, sin turned the Law into a heavy burden (Romans 7:7–11), but God's expressed purpose in giving the Law was to bless His people.[18] As Moses predicted:

> See, I have taught you decrees and laws as the Lord my God commanded me. . . . Observe them carefully, for this will show your wisdom and understanding to the nations, who will hear about all these decrees and say, "Surely this great nation is a wise and understanding people" (Deuteronomy 4:5, 6).

Israelite Law was not completely different from the laws and customs of other nations.[19] Archaeological research has shown many similarities between Israel and the practices of other nations. But God gave these common practices special significance for His people. For example, many nations practiced circumcision,[20] observed covenant rituals similar to those in Old Testament Law,[21] and had built temples like Solomon's.[22] But in the Old Testament these norms were reinterpreted by the revelation of Yahweh. The beliefs associated with circumcision, the temple, covenant rituals, and the like set Israel apart from other societies in many ways.

Beyond this, God prescribed cultural norms contrary to the practices of other nations. Cultic prostitution was prohibited (Deuteronomy 23:17); Israelites were not to eat food others considered acceptable (Leviticus 11:1–47); Mosaic Law prohibited forms of economic oppression that were widespread among Israel's neighbors.[23] God prescribed many practices for His people that distinguished Israel as a holy people separate from the common customs in the ancient Near East.

In sum, God granted Israel areas of cultural freedom, but many aspects of life were also directly governed by God's Law. This high degree of cultural regulation distinguished Israel from other nations, forming Israel into a geo-political expression of the rule of God in the Old Testament age.

Culture in the New Testament

The coming of Christ had a dramatic effect on the relationship between faith and culture. As we have seen, God's ultimate design in Christ was to expand Israel's national theocracy into a universal kingdom.[24] The theocracy was to be a worldwide cultural reality, but this destiny will be reached only in the second coming of Christ. Between the resurrection and Christ's return, the church has been set free from its nationalistic moorings and has set sail for the glorious universal Kingdom. Now the Christian community is between ports, existing as a sub-culture among the nations of the world.

Many questions are raised by this epochal change. What cultural norms are required in the Christian theocratic sub-culture? How are Christians to express their faith within the various nations to which they belong? Christ has ordained flexibility and legislation for His people today as in Old Testament Israel, but these facets of theocratic life have shifted significantly. We will look at *cultural legislation* and *cultural flexibility* in the Christian theocracy.

Cultural legislation. God has established cultural legislation for the Christian community wherever it exists. These patterns of life are not as extensive as Old Testament regulations, but Christians must observe them in every nation and age. Paul exhorted the Roman believers, "Do not conform any longer to the pattern of this world" (Romans 12:2). Followers of Christ are expected to adopt a new culture for themselves, a way of life ordained by divine revelation. Consequently, the Christian community should stand out among all the kingdoms of the world.

Evangelicals often have difficulty recognizing the distinctive manner of life within the Christian theocracy. In centuries past, the Kingdom of Christ has been so closely identified with Western culture at large that the uniqueness of the Christian community has been obscured. For better or worse, Christian ideals have intertwined with European and American ideals for centuries. [25]

In recent decades many missiologists have emphasized the need to separate Christianity from its Western setting by putting the gospel in the context of various world cultures.[26] The call to contextualization offers a healthy corrective. Missionaries have been guilty of forcing their converts to accept norms that go beyond the teaching of Scripture. Nevertheless, current proposals of contextualization run the risk of simply replacing Western ideals with the mores of other cultures. Instead of emphasizing the distinctive patterns of life ordained for the church, the Christian message is often buried beneath the cultural norms existing outside the European and North American context.

One of the greatest difficulties facing advocates of contextualization is the distinction they often make between the cultural "form" and normative "meaning" of the New Testament teaching.[27] In this outlook only the principles of the New Testament carry from one nation to another; cultural patterns are discarded for forms more appropriate within different societies. For instance, Kraft argues:

> An anthropologically informed approach, however, identifies as the constants of Christianity the functions and meanings behind such forms rather than any given set of doctrinal or behavioral forms. It would leave the cultural forms in which these constant functions are expressed largely negotiable in terms of the cultural matrix of those with whom God is dealing at the time . . . . It is the meaning conveyed by a particular doctrine (e.g., consumption of alcoholic beverages, baptism) that is of primary concern of [sic] God.[28]

This position certainly has an element of truth. Modern Christians do not have to carry swords (Luke 22:36) or wear sandals (Mark 6:9) to obey the teachings of Christ. We may greet each other with an embrace or a hearty handshake instead of a kiss (1 Peter 5:14). Yet in many cases a sharp distinction between form and meaning cannot be justified.[29] The New Testament does not merely insist that believers affirm abstract theological principles; it also requires us to follow forms and structures in the church. In many cases the forms and the principles are largely inseparable. We do not need to contextualize such Biblical teaching; we need to teach and explain the requirements of Scripture.

The distinctive norms of the Christian community touch many areas of life. Above all, the church builds upon Christ as the fulfillment of Old Testament redemptive structures. We follow the Son of David, who has taken His eternal heavenly throne; we trust in His sacrifice as payment for our sins; we worship through Christ's priestly mediation. These beliefs and practices have distinctively Israelite contours, but they remain normative for Jewish and Gentile believers. Gentiles are to adopt these Jewish outlooks as their own, even though they were foreign to their native cultures. These concepts and practices are essential for salvation; no other cultural definitions of sin and salvation may substitute in the Christian theocracy.

Many other requirements are always incumbent upon the life of the theocratic subculture. For instance, proper observance of baptism and holy communion are specifically prescribed by God. They are not to be exchanged for other rites.[30] The authority structure and discipline of the church has been ordained for believers in all ages. The service of mercy is established for the Christian community. Mutual harmony, forgiveness, and submission are regulated by divine prescription. The list goes on and on. These patterns also stem from Jewish culture, but they are not negotiable for the Christian church. To be sure they must be applied with wisdom to particular circumstances. But no matter where we live, all Christians are called to observe these regulations.

The Biblical norms governing the Christian subculture form us into a holy people. Although we are scattered throughout the world, God has given us special guidelines that make us His treasured possession. We live as His people only as we follow these New Testament theocratic regulations throughout the world.

Cultural flexibility. At the same time, however, the New Testament significantly expands cultural flexibility for Christians. Christ sent His disciples beyond the borders of Israel to all the nations of the earth (Matthew 28:18–19). In the early decades after Christ, the Kingdom moved away from the Jews to the Gentiles (Acts 13:46; 18:6). This international shift was not a simple matter; it raised difficult questions among the apostles. How should Gentile Christians relate to the regulations of Old Testament Israel? Do they have to observe the patterns of life prescribed for the national theocracy? New Testament writers answered with one voice: the international expansion of the Kingdom calls Christians to cultural flexibility.

Christ broke down the wall dividing Jews and Gentiles by "abolishing in his flesh the law with its commandments and regulations" (Ephesians 2:14–15). Now there is "neither Jew nor Greek, slave nor free, male nor female" (Galatians 3:28). Consequently many of the extensive regulations designed to separate Israel from the other nations no longer serve to separate the people of God from unbelievers today. Many of these norms were reduced to the status of natural cultural diversities. They became matters regulated by the general principles of Scripture instead of specific legislation.

For example, Genesis 17:1–27 taught Moses' readers that circumcision had to be observed as the sign of the covenant people. The New Testament, however, teaches that in Christ Jesus "neither circumcision nor uncircumcision has any value" (Galatians 5:6). It is not that circumcision is evil; Paul felt free to circumcise in some instances (Acts 16:3) and to refuse in others (Galatians 2:3–5). With the coming of Christ, the relative isolation of Israel as a national theocracy ended. So the rite of circumcision was reduced to a matter of cultural diversity.

Old Testament believers were to observe an annual cycle of holy days. To break with this arrangement in Old Testament times was to violate the will of God. Yet Paul instructed the Colossians not to allow anyone to "judge you . . . with regard to a religious festival . . ." (Colossians 2:16). These Old Testament directives were but "shadow[s] of the things that were to come" (Colossians 2:17). As he said to the Romans, "Each one should be fully convinced in his own mind" (Romans 14:5). The observance of holy days became a matter of cultural freedom for the Christian subculture.

In much the same way, Paul instructed the Corinthians to refrain from eating meat offered to idols. Nothing was wrong with the practice itself, but to avoid offending weaker brothers and sisters, he advised against it (1 Corinthians 8:7–13). The directive of the Jerusalem council (Acts 15:1–35) followed the same line of thought. The apostles recognized that Gentile converts were free from the theocratic policies designed to separate Jews from Gentiles before Christ. So they only required that the Gentiles restrain themselves out of regard for their Jewish brothers (Acts 15:24–29).

Broad cultural flexibility is not an option for Christians; Scripture requires it. The New Testament directs us to rise above the patterns of every world culture. Paul's description of his own life style illustrates this responsibility: "I have become all things to all men so that by all possible means I might save some" (1 Corinthians 9:22).

Christians have been sent into the world as witnesses for Christ. To reach this end, we must accommodate ourselves to the natural variations among cultures as much as possible. So long as we do not violate the principles of Scripture, we must exercise cultural flexibility in order to win others to Christ.

To sum up, the shift between the Old Testament and New Testament has significantly affected the ways God expects His people to apply His Word to culture. God ordained a level of cultural flexibility in the Old Testament, but He strictly regulated many areas of life to form Israel into a national theocracy. God now calls the church to maintain certain norms as a theocratic subculture, but He also requires far-reaching cultural flexibility so that the Kingdom may spread unhindered throughout the world (see figure 62).

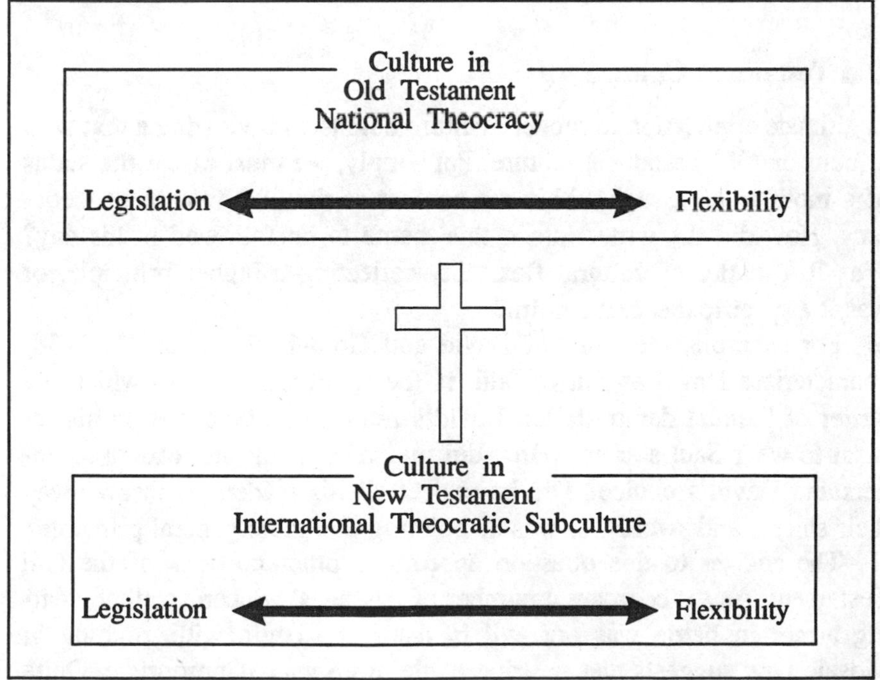

Fig. 62: Culture in the Old and New Testaments

Application to Modern Culture

Parents of young children give out lots of rules. "Don't touch the stove." "Stay out of the street." As children grow up, the limits of acceptable behavior change, but the lessons learned from early childhood remain with them. An eighteen-year-old may not have to keep away from the stove, but he had better remember that stoves are dangerous. A fifteen-year-old may not keep out of the street, but she should still be wary of cars.

In much the same way, God guided the practices of Israel as a father teaching young children.[31] In our age Christ has taken God's people beyond the immature stages of the Old Testament theocracy. Nevertheless, Old Testament regulations must not be forgotten. Just as childhood rules continue to inform adults of important principles, the cultural norms of the Old Testament theocracy have much to offer us in our day.

Applying Old Testament stories to the modern culture requires all the basic considerations we have outlined in this chapter. But we may organize these perspectives into three steps: focusing on *Old Testament culture, focusing on New Testament teaching,* and focusing on *our subculture.*

Old Testament Culture

Legitimate application to modern culture begins with viewing a text with a focus on Old Testament culture. Put simply, we must assess the status of a motif in a passage within the context of the Old Testament theocracy. How did the writer intend this theme to be followed in his day? Was it a matter of cultural flexibility reflecting a higher principle, or was it a specific theocratic norm?

For example, the story of David and Goliath (1 Samuel 17:1–58) characterizes David as full of faith in the Lord. One way in which the writer of Samuel demonstrated David's reliance on God was in his refusal to wear Saul's armor. How did the writer want his readers to understand David's choice? Did he expect all his readers to throw away their shields and swords, or was he pointing to a more general principle?

The answer to this question appears in other portions of the Old Testament. As we compare a number of passages, we can see that wearing armor in battle was not evil in itself. To begin with, nothing in Mosaic Law suggests that wearing battle attire was inappropriate. Quite to the contrary, the Israelites entered the conquest equipped for war.

Other kings used shields and swords. The writer of Samuel even reported that David used weapons other than a sling (1 Samuel 25:13).

These observations indicate rather plainly that the writer was not pointing to David's specific choice as a theocratic norm. Instead he focused on David's choice of a sling as an example of the principle of trusting God in battle. David exemplified reliance on God instead of human strength. On this level his choice was normative for all Israel, but his particular action was not a specific requirement for all time.

In a similar way, God commanded Joshua to march around Jericho for seven days (Joshua 6:2–5). Joshua's performance at Jericho was a direct command from God, but was it a categorical theocratic regulation? Did the writer expect the Israelites always to follow this specific prescription, or were they to look for a broader principle?

Other battle accounts indicate that this precise pattern of warfare was never prescribed again. So we may conclude that Joshua simply illustrated the principle of following divine direction in battle. This concept appears throughout the Old Testament as a requirement for Israel. When God revealed a battle plan, faithful Israelites were to obey. Only the principle was normative for the Old Testament theocracy.

Comparisons with other portions of Scripture reveal that many events reported in Old Testament stories were not normative practices for Israel. In these cases we should look beyond the particular instances to the concepts or principles that concerned the writers. Application to the church must rest on the particular events as illustrations of more general truths.

At other times comparisons with the rest of the Old Testament will reveal that a particular event depicts specific norms for Old Testament believers. For example, in his account of Shishak's invasion (2 Chronicles 12:1–12),[32] the Chronicler reported that the "leaders of Israel and the king humbled themselves and said, 'The Lord is just.'" This verse reflected a practice to be imitated by every Old Testament Israelite who heard words of judgment. Humility in prayer before God was a specific norm to be followed. In this passage we do not have to look for a broader theocratic principle. The particular action of Rehoboam and the leaders should be our concern.

Similarly, in Exodus 32:1–35 Moses reported how Israel suffered the wrath of God for worshipping the golden calf at Sinai.[33] When we compare this story with the Mosaic Law (Exodus 20:4–6; Deuteronomy 4:15–31), it is evident that Moses presented this event to condemn the introduction of idols into Israel's worship. Israel had violated specific legislation governing worship. This passage focused on the particular issue of idolatry in worship, a norm that all Israelites had to observe with care.

As we bridge the gap between Old Testament culture and our culture, we should begin with assessing a text in the light of Old Testament theocratic norms. If a passage deals with matters of flexibility, we must look beyond particulars to the more general principles involved. But when texts present more specific actions and ideas that were binding in the Old Testament theocracy, we should orient our attention more toward the particular actions in view.

New Testament Teaching

Once we have decided that a passage points to specific or general norms for Old Testament culture, we may move toward application to our culture by focusing on New Testament teaching. The New Testament elaborates on Old Testament themes in many ways, sometimes directly and other times indirectly. Whatever the case, New Testament teaching offers indispensable guidance for moving from Old Testament culture to our day.

Many general principles in Old Testament stories are affirmed and applied in the New Testament. For example, the principle we derived from David's refusal to wear Saul's armor (1 Samuel 17:38–39) resonates with Paul's instruction on our spiritual warfare. Paul expresses the need for putting on "the full armor of God" (Ephesians 6:11)—not human armor. Within the Christian theocracy we take up "truth . . . righteousness . . . the gospel of peace . . . faith . . . salvation . . . and the sword of the Spirit" (Ephesians 6:14–17). If ever the church discards these tools of warfare for human wisdom, political power, or physical coercion, we have violated Paul's instructions as well as David's exemplary fight against Goliath.

New Testament texts also help us adjust specific theocratic legislation for modern culture. For example, New Testament writers strictly forbade idolatry (2 Corinthians 6:16; 1 John 5:21; Revelation 2:20; 9:20) just as Moses prohibited it in the story of the golden calf (Exodus 32:1–35). Our worship of God is regulated by the holiness of the heavenly temple in which we now worship (Hebrew 9:11–27). No syncretism is permitted in our worship either. New Testament writers plainly affirm Moses' teaching.

New Testament texts mediate between Old Testament culture and our world, offering fundamental guidelines for the adjustments we must make. As we see how New Testament authors handled Old Testament texts for the church, we discover many insights into the kinds of applications we should pursue.

Our Subculture

Legitimate applications also require a focus on our subculture. God originally designed Old Testament stories to direct life in national Israel. He did not inspire them primarily for Egyptian, Hittite, or Babylonian societies. To be sure, Scripture had implications for these nations, but their principal focus was the culture of Israel. In much the same way, Old Testament stories speak especially to the continuing theocracy in Christ. These texts have implications for the world at large, calling the world to repentance and faith and revealing the standards of justice that should exist in all nations. But Christians are the principal heirs of Old Testament stories. We have been adopted into the family of Abraham and inherit the promises given to his descendants (Romans 4:1–25); therefore, Old Testament narratives belong to us and benefit us in ways the world will never enjoy.

For this reason application to modern life requires careful attention to the Christian subculture. We must concentrate on the ways these texts challenge the church in areas of legislation and flexibility. We have been called to a distinctively holy life style, but we have also been called to cultural flexibility. Old Testament themes apply to our lives on both levels. Confusing one for the other can lead to serious errors in application.

Just as Exodus 32:1–35 required Israelites to forsake all forms of idolatry, the Christian subculture must without exception resist idolatry. Similarly, we must humble ourselves before God in repentance as Rehoboam and the leaders did in their day (2 Chronicles 12:1–12). This is not a matter of cultural flexibility. Nevertheless, our applications to the Christian community must acknowledge legitimate differences among God's people. Although some aspects of our subculture leave little room for variations, many facets of Christian practice are open to wide diversity. For instance, we noted above that David's refusal of Saul's armor (1 Samuel 17:38–40) directs us to take the armor of God into our spiritual warfare. All Christians must comply with this directive, but we go beyond the limits of legitimate application if we do not acknowledge that different cultural settings require the church to fight this war in different ways. Believers in the Soviet Union may spread the faith differently than American Christians. Urban Christians respond to God's call differently than believers in rural environments. Whatever the circumstance we must always remember our call to cultural flexibility as we apply Old Testament stories to the Christian community (see figure 63).

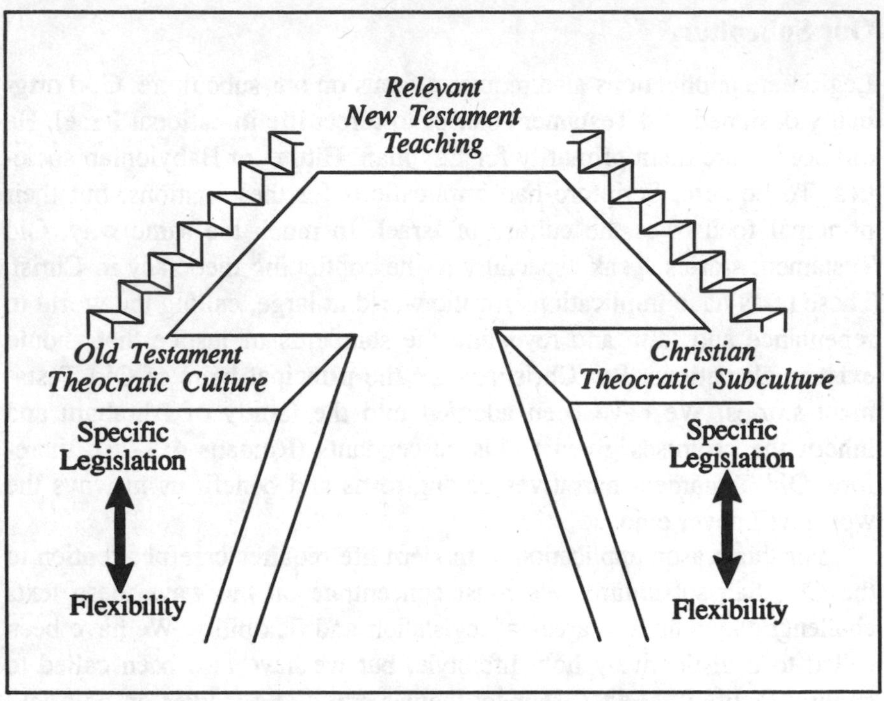

Fig. 63: Basic Steps for Cultural Adjustments

Conclusion

In this chapter we have examined several dimensions of applying Old Testament stories to modern culture. As we bridge the cultural gap between ourselves and Old Testament texts, we must keep a number of factors in mind. Many cultural variations result from natural diversities God has established in the world, but God's revelation is the standard for evaluating all patterns of life. Significant changes in the relation of faith and culture have taken place in Christ. The Christian community has its own cultural norms, but we have also been called to radical cultural flexibility as we live in different parts of the world. To bridge the cultural gap between us and the Old Testament, we must assess a passage in the light of Old Testament culture, New Testament teaching, and the structure of the modern Christian subculture. These principles will help us make legitimate applications of Old Testament stories from culture to culture.

Review Questions

1. How is culture influenced by religion and nature? Why must we keep these influences in mind as we assess Old Testament culture and modern culture?
2. Compare and contrast theocratic culture in the Old Testament and New Testament. How are areas of legislation and flexibility facets of cultural life in both eras?
3. What are three practical steps for bridging the culture gap between Old Testament stories and modern believers?

Study Exercises

1. Make a list of ten practices that God specifically legislated for the Old Testament theocracy. How do each of these regulations apply to the Christian subculture?
2. Make a list of ten areas of cultural flexibility in the Christian theocracy that result from the international character of Christ's Kingdom. What broad principles apply to these areas?
3. Examine the story of Abram's call (Genesis 12:1–9). What were two ways this passage spoke to culture in the Old Testament? What New Testament teaching helps us apply these motifs? How should Christians respond as participants in the theocratic subculture?

16

FROM PEOPLE TO PEOPLE

I hope I can see Chuck and his family," I said to my wife as I left for the plane. It had been five years since I had seen my friends, and I was leading a week-long conference in their city. "I'll call them on the phone when I get there." I called every day but never got an answer. At the end of the week, I left without seeing them. I had come close but not close enough.

In the two preceding chapters, we have explored ways to span the epochal and cultural distances that separate us from Old Testament stories. Adjusting to our age and culture permits us to bring Old Testament narratives closer to modern believers, but these large-scale concerns alone will not bring them close enough. We must also give attention to personal adjustments, addressing the needs of specific groups, and individuals.

The personal dimension of application involves a number of crucial issues. We will focus on three: *obstacles to personal application,* the *process of personal application,* and the *levels of personal application.* What hinders our attempts to apply Old Testament narratives to people's lives? What processes will help us reach our goal? What changes are we trying to bring about in the lives of modern believers?

Obstacles to Personal Application

When I visit churches, I often hear the same complaints. "Our pastor is too abstract." "He doesn't know what's going on in my life." "He's not practical." "He doesn't care about people, only ideas."

I'm never quite sure how to handle these criticisms, especially when they come against my students and friends. Sometimes the charges simply reflect the critic's lack of interest in learning. But I have to admit that frequently the appraisals are accurate; many church leaders are more interested in ideas than people.

Why do we find it difficult to address practical needs as we interpret Old Testament narratives? Three hindrances play a central role: *our inadequacies, abuses by others,* and the *nature of Old Testament narratives.*

Our Inadequacies

In many cases our own inadequacies form the greatest obstacle to personal application. Church leaders must overcome serious deficiencies in themselves before they can discern the practical dimensions of Old Testament narratives.

On the one hand, we neglect personal application because of our own spiritual condition.[1] We all face this difficulty from time to time. When our hearts are cold to Scripture, it is nearly impossible to see the value of Old Testament stories for practical living. If we are in rebellion against God, we avoid specific applications for fear of having to change ourselves. Teachers of the Word must look for ways to conform their own lives to Scripture. Otherwise their attempts to minister to others will always be hampered.

A few years ago I asked an experienced pastor what he found to be the most difficult part of sermon preparation. I expected him to say, "Understanding the Hebrew," or "Coming up with a simple outline." Instead he confessed, "The hardest part is applying the passage to my own life . . . I spend hours asking how I need to change. Once I do that, I can see what my church needs to hear." That pastor recognized one of the greatest obstacles to effective application, his own spiritual condition.

Every interpreter must learn this lesson. To meet the needs of others, we begin with ourselves. Every time we read an Old Testament story, we must ask, "How does this text challenge *me?*" "How must I apply it to *my life?*" Then we can turn to others.

On the other hand, teachers may want to make practical applications, but they may not know how. With few exceptions formal theological education gives little attention to these matters. Students learn about basic exegetical skills and ecclesiastical doctrines. These topics are essential for sound interpretation, but too little time is spent on the ways Old Testament texts address the particular issues confronting people today.[2]

Neglecting personal application causes many church leaders to approach Old Testament stories with that agenda are largely irrelevant to ordinary believers. We are preoccupied with textual variants and enamored with the literary structures; we have interest in historical backgrounds; we want to know how passages have been handled throughout church history. These are important issues, but they often distract us from dealing with the needs of believers in the pew.

What do modern Christians need? Although the list varies from person to person, most believers long for similar things. They need to be corrected in their errors and assured of forgiveness. They look for guidance in making difficult choices. They yearn to be encouraged in their trials. They want their relationships strengthened. They look for healing of the past and courage for the future.

If we are to convey the relevance of Old Testament narratives to modern people, we have to place issues such as these at the forefront of our minds. Instead of focusing so much on matters emphasized by formal education, we should concentrate more on meeting the needs of the people we teach. We must ask ourselves, "Am I pursuing my own agenda too much?" "How does this passage address the practical needs of others?"

Abuses by Others

Pastors and teachers also tend toward irrelevance because of abuses by others. Many Christians are so concerned with personalizing Old Testament stories that they fail to give careful attention to the text in its original setting. In reaction many leaders turn completely away from all personal considerations.

We have all encountered well-meaning believers who treat Old Testament stories as their own personal communiques from heaven. They select a passage and intuitively sense God speaking to them in ways that often have little to do with the original meaning.

I once heard about a young man who approached a professor with great excitement. He had been wrestling with the possibility of attending seminary for several months. "God told me what to do yesterday," he said with joy. "I read 1 Samuel 14:12, 'Come up to us and we'll teach you a lesson' . . . God told me through this passage to go to seminary to learn my lessons from you."

The teacher was glad that the fellow was coming to school, but the passage he cited had little to do with learning lessons in seminary. In the context of the verse, the Philistines were mocking Jonathan as he approached them in battle (1 Samuel 13:23—14:14). They planned to teach him a lesson by killing him.

"I didn't know what to think," the professor said to me with a smile. "He was either calling me a Philistine or a murderer!"

In reaction to such abuses, we rightly emphasize the basic rules of interpretation we have been discussing throughout this book. The original meaning is the guide to all legitimate applications.[3] Because so many believers mishandle Scripture in this way, it is wise to indicate how our applications are rooted in the original meaning.[4] This practice will help others see the importance of careful exegesis.

Yet underscoring the original meaning can easily lead to neglect of personal application, if for no other reason than simply not having the time to consider both sides extensively. We have so many minutes in a day and hours in a week to study. If we spend too much time expounding the original meaning, we may never deal with application. At the same time, we must also resist the temptation to deal exclusively with application. Neither extreme is acceptable. We should always ask ourselves, "How have I balanced my presentation between the original meaning and modern application?" "Have I stressed one to the neglect of the other?"

Nature of Old Testament Narratives

We face another serious obstacle to personal application: the nature of Old Testament narratives themselves. As far as we can tell, most Old Testament books were not written for a specific person but for Israel as a nation. They deal with general matters such as the mighty acts of God, politics, worship, and warfare.

For instance, the patriarchal stories in the book of Genesis call the nation of Israel to forsake Egypt and to move forward toward the conquest of Canaan.[5] In Moses' view the patriarchs were more than mere individuals; they represented the nation as a whole. The blessings of God for Abraham, Isaac, and Jacob took place on behalf of all Israelites. The experiences of the sons of Jacob had implications for all of their tribal descendants.

In much the same way, Chronicles directed the entire post-exilic community in the restoration program.[6] The extensive genealogies (1 Chronicles 1:1—9:44) covered the backgrounds of all the tribes.[7] The Chronicler's emphasis on "all Israel" indicated his interest in all the people of God, not in a small segment.[8]

The broad focus of Old Testament narratives makes it easy to remain on the level of generalities when we apply these texts. Pastors encourage their congregations to love God, obey the Lord, have faith, and be kind to their neighbors. These applications are important, but they often leave people with little idea of specific things to do in response to God's Word.

Nevertheless, we must remember that Old Testament stories were also designed for application to groups and individuals in Israel. In the Old Testament period, priests, Levites, and prophets taught the Law and brought out the implications of texts for the people (Leviticus 10:11; 2 Kings 22:11–20; 2 Chronicles 15:3; 17:7–9; Ezra 7:27; Nehemiah 8:7–8, 11; Malachi 2:7–9). Heads of households were commanded to "impress them on your children. Talk about them when you sit at home and when you walk along the road, when you lie down and when you get up" (Deuteronomy 6:7–8). Kings were to have personal copies of the Law (Deuteronomy 17:18–20). Josiah heard the Law of Deuteronomy and saw his personal responsibility (2 Kings 22:1—23:25). Nehemiah recalled the words of Scripture and realized the implications for his life (Nehemiah 1:5–11). In much the same way, teachers of Scripture today have the responsibility to apply Old Testament stories to the specific needs of people. We must work hard to show the implications of these books on the lives of groups and individuals. We should pause occasionally and ask, "Am I too general in my applications?" "Am I addressing the specific needs of my audience?"

Interpreters who desire to be relevant in their ministries face many difficulties. Our own inadequacies, abuses by others, and the nature of Old Testament stories themselves pose formidable obstacles. If we hope to reach the goal of personal application, we must recognize these difficulties and be determined to overcome them (see figure 64).

Process of Personal Application

What practical steps can we take to overcome the obstacles against personal application? The process of personal application may follow many paths, but in one way or another, we should deal with at least three matters: the *original audience, inferring principles,* and the *modern audience.*

Original Audience

The first step toward personal application is to acknowledge variations in the original audience. All too often we think of Old Testament au-

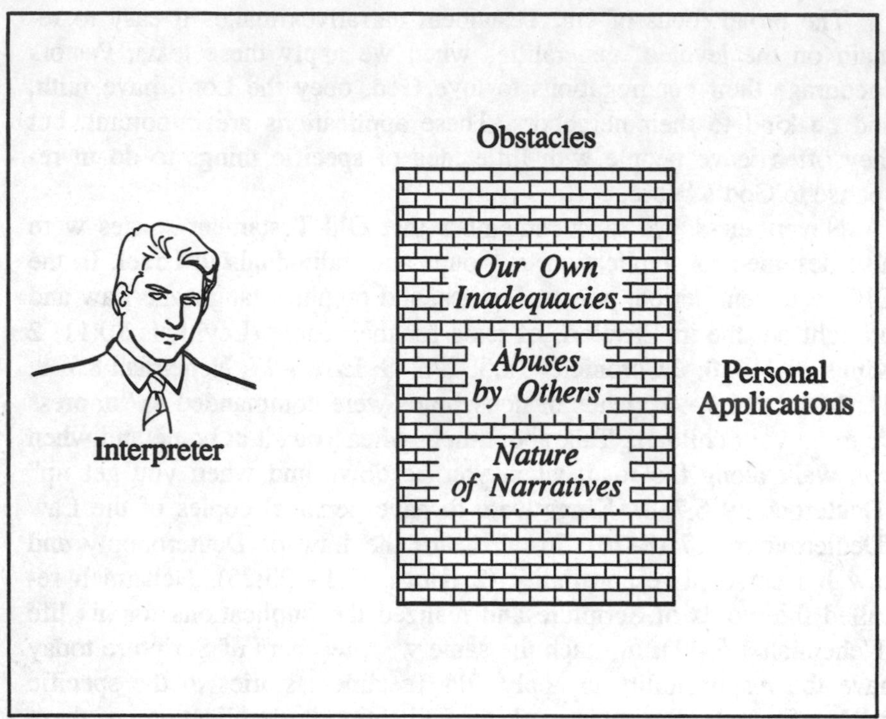

Fig. 64: Obstacles to Personal Application

thors writing eternal truths to faceless audiences. Throughout this book we have tried to dispel this oversimplification. Old Testament writers composed their accounts with pastoral intentions, directing their writings to all sorts of people. Their audiences included men and women, young and old, rich and poor, the faithful and the unfaithful. Old Testament stories were designed to address these and other segments of Israelite society.

Even so, it soon becomes apparent that certain Old Testament stories focused on some elements of the nation more directly than others. Sometimes the texts were very general; at other times, specific. To explore these matters, we will look at three levels of focus: *general, multiple group,* and *specific.*

General focus. On one end of the scale, many texts present a general focus on the nation. No one group is highlighted; the whole nation is in view. Consider the story of Abraham's test (Genesis 22:1–19) in which God called Abraham to sacrifice his son. This passage had many implications for the original audience, but one prominent theme appeared in the words of the angel of the Lord. Abraham's obedience established the certainty of Israel's victory in Canaan.

This motif of confidence and assurance applied to the whole community of Israel. The text gives no indication of a specific focus on leaders, priests, prophets, or any other particular group. Moses wanted the whole exodus audience to draw confidence about the future from God's promise to Abraham.

Despite its general focus, the original implications of this story were quite varied. Each tribe was to take its assigned place in the arrangement of the holy army (Numbers 2:1–34; 10:11–36); priests were to show their confidence by bearing the ark before the tribes (Numbers 10:33–36); commanders were to fulfill their duties in organizing and training; men of fighting age were expected to prepare themselves for specific roles in battle; women and children were to pray and to encourage the soldiers. Although the story itself was very general, its implications for the different kinds of people in the original audience were diverse.

Multiple group focus. Toward the middle of the scale, some Old Testament stories had a multiple group focus. They pointedly dealt with several portions of Israelite society. For example, 1 Chronicles 29:1–9 gives an account of the temple contributions collected in the latter days of David's life. This passage offered the post-exilic community a model of dedication to the service of the temple.[9] But the Chronicler did not leave matters in general terms; he recorded the event in a way that touched on particular groups of people within the Israelite community.

The passage begins with David's words about his own gifts (1 Chronicles 29:1–5a): "With all my resources I have provided for the temple of my God . . . in my devotion to the temple of my God I now give my personal treasures" (1 Chronicles 29:2–3). Then David turns to the assembly with a challenge: "Now, who is willing to consecrate himself today to the Lord?" In response, "the leaders of the families, the officers of the tribes of Israel, the commanders of thousands and commanders of hundreds, and the officials in charge of the king's work gave willingly." At the conclusion of the passage, the Chronicler added that "the people rejoiced at the willing response of their leaders, for they had given freely and wholeheartedly to the Lord."

Each portion of this passage addressed different groups of people in the Chronicler's audience. If we assume an early date for the book, David's own example demonstrated the need for Zerubabbel and other members of the Davidic line to support the temple reconstruction.[10] The actions of the officials pointed to the role of leaders in the post-exilic community; the joyful reactions of the people turned attention to the responsibilities of commoners among the returnees. By focusing his account on specific kinds of people in the days of David, the Chronicler addressed the needs of the various segments of his audience.

Specific focus. At the other end of the scale, some Old Testament narratives specifically focus on one group or class of people. For instance, the death of Nadab and Abihu (Leviticus 10:1–20) appears after a section of Leviticus that focuses primarily on the duties of priests in the ceremonies of the tabernacle (Leviticus 6:8—9:24). When Nadab and Abihu present "unauthorized fire" before the Lord, He destroys them. The priestly focus of the passage continues as Moses warns Aaron and his sons not to mourn and to remain separate from the people. The Lord then tells Aaron that he and his sons are to avoid strong drink, because they must "distinguish between the holy and the common, between the clean and unclean, and [they] must teach the Israelites all the decrees the Lord has given them through Moses." These aspects of the story indicate that Moses intended this passage to speak primarily to the priests of Israel.

But this story also had implications for people who were not priests. The book of Leviticus also addressed many matters that concerned ordinary people (1:1—6:7; 18:1—20:27; 26:1—27:34).[11] Consequently, we may assume that Moses did not intend the story of Nadab and Abihu solely for priestly instruction. The men, women, and children of Israel were also to learn about the holiness of tabernacle services. This passage spoke to their concept of worship, their actions in service to God, and their attitude toward all holy matters.

Making personal applications of Old Testament stories to modern readers begins with recognizing the variations within the original audience. To understand the many original implications of these texts, it helps to ask a few basic questions. "What were the implications of this passage for the whole nation of Israel?" "What specific responses were appropriate from different groups and individuals within the nation?" As we recognize these original diversities, we begin to see some of the many ways in which we may form personal applications for our day.

Inferring Principles

The second basic step for reaching personal applications is inferring principles from the original meaning that readily apply to contemporary life. If we have made careful summaries of the original meaning, our assessments will be closely tied to the epochal and cultural circumstances of the writer's day. We will have a rather specific understanding of how the text was intended to be used at that time. But the more tightly we connect a passage to its original setting, the more difficult it is to apply it to modern life. Our interpretation will be bound to the specifics of the original situation.

To move toward the modern world, we must restate the original implications in ways that fit with our age and culture. This aspect of application is similar to what Kaiser calls "principalization."[12] He mentions, "To 'principalize' is to state the author's propositions, arguments, narrations, and illustrations in timeless abiding truths with special focus on the application of those truths to the current needs of the Church."[13]

To accomplish this end, we must look at original implications in the light of epochal and cultural changes that have taken place between the original setting and our day.[14] We may ask, "How has the coming of Christ developed this motif?" "What cultural developments help us adjust the meaning for our day?"

By way of illustration, let us review three passages we have already considered in this chapter. First, we have seen that Abraham's test (Genesis 22:1–19) focused on the particular needs of the exodus audience. Moses encouraged the nation to be confident of victory in their conquest of Canaan because of God's response to Abraham's obedience.

To apply this aspect of the original meaning to our day, we must restate Moses' intentions. We do not face Canaanite cities; we have no physical holy war to pursue. In the light of the New Testament, we must say that the church should gain confidence of victory *in her spiritual warfare* because Christ has secured God's promise to Abraham. Christ gained the initial victory in His death and resurrection (Colossians 2:13–15); He is winning the battle today through the church (Ephesians 6:10–18); and He will complete the battle when He returns (Revelation 19:11–21). When we take these epochal considerations into account, we move from the original meaning toward our day.

Beyond this we should also assess cultural developments. The spiritual warfare of the church varies in different cultures. In some the church is socially and physically oppressed. Other religions boldly attack the beliefs of the Christian church. We wrestle with the subtleties of syncretism within the church. Our spiritual warfare takes on many different forms. For this reason we must reformulate Moses' message in Genesis 22:1–19 in a way that acknowledges the need for *confidence in whatever spiritual battle our culture presents.*

Second, we saw that 1 Chronicles 29:1–9 was designed to call the different segments of the post-exilic community to support the temple.

The Chronicler taught his readers to give of themselves and their resources to the temple services so that the blessings of God would come to the restored community. But this summary of the text does not easily transfer to modern audiences. The Chronicler's concern reflected the specific issues faced by the post-exilic community. We do not live in Jerusalem; we have no temple project before us.

To move toward modern application, Christian interpreters must restate the Chronicler's aim in ways that replace Old Testament distinctives with the characteristics of our epoch. In this case we may simply say that the passage teaches the people of God to be devoted to worship *in Christ* to receive God's blessings. We give all that we are to Him because He "made his dwelling among us" (John 1:14) and offered Himself as our sacrifice (Romans 3:25–26; Hebrews 9:14). He mediates in the heavenly temple for us (Hebrews 9:11–15) and will bring us into the presence of God in His second coming (Revelation 21:3–4). This reformulation opens the way for bringing this passage to bear on people's lives today.

We also pave the way to personal applications by exploring the cultural features of our day. How are Christians in various cultures called upon to devote themselves to worship? What aspects of worship are matters of cultural flexibility and theocratic requirement?[15] In a word the Chronicler's text teaches us to be devoted to worship in Christ *as our cultural circumstances require*. Some situations require monetary contributions; others may demand our jobs, property, even our lives. In situations of widespread apostasy, devotion to true worship means separation from established churches. In other circumstances, we respond in obedience by supporting existing structures. We must ask how cultural variations affect our application of the Chronicler's message.

Third, the story of Nadab and Abihu (Leviticus 10:1–20) may be handled in a similar fashion. Originally, the passage warned priests and the people against violating the holy tabernacle services. Once again, to apply this text to our day, we must see Christ as the fulfillment of the tabernacle. His death and resurrection, His constant intercession in heaven, and the future blessing of God's presence dramatically shift the emphasis of this text for us. Today the story warns us not to violate the *holiness of our Savior*. We must always approach the Father in devotion to all His prescriptions.

The cultural variations in our age also call us to regard Christ as holy *in every cultural setting*. We must resist the world's attempts to turn us away from the pure devotion of honoring and worshipping Him.

Modern Audience

If we remain on the level of large-scale epochal and cultural adjustments, our applications will still tend to be general and impersonal. Individual and group needs are only indirectly addressed by these considerations. For this reason the third basic step toward personal application is to give detailed attention to variations within the modern audience. The contemporary community exhibits many kinds of variations. Just as Old Testament writers addressed diverse needs, modern interpreters must acknowledge varieties among modern believers. "Ultimately the expository preacher does not address all mankind; he speaks to a particular people and calls them by name."[16]

To address the diversity of modern audiences, we must be careful not to focus on one segment of the believing community. For instance, I don't know how often I have heard sermons directed exclusively to the needs of adult males. On occasion women come into the picture, but seldom do pastors reflect on the implications of passages for adolescents, young children, the sick, or the physically and mentally handicapped. To bring Old Testament stories to bear on the lives of believers, we must consider not just one facet of the community of faith. From time to time, different kinds of people must be addressed.

What kinds of people are in the church? Most congregations represent various spiritual, emotional and physical conditions, ages, sexes, roles in the church, occupations, and economic status. These are but a few of the diversities in the church, but they often require significantly different applications.

What does the account of Abraham's test say to different kinds of modern believers? In general, it gives assurance of our ultimate victory in Christ. But how does this theme apply to those who do not believe? It warns them of the judgment of God and encourages them to turn to Christ for victory over evil and death. How does it speak to believers who are discouraged and troubled? It offers them hope despite their present circumstances. How does this passage speak to the rich? Do not trust in your wealth to secure your future. What message does it offer to the poor? Our eternal riches in Christ far outweigh any suffering we experience today. How does it address believers who are in good physical condition? Use all your energy in the spiritual battles ahead. What does it say to those who are ill and dying? Victory over death is certain because of God's promise to Abraham and the work of Christ.

The Chronicler's account of Israel's devotion to the temple (1 Chronicles 29:1–9) also addresses different needs. The passage rebukes those who have neglected contributing to the worship of God, encouraging church leaders to lead by their own example as David did, and instructing lay people to follow the examples of their leaders. It calls for the rich to give generously to the work of the kingdom and even requires children to worship attentively.

Moses' story of Nadab and Abihu (Leviticus 10:1–20) admonishes those who treat the holiness of God lightly. The passage brings joy to believers who find acceptance in the presence of God. It applies rather directly to leaders, commanding them to examine their hearts as they lead God's people in worship. The old are warned against maintaining traditional practices that displease God. The young see the caution they should exercise as they introduce new practices into worship. As we permit this story to shed its light on different people, we see its vast potential for practical application.

To uncover the personal applications of Old Testament stories for modern believers, we must first examine the diversities within the original audience. We then infer principles in light of epochal and cultural changes. Finally we adjust the implications of these texts to the diverse needs of the modern audience (see figure 65).

Levels of Personal Application

In an earlier chapter, we saw that sanctification and interpretation are interdependent.[17] On the one hand, our struggles with sin and the flesh dramatically affect our investigation of Old Testament stories. Personal growth in the faith is the ground upon which successful interpretation rests. On the other hand, sanctification is our goal in reading these texts. Unless we apply Scripture to our lives, our spiritual condition rapidly deteriorates.

Often I ask people, "What is the most important benefit you receive from Scripture?" Of course, I get many different responses, but I have noticed over the years that they tend to fall into one of three basic categories. Some people say "I learn how to *think.*" Others respond, "It changes the way I *act.*" Still others answer, "Scriptures make me *feel* God in my life." These answers point out the depths to which personal application should reach. Old Testament narratives sanctify us in our thinking, actions, and emotions.

Christ taught that the greatest commandment is to "love the Lord your God with all your heart and with all your soul and with all your mind" (Matthew 22:37; see Deuteronomy 6:5). In a word, He called us

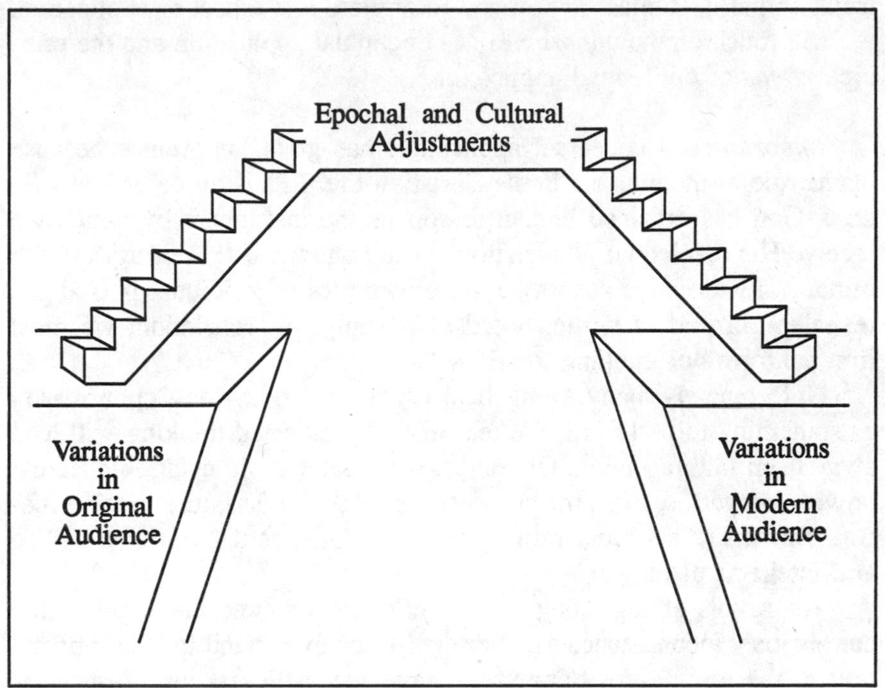

Fig. 65: Basic Steps for Personal Adjustments

to submit our whole being in loyal service to God. Consequently, the *summum bonum* (highest good) of interpretation is to apply Scripture to our whole existence. As Van Til summarized the matter, "The consistency that is found in the believer is correspondent to the consistency that is found in God. This consistency in the believer consists in willingness to think God's thoughts after him, in willingness to do God's will after him, and to feel God's feelings after him."[18]

We will speak of three levels of personal application: *conceptual, behavioral,* and *emotional.* How should Old Testament stories change the way we think? How must we modify our behavior? How are these passages to influence our emotions? These aspects of application are fully interdependent. The sanctification of our thinking, behavior, and emotions depend on each other in countless ways. Yet, for the sake of discussion, we will look at each facet of our lives separately.

Conceptual Application

Conceptual application is the process of conforming our understanding of life to Old Testament stories. We reject falsehoods and receive the truths found in Biblical revelation. To explore this aspect of application, we will touch on the *importance* of conceptual application and the principal *areas* of conceptual application.

Importance. Conceptual application has great importance because of the role of the intellect in the Christian life. In His unsearchable wisdom, God has ordained human reason as the instrument by which we receive His revelation: "Revelation is the communication of truth to the mind. . . . Revelation cannot be made to brutes or to idiots."[19] God has revealed Himself in written words. To apply this revelation, we must first conform our thinking to His will.

Unfortunately many evangelical Christians today look upon reason as something to be feared. We fear that sophisticated thinking will lead away from faithful living. Of course, we cannot avoid using intellectual powers altogether. Even the simplest responses to Scripture involve reason. But many believers turn away from "intellectual Christianity" to anti-intellectualism.

The results of neglecting serious reflection on conceptual application are obvious. Inconsistencies and errors in our lives stand in clear opposition to the teaching of Scripture. I have met believers who justify involvement in blatant sin by saying that they did not "feel the Holy Spirit convicting them." Others defend their views because they "get the job done." Feelings and pragmatics are important considerations, but in the final analysis we must shape our outlooks on life through conceptual application of Scripture.

It is easy to confuse understanding Scripture with genuine conceptual application. We often think that once we know what the Scriptures teach, we have completed the hard thinking that needs to be done. But this is not so. We have not applied Old Testament narratives until we *accept* their teaching and adjust our concepts of reality accordingly. We know that Old Testament stories teach us to observe the Sabbath, but many believers think it is a heavy burden. We understand the Old Testament view of God's justice but doubt that He is just in all His ways today. Understanding a text is not sufficient; we have made conceptual application only when we change our thinking to conform to the teaching of Scripture.

Areas. Conceptual application focuses on three principal areas. As we have seen, Old Testament stories offer informative, directive, and affective implications for modern life.[20] Applying Old Testament narratives to our thinking involves each kind of application.

First, we must believe the information that these texts give us about modern life. All believers have misconceptions about God, the world, and humanity. We think that God is one way, when, in fact, He is just the opposite. We believe we have understood ourselves when we have actually misunderstood. For instance, many Christians find it difficult to believe that God would command someone to sacrifice his child. But the story of Abraham's test tells us this was precisely what He did. As hard as it may be, we must give up our outlooks and accept this information about God. Old Testament stories present proper perspectives on all facts. It is our responsibility to receive this information and to change the way we think.

Second, conceptual application includes adopting the directive implications of texts. Old Testament stories have much to say about our moral responsibilities. We may think that a course of action is proper but discover that Scriptures teach otherwise. We may also find our standards confirmed by the teaching of a text. Joseph's attitude toward his brothers in the last chapter of Genesis directs us to be humble and forgiving toward others. We often face circumstances that pressure us to ignore this obligation. Yet, we have applied these directives only when we acknowledge that this mandate is appropriate.

Third, conceptual application consists of accepting the affective implications of Old Testament stories. We may think that an attitude is appropriate and discover that a text tells us differently. At other times we may find our assessments confirmed. The Chronicler's record of contributions to the temple (1 Chronicles 29:1–9) teaches us to support worship cheerfully. We may not think that giving our money is a joyous event, but the Chronicler's story teaches otherwise. We must go beyond merely understanding what this text says about human feelings and agree with its teaching.

Conceptual application of Old Testament stories consists of giving mental assent. Through careful study we discover the informative, directive, and affective teachings of these texts for contemporary life. In response we affirm these texts are true. Several questions guide us through the process of conceptual application. How should we adjust our thinking to conform to the informative implications of this text? How do the moral directives of the passage challenge our views? How do we need to concur with the affective implications of the passage?

Behavioral Application

Applying Old Testament narratives to modern life entails more than cerebral concurrence; this is just the beginning. God also requires that our *actions* conform to His revelation. We will touch on the *importance* of behavior and *areas* of behavioral application.

Importance. The importance of emphasizing behavioral application becomes clear when we realize how easily we fail to live what we believe. All believers know more than they actually do. To some degree these failures are unavoidable; we always face behavioral shortcomings. Nevertheless, as we apply Old Testament stories to modern life, we must not be satisfied simply to affirm their truths. We must also translate those affirmations into actions. As James put it, "Do not merely listen to the word, and so deceive yourselves. Do what it says" (James 1:22).

Many evangelicals fail to see the importance of living a holy life because of a fundamental theological misunderstanding. Fully convinced that salvation is "by grace . . . through faith" (Ephesians 2:8), they take the mercy of God as license for sin. The Scriptures clearly teach that our works do not merit salvation; the work of Christ is our only hope for eternal life. Nevertheless, Scriptures are just as plain that those redeemed by Christ will bear the fruit of righteous living: "We are God's workmanship, created in Christ Jesus to do good works, which God prepared in advance for us to do" (Ephesians 2:10). Trusting Christ for salvation places us on the path of good works. Saving faith will not produce perfection, but it orients our behavior toward deeds of righteousness.

Areas. Behavioral applications also focus on three principal areas. We conform our behavior to the informative, directive, and affective implications of Old Testament stories.

First, the information that Old Testament texts give us teaches us how to behave. Consider Genesis 1:1—2:3. This text teaches that God is the Creator. Whenever we live in ways that obscure or deny this truth, we have failed to apply this information to our behavior. The passage also tells us that God viewed His original created order as good. We must always behave in ways that affirm this reality. The text reveals that human beings are the image of God. When we treat others or ourselves as something less, we have violated this information. Our behavior must conform to the information we receive from Old Testament narratives.

Second, the directive implications of Old Testament stories must also be translated into appropriate actions. The story of Shishak's invasion (2 Chronicles 12:1–12) teaches that sinners should humble themselves and seek God's mercy.[21] To apply this story behaviorally entails praying and seeking forgiveness. Similarly, the Tower of Babel (Genesis 11:1–9) directs us not to exalt our own name in defiance of God.[22] Modern Christians must behave in ways that bring glory only to the name of God.

Third, the affective implications of Old Testament passages often require particular behaviors. The death of Nadab and Abihu (Leviticus 10:1–20) teaches the importance of fear and high regard for the holiness of God in worship.[23] Applying this passage on a behavioral level requires that we perform our worship in ways that reflect a wholesome reverence for God. As we bring Old Testament stories to bear on modern life, we should focus on the behavioral changes required by their informative, directive, and affective implications. To accomplish this end, we may ask several pertinent questions. What actions does the information of this passage demand of us? How should our life styles change in light of the text's directives? How must our behavior exhibit the affective implications of this text?

Emotional Application

Old Testament stories were also designed to be applied on an emotional level. They were meant to affect our attitudes, motivations, and dispositions.

Importance. The importance of emotional application rests in our need for guidance on the level of our feelings. God made us emotional creatures, and He renews this aspect of our lives in Christ. But when our feelings go awry, Old Testament stories offer us indispensable guidance.

Unfortunately many Christians think emotions are untouchable. We permit our feelings to go in whatever direction they like. Yet in Christ we are not simply called to accept the truths of Scripture and to behave according to them; we are called to love God and His ways and to hate sin.[24] As Christians we must bring our emotions under the control of the Holy Spirit just as we bring our thinking and behavior.

Neglecting emotional applications creates serious problems for believers. We cannot go for long without the encouraging words and stern warnings found in Scripture. We live in a world full of disappointments and difficulties. At one time or another, every believer feels a void within—no more zeal, no more love, no more courage. In these situations the positive emotional dimensions of Old Testament stories speak directly to us, warming our hearts and spurring us toward renewed zeal for Christ. At other times our hearts become hardened toward God. When we become entangled in sin, we find ourselves unconcerned with matters of faith. Our affections turn from God toward the world. When this occurs redirection comes as we apply Old Testament texts on an emotional level.

Areas. The areas of emotional application include all the major implications of Old Testament stories. When we read these texts sensitively, we find that their informative, directive, and affective implications have a bearing on our feelings.

First, the information we derive from Old Testament texts has the potential for an emotional effect. For example, we learn from the book of Judges that Christ has fulfilled our need for a godly king to rule over us.[25] This implication is not a sterile fact; it reminds us that Christ is our only hope. What brings greater joy and confidence than the realization that He has provided our deliverance and security? Genesis 2:4—3:24 teaches us that difficulties in life come from our rebellion against God.[26] We can hardly be reminded of this fact without a sense of humility and gratitude for God's redeeming grace. These informative implications should touch us emotionally.

Second, the directive implications of these texts spawn emotional reactions as well. We learn from Asa's reign (2 Chronicles 14:2—16:14) that God's people should heed the word of His prophets.[27] How does this make us feel? Perhaps we are encouraged that God has not left us without direction. Or we may be mortified at our own refusal to obey His Word. We understand the requirement of sexual purity from the story of Judah and Tamar (Genesis 38:1–30).[28] What emotional response should we have? Those who are chaste rejoice; those who are immoral ought to tremble with fear.

Third, the affective implications of Old Testament stories must also be applied emotionally. Application of the affective dimensions of these texts goes beyond understanding to actual feeling. Abraham's test gives us reason for confidence in the future. We have applied this truth emotionally, however, only when we genuinely feel confident about the future. David's joy at bringing the ark into Jerusalem (2 Samuel 6:12–19) reveals the joy for all God's people as they encounter His presence. We must not only be convinced that this is true but also experience the joy.

Application on conceptual, behavioral, and emotional levels calls for great care on the part of interpreters. We must learn how to adjust our emphases according to the needs of those whom we are teaching. Believers have different strengths and weaknesses at various points in their lives. If a group or individual requires attention to one type of application more than the others, then we should highlight that dimension of the text. As interpreters of the Word, we must be sensitive to these variations. When intellectual corrections are necessary, we ought to emphasize conceptual application. If people are weak in their behavior, we must address this area more. Believers who have emotional needs should be served with application on that level.

Overlooking the specific needs of believers can cause serious problems in the Christian life. Overemphasis on conceptual application leads to intellectualism; our faith is reduced to mere ideas. Too much stress on behavioral application results in legalism; religious life amounts only to doing what is right. Exaggerating emotional application to the neglect of other levels leads to emotionalism; believers become entirely focused on their feelings.

Each level of application is essential for sanctification in Christ. We should neither overemphasize nor neglect any dimension. We must address thoughts, actions, and attitudes as the need arises. As we prepare

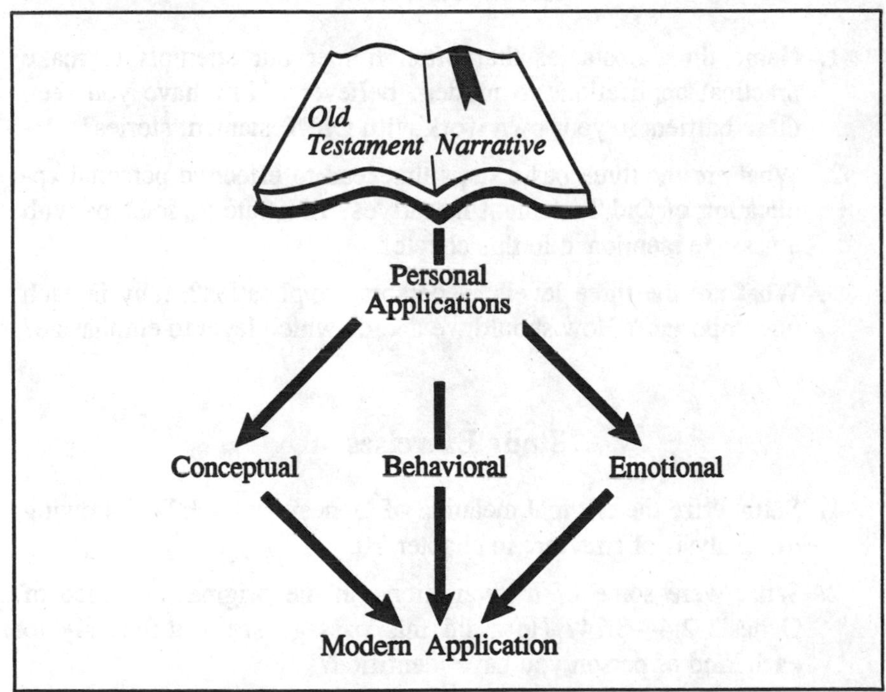

Fig. 66: Levels of Personal Application

to teach an Old Testament story, we may avoid extremes by asking three simple questions. What modern conceptual issues does this text address for my audience? How is modern behavior challenged by this text? What emotional needs in my audience does this text meet (see figure 66)?

Conclusion

In this chapter we have looked at personal applications of Old Testament narratives. We have seen that many obstacles stand in the way of this aspect of interpretation. But we can overcome these hindrances by noting the varieties of applications in the original setting, making epochal and cultural adjustments, and addressing the varieties of need in the modern setting. In the end we must bring to light the concepts, behavior, and emotions that Old Testament stories address. As we keep these basic considerations in mind, we will be able to apply Old Testament stories in ways that further the sanctification of God's people and bring glory to God.

Review Questions

1. Name three obstacles that often hinder our attempts to make practical applications to modern believers. How have you seen these barriers in your own work with Old Testament stories?
2. What are the three basic steps that lead to effective personal application of Old Testament narratives? Illustrate these steps with a passage mentioned in this chapter.
3. What are the three levels of personal application? Why is each one important? How should we decide which level to emphasize?

Study Exercises

1. Summarize the original meaning of Genesis 2:4—3:24, following the analysis of structure in chapter 10.
2. What were some of the variations in the original audience of Genesis 2:4—3:24? How did this passage speak differently to each kind of person you have identified?
3. What epochal and cultural adjustments should be made when applying Genesis 2:4—3:24 to modern audiences?
4. What variations in modern audiences require different kinds of applications of Genesis 2:4—3:24. What conceptual, behavioral, and emotional applications can be highlighted according to the needs of modern audiences?

ENDNOTES

Introduction

1. In his influential work at the end of the last century, Terry summarized traditional divisions in the field of hermeneutics saying, "General hermeneutics is devoted to the general principles which are applicable to the interpretation of all languages and writing. . . . Special hermeneutics is devoted . . . to the explanation of particular books and classes of writings. . . . Sacred hermeneutics is the science of interpreting the Holy Scripture of the Old and New Testaments." M. S. Terry, *Biblical Hermeneutics* (New York: Eaton and Mains, 1890), 17–8. These distinctions have largely fallen into disuse. For more recent discussions of the meaning of hermeneutics see *New International Dictionary of New Testament Theology* 1.579–84; R. Palmer, *Hermeneutics* (Evanston: Northwestern, 1969), 14–45; R. Soulen, *Handbook of Biblical Criticism* (2d ed.; Atlanta: John Knox, 1981), 82–6.

2. Unless noted otherwise, all Biblical quotations are taken from the Holy Bible, New International Version, 1973, 1978 by the International Bible Society, used by permission of Zondervan Bible Publishers.

3. For a helpful summary of the classical Protestant doctrine of inspiration see B. B. Warfield, *The Inspiration and Authority of the Bible* (ed. S. G. Cross; Phillipsburg: Presbyterian and Reformed, 1970), 153–4, 422. Also see C. G. Berkouwer, *Holy Scripture* (Grand Rapids: Eerdmans, 1975), 139–94.

4. For a summary of the Spirit's role in relation to Scripture itself see J. M. Frame, "The Spirit and the Scriptures," *Hermeneutics, Authority, and Canon* (eds. D. A. Carson and J. D. Woodbridge; Grand Rapids: Zondervan, 1986), 217–35.

5. See Berkouwer, *Holy Scripture,* 267–98; M. Silva, *Has the Church Misread the Bible?* (*Foundations of Contemparary Interpretation* 1; Grand Rapids: Zondervan, 1987), 80–9.

6. "Those things which are necessary to be known, believed, and observed, for salvation, are so clearly propounded and opened in some place of Scripture or other, that not only the learned but the unlearned, in a due use of ordinary means, may attain unto a sufficient understanding of them." *Westminster Confession of Faith* 1.7.

7. See previous note, *Westminster Confession of Faith* 1.7.

8. *Westminster Confession of Faith* 1.7.

9. See J. Calvin, *Institutes of the Christian Religion* (ed. J. T. McNeill and tr. F. L. Battles; Philadelphia: Westminster, 1967), 1.7.5; J. Owen, *The Works of John Owen* (16 vols.; London: Banner of Truth, 1966 [1850–53]), 4.121–73; J. Buchanan, *The Office and Work of the Holy Spirit* (London: Banner of Truth, 1966 [1843]), 46-58; *Westminster Confession of Faith* 1.6.

10. Owen, *Works of John Owen*, 4.124–5.

11. W. Wink, *The Bible in Human Transformation: Toward a Paradigm for Biblical Study* (Philadelphia: Fortress, 1973), 10.

12. Occasionally critical scholars affirm an important role for the Spirit in interpretation. For example, see Thiselton's discussion of Barth and Grech in *A. Thiselton, The Two Horizons* (Grand Rapids: Eerdmans, 1980), 85–92. See also B. S. Childs, *Biblical Theology in Crisis* (Philadelphia: Westminster, 1970), 219. These positions represent a minority among critical scholars.

13. See Calvin, *Institutes* 1.9.1–3; W. Ames, *The Marrow of Theology* (tr. and ed. J. D. Eusden; Boston: Pilgrim, 1968 [1629]), 1.34.26; J. A. Ernesti, *Elementary Principles of Interpretation* (ed. and tr. M. Stuart; 4th ed.; New York: Dayton and Saxton, 1842), 27 [1.1.31]; Terry, *Biblical Hermeneutics*, 30.

14. For the most part, the work of the Spirit in hermeneutical preparation is assumed by modern evangelical writers and thus receives little mention. See W. Kaiser, *Toward an Exegetical Theology* (Grand Rapids: Baker, 1981), 235–47. See also A. B. Mickelsen, *Interpreting the Bible* (Grand Rapids: Eerdmans, 1972), 4, 39, 42, 361, 378; H. A. Virkler, *Hermeneutics: Principles and Processes of Biblical Interpretation* (Grand Rapids: Baker, 1981), 31; Silva, *Has the Church Misread the Bible?*, 86–9. For recent discussions of the Spirit in interpretation, see the three articles in *Hermeneutics, Inerrancy, and the Bible* (eds. E. Radmacher and R. Preus; Grand Rapids: Zondervan, 1985): F. Klooster, "The Role of the Holy Spirit in the Hermeneutic Process: The Relationship of the Spirit's Illumination to Biblical Interpretation," 451–72; W. Dayton, "A Response to The Role of the Holy Spirit in the Hermeneutic Process," 475-84; A. Lindsley, "A Response to The Role of the Holy Spirit in the Hermeneutic Process," 487–92. See also R. B. Zuck, "The Role of the Holy Spirit in Hermeneutics," *Bibliotheca Sacra,* 141 (1984), 120–9.

15. As Owen wrote so forcefully, "For a man solemnly to undertake the interpretation of any portion of Scripture without invocation of God, to be taught and instructed by his Spirit, is a high provocation of him; nor shall I expect the discovery of truth from any one who thus proudly engages in a work so much above his ability." J. Owen, *Pneumatology: Or a Discourse Concerning the Holy Spirit* (Philadelphia: Towar and Hogan, 1827), 204–5. See also Owen, *Works of John Owen,* 4.121–234.

16. Thiselton, *Two Horizons,* 92.

17. "God, in his ordinary providence, maketh use of means, yet is free to work without, above, and against them, at his pleasure." *Westminster Confession of Faith* 5.3. These categories are limited, but they represent the principal ways in which divine activity relates to creaturely means. We are applying these basic categories to hermeneutical processes.

18. For a discussion of Mosaic authorship of the Pentateuch see chapter 12.

19. For a discussion of the date of Samuel see chapter 12.

20. For a discussion of the date of Kings and Chronicles see chapter 12.

21. L. Berkhof, *Principles of Biblical Interpretation* (Grand Rapids: Baker, 1950), 11. Also note Terry, *Biblical Hermeneutics*, 17–9; Virkler, *Hermeneutics*, 77–81.

22. Terminology has varied in recent years. Kaiser, for instance, prefers the term "syntactical-theological." Kaiser, *Exegetical Theology*, 88. Mickelsen adopts the term "grammatical-historical-contextual." Mickelsen, *Interpreting the Bible*, 159, 299. Virkler speaks of "historical-cultural" and "lexical-syntactical" analyses. Virkler, *Hermeneutics*, 76–112. Even so, "grammatico-historical" has been used widely and adequately represents the main concerns of the approach that most evangelicals follow.

23. See Berkhof, *Principles of Biblical Interpretation*, 25; F. Farrar, *History of Interpretation: Bampton Lectures*, 1885 (Grand Rapids: Baker, 1961; [1886]), 15–6; Kaiser, *Exegetical Theology*, 44–5, 60–1; B. Ramm, *Protestant Biblical Interpretation* (Grand Rapids: Baker, 1970), 1–19. Recent studies have pointed to many continuities between the Reformers and medieval interpreters. See J. S. Preus, *From Shadow to Promise: Old Testament Interpretation from Augustine to the Young Luther* (Cambridge: Harvard University, 1969), 3; D. C. Steinmetz, "The Superiority of Practical Exegesis," *A Guide to Contemporary Hermeneutics: Major Trends in Biblical Interpretation* (ed. D. K. McKim; Grand Rapids: Eerdmans, 1986), 71, and Silva's discussion of medieval reaction to Origen's allegorical method in *Has the Church Misread the Bible?*, 52–7.

24. See, for example, Farrar, *History of Interpretation*, 323–54; Ramm, *Protestant Biblical Interpretation*, 51–9; H. Frei, *The Eclipse of Biblical Narrative: A Study in Eighteenth and Nineteenth Century Hermeneutics* (New Haven: Yale University, 1974), 18–37; Terry, *Biblical Hermeneutics*, 47–9; Mickelsen, *Interpreting the Bible*, 39-41; Berkhof, *Principles of Biblical Interpretation*, 25–7.

25. As Schaff suggested, "Calvin, like Melancthon and Zwingli, started as a humanist, and like them, made the linguistic and literary culture of the Renaissance tributary to the Reformation." P. Schaff, *History of the Christian Church* (8 vols.; Grand Rapids: Eerdmans, 1910), 8.309. See also H. J. Kraus, "Calvin's Exegetical Principles," (tr. K. Crim) *Interpretation* 31 (1977), 12–8; T. F. Torrance, *The Hermeneutics of John Calvin* (Edinburgh: Scottish Academic, 1988).

26. See P. O. Kristeller, *Renaissance Thought* (New York: Harper, 1961) for a discussion of Renaissance treatment of classical literature.

27. K. A. G. Keil, *De historica librorum sacrorum interpretatione ejusque necessitate* (Leipzig, 1788); *Lehrbuch der Hermeneutik des neuen Testamentes nach*

Grundsätzen der grammatisch-historischen Interpretation (Leipzig: Vogel, 1810). The importance of Keil in the history of Biblical interpretation has been noted in several works; for example Kaiser, *Exegetical Theology*, 87, 197; Terry, *Biblical Hermeneutics*, 101; Berkhof, *Principles of Biblical Interpretation*, 37; Frei, *Eclipse of Biblical Narrative*, 339 n.5.

28. J. A. Ernesti is frequently noted as a pivotal figure in the history of interpretation. See Terry, *Biblical Hermeneutics*, 53–4; Frei, *Eclipse of Biblical Narrative*, 39, 95, 108, 246; Ramm, *Protestant Biblical Interpretation*, 59–60.

29. See *The New Schaff-Herzog Encyclopedia of Religious Knowledge*, s.v. "Grotius (De Groot), Hugo"; Terry, *Biblical Hermeneutics*, 51. For a discussion of Ernesti's dependence on Grotius, see Terry, *Biblical Hermeneutics*, 54.

30. See Ernesti, *Elementary Principles*, 27 [1.1.31].

31. See G. Hasel, *Old Testament Theology: Basic Issues in the Current Debate* (Grand Rapids: Eerdmans, 1972), 84–6; Frei, *Eclipse of Biblical Narrative*, 60–5; Farrar, *History of Interpretation*, 397–437; Terry, *Biblical Hermeneutics*, 57, 62–8.

32. The conventional character of language has been a major emphasis in modern linguistics. See, for instance, L. Wittgenstein, *Tractatus Logico-Philosophicus* (London: Routledge and Kegan Paul, 1961), 4.0031; B. Russell, "On Denoting," *Mind* 14 (1905), 479–93; F. de Saussure, *Course in General Linguistics* (tr. W. Baskin, eds. C. Bally and A. Sechehaye, in collaboration with A. Reidlinger; New York: Philosophical Library, 1959; originally published as *Cours de linguistic générale* posthumously in 1915), 9, 13–4; J. L. Austin, *How to Do Things with Words* (ed. J. O. Urmson; London: Oxford University, 1962). As Stubbs has put it, "On the one hand, therefore, there is no use of language which is not embedded in the culture; on the other hand, there are no large-scale relationships between language and society which are not realized, at least partly, through verbal interaction." M. Stubbs, *Discourse Analysis: The Sociolinguistic Analysis of Natural Language* (Chicago: University of Chicago, 1983), 8. For a fuller discussion see chapter 5.

33. See M. Silva, *Biblical Words and their Meaning* (Grand Rapids: Zondervan, 1983), 35–51; E. A. Nida, *Language Structure and Translation* (Stanford: Stanford University, 1975), 27.

34. For a helpful discussion of these matters, see Berkouwer, *Holy Scripture*, 151-7. The term "organic inspiration" has also been used in evangelical circles outside the Reformed Tradition. See, for example, L. S. Chafer, *Systematic Theology* (8 vols.; Dallas: Dallas Seminary, 1964), 1.71–6.

35. Warfield, *Inspiration and Authority*, 154–5.

36. See chapter 12 for a treatment of the purpose of Kings.

37. See R. L. Pratt, Jr., "Royal Prayer and the Chronicler's Program" (unpublished dissertation: Harvard University, 1987), 347–50; H. G. M. Williamson, *1 and 2 Chronicles* (*New Century Bible Commentary*; Grand Rapids: Eerdmans, 1982),

388–90; R. Dillard *2 Chronicles* (*Word Biblical Commentary* 15; Waco: Word, 1988), 76–8.

38. As the exposition of the Chicago Statement on Biblical Inerrancy has put it, "although the human writers' personalities were expressed in what they wrote, the words were divinely constituted. Thus, what Scripture says, God says . . . having given it through the minds and words of chosen and prepared men who in freedom and faithfulness spoke from God as they were carried along by the Holy Spirit (2 Peter 1:21)." *The Chicago Statement on Biblical Inerrancy* as found in J. M. Boice, *Standing on the Rock* (Wheaton: Tyndale, 1978), 132. Also see Warfield, *Inspiration and Authority*, 154–7; J. I. Packer, *"Fundamentalism" and the Word of God* (Grand Rapids: Eerdmans, 1958), 78; Berkouwer, *Holy Scripture*, 19; C. Hodge, *Systematic Theology* (3 vols.; Grand Rapids: Eerdmans, 1970 [1873]), 1.156–7.

39. See Calvin, *Institutes*, 1.17.13. For a discussion of accommodation in relation to Scripture and modern science see R. Hooykaas, *Religion and the Rise of Modern Science* (Grand Rapids: Eerdmans, 1974), 122–4; Warfield, *Inspiration and Authority*, 189–95; J. M. Frame, *The Doctrine of the Knowledge of God* (Phillipsburg: Presbyterian and Reformed, 1987), 24. For the doctrine of accommodation in critical circles, see F. L. Battles, "God Was Accommodating Himself to Human Capacity," *Interpretation* 31 (1977), 19–38; Frei, *Eclipse of Biblical Narrative*, 60–5.

40. For a discussion of the covenant-treaty form and the book of Deuteronomy see M. G. Kline, *Treaty of the Great King* (Grand Rapids: Eerdmans, 1963), 13 and *The Structure of Biblical Authority* (Grand Rapids: Eerdmans, 1972), 27–43; J. McCarthy, *Treaty and Covenant* (Rome: Pontifical Biblical Institute, 1963), 11; G. E. Mendenhall, "Ancient Oriental and Biblical Law," *Biblical Archaeologist* 17 (1954), 26–46 and "Covenant Forms in Israelite Tradition," *Biblical Archaeologist* 17 (1954), 50–76; K. Baltzer, *The Covenant Formulary* (tr. D. E. Green; Philadelphia: Fortress, 1971); K. A. Kitchen, *Ancient Orient and Old Testament* (Chicago: Inter-Varsity, 1966), 20–102; P. C. Craigie, *The Book of Deuteronomy* (Grand Rapids: Eerdmans, 1976), 79–83. See also the discussion of Deuteronomy in chapter 12.

41. See the discussion of Kings in chapter 12.

42. Janzen points out Job's role as "everyman" (*'dm*) concerned the perennial questions of life. See J. G. Janzen, *Job* (*Interpretation*; Atlanta: John Knox, 1985), 12–4.

43. Kaiser has noted, "Grammatico-historical exegesis has failed to map the route between the actual determination of the authentic meaning and the delivery of the word to modern men and women who ask that meaning be translated into some kind of normative application or significance for their lives." Kaiser, *Exegetical Theology*, 88.

44. Application has been at least nominally acknowledged as part of hermeneutical procedure. From the time of Origen's allegorical method to the traditional threefold distinction (*explicatio, meditatio,* and *applicatio*), its importance has been

acknowledged. See K. Barth, *Church Dogmatics* (eds. G. W. Bromiley and T. F. Torrance; Edinburgh: T. and T. Clarke, 1956), 1.2.721–7; Silva, *Has the Church Misread the Bible?*, 63–9; C. M. Wood, *The Formation of Christian Understanding: An Essay in Theological Hermeneutics* (Philadelphia: Westminster, 1981), 60, 75.

45. For a brief history of the shift see Soulen, *Handbook*, 82–6. See also P. Ricoeur, *Essays on Biblical Interpretation* (ed. L. S. Merdge; Philadelphia: Fortress, 1980); *The Encyclopedia of Religion* (ed. M. Eliade; New York: Macmillan, 1978) s.v. "Hermeneutics." See the fuller discussion of these matters in chapter 1.

46. See chapter 1 for a fuller treatment of Heidegger and Gadamer.

47. See Virkler, *Hermeneutics*, 211–32; Mickelsen, *Interpreting the Bible*, 169–76; E. A. Nida, *Message and Mission: The Communication of the Christian Faith* (New York: Harper and Row, 1960); Kaiser, *Exegetical Theology*, 185–231.

48. Thiselton, *Two Horizons*, xix.

49. See S. B. Berg, *The Book of Esther* (*Society of Biblical Literature* 44; Missoula: Scholars, 1977), 2–3; also see H. Lamparter, *Das Buch Der Sehnsucht* (Druck: Gutmann, 1977), 13 and W. L. Humphreys, "Novella," in *Saga, Legend, Tale, Novella, Fable* (ed. G. W. Coats; *Journal for the Study of the Old Testament Supplements* 35; Sheffield: Journal for the Study of the Old Testament Press, 1985), 85.

50. Opinions on this text often go to extremes. DeVries, for example, remarks that these are "elements derived not from revelation but from the culture," which "represent a drastic departure from Israel's traditional ideals." S. J. DeVries, *1 Kings* (*Word Biblical Commentary* 12; Waco: Word, 1985), 20–1.

51. For a popular discussion of the ethical implications of "holy war" (*hrm*) see P. Craigie, *The Problem of War in the Old Testament* (Grand Rapids: Eerdmans, 1978), 45–54.

52. See A. Weiser, *The Old Testament: Its Formation and Development* (tr. D. Barton; New York: Association, 1961), 172; J. Gray, 1 and 2 Kings (*Old Testament Library*; 2d ed.; Philadelphia: Westminster, 1964), 37–43. See also the discussion of the Deuteronomistic History in chapter 12.

53. According to the Index of Quotations, Allusions, and Verbal Parallels in *The Greek New Testament* (ed. K. Aland et al.; United Bible Societies 3d ed.; Stuttgart: Biblia-Druck, 1983), 897–911.

54. For general discussions of Jesus' view of OT Law see G. Knight, *Law and Grace* (Philadelphia: Westminster, 1962), 66–75; G. Sloyan, *Is Christ the End of the Law?* (Philadelphia: Westminster, 1978), 38–69; P. Fairbairn, *The Revelation of Law in Scripture* (Grand Rapids: Zondervan, 1957 [1869]), 214–53.

55. See Kaiser, *Exegetical Theology*, 18–23 and J. Murray, *Collected Writings of John Murray* (4 vols.; Carlisle: Banner of Truth, 1976), 1.21–2.

56. For a discussion of the eschatological dimensions of this passage see H. Ridderbos, *Paul: An Outline of His Theology* (tr. J. DeWitt; Grand Rapids: Eerdmans, 1975), 52–3 and G. Vos, *The Pauline Eschatology* (Grand Rapids: Eerdmans, 1972), 1–41.

Chapter One

1. Van Til has provided a helpful evangelical assessment of Kant's influence in the history of western philosophy. See for instance C. Van Til, *The New Hermeneutic* (Phillipsburg: Presbyterian and Reformed, 1974), 2, 30, 50–1. For a bibliography and brief description of Hume and Kant see T. V. Smith and M. Greene, eds., *Philosophers Speak for Themselves: Berkeley, Hume, and Kant* (Chicago: University of Chicago, 1940 and 1957), 253. For a brief discussion of the significance of Kant's views on hermeneutics, see E. D. Hirsch, *Aims of Interpretation* (Chicago: University of Chicago, 1976), 45–9.

2. See R. H. Popkin, "David Hume: His Pyrrhonism and his Critique of Pyrrhonism," *Modern Studies in Philosophy: Hume* (ed. V. C. Chappell; Notre Dame: University of Notre Dame, 1966), 53. See also B. Stroud, *Hume* (London, Henley, and Boston: Routledge and Kegan Paul, 1977), 1–6. Kant resisted Hume's skepticism by attempting to elaborate the universal human principles of thought which he called "Synthetic a priori judgments." See F. Copleston, *A History of Philosophy* (9 vols.; London: Search, 1960), vol. 6, *Wolff to Kant*, 227–8; see also pp. 225–6; A. C. Ewing, *A Short Commentary on Kant's Critique of Pure Reason* (Chicago: University of Chicago, 1938), 99-105.

3. For Kant, these categories included the basic notions of time and space, quantity and quality, relation and modality. As Kant put it, "Hence if pure concepts of the understanding do not refer to objects of experience but to things in themselves (noumena), they have no signification whatever. They serve, as it were, only to decipher appearances, that we may be able to read them as experience." I. Kant, *Prolegomena to Any Future Metaphysics* (tr. P. Carus; Chicago: Open Court, 1933) paragraph 30.

4. For a concise review of Kantian categories, see B. Russell, *Wisdom of the West: A Historical Survey of Western Philosophy in its Social and Political Setting* (ed. P. Foulkes; London: MacDonald, 1959), 240.

5. This basic model has been expanded far beyond Kant's original thinking. For instance, See T. S. Kuhn, *The Structure of Scientific Revolutions* (2d ed.; Chicago: University of Chicago, 1970), 10–20. See, however, Russman's response to Kuhn, T. A. Russman, *A Prospectus for the Triumph of Realism* (Macon, Ga.: Mercer University, 1987) and also Popper's response to Kuhn: K. Popper, "Normal Science and its Dangers," in *Criticism and the Growth of Knowledge* (eds. I. Lakatos and A. Musgrave; Cambridge: Cambridge University, 1970), 56–7. For an evangelical perspective on some of these matters see V. S. Poythress, *Science and Hermeneutics* (*Foundations of Contemparary Interpretation* 6; Grand Rapids: Zondervan, 1988), 39–63.

6. For a discussion of these developments see Palmer, *Hermeneutics*, 84–127; H. G. Gadamer, *Truth and Method* (New York: Seabury, 1975), 162–79, 192–225; En-

glish translation copyright 1975 by Sheed and Ward Ltd., based on the second (1965) edition of *Warheit und Methode* (Tübingen: J. C. B. Mohr, 1960); Thiselton, *Two Horizons*, 103-14; Hirsch, *Aims of Interpretation*, 17–35.

7. See M. Heidegger, *Being and Time* (tr. J. Macquarrie and E. Robinson; New York: Harper and Row, 1962), 191–2; English translation copyright 1962 by Harper and Row, based on the seventh edition of *Sein und Zeit* (Tübingen: Neomarius, 1926).

8. Gadamer's major works include *Warheit und Methode: Grundzüge einer philosophischen Hermeneutik* (2d ed.; Tübingen: Mohr, 1965; English translation *Truth and Method* [New York: Seabury, 1975]); *Kleine Schriften* (4 vols.; Tübingen: Mohr, 1977; vols. 1–3 are partially translated in *Philosophical Hermeneutics* [Berkeley: University of California, 1976]); *Platos und die Dichter* (Frankfurt: Klosterman, 1934).

9. Gadamer, *Truth and Method*, 239–40.

10. As Gadamer said, "A person who is trying to understand a text is always performing an act of projecting. He projects before himself a meaning for the text as a whole as soon as some initial meaning emerges in the text. Again, the latter emerges only because he is reading the text with particular expectations in regard to a certain meaning." Gadamer, *Truth and Method*, 236.

11. Prominent literary critics in this movement include David Bleich, Stanley Fish, Robert Fowler, Norman Holland, and Wolfgang Iser. See R. Fowler, "Who is 'The Reader' in Reader Response Criticism?" *Semeia* 31 (1985), 5–26 for bibliography. Also see T. Longman, *Literary Approaches to Biblical Interpretation* (*Foundations of Contemparary Interpretation*; vol. 3; Grand Rapids: Zondervan, 1987), 38–41.

12. Bultmann's seminal article "Is Exegesis without Presuppositions Possible?" was an early attempt to apply a subjective model to the Bible. See R. Bultmann, "Is Exegesis without Presuppositions Possible?" *New Testament and Mythology* (tr. S. Ogden; Philadelphia: Fortress, 1984 [1957]), 145–54.

13. Gadamer, *Truth and Method*, 236. Heidegger commented similarly, "Our first, last and constant task is never to allow our fore-having, foresight and fore-conception to be presented to us by fancies and popular conception, but rather to make the scientific theme secure . . . in terms of the things themselves." Heidegger, *Being and Time*, 125.

14. For example, J. Miranda, *Communism in the Bible* (tr. R. R. Barr; Maryknoll, New York: Orbis, 1982) and *Marx and the Bible: a Critique of the Philosophy of Oppression* (tr. J. Eagleson; Maryknoll, N.Y.: Orbis, 1974); J. L. Segundo, *Liberation of Theology* (Maryknoll, N.Y.: Orbis, 1976), 39–95; J. M. Bonino, *Doing Theology in a Revolutionary Situation* (Philadelphia: Fortress, 1975), 81.

15. Croatto, *Exodus: A Hermeneutic of Freedom* (tr. S. Attansio; Maryknoll, N.Y.: Orbis, 1981), 2.

16. Croatto, *Exodus*, 3.

17. N. K. Gottwald, *The Tribes of Yahweh: A Sociology of the Religion of Liberated Israel 1250–1050 B. C. E.* (Maryknoll, N.Y.: Orbis, 1979), 35–40, 214–5.

18. Gottwald, *Tribes of Yahweh*, 210–9.

19. Liberationists are often accused of subjecting the Bible to Marxist ideology. As Witvliet has suggested, Liberationists have "replaced Aristotle with Marx." T. Witvliet, *A Place in the Sun: An Introduction to Liberation Theology in the Third World* (tr. J. Bowden; Maryknoll, N.Y.: Orbis, 1985), 130. See also Bonino, *Doing Theology in a Revolutionary Situation*, 87 and Gadamer, *Truth and Method*, 296.

20. There are evangelical feminists who view the entire Bible as authoritative. See E. Storkey, *What's Right with Feminism* (Grand Rapids: Eerdmans, 1985), 151–9, and the issue of *Journal of the Evangelical Theological Society* devoted to the role of women in the church. *Journal of the Evangelical Theological Society* 30/1 (1987). See also the evangelical magazine *Daughters of Sarah*. Even so, many feminists speak boldly of limited authority for the Bible. For examples see A. Y. Collins, "New Testament Perspectives: The Gospel of John," *Journal for the Study of the Old Testament* 22 (1982), 47–53; E. S. Fiorenza, "Feminist Theology and New Testament Interpretation," *Journal for the Study of the Old Testament* 22 (1982), 32–46 and "The Ethics of Interpretation: De-Centering Biblical Scholarship," *Journal of Biblical Literature* 107 (March 1988), 3–17; R. R. Ruether, "Feminism and Patriarchal Religion: Principles of Ideological Critique of the Bible," *Journal for the Study of the Old Testament* 22 (1982), 54–66; L. M. Russell, "Feminist Critique: Opportunity for Cooperation," *Journal for the Study of the Old Testament* 22 (1982), 67–71; K. D. Sakenfeld, "Old Testament Perspectives: Methodological Issues," *Journal for the Study of the Old Testament* 22 (1982), 13–20; M. K. Wakeman, "Sacred Marriage," *Journal for the Study of the Old Testament* 22 (1982), 21–31. Gay/Lesbian theologians make a similar appeal to their governing presuppositions in Biblical interpretation. See G. R. Edwards, *Gay/Lesbian Liberation: A Biblical Perspective* (New York: Pilgrim, 1984) and M. Johnson, *Gays under Grace: A Gay Christian's Response to the Moral Majority* (Nashville: Winston-Derek, 1983).

21. E. Fiorenza, "Toward a Feminist Biblical Hermeneutics: Biblical Interpretation and Liberation Theology," in *The Challenge of Liberation Theology* (eds. B. Mahan and C. Richesin; Maryknoll, N.Y.: Orbis, 1981), 107–8.

22. "The hermeneutical phenomenon is basically not a problem of method at all. It is not concerned with a method of understanding, by means of which texts are subjected to scientific investigation like all other objects of experience." Gadamer, *Truth and Method*, xi.

23. For instance, Fiorenza remarks, "I would suggest that the canon and norm for evaluating Biblical traditions and their subsequent interpretations cannot be derived from the Bible or the Biblical process of learning within and through ideologies, but can only be formulated within and through the struggle for the liberation of women and all oppressed people." Fiorenza, "Feminist Biblical Hermeneutics," 107. Similarly, Croatto says, "We wish to establish a hermeneutical perspective with a view to a 're-reading' of the Biblical message of liberation

on the basis of our experience as oppressed peoples or persons. It will be up to the readers to 'situate' themselves vis-a-vis the Word of God, to explore its conscientizing and liberative meaning for themselves or in order to dialogue with their oppressed brothers and sisters." Croatto, *Exodus 11* (emphasis his).

24. One of the most fruitful benefits of this emphasis can be seen in recent discussions of evangelical missiology. For an evangelical discussion of contextualization, see A. Glasser and D. McGavran, *Contemporary Theologies of Mission* (Grand Rapids: Baker, 1983), 139–49. As Conn has put it, in modern missiology, "the possibility of a trialogue now exists—missiology, cultural anthropology and theology in simultaneous interchange." H. Conn, *Eternal Word and Changing Worlds* (Grand Rapids: Zondervan, 1984), 130. See also D. J. Hesselgrave, *Communicating Christ Cross-Culturally* (Grand Rapids: Zondervan, 1978), 110–40. See the discussion of contextualization in chapter 15.

25. See R. Lundin, A. C. Thiselton, C. Walhout, *The Responsibility of Hermeneutics* (Grand Rapids and London: Eerdmans and Paternoster, 1985), 4–14.

26. In describing his epistemological goal Descartes said, "Today, then, since very opportunely for the plan I have in view I have delivered my mind from every care [and am happily agitated by no passions] and since I have procured for myself an assured leisure in a peaceable retirement, I shall at last seriously and freely address myself to the general upheaval of all my former opinions." R. Descartes, "Meditations on First Philosophy," in *The Philosophical Works of Descartes* (tr. E. S. Haldane and G. R. T. Ross; 2 vols.; Cambridge: Cambridge University, 1911), 1.144.

27. For a discussion of Cartesian epistemology in relation to developments in the Enlightenment, see A. Glucksmann, *The Master Thinkers* (tr. B. Pearce; New York: Harper and Row, 1980), 179. See also P. Gay, *The Enlightenment, The Rise of Modern Paganism* (New York: Norton, 1977), 139 and *The Enlightenment, The Science of Freedom* (New York: Norton, 1977), 6.

28. Bacon's Tables of Investigation are often referred to as the Tables of Affirmation, Negation, and Comparison. See F. Bacon, *Novum Organum* (ed. T. Fowler; Oxford: Clarendon, 1889) and *The Advancement of Science* (ed. W. A. Wright; Oxford: Clarendon, 1900). For a popular discussion of Bacon's inductive method, see W. T. Jones, *A History of Western Philosophy* (2d ed.; New York: Harcourt, Brace, and World, 1952 and 1969), vol. 3, *Hobbes to Hume*, 82–7.

29. For a summary of Reid's views see S. A. Grave, *The Scottish Philosophy of Common Sense* (Oxford: Oxford University, 1960) and M. Evans, "Perception and Common Sense in the Writings of Thomas Reid," (unpublished dissertation, Princeton University, 1955). For a discussion of the widespread influence of Common Sense Realism in hermeneutics see M. Noll, "Evangelicals and the Study of the Bible," in *Evangelicalism and Modern America* (ed. G. Marsden; Grand Rapids: Eerdmans, 1984), 103–21 and G. Marsden, "Everyone One's Own Interpreter?: The Bible, Science, and Authority in Mid-Nineteenth-Century America," in *The Bible in America* (eds. N. Hatch and M. Noll; New York: Oxford, 1982), 79–100. See also T. Reid, *Essays on the Intellectual Power of Man* (ed. B. A. Brady; Cambridge: Harvard University, 1969 [1785]).

30. See Lundin, Walhaut, and Thiselton, *Responsibility of Hermeneutics*, 20.

31. See J. Immerwahr, "Thomas Reid: Theory of Perception," (unpublished dissertation, University of Michigan, 1972), 113.

32. As Reid himself put it, "It is vain to reason with a man who denies the first principles on which the reasoning is grounded." T. Reid, *Inquiry and Essays* (eds. R. Beenblossum and R. Leher; Indianapolis: Hackett, 1983), 257.

33. See, for instance, Terry, *Biblical Hermeneutics*, 70.

34. R. C. Sproul, "A Response to Philosophical Presuppositions Affecting Biblical Hermeneutics," in *Hermeneutics, Inerrancy, and the Bible* (eds. E. Radmacher and R. Preus; Grand Rapids: Zondervan, 1984), 518.

35. Berkhof, *Principles of Biblical Interpretation*; R. T. Chafer, *The Science of Biblical Hermeneutics* (Dallas: Bibliotheca Sacra, 1939).

36. See Ramm, *Protestant Biblical Interpretation*, 11. See also Virkler, *Hermeneutics*, 16 and Mickelsen, *Interpreting the Bible*, 19.

37. Kaiser speaks in terms quite reminiscent of Scottish Common Sense philosophy when he argues that reliable hermeneutics has called for "a return to rules that do not violate what God-given nature has taught, art has practiced, and science has collected and arranged in systems." W. Kaiser, "Legitimate Hermeneutics," in *A Guide to Contemporary Hermeneutics: Major Trends in Biblical Interpretation* (ed. D. McKim; Grand Rapids: Eerdmans, 1986), 115 (emphasis his). Similarly, Ramm states: "The theologian is the scientist; the 'facts' to be examined are Scripture; and the procedure is inductively directed. The theologian is to be a careful collector of facts. He tries to be as thorough and systematic as any scientist. His rules of evidence, however, are not experimentation and observation but Biblical hermeneutics." Ramm, *Protestant Biblical Interpretation*, 173 (emphasis mine).

38. Heidegger, *Being and Time*, 61–2 and Gadamer, *Truth and Method*, 431–47.

39. See, for instance, *Westminster Confession of Faith* 1.6; *Belgic Confession*, 5; *Formula of Concord*, Epitome 1; *Thirty-Nine Articles of England*, 6.

40. See 2 Samuel 7:28; 1 Kings 17:24; Matthew 22:43; Mark 12:24; John 10:34–35; Acts 4:25; Romans 4:23–24; 1 Corinthians 14:37; 1 Thessalonians 2:13; 2 Timothy 3:15–16; 2 Peter 1:21; 1 John 5:10.

41. See N. L. Geisler and J. I. Packer, *Summit II Hermeneutics: Understanding God's Word* (Oakland: International Council on Biblical Inerrancy, 1977) Article 19. See also Kaiser, "Legitimate Hermeneutics", 86–9; M. Silva, "Historical Reconstruction in New Testament Criticism," in *Hermeneutics, Authority, and Canon* (eds. D. A. Carson and J. D. Woodbridge; Grand Rapids: Zondervan, 1986), 131; Sproul, *Knowing Scripture*, 40.

42. Here we use the term "ethic" following Hirsch. See Hirsch, *Aims of Interpretation*, 7–8, 74–95.

43. R. Grant and D. Tracy, *A Short History of the Interpretation of the Bible* (Philadelphia: Fortress, 1946), 164.

44. "Explanation, then, will appear as the mediation between two stages of understanding. If isolated from this concrete process, it is a mere abstraction, an artifact of methodology." P. Ricoeur, *Interpretation Theory: Discourse and the Surplus of Meaning* (Fort Worth: Texas Christian University, 1976), 75.

45. For a discussion of the origins of this terminology see Soulen, *Handbook*, 82–4. See also Thiselton, *Two Horizons*, 104.

46. For example, Hirsch, *Aims of Interpretation* 1–13 and Thiselton, *Two Horizons*, 104.

47. Many others have adopted this terminology. See D. A. Carson, *Exegetical Fallacies* (Grand Rapids: Baker, 1984), 129, and Thiselton, *Two Horizons*, 104.

48. Harvey regards Schleiermacher as the "originating figure" of modern hermeneutics. See V. A. Harvey, s.v. "Hermeneutics," in *The Encyclopedia of Religion* (ed. M. Eliade; New York: Macmillan, 1978), 6.280. See also introduction to F. D. E. Schleiermacher, *Hermeneutics* (ed. H. Kimmerle, trs. J. Duke and J. Forstman; Atlanta: Scholars, 1986), 1 and Palmer, *Hermeneutics*, 97. Schleiermacher's major works on hermeneutics include *Hermeneutik* (ed. H. Kimmerle; Heidelberg: Carl Winter, Universitätsverlag, 1959); *Hermeneutik und Kritik: mit besonderer Beziehung auf das Neue Testament* (ed. F. Lucke; vol. 7 of the First Division of his Sammtliche Werke; Berlin: Reimer, 1838); "Über die verschiedenen Methoden des Übersezens," in *Akademie der Wissenschaften*, 24 (Juni 1813), 207–45; *The Christian Faith* (Edinburgh: T. and T. Clark, 1928).

49. See Palmer, *Hermeneutics*, 94.

50. Dilthey, Heidegger, Gadamer, Riceour and many other comtemporary scholars follow Schleiermacher by looking at hermeneutics in terms of basic epistemological questions. See Palmer, *Hermeneutics*, 100, 124, 164. Palmer summarizes the shift in Schleiermacher's work: "His contribution to hermeneutics marks a turning point in its history. For hermeneutics is no longer seen as a specifically disciplinary matter belonging to theology, literature, or law; it is the art of understanding any utterance in language." Palmer, *Hermeneutics*, 94.

51. Silva acknowledges the growing interdisciplinary nature of hermeneutics. The topics covered in the Zondervan Series Foundations of Contemporary Interpretation in the areas of philosophy, literary criticism, linguistics, history, science, and theology, give evidence of the integration of a variety of disciplines into the field of Biblical hermeneutics. See Silva, *Has the Church Misread the Bible?*, 1–19.

52. See Berkouwer, *Holy Scripture*, 106, 192, 267–8, 320; Grant and Tracy, *A Short History*, 133; Ramm, *Protestant Biblical Interpretation*, 104–6.

53. Berkouwer points out that the doctrine of *Sacra Scriptura sui ipsius interpres* serves to establish the authority of Scripture against "all forms of subjectivism which do not openly conform to it." Berkouwer, *Holy Scripture*, 106.

54. The importance of this principle in contemporary evangelical hermeneutics is reflected in *The Chicago Statement on Biblical Hermeneutics.* "We affirm the unity, harmony, and consistency of Scripture and declare that it is its own best interpreter" (emphasis mine). Geisler and Packer, *Summit II Hermeneutics,* Article 17.

55. See The Belgic Confession 2.1–2; *Westminster Confession of Faith* 1.1; Calvin, *Institutes,* 1.5–6.

56. As Berkouwer has said, "General and special revelation do not stand beside or opposite each other as a duality in a relationship of rivalry and competition . . . but they find their unity in the sovereign activity of God." G. C. Berkouwer, *General Revelation* (Grand Rapids: Eerdmans, 1955), 292.

57. As Calvin said, "For just as eyes, when dimmed with age or weakness or by some other defect, unless aided by spectacles, discern nothing distinctly; so, such is our feebleness, unless Scripture guides us in seeking God, we are immediately confused." Calvin, *Institutes,* 1.14.1; see also *Institutes,* 1.6.1.

58. Frame, *Knowledge of God,* 138, 144–9.

59. See Hooykaas, *Religion and the Rise of Modern Science,* 130–5. For a more extensive discussion, see J. Dillenberger, *Protestant Thought and Natural Science: A Historical Interpretation* (Garden City, N.Y.: Doubleday, 1960), 21–49.

60. Packer writes: "[The Bible] speaks of natural phenomena as they are spoken of in ordinary language." See N. L. Geisler and J. I. Packer, *Explaining Hermeneutics: A Commentary* (*International Council on Biblical Inerrancy* Foundation Series 6; Oakland: International Council on Biblical Inerrancy, 1983), 32.

61. I find this tendency to be one of the best ways to distinguish between theological liberals and conservatives. Conservatives tend to rely on their understanding of Scripture until their assessment of general revelation compels them to change. Liberals favor their interpretation of general revelation (history, science, experience, etc.) over their understanding of the Bible.

62. Packer, *Explaining Hermeneutics* (emphasis his), 32.

Chapter Two

1. For a helpful survey of different views of sanctification see M. Dieter, et al., *Five Views on Sanctification* (Grand Rapids: Zondervan, 1987). See also *New International Dictionary of New Testament Theology,* 2.223-38 and *Theological Wordbook of the Old Testament,* 1.305–7, 2.786–8. Our definition of sanctification follows the mainline Reformed and Lutheran views. See Augsburg Confession 6 and 20; Formula of Concord 4; Second Helvetic Confession 16; Heidelberg Catechism 24, 62, 63; Belgic Confession 24; *Westminster Confession of Faith* 13.

2. A. Hoekema, "The Reformed Perspective," in *Five Views on Sanctification* (ed. M. Dieter, et al; Grand Rapids: Eerdmans, 1987), 61. See also Hodge, *Systematic Theology,* 3.213–258; B. B. Warfield, *Selected Shorter Writings of Benjamin B. Warfield* (ed. J. E. Meeter; 2 vols.; Nutley: Presbyterian and Reformed, 1973),

2.325–8 and G. C. Berkouwer, *Faith and Sanctification* (tr. J. Vriend; Grand Rapids: Eerdmans, 1952), 71–113.

3. For rare exceptions see Owen, *Works of John Owen*, 3.150, 4.199–234; 14.40; Ames, *Marrow of Theology*, 191 [1.35.13] and A. Pink, *Interpretation of the Scriptures* (Grand Rapids: Baker, 1972), 18–9. Note also the addition of E. Henderson's "On the Moral Qualifications of the Interpreter of the Scriptures" to *Ernesti's Elementary Principles*, 136–42.

4. Examples include Berkhof, *Principles of Biblical Interpretation*; Virkler, *Hermeneutics*; Mickelson offers two paragraphs on "The One to Whom We Must Give an Account," in *Interpreting the Bible*, 378–9; Kaiser devotes one page to the exegete's sanctification in *Toward an Exegetical Theology*, 241–2. See also Ernesti, *Elementary Principles*, 136–42. and G. C. Berkouwer, *Faith and Sanctification* (tr. J. Vriend; Grand Rapids: Eerdmans, 1952), 71–113.

5. As Frame writes, ". . . the believer's knowledge of God is inseparable from godly character . . . the qualifications for the ministry of teaching (theology) in Scripture are predominantly moral qualifications (1 Timothy 3:1ff; 1 Peter 5:1ff)." Frame, *Knowledge of God*, 322.

6. Hoekema describes how sanctification affects the mind, will, and emotions: "Sanctification empowers us to think, will, and love in a way that glorifies God, namely, to think God's thoughts after Him and to do what is in harmony with His will." Hoekema, "The Reformed Perspective", 62.

7. See, for instance, the differences between M. Woudstra, *Joshua* (*New International Commentaries on the Old Testament*; Grand Rapids: Eerdmans, 1981), 76–89 and F. A. Soggin, *Joshua* (tr. R. A. Wilson; *Old Testament Library;* Philadelphia: Westminster, 1972 [1970]), 43–64.

8. The subtle influence of racism on Biblical interpretation can be seen in the work of R. L. Dabney. While Dabney is known for his keen insights and clear thinking, he exhibits the blindness of his day in his attempt to find Biblical justification for African slave trade in America. See his appeal to the curse of Canaan, Abraham's slaves, etc. in *A Defense of Virginia and the South* (New York: E. J. Hale and Son, 1867 reprinted by Sprinkle Publications, 1977), esp. 92–198. See also the helpful discussion in D. Kelly, "Robert Lewis Dabney," in *Reformed Theology in America* (ed. D. F. Wells; Grand Rapids: Eerdmans, 1985), 225–6.

9. See Van Til's contrast of non-Christian and Christian thought in *The Defense of the Faith* (Philadelphia: Presbyterian and Reformed, 1955), 64–5. See also Van Til, *Introduction to Systematic Theology* (unpublished class syllabus; Westminster Theological Seminary, 1971), 245.

10. "Prayer is an integral part in the study of Scripture because it anticipates the Spirit's carrying its reader through the written page to God himself." Childs, *Biblical Theology in Crisis*, 219.

11. See, however, Kaiser, *Exegetical Theology*, 240 and Virkler, *Hermeneutics*, 233–44.

12. See Owen, *Works of John Owen*, 4.201–9.

13. See D. G. Myers, *The Human Puzzle: Psychological Research and Christian Belief* (San Francisco: Harper and Row, 1978), 96–117.

14. Myers, *The Human Puzzle*, 124–31.

15. Gutiérrez writes, "Only by doing this truth will our faith be 'verified,' in the etymological sense of the word." G. Gutiérrez, *A Theology of Liberation* (tr. C. Inda and J. Eagleson; Maryknoll, N.Y.: Orbis, 1973), 10. Note the introductory section, "Theology as Critical Reflection on Praxis", 6–13.

16. For examples see Bonino, *Doing Theology in a Revolutionary Situation* and L. Magesa, *The Church and Liberation in Africa* (Nakuru, Kenya: Nakuru, 1976).

17. See Ridderbos, *Paul: An Outline of His Theology*, 259 and *Galatians* (*New International Commentaries on the New Testament*; Grand Rapids: Eerdmans, 1953), 206–8.

18. See R. Roberts, *Spirituality and Human Emotions* (Grand Rapids: Eerdmans, 1982), 1.

19. During the course of his earthly ministry, Jesus exhibited a wide variety of emotions such as compassion (Matthew 20:34), indignation and anger (Matthew 23:13–36; Mark 3:15; 11:15–17), sadness (John 11:35), and joy (John 17:13). See B. B. Warfield, *The Person and Work of Christ* (Philadelphia: Presbyterian and Reformed, 1970), 93–145.

20. While "fear" (*yr'h*) may refer to emotional terror (Psalm 55:5 [6]; Ezekiel 30:13), it carries the emphasis of reverence and awe when God is its object. In Proverbs, this attitude of awe toward God is the basis of wisdom which manifests itself in righteous living. See *Theological Wordbook of the Old Testament*, 1.401.

21. Pervin offers this general definition: "Personality represents those characteristics of the person or of people generally that account for consistent patterns of behavior." See L. A. Pervin, *Personality: Theory and Research* (4th ed.; New York: John Wiley and Sons, 1984), 2–5. See also L. A. Fehr, *Introduction to Personality* (New York: Macmillan, 1983), 3–9.

22. In this section I am indebted to C. B. Johnson, *The Psychology of Biblical Interpretation* (Grand Rapids: Zondervan, 1983), 41–66.

23. Pervin writes: "All theories of personality recognize that factors inside the organism, and events in the surrounding environment, are important in determining behavior. However, the theories differ in the level of importance given to internal and external determinants and in their interpretation of the relationship between the two." Pervin, *Personality*, 13. See also Fehr, *Introduction to Personality*, 318-9.

24. See the summary of earlier studies in K. F. Bernheim and R. R. J. Levine, *Schizophrenia: Symptoms, Causes, and Treatments* (New York: W. W. Norton and Company, 1979), 81–4.

25. See for instance B. W. P. Wells, *Personality and Heredity: An Introduction to Psychogenetics* (London: Longman Group, 1980), 33–64, 115–20.

26. For a helpful summary of studies see Fehr, *Introduction to Personality*, 335–41.

27. See Johnson, *Psychology of Biblical Interpretation*, 46. For helpful discussions of cognitive selectivity see M. W. Eysenck, *A Handbook of Cognitive Psychology* (London: Lawrence Erlbaum Associates, 1984), 49–74 and J. R. Royce and A. Powell, "The Cognitive and Affective Transformation Systems," in *Theory of Personality and Individual Differences: Factors, Systems, and Processes* (Englewood Cliffs, N.J.: Prentice-Hall, 1983), 107–32.

28. Shevarin and Dickman write: "At least part of the cognition related to attention takes place outside the awareness." H. Shevarin and S. Dickman, "The Psychological Unconscious: A Necessary Assumption for all Psychological Theory," in *American Psychologist* (May 1980), 422 as cited in Johnson, *Psychology of Biblical Interpretation*, 46.

29. For a helpful evangelical outlook on these matters see V. M. Stewart [Van Leeuwen], "Cognitive Style, North American Values, and the Body of Christ," in *Journal of Psychology and Theology* 2 (1974), 77–88.

30. See Stewart [Van Leeuwen], "Cognitive Style", 80.

31. Stewart [Van Leeuwen] writes, "Witkin et al. . . . refer to articulated (analytic, or field-independent) functioning when the person can 'disembed' a figure from a context perceptually, has a well-developed sense of separate identity socially, and is relatively self-contained emotionally. By contrast, those with a global (or field-dependent) style have trouble isolating detail from context perceptually, have a much greater sense of dependence socially, and are relatively open and expressive emotionally." See Stewart [Van Leeuwen], "Cognitive Style", 80–1.

32. Keil's commentary on Jonah exhibits a cognitive-factual focus with little sensitivity to the emotive content. See C. F. Keil and F. Delitzsch, *Commentary on the Old Testament: Minor Prophets* (Grand Rapids: Eerdmans, 1946), 379–417. Calvin's comments show more sensitivity to the emotional qualities, but tend to be microscopic. See J. Calvin, *A Commentary on the Twelve Minor Prophets*, Vol. 3: Jonah, Micah and Nahum (tr. J. Owen; Edinburgh: Banner of Truth, 1986), 19–145. By contrast the more recent work of Fretheim demonstrates an awareness of the use of irony within the overall structure and unity of Jonah. See T. E. Fretheim, *The Message of Jonah: A Theological Commentary* (Minneapolis: Augsburg, 1977).

33. See Poythress' discussion of the "Advantages and Liabilities of Perspectives" in the context of his test case—Pastoral Healing and the Miracles Controversy—in V. S. Poythress, *Symphonic Theology: The Validity of Multiple Perspectives in Theology* (Grand Rapids: Zondervan, 1987), 112–9.

34. E. D. Hirsch, *Validity in Interpretation* (New Haven: Yale University, 1967), 249–58.

35. For a discussion of the purpose of the writer of Judges, see E. J. Young, *An Introduction to the Old Testament* (Grand Rapids: Eerdmans, 1949), 176; A. E. Cundall, *Judges* (*Tyndale Old Testament Commentaries*; Downers Grove: InterVarsity, 1968), 18, 26, 36–7, 182. See also D. W. Gooding, "The Composition of

the Book of Judges," *Ereṣ Israel* 16 (1982), 70–9. Most students come to seminary with the mistaken notion that every kind of human king was forbidden to Israel. But see E. H. Merrill, *Kingdom of Priests: A History of Old Testament Israel* (Grand Rapids: Baker, 1987), 186–7, 190, 208–9; R. W. Klein, *1 Samuel* (*Word Biblical Commentary*, 10; Waco: Word, 1983), 79; R. E. Clements, "The Deuteronomistic Interpretation of the Founding of the Monarchy in 1 Samuel VIII," *Vetus Testamentum* 24 (1974), 398–410. See also the treatment of Judges in chapter 12.

36. This concept of reading-for-a-purpose is similar to what Lundin, Walhout, and Thiselton have recently called a "hermeneutic of action." See Lundin, Thiselton and Walhout, *Responsibility of Hermeneutics*, 42–4.

37. See Pratt, "Royal Prayer," 355–7. "These motifs find their center in the Chronicler's own hopes for the restoration community, his picture of a reunited, reestablished nation." Dillard, *2 Chronicles*, 243.

38. See Lundin, Thiselton, and Walhout, *Responsibility of Hermeneutics* 113.

Chapter Three

1. Berkhof describes the fruit of common grace as (a) the general operation of the Holy Spirit which restrains sin and, thereby, preserves social order and promotes "civil righteousness," and (b) the general blessings necessary for life (i.e. rain, sunshine, food, shelter, etc.) that God distributes to all men indiscriminately in the measure which seems good to Him. See Berkhof, *Systematic Theology* (4th rev. ed.; Grand Rapids: Eerdmans, 1977 [1938]), 432–46. See also, C. Van Til, *Introduction to Systematic Theology*, 240–4 and G. C. Berkouwer, *The Providence of God* (Grand Rapids: Eerdmans, 1972 [1952]), 70–82.

2. Frame, *Knowledge of God*, 66–8.

3. See Van Til, *Introduction to Systematic Theology*, 101; *Defense of the Faith*, 125, 158–9.

4. See Van Til, *Introduction to Systematic Theology*, 194–9 and Frame, *Knowledge of God*, 20–2; Berkhof, *Systematic Theology*, 233; G. C. Berkouwer, *Sin* (Grand Rapids: Eerdmans, 1971); Calvin, *Institutes*, 2.1.9.

5. Van Til makes the point that "No Christian can escape facing the fact that many non-Christian scientists have discovered much truth about nature. If he does not explain this fact with Calvin by virtually saying that this is true in spite of their immanentistic view of life and because of the fact that they cannot help but work with the 'borrowed' capital of Christianity, then he must grant that the naturalist is partially right." See Van Til, *Introduction to Systematic Theology*, 81.

6. Calvin refers to this operation of the Spirit as "for the common good of mankind." Calvin, *Institutes*, 2.2.16.

7. For a discussion of the interaction of Proverbs with ancient Near Eastern wisdom, see B. Childs, *Introduction to the Old Testament as Scripture* (Philadelphia: Fortress, 1979), 548. See also A. Erman, "Eine agyptische Quelle der Spruche Salomos," *Sitzungsberichte der Deutschen (Preussischen) Akademie der*

Wissenschaften zu Berlin 15 (1924), 86–93. For an evangelical contribution see B. Waltke, "The Book of Proverbs and Ancient Wisdom Literature," *Bibliotheca Sacra* 136 (1979), 221–38.

8. See D. Kidner, *Proverbs* (*Tyndale Old Testament Commentaries*; London: Tyndale, 1964), 24, 178; C. H. Toy, *A Critical and Exegetical Commentary on the Book of Proverbs* (*International Critical Commentary*; Edinburgh: T. and T. Clark, 1899), 518, 539.

9. Aratus, Phaenomena 5. See "Index of Allusions and Verbal Parallels," 911.

10. Epimemides, de Oraculis 1.12. See "Index of Allusions and Verbal Parallels," 911.

11. Menander, *Thais*, 218. See "Index of Allusions and Verbal Parallels," 911.

12. Calvin, *Institutes*, 2.2.15; see also 2.2.16.

13. See chapter 2.

14. This doctrine is described in chapters 5, 7, and 8 of the *Augsburg Confession*, as well as chapter 18 of *The Second Helvetic Confession*. See also the helpful study of the priesthood of believers by C. Eastwood in *The Priesthood of All Believers: An Examination of the Doctrine from the Reformation to the Present Day* (Minneapolis: Augsburg, 1962) and *The Royal Priesthood of the Faithful: An Investigation of the Doctrine from Biblical Times to the Reformation* (Minneapolis: Augsburg, 1963).

15. See Eastwood, *Priesthood of All Believers*, 242.

16. "To be sure, the wisdom of the whole church and not just of the preacher is needed to apply the Word of God to the dismaying complexity of the modern world. . . . The wise preacher will encourage discriminating wisdom on the part of those who daily live and struggle with the ethical issues of politics, biological research, medical procedures, and environmental stewardship. He must learn from them the nature of Christian engagement with the issues that confront us all." E. P. Clowney, "Preaching the Word of the Lord: Cornelius Van Til, V. D. M.," *Westminster Theological Journal* 46 (1984), 252.

17. For a discussion of the value of the creeds and councils in the church, see P. Schaff, *The Creeds of Christendom* (3 vols.; New York and London: Harper Brothers, 1919), 1.8–9. See also J. H. Leith, ed., *Creeds of the Churches* (Atlanta: John Knox, 1982), 1–11.

18. For a popular treatment see J. I. Packer, "Sola Fide: The Reformed Doctrine of Justification," in *Sola Deo Gloria* (ed. R. C. Sproul; Phillipsburg: Presbyterian and Reformed, 1976), 11–25.

19. For a history of these creeds see Schaff, *Creeds of Christendom*, vol. 3.

20. *The Book of Mormon* (1 Nephis 13:23f) refers to the Bible as a basis for truth: "The book that thou beheldest is a record of the Jews, which contains the covenant of the Lord, which he hath made unto the house of Israel." Also, in the Forward to *Aid to Biblical Understanding* (New York: Watchtower Bible and

Tract Society, 1971), a Jehovah's Witness publication, the authors state, "The principal authority on which all the articles are based is the Bible itself" (p. 5).

21. For a helpful discussion of private judgment, see P. Toon, *The Right of Private Judgment: The Study and Interpretation of Scripture in Today's Church* (Portland: Western Conservative Baptist Seminary, 1975).

22. We use the term "cognitive rest" following Frame: "Coming to cognitive rest about Christianity is achieving a 'godly sense of satisfaction' with the message of Scripture. . . . Whether the feeling is intense or not, however, every Christian comes to the point where he can say, 'Yes, this is for me, I can live with this.'" Frame, *Knowledge of God*, 153. For a fuller discussion of Frame's doctrine of "cognitive rest" from a corporate existential perspective see Frame, *Knowledge of God*, 158–60.

23. For an historical description of *Sola Scriptura* see G. Ebeling, *The Word of God and Tradition* (Philadelphia: Fortress, 1968), 102–47; J. L. Gonzáles, *A History of Christian Thought* (3 vols.; Nashville: Abingdon, 1975), 3.41–55; H. Oberman, *The Harvest of Medieval Theology* (Grand Rapids: Eerdmans, 1967), 361–412. For a related discussion of the sufficiency of Scripture see Berkouwer, *Holy Scripture*, 299–326 and N. Weeks, *The Sufficiency of Scripture* (Carlisle: Banner of Truth, 1988), 3–7.

24. See R. E. Brown, *Biblical Exegesis and Church Doctrine* (New York: Paulist, 1985), 40–5.

25. "The purest churches under heaven are subject both to mixture and error." *Westminster Confession of Faith*, 27.5.

26. For a helpful discussion of the Reformers' attitude toward Scripture and tradition, see A. E. McGrath, "The Theological Method of the Reformers," in *The History of Christian Theology* (ed. P. Avis; Grand Rapids: Eerdmans, 1986) vol. 1, *The Science of Theology*, 131–41.

27. See McGrath, *The Science of Theology*, 121–2.

28. See especially Calvin, *Institutes*, 2.2. For a detailed comparison of Calvin and Augustine see B. B. Warfield, *Calvin and Augustine* (Philadelphia: Presbyterian and Reformed, 1971).

29. As Parker says, "One of the most striking improvements in the editions since 1543 has been the vastly increased reference to the Church fathers. . . . Ambrose, Cyprian, Theodoret, Jerome, Leo, Gregory I, and Bernard of Clairvaux all figure largely, but with Augustine far and away taking the leading place." T. H. L. Parker, *John Calvin: a Biography* (Philadelphia: Westminster, 1975), 106, 132.

30. In his own words, "We willingly embrace and reverence as holy the early councils, such as those of Nicea, Constantinople, Ephesus I, Chalcedon, and the like, which were concerned with refuting errors—in so far as they relate to the teachings of faith." Calvin, *Institutes*, 4.9.8.

31. Although the modern Biblical Theology movement may be traced to Johann Gabler's address at Altdorf in 1787, its development was heavily influenced by

Hegelian philosophy. See W. Kümmel, *The New Testament: The History of the Investigation of Its Problems* (tr. S. Gilmour and H. Kee; New York: Abingdon, 1972), 98, 120, 132; E. P. Clowney, *Preaching and Biblical Theology* (Grand Rapids: Eerdmans, 1961), 11; *Interpreter's Dictionary of the Bible* s.v. "Biblical Criticism, History of."

32. As Hegel said, "The spirit and the course of its development are the true substance of history." G. W. F. Hegel, *Lectures of the Philosophical of World History* (tr. H. B. Nisbet; London: New York, 1975), 44.

33. Scholars from this school included J. J. Beck (1804–1878) and E. W. Hengstenberg (1802–1869). J. Bengel (1687–1752) is usually recognized as the father of the movement.

34. G. E. Ladd, *A Theology of the New Testament* (Grand Rapids: Eerdmans, 1974), 15-6.

35. Kittle's *Theological Dictionary of the New Testament* was the crowning achievement. J. Barton, *Reading the Old Testament* (Philadelphia: Westminster, 1984), 208–9.

36. Childs, *Biblical Theology in Crisis*, 62.

37. Childs, *Biblical Theology in Crisis*, 21. See the representative works in *Essays on Old Testament Interpretation* (ed. C. Westermann; London: SCM, 1963).

38. Note the selective works of these Biblical theologians: G. von Rad, *Old Testament Theology* (tr. D. M. G. Stalker; 2 vols.; New York: Harper and Row, 1962 [1957]) and *God at Work in Israel* (tr. J. Marks; Nashville: Abingdon, 1980); O. Cullmann, *Christ and Time: the Primitive Christian Conception of Time and History* (tr. F. Filson; Philadelphia: Westminster, 1950) *Salvation in History* (tr. S. Sowers; New York: Harper and Row, 1967); O. Piper, *God in History* (New York: Macmillin, 1939) and *New Testament Interpretation of History* (Princeton: Theological Book Agency, 1963); F. Filson, *One Lord, One Faith* (Philadelphia: Westminster, 1943), *Jesus Christ: The Risen Lord* (New York: Abingdon, 1956) and *A New Testament History* (Philadelphia: Westminster, 1964); J. W. Bowman, *Prophetic Realism and the Gospel: A Preface to Biblical Theology* (Philadelphia: Westminster, 1955) and *Which Jesus?* (Philadelphia: Westminster, 1970); G. E. Wright, *The Book of the Acts of God with R. Fuller* (Garden City: Doubleday, 1960), *God Who Acts: Biblical Theology as Recital* (Chicago: Regnery, 1952), and *The Rule of God: Essays in Biblical Theology* (Garden City: Doubleday, 1960). Late in life, Wright altered his position and moved toward Eichrodt's view. See G. E. Wright, *The Old Testament and Theology* (New York: Harper and Row, 1969), 61–7.

39. The structuring categories of systematic theology were shaped by Aristotelian philosophy largely through the influence of Thomas Aquinas' *Summa Theologica.* For a popular treatment see W. T. Jones, *The Medieval Mind* (2d ed.; New York: Harcourt, Brace, Jovanovich, 1969), 211–2.

40. D. M. Beegle, *Moses the Servant of Yahweh* (Grand Rapids: Eerdmans, 1972), 69. As Barr summarizes the Biblical theological viewpoint, "The dynamic ap-

proach of the Hebrews to reality is expressed in their interest in history. Their God is characteristically one who acts in history, and these actions in history are the core of the religious tradition of Israel." J. Barr, *Semantics of Biblical Language* (London: Oxford University, 1961), 11.

41. See J. Barr, "Revelation through History in the Old Testament and Modern Theology," *The Princeton Seminary Bulletin* 56 (1963), 4–14. L. Gilkey, "Cosmology, Ontology, and The Travail of Biblical Language," *Journal of Religion* 41 (1961), 194–205.

42. Gilkey, "Cosmology, Ontology," 199.

43. Barr, *Semantics of Biblical Language*, 263–96.

44. Barr, *Semantics of Biblical Language*, 202–62. See G. Hasel for a brief summary of the critical Biblical Theology movement, *Evangelical Dictionary of Theology* (ed. W. Elwell; Grand Rapids: Baker, 1984) s.v. "Biblical Theology Movement."

45. G. Vos, *Biblical Theology: Old and New Testaments* (Grand Rapids: Eerdmans, 1948). For the most complete bibliography of the works of Vos, see "A Bibliography of the Writings of Geerhardus Vos (1862–1949)," compiled by J. T. Dennison, Jr., *Westminster Theological Journal* 38 (1976), 350–67.

46. See Vos, *Biblical Theology*, 17–8.

47. For a good summary of Gabler's views, see H. Boers, *What is New Testament Theology?* (Philadelphia: Fortress, 1979), 23–38.

48. According to Vos, "Gabler correctly perceived that the specific difference of Biblical Theology lies in its historical principle of treatment." Vos, *Biblical Theology*, 9. This emphasis upon the historical element is foundational to his own description of Biblical Theology as "the study of the actual self-disclosures of God in time and space which lie back of even the first committal to writing of any Biblical document, and which for a long time continued to run alongside of the inscripturation of revealed material" (p. 5). He thus defines Biblical Theology as "that branch of Exegetical Theology which deals with the process of the self-revelation of God deposited in the Bible" (p. 5); see also pp. 3–11; G. Vos, *Redemptive History and Biblical Interpretation* (Phillipsburg, N.J.: Presbyterian and Reformed, 1980), 15.

49. Vos, *Biblical Theology*, 15–6.

50. Hasel has put it boldly: "The Biblical theologian draws his categories, themes, motifs, and concepts from the Biblical text itself." Hasel, *Old Testament Theology*, 101–3, 130. See also J. Murray, "Systematic Theology II," *Westminster Theological Journal* 26 (1963), 43 and R. B. Gaffin, "Systematic Theology and Biblical Theology," *Westminster Theological Journal* 38 (1975–1976), 294.

51. Ladd, *A Theology of the New Testament*, 25.

52. For example, Clowney, *Preaching and Biblical Theology*, 16 and Gaffin, "Systematic Theology and Biblical Theology," 294–5.

53. See Gaffin, "Systematic Theology and Biblical Theology," 293–4.

54. See Barr, "Revelation through History in the Old Testament and in Modern Theology," 6–7.

55. Kline, *Structure of Biblical Authority*, 47.

56. Vos states, "There is no difference in that one would be more closely bound to the Scriptures than the other. In this they are wholly alike. Nor does the difference lie in this, that one transforms the Biblical material, whereas the other would leave it unmodified. Both equally make the truth deposited in the Bible undergo a transformation: but the difference arises from the fact that the principles by which the transformation is effected differ. In Biblical Theology the principle is one of historical; in Systematic Theology it is one of logical construction." Vos, *Biblical Theology*, 15–6.

57. See Murray, "Systematic Theology II," 43–4 n.23.

58. For example, Robertson develops the seven periods of redemption history based upon the covenants of Scripture. See O. P. Robertson, *The Christ of the Covenants* (Grand Rapids: Baker, 1980), 62–3.

59. See W. C. Kaiser, *Toward an Old Testament Theology* (Grand Rapids: Zondervan, 1978), 41–54; W. A. VanGemeren, *The Progress of Redemption* (Grand Rapids: Zondervan, 1988), 33.

60. Murray argued that "The Bible is itself conscious of the distinct periods into which the history of revelation falls. Although there could be more detailed subdivision within certain periods . . . ." Murray, "Systematic Theology II," 43. Yet, the variances among different Biblical Theologians suggest that divisions may not be so obvious.

61. See Frame, *Knowledge of God*, 251–4.

62. "Thus the three forms of theology—exegetical, biblical, systematic—are mutually dependent and correlative; they involve one another. They are 'perspectives' on theology, not independent disciplines." Frame, *Knowledge of God*, 213.

Chapter Four

1. Many aspects of this chapter appeared in preliminary form in R. L. Pratt, Jr., "Pictures, Windows, and Mirrors in Old Testament Exegesis," *Westminster Theological Journal* 45 (1983), 156–67. Similar approaches may be found in L. Ryken, *Words of Delight: A Literary Introduction to the Bible* (Grand Rapids: Baker, 1987), 12; M. Sternberg, *The Poetics of Biblical Narrative* (Bloomington: Indiana University, 1985), 1–57.

2. I am borrowing loosely from the terminology of transformational grammarians. See, for instance, N. Chomskey, *Aspects of the Theory of Syntax* (Cambridge: Harvard University, 1965 and 1970). See also E. A. Nida and C. R. Taber, *The Theory and Practice of Translation* (Leiden: E. J. Brill, 1969), 53–4.

3. For a fuller treatment of this passage see chapter 8.

4. See, for example, H. Robinson, *Biblical Preaching: The Development and Delivery of Expository Messages* (Grand Rapids: Baker, 1980), 66–70. See also J. E.

Adams, *Preaching With Purpose: A Comprehensive Textbook on Biblical Preaching* (Phillipsburg, N.J.: Presbyterian and Reformed, 1982), 27–8; Kaiser, *Exegetical Theology*, 150–6.

5. See R. A. Carlson, *David, the Chosen King* (tr. E. J. Sharpe and S. Rudman; Stockholm: Almquist and Wiksell, 1964), 7, 20–34. See also H. W. Hertzberg, *1 and 2 Samuel* (tr. J. S. Benden; *Old Testament Library*; Philadelphia: Westminster, 1964), 8–9, 295–7, 375–9.

6. The writer of Samuel presents the initial troubles of the Davidic kingdom in 2 Samuel 9:1–12:31 as an adumbration of the more significant troubles recorded in 2 Samuel 13–20. The placement of Nathan's oracle (2 Samuel 12:1–25) between the initial troubles and the further troubles in David's house and kingdom (2 Samuel 13–20) demonstrate the Deuteronomistic view that David himself had brought these troubles on his house. See Carlson, *David, the Chosen King*, 162.

7. As both Williamson and Japhet have pointed out, the Chronicler in his "idealization" of David is not unaware of shortcomings that remain in his account. See S. Japhet, "The Ideology of the Book of Chronicles and its Place in Biblical Thought," [Hebrew] (unpublished dissertation, The Hebrew University, 1973), 468–72; H. G. M. Williamson, "Eschatology in Chronicles," *Tyndale Bulletin* 28 (1977), 132–3; Pratt, "Royal Prayer," 94–9.

8. Beyond this, the Chronicler also idealized David by adding information not in Samuel. In one case, he drew a sharp contrast between David and Saul (1 Chronicles 10:13-14); in another he expounded on the spread of David's fame (1 Chronicles 14:17). From the Chronicler's point of view, David exemplified ideal kingship for his post-exilic audience.

9. For example, see *The Gallican Confession*, 39 (Exodus 18:20–21); *The Belgic Confession*, 28 (Daniel 3:17–18; 6:8–10); *The First Scotch Confession*, 14 (1 Samuel 15:22); the *Westminster Confession of Faith* 26.6 (Ezra 10:3).

10. Hodge, *Systematic Theology*, 3.144 and Berkhof, *Systematic Theology*, 169.

11. Kaiser denounces proof-texting as "reprehensible" and calls for a swift end to it. See Kaiser, *Exegetical Theology*, 82.

12. Frame, *Knowledge of God*, 197.

13. Clowney criticizes the abuses of the exemplary approach by arguing that the usual stress on David's faith and God's faithfulness is inadequate. See Clowney, *Preaching and Biblical Theology*, 82–4. See also Greidanus' negative evaluation that "one hardly needs the Bible for exemplary sermons. Ironically, the exemplary preacher . . . motivated by the search for analogy (relevance) . . . loses precisely that distinctiveness which occasioned the appearance in the Bible of the man in the text." S. Greidanus, *Sola Scriptura: Problems and Principles in Preaching Historical Texts* (Toronto: Wedge, 1970), 70. See also S. Greidanus, *The Modern Preacher and the Ancient Text* (Grand Rapids: Eerdmans, 1989), 114–8.

14. See C. Swindoll, *Hand Me Another Brick* (Waco: Word, 1981) and Kaiser, *Exegetical Theology*, 206–8. Interestingly enough, Kaiser describes Nehemiah 6 as

a study in godly leadership, while Robinson implies that the writer of Nehemiah did not intend for his book to be used that way. See Kaiser, *Exegetical Theology*, 207–10.

15. See H. G. M. Williamson, *Ezra, Nehemiah* (*Word Biblical Commentary* 16; Waco: Word, 1985), 402.

16. In discussing how the preacher is to select "the preaching portion" of Scripture, Adams gives a helpful description of the starting place: "'Do I begin with the preaching portion or the congregation?' . . . you must begin with both, but with an emphasis on the congregation." Adams, *Preaching With Purpose*, 21. Robinson gives a less balanced evaluation of exemplary preaching by describing "case studies in morals, virtues, or spiritual struggles" as "harmful" and "outside the original purpose of the Biblical writer." H. Robinson, "Homiletics and Hermeneutics," in *Hermeneutics, Inerrancy, and the Bible* (eds. E. Radmacher and R. Preus; Grand Rapids: Zondervan, 1985), 809.

17. C. H. Spurgeon, *The Treasury of Charles H. Spurgeon* (London: Revell, 1955), 144.

18. J. Buszko, ed., *Auschwitz: Nazi Extermination Camp* (2d ed.; Warsaw: Interpress Publishers, 1985).

19. "We affirm that Scripture in its entirety is inerrant . . . .We deny that Biblical infallibility and inerrancy are limited to spiritual, religious, or redemptive themes, exclusive of assertions in the fields of history and science." *The Chicago Statement on Biblical Inerrancy*, Article 12.

20. See the articles by D. J. Moo, R. H. Gundry and N. L. Geisler, *Journal of the Evangelical Theological Society* 26 (1983), 31–115.

21. See G. L. Archer, *Encyclopedia of Bible Difficulties* (Grand Rapids: Zondervan, 1982), 15–44 and Merrill, *Kingdom of Priests*, 17–8.

22. For example, Archer writes, "In dealing with Bible problems of any kind . . . be fully persuaded in your own mind that an adequate explanation exists, even though you have not yet found it." Archer, *Encyclopedia*, 15.

23. "We affirm that the text of Scripture is to be interpreted by grammatico-historical exegesis, taking account of its literary forms and devices, and that Scripture is to interpret Scripture." See the *The Chicago Statement on Bible Inerrancy* Article 18 (emphasis mine).

24. Many interpreters have discussed developments in genre theory from Herman Gunkel's early work to the present day. See G. M. Tucker, *Form Criticism of the Old Testament* (Guides to Biblical Scholarship; Philadelphia: Fortress, 1971); R. Knierim, "Old Testament Form Criticism Reconsidered," *Interpretation* 27 (1973), 435–68; G. W. Coats, *Genesis: with an Introduction to Narrative Literature* (*The Forms of Old Testament Literature* 1; Grand Rapids: Eerdmans, 1983), 3–10. More recently, T. Longman, "Form Criticism, Recent Developments in Genre Theory, and the Evangelical," *Westminster Theological Journal* 47 (1985), 46–67; L. Coppes, "The Contribution of Herman Gunkel to Old Testament Historical Research," in *The Law and the Prophets* (ed. J. Skilton; Phillipsburg:

Presbyterian and Reformed, 1974), 174–94; G. W. Coats, ed., *Saga, Legend, Tale, Novella, Fable: Forms in Old Testament Literature* (*Journal for the Study of the Old Testament Supplement Series* 35; Sheffield: Journal for the Study of the Old Testament Press, 1985).

25. For helpful discussions of some of the uncertainties involved in these matters see the various discussions in Coats, *Saga, Legend, Tale, Novella, Fable.*

26. Westermann argues that the *wyhy* in Gen. 11:1 is formulaic "like our 'once upon a time,' which introduces the situation at the beginning of the tale." But he offers little support for this view. See Westermann, *Genesis 1–11* (tr. J. J. Scullion; Minneapolis: Augsburg, 1984), 542.

27. He continues, "Or if a certain king is said to have reigned twenty-two years (cf. 1 Kings 14:20), we must not impose upon such a statement the necessity of his having reigned precisely twenty-two years in terms of twenty-two times three hundred and sixty-five days. . . . We need not doubt that it was this distinction between the demands of pedantic precision, on the one hand, and adequate statement, that is, statements adequate to the situation and the intent, on the other, that Calvin had in mind when he said that 'the apostles were not so punctilious as not to accommodate themselves to the unlearned.'" Murray, *Collected Writings*, 4.174–5 (emphasis mine). Young comments similarly that infallibility "does not insist that the writers, whenever they happen to record the same event, must be in actual verbal agreement with one another. It does not necessarily require that events be narrated in the same order. Sometimes, for reasons of emphasis, where the order is not intended to be chronological, that order may vary in differing accounts of the same events." E. J. Young, *Thy Word is Truth* (Grand Rapids: Eerdmans, 1957), 139.

28. *The Chicago Statement on Biblical Inerrancy,* Article 13.

29. For helpful discussions of these matters, see D. W. Bebbington, *Patterns in History* (Downers Grove: Inter-Varsity, 1979), 5; G. J. Renier, *History: Its Purpose and Method* (New York: Harper and Row, 1965), 249–55; H. H. Rienstra, "History, Objectivity, and the Christian Scholar," in *History and Historical Understanding* (Grand Rapids: Eerdmans, 1984), 69–82.

30. W. S. LaSor, A. Hubbard, and F. W. Bush, *Old Testament Survey: The Message, Form, and Background of the Old Testament* (Grand Rapids: Eerdmans, 1982), 191. As Merrill comments, "Selectivity is eminently discernible in the Old Testament account of Israel's history because the author (and authors) had particular objectives in mind. The real thrust of the Old Testament is theological." Merrill, *Kingdom of Priests*, 17.

31. See Young, *Introduction*; G. L. Archer, *A Survey of Old Testament Introduction* (Moody: Chicago, 1964); Harrison, *Introduction to the Old Testament.*

32. For example, see Woudstra, *Joshua* 66–76; H. C. Leupold, *Exposition of Genesis* (Grand Rapids: Baker, 1942), 1.381–93; C. F. Keil and F. Delitzsch, *Commentary on the Old Testament: Joshua, Judges, Ruth, 1 and 2 Samuel* (Grand Rapids: Eerdmans, 1949), 249–66.

33. See the discussion of Biblical Theology in chapter 3.

34. Greidanus, *Modern Preacher*, 50.

35. J. Skinner, *A Critical and Exegetical Commentary on Genesis* (*International Critical Commentary*; Edinburgh: T. and T. Clark, 1910), 248.

36. Skinner, *Genesis*, 250.

37. G. von Rad, *Genesis: A Commentary* (*Old Testament Library*; Philadelphia: Westminster, 1972), 168.

38. von Rad, *Genesis*, 169.

39. C. F. Keil and F. Delitzsch, *Commentary on the Old Testament: The Pentateuch* (Grand Rapids: Eerdmans, 1949), 197.

40. Keil and Delitzsch, *Pentateuch*, 197.

41. D. Kidner, *Genesis* (*Tyndale Old Testament Commentaries*; Downers Grove: Inter-Varsity, 1967), 117.

42. Kidner, *Genesis*, 116.

43. For the distinction between intrinsic and extrinsic inquiry see R. Wellek and A. Warren, *Theory of Literature* (rev. ed.; New York: Harcourt, Brace, and World, 1962), 73–4, 139–41.

44. For a fuller discussion of the interpretative techniques applied to this narrative see chapters 5–12.

45. The early portions of the narrative divide into four sections, each introduced by the marker "and it came about" (*wyhy*). Verse 10 opens the story in this manner. The word occurs again in v. 11, and again in v. 14. The last appearance (*wyhy lw*) is found in v. 16b. Verses 16b-17 are best understood as a contrast between the prosperity of Abram and the plagues on Pharaoh. The next sequence begins with v. 18. Without a doubt, v. 20 is to be closely associated with vv. 18–19, but the resumption of consecution after lengthy simultaneity (*wyṣw*) gives it some degree of independence.

46. For a discussion of the date and circumstances of Genesis see chapter 12.

47. As Ross put it recently, "Moses has carefully worded the account of Abram's sojourn in, and deliverance from, Egypt with the greater sojourn and deliverance in mind. The effect was the demonstration that the great deliverance out of bondage by the plagues that Israel experienced had previously been accomplished in the life of the ancestor of the nation." A. P. Ross, *Creation and Blessing* (Grand Rapids: Baker, 1988), 273–4. Before him, Cassuto argued similarly. See U. Cassuto, *A Commentary on the Book of Genesis* (tr. I. Abraham; 2 vols.; Jerusalem: Magnes, 1984 [1949]), 2.336. See also M. Henry, *Commentary on the Whole Bible* (6 vols.; New York: Revell, n.d.), 1.89. Most commentaries do not note the connection between Genesis 12:10–20 and the events of the Israelite nation. Westermann's reliance on form critical reconstruction leads him to conclude that "there is certainly no direct link" between this story and the exodus

events. C. Westermann, *Genesis 12–36* (tr. J. J. Scullion; Minneapolis: Augsburg, 1985), 166.

48. For some interesting examples of literary sensitivity in exegesis before the Reformation see J. Kugel, *The Idea of Biblical Poetry* (New Haven: Yale University, 1981), 135–70.

49. In his *Institutes* and commentaries Calvin acknowledges that Biblical writers used figures of speech. For example, synecdoche (Institutes 1.15.4 and 2.8.10; Matthew 9:2), hyperbole (1 Corinthians 13:1), and metaphor (Exodus 15:17). He comments on the style of Scripture, acknowledging that some portions are elegant and others are unrefined (Institutes 1.8.2). He distinguishes between the writing style of the synoptics and the gospel of John (Institutes 1.8.11). He differentiates between the preface and laws of Exodus 20 (Exodus 20:1). Calvin notices the change of style from prose to poetry (Micah 1:2).

50. For a brief history see Frei, *Eclipse of Biblical Narrative*, 1–16.

51. For example, see Terry, *Biblical Hermeneutics*, 144–87 and Mickelsen, *Interpreting the Bible*, 179–230. Also note E. W. Bullinger, *Figures of Speech Used in the Bible* (Grand Rapids: Baker, 1968 [1898]).

52. For a summary of these developments see the survey in Barton, *Reading the Old Testament*, 20–154; Longman, *Literary Approaches*, 13–45; Greidanus, *Modern Preacher*, 48–79.

53. For a basic introduction to source criticism see N. Habel, *Literary Criticism of the Old Testament* (Guides to Biblical Scholarship; Philadelphia: Fortress, 1971).

54. For a basic introduction to form criticism see Tucker, *Form Criticism of the Old Testament.*

55. For a basic introduction to redaction criticism see N. Perrin, *What is Redaction Criticism?* (Guides to Biblical Scholarship; Philadelphia: Fortress, 1969).

56. For helpful evangelical evaluations of these methods see C. E. Armerding, *The Old Testament and Criticism* (Grand Rapids: Eerdmans, 1983), 21–66; Greidanus, *Modern Preacher*, 51–7.

57. For a fuller discussion see chapter 10.

58. James Muilenburg is generally credited with initiating rhetorical criticism with his presidential address to the Society of Biblical Literature in 1968. See J. Muilenburg, "A Study in Hebrew Rhetoric: Repetition and Style," *Journal of Biblical Literature* 88 (1969), 1–18. For recent discussions and examples of rhetorical criticism in Biblical studies, see D. J. A. Clines, D. G. Gunn, and A. J. Houser, eds., *Art and Meaning: Rhetoric in Biblical Literature* (*Journal for the Study of the Old Testament Supplement Series* 19; Sheffield: Journal for the Study of the Old Testament Press, 1982). See also E. P. J. Corbett, *Rhetorical Analyses of Literary Works* (London: Oxford University, 1969).

59. D. Patte, *What is Structural Exegesis?* (Philadelphia: Fortress, 1988).

60. For helpful discussions of the background of these, see Barton, *Reading the Old Testament*, 104–37 and Longman, *Literary Approaches*, 27–35.

61. For a basic introduction to canonical criticism see Barton, *Reading the Old Testament*, 140–57. For further discussions see Childs, *Biblical Theology in Crisis and Introduction to the Old Testament*, 46–83; J. A. Sanders, *Torah and Canon* (Philadelphia: Westminster, 1972).

Chapter Five

1. See L. Jacobs, *Jewish Biblical Exegesis* (New York: Behrman House, 1973), 8–18. Farrar traces the history of *multiplex intelligentia* to Rabbi Aqiba. See Farrar, *History of Interpretation*, 294–6.

2. R. Williamson, *Philo and the Epistle to the Hebrews* (Leiden: E. J. Brill, 1970), 519–38. See also H. A. Wolfson, *Philo* (2 vols.; Cambridge: Harvard University, 1962), esp. 1. 55–138.

3. See R. P. C. Hanson, "Biblical Exegesis in the Early Church," in *The Cambridge History of the Bible* (eds. P. R. Ackroyd and C. F. Evans; 3 vols.; Cambridge: Cambridge University, 1970), 1.412–53. See Farrar, *History of Interpretation*, 294.

4. For an extensive treatment of the developments from the early to the medieval church see H. De Lubac, *Exégèse Médiévale* (3 vols.; Paris: Aubier, 1961), 1.1–118. See also Farrar, *History of Interpretation*, 245–303; W. S. LaSor, "The Sensus Plenior and Biblical Interpretation," in *A Guide to Contemporary Hermeneutics* (ed. D. McKim; Grand Rapids: Eerdmans, 1986), 54–6.

5. See Steinmetz, "The Superiority of Precritical Exegesis," 68–9.

6. Augustine, *On Christian Doctrine*, 3.27 in *The Nicene and Post-Nicene Fathers* (ed. P. Schaff and tr. J. F. Shaw; 10 vols.; Grand Rapids: Eerdmans, 1956), 2.567.

7. A number of Roman Catholic and Protestant interpreters today have reaffirmed the traditional view of polyvalency on the basis of divine inspiration. See Steinmetz, "The Superiority of Precritical Exegesis," 76–7. See also R. E. Brown, *The Critical Meaning of the Bible* (New York: Paulist, 1981), 23–44. For helpful discussions of the concept of *sensus plenior* and its development see R. E. Brown, "The History and Development of the Theory of a Sensus Plenior," *Catholic Biblical Quarterly* 15 (1953), 141-62.

8. Schleiermacher, *Hermeneutik*, 31; *Hermeneutics: the Handwritten Manuscripts*, 42.

9. Schleiermacher divided the hermeneutical process into two basic activities: "the historical [grammatical] and divinatory [psychological], objective and subjective reconstruction of a given statement." Schleiermacher, *Hermeneutik*, 83. See also Schleiermacher, *Hermeneutics: the Handwritten Manuscripts*, 111. Grammatical investigation involved the more objective task of examining actual linguistic expressions of a text. The psychological investigation entailed a more subjective process of entering into the mental processes of the writer as he or she wrote.

10. New critics such as Cleanth Brooks, I. A. Richards, Robert Penn Warren, and F. R. Leavis emphasized the self-sufficiency of the literary work. In their approach the text becomes a "verbal icon" with the result that author-centered approaches, following Schleiermacher, are reduced to relative unimportance. See also Longman, *Literary Approaches*, 25–37. Barton, *Reading the Old Testament*, 140–56. For a helpful discussion of the character of New Criticism see D. H. Hesla, "Religion and Literature: the Second Stage," *Journal of the American Academy of Religion* 46 (1978), 2, 181–92.

11. "It is likely that the signified owes as much to the meaning system in the mind of the perceiver as it does to the signifier itself." Wittig, "A Theory of Multiple Meanings," *Semeia* 9 (1977), 89, also 90–1.

12. S. Wittig, in "A Theory of Multiple Meanings," 88.

13. See W. Iser, *The Act of Reading: A Theory of Aesthetic Response* (Baltimore and London: Johns Hopkins, 1978), esp. 20–52, 107–34. See also the discussion of subjectivism in hermeneutics in chapter 1.

14. See Farrar, *History of Interpretation*, 294–9; Ramm, *Protestant Biblical Interpretation*, 38–45; Grant and Tracy, *A Short History*, 73–99. For a related discussion, see G. W. Bromiley, "The Church Fathers and Holy Scripture," in *Scripture and Truth* (eds. D. A. Carson and J. D. Woodbridge; Grand Rapids: Zondervan, 1983), 199–220.

15. J. Calvin, *The Epistles of Paul the Apostle to the Galatians, Ephesians, Philippians and Colossians* (tr. T. H. L. Parker; Grand Rapids: Eerdmans, 1965), 84-5.

16. See Ernesti, *Elementary Principles*, 21–9; Terry, *Biblical Hermeneutics*, 101–8, esp. 108; Kaiser, *Exegetical Theology*, 87–8.

17. Ames, *Marrow of Theology*, 88.

18. *Westminster Confession of Faith* 1.9.

19. See J. Macpherson, *The Westminster Confession of Faith* (Edinburgh: T. and T. Clark, 1881, 1951), 41.

20. See Berkhof, *Principles of Biblical Interpretation*, 114; Mickelsen, *Interpreting the Bible*, 5; Virkler, *Hermeneutics*, 45; Ramm, *Protestant Biblical Interpretation*, 1237.

21. See Hirsch, *Validity in Interpretation*, 5–6.

22. See Kaiser, *Exegetical Theology*, 113; Kaiser, "Legitimate Hermeneutics," 112.

23. W. C. Kaiser, "A Response to Author's Intention and Biblical Interpretation" in *Hermeneutics, Inerrancy, and the Bible* (eds. E. D. Radmacher and R. D. Preus; Grand Rapids: Zondervan, 1985), 441.

24. *Chicago Statement on Biblical Hermeneutics*, Article 7.

25. For example, Poythress has recently argued that the meaning of a passage is manifold as it is viewed from the perspectives of speaker, discourse, and audi-

ence. V. S. Poythress, "Analyzing a Biblical Text: Some Important Linguistic Distinctions," *Scottish Journal of Theology* 32 (1979), 113–30; V. S. Poythress, "Analyzing a Biblical Text: What Are We After?" *Scottish Journal of Theology* 32 (1979), 324–6. He argues elsewhere that divine authorship of Scripture implies that the "meaning" of a passage often goes well beyond the intentions of the human writer. For example, commenting on Malachi 3:8–12 he writes, "We may say that . . . God intends us to apply Malachi to our proportional giving. But if we say that God intends(!) each valid application of Malachi, then in an ordinary sense each valid application is part of God's meaning (=intention), even if it was not immediately in the view of the human author of Malachi. This seems to break down the idea that there is an absolute, pure equation between divine intention and human author's meaning." V. S. Poythress, "Divine Meaning of Scripture," *Westminster Theological Journal* 48 (1986), 246-7. In discussing the relationship between meaning and application Frame asserts that, "There is, in fact, no important distinction to be made at all between meaning and application, and so I shall use them interchangeably." See Frame, *Knowledge of God*, 82–3. I agree substantially with these observations on a conceptual level. My hesitation has to do with the choice of terms.

26. Frame, *Knowledge of God*, 95–6. See also Poythress, "Divine Meaning of Scripture," 241–79.

27. See Kaiser, *Exegetical Theology*, 45–6.

28. I am using the concept of full value similar to the Protestant understanding of *sensus plenior*. For a discussion of the concept of *sensus plenior* in Roman Catholic thought, see R. E. Brown, *The Sensus Plenior of Sacred Scripture* (Baltimore: St. Mary's University, 1955) and Brown, in "The History and Development of the Theory of a Sensus Plenior", 141–62. A number of Protestant interpreters, as well, have discussed the implications of *sensus plenior* for contemporary hermeneutics. For example, see LaSor, "The Sensus Plenior and Biblical Interpretation", 260–77; Poythress, "Divine Meaning of Scripture", 241–79; D. J. Moo, "The Problem of Sensus Plenior," in *Hermeneutics, Authority, and Canon* (eds. D. A. Carson and J. D. Woodbridge; Grand Rapids: Zondervan, 1986), 179–211; B. K. Waltke, "A Canonical Process Approach to the Psalms," in *Tradition and Testament: Essays in Honor of Charles Lee Feinberg* (eds. J. S. Feinberg and P. D. Feinberg; Chicago: Moody, 1981), 3–18. My own view of a text's full value is similar to that of Poythress and Waltke. See Kaiser's helpful bibliography as cited in Virkler, *Hermeneutics*, 249–50.

29. Ramm, *Protestant Biblical Interpretation*, 1–4. See also Poythress, "Divine Meaning of Scripture," 227–9; J. R. McQuilkin, *Understanding and Applying the Bible* (Chicago: Moody, 1983), 236, 255–6.

30. See Introduction, n. 32.

31. Saussure, *Course*, 9, 13.

32. For extensive discussions of the three controls for meaning, see Longman, *Literary Approaches*, 63–71; Wellek and Warren, *Theory of Literature*, 73–135; L. Ryken, *Windows to the World: Literature in Christian Perspective* (Grand Rap-

ids and Dallas: Zondervan, Probe Ministries International, 1985), esp. 83–130; Poythress, "Analyzing a Biblical Text: Some Important Linguistic Distinctions", 120–9; D. Patte, "Speech Act Theory and Biblical Exegesis," *Semeia* 41 (1988), 88–92; Barton, *Reading the Old Testament*, 198–204. Also see the various viewpoints represented in *On Literary Intention* (ed. D. Newton-De Molina; Edinburgh: Edinburgh University, 1976).

33. See Hirsch, *Validity in Interpretation*, 1–23; Kaiser, *Exegetical Theology*, 17–33; Barton, *Reading the Old Testament*, 147–51; W. K. Wimsatt and Beardsley, "The Intentional Fallacy," in *The Verbal Icon: Studies in the Meaning of Poetry* (University of Kentucky, 1954).

34. For example see M. Weiss, *The Bible from Within: The Method of Total Interpretation* (Jerusalem: Magnes, 1984), 47–73 and Ryken, *Words of Delight* 20, 81–6. New Critics are often characterized as being entirely unconcerned with authorial intentions. See Barton, *Reading the Old Testament*, 154 and Longman, *Literary Approaches*, 25–7. New Critics emphasized the text over psychological and biographical methods, but they did not reject all concern for authorial intentions. Upon closer examination it becomes plain that New Critics did not ignore these considerations. See D. Brown, "Barton, Brooks and Childs: A Comparison of the New Criticism and Canonical Criticism," (unpublished Th.M. thesis: Reformed Theological Seminary, Jackson; 1989). Only rarely does the typical literary distinction between "narrator" and "writer" apply to OT narratives. For discussions of the distinctions between writer and narrator see Longman, *Literary Approaches*, 83–7 and Sternberg, *Poetics*, 32-5, 58–85.

35. See Poythress, "Analyzing a Biblical Text," 125. Even though few people have argued for an exclusively reader-oriented approach, a number of scholars have argued for the primacy of the reader in interpretation. For related discussions see E. V. McKnight, *The Bible and the Reader: An Introduction to Literary Criticism* (Philadelphia: Fortress, 1985); Thiselton, "Reader-Response Hermeneutics, Action Models, and the Parables of Jesus," in *Responsibility of Hermeneutics*, 79–113; Fowler, "Who is 'the Reader' in Reader Response Criticism?," 5–21; K. Dauber, "The Bible as Literature: Reading Like the Rabbis," *Semeia* 31 (1985), 27–45; Longman, *Literary Approaches*, 38–45; Iser, *The Act of Reading*, 20–7.

36. For a helpful discussion see Ryken, *Windows*, 83–130.

37. Saussure focused especially on associative (paradigmatic) and syntagmatic relations. He argued, "The syntagmatic relation (*le rapport syntagmatique*) is in praesentia. It is based on two or more terms that occur in effective series. Against this, the associative relation (*le rapport associatif*) unites terms in absentia in a potential mnemonic series." Saussure, *Course*, 123. Many linguists have also addressed the pragmatic (contextual, situational) angle on meaning. Even though different terms have been employed to explore this aspect of meaning, understanding meaning involves extra-linguistic factors. For example, see G. B. Caird, *The Language and Imagery of the Bible* (Philadelphia: Westminster, 1980), 49–50; J. Lyons, *Introduction to Theoretical Linguistics* (London and New York: Cambridge University, 1968), 412–4; Stubbs, *Discourse Analysis*,

1–7; Silva, *Biblical Words*, 144–7; S. Ullmann, *The Principles of Semantics* (2d ed.; Oxford: Basil Blackwell and Glasgow: Jackson, Son and Co., 1957), 61–5.

38. For a helpful discussion of meaning and use, see L. Wittgenstein, *Philosophical Investigations* (tr. G. E. M. Anscombe; 3d ed.; New York: Macmillan, 1968), 1.43, 2.2; J. Searle, *Speech Acts* (London: Cambridge University, 1970), 146–9; Frame, *Knowledge of God*, 97–8; W. P. Alston, "Meaning and Use," in *The Theory of Meaning* (ed. G. H. R. Parkinson; London: Oxford University, 1968), 141–65; J. N. Findlay and Gilbert Ryle, "Use, Usage and Meaning," in *The Theory of Meaning* (ed. G. H. R. Parkinson; London: Oxford University, 1968), 109–27; Silva, *Biblical Words*, 106 and 138–47.

39. See Lyons, *Introduction*, 413 and G. T. Polletta, ed., *Intention and Choice* (New York: Random House, 1967), 5–6.

40. For a discussion of problems associated with this distinction, see Lyons, *Introduction to Theoretical Linguistics*, 402–3, 448–50 and *The Meaning of Meaning* (eds. C. K. Ogden and J. A. Richards; New York: Harcourt, Brace and World, 1923), 187–90. See M. H. Abrams, *A Glossary of Literary Terms* (4th ed.; New York: Holt, Rinehart and Winston, 1981), 32–3. See also C. Brooks and R. P. Warren, *Modern Rhetoric* (New York: Harcourt, Brace and World, 1949), 177–9, 249–50, 263–5; Nida and Taber, *The Theory and Practice of Translation*, 59–78.

41. See Silva, *Biblical Words*, 148–51; Caird, *Language*, 95–108.

42. See Silva, *Biblical Words*, 103–8, 121–5.

43. See I. M. Copi, *Introduction to Logic* (4th ed. New York: Macmillan, 1972), 59.

44. An example offered by Bertrand Russell, as cited in Copi, *Introduction*, 60.

45. Cassuto points to the satirical force, "Even if you were to raise the summit of your ziggurat even so high, you would not be nearer to Him than when you stand upon the ground; nor did you comprehend that He who in truth dwells in heaven, if He wishes to take a closer look at your lofty tower, must needs come down." Cassuto, *Genesis*, 2.229–30 (emphasis his). See also Westermann, *Genesis 1–11*, 549–50 and von Rad, *Genesis*, 149.

46. See Silva, *Biblical Words*, 119–35 and Lyons, *Introduction*, 443–81.

47. See A. C. Thiselton, "Semantics and New Testament Interpretation," in *New Testament Interpretation* (ed. I. H. Marshall; Grand Rapids: Eerdmans, 1977), 83–9.

48. See the discussion of organic inspiration in the Introduction.

49. For example, compare the differences between 2 Kings 23:21–23 and 2 Chronicles 35:1–19; 2 Chronicles 20:1–30 and 2 Kings 3:4–27.

50. See Saussure, *Course*, 122–7. Nida makes an additional distinction between syntactic and semotactic structures. See Nida, *Language Structure and Translation*, 89–110.

51. See Silva, *Biblical Words*, 142–3 and Lyons, *Linguistics*, 452–3.

52. See Silva, *Biblical Words*, 143–4. See also the related discussion in Hirsch, *Validity in Interpretation*, 71–4.

53. See B. Malinowski, "The Problem of Meaning in Primitive Languages," in *The Meaning of Meaning* (eds. C. K. Ogden and I. A. Richards; New York: Harcourt, Brace and World, 1923), 306–7; Thiselton, "Semantics and New Testament Interpretation," 75; Silva, *Biblical Words*, 144–7. For a related discussion, see P. Watzlawick, J. B. Bavelas and D. D. Jackson, *Pragmatics of Human Communication* (New York and London: W. W. Norton and Company, 1967), 19–23 and D. S. Palermo, "Theoretical Issues in Semantic Development," in *Language Development* (ed. S. A. Kuczaj; Hillsdale: Laurence Erlbaum Associates, 1982), 1.338–42. I am using the term 'pragmatic' to refer to the "spatio-temporal situation which includes the speaker and hearer, the actions they are performing at the time and various external objects and events." See Lyons, *Introduction*, 413. Similar expressions used to convey the same idea include, "extra-linguistic," "situational," and "context of situation."

54. For a discussion of the various uses of the imperative mood, see W. Gesenius, *Hebrew Grammar* (ed. E. Kautzsch and tr. A. E. Cowley; 2d rev. ed.; Oxford: Clarendon, 1910), 324–6 and R. J. Williams, *Hebrew Syntax* (2d rev. ed.; Toronto: University of Toronto, 1974), 35, 37–8, 41, 86.

55. This tendency can be seen in Kaiser's reticence to depend on semantic structures underlying the surface structure of a text. See Kaiser, *Exegetical Theology*, 97, 103. See also McQuilkin, *Understanding and Applying the Bible*, 107–21. For a simple introduction to the concepts of deep structure and surface structure, see J. Beekman and J. Callow, *Translating the Word of God* (Grand Rapids: Zondervan, 1974), 268–71.

56. For a helpful discussion of logico-grammatical isomorphism see Thiselton, "Semantics and New Testament Interpretation," 76–8 and Ullmann, *Principles of Semantics*, 16.

57. See Berkhof, *Principles of Biblical Interpretation*, 133–4; W. M. Dunnett, *The Interpretation of Holy Scripture* (Nashville: Thomas Nelson, 1984), 142–50.

58. For the distinction between intrinsic and extrinsic summaries see chapter 4, n. 43.

Chapter Six

1. For a discussion of some of these issues see S. Chatman, *Story and Discourse* (Ithaca: Cornell University, 1978), 108–10.

2. Chatman's advice is correct. "Let us argue that plot and character are equally important." Chatman, *Story and Discourse*, 110. As Ryken has put it, "Some stories are more thoroughly plot stories, others more thoroughly character stories, but stories are finally an interaction between plot and character." Ryken, *Words of Delight*, 71.

3. In several recent studies of characterization in Old Testament narratives, little attention is given to God and supernatural creatures as characters. See Ryken, *Words of Delight*, 71–81, Longman, *Literary Approaches*, 88–93, A. Berlin, *Po-*

etics and Interpretation of Biblical Narrative (*Bible and Literature Series* 9; Sheffield: Almond, 1983), 23–42, R. Alter, *The Art of Biblical Narrative* (New York: Basic Books, 1981), 114–30, Greidanus, *Modern Preacher*, 200–1. But see Sternberg's helpful analysis of divine and human characterization. Sternberg, *Poetics*, 322–5.

4. As the Westminster Shorter Catechism puts it, "The Scriptures principally teach what man is to believe concerning God, and what duty God requires of man." *Westminster Shorter Catechism* Answer 4.

5. See the discussion of this passage in chapter 7.

6. This terminology originated as a description of a machine used in Greek drama by which a god was lowered to the stage in order to solve the problems of the drama. We use the term to indicate the sudden entry and exit of God as He causes a major shift in a story. See Abrams, *Glossary*, 41.

7. For a discussion of the theological implications of God's absence from Esther see Young, *Introduction*, 357–8 and Baldwin, *Esther*, 36–42.

8. For a discussion of the identities of the three visitors see Ross, *Creation and Blessing*, 41.

9. W. F. Thrall and A. Hibbard, *A Handbook to Literature* (New York: Harper and Row, 1936), 74. Or as Abrams has put it, "the moral and dispositional qualities" of characters. Abrams, *Glossary*, 20.

10. See the discussion of Judges in chapters 1 and 12.

11. See the discussion of Jephthah and Samson in chapter 4.

12. Cundall comments correctly, "He showed his lack of appreciation of the character and requirements of the Lord, and also a lack of confidence in the divine enablement, by seeking to secure the favour of God by his rash *vow*." Cundall, *Judges*, 146 (italics his).

13. Other authors refer to similar techniques for characterization. Alter speaks of "actions or appearances," "direct speech" and the "reliable narrator's explicit statement." Alter, *Art of Biblical Narrative*, 117. Berlin refers to "description," "inner life," "speech and actions" and "contrast." Berlin, *Poetics and Interpretation*, 34–40. Ryken expands the list to include "actions," "personal traits and abilities," "thoughts and feelings," "relationships and roles," "responses to events or people" and "archetypal character types." Ryken, *Words of Delight*, 74.

14. Alter, *Art of Biblical Narrative*, 116.

15. See Sternberg's treatment of the metonymic inference. Sternberg, *Poetics*, 342-9.

16. See Sternberg's discussion and proleptic epithets, *Poetics*, 328–41.

17. For helpful discussions of the names Jacob and Israel see Ross, *Creation and Blessing*, 441,554–6.

18. Ross notes the dramatic effect of this designation. "Jacob perceived only that a male antagonist was closing in on him. The reader gradually learns his identity

as Jacob did." Ross, *Creation and Blessing*, 552–3 and Westermann, *Genesis 12–36*, 142, 264.

19. For discussions of these distinctions see Abrams, *Glossary*, 20–1 and Berlin, *Poetics and Interpretation*, 23.

20. Berlin, *Poetics and Interpretation*, 23.

21. Berlin, *Poetics and Interpretation*, 23.

22. Abrams, *Glossary*, 21.

23. Ryken, *Words of Delight*, 72.

24. Ryken, *Words of Delight*, 72.

25. See the discussion of thematic analysis in chapter 4.

26. For instance, Durham designates Exodus 1–18 as "Israel in Egypt" and "Israel in the Wilderness." J. I. Durham, *Exodus* (*Word Biblical Commentary*; Waco: Word, 1987) vii-viii. Hyatt suggests "Preparation for Deliverance," "The Ten Plagues" and "The Exodus from Egypt and Crossing of the Sea." J. P. Hyatt, *Exodus* (*New Century Bible Commentary*; Grand Rapids: Eerdmans, 1971), 15–6.

27. See chapter 12 for a defense of the position that Exodus was written primarily to support Moses' authority over Israel.

28. See the discussions of plot and dramatic flow in chapters 8–9.

29. See the discussion of Jonah in chapter 12.

30. See the treatment of original observations, anticipations, and implications of Old Testament stories in chapter 11.

31. See the discussion of the emotional quality of this event in chapter 11.

Chapter Seven

1. The term "scene" is used differently by various literary critics. Licht, for instance, defines scene as that which "presents the happenings of a particular place and time, concentrating the attention of the audience on the deeds or the words spoken." J. Licht, *Storytelling in the Bible* (Jerusalem: Magnes, 1978), 29. To allow for the variety presented in OT narratives we have adopted a fairly flexible definition: "a set of closely related circumstances, characters, and actions." Our definition is similar to Gunkel "'Szenen' nennen wir diejenigen kleineren Teile einer Erzählung, die durch den Wechsel der Personen, des Schauplatzes oder der Handlung von einander unterschieden sind." H. Gunkel, *Genesis* (8th ed.; Göttingen: Vandenhoeck and Ruprecht, 1969), xxxiv.

2. Robinson correctly notes that the interpretative focus in narratives must be on larger units than in didactic materials. Robinson, *Biblical Preaching*, 54–5.

3. See Chatman, *Story and Discourse*, 37–41.

4. Interpreters who rely entirely on translations of the Hebrew text should be aware that scene divisions will be affected by the version they follow.

5. See, for instance, Exodus 9:6; 18:13; Numbers 16:41 [17:6]; 16:8 [17:23]; 33:3; Judges 6:38; 9:42; 21:4; 1 Samuel 5:3–4; 11:11; 18:10, et al.

6. See, for instance, Genesis 19:27; 20:8; 21:14; 1 Samuel 20:35; 25:37; 2 Kings 10:9, et al.

7. See, for instance, Genesis 19:1; 24:11; Joshua 5:10; Judges 19:16; 2 Samuel 11:2,13; Esther 6:1, et al.

8. See, for instance, Genesis 8:13,14; Exodus 19:1; Joshus 4:19; Ezra 3:1, et al.

9. See, for instance, Genesis 7:11; 16:3; 10:8; 1 Samuel 7:2; 1 Kings 2:39; 15:1; 2 Chronicles 18:2; Esther 1:3; 3:7, et al.

10. See, for instance, Genesis 16:3; 1 Kings 2:39; 2 Chronicles 8:1; Judges 11:39; Genesis 22:1,20; 39:7; Joshua 24:29; Genesis 23:19; 2 Samuel 15:1; Genesis 25:11; Numbers 26:1; Judges 10:1; Joshua 23:1; Judges 11:4, et al.

11. See, for instance, Genesis 19:27; 20:8; 31:55 [32:1]; Exodus 24:4; 32:6; Joshua 3:1; 6:12; 8:10; 1 Samuel 1:19; 5:3; 2 Chronicles 20:20; 29:20, et al.

12. See, for instance, Genesis 29:25; 41:8; 22:1; 22:20; Numbers 26:1; Joshua 24:29; Judges 11:4; 2 Samuel 21:18; 2 Chronicles 18:2, et al.

13. See Gesenius, *Hebrew Grammar*, 132–3; Williams, *Hebrew Syntax*, 33–4; P. Joüon, *Grammaire de L'hébreu Biblique* (2d ed.; Rome, 1965), 115–9.

14. Critics use different terms to refer to this distinction. Chatman refers to "discourse-time" and "story-time." Rimmon-Kenan refers simply to "text-time"—which is "inescapably linear"—and to the "multilinearity" of "story-time." Genette distinguishes between the order, duration and frequency of events within the narrative. The tension between simultaneity and narrative order falls under Genette's heading of order. "To study the temporal order of a narrative is to compare the order in which events or temporal sections are arranged in the narrative discourse with the order of succession these same events or temporal segments have in the story, to the extent that story order is explicitly indicated by the narrative itself or inferable from one or another indirect clue." G. Genette, *Narrative Discourse* (Ithaca: Cornell University, 1980), 35. See also Chatman, *Story and Discourse*, 62–7; S. Rimmon-Kenan, *Narrative Fiction* (New York: Methuen, 1983), 43–58; Longman, *Literary Approaches*, 93–4.

15. Chatman succinctly summarizes Genette's observations. "Genette distinguishes between normal sequence, where story and discourse have the same order (1 2 3 4), and 'anachronous' sequences. And anachrony can be of two sorts: flashback (analepse), where the discourse breaks the story-flow to recall earlier events (2 1 3 4), and flashforward (prolepse) where the discourse leaps ahead, to events subsequent to intermediate events." Chatman, *Story and Discourse*, 64. See also Rimmon-Kenan, *Narrative Fiction*, 46–51 and Genette, *Narrative Discourse*, 39–40.

16. Often OT narratives indicate simultaneous action by simple waw constructions: e.g. Genesis 24:21; 37:36; Exodus 24:17; 2 Samuel 6:5. See Gesenius, *Hebrew Grammar*, 132–5 and Williams, *Hebrew Syntax*, 33–4. Also note that in a series

of *waw* consecutives the first verb may indicate a simultaneous circumstance. See Williams, *Hebrew Syntax*, 33–4.

17. In light of the grammatical construction this verse may be translated "Meanwhile he treated Abram well for her sake."

18. Calvin states that the edict of the King was the cause for the Ninevites' fast. It was "not any movement among the people, capriciously made, as it sometimes happens." Calvin, *Minor Prophets* III, 102. Conversely, however, Allen argues that 3:5–6 refers to subsequent action. L. Allen, *The Books of Joel, Obadiah, Jonah, and Micah (New International Comm; Grand Rapids: Eerdmans, 1976), 223–4.*

19. Licht calls this a "partial flashback," a "simple comment which explains the action by reference to some earlier event." Licht, *Storytelling in the Bible*, 109. See also Genette, *Narrative Discourse*, 48–67.

20. As Licht has put it, "'Teichoscopy' is a device of Greek drama, used to inform the spectators about events off-stage; it is used to present elements of the plot that cannot be effectively staged. No such constraint exists in narrative, which uses teichoscopy purely for aesthetic effect. Its basic function is to heighten the mimetic value of the storytelling by making the reader participate, through the reaction of witnesses, in the 'shown' event." Licht, *Storytelling in the Bible*, 45.

21. For instance, the stories of 1 Samuel 2 and 3 occur within the bounds of Shiloh. See also Nehemiah 2:11–13:31.

22. See Genesis 15:1–21; 32:24–31; 1 Samuel 3:15.

23. See Genesis 15:11.

24. See discussion of spatio-temporal variations below in this chapter.

25. For a helpful discussion of character placement see D. Gropp, "Toward a Discourse Grammar of Biblical Hebrew Narrative: The Abraham Story," (unpublished Th.M. thesis, Westminster Theological Seminary, 1979), 34.

26. For example note the shift in Exodus 24:15–18.

27. See, for instance, Exodus 5:1–5,6–21; Joshua 1:1–9,10–18 and 1 Samuel 10:1–8,9–27.

28. See, for instance, Judges 4:17–21,22; Ruth 2:1–3,4–23.

29. For helpful discussions of the four modes of narration see Licht, *Storytelling in the Bible*, 29–30; Berlin, *Poetics and Interpretation*, 46; Ryken, *Words of Delight*, 43–5. See also Chatman's discussion of the differences between diegesis and mimesis (telling and showing). Chatman, *Story and Discourse*, 31–4.

30. "Storytellers can do two basic things to impose their interpretive point of view on the material. They can enter the story and comment on characters and events in their own voice. I call this authorial assertion." Ryken, *Words of Delight*, 84.

31. In the descriptive mode of narration "the storyteller stops the flow of events, taking his time to tell the audience how persons, places and objects looked or

sounded or smelled. No proper tale can be all description, but a storyteller can convey much relevant information, or create the atmosphere he wants, by leaning heavily on the descriptive mode." Licht, *Storytelling in the Bible*, 29–30.

32. Licht and Berlin speak of "scenic narrative." "Each scene presents the happenings of a particular place and time, concentrating the attention of the audience on the deeds and the words spoken. Conflicts, direct statements of single acts, and direct speech are preeminent." Licht, *Storytelling in the Bible*, 29. See also Berlin, *Poetics and Interpretation*, 24.

33. Dialogue often predominates, with narration acting as a bridge to another portion of dialogue. See Berlin, *Poetics and Interpretation*, 63–4.

34. For a discussion of the Hebrew *tnwr* ("smoking firepot") see E. A. Speiser, *Genesis* (*The Anchor Bible* 1; Garden City: Doubleday, 1964), 113–4; von Rad, *Genesis*, 188.

35. For a discussion of S(pace) and T(ime) ratings see below.

36. The complexity of temporal shifts may be due in part to the fact that the Chronicler has expanded his Vorlage into a full scale narrative. See Pratt, "Royal Prayer," 277–88, 321–2.

37. The Chronicler divides Rehoboam's reign into three years of blessing (11:17), one of rebellion (12:1), and punishment in the fifth year (12:2).

38. ". . . he came about as far as Jerusalem" (2 Chronicles 12:4) indicates the extent of his campaign.

39. In light of the temporal regression, 2 Chronicles 12:4 should be translated "he had captured . . . and he had come."

40. Note the explicit marking of simultaneity by the simple *waw* (*wšm'yh hnby' b'*).

41. For a discussion of S(pace) and T(ime) ratings in this story see below.

42. For helpful discussions of spatiality in narratives see Chatman, *Story and Discourse*, 101–7; Rimmon-Kenan, *Narrative Fiction*, 77–8; Ryken, *Words of Delight*, 54-62.

43. See Berlin, *Poetics and Interpretation*, 38, 61–2; Wellek and Warren, *Theory of Literature*, 223–4.

44. Concerning the use of close-ups in filmmaking, Coynik says, "The close-up magnifies an action or object and separates it from its surroundings. By making the object or action the entire content of his picture, a director also magnifies its importance." D. Coynik, *Film: Real to Reel* (Winona: St. Mary's College, 1972), 11.

45. Coynik, *Film: Real to Reel*, 98.

46. For example, "Arthur Penn shows the death of Bonnie and Clyde in that film in slow motion in order to make the horror of the moment last longer and have more of an impact on his audience. It works." Coynik, *Film: Real to Reel*, 102.

47. For a fuller discussion of temporal variations see Chatman, *Story and Discourse*, 79–84; G. Genette, "Time and Narrative in A la recherche du temps perdu," in *Aspects of Narrative* (ed. J. H. Miller; New York: Columbia University, 1971), 99–103; Licht, *Storytelling in the Bible*, 96–120.

48. Licht uses the term "retardation." Other literary critics speak of "deceleration." For fuller discussions see Licht, *Storytelling in the Bible*, 105–7; Rimmon-Kenan, *Narrative Fiction*, 51–6; Genette, "Time and Narrative," 99–102.

49. See Alter, *Art of Biblical Narrative*, 39.

50. See von Rad, *Genesis*, 241–2.

51. Scholes and Kellogg speak of "mimesis" to describe a story's attention "to truth of sensation and environment . . . .Its ultimate form is the 'slice of life.'" R. Scholes and R. Kellogg, *The Nature of Narrative* (New York: Oxford, 1966), 13. They use this term similar to my use of the term "imagery." For a fuller discussion of mimesis, see Aristotle, *Poetics*, 1.1–2. See also Licht, *Storytelling in the Bible*, 9–11; R. Scholes, *Structuralism in Literature* (New Haven: Yale, 1974), 119–23.

52. See Berlin, *Poetics and Interpretation*, 138–9; E. Auerbach, *Mimesis* (Princeton: Princeton University, 1953), 8–15. A notable exception to this general rule may be found in Esther 1:5ff.

53. As Alter has put it, "There is not a great deal of narrative specification in the Bible, and so when a particular descriptive detail is mentioned—Esau's ruddiness and hairiness, Rachel's beauty, King Eglon's obesity—we should be alert for consequences, immediate or eventual, either in plot or theme." Alter, *Art of Biblical Narrative*, 180.

54. Abrams distinguishes between tactile imagery (touch), thermal imagery (heat and cold), as well as kinesthetic imagery (sensations of movement). Wellek and Warren distinguish between thermal images and pressure images ('kinesthetic,' 'haptic,' 'empathic'). See Abrams, *Glossary*, 78–9 and Wellek and Warren, *Theory of Literature*, 187.

Chapter Eight

1. "By 'plot' I mean here the arrangement of the incidents." Aristotle, *Poetics*, 6.8.

2. Plot has been defined differently. For example, "The plot . . . in a narrative work is the structure of its actions, as these are ordered and rendered toward achieving particular emotions and artistic effects." Abrams, *Glossary*, 137. "The plot of a story is the arrangement of events. Three time-honored principles on which plot is constructed are unity, coherence and emphasis. A plot is not simply a succession of events but a sequence of related events." Ryken, *Words of Delight*, 62 (emphasis his). See also Scholes and Kellogg, *Nature of Narrative*, 207. For a bibliography of contemporary views of plot, see F. J. Matera, "The Plot of Matthew's Gospel," *Catholic Biblical Quarterly* 49 (1987), 233–53.

3. For instance, Bar-Efrat distinguishes four different levels: "1) the verbal level; 2) the level of narrative technique; 3) the level of narrative world; 4) the level of

conceptual content." S. Bar-Efrat, "Some Observations on the Analysis of Structure in Biblical Narrative," *Vetus Testamentum* 30 (1980), 157.

4. For the sake of convenience I have adopted the following terminology. In ascending order, narrative materials consist of scenes, phases, steps, episodes, sections and whole books. Variations among texts force some inconsistencies in use, but this scheme is roughly maintained throughout this study. Episodes display relative independence from their surrounding context. Thus, they may rightly be called "stories." As opposed to sections and whole books, episodes are relatively simple. Various critics and commentators use these terms and other terms in different ways.

5. Here I follow Stubbs (following Labov) who defines story as "a sequence of two clauses which are temporally ordered." M. Stubbs, *Discourse Analysis*, 31; 23–37. See also W. Labov, *Sociolinguistic Patterns* (Philadelphia: University of Pennsylvania, 1972), 354–96; Rimmon-Kenan, *Narrative Fiction*, 16–9. Many interpreters begin with Aristotle's tripartite scheme: beginning, middle, and end (Aristotle, *Poetics*, 7.1-3). For example, see Ryken, *Words of Delight*, 62. See also Scholes, *Structuralism in Literature*, 97; Longman, *Literary Approaches*, 93; Greidanus, *Modern Preacher*, 203. We should note, however, that Aristotle's discussion focused on tragedies, not the minimal definition of a story. A three-part scheme appears frequently in the Old Testament, but is too complex to serve as a minimum.

6. For similar categories see Chatman's distinction between "narrative of resolution" which reveals "a kind of ratiocinative or emotional teleology" and "plot of revelation" which reveals "a state of affairs." Chatman, *Story and Discourse*, 48. I suggest that episodes tend to fall somewhere on a continuum between these types. Thus my three categories of plot.

7. For helpful discussions of the contribution of this passage to its larger context see Childs, *Introduction to Old Testament*, 259; J. Gray, *Joshua, Judges, Ruth* (*New Century Bible Commentary*; Grand Rapids: Eerdmans, 1986), 188.

8. Biblical genealogies contain brief episodes of resolution (1 Chronicles 4:9–10), unresolved tension (1 Chronicles 5:7–10), and report (1 Chronicles 5:1–6).

9. For helpful discussions of the significance of this passage see Ross, *Creation and Blessing*, 583; Westermann, *Genesis 12–36*, 556.

10. Licht argues that this episode is resolved by "re-establishing calm" in 2 Kings 6:7, but this analysis seems less than adequate. See Licht, *Storytelling in the Bible*, 25.

11. To use the terminology we will introduce later in this chapter, 2 Kings 6:1–4a forms the dramatic problem of the story; 2 Kings 6:4b-7 comprises the turning point of the story. Each of these steps has its own dramatic tension and resolution, but together they form an episode that remains unresolved.

12. As Nelson put it, "The problem of a new house has served its narrative purpose and is dropped." R. D. Nelson, *First and Second Kings* (*Interpretation*; Atlanta: John Knox, 1987), 185.

13. The scheme offered in this study is a blend of several different approaches. Aristotle's categories of "simple" action, "complex" action, "reversal," and "discovery" are somewhat similar. See Aristotle, *Poetics,* 10 and 11. Kort refers to these distinctions as rhythmic (or circular), conflict and competition, and melodic ("a strong forward-moving direction to events"). See W. A. Kort, *Story, Text, and Scripture* (University Park: Pennsylvania State, 1988), 26.

14. "In many plots the denouement involves a reversal, or in Aristotle's terms, peripety, in the hero's fortunes, whether to his failure or destruction, as in tragedy, or to his success, as in comic plots." Abrams, *Glossary,* 139. Both comedies and tragedies fall within this category. Simply put, comedy moves from disorder to order, while tragedy moves from order to disorder. Ryken notes that comedy is usually "a u-shaped story that begins in prosperity, descends into tragedy, and rises again to end happily." On the other hand, "tragedy is the story of exceptional calamity. It portrays a movement from prosperity to catastrophe." Ryken, *How to Read the Bible as Literature* (Grand Rapids: Zondervan, 1985), 82–3.

15. Aristotle, *Poetics,* 7.3.

16. For a helpful analysis of the structural symmetry of this narrative see I. M. Kikawada, "The Shape of Genesis 11:1–9," in *Rhetorical Criticism: Essays In Honor of James Muilenburg* (eds. J. J. Jackson and M. Kessler; Pittsburgh: Pickwick, 1974), 18–32.

17. As Chatman remarks, "the notion that all narratives can be successfully grouped according to a few forms of plot-content seems to me highly questionable." Chatman, *Story and Discourse,* 95, 84–95.

18. Throughout this discussion we will be using terms that have been adopted in a variety of ways. For instance, Aristotle uses the term complication (désis) to describe the action from the beginning to the point immediately preceding the reversal. The denouement (lusis) includes the reversal and continues to the end. See Aristotle, *Poetics,* 18. Abrams suggests 1) exposition, 2) rising action which ends at the climax, 3) falling action which is inaugurated by the crisis or turning point, and 4) denouement. In his discussions of plot structures, Abrams distinguishes between the climax (the height of the rising action) and the "crisis," or "turning point" (the inauguration of the falling actions). See Abrams, *Glossary,* 139. Ryken is similar to Abrams, but he reverses the terms turning point and climax. Ryken, *Words of Delight,* 117. Longman uses the term "climax" in yet a third way. Longman, *Literary Approaches,* 92.

19. For a discussion of this passage in its context see chapter 8.

20. It should be noted that three, four and five step resolution follow chiastic patterns (ABA') (ABB'A') (ABCB'A'). See J. Breck, "Biblical Chiasmus: Exploring the Biblical Structure for Meaning," *Biblical Theology Bulletin* 17 (1987), 71.

21. The Masoretic Text begins a new chapter at English Translation 1:17.

22. Many critical scholars consider the psalm of Jonah 2:2–10 [English Translation 2:1–9] intrusive and not important for the interpretation of the passage. See H. W. Wolff, *Obadja und Jona* (*Biblischer Kommentar Altes Testament* 14; Neu-

kirchen-Vluyn: Neukirchener Verlag, 1977), 62, 101–17. Magonet considers the psalm integral to the book but sees 2:1 [English Translation 1:17] as a "transition" and 2:2–11 [English Translation 2:1–10] as a unit. See J. Magonet, *Form and Meaning* (Sheffield: Almond, 1983), 43, 55. Landes sees 2:1–10 [English Translation 1:17–2:9] as a unit and 2:11 [English Translation 2:10] as a transition. He believes that the salvation occurred when the fish swallowed Jonah (hence solving the problem stated in 1:15). See G. M. Landes, "The Kerygma of the Book of Jonah," *Interpretation* 21 (1967), 13–6. Stuart and Allen argue correctly that 2:1-11 [English Translation 1:17–2:10] is one unit. See D. Stuart, *Hosea-Jonah* (*Word Biblical Commentary* 31; Waco: Word, 1987), 469 and L. C. Allen, *The Books of Joel, Obadiah, Jonah and Micah* (*New International Comm; Grand Rapids: Eerdmans, 1976*), *213*.

23. Westermann correctly designates it a "Declarative Psalm of Praise of the Individual." See Westermann, *The Praise of God in the Psalms* (tr. K. R. Crim; Richmond: John Knox, 1965 [1961]), 102. For the structural breakdown of the prayer see Stuart, *Hosea-Jonah*, 472.

24. Jonah's time in the fish should be understood as probationary. His thanksgiving is in response to being swallowed, but it also anticipates his escape and temple sacrifices (Jonah 2:9). For contrary views see Landes, "The Kerygma of the Book of Jonah" 13; Stuart, *Hosea-Jonah*, 472; Allen, *Joel, Obadiah, Jonah and Micah*, 215.

25. Westermann correctly observes that this narrative contains typical features of "testing" genre. The task is given; the task is carried out; approval or disapproval follows. Westermann, *Genesis 12–36*, 354–5. See also Ross, *Creation and Blessing*, 392-6. These elements do not correspond, however, to the rise and fall of dramatic tension. My outline is similar to Ross, except that I have batched scenes more along the lines of temporal and geographical movement. See Ross, *Creation and Blessing*, 393-6.

26. See the diagrams in Longman, *Literary Approaches*, 92; Greidanus, *Modern Preacher*, 204.

27. For a helpful discussion of the role of self-malediction in Ancient Near Eastern treaties and Scripture see M. G. Kline, *By Oath Consigned* (Grand Rapids: Eerdmans, 1968), 16–7; *Structure of Biblical Authority*, 126; Westermann, *Genesis 12–36*, 225; von Rad, *Genesis*, 186.

28. See von Rad, *Genesis*, 181 for a helpful discussion of the theophany.

Chapter Nine

1. For treatments of this passage see chapters 7 and 8.

2. See Westermann, *Genesis 12–36*, 224 and von Rad, *Genesis*, 186.

3. Many commentators have acknowledged the parallels between 15:1–6 and 15:7–21. See Westermann, *Genesis 12–36*, 216; Ross, *Creation and Blessing*, 305–6.

4. The Chronicler frequently makes temporal references to divide a king's reign into periods of obedience and disobedience. See Dillard, *2 Chronicles*, 122–3.

5. The terms "to seek" (*drš*) and "to forsake" (*'zb*) relate to the Chronicler's doctrine of divine retribution. If the kings (or people) sought the Lord, they benefited; if they forsook the Lord, punishment followed (1 Chronicles 28:9; 2 Chronicles 7:14; 12:5; 15:2; 26:5). See G. E. Schaeffer, "The Significance of Seeking God" (unpublished dissertation; Southern Baptist Theological Seminary in Louisville, KY).

6. Kings has other instances where the king of Judah gives away the "treasures of the Lord's temple" (Asa, 1 Kings 15:18; Joash, 2 Kings 12:18; Ahaz, 2 Kings 16:8; Hezekiah, 2 Kings 18:15). The Chronicler only records the offense of Asa. For possible rationales for this modification see Williamson, *Chronicles*, 273.

7. Not all commentators agree, but see J. M. Myers, II Chronicles *(The Anchor Bible 13,* Garden City: Doubleday, 1965), 95.

8. "The Lord was with Joseph" emphasized that the blessings given to Joseph were due to special divine providence. It occurs here four times (Genesis 39:2, 3, 21, 23).

9. Many commentators note the moral issues in these chapters but focus little on the deliberate juxtaposition of Judah and Joseph. See D. S. Briscoe, *Genesis* (*Communicator's Commentary 1*; Waco: Word, 1987), 312; Kidner, *Genesis*, 187–9.

10. As the *Chicago Statement on Biblical Inerrancy* puts it, "We further deny that inerrancy is negated by . . . the topical arrangement of material . . .", 13.

11. For a helpful discussion of the chronology of these passages see P. K. McCarter, II Samuel (*The Anchor Bible* 9; Garden City: Doubleday, 1984), 443. For an evangelical outlook see Keil and Delitzsch, *1 and 2 Samuel*, 459.

12. For a similar assessment see Childs, *Introduction to Old Testament*, 273–275; Hertzberg, *1 and 2 Samuel*, 415–6; McCarter, *II Samuel*, 16–9.

13. As DeVries comments, Adonijah's request demonstrates that he "remains firmly convinced of the right of primogeniture and has no misgivings about the rightness of his move to seize the throne." As a result, King Solomon gives the death order for Adonijah. See DeVries, *1 Kings*, 37–8.

14. As Long states, "the episodes . . . give careful justification for each of Solomon's actions, as though to remove any doubt as to the legitimacy of his attempts to consolidate authority." B. O. Long, *1 Kings with an Introduction to Historical Literature* (*The Forms of Old Testament Literature* 9; Grand Rapids: Eerdmans, 1984), 49.

15. An inclusion is "a passage of Scripture in which the opening phrase or idea is repeated, paraphrased, or otherwise returned to at the close (also called a cyclic or ring composition)." Soulen, *Handbook*, 94 and 169. For a fuller discussion see J. J. Jackson and M. Kessler, eds., *Rhetorical Criticism* (Pittsburgh: Pickwick, 1974), 63–9.

16. The division of this material into "national" and "international" wisdom is not intended to be an absolute distinction (cf. 4:29–34) but a reflection of primary emphasis.

17. See Longman, *Literary Approaches*, 146; A. R. Ceresko, "The Chiastic Word Pattern in Hebrew," *Catholic Biblical Quarterly* 38 (1976), 303–11.

18. See the discussion of this passage earlier in this chapter.

19. See R. B. Dillard, "David's Census: Perspectives on II Samuel 24 and I Chronicles 21," in *Through Christ's Word* (eds. W. R. Godfrey and J. L. Boyd III; Phillipsburg: Presbyterian and Reformed Publishing Company, 1985), 94–107.

20. See the treatment of individual episodes in chapter 7.

21. In recent years, evangelicals have viewed the relationship between the covenant in Genesis 15:7–21 and Genesis 17:1–27 in a number of ways. See M. G. Kline, *By Oath Consigned*, 24, 39–49; Robertson, *Christ of the Covenants*, 127–66; T. E. McComiskey, *The Covenants of Promise: A Theology of the Old Testament Covenants* (Grand Rapids: Baker, 1985), 59–66. It seems best to see these passages as two ratifications of the same covenant relationship. The first emphasizes divine promise and the second emphasizes human obligation. The tendency to treat Genesis 15:7–21 as more essential covenantal structures in the patriarchal period hardly accords with the importance placed on circumcision and obligation throughout the Old Testament. Both passages should be given equal weight when reconstructing the features of the Abrahamic covenant.

22. The use of emphatic *'ny* (Genesis 17:4) as well as the repetition of first person singular verbs points to the divine side of the covenant relationship.

23. For a helpful discussion of circumcision as a ceremony of self-malediction see Kline, *By Oath Consigned*, 40.

24. Note the contrastive *w'th* (Genesis 17:10) and the series of imperatives. For a discussion of the use of the imperative in conjunction with the covenant stipulations see von Rad, *Genesis*, 197–201; Westermann, *Genesis 12–36*, 256–267; Ross, *Creation and Blessing*, 330–4.1

25. For discussions of the practice of surrogate motherhood see Westermann, *Genesis 12–36*, 238–9; von Rad, *Genesis*, 191; Kidner, *Genesis*, 126; Speiser, *Genesis*, 119–21; Ross, *Creation and Blessing*, 319.

26. Here the NASB is far superior to the NIV's "born in the ordinary way."

27. Williamson divides this portion of 2 Chronicles into seven main parts. See Williamson, *Chronicles*, 255–77.

28. "The whole event in Genesis 2–3 reveals a carefully constructed arch which begins with the command that God gives to his human creatures, and ascends to a climax with the transgression of the command. It then descends from the climax to the consequences of the transgression the discovery, the trial and the punishment. The conclusion, the expulsion from the garden where God has put the man and woman, calls to mind again the beginning. There is a well-rounded, clear and polished chain of events." See Westermann, *Genesis 1–11*, 190.

29. For a similar analysis see J. Walsh, "Genesis 2:46–3:24: A Synchronic Approach," *Journal of Biblical Literature* 96 (1977), 161–77.

Chapter Ten

1. This has been a longstanding conviction among evangelicals. For example see Young, *Introduction*, 26–31; Berkouwer, *Holy Scripture*, 240–66.

2. Many ancient texts outside Scripture, especially from the inter-testamental period, were pseudopigraphic. See, for example, the discussion of 'The Wisdom of Solomon' and 'The Enoch Tradition' in D. G. Meade, *Pseudonymity and Canon: An Investigation into the Relationship of Authorship and Authority in Jewish and Earliest Christian Tradition* (Grand Rapids: Eerdmans, 1986), 62–6 and 91–101. Yet, there is little evidence that this practice was carried on by Biblical writers. Pseudonymity was primarily designed to give a book authority by attaching it to an authoritative figure. But to do so, it conveyed more than a "literary fiction." It asserted a literary deception, misleading unsuspecting readers. As Packer writes, "We may lay it down as a general principle that, when Biblical books specify their own authorship, the affirmation of their canonicity involves a denial of their pseudonymity. Pseudonymity and canonicity are mutually exclusive." See Packer, *Fundamentalism and the Word of God*, 184. See also Meade, *Pseudonymity and Canon*, 1–2. For a brief discussion of the phenomenon of pseudonymity see D. Guthrie, "Pseudonymity," in *The Illustrated Bible Dictionary* (ed. J. D. Douglas; Leichester: Inter-Varsity, 1980), 3.1301–3; D. S. Russell, *The Old Testament Pseudopigrapha: Patriarchs and Prophets in Early Judaism* (Philadelphia: Fortress, 1987), 8–12 and Meade, *Pseudonymity and Canon*, 1–16.

3. *Chicago Statement on Biblical Inerrancy: A Short Statement* (1978), Article 4 (emphasis mine).

4. See R. E. Clements, *One Hundred Years of Old Testament Interpretation* (Philadelphia: Westminster, 1976). See also Childs, *Introduction to Old Testament*, 30–45 and Young, *Introduction*, 123–53.

5. As Sternberg observed, "Rarely have so many worked so long and so hard with so little to show for their trouble. Not even the widely accepted constructs of geneticism, like the Deuteronomist, lead an existence other than speculative. Small wonder, then, that literary approaches react against this atomism by going to the opposite extreme of holism." See Sternberg, *Poetics*, 13. See also chapter 5.

6. See Kaiser, *Exegetical Theology*, 64–6. See also the related discussions in Mickelsen, *Interpreting the Bible*, 44–5; Young, *Introduction*, 19–31, Ramm, *Protestant Biblical Interpretation*, 63–9 and Armerding, *Old Testament and Criticism*, 1–15.

7. For helpful treatments of these parallel texts see T. R. Hobbs, *2 Kings (Word Biblical Commentary* 13; Waco: Word, 1985), 241–64; Dillard, *2 Chronicles*, 298, 302; H. G. M. Williamson, *Israel in the Books of Chronicles* (Cambridge: Cambridge University, 1977), 7–11.

8. For the discussion of organic inspiration see the Introduction.

9. For an in-depth study of the Chronicler's sources see S. L. McKenzie, *The Chronicler's Use of the Deuteronomistic History* (*Harvard Semitic Monographs* 33; Atlanta: Scholars Press, 1985).

10. See Gray, *Kings*, 28–32.

11. See C. Westermann, *Genesis 37–50* (tr. J. J. Scullion; Minneapolis: Augsburg, 1986), 15–30. See also Coats, *Genesis*, 264–6.

12. See G. H. Jones, *1 and 2 Kings* (2 vols.; New Century Bible Commentary; Grand Rapids: Eerdmans and London: Marshall, Morgan and Scott, 1984), 1.31; J. Robinson, *The First Book of the Kings* (London: Cambridge University, 1972), 95 and J. R. Lumby, *The First Book of the Kings* (London: Cambridge University, 1886), 85. For a more detailed analysis see B. S. Childs, "A Study of the Formula 'Until this day'," *Journal of Biblical Literature* 82 (1963), 279–92 and "The Etiological Tale Re-examined," *Vetus Testamentum* 24 (1974), 387–97. Similar explanations hold for the temporal references in 1 Kings 9:20–21; 12:19 and 2 Kings 8:22.

13. Inerrantists by and large acknowledge that the extant Hebrew texts are not identical with the autographa. We speak of our transmitted texts as "reliable" not "inerrant." See *Chicago Statement on Biblical Inerrancy* (1978), Articles 10 and 11.

14. For simple introductions to Old Testament textual criticism see D. Stuart, *Old Testament Exegesis* (Philadelphia: Westminster, 1980), 88–96 and E. Wurthwein, *The Text of the Old Testament* (tr. P. Ackroyd; Oxford: Basil Blackwell, 1957), 70–82.

15. For a discussion of these and related topics, see LaSor, Hubbard, and Bush, *Old Testament Survey*, 30–4 and Armerding, *Old Testament and Criticism*, 21–42 and 123–5. For an extended discussion see also Harrison, *Introduction to the Old Testament* (Grand Rapids: Eerdmans, 1969), 201–59.

16. See Young, *Introduction*, 59.

17. While admitting the textual problems associated with this passage, Williamson argues that the genealogy "requires a date at least two generations later than Zerubbabel, and possibly more." See Williamson, *Chronicles*, 15–7. The significance of this genealogy for the dating of Chronicles has been interpreted a number of different ways. For other viewpoints see J. M. Myers, *I Chronicles* (*The Anchor Bible*; Garden City: Doubleday and Company, 1965) LXXXIX; E. L. Curtis and A. A. Madsen, *A Critical and Exegetical Commentary on the Books of Chronicles* (*International Critical Commentary*; Edinburgh: T. and T.Clark, 1910), 5 and Young, *Introduction*, 391.

18. See C. F. Keil, *Commentary on the Old Testament: 1 and 2 Kings, 1 and 2 Chronicles, Ezra, Nehemiah, Esther* (Grand Rapids: Eerdmans, 1964), 84.

19. For arguments in favor of an early date see Pratt, "Royal Prayer," 20–8.

20. Young, *Introduction*, 386. Williamson notes, "This list of high priests has been seen to be one of the latest elements in the chapter. It was apparently inserted in order to show the connection between Jeshua (vv 1–9) and Joiakim (v. 12)." See

Williamson, *Ezra, Nehemiah*, 362–3. See also D. J. A. Clines, *Ezra, Nehemiah, Esther* (*New Century Bible Commentary*; Grand Rapids: Eerdmans, 1984), 224–6.

21. The Talmud reads, "Who wrote the Scriptures?—Moses wrote his own book and the portion of Balaam and Job. Joshua wrote the book which bears his name and [the last] eight verses of the Pentateuch. Samuel wrote the book which bears his name and the Book of Judges and Ruth. David wrote the book of Psalms, including in it the work of the elders, namely, Adam, Melchizedek, Abraham, Moses, Heman, Yeduthun, Asaph, and the three sons of Korah. Jeremiah wrote the book which bears his name, the Book of Kings, and Lamentations. Hezekiah and his colleagues wrote Isaiah, Proverbs, the Song of Songs, and Ecclesiastes. The men of the Great Assembly wrote Ezekiel, the Twelve Minor Prophets, Daniel, and the Scroll of Esther. Ezra wrote the book that bears his name and the genealogies of the book of Chronicles up to his own time . . . .Who then finished it?—Nehemiah the son of Hachaliah." B. Baba, *Bathra*, 14b-15a.

22. See the discussion of each book in chapter 12.

23. Some attempts have also been made to identify the dates of extrinsic agents on the basis of grammatical considerations. Analysis of grammatical features may be helpful at times, but these approaches are highly problematic and yield few solid conclusions.

24. For extensive discussions of the "daric"-"drachma" difficulty see Williamson, "Eschatology in Chronicles," 115–54, Archer, *Survey of Old Testament*, 406–7 and Pratt, "Royal Prayer", 33.

25. For a fuller discussion see chapter 12.

26. For a brief discussion of this custom see Cundall, *Judges*, 305–8. See also H. W. Hertzberg, *Die Bücher Josua, Richter, Ruth* (*Das Alte Testament Deutsch* 9; Göttingen: Bandenhoed and Ruprecht, 1954), 279.

27. See Gray, *Kings*, 8–9.

28. See the discussion of this matter in chapter 12.

29. See the discussion of a writer's ideological point of view later in this chapter.

30. See Pratt, "Royal Prayer," 28–44, 261–4.

31. See D. R. Davis, "A Proposed life Setting for the Book of Judges," (unpublished dissertation, Southern Baptist Theological Seminary in Louisville, 1978), 84–90 and 128–30; B. G. Webb, *The Book of Judges: An Integrated Reading* (*Journal for the Study of the Old Testament Supplements* 46; Sheffield: Journal for the Study of the Old Testament Press, 1987), 182–7.

32. For a sampling of viewpoints see Newton-De Molina, ed., *On Literary Intentions*; E. E. Johnson, "Author's Intention and Biblical Interpretation," in *Hermeneutics, Inerrancy and the Bible* (eds. E. D. Radmacher and R. D. Preus; Grand Rapids: Zondervan, 1984), 407–29; Sternberg, *Poetics*, 7–23; Barton, *Reading the Old Testament*, 140–57; Virkler, *Hermeneutics*, 22–7; Hirsch, *Validity in In-*

terpretation, 1–67, *Aims of Interpretation*, 1–21; Kaiser, *Exegetical Theology*, 113–4.

33. For related discussions see Berlin, *Poetics and Interpretation*, 55–7 and Longman, *Literary Approaches*, 87–8. See also Abrams, *Glossary*, 142–5; R. Fowler, *Linguistics and the Novel* (London: Methuen and Co. Ltd., 1977), 72–8; Chatman, *Story and Discourse*, 151–61 and Scholes and Kellogg, *Nature of Narrative*, 240–82.

34. In this discussion I follow Uspensky who distinguishes five "planes" of point of view: spatial, temporal, phraseological, psychological and ideological. See B. Uspensky, *A Poetics of Composition* (Berkeley: University of California, 1973). See also Berlin, *Poetics and Interpretation*, 55–6 and Longman, *Literary Approaches*, 87–8.

35. See the discussion of prominence in chapter 6.

36. See the related discussion of variations in the original audience in chapter 16.

37. See Polletta, ed., *Intention and Choice: The Character of Prose*, 14–15.

38. As Cotterell and Turner comment, "My utterance successfully conveys much more than I actually say because I share with my hearer a 'Presupposition Pool' . . . as well as new information from the completed part of the discourse itself." P. Cotterell and M. Turner, *Linguistics and Biblical Interpretation* (Downers Grove: Inter-Varsity, 1989), 90.

39. Frame, *Knowledge of God*, 96. For a fuller discussion see Poythress, "Divine Meaning of Scripture," 241–79.

40. See figure 41.

41. For a fuller discussion see chapter 12.

42. As Ryken has put it, "Clarity and mystery mingle as we move through these stories. . . . What they tell us is reliable, but they leave so much unsaid. For the most part they describe but do not explain what happened." Ryken, *Words of Delight*, 43.

43. See chapter 6.

44. See chapter 7.

45. See chapters 8 and 9.

46. For more complete discussions of repetition see Licht, *Storytelling in the Bible*, 51–95; Sternberg, *Poetics*, 365–440; Alter, *Art of Biblical Narrative*, 88–113; G. W. Savran, *Telling and Retelling: Quotation in Biblical Narrative* (Bloomington and Indianapolis: Indiana University, 1988), 1–17; Longman, *Literary Approaches*, 95–6.

47. R. L. Braun, *1 Chronicles* (*Word Biblical Commentary* 14; Waco: Word, 1986), 132. See also Curtis and Madsen, *Chronicles*, 180–4.

48. Abrams defines allusion as "a reference, explicit or indirect, to a person, place, or event, or to another literary work or passage." Abrams, *Glossary*, 8. Perrine com-

ments, "Allusions are a means of re-inforcing the emotion or the ideas of one's own work with the emotion or ideas of another work or occasion." Perrine, *Sound and Sense: An Introduction to Poetry* (New York: Harcourt, Brace and Company, 1956), 106-13. Ryken defines allusion more broadly. "By this I mean that various Biblical writers allude to earlier works in the same canon, or to the same historical events, or to the same religious beliefs and experiences, or to the same cultural context." See Ryken, *Words of Delight*, 30.

49. For example, Abrams discusses verbal, structural, Socratic, dramatic, cosmic, invective, and romantic irony. There is, however, little agreement on these distinctions. See Abrams, *Glossary*, 89–93. For a helpful comparison, as well as some important distinctions between irony and related devices such as sarcasm, parody, satire, etc., see E. M. Good, *Irony in the Old Testament* (Philadelphia: Westminster, 1965), 13–38. See also the study of W. C. Booth, *A Rhetoric of Irony* (Chicago and London: University of Chicago, 1974).

50. See Abrams, *Glossary*, 89.

51. See Good, *Irony in the Old Testament*, 22–4.

52. See Abrams, *Glossary*, 91–2 and Good, *Irony in the Old Testament*, 17–9.

53. See Lundin, Thiselton and Walhout, *Responsibility of Hermeneutics*, 79–113, esp. 90–6.

54. See Alter, *Art of Biblical Narrative*, 63–87; Berlin, *Poetics and Interpretation*, 64–72; Auerbach, *Mimesis*, 39–49; Sternberg, *Poetics*, 7–23; Savran, *Telling and Retelling*, 7–17, 24–5.

55. As Alter comments, "The Biblical writers . . . are often less concerned with actions in themselves than with how an individual character responds to actions or produces them; and direct speech is made the chief instrument for revealing the varied and at times nuanced relations of the personages to the actions in which they are implicated." Alter, *Art of Biblical Narrative*, 66.

56. See the discussion of these matters in chapter 6.

57. See chapter 5, n. 8.

58. For a fuller discussion of the importance of past events and contemporary circumstances see chapter 10.

59. For a discussion of the date of Genesis see chapter 12.

60. For a fuller discussion of this passage see chapter 4.

61. Compare 2 Kings 20:12–19 with 2 Chronicles 32:31. The Chronicler summarizes the entire account, "But when envoys were sent by the rulers of Babylon to ask him about the miraculous sign that had occurred in the land, God left him to test him and to know everything that was in his heart."

62. "The writer's final judgment on Hezekiah is that he cuts a negative figure on the stage of Judah's history. The reign, which clearly began with promise and which received a demonstration of Yahweh's grace and deliverance, now ends on a note of potential disaster." Hobbs, *2 Kings*, 296.

Chapter Eleven

1. For a fuller discussion of this passage see chapter 4.
2. See the discussion of human characters in chapter 6.
3. For discussions of the continuing struggle between the families of Saul and David see J. Bright, *A History of Israel* (3d ed., Philadelphia: Westminster, 1981), 191–2 and Merrill, *Kingdom of Priests*, 271–2.
4. See P. K. McCarter, *I Samuel* (*The Anchor Bible* 8; Garden City: Doubleday, 1980), 58.
5. See the discussion of God's character in chapter 6.
6. See Frame's discussion of the integrality of normative and situational perspectives. Frame, *Knowledge of God*, 74.
7. See the discussions of dating for each book in chapter 12.
8. For a fuller discussion of the nature of progressive revelation with respect to the Mosaic moral code see W. Kaiser, *Toward Old Testament Ethics* (Grand Rapids: Zondervan, 1983), 60–4.
9. For discussions of the customs related to Abraham's actions see Westermann, *Genesis 12–36*, 237 and Ross, *Creation and Blessing*, 319.
10. As Robertson remarks, "Law functioned significantly in the period preceding Moses, and law functions significantly in the period succeeding Moses. While the summation of the law in an externalized form may remain as the distinctive property of the Mosaic era, the presence of law throughout the history of redemption must be recognized." Robertson, *Christ of the Covenants*, 175. See also Calvin, *Institutes*, 2.7.1 and 2.8.1.
11. For similar positive references to the Law of Moses see Joshua 8:31,32; 2 Kings 23:25; 2 Chronicles 23:18; 25:4; Ezra 3:2.
12. For similar negative evaluations based on the Law of Moses see 1 Kings 18:18; 2 Kings 18:12–13.
13. See Hanson's helpful discussion of the royal ideology behind Ahab's actions. P. D. Hanson, *The People Called: The Growth of Community in the Bible* (New York: Harper and Row, 1986), 140–7. As DeVries comments, "Ahab offers money or compensation in kind for Naboth's vineyard, but Naboth refuses on the grounds of ancestral law (see Leviticus 25). With the loss of land would have gone the loss of position, and before long Naboth and his posterity would have been reduced to the status of royal pensioners." DeVries, *I Kings*, 256.
14. For a discussion of the legal implications of the term *nahala* see, *Theological Wordbook of the Old Testament* 2.569–70 and *The International Standard Bible Encyclopedia (rev. ed.)* (ed. G. W. Bromiley; rev. ed.; 4 vols.; Grand Rapids: Eerdmans, 1982) s. v. "inherit."
15. For a fuller discussion of this passage see chapter 9.

16. von Rad correctly observes "Our narrator exercises a chaste reticence on the emotional side and manages to use that indirect method in the presentation or suggestion of inner emotional circumstances with great skill. Thus he shows us, for example, Abraham's attentive love for the child in the division of the burdens. He himself carries the dangerous objects with which the boy could hurt himself, the torch and the knife." von Rad, *Genesis*, 240.

17. See the analysis of this passage in chapter 9.

18. See the discussion of this passage in chapter 6. See also Kidner, *Genesis*, 168-9.

19. Some interpreters have argued that establishing Purim was the central purpose of the book of Esther (see the discussion of Esther in chapter 12). Even though the book has a different focus, it is clear that this passage was designed to establish the practice of the feast.

20. See the treatment of Genesis in chapter 12.

21. See the analysis of Exodus in chapter 12.

22. See W. Brueggemann, *Genesis* (*Interpretation*; Atlanta: John Knox, 1982), 40.

23. The apostle Paul pointed to the establishing function of this text when he described how Adam cast the entire human race into sin (Romans 5:12–21). He also drew upon the modeling function when he warned the Corinthians, "But I am afraid that just as Eve was deceived by the serpent's cunning, your minds may somehow be led astray from your sincere and pure devotion to Christ" (2 Corinthians 11:3).

24. See Nelson, *Kings*, 249.

25. See Bright, *History*, 426.

26. See the discussion of Chronicles' idealized monarchs in chapter 12.

27. See the discussion of the purpose of Esther in chapter 12.

28. See the analyses of this passage in chapters 8 and 9.

29. See von Rad, *Genesis*, 188.

30. For the date and purpose of Chronicles see chapter 12.

31. See Dillard, *2 Chronicles*, 270–1.

32. See the analysis of this passage in chapter 4.

33. See the analysis of this passage in chapter 8.

34. It seems likely that "the Lord scattered" (*hpysm*) is used in the military sense of scattering the enemy after battle (Numbers 10:35; 1 Samuel 11:11; 2 Samuel 18:8; 2 Kings 25:5; Psalm 68:1). The military imagery is especially important for seeing the connection with the conquest of Canaanite cities in the days of Moses.

35. See Ross, *Creation and Blessing*, 363.

36. See the analysis of this passage in chapter 8.

37. See the analysis of this passage in chapter 9.

38. See the discussion of moral standards earlier in this chapter.

39. See the analysis of this passage in chapter 9.

40. See Dillard, *2 Chronicles*, 129; Williamson, *Chronicles*, 259–75.

41. See the analysis of this passage in chapter 9.

42. See the earlier treatment of Genesis 48:1–22 in chapter 10.

43. See the discussion of Kings in chapter 12.

44. See the analysis of this passage in chapter 9.

45. "'What right do you have to be angry?' constitutes the challenge of chap. 4 for the hearer/reader." Stuart, *Hosea-Jonah*, 508–9.

Chapter Twelve

1. We will not include Leviticus due to the abundance of ceremonial legislation.

2. See Childs, *Introduction to Old Testament*, 129ff. Harrison's characterization of the Pentateuch as "a single work in five volumes" overstates the unity displayed by the books. See Harrison, *Introduction*, 496.

3. We speak of "fundamental Mosaic authorship" in the sense in which Young used the expression. "When we affirm that Moses wrote, or that he was the author of, the Pentateuch, we do not mean that he himself necessarily wrote every word. To insist upon this would be unreasonable. . . . The witness of sacred Scripture leads us to believe that Moses was the fundamental or real author of the Pentateuch. In composing it, he may indeed, as Astruc suggested, have employed parts of previously existing written documents. Also, under divine inspiration, there may have been later minor additions and even revisions. Substantially and essentially, however, it is the product of Moses." See Young, *Introduction*, 45. See also LaSor, Hubbard, and Bush, *Old Testament Survey*, 62–3.

4. For explanations and evaluations of the documentary hypothesis of the Pentateuch see Young, *Introduction*, 19–32, 495–541. For a more detailed analysis see O. T. Allis, *The Five Books of Moses* (Phillipsburg: Presbyterian and Reformed, 1973; U. Cassuto, *The Documentary Hypothesis: and the Composition of the Pentateuch* (tr. I. Abrahams; Jerusalem: Magnes, 1961 [1941]).

5. Ross observes, "Sources were probably used in the writing of Genesis—sources that were brought by ancestors from Mesopotamia, sources and records of the ancestral families kept by the patriarchs, genealogical records, and the like. It is reasonable to suggest that Moses gathered ancient records and traditions, and it makes better sense for the message of the book in the Pentateuch." Ross, *Creation and Blessing*, 35.

6. "It may well be that the presence of third person pronouns in various sections of the Mosaic enactments indicate that these sections were dictated." Harrison, *Introduction*, 538.

7. See the discussion of Deuteronomy later in this chapter.

8. See Matthew 19:8; Luke 5:14; John 5:45–47. As Archer argues, "It is hard to see how anyone can embrace the documentary theory (that Moses wrote not a word of the law) without attributing either falsehood or error to Christ and the apostles." Archer, *Survey of Old Testament*, 110. See also Allis, *Five Books of Moses*, 280–8.

9. For example, see the discussion on Genesis 14:14 and 36:31 in Young, *Introduction*, 59–60.

10. See Childs, *Introduction to Old Testament*, 145–6; LaSor, Hubbard, and Bush, *Old Testament Survey*, 68–70; VanGemeren, *Progress of Redemption*, 70–3.

11. The *twldwt* formula represents a significant element in the structure of Genesis, but, placing too much emphasis can obscure other aspects of the text. For other approaches see von Rad, *Genesis*, 70 and Westermann, *Genesis 1–11*, 355–6.

12. For similar divisions see von Rad, *Genesis*, 5–7; Ross, *Creation and Blessing*, 7-9, 35 and Westermann, *Genesis 1–11*, ix-x. The unity of Genesis 37–50 has long been recognized and in recent years has attracted considerable attention. For instance, see Coats, *Genesis 8*, 259–315.

13. Many of the Israelites were ambivalent about the departure from Egypt. See, for example, Exodus 3:11–14; 6:9–12; 14:10–12; 16:1–3; 17:3.

14. The need to encourage the people toward this goal is evident. See Numbers 13:1-14:45; Deuteronomy 1:19–46.

15. See Harrison's discussion of Exodus 6:26; 11:3; 12:42; 16:26,33ff. Harrison, *Introduction*, 569–73.

16. This outline is similar to J. Durham, *Exodus* (*Word Biblical Commentary* 3; Waco: Word, 1987) vii-x. For alternatives see R. Cole, *Exodus: An Introduction and Commentary* (*Tyndale Old Testament Commentaries*; Downer's Grove: Inter-Varsity, 1973), 52; Hyatt, *Exodus*, 14–8. The two sections concerning the law and the cult are closely connected by their common setting at Mount Sinai.

17. This theme has largely gone unnoticed. Durham mentions the legitimization of Moses in certain sections of the book, but does not treat this as an overarching theme. He writes concerning 4:1–9, "As theophany and call (3:1–12) have been followed by assertion and illustration of God's authority (3:13–22), so now the compiler addresses the question of Moses' authority and how that authority is to be made credible" (p. 43). Durham also notes that the genealogy serves a legitimizing function for both Aaron and Moses (6:14–27). He mentions this function again in 14:21–31. Nevertheless, Durham says that the primary purpose of the book is a theological one. He writes, "The centerpiece . . . is the theology of Yahweh present with and in the midst of his people Israel." Durham, *Exodus*, xxi.

18. Kline points to a number of ways in which the New Testament gospels reflect the genre of Exodus. See M. G. Kline "Old Testament Origins of the Gospel Genre," *Westminster Theological Journal* 38 (1975-76), 1–27.

19. See Harrison, *Introduction*, 615–22 and Young, *Introduction*, 91–2.

20. This outline is similar to Budd's proposal. See P. Budd, *Numbers* (*Word Biblical Commentary* 5; Waco: Word, 1984), xvii. For alternatives see Young, *Introduction*, 84; Harrison, *Introduction*, 614–5; Archer, *Survey of Old Testament*, 245–6.

21. See Archer, *Survey of Old Testament*, 109–18, 253–62; Harrison, *Introduction*, 237-53; P. C. Craigie, *Deuteronomy*, 24–9.

22. See Craigie, *Deuteronomy*, 30–2.

23. See Kline, *Structure of Biblical Authority*, 27–44; Craigie, *Deuteronomy*, 24–9.

24. Craigie writes, "Both the form of the book and the religious significance of that form make it not unreasonable to assume that the book comes from the time of Moses or shortly thereafter . . . . It is probable, therefore, that Deuteronomy, as a covenant renewal document, was written down soon after the renewal ceremony." Craigie, *Deuteronomy*, 28.

25. For outlines that focus primarily on Mosaic speeches see J. A. Thompson, *Deuteronomy: An Introduction and Commentary* (*Tyndale Old Testament Commentaries*; London: Inter-Varsity, 1974), 78-80; Young, *Introduction*, 94–105; Archer, *Survey of Old Testament*, 251–2.

26. This outline is similar to Craigie's proposal. See Cragie, *Deuteronomy*, 67–9.

27. Ruth is counted among the writings, the third division of the Hebrew canon. See the treatment of Ruth later in this chapter.

28. For example see S. R. Driver, *An Introduction to the Literature of the Old Testament* (rev. ed.; New York: Charles Scribner's Sons, 1925), 5–6; H. Creelman, *An Introduction to the Old Testament: Chronologically Arranged* (New York: Macmillan, 1927), 13–29. For a further discussion see Young, *Introduction*, 123–53.

29. See M. Noth, *Überlieferungsgeschichtliche Studien* (2d. ed.; Tübingen: Max Niemeyer, 1957). English Translation *The Deuteronomistic History* (ed. D. J. A. Clines; *Journal for the Study of the Old Testament Supplement Series* 15; Sheffield: *Journal for the Study of the Old Testament* Press, 1981).

30. Noth, *Deuteronomistic History*, 4–11.

31. Noth, *Deuteronomistic History*, 89–99.

32. See von Rad, *Old Testament Theology*, 2.334–47.

33. F. M. Cross, *Canaanite Myth and Hebrew Epic* (Cambridge: Harvard University, 1973), 274–89. See also the refinement of this view in K. D. Nelson, *The Double Redaction of the Deuteronomistic History* (*Journal for the Study of the Old Testament Supplement Series* 18; Sheffield: *Journal for the Study of the Old Testament* Press, 1981).

34. See H. W. Wolff, "Das kerygma des deuteronomistischen Geschictswerks," *Zeitschrift für die Alttestamentliche Wissenschaft* 73 (1961), 171–86.

35. For summaries of critical and conservative views of Deuteronomy's compositional history see Harrison, *Introduction*, 637–53; Childs, *Introduction to Old Testament*, 204–10.

36. For an extensive discussion of connections and developments see M. Weinfeld, *Deuteronomy and the Deuteronomistic School* (Oxford: Clarendon, 1972).

37. See Woudstra, *Joshua 10–11*; Archer, *Survey of Old Testament*, 264; Harrison, *Introduction*, 672.

38. It is possible to understand "Rahab" as a reference to her descendants. See R. G. Boling, *Joshua* (*The Anchor Bible* 6; Garden City: Doubleday and Company, 1982), 209.

39. For the history of Tyre and Sidon in relation to this evidence see Woudstra, *Joshua 11*.

40. One passage distinguishes between "the hill country of Judah" and "the hill country of Israel" (Joshua 11:21), but the text critical problems in this passage render this evidence questionable. See Boling, *Joshua*, 313.

41. Of course, it must be admitted that 1 Kings 16:34 may be based on other traditions.

42. See the discussion of the date of Kings later in this chapter.

43. A similar outline appears in T. C. Butler, *Joshua* (*Word Biblical Commentary* 7; Waco: Word, 1983) v. For alternative two part outlines see Young, *Introduction*, 163; Harrison, *Introduction*, 665.

44. See Woudstra, *Joshua 11*.

45. See D. R. Davis, "A Proposed Life-setting for the Book of Judges" 22–30; Young, *Introduction*, 170; Archer, *Survey of Old Testament*, 274; Harrison, *Introduction*, 690 place the writing during the early monarchy. See also Cundall, *Judges*, 26–8.

46. See Archer, *Survey of Old Testament*, 275–6; Young, *Introduction*, 169–70.

47. See Davis, "Proposed Life-setting," 92–6 for his argument concerning the stress on Judah in the first chapter of Judges.

48. See Gray, *Joshua, Judges, Ruth*, 218–9.

49. See Davis, "Proposed Life-setting," 1–24 and A. E. Cundall, "Judges—an Apology for the Monarchy?" *Expository Times* 81 (1970), 178–81.

50. For a discussion of various source theories see R. W. Klein, 1 Samuel (*Word Biblical Commentary* 10; Waco: *Word Biblical Commentary*, 1983), xxviii-xxxii; McCarter, *I Samuel*, 12–30; Harrison, *Introduction*, 696-709.

51. S. Goldman, *1 and 2 Samuel* (London: Soncino Press, 1966), ix. See also Harrison, *Introduction*, 709; Archer, *Survey of Old Testament*, 283–285; Young, *Introduction*, 178.

52. For alternative outlines see D. F. Payne, *1 and 2 Samuel* (*Daily Study Bible*; Philadelphia: Westminster, 1982), 2–3; Harrison, *Introduction*, 695–696.

53. For a discussion of this theme see Hertzberg, *1 and 2 Samuel*, 414–6; Childs, *Introduction to Old Testament*, 273–5.

54. For discussions of the sources of Kings see Gray, *Kings*, 9–35; DeVries, *I Kings* xxxviii-lii; J. A. Montgomery and H. S. Gehman, *A Critical and Exegetical Commentary on the Books of Kings* (*International Critical Commentary*; Edinburgh: T. and T. Clark, 1976), 24–45.

55. See the discussion of this matter in chapter 10.

56. Opinion is divided concerning the statement, "for the rest of his life" (2 Kings 25:29). Hobbs states that the "parallel in Jeremiah 52:34 adds the reference to the day of Jehoiachin's death, possibly indicating that its perspective is a later one than [25:27f] . . . . It is fair to conclude that Jehoiachin was still alive when 2 Kings 25 was written." Hobbs, *2 Kings*, 368. On the other hand, Montgomery and Gehman conclude that "it was composed after Jehoiachin's death, but before the Persian conquest." Montgomery and Gehman, *Kings*, 567.

57. See Wolff, "Das kerygma", 171–86.

58. See chapter 10, n. 21.

59. For a discussion of the limits of Ezra's memoirs see Clines, *Ezra, Nehemiah, Esther*, 6–8; Williamson, *Ezra, Nehemiah*, xxviii-xxxii.

60. Myers summarizes the consensus of most interpreters in recent decades. "Chronicles, Ezra, and Nehemiah are so closely related in thought, language, and theology that . . . they [must] have come from a single hand." Myers, *I Chronicles*, xviii.

61. For various outlooks on this parallel material see Dillard, *2 Chronicles*, 298; Williamson, *Israel in the Books of Chronicles*, 9; Curtis and Madsen, *Chronicles*, 525.

62. See Young, *Introduction*, 378. For a further discussion see Harrison, *Introduction*, 1149–50.

63. Williamson, *Ezra, Nehemiah*, xxiii. Fensham attributes the division of Ezra and Nehemiah to Origen. See F. C. Fensham, *The Books of Ezra and Nehemiah* (*New International Commentaries on the Old Testament;* Grand Rapids: Eerdmans, 1982), 1.

64. See S. Japhet, "The Supposed Common Authorship of Chronicles and Ezra-Nehemiah Investigated Anew," *Vetus Testamentum* 18 (1968), 330–71; Williamson, *Israel in the Books of Chronicles*, 5–70; Williamson, *2 Chronicles*, 5–11; Pratt, "Royal Prayer," 6–20.

65. Williamson and Braun have pointed out that the prayers of Ezra 9:5–15 and Nehemiah 9:5–37 reflect an idea of retribution that parallels Chronicles to some degree. See Williamson, *Chronicles*, 31–33; R. L. Braun, "Chronicles, Ezra, and Nehemiah: Theology and Literary History," in *Studies in the Historical Books of*

the Old Testament (ed. J. A. Emerton; *Vetus Testamentum Supplements* 30; Leiden: E. J. Brill, 1979), 52–64. Croft argues that this variation in theological themes may be due to a difference in the source materials used for the respective books. See S. J. L. Croft, "Review of Israel in the Books of Chronicles," *Journal for the Study of the Old Testament* 14 (1979), 68–72.

66. See Pratt, "Royal Prayer," 14–5.

67. See Williamson, *Israel in the Books of Chronicles*, 66–67; Pratt, "Royal Prayer," 14–5.

68. "Finally, although Nehemiah 13:26 is probably to be attributed to the [Nehemiah memoirs], yet it still contrasts strikingly with the Chronicler's own portrayal of Solomon's reign (2 Chronicles 1–9)." Williamson, *Chronicles*, 11.

69. Williamson also refers to the lack of Levitical sermons in Ezra and Nehemiah as an example of theological differences. But this difference may be attributed to differences in sources. See Pratt, "Royal Prayer," 16–7. See also Williamson, *Chronicles*, 11.

70. For a survey of proposals of sources used by the Chronicler see Williamson, *Chronicles*, 17–24. See also A. M. Brunet, "Le Chroniste et ses Sources," *Revue biblique* 60 (1953), 481–508.

71. For discussions related to the complexities of textual traditions involved in the Chronicler's use of Samuel and Kings see Pratt, "Royal Prayer," 63–8; Williamson, *Chronicles*, 17–33.

72. See McKenzie, *The Chronicler's Use of the Deuteronomistic History* and Myers, *1 Chronicles*, xiv-xlviii.

73. See D. N. Freedman, "The Chronicler's Purpose," *Catholic Biblical Quarterly* 23 (1961), 437–8; A. Welch, *The Work of the Chronicler, Its Purpose and Its Date* (London: Oxford University, 1939), 155–60; J. D. Newsome, Jr., "Toward a New Understanding of the Chronicler and his Purposes," *Journal of Biblical Literature* 94 (1975), 214–7; F. M. Cross, Jr., "A Reconstruction of the Judean Restoration," *Interpretation* 29 (1975), 198.

74. See Williamson, *Chronicles*, 16.

75. See the earlier discussion in chapter 10.

76. See Williamson's discussion of the Chronicles' citation by Eupolemos. Williamson, *Chronicles*, 15–7.

77. See Williamson, *Chronicles*, 16; Braun, *1 Chronicles*, xxix; Harrison, *Introduction*, 1157.

78. See Braun, "Theology and Literary History," 59–62. See also Williamson, *Chronicles*, 24–31.

79. Bright, *History*, 392–403; Cross, "Reconstruction," 187–203; G. Widengren, "The Persian Period," in *Israelite and Judean History* (eds. J. H. Hayes and J. M. Miller; *Old Testament Library*; Philadelphia: Westminster, 1977), 503–9.

80. See Williamson, *Ezra, Nehemiah*, xxiii-xxiv; Clines, *Ezra, Nehemiah, Esther*, 4–9.

81. See n. 59 above.

82. These lists may have included: 1) list of exiles who returned with Zerubbabel, 2) list of heads of families who returned with Ezra, 3) inventory of temple vessels returned to Sheshbazzar by the Persian court, 4) list of those who married foreign wives and 5) list of builders of the wall. See LaSor, Hubbard, and Bush, *Old Testament Survey*, 645.

83. See note 79 above.

84. See chapter 10.

85. See the discussion on authorship and date in LaSor, Hubbard, and Bush, *Old Testament Survey*, 646–8; Archer, *Survey of Old Testament*, 411–6; Harrison, *Introduction*, 1149–50.

86. For a contrary view see Young, *Introduction*, 387.

87. For alternative outlines see Clines; *Ezra, Nehemiah, Esther*, 31–32; Young, *Introduction*, 384–388; Archer, *Survey of Old Testament*, 411.

88. Williamson concludes his introduction to *Ezra, Nehemiah* by stating "Rather, the narrative structure itself points to past achievements as a model for future aspiration." See Williamson, *Ezra, Nehemiah*, lii.

89. This genre designation was first made by H. Gunkel "Ruth," in *Reden und Aufsatze* (Göttingen: Vanderhoeck and Ruprecht, 1913), 65–92.

90. See Archer, *Survey of Old Testament*, 285. Also L. Morris, *Judges Ruth* (*Tyndale Old Testament Commentaries*; Downer's Grove: Inter-Varsity, 1968), 232–9; Young, *Introduction*, 338–9; Harrison, *Introduction*, 1060–3.

91. These and other themes have been proposed as the main purpose of the book. See Gunkel, "Ruth," 65–92 (Ruth's Heroism); S. R. Driver, *Introduction to the Literature of the Old Testament* (New York: Scribners, 1914) (Levirate Marriage); W. Rudolph, *Das Buch Ruth* (*Kommentar zum Alten Testament*; Neukirchen: Neukirchener-Vluynm 1939) (Providence); Hertzberg, *Die Bucher Josua, Richter, Ruth*; R. Gerleman, *Ruth* (*Biblischer Kommentar Altes Testament*; Kreis Moers, 1960) (Royal Apologetic).

92. See Archer, *Survey of Old Testament*, 279. See also Young, *Introduction*, 340; Keil and Deilitzsch, *Ruth*, 466.

93. For a similar outline see Gray, *Joshua, Judges, Ruth*, 384–403. For alternative see Young, *Introduction*, 341; Morris, *Ruth*, 244.

94. For helpful discussions of the historical background of these events see Merrill, *Kingdom of Priests*, 497–502; Bright, *History*, 374–380; Baldwin, *Esther*, 16–24.

95. For a discussion of these sources see Clines, *Ezra, Nehemiah, Esther*, 266–8; Young, *Introduction*, 354.

96. See Introduction, n. 49.

97. For a similar outline see J. G. Baldwin, *Esther: An Introduction and Commentary* (*Tyndale Old Testament Commentaries*; Downer's Grove: Inter-Varsity, 1984), 53–4; C. A. Moore, *Esther* (*The Anchor Bible* 7B; Garden City: Doubleday, 1971), 128; Clines, *Ezra, Nehemiah, Esther*, 272.

98. See Baldwin, *Esther*, 48–9.

99. As Archer put it, "Whoever the author may have been, he shows such intimate knowledge of Persian customs and of the 5th century historical situation that he may well have lived in Persia and been an eyewitness of the events recorded" Archer, *Survey of Old Testament*, 419. For a discussion of Persian linguistic influence see R. J. Coggins and S. P. Re'emi, *Israel Among the Nations: A Commentary on the Books of Nahum and Obadiah and Esther* (*International Theological Commentary*; Grand Rapids: Eerdmans, 1985), 110.

100. See Childs, *Introduction to Old Testament*, 599.

101. See Harrison, *Introduction*, 1099.

102. For discussions of the similarities see Young, *Introduction*, 358; Humphreys, "Novella," 85.

103. See Young, *Introduction*, 261. More recent views have elaborated on chronological problems within the text. For example, see Gray, *Kings*, 72–3, 614; Hobbs, *2 Kings*, 184-5.

104. See, for instance, Young, *Introduction*, 261.

105. See Allen, *Joel, Obadiah, Jonah and Micah*, 186. For an alternative interpretation of 3:3 see Stuart, *Hosea-Jonah*, 432.

106. Stuart gives the range of composition from (750–250 B.C.). See Stuart, *Hosea-Jonah*, 432–3. See also Allen, *Joel, Obadiah, Jonah and Micah*, 186–7.

107. We must disagree with Young who says "The fundamental purpose of the book of Jonah is . . . to show that Jonah being cast into the depths of sheol and yet brought up alive is an illustration of the death of the Messiah for sins not His own and of the Messiah's resurrection." Young, *Introduction*, 263. For different views see Allen, *Joel, Obadiah, Jonah and Micah*, 188–90; Stuart, *Hosea-Jonah*, 130, 434.

108. See also Stuart, *Hosea-Jonah* and Allen, *Joel, Obadiah, Jonah and Micah*, 200.

Chapter Thirteen

1. See the discussion of legitimate application in chapter 5.

2. See Frame, *Knowledge of God*, 81–5; Greidanus, *Modern Preacher*, 120–1.

3. See the discussion of original observations, anticipations, and implications in chapter 11.

4. For a fuller discussion of the relationship between meaning and application see chapter 5.

5. Adams, *Preaching with Purpose*, 27; Greidanus, *Modern Preacher*, 106–7.

6. For the discussion of the complexities of writers' intentions see chapter 5.

7. "Just as exegesis of the text of Scripture illuminates the text of life, so exegesis of the text of life can illumine the text of Scripture. It does so as, in the identification of the great conceptual truths of the Christian faith, we find them pictured and storied in the commonplace of human experience." I. P. Watson, *A Primer for Preachers* (Grand Rapids: Baker, 1986), 46.

8. See the discussion of the three basic forms of analysis in chapter 4.

9. For recent discussions of the Sabbath institution and its relation to Genesis 1 and 2 see Murray, *Collected Writings*, 1.205–7; J. Murray, *Principles of Conduct* (Grand Rapids: Eerdmans, 1981 [1957]), 30–5.

10. See the discussion of this passage in chapter 11.

11. Or "bless themselves" as the RSV translates the Niphal verb (*nbrkw*). See the discussion in Westermann, *Genesis 12–36*, 151–2.

12. For a discussion of analogy in application see Greidanus, *Modern Preacher*, 172-5.

13. For helpful warnings concerning moralizing see Greidanus, *Modern Preacher*, 163-6; L. E. Keck, *The Bible in the Pulpit* (Nashville: Abingdon, 1978), 100–5. See also the earlier discussions of the exemplary approach in chapter 4 and characters as models in chapter 6.

14. Williamson writes, "The Chronicler has gone out of his way to present Hezekiah as a second Solomon. . . . Thus in Hezekiah's recapitulation of Solomon's achievements it is as though the Chronicler is taking us back prior to the point of division where the one Israel is united around a single temple under the authority of the Davidic king." Williamson, *Chronicles*, 350–1.

15. Again, Williamson comments, "While Kings devotes only a single verse to his religious reform . . . in Chronicles the reform occupies three chapters, and deals with the cleansing and rededication of the temple (Ch. 29), the celebration of the passover by representatives of all Israel (Ch. 30) and subsequent arrangements for the continuing temple worship (Ch. 31)." Williamson, *Chronicles*, 350.

16. See Williamson, *Chronicles*, 365, 373.

17. See Pratt, "Royal Prayer," 362.

18. See the discussion of Samuel in chapter 12.

19. Greidanus writes that "allegorizing is a bridge from then to now that fails to bear the weight of the text: it fails to bring across the plain meaning of a passage in its historical context and thus falsifies the message." Greidanus, *Modern Preacher*, 160.

20. See the analysis of this passage in chapter 4.

21. See the discussion of this connection in chapter 11.

22. See the discussion of this passage in chapter 11.

23. See the analysis of this passage in chapter 9.

24. See the discussion of this passage in chapter 9.

25. See the analysis of this passage in chapter 9.

26. See the analysis of this passage in chapter 8.

27. G. E. Lessing, *Lessing's Theological Writings* (tr. H. Chadwick; London: Adam and Charles Black, 1983 [1956]), 31.

28. J. Barr, *The Bible in the Modern World* (New York: Harper and Row, 1973), 39–41.

29. See the discussion of these matters in Introduction.

30. See E. Troeltsch, *The Absoluteness of Christianity and the History of Religions* (tr. D. Reid; Richmond: John Knox, 1971 [1929]), 85–106.

31. For a brief discussion of Bultmann's hermeneutic, see K. Hamilton, *Words and the Word* (Grand Rapids: Eerdmans, 1971), 36–41; Grant and Tracy, *A Short History*, 145-6; J. D. G. Dunn, "Demythologizing—The Problem of Myth in the New Testament," in *New Testament Interpretation* (ed. I. H. Marshall; Grand Rapids: Eerdmans, 1977), 294-300.

32. For a recent evangelical explanation and critique of process theology, see R. G. Gruenler, *The Inexhaustible God* (Grand Rapids: Baker, 1983).

33. See my treatment of Liberation theology in chapter 1.

34. For a fuller discussion of the Spirit's work in illumination see Introduction.

35. As Bloesch comments, "We allow for the fact that both induction and deduction will be used both prior to faith and in the service of faith, but the truth of revelation can be apprehended only by faith. Moreover, the processes of reason before faith can only lead to dead ends, since it is not until reason is turned around by the Spirit that it becomes fruitful in a Christian sense." See D. G. Bloesch, "Crisis in Biblical Authority," *Theology Today* (1979), 462; W. J. Larkin, *Culture and Biblical Hermeneutics* (Grand Rapids: Baker, 1988), 100, 287–92; K. Hamilton, *Words and the Word* (Grand Rapids: Eerdmans, 1971), 83.

36. Kaiser writes, "All men and women in all cultures are made in the image of God. And when this fact is joined with a Biblical concept of truth as having an objective grounding and reference point in *the nature of God* and in the doctrine of creation, the possibility for adequate (even if no one knows comprehensively except God) transcultural communication has been fairly provided and secured." See W. Kaiser, "Meanings from God's Message: Matters for Interpretation," *Christianity Today* 23 (1979), 1321 (emphasis mine).

37. See Hodge, *Systematic Theology*, 1.390–1; L. Berkhof, *Systematic Theology*, 58–9; R. L. Dabney, *Lectures in Systematic Theology* (Grand Rapids: Zondervan, 1972 [1878]), 152–4; J. I. Packer, *Knowing God* (Downers Grove: Inter-Varsity, 1985 [1973]), 67–72; B. Ware, "An Evangelical Reformation of the Doctrine of the Immutability of God," *Journal of the Evangelical Theological Society* 29 (1986), 431–46.

38. See Berkhof, *Systematic Theology*, 58.

39. As Larkin summarizes the matter, "In applying this message to a given time, we can assume that God deals the same way with men and women in every age, which makes the transhistorical understanding and application of the message possible." Larkin, *Culture and Biblical Hermeneutics*, 100. For a more detailed discussion see P. Wells, *James Barr and the Bible* (Phillipsburg: Presbyterian and Reformed, 1980), 354–62.

40. See Robertson, *Christ of the Covenants*, 25.

41. From the reports of missionaries, general revelation prepares some people for the message of Scripture in rather dramatic ways. See D. Richardson, *Eternity in their Hearts* (Ventura: Regal Books, 1984), 151–97.

42. See the discussion of anticipation through modelling and adumbration in chapter 11.

43. As Nixon writes, "The principles of human nature, human conduct and human relationships do not change from age to age and the New Testament principles are available for translation into our situation." R.E. Nixon, "The Authority of the New Testament," in *New Testament Interpretation: Essays on Principles and Methods* (ed. I. H. Marshall; Grand Rapids: Eerdmans, 1977), 345.

44. Frame states that language "likens us to God, who does all things by His powerful Word and who is identical with his Word (John 1:1ff). (2) It distinguishes us from the animals, giving us a powerful tool of dominion." Frame, *Knowledge of God*, 240.

45. For helpful discussions of the adequacies of human language for communicating religious truth see K. Pike, "The Linguist and Axioms Concerning the Language of Scripture," in *Journal of the American Scientific Affiliation*, 26 (1974), 48, V. S. Poythress, "Adequacy of Language and Accommodation," in *Hermeneutics, Inerrancy, and the Bible* (eds. E. Radmacher and R. Preus; Grand Rapids: Zondervan, 1984), 349-76; J. Frame "God and Biblical Language: Transcendence and Immanence," in *God's Inerrant Word* (ed. J. W. Montgomery; Minneapolis: Bethany Fellowship Inc., 1973), 159–75.

46. See Larkin, *Culture and Biblical Hermeneutics*, 70–6. See also E. A. Nida, "Implications of Contemporary Linguistics for Biblical Scholarship," *Journal of Biblical Literature* 91 (1972), 73–89; J. F. A. Sawyer, *Semantics in Biblical Research: New Methods of Defining Hebrew Words for Salvation* (Studies in *Biblical Theology* 24, 2d Series, vol., 24 London: SCM, 1972), 112; Cotterell and Turner, *Linguistics and Biblical Interpretation*, 19–25.

47. For helpful discussions of rationality as a quality of the image of God see P. Hughes, *The True Image* (Grand Rapids: Eerdmans, 1989), 57–8; C. Henry, *God, Revelation, and Authority* (Waco: Word, 1976–79), 3.389.

48. For helpful discussions on human moral nature, see Hughes, *Image*, 59–61; Dabney, *Lectures on Systematic Theology*, 96–112.

49. Murray writes, "Some Reformed theologians regard this dominion as an element of the divine image. It would appear preferable, however, to regard dominion as a function or office based upon the specific character defined as the image of God. The latter fits him for the dominion to be exercised. Man is made in God's image. He is, therefore, constituted God's vice regent. It belongs to God's being to be sovereign over all creation. It belongs to man's being to execute delegated dominion." See Murray, *Collected Writings*, 2.41. For other discussions see also Hall, *Imaging God* (Grand Rapids: Eerdmans, 1986), 192–205; G. C. Berkouwer, *Man: The Image of God* (Grand Rapids: Eerdmans, 1962), 70–4.

50. For a discussion of the moral character of human beings as a hermeneutical bridge see Larkin, *Culture and Biblical Hermeneutics*, 204–5.

51. As Adams has summarized the matter, "Basically people and their problems (as well as God's solutions to them) remain the same in all generations, there *is* a circumstance today that corresponds to the original one, to which God also directed His word." Adams, *Preaching with Purpose*, 133 (emphasis his).

52. See the discussion of the purpose of Exodus in chapter 12.

53. See the discussion of Numbers in chapter 12.

54. See the discussion of Christian living in chapter 2.

55. See the discussion of interaction in chapter 3.

56. *Westminster Confession of Faith* 1, 9.

57. For the discussion of the distinction between original meaning and Biblical elaborations see chapter 5.

58. Greidanus writes, "First, the original message of the text will have to be traced throughout the Scriptures. Since revelation progresses within the Testament and especially from the Old to the New Testament, and since preachers must aim the message at New Testament congregations in the twentieth century, the theme of the text must be traced from Genesis 1 to Revelation 22." Greidanus, *Modern Preacher*, 167–8. See also Kaiser, *Exegetical Theology*, 134–40.

59. For a discussion of the Deuteronomistic history and its dependence on Deuteronomy see chapter 12.

60. See the discussion of the Old Testament in the New Testament in Introduction.

61. See B. B. Warfield, *Biblical Foundations* (Grand Rapids: Eerdmans, 1958), 19–23; Vos, *Biblical Theology*, 15–7.

62. For a fuller discussion of the organic quality of progressive revelation see chapter 14.

63. For helpful discussions see Greidanus, *Modern Preacher*, 158–181; J. R. McQuilkin, "Limits of Cultural Interpretation," *Journal of the Evangelical Theological Society* 23 (1980), 113–124; J. R. W. Stott, *Between Two Worlds: The Art of Preaching in the Twentieth Century* (Grand Rapids: Eerdmans, 1982), 137–139; Larkin, *Culture and Biblical Hermeneutics*.

Chapter Fourteen

1. For a helpful discussion of Peter's redemptive-historical categories see M.G. Kline, *Kingdom Prologue* (unpublished syllabus: Gordon-Conwell Theological Seminary, 1981), 1.15–24. See also J. N. D. Kelly, *A Commentary on the Epistles of Peter and of Jude* (Black's New Testament Commentaries; London: Adam and Charles Black, 1976), 359; R. J. Bauckham, *Jude, 1 and 2 Peter* (*Word Biblical Commentary* 50; Waco: Word, 1983), 299.

2. See Robertson, *Christ of the Covenants*, W. J. Dumbrell, *Covenant and Creation* (Nashville: Thomas Nelson, 1984); McComiskey, *Covenants of Promise*.

3. See the discussion of this passage in chapter 9.

4. For helpful discussions of this passage see Ladd, *A Theology of the New Testament*, 364; Ridderbos, *Paul: An Outline of His Theology*, 52–3; Vos, *Pauline Eschatology*, 1-41.

5. For discussion of the Rabbinic background of this phraseology, see W. D. Davies, *Paul and Rabbinic Judaism* (London: *Society for the Propagation of Christian Knowledge*, 1948), 314–7.

6. For discussions on dualism in the synoptic gospels, see Ladd, *A Theology of the New Testament*, 68–9; H. Ridderbos, *The Coming of the Kingdom* (ed. R. D. Zorn and tr. H. deJongste; Philadelphia: Presbyterian and Reformed, 1962), 36–59.

7. For a discussion of Johannine dualism see J. L. Price, "Light from Qumran upon Some Aspects of Johannine Theology," in *John and Qumran* (ed. J. H. Charlesworth; London: Geoffrey Chapman, 1972), 18–24; Ladd, *A Theology of the New Testament*, 223-36.

8. As Ladd writes, "There is a twofold dualism in Hebrews: a dualism of the above and below—the real heavenly world and the transient earthly world; and there is an eschatological dualism: the present age versus the world to come." Ladd, *A Theology of the New Testament*, 572–7.

9. See E. G. Selwyn, "Eschatology in I Peter," in *The Background of the New Testament and its Eschatology* (eds. W. D. Davies and D. Daube; Cambridge: Cambridge University, 1964), 394–401; Ladd, *A Theology of the New Testament*, 595.

10. For a helpful discussion on the eschatological significance of Christ's first coming see Cullman, *Christ and Time*, esp. 61–93.

11. See also Matthew 13:17; Luke 10:24; 24:27; 24:44; Acts 2:29–31.

12. See Greidanus, *Modern Preacher*, 119, 220–1, 305–6, 331–2; Frame, *Knowledge of God*, 191–4.

13. For example, *Westminster Confession of Faith* 7.1–6.

14. See the discussion of the date of Samuel in chapter 12.

15. See, for instance, Vos, *Biblical Theology*, 7; VanGemeren, *Progress of Redemption*, 31–4.

16. See C. I. Scofield, *The Scofield Bible Correspondence Course* (Chicago: Moody Bible Institute, 1907), 1.17–21.

17. See C. I. Scofield, *Rightly Dividing the Word of Truth* (New York: Loizeaux Brothers, n.d.), esp. 1–18.

18. L. S. Chafer, *Grace* (Chicago: Moody, 1947), 215–44.

19. See chapter 11.

20. For some representative works from this perspective see G. L. Bahnsen, *Theonomy in Christian Ethics* (Nutley: Craig, 1977); G. L. Bahnsen, *By This Standard* (Tyler: Institute for Christian Economics, 1985); R. J. Rushdoony, *The Institutes of Biblical Law* (Nutley: Craig, 1973); G. North, *Backward Christian Soldiers: an action manual for Christian Reconstruction* (Tyler: Institute for Christian Economics, 1984); J. B. Jordan, *The Law of the Covenant: An Exposition of Exodus*, 21–23 (Tyler: Institute for Christian Economics, 1984). For responses to this position see W. S. Barker and W. R. Godfrey, eds., *Theonomy: A Reformed Critique of the Movement* (Grand Rapids: Zondervan, 1990); J. Frame, "Review of Institutes of Biblical Law," *Westminster Theological Journal* 38 (1976), 195–217. For an interesting critique from a dispensational posture see H. W. House and T. Ice, *Dominion Theology: Blessing or Curse? An Analysis of Christian Reconstructionism* (Portland, Oregon: Multnomah, 1988).

21. For example, see Bahnsen, *By This Standard*, 276–84; Bahnsen, *Theonomy in Christian Ethics*, 435–68.

22. *Westminster Confession of Faith* 7.6.

23. For more detailed explanations of the covenant of grace see McComiskey, *Covenants of Promise*, 179–92; Robertson, *Christ of the Covenants*, 54–7. See also Dumbrell, *Covenant and Creation*, esp. 44–6.

24. See the discussion of God, the world, and people as continuities throughout the ages in chapter 13.

25. See the discussion of the purpose of Genesis in chapter 12.

26. See n. 22 above.

27. Calvin, *Institutes*, 2.11.13. See also C. Van Til, *Christian Theistic Ethics* (n.p.: den Dulk Christian Foundation, 1971), 3.92–105.

28. Kaiser is correct when he says, "The material question eventually reduces itself to one of the following methodologies: (1) everything the New Testament does not repeat from the Old Testament is passé for the Christian or (2) everything that the New Testament has not changed in principle still remains in force for the Christian." W. C. Kaiser, *Toward Rediscovering the Old Testament* (Grand Rapids: Zondervan, 1987), 147. But I must add a third option. Everything in the Old Testament remains in force for the Christian, but the teachings of the New Testament lead to adjustments of everything in the Old Testament for the Christian.

29. For discussions of the offices of Christ see Calvin, *Institutes*, 2.15.1–6; Berkhof, *Systematic Theology*, 356–411; Hodge, *Systematic Theology*, 367–76 and 401–9; H. Hoeksema, *Reformed Dogmatics* (Grand Rapids: Reformed Free Publishing Association, 1966), 363–97; H. Bavinck, *Our Reasonable Faith* (Grand Rapids: Eerdmans, 1956), 332.

30. See *Westminster Shorter Catechism* Question 24.

31. See *Westminster Shorter Catechism* Question 25.

32. See the discussion of Chronicles in chapter 12.

33. See *Westminster Shorter Catechism* Question 26.

34. See the related discussion of kingship in W. Eichrodt, *Theology of the Old Testament* (tr. J. A. Baker; Philadelphia: Westminster, 1961), 1.436–56; Merrill, *Kingdom of Priests*, 208–9.

35. As Merrill writes, "The alleged tension, then, between Samuel's negative attitude toward kingship in response to the people's demand (1 Samuel 8; 10:17–27) and his positive support of Saul at the time of his selection and anointing (1 Samuel 9:1–10:16) is without historical foundation. Samuel's quarrel is not with kingship but, as has been suggested, with the character of kingship demanded by the people—'such as all the other nations have'—and with their refusal to wait for the man of God's own choosing." See Merrill, *Kingdom of Priests*, 190. See also Kaiser, *Old Testament Theology*, 145.

36. See the discussion of this passage in chapter 9.

37. Ladd writes, "A mighty leader who would overthrow Rome is precisely what the people desired of their messiah. . . . Had it been Jesus' purpose to offer to the Jews such an earthly, political Davidic kingdom, they would have accepted it on the spot and [would] have been willing to follow him to death if need be to see the inauguration of such a kingdom. However, when Jesus refused this and indicated that his mission was of an entirely different character and that his kingdom was to be a spiritual kingdom in which men were to eat his flesh and drink his blood, the crowds turned against him and his popularity waned (John 6:66). They wanted a king to deliver them from Rome, not a saviour to redeem them from their sins." Ladd, *A Theology of the New Testament*, 139–40.

38. See Ladd, *A Theology of the New Testament*, 38 and Vos, *Biblical Theology*, 315. For a related discussion see Ridderbos, *The Coming of the Kingdom*, 18–56.

39. See I. H. Marshall, *Eschatology and the Parables* (London: Tyndale, 1963), 34; S. T. Kistemaker, *The Parables of Jesus* (Grand Rapids: Baker, 1980), 35–43 (wheat and tares) and 44–7 (mustard seed).

40. See Ridderboss, *Paul: An Outline of His Theology*, 43.

41. See the discussion of the Mosaic History in chapter 12.

42. See the discussion of the Deuteronomistic History in chapter 12.

43. See the discussion of the Chronistic History in chapter 12.

44. For a discussion of these books see chapter 12.

Chapter Fifteen

1. P. G. Hiebert, *Cultural Anthropology* (2d ed.; Grand Rapids: Baker, 1983 [1976]), 25.

2. See the discussion of organic inspiration in the Introduction.

3. See S. C. Neill, "Religion and Culture—A Historical Introduction," in J. R. W. Stott and R. Coote, eds., *Down to Earth: Studies in Christianity and Culture* (Grand Rapids: Eerdmans, 1980), 1.

4. As Tillich said, "Religion as ultimate concern is the meaning-giving substance of culture, and culture is the totality of forms in which the basic concern of religion expresses itself. In abbreviation: religion is the substance of culture, culture is the form of religion." P. Tillich, *Theology of Culture* (ed. R. C. Kimball; New York: Oxford University, 1959), 42.

5. For helpful discussions of the interaction of pagan and Christian influences see C. Dawson, *Religion and the Rise of Western Culture* (Garden City: Image Books, 1958), 140–60; W. B. Glover, *Biblical Origins of Modern Secular Culture* (Macon, Ga.: Mercer University, 1984), 23–6; E. E. Cairns, *Christianity Through the Centuries* (rev. ed.; Grand Rapids: Zondervan, 1981 [1954]), 192–4.

6. "The reason humanism adjusts naturalistic beliefs experientially to universal ethical imperatives is that like every other human being the humanist is related to a larger realm of being and life and value, one that he neither creates nor controls. He cannot wholly escape God in his revelation nor wholly suppress the claim of the imago Dei upon his psyche. He is informed about inescapable moral obligation far more than the naturalistic theory implies. . . . Despite his intellectual and moral revolt against the supernatural, fallen man is unable to fully free himself of God's counterclaim upon his mind and conscience." See C. F. H. Henry, *The Christian Mindset in a Secular Society* (Portland, Oregon: Multnomah, 1984), 89–90.

7. For a discussion of "civil good" within the cultures of the world see R. L. Dabney, *Lectures in Systematic Theology*, 323–4 and L. Berkhof, *Systematic Theology*, 247–8.

8. See W. A. Haviland, *Anthropology* (5th ed.; New York: Holt, Rinehart and Winston, Inc., 1989 [1974]), 296–7. For additional discussions on cultural relativism see P. Hiebert, *Cultural Anthropology*, 364–9; Larkin, *Culture and Biblical Hermeneutics*, 20-1; D. McGavran, *The Clash Between Christianity and Cultures* (Washington, D.C.: Canon, 1974), 2–15.

9. Soggin writes, "The Canaanite city-state and Egyptian royal administrative systems have been considered the most likely areas for Davidic borrowing. About the organization of the former at the end of the second millennium we know practically nothing. This explains why scholars have sought to find the strong influence of Egyptian governmental organization on the David-Solomonic bureaucratic structure." See J. A. Soggin, "The Davidic-Solomonic Kingdom" in

Israelite and Judean History (eds. J. H. Hayes and J. M. Miller; Philadelphia: Westminster, 1977), 356–9. See also T. N. D. Mettinger, *Solomonic State Officials: A Study of the Civil Government Officials of the Israelite Monarchy* (Lund: C. W. K. Gleerup, 1971).

10. See the discussion of the moral implications of this event in chapter 9.

11. For a brief but helpful history of various viewpoints see M. Harris, *Culture, People, Nature: An Introduction to General Anthropology* (5th ed.; New York: Harper and Row, 1988), 585–93. Anthropologists have noted that cultural variety often rises out of different responses to an identical need. Bronislaw Malinowski has gone on to describe some of the basic needs of men in every society. For a useful summary of Malinowski's contribution see S. A. Grunlan and M. K. Mayers, *Cultural Anthropology: A Christian Perspective* (Grand Rapids: Zondervan, 1979), 43–53.

12. See A. Kuyper, *Calvinism: Six Stone Foundation Lectures* (Grand Rapids: Eerdmans, 1943), 117–8, 125, 163.

13. "Knowledge of creation is necessary if we are to apply Scripture properly." Frame, *Knowledge of God*, 75. See also J. M. Frame, *Medical Ethics* (Phillipsburg, N.J.: Presbyterian and Reformed, 1988), 19–25, 53–74.

14. Conn, *Eternal Word*, 331.

15. As Williamson comments on 1 Chronicles 6:32–47, "The Chronicler's presentation both here and in comparable passages implies the claim that the guilds of singers of his own day . . . stand in legitimate and unbroken community with the innovations of David." Williamson, *Chronicles*, 73.

16. See Murray, *Collected Writings*, 1.205–8.

17. As Cassuto observed, "The legal sections of the Pentateuch should not be regarded as a code of laws . . . but only as separate instructions on given matters . . . the Torah does not deal at all with several subjects that constitute basic legal themes: for example, the laws of marriage, apart from forbidden relations and the reference to the marriage price of virgins, which occurs incidentally; or with laws of divorce, which are also mentioned incidentally." Cassuto, *A Commentary on the Book of Exodus* (tr. I. Abrahams; Jerusalem: Magnes, 1967 [1951]), 262.

18. As Calvin comments on Romans 7:10, "It is incidental that the law inflicts on us a deadly wound . . . it is not in its own nature hurtful to us, but it is so because our corruption provokes and draws upon us its curse." Calvin, *The Epistle of Paul to the Romans and Thessalonians* (tr. R. Mackenzie; Grand Rapids: Eerdmans, 1965), 256. See also Calvin's discussion of the benefits of the Law of Moses in Calvin, *Institutes*, 2.7.1–2.8.10.

19. For introductory comparisons between OT Law and ancient Near Eastern laws see Cassuto, *Exodus*, 261–4; S. M. Paul, *Studies in the Book of the Covenant in the Light of Cunieform and Biblical Law* (*Vetus Testamentum Supplements* 18; Leiden: E. J. Brill, 1970); Kaiser, *Old Testament Ethics*, 96–111.

20. See Westermann, *Genesis 12—36*, 265.

21. See the bibliographical information in Westermann, *Genesis 12–36,* 210–12.

22. See Bright, *History,* 217–19.

23. For instance, note the remarkable contrast between the views of real estate in Israel and other nations as exemplified in the story of Naboth's vineyard (1 Kings 21:1–29). See Hanson, *The People Called,* 143–4.

24. For a fuller discussion of this matter see chapter 14.

25. As Bright comments, "Will we, like Israel, imagine that our destiny under God and God's purpose in history are to be realized in terms of the society we have built?" J. Bright, *Kingdom of God* (Nashville: Abingdon, 1981), 68–70.

26. For example, see P. G. Hiebert, *Anthropological Insights for Missionaries* (Grand Rapids: Baker, 1985), 171–92; D. J. Hesselgrave, *Communicating Christ Cross-Culturally* (Grand Rapids: Zondervan, 1978), 82–6; L. E. Reed, *Preparing Missionaries For Intercultural Communication: A Bi-cultural Approach* (Pasadena: William Carey Library, 1985), 138–9.

27. Kraft so separates meaning from form that he overlooks the importance of the form associated with that meaning. See, for example, C. H. Kraft, *Communication Theory for Christian Witness* (Nashville: Abingdon, 1986), 115–9, 238–9. For further discussion of this see Larkin, *Culture and Biblical Hermeneutics,* 105–6, 314–5.

28. C. H. Kraft, "Supracultural Meanings via Cultural Trends in Biblical Interpretation," in *A Guide to Contemporary Hermeneutics: Major Trends in Biblical Interpretation* (ed. D.K. McKim; Grand Rapids: Eerdmans, 1986), 312 (emphasis his).

29. For helpful discussions of some of the problems associated with this distinction, see J. R. McQuilkin, "Limits of Cultural Interpretation," *Journal of the Evangelical Theological Society* 23 (1980), 113–24 and R. P. Richard, "Methodological Proposals for Scripture Relevance, Part 3: Application Theory in Relation to the New Testament," *Bibliotheca Sacra* 143 (1986), 205–15.

30. Some, however, have denied the transcultural normativity of water baptism. See, for example, C. H. Kraft, *Christianity in Culture* (Maryknoll, N.Y.: Orbis, 1979), 331-2.

31. See the discussion of this matter in chapter 14.

32. See the treatment of this passage in chapter 8.

33. See the discussion of this passage in chapter 9.

Chapter Sixteen

1. See chapter 2 for a discussion on the effect of personal sanctification on interpretation.

2. For a similar assessment see Stuart, *Exegesis,* 71–2.

3. See the discussion of the relation between original meaning and legitimate applications in chapter 5.

4. As Stuart comments, "You can hardly expect your congregation to accept your suggested application of a passage solely on your own authority. They need to be shown how the application is based on a proper comprehension of the passage's meaning." Stuart, *Exegesis*, 86–7.

5. See the description of the purpose of Genesis in chapter 12.

6. See the discussion of the original meaning of Chronicles in chapter 12.

7. As Williamson argues, "Quite in contrast with what is generally regarded as the narrow-mindedness of the Chronicler's community, we are presented with an effort to include within the family of Israel all who could mount any legitimate claim to participation." Williamson, *Chronicles*, 38.

8. See Williamson's seminal study of the Chronicler's view of Israel. Williamson, *Israel in the Books of Chronicles*, esp. 87–132.

9. "David also serves as a model in making his own contribution from his personal treasury, and his example is followed by both leaders and people." Braun, *1 Chronicles*, 280.

10. See chapter 12 for a discussion of the date and purpose of Chronicles.

11. As Wenham points out that instructions for sacrifice in 1:1–6:7[8] are repeated in 6:8[1]-7:38[36] because the latter concerns priestly duties and the former focuses on the responsibilities of the laity. See G. J. Wenham, *The Book of Leviticus* (*New International Commentaries;* Grand Rapids: Eerdmans, 1979), 116–8.

12. See Kaiser, *Exegetical Theology*, 92, 121, 150–63, 194, 197–8, 205–6, 231, 236.

13. Kaiser, *Exegetical Theology*, 152.

14. See the treatments of these matters in chapters 14 and 15.

15. For this distinction see chapter 15.

16. Robinson, *Biblical Preaching*, 78.

17. See the discussion of the influence of sanctification on interpretation in chapter 2.

18. C. Van Til, *Introduction to Systematic Theology*, 245 (emphasis mine).

19. Hodge, *Systematic Theology*, 1.49.

20. See the discussion of these matters in chapter 13.

21. See the treatments of this passage in chapter 8.

22. See the discussion of this passage in chapter 11.

23. See the treatment of this passage earlier in this chapter.

24. Roberts expresses the matter rather pointedly. "For the person in whom justice is a character trait rather than just a duty, seeing injustice will be a painful thing.

He will love justice, desire it and in its absence long for it." Roberts, *Spirituality and Human Emotion*, 49 (emphasis his).

25. See the discussion of the purpose of Judges in chapter 12.

26. See the discussion of this passage in chapter 9.

27. See my treatment of this passage in chapter 9.

28. See the analysis of this text in conjunction with Genesis 39:1–23 in chapter 9.

SUBJECT INDEX

SCRIPTURE INDEX

Exodus

Leviticus

Numbers

Deuteronomy

Joshua

Judges

Ruth

1 Samuel

2 Samuel

1 Kings

Ezra

Nehemiah

Esther

Job

Psalm

ABOUT THE AUTHOR

Richard L. Pratt, Jr. is associate professor of Old Testament at Reformed Theological Seminary, in Orlando, Florida. He holds a Th.D. degree in Old Testament studies from Harvard University, a M.Div. degree from Union Theological Seminary, and a B.A. degree in Philosophy and Religion from Roanoke College.

Dr. Pratt has published articles in several theological journals and is the author of two previous books, *Every Thought Captive* (Presbyterian and Reformed), and *Pray with Your Eyes Open* (Presbyterian and Reformed). He brings to his writing not only the clarity and precision of the theological disciplines but also his experiences as a pastor and a Christian education director.

Richard, his wife, Gena, and their daughter, Becky, live in Longwood, Florida and worship at the Orangewood Presbyterian Church.